The Official
SAT
Study Guide™

THE COLLEGE BOARD, NEW YORK

ABOUT THE COLLEGE BOARD

The College Board is a mission-driven not-for-profit organization that connects students to college success and opportunity. Founded in 1900, the College Board was created to expand access to higher education. Today, the membership association is made up of over 6,000 of the world's leading educational institutions and is dedicated to promoting excellence and equity in education. Each year, the College Board helps more than seven million students prepare for a successful transition to college through programs and services in college readiness and college success — including the SAT® and the Advanced Placement Program®. The organization also serves the education community through research and advocacy on behalf of students, educators, and schools. For further information, visit collegeboard.org.

Copies of this book are available from your bookseller or may be ordered from College Board Publications at store.collegeboard.org or by calling 800-323-7155.

Editorial inquiries concerning this book should be submitted at sat.collegeboard.org/contact.

This publication was written and edited by the College Board, with primary authorship by Carolyn Lieberg, Jim Patterson, Andrew Schwartz, Jessica Marks, and Sergio Frisoli. Cover and layout design: Iris Jan. Project manager: Jaclyn Bergeron. Product owner: Aaron Lemon-Strauss. Invaluable contributions and review from the College Board's Assessment Design & Development team led by Sherral Miller, Laurie Moore, and Nancy Burkholder.

ISBN-13: 978-1-4573-0430-9

ISBN-10: 1-4573-0430-9

Distributed by Macmillan

Dear Student:

Congratulations on taking an important step toward preparing for the redesigned SAT®. *The Official SAT Study Guide*™ is a tool to help you practice for the newest version of the exam. By investing in SAT practice, you are making a commitment to your college, career, and life success.

As you start to familiarize yourself with the new exam, we are excited to share with you some of the many benefits it has to offer. It is important to remember that the questions that make up the exam are modeled on the work you are already doing in school. You will recognize topics and ideas from your math, English language arts, science, history, and social studies classes. These questions are also aligned with the skills that research says matter most for college and career readiness. This means that, by practicing for the redesigned SAT, you are reinforcing the knowledge and skills that will help you excel both in your course work and in your future pursuits.

The new SAT is clearer than ever. The questions will not be tricky, nor will there be any obscure vocabulary or penalties for guessing. By being transparent about what is on the test and making materials easily available, we are providing you the foundation for successful practice. The best source of information about the SAT is found right here in the pages of this book, and you have taken an important step by equipping yourself with these key facts.

The redesigned SAT is just one component of the College Board's commitment to increasing students' access to and success in college and career. We have also partnered with colleges and universities to offer college application fee waivers to every income-eligible senior who takes the SAT using a fee waiver. The College Board wants you to succeed in your pursuits, and defraying the cost of admission for eligible students is just one way that we can make it easier for you to reach your goals.

Now that you have this great study guide as a tool, we encourage you to begin practicing today.

Keep up the good work.

Cynthia B. Schmeiser

Cynthia B. Schmeiser
Chief of Assessment
The College Board

Dear Student:

I took the SAT more than 20 years ago. But even back in the prehistoric times of the early '90s, an earlier version of this book played a big role in helping me prepare not just for the SAT, but for life. For several weeks, I would wake up early on Saturday mornings, do push-ups while blasting "Eye of the Tiger," take a practice test, and review the items I found difficult. Eventually, I worked through every test in the book. By the time test day came around, I found I was just as prepared as anyone to put my best foot forward for the SAT. I also showed myself that I could develop a plan and stick to it to reach a goal, and that skill has proven essential ever since.

But you have much more than even I had at your disposal.

The Khan Academy® is a nonprofit with the mission of providing a free, world-class education for anyone, anywhere, and we've partnered with the College Board to create the world's best online SAT practice program, which also happens to be free. Yes, FREE! On Khan Academy (khanacademy.org/sat), we've designed a program that gives you unlimited practice and help with the skills you find challenging so you can show up on test day ready to rock the SAT.

So take a breath. Force a smile. Strike a power pose (look that up on YouTube if you don't know what a "power pose" is). Realize that your brain is like a muscle: The more you practice and get feedback, the stronger it gets. Realize that when you get a question wrong in practice, that is when your brain actually grows and strengthens. Realize that the SAT is just a measure of college readiness, and the best way to get college ready is to really hone your language and math abilities through deliberate practice. No matter how long you have until the exam, realize that you have the power to create a study plan for yourself and stick to it. This isn't about SAT prep, but life prep. And of course, the more practice, the better; so if you can, start regularly practicing with this book and the resources on Khan Academy weeks or months before the exam.

I envy you. You're at the most exciting stage of your life. Embrace the challenge. Enjoy the process. As you prepare, remember that you can arm yourself now with tools and habits that will help you be the best version of yourself, not just on the SAT but throughout your life.

And don't forget to smile!

Onward,

Sal Khan
Founder, Khan Academy
◆KHANACADEMY

Contents

PART 4   Four Official Practice Tests with Answer Explanations

PART 1

The Path to Opportunity

Chapter 1

Introduction

Welcome to the *Official SAT Study Guide*! Browse through the guide to gain a sense of the information in it, and begin marking sections that get your attention. This guide is designed for you. Return to it again and again in the coming weeks and months. Reading it is an excellent way to become familiar with the SAT — its content, structure, timing, question types, and more. The information, advice, and sample questions will help you prepare to take the test with confidence.

New and important undertakings put most of us on edge — at least a little — and raise our adrenaline. This happens whether it's an audition or the first day in a new school. But if we feel prepared for the adventure, we can use that adrenaline rush for a focused energy boost.

Tackling new things makes most of us nervous, but when we can learn a great deal about a new situation in advance, we feel much more able to take a deep breath and meet the challenge. Learning about the SAT through this guide and trying out some timed sample tests will contribute to being well prepared when your test date arrives.

How Does the SAT® Measure Academic Achievement?

Questions on the SAT will not ask you to recall details of *Hamlet* or to simply find the answer to 11×11 or to name the capital of Nevada or the location of the Platte River. If you recall those facts, good for you, but the SAT will ask for something different. Instead of asking you to show what you've memorized, the questions invite you to exercise your thinking skills.

All of the learning you've done — from childhood to now — contributes to how you think, how your mind manages information. Even if you don't recall the details of a history or science lesson, the process of learning information and blending it with previously learned information is key to becoming a skilled thinker. A chef knows a half-teaspoon of salt just by looking. You're reading this page easily because you've had a lot of practice reading.

REMEMBER

The SAT isn't designed to assess how well you've memorized a large set of facts. Rather, the SAT assesses your ability to apply the knowledge and skills you'll need in college and career.

You also evaluate, analyze, and make assumptions all the time. We humans love to figure out puzzles, and finding our way through unfamiliar places or comprehending a text requires discovering a solution, just as playing Candy Crush or Sudoku does. It should be no surprise to discover that the best preparation for success on the SAT aligns with the learning you've done in your classes and perhaps in your extracurricular interests, too. If you've challenged yourself again and again with complex problems — whether in literature, programming, physics, or other domains — you've exercised your thinking skills, just as athletes exercise their muscles by running.

Who's Responsible for the SAT?

The SAT is developed by the College Board, a not-for-profit organization that was founded more than a century ago to expand access to higher education.

▶ Membership: Over 6,000 schools, colleges, and universities

▶ SAT: Administered 3.3 million times annually

The mission of the College Board is to connect students with the opportunities in higher education that they've earned through their own hard work. Each year, College Board programs and initiatives serve more than 7 million students and their parents, 24,000 high schools, and 3,800 colleges by assisting with:

▶ College and career readiness

▶ College admission and placement

▶ College recruitment

▶ Financial aid

▶ Scholarship and recognition programs

The best-known programs offered or delivered by the College Board are the SAT, the PSAT/NMSQT®, and the Advanced Placement Program® (AP®).

How Is the SAT Developed?

The process of developing a test given to students around the world is complex and involves many people. Test developers are content experts who majored in physics, biology, statistics, math, English, history, computer science, sociology, education, psychology, and other disciplines. Their goals are to craft questions — and answer choices — that allow students to demonstrate their best thinking. The people who work on the SAT are not only content experts, but most have also been classroom teachers. A majority of the test developers took the SAT themselves when they were in high school. So in addition to all of the knowledge they've gained since taking the test, they share the experience of preparing for, being anxious about, and then taking the SAT. It's part of the knowledge they bring to test development now.

Many other experts are involved in the development of SAT test questions. Committees of high school and college instructors review every question to ensure that each one measures important knowledge, skills, and understandings; that the questions are fair to all students; and that they're written in a way that models what students are learning in the best high school classrooms.

Good standardized test development links scores and test questions to actual outcomes. In other words, because the SAT is developed according to rigorous specifications and assesses the content that matters most for college and career readiness and success, test results provide meaningful information about a student's readiness for and likelihood of succeeding in college. And, of course, that is the information that colleges seek. After all, they want to admit students who will have successful college experiences and successful careers. Everyone knows that the SAT gives colleges one indicator of college readiness and success; other factors that colleges typically consider include grade point average (GPA), class standing, extracurricular activities, and traits that are hard to measure, such as grit and perseverance. Independent research demonstrates that the single most important factor for demonstrating college readiness is high school GPA. Even more predictive than GPA, though, is GPA combined with an SAT score. That's why colleges often require SAT (or ACT) scores, since the scores help them gauge your readiness for and likelihood of succeeding at their school.

Why Has the SAT Changed?

The world needs more people who can solve problems, communicate clearly, and understand complex relationships — whether those relationships involve nations, cells, futures markets, or novels. Recent research has revealed that far too few students are fully prepared to participate in careers that require such skills.

The goal of strengthening education in the United States and around the world inspired the College Board to align the SAT with the latest research about what students need in order to succeed after high school. The changes in the SAT are intended to provide a better, more complete picture of student readiness for college-level work while focusing the test more clearly on the knowledge, skills, and understandings that research shows are essential for college and career readiness and success. In addition, by reflecting the relevant, focused, engaging, and rigorous work offered in the best high school courses taught today, the redesigned SAT creates a stronger bond between the assessment and what students are learning in their classrooms.

While research is ongoing, we believe that the redesign of the SAT meets these goals while maintaining the test's traditional value as a predictor of readiness for success in college and career.

 **REMEMBER**

The SAT has been carefully crafted by many people, experts in their fields, to ensure that it's a fair test that assesses the knowledge and skills you'll need to succeed in college and career.

REMEMBER

Colleges care about your SAT score because it's a strong predictor of how you'll perform in college. By doing well on the SAT, you can show colleges that you're ready to succeed.

REMEMBER

The redesigned SAT is more closely aligned with the knowledge and skills that are taught in high school classes around the country.

How Is the Test Organized?

The redesigned SAT has four tests, with the Essay being optional. The three tests that everyone will take are (1) the Reading Test, (2) the Writing and Language Test, and (3) the Math Test. The breakdown is structured as follows:

Component	Time Allotted (min.)	Number of Questions/ Tasks
Reading	65	52
Writing and Language	35	44
Essay (optional)	50	1
Math	80	58
Total	180 (230 with Essay)	154 (155 with Essay)

The Essay, which formerly lasted 25 minutes, now lasts 50 minutes; the longer period reflects the fact that the task is different from what it used to be. You'll be asked to read a passage and to write an analysis of what you've read, which will require more time. Some high schools and colleges require the Essay, and some don't. Depending on your high school and your college choice, you may already know whether or not you will take the Essay. If you have any uncertainty — for instance, if you can imagine that you might transfer from a school that doesn't require it to one that does — consider taking the SAT with Essay. Then you won't have to make arrangements to take it later.

How Is the Test Scored?

As you know, numbers often represent information in a straightforward manner, but we need context to give meaning to those numbers. When we see 32 degrees Fahrenheit, we may think "water freezes," but if the topic is seawater, we need a different number. Similarly, SAT test results show scores (numbers) in different contexts; several of the scores describe the same parts of the test in different ways or combinations, as explained below.

SECTION SCORES AND TOTAL SCORE

The redesigned SAT includes two section scores: (1) Evidence-Based Reading and Writing, which combines the results on the Reading Test and the Writing and Language Test, and (2) Math, which is derived from the results on the Math Test's calculator and no-calculator portions. Each of the two section scores will be reported on a scale ranging from 200 to 800. The scores for the Essay will be reported separately and will not be factored into the section scores.

The total score is the best-known number attached to the SAT. Your total score will range from 400 to 1600 and will be the sum of your scores on the

REMEMBER

Thoroughly research schools you're interested in before deciding whether to sign up for the Essay.

REMEMBER

You'll receive two section scores — Evidence-Based Reading and Writing and Math — which are each reported on a scale ranging from 200 to 800. Together, these two scores make up your total score. Your scores on the optional Essay are reported separately.

two sections of the SAT: the Evidence-Based Reading and Writing section and the Math section (discussed above).

TEST SCORES

In addition to the total score and section scores, the redesigned SAT reports three test scores that range from 10 to 40. Those scores reflect your achievement in the following:

1. Reading Test

2. Writing and Language Test

3. Math Test

Each test score is determined by adding up the number of questions you answered correctly on that test and then converting that to a scaled score of 10 to 40. Because different questions are asked every time the SAT is administered, a scaled score is determined so that student performance can be compared across test dates. If you take the optional Essay, you'll receive three separate Essay scores: Reading, Analysis, and Writing.

CROSS-TEST SCORES

Within each of the tests that make up the SAT, some questions require analysis grounded in history/social studies and science contexts. Your responses will illustrate your ability to apply analytical thinking — by using reading, writing, language, and math skills — to texts and problems in these subject areas. Results on these questions contribute to two cross-test scores:

1. Analysis in History/Social Studies

2. Analysis in Science

Each cross-test score is reported on a 10 to 40 scale.

SUBSCORES

Just as your responses to certain questions contribute to the cross-test scores described above, your responses to various questions also contribute to seven subscores, which provide even more detail about your achievement. Responses to select questions on the Reading and the Writing and Language Tests contribute to the following subscores:

1. Command of Evidence

2. Words in Context

Responses to questions on the Writing and Language Test also contribute to the following subscores:

1. Expression of Ideas

2. Standard English Conventions

 **REMEMBER**

Test scores will reflect your performance on each of the three required tests on the SAT. The three different Essay scores serve a similar role.

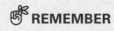 **REMEMBER**

Subscores provide additional insights into your performance on specific topics and skills.

Responses to select questions on the Math Test contribute to three subscores:

1. Heart of Algebra

2. Problem Solving and Data Analysis

3. Passport to Advanced Math

Each subscore is reported on a 1 to 15 scale.

The SAT Score Report

You'll be able to access all of your scores online through your free College Board account. This account will be the same one you use to register for the SAT. Learn more at sat.org.

SCORE RANGE

In addition to the scores described above, the SAT Score Report includes a score range for each score. This range indicates where your scores would likely fall if you took the test several times within a short period of time (for instance, on three consecutive days). If you were to do that, you would see numbers that differ, but not by much.

PERCENTILES

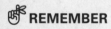

REMEMBER

Your percentile rank indicates the percentage of test-takers who scored at or below your score.

Your SAT Score Report includes the percentile rank for each score and subscore. As you may know, percentile ranks are a way of comparing scores in a particular group. For the SAT, separate percentile ranks are reported based on your state and on the total group of test-takers. Each percentile rank can range from 1 to 99 and indicates the percentage of test-takers who attained a score equal to or lower than yours. For instance, a perfect total score of 1600 would have a percentile rank of 99, meaning that 99 percent of people taking the test achieved a 1600 or lower score. A percentile rank of 50 means that half of students taking the test scored at or below your score.

ONLINE SCORE REPORT

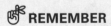

REMEMBER

You'll be able to access your online score report through your free College Board account. This report will give you a detailed breakdown of your performance.

This Web-based report gives you the meaning behind your numbers by providing a summary of how you did on each section with how many answers you got right, got wrong, or omitted. The tool offers insight into your strengths and weaknesses by showing your results grouped by content area and level of difficulty. The SAT Online Score Report provides other information as well:

▶   Percentiles to help you see how your results compare with those of other students like you

▶   A search tool for career and college majors, with suggestions based on information you provide in your profile

▶   If you completed the Essay, a scanned copy of your response and the question

Being able to review your response to the Essay gives you an opportunity to reconsider how well you understood the passage, the effectiveness of your analysis, and the quality of your writing. You can reflect on whether your points were clear, how well you provided support for your points, and how effectively you structured your essay. Reading a passage and writing an essay under time pressure are not easy tasks. Reviewing your essay to assess what was effective and what could've been more effective will serve you well. Each essay written under pressure provides good practice in composing your thoughts and writing under time constraints.

Additional Services

When you register for the SAT, you'll be able to choose reports and services that will be helpful in a number of ways. Review the types and availability so that you can decide which ones you want. Depending on which date you test on, there are different options for receiving detailed feedback on the questions from your test. Browse through the types of information that each of the following reports and services offers you.

ADDITIONAL SCORE REPORTS

Registering for the SAT allows you to send your results to up to four institutions; you can identify these institutions within nine days of taking the test. Take advantage of all four score reports, whether you send them to colleges or to scholarship sites. Sending your scores to colleges and universities early in the college application process is a great way to show your interest. Use your online account to order additional score reports.

SCORE CHOICE™

If you take the SAT more than once, you can utilize the Score Choice service. Score Choice allows you to select which score, by test date (or by test for SAT Subject Tests™), to send to your chosen colleges, in accordance with each institution's individual score use practices. Note that this service is optional. If you do not select Score Choice when registering, all of your scores will be sent to institutions receiving your results. Colleges consider your best scores when they review your application, so having them all sent will not have a negative impact. However, if you want only the top numbers to be seen, you should elect Score Choice.

Each school or program has its own deadlines and policies for how scores are used. Information is listed on the Score Choice site for each participating institution, but check with the individual school or scholarship program to make sure you're following its guidelines.

Note that you cannot select one section score from one test date and another section score from another date. (For example, you won't be able to send your Evidence-Based Reading and Writing score from one date and your Math score from a different date.) Also, if you took the SAT with Essay, you won't be able to send a score without the Essay scores as well.

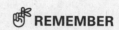 **REMEMBER**

Within nine days of taking the test, you can decide to have your SAT results sent, free of charge, to four institutions.

REMEMBER

The Score Choice service allows you to select which score (by test date) to send to your chosen colleges. Keep in mind, however, that you can't choose to submit specific section scores or subscores from different test dates.

If you haven't selected to have any scores mailed by the customary college application deadlines, the SAT site will send you an email reminder.

STUDENT ANSWER VERIFICATION SERVICES

The SAT Program offers two answer verification services for the SAT. (These services aren't available for SAT Subject Tests.) These services are intended to help you feel comfortable that your test was scored accurately by providing information about the types of questions and their content as well as how you answered them. Depending on when and where you take the SAT, you can either order the Student Answer Service (SAS) or the Question-and-Answer Service (QAS). You can order the services when you register for the SAT or up to five months after your test date.

Both SAS and QAS tell you which questions you answered correctly, which ones you didn't answer correctly, and which ones you didn't answer. You'll see information about the type of questions and the associated content. QAS provides additional information, including the actual test questions themselves. The Essay prompt will only be released as part of the Question and Answer Service.

STUDENT SEARCH SERVICE®

All students who take the SAT, the PSAT/NMSQT, PSAT 10, or any AP Exam are eligible to opt into this service, which helps colleges and scholarship recognition organizations find you. If you sign up during registration, your name and contact information, plus your GPA, date of birth, grade level, high school, e-mail address, extracurricular activities, and intended college major, will all be put into a database that colleges and scholarship programs use when they want to locate and recruit students with particular characteristics or interests.

Please note:

▶ Joining the Student Search Service is voluntary.

▶ Colleges that participate in the program don't receive your scores as part of their membership. They may request information about students whose scores lie in a particular range, but your scores will not be provided through this service.

▶ Colleges that may contact you are doing so to invite you to apply. Going through the application process is the only way to be admitted to a college. Colleges use the service to locate potential students who may not have thought to apply there.

▶ The Student Search Service is restricted to colleges, universities, and scholarship programs that sign up. Your information will never be sold to a commercial marketing firm or retailer of merchandise or services (such as a test preparation company).

☞ **REMEMBER**

Enrolling in the optional Student Search Service allows colleges and scholarship programs to contact you to invite you to apply.

INCREASING ACCESS TO THE SAT WITH FEE WAIVERS

Students who are the first in their families to consider attending college, who come from low-income families, or whose ethnicities are underrepresented in colleges may feel that college isn't for them. The College Board is committed to identifying and breaking down barriers that prevent such students from applying to and enrolling in colleges that are the best academic, social, and financial fit. Visit youcango.collegeboard.org for more information about ways to achieve your dreams.

Students who face financial barriers to taking the SAT can be granted College Board fee waivers through schools and authorized community-based organizations to cover the cost of testing. Seniors who use a fee waiver to take the SAT will automatically receive four college application fee waivers to use in applying to colleges and universities that accept the waivers. You can learn about eligibility and the other benefits offered to help you in the college application process at sat.org/fee-waivers.

REMEMBER

Visit sat.org/fee-waivers to learn more about SAT fee waivers as well as college application fee waivers.

Time to Get Started

Want to know the difference between "good" test-takers and "bad" test-takers? It's not biochemical or genetic. Successful test-takers understand that the SAT is a unique opportunity to demonstrate readiness for college and career success. They approach the SAT as an opportunity, not a hurdle, confident that with the right amount of practice they can achieve a strong outcome. In this way, taking the SAT increases the opportunities you have in your life.

Increasing opportunity is at the heart of the College Board's work with Khan Academy®. Beyond sharing the detailed test plans with Khan Academy, College Board's test developers are reviewing every SAT-like item that appears within Khan Academy's program and are providing in-depth feedback on Khan Academy practice tests. This means that time spent on Khan Academy practicing for the SAT is like having a sneak peak at what you'll see on test day. College Board test developers helped train Khan Academy's content experts in how to develop test questions like those that appear on the SAT and provide ongoing guidance and support of Khan Academy's practice test content. And it's all free for you.

As you learn more about the SAT from this guide, you should also use the resources and practice available on Khan Academy at khanacademy.org/sat to refresh and improve your skills. On the Khan Academy site, you will receive personalized guidance and instruction that is focused specifically for you.

Throughout this guide you'll see a lot of references to "practice" where you may be used to seeing "test prep." That's intentional. The redesigned SAT, PSAT/NMSQT and PSAT 10, and the new PSAT 8/9 focus on what matters most for college and career readiness. The act of preparing for the SAT, therefore, is not just a one-time hurdle that must be overcome, but part of a deep engagement in improving your fluency with mathematics, literacy, and other skills that will serve you well in college, career, and life.

As you embark on this important transition in your life, we ask that you commit yourself to a growth mindset that will help you improve your performance and your results. Colleges are looking for students like you. The SAT is a major tool that they use to find you. Commit yourself to the kind of productive practice that will earn you a strong SAT score and increased options for the next step in your journey.

Congratulations on taking this important step.

Chapter 2
Eight Key Changes to the SAT

This chapter describes the major changes in the SAT that make it more focused and useful than ever before. You may not have taken the SAT before the changes, but it's still worth knowing about the key design decisions that went into creating the test. The redesigned SAT, which parallels changes in the PSAT/NMSQT and PSAT™ 10 and the new PSAT™ 8/9, tests the few things that research shows have strong connections to college and career readiness and success. The eight key changes are described below.

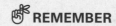 Relevant Words in Context

Rather than testing you on seldom-used words and phrases in very limited contexts (say, a sentence or two), the redesigned SAT will test your understanding of relevant words and phrases, the precise meanings of which largely depend on how they're used in the passages in which they appear. By "relevant" we mean that the words and phrases you'll be tested on aren't the kinds you'd see only on a test such as the SAT. Instead, they're representative of the language used in college and careers, the kind of vocabulary that you'll use throughout your life — in high school, college, and beyond.

As people advance through school, their vocabulary expands. Some of this expansion comes in the form of new words and phrases important to particular courses. You might, for example, learn in a biology class that "gorse" is a European shrub or that a "philtrum" is that shallow little valley from the bottom of your nose to the top of your upper lip. Not all of your vocabulary growth will come in the form of specialized terms, however. More important is a growing understanding of words and phrases that are found in many kinds of course readings — from literature to history to science — that are key to unlocking the meaning of those texts. It's just this sort of vocabulary — words and phrases such as "channeled," "intense," and "departed from" — that's assessed on the redesigned SAT.

On the test, you may encounter words or phrases that are new to you. Don't worry. The passages containing those words and phrases will provide

> **REMEMBER**
>
> The redesigned SAT won't test you on the meaning of obscure, seldom-used words and phrases presented with little context. Rather, you'll be tested on contextually based words and phrases that often appear in college courses and beyond.

REMEMBER

If you encounter words or phrases that you're not familiar with on the SAT, use the many context clues in the passage to help you develop a general sense of what the word or phrase means.

important clues to their meaning. In some cases, you may see familiar words and phrases used in ways that are different from how you might normally use them. Take the word "husband." Most people think of a husband as a marriage partner, but "husband" can also be used as a verb that means to use carefully or in a limited way, as in "Salina asked her friend to husband the supplies so that they would not run out." Here, too, context provides a critical clue to meaning even if you'd never heard of "husband" being used in this way. Note that "husband" in the "use carefully" sense might show up in practically any kind of text, making this word (and this meaning) valuable to know. It's just this sort of word that's become the focus of vocabulary-related questions on the redesigned SAT.

≣Q Command of Evidence

"Showing command of evidence" is probably not how you describe what you do when you write a research paper, but it's a good description nonetheless. When you demonstrate such command, you gather the best evidence to support your thesis or hypothesis; you interpret that evidence, putting it into your own words or quoting selectively from sources; and you consider the kinds of questions and criticisms that your audience is likely to have. This sort of process is what all writers do when they compose texts of any sort. Even writing stories follows a similar method, as authors have to figure out what scenes, characters, and details to use to further their goal for the narrative.

REMEMBER

Using evidence to craft an argument or defend your position is something you'll be asked to do repeatedly in college and career. That's why you'll be asked to demonstrate this skill on the SAT.

On the SAT, you'll be asked to consider these same kinds of issues as you read various passages. Which part of the passage provides the best textual evidence for a particular conclusion? Can the focus of a piece of writing be sharpened by getting rid of a detail that may be interesting but isn't particularly relevant? Has the writer accurately incorporated information from a graph into the text? These kinds of questions are key parts of what the College Board means by demonstrating command of evidence.

One common way that the SAT assesses your command of evidence on the Reading Test is by asking you to determine the best evidence for the answer to a previous question. After answering the first question in such a pair, you'll have to identify the part of the passage that provides the clearest support for the answer to the first question. Your options will usually come in the form of short quotations from the passage. While this sounds challenging — and it can be — it's a lot like what you'd normally do when a teacher asks you to explain your interpretation of a text. If you say, for example, that you thought two characters in a story strongly disliked each other, your teacher might well ask you to explain why you feel that way. To do that, you'd cite textual evidence, such as what a character says or the words the author uses to describe that character's attitude or actions. In this way, then, the SAT is really just asking you to do what you do all the time in your classes and to show that you've mastered a skill that is critical for success in your future postsecondary work.

📖 Essay Analyzing a Source

In the redesigned SAT, the Essay — which is now optional — is quite different from many other essay tests, including the one that was on the SAT from 2005 until January 2016. While many tests ask you to take and defend a position on an issue, the Essay portion of the redesigned SAT takes a different approach. You'll be presented with a passage and asked to explain how the author of that passage builds an argument to persuade an audience.

As you're reading the passage, you'll want to consider such things as how the author uses evidence (such as facts and examples) to support claims, reasoning to develop ideas and connect claims and evidence, and stylistic or persuasive elements (such as word choice or appeals to emotion) to add power to ideas. You may also find that the author uses other techniques in an attempt to persuade an audience; you're encouraged to write about those as well. When you write your response, you'll want to focus on those techniques that are the most important to making that passage persuasive. If the author doesn't use a lot of facts and figures, for instance, you'll want to talk about what the author does instead, such as attempt to appeal to the audience's feelings of pity or sense of duty. It's your choice what to focus on, but however you develop your essay, it should demonstrate that you understand how the author puts his or her text together.

To give this another name, you'll be performing a rhetorical analysis of a passage, explaining how the passage "works" as a piece of writing. Rhetorical analysis is different from summary, where you simply restate in your own words what an author has written. Rhetorical analysis is also different from taking a position on an issue. While the author will argue a case, it's not your job to explain whether you agree or disagree. (The test directions remind you of this.) Instead, you are to explain what the author is doing and why, and how the writerly techniques the author is using attempt to persuade the audience. Responses that just summarize the passage or that simply take one side on an issue won't receive the best scores.

Speaking of scores, the Essay has three of them: Reading, Analysis, and Writing. Each score is on a 2 to 8 scale, and the scores aren't combined together or blended with other scores on the SAT. Your Reading score tells you how well you did in showing that you understood the passage; you can show that understanding by doing such things as discussing the passage's central ideas and important details and selectively quoting or paraphrasing from the passage. Your Analysis score reflects how effectively you explained how the author builds an argument to persuade an audience. Your Writing score describes how effective your essay was as a piece of writing in terms of such things as organization, word choice, grammar, usage, and mechanics. One great thing about getting three scores instead of one (as on the previous SAT Essay) is that this more clearly rewards you for what you've done well and identifies areas that might need work. If, for example, you get a high

👉 REMEMBER

Your task on the redesigned SAT Essay is quite different from tasks directing many essays you've been asked to write before. Rather than developing your own persuasive argument, you'll be asked to analyze how another author builds an argument to persuade an audience.

👉 REMEMBER

Your response on the Essay should neither simply summarize the argument presented nor present your opinion on an issue. Rather, your response should focus primarily on analyzing the techniques the author uses to persuade an audience.

score in Reading and Writing but a low score in Analysis, you showed that you understood what you read and could write about it effectively but struggled with examining the passage rhetorically.

One other important feature of the redesigned Essay is that the task you'll be presented with is the same every time. You'll always be asked to consider how an author builds an argument to persuade an audience. That's it. Only the passage and a sentence in the prompt describing that passage change on each administration of the SAT. No more trying to guess what the College Board is going to ask this time around — which makes preparing for the test that much easier. Because the redesigned Essay includes a reading and requires careful analysis of that text, the time limit has gone up to 50 minutes (from the previous 25 minutes) to give you adequate time for your response.

⧉ Focus on Math that Matters Most

The SAT Math Test focuses on three areas where numbers help us to manage and understand the world. The questions in Problem Solving and Data Analysis are grounded in daily situations that many of us are familiar with. Percentages (who pays which portion of a meal at a restaurant), ratios (how much additional paint is needed if half a quart covered one wall of your bedroom), and proportional reasoning are all part of a repertoire of basic math strategies for solving problems in science, social studies, careers, and life.

For example, when a natural disaster occurs, professionals immediately begin gathering information — data — about the number of roads open, people stranded, helicopters available, supplies needed, emergency responders on call, and more. Analyzing the conditions that impact an area because of a natural calamity helps workers learn more and improves their capabilities in future disasters. Each person's story is important, but it's the numbers taken together that help relief agencies and government officials make the decisions that will help the most people as quickly as possible. (Perhaps it's occurred to you that this description offers a mathematical version of demonstrating command of evidence, as discussed previously. What we do with numbers and with words isn't as different as many people think.)

The second area in math covered on the SAT is Heart of Algebra. As you might guess, the goal is mastery of linear equations and systems. This mastery is part of developing your skill in thinking abstractly. You've been building this capacity since infancy as you worked with symbols. A smile is a well-known symbol, as is a nod. You learned to read, and your skills with abstract symbols grew by leaps and bounds. Take the word "chair." It's composed of curves, straight lines, and a dot. It stands for a physical chair, but it's a constructed abstract representation. If you have a friend or relative who knows another form of writing besides the English alphabet, ask him or her to write "chair" and see how the two representations compare. As you know, math, like language, relies on symbols to create relationships.

☞ **REMEMBER**

The redesigned SAT Math Test focuses on the topics that research has shown matter most for college and career readiness and success.

☞ **REMEMBER**

The Math Test emphasizes the application of essential math skills to real-world situations and problems.

Becoming skilled in linear equations and systems gives you practice in thinking abstractly — how things relate or don't relate. Such abstract thinking as is routinely called on when solving problems in algebra is another important element of becoming prepared to succeed in college and career.

The final area covered on the SAT is Passport to Advanced Math. Questions of this sort will test your skill in managing more complex equations.

Although there are only three subscore areas in the Math Test (Problem Solving and Data Analysis, Heart of Algebra, and Passport to Advanced Math), there are actually four areas covered in total. Geometry and trigonometry are addressed under the heading of Additional Topics in Math.

Problems Grounded in Real-World Contexts

Throughout the redesigned SAT, you'll engage with questions grounded in the real world, questions directly related to the work performed in college and career.

In the Evidence-Based Reading and Writing section, the Reading Test will include literature and literary nonfiction, but also feature readings and graphics like ones you're likely to encounter in science and social science courses and in various majors and careers. On the Writing and Language Test, you'll be asked to do more than identify errors; you'll revise and edit to improve texts on career-related topics and in the subject areas of history/social studies, the humanities, and science.

Included on the Math Test are a number of questions situated in science, social science, career, and other real-world scenarios. Some of these questions are discrete, meaning that they're independent of the other questions on the test, while others will be grouped in small sets, with each set's questions based in a common context. Some real-world questions are application problems that require you to perform multiple steps to reach the correct solution — problems that ask you to dig in, think through and carry out a sequence of tasks, and model a situation mathematically.

REMEMBER

You'll be asked to analyze and interpret informational graphics such as tables, graphs, and charts on the SAT, as these skills are essential in college, career, and everyday life.

Analysis in History/Social Studies and in Science

The SAT has always included a range of different passages and questions, but the redesigned SAT has a sharper and more consistent focus on two important areas of study: history/social studies and science. Although you may not always notice them because they're not marked as such, questions on history/social studies and science topics can be found throughout the Reading, Writing and Language, and Math Tests of the redesigned SAT.

REMEMBER

While you won't be tested on history/social studies or science facts on the SAT, you will be asked to apply skills you should have learned in these classes, like identifying a researcher's conclusion.

It's important to note that these questions don't ask you to provide history/social studies or science facts, such as the year the Battle of Hastings was fought or the chemical formula for a particular molecule. Instead, these questions ask you to apply the knowledge and skills that you should have picked up in your history, social studies, and science courses to problems in reading, writing, language, and math. On the Reading Test, for example, you'll be given two history/social studies and two science passages to analyze. You might be asked to identify the conclusion a researcher drew or the evidence used to support that conclusion. On the Writing and Language Test, you could be asked to revise a passage to incorporate data from a table into the writer's description of the results of an experiment. On the Math Test, some questions will ask you to solve problems grounded in social studies or science contexts. Your scores in Analysis in History/Social Studies and in Analysis in Science, which are drawn from questions on all three of those tests, will help you see how well you're doing in these areas and whether you need additional practice.

U.S. Founding Documents and the Great Global Conversation

The founding documents of the United States, including the Declaration of Independence, the Bill of Rights, and the Federalist Papers, continue to influence discussions and debates about the nature of civic life and of individual and collective rights and responsibilities. We see this not only in the speeches of politicians and the decisions of members of the judiciary but also in literature and popular culture. The ideas articulated centuries ago by the U.S. founders have, over time, mingled with and been enriched by those of more recent authors from the United States and across the globe. The writings of people such as Mahatma Gandhi, Mary Wollstonecraft, and Edmund Burke have both broadened and deepened the conversation around the central question of how we are all to live together.

These founding documents and texts in the Great Global Conversation often do present some challenges for the reader. The vocabulary is often elevated, the sentences can be long and involved, and the ideas discussed are often more abstract than we're used to dealing with on a daily basis. The rewards of a close reading of these texts, though, are significant, as we exercise the privilege of engaging with some of the most important and influential works ever written.

The SAT Reading Test includes a passage from either a U.S. founding document or a text in the Great Global Conversation. The questions will ask you to think about such things as the author's main points, word choice, and persuasive techniques. Although your appreciation for the text may be increased if you've read it before, the questions don't assume that you have.

Everything you need to know to answer the questions can be found in the passage itself or in supplementary material, such as an explanatory note.

☺ No Penalty for Wrong Answers

In the past, the SAT gave a point for each correct answer and took away a quarter of a point for each incorrect answer to a multiple-choice question. The decision to eliminate the penalty for wrong answers was made to encourage you to try your best on all questions, even ones you're not sure of the answer to, without the added pressure of having to decide whether it would be best to take the risk and possibly lose a fraction of a point for an incorrect answer.

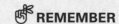 **REMEMBER**

Since there's no penalty for wrong answers, you should answer every question on the SAT. Never leave a question blank!

Chapter 3

Read This! Keys to Doing Your Best on the SAT

If you're like most test-takers, you see the SAT as an important exam, one that can have a big impact on your future. It's only natural, then, that you want to prepare for it as well as you can. Presumably that's why you're reading this book right now. You may be thinking that getting ready for the SAT is some kind of mysterious process that has little or nothing to do with what you've been learning in school. Maybe you've heard that the SAT is an aptitude test — a test of how well you can learn, not what you already know. Or maybe someone told you that the SAT is like an IQ test.

It's true that the "A" in "SAT" used to stand for "aptitude," but for many years now, the SAT has been what's called an achievement test — a test of how well you've mastered important knowledge and skills. The SAT is, in short, a test about what you've learned in school. It's a test you can — and should — prepare for. That still leaves the question of how best to prepare.

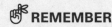 **REMEMBER**

The SAT is an achievement test rather than an aptitude test. You can improve your score on this test by practicing for it!

This chapter offers some ideas about that. The information is divided into three main chunks:

▶ Helping you develop the knowledge and skills measured on the test

▶ Identifying ways that you can familiarize yourself with the test itself

▶ Discussing some things to do (and not do) on test day

All three areas are important. Even if you have a strong grasp of the content included on the test, you still can benefit from becoming familiar with the test format and picking up some test day strategies.

This chapter covers the following topics:

Building Important Knowledge and Skills Measured on the SAT

▶ The big key: working hard in school

▶ Reading and vocabulary

▶ Writing and language

▶ Creating a personalized study plan through Khan Academy

Getting Familiar with the SAT

▶ Practicing: it can make a difference

▶ Understanding the test directions

▶ Getting to know the test question formats

▶ Taking the PSAT/NMSQT® or PSAT™ 10

▶ Using sample SAT questions and tests

▶ Exploring other resources

— Online Score Report

— The College Board on social media

Test Day and Beyond

▶ Counting down to the test

▶ Readying yourself the day before the test

▶ What to pack

▶ What NOT to pack

▶ Avoiding problems on test day

▶ Using good test-taking strategies

▶ Dealing with nerves and distractions

▶ Taking the test again?

Building Important Knowledge and Skills Measured on the SAT

THE BIG KEY: WORKING HARD IN SCHOOL

The SAT has had a reputation for testing students on obscure bits of knowledge, the kinds of things you'd find on the SAT and nowhere else. This has fed into a perception that the way to do well is to learn things specifically for the SAT. One of the most important goals in the redesign of the SAT has been to change that perception by making what's on the test more clearly reflect what's being taught in the best high school classrooms in the country and what's needed to be ready for and to succeed in college and workforce training programs.

This means that, more than ever before, the best way to prepare for the SAT is as simple and as difficult as working hard in high school: taking challenging courses, diligently doing your homework, carefully preparing for tests and quizzes, asking and answering lots of questions . . . in short, learning as much as you can. In a very real sense, preparing for the SAT is something you do every day in school as part of your regular course work. Because what's on the redesigned SAT is a good reflection of rigorous curricula, the hard work you put into your studies is likely to yield strong results on the test.

READING AND VOCABULARY

You've been reading for many years, of course, but being able to read well enough to be ready to succeed in college and career (and, not coincidentally, to do well on the SAT) requires both a range of skills and the ability to apply them to challenging texts in a wide range of subjects.

In terms of skills, you'll need to be able to determine both what's stated and what's implied in a text. Authors often make information and ideas explicit by stating them directly. Some questions on the SAT will ask you to locate a piece of information or an idea presented in such a way. Often, though, authors are more subtle, requiring readers to make reasonable inferences or to draw logical conclusions on their own to reach a deeper level of meaning or just to follow the author's train of thought. Some SAT questions will ask you to work out the implications of a text by using what's made clear by an author to figure out suggested meanings. You'll also work with stated and implied information and ideas when the SAT presents you with a pair of related passages and asks you to make connections between them.

Reading skills are obviously important, but they're not enough by themselves. It's also critical to be able to apply those skills to the kinds of readings you're likely to see in college or workforce training programs (and in many challenging high school classes such as AP courses). The more complex texts you'll see in high school and postsecondary courses will often contain uncommon vocabulary, use sophisticated sentence structures, present large amounts of information and ideas quickly, discuss abstract ideas (such as justice or duty),

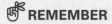
REMEMBER

The best way to prepare for the SAT is to work hard in school. The SAT has been designed to reflect what you're being taught in school, as well as the skills and knowledge you need to succeed in college and workforce training programs.

PRACTICE AT

khanacademy.org/sat

Throughout this book you'll see notes like this one that give you specific ideas on how to improve your SAT score. To learn more about College Board's partnership with Khan Academy and what it means for your success on the SAT, go to khanacademy.org/sat.

PRACTICE AT

khanacademy.org/sat

SAT passages are drawn from high-quality, previously published sources in the subject areas of U.S. and world literature, history/social studies, and science. Practice reading and analyzing essays or articles from each of these areas to prepare yourself for the SAT.

and identify subtle or complex relationships among concepts. Because these types of readings are going to be required in your earliest classes post-high school, you'll also see complex texts included in each SAT. Not all passages on the SAT are that difficult, but you should be ready to use your reading skills to draw out meaning from them when they appear.

Although the redesigned SAT doesn't have a vocabulary section, the test does assess your knowledge of and skill with words and phrases in numerous ways. On the Reading Test, you'll be asked to figure out the precise meaning of words and phrases as they are used in particular passages. Generally, these words and phrases will have more than one dictionary-type meaning, and you'll have to use context clues (and possibly other word knowledge, such as an understanding of common prefixes and suffixes) to determine exactly what the tested word or phrase means in a given passage. Both the Writing and Language Test and the optional Essay assess whether you're able to use words and phrases appropriately and precisely. On the Writing and Language Test, for example, you might be asked to choose from among four words or phrases the one that expresses an idea most clearly or that best accomplishes a given goal, such as evoking a particular mood or tone.

PRACTICE TIP

Read one essay or article each week in an online or print publication that's new to you. Ask your teachers, parents, or school or public librarian for ideas. If you can print the essay or make a copy, then you'll be able to mark it up. Read it once for the overall sense of the piece. The second time, read it more slowly or in chunks, and examine the language and the structure. Why did the author present the evidence in the way he or she did? What viewpoint was taken, and why do you think the author chose that one instead of another one?

Read the chapters later in the book on reading (8 to 12), and then review this practice tip again to imagine the ways that you can improve your reading skills.

WRITING AND LANGUAGE

Writing is a central component of your post–high school future. As with reading, effective writing is about more than just developing skills, although that's clearly essential. You must also learn to use writing to accomplish various tasks and purposes for different audiences; to write under varied conditions, including timed writing; and to take your writing through multiple phases.

The SAT divides the skills assessed on the Writing and Language Test into two broad categories: Expression of Ideas and Standard English Conventions. Although there are other ways to divide writing and language skills, this approach draws attention to the fact that skilled writing involves both conveying information and ideas in an effective way and observing the conventions of standard written English to help ensure that the messages you're trying to send are received and understood as you intended. On the SAT, Expression of Ideas questions focus on topic development (matters such as support and focus), organization (matters such as introductions, conclusions, transitions, and logical sequence), and effective language use (matters such as precision, style, and tone). These questions focus on the content of writing, and when answering them, you must consider how a piece of writing could be improved in order to weed out extraneous material, create a smooth progression of ideas, and eliminate wordiness and redundancy, to name a few examples. Other questions deal with sentence structure, usage, and punctuation — elements of the conventions of standard written English. When answering these Standard English Conventions questions, typically you must recognize and correct errors (or figure out that no error has been made), drawing on your knowledge of language practices.

Your writing will also be evaluated should you choose to take the optional Essay Test. The Essay, in part, will be scored according to how well you've expressed and fleshed out your ideas and to what extent, if any, mistakes in applying standard written English conventions impair the quality of your expression.

Good writers are also able to tailor what they produce to particular tasks, purposes, and audiences. The Essay is the clearest example on the SAT of the importance of these considerations. To score well on this part of the exam, you not only have to read and write skillfully, but also create a response that's appropriate to the task of analyzing a source text for the purpose of explaining to a reader how an author tries to build an argument to persuade an audience. If you fail to appreciate the nature of the analytical task — by merely summarizing the source text, for instance, or by arguing for the rightness or wrongness of the author's position — your response won't receive a high score on the Essay's Analysis dimension.

Strong writers are also able to take the texts that they're working on through a flexible, sometimes recursive process that generally includes planning, drafting, revising, editing, and publishing (or at least sharing with a broader audience). While the SAT doesn't simulate all aspects of this process, you'll be expected to revise and edit text produced by others on the Writing and Language Test and to plan and draft text if you choose to take the Essay (although your planning won't be scored).

PERSONALIZED PRACTICE THROUGH KHAN ACADEMY

While a lot has changed about the SAT itself during its most recent redesign, just as important have been the College Board's efforts to bring world-class test practice to students everywhere — for free. Through the College Board's partnership with Khan Academy, you and your fellow test-takers have access not only to a wide range of practice materials, but also to Khan Academy's personalized study planning aimed at helping you acquire the knowledge and skills you need to do well on the test and, more importantly, in college and career.

Part of the reason the College Board decided on this partnership is the commitment of the founder of Khan Academy to sharing knowledge with the world. Before Salman Khan launched his nonprofit in 2008, he worked as a

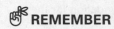 **REMEMBER**

The redesigned SAT Essay is optional for students. Some school districts and colleges, however, will require it. The Essay has been designed to mirror some of the kinds of work often required in college and career.

hedge fund analyst in Boston. At home, he made YouTube videos and online practice problems for his cousins in New Orleans to help them understand math. The videos gained a wide audience, Sal left the hedge fund to work on Khan Academy full-time, and now the website offers a wide variety of resources on many subjects for learners of all ages. From its initial focus on math, Khan Academy has branched out to include science, history, art, and more. In addition, Khan Academy has created brand-new resources in both math and reading and writing specifically to support practice for the redesigned SAT. Everything on the site, at all levels of learning, is free.

The partnership between the College Board and Khan Academy means you have more choices than ever before in terms of how you refresh or increase your knowledge and skills in various areas. On the Khan Academy website (khanacademy.org/sat), you'll find interactive practice materials that provide instant feedback and personalized recommendations. Start by importing your actual PSAT/NMSQT, PSAT 10, or SAT results into the Khan Academy system, and then learn exactly what you need to work on next. Maybe it's linear equations word problems or subject-verb agreement. The system will make personalized recommendations as you answer problems. As you grow in knowledge and confidence, you'll be able to take full-length practice tests and see your progress.

Getting Familiar with the SAT

PRACTICING: IT CAN MAKE A DIFFERENCE

As we hope we've made clear in the preceding sections, the single best way to prepare for the SAT is to evaluate and, where needed, improve your grasp of the important knowledge and skills included on the test. Doing so will mean more to you in the long run than any sort of test-taking strategy we or someone else could give you.

That said, there's still something to be gained from understanding how the SAT itself works and how you'll be tested. Reducing the mystery of the test is an important aim of this book and of the College Board more generally. We want the test to be about what you know and can do, not about your test-taking skills per se. By coming into test day with a solid understanding of what's on the exam, you'll be more comfortable with the format, better able to focus on the particular questions, and more certain that you'll do your absolute best in answering them.

UNDERSTANDING THE TEST DIRECTIONS

It's worth spending some time acquainting yourself with the directions for each portion of the SAT — and to do so before test day. By learning in advance what the directions say, you can minimize the amount of time you spend reading them on test day. Moreover, the directions give you important information about how to answer the questions, when a calculator is permitted or not permitted, and so on — all of which are important to informing your preparation.

PRACTICE AT

khanacademy.org/sat

By using the personalized practice on the Khan Academy website, you'll be able to focus on the skills likely to have the biggest impact on your performance, building a solid foundation for the SAT and beyond.

PRACTICE AT

khanacademy.org/sat

Know exactly what to expect on test day. By knowing how long the test is, when the breaks are scheduled, what formats the questions come in, what the test directions are, and how the test is scored, you won't have any surprises and will be able to focus on performing your best.

Reading Test

65 MINUTES, 52 QUESTIONS

Turn to Section 1 of your answer sheet to answer the questions in this section.

DIRECTIONS

Each passage or pair of passages below is followed by a number of questions. After reading each passage or pair, choose the best answer to each question based on what is stated or implied in the passage or passages and in any accompanying graphics (such as a table or graph).

Writing and Language Test

35 MINUTES, 44 QUESTIONS

Turn to Section 2 of your answer sheet to answer the questions in this section.

DIRECTIONS

Each passage below is accompanied by a number of questions. For some questions, you will consider how the passage might be revised to improve the expression of ideas. For other questions, you will consider how the passage might be edited to correct errors in sentence structure, usage, or punctuation. A passage or a question may be accompanied by one or more graphics (such as a table or graph) that you will consider as you make revising and editing decisions.

Some questions will direct you to an underlined portion of a passage. Other questions will direct you to a location in a passage or ask you to think about the passage as a whole.

After reading each passage, choose the answer to each question that most effectively improves the quality of writing in the passage or that makes the passage conform to the conventions of standard written English. Many questions include a "NO CHANGE" option. Choose that option if you think the best choice is to leave the relevant portion of the passage as it is.

Math Test – No Calculator

25 MINUTES, 20 QUESTIONS

Turn to Section 3 of your answer sheet to answer the questions in this section.

DIRECTIONS

For questions 1-15, solve each problem, choose the best answer from the choices provided, and fill in the corresponding circle on your answer sheet. **For questions 16-20,** solve the problem and enter your answer in the grid on the answer sheet. Please refer to the directions before question 16 on how to enter your answers in the grid. You may use any available space in your test booklet for scratch work.

NOTES

1. The use of a calculator **is not permitted**.

2. All variables and expressions used represent real numbers unless otherwise indicated.

3. Figures provided in this test are drawn to scale unless otherwise indicated.

4. All figures lie in a plane unless otherwise indicated.

5. Unless otherwise indicated, the domain of a given function f is the set of all real numbers x for which $f(x)$ is a real number.

REFERENCE

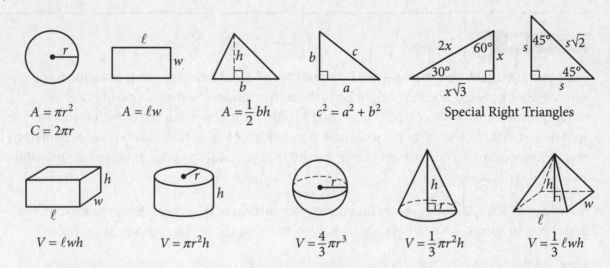

$A = \pi r^2$
$C = 2\pi r$

$A = \ell w$

$A = \dfrac{1}{2} bh$

$c^2 = a^2 + b^2$

Special Right Triangles

$V = \ell w h$

$V = \pi r^2 h$

$V = \dfrac{4}{3}\pi r^3$

$V = \dfrac{1}{3}\pi r^2 h$

$V = \dfrac{1}{3}\ell w h$

The number of degrees of arc in a circle is 360.
The number of radians of arc in a circle is 2π.
The sum of the measures in degrees of the angles of a triangle is 180.

Math Test – Calculator

55 MINUTES, 38 QUESTIONS

Turn to Section 4 of your answer sheet to answer the questions in this section.

DIRECTIONS

For questions 1-30, solve each problem, choose the best answer from the choices provided, and fill in the corresponding circle on your answer sheet. **For questions 31-38,** solve the problem and enter your answer in the grid on the answer sheet. Please refer to the directions before question 31 on how to enter your answers in the grid. You may use any available space in your test booklet for scratch work.

NOTES

1. The use of a calculator **is permitted**.

2. All variables and expressions used represent real numbers unless otherwise indicated.

3. Figures provided in this test are drawn to scale unless otherwise indicated.

4. All figures lie in a plane unless otherwise indicated.

5. Unless otherwise indicated, the domain of a given function f is the set of all real numbers x for which $f(x)$ is a real number.

REFERENCE

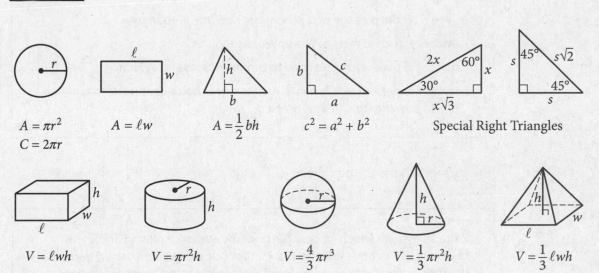

$A = \pi r^2$
$C = 2\pi r$

$A = \ell w$

$A = \frac{1}{2} bh$

$c^2 = a^2 + b^2$

Special Right Triangles

$V = \ell wh$

$V = \pi r^2 h$

$V = \frac{4}{3}\pi r^3$

$V = \frac{1}{3}\pi r^2 h$

$V = \frac{1}{3}\ell wh$

The number of degrees of arc in a circle is 360.
The number of radians of arc in a circle is 2π.
The sum of the measures in degrees of the angles of a triangle is 180.

Essay

DIRECTIONS

The essay gives you an opportunity to show how effectively you can read and comprehend a passage and write an essay analyzing the passage. In your essay, you should demonstrate that you have read the passage carefully, present a clear and logical analysis, and use language precisely.

Your essay must be written on the lines provided in your answer booklet; except for the Planning Page of the answer booklet, you will receive no other paper on which to write. You will have enough space if you write on every line, avoid wide margins, and keep your handwriting to a reasonable size. Remember that people who are not familiar with your handwriting will read what you write. Try to write or print so that what you are writing is legible to those readers.

You have <u>50 minutes</u> to read the passage and write an essay in response to the prompt provided inside this booklet.

REMINDERS:

— Do not write your essay in this booklet. Only what you write on the lined pages of your answer booklet will be evaluated.

— An off-topic essay will not be evaluated.

As you read the passage below, consider how [the author] uses

- evidence, such as facts or examples, to support claims.

- reasoning to develop ideas and to connect claims and evidence.

- stylistic or persuasive elements, such as word choice or appeals to emotion, to add power to the ideas expressed.

The passage follows the box above.

Write an essay in which you explain how [the author] builds an argument to persuade [his/her] audience that [author's claim]. In your essay, analyze how [the author] uses one or more of the features listed above (or features of your own choice) to strengthen the logic and persuasiveness of [his/her] argument. Be sure that your analysis focuses on the most relevant aspects of the passage.

Your essay should not explain whether you agree with [the author's] claims, but rather explain how the author builds an argument to persuade [his/her] audience.

GETTING TO KNOW THE TEST QUESTION FORMATS

In addition to understanding the test directions, you should also get a sense of how questions on the various sections of the test are asked. Doing so will help prevent surprises on test day and free you up to focus on the content rather than the format. For example, you'll want to become familiar with the two-column format and the underlined portions of text in the Writing and Language Test. For the Math Test, you'll definitely want to become familiar with the format of the student-produced response questions, or SPRs. For these questions, you won't have answer choices to select from. Rather, you must solve the problem and "grid" the answer you came up with on the answer sheet. Be sure to read through this book's information about the format of each test and work through the sample questions in Chapter 12 (the Reading Test), Chapter 16 (the Writing and Language Test), and Chapters 23 and 24 (the Math Test).

TAKING THE PSAT/NMSQT OR PSAT 10

Taking the PSAT/NMSQT has a number of benefits. Probably the best-known one is that the PSAT/NMSQT serves as the qualifying test for the National Merit Scholarship Program (hence the abbreviation "NMSQT"). But the test also gives you an early opportunity to take an exam very similar to the SAT and under similar conditions. While the PSAT/NMSQT test is a little shorter than the multiple-choice portion of the SAT, and the material is geared to high school sophomores and juniors, the PSAT/NMSQT covers the same broad subjects as the SAT and uses questions that are in the same general formats as those found on the SAT. (There is, however, no Essay on the PSAT/NMSQT.)

Note: Your school may also offer a test called the PSAT 10 in the spring in addition to the PSAT/NMSQT in the fall. The content is identical on both tests. The only important differences are the time of the year that the test is given and the fact that the PSAT 10 isn't associated with the National Merit Scholarship Program.

USING SAMPLE SAT QUESTIONS AND TESTS

The College Board and Khan Academy are making hundreds of sample SAT questions and numerous sample SAT tests available to test-takers for practice. By using these materials, along with other forms of preparation, you can familiarize yourself with the particular question formats you'll encounter on test day and identify areas of strength and weakness in your understanding of the knowledge and skills measured on the SAT.

In addition to the samples in this book and on the Khan Academy website, practice materials can be found at http://sat.org.

EXPLORING OTHER RESOURCES

Online Score Report

The introduction to this book described your Online Score Report. To view this report, you'll need to register for a free account if you haven't already done so. Registering gives you access to many services, including the opportunity to register for the SAT electronically. When you register for the SAT, you must upload a digital photo of yourself that will be printed on your admission ticket as a form of identification (so make sure it accurately represents how you'll look on test day).

The College Board on Social Media

The College Board uses a variety of social media to share information with students, teachers, parents, counselors, and others. To stay up-to-date on the latest SAT news and happenings, consider following one or more of our official Twitter accounts: @CollegeBoard, @OfficialSAT, and @SATQuestion. We also regularly update content on Facebook (facebook.com/thecollegeboard) and Instagram (@collegeboard). You can use these accounts and pages to ask questions about the SAT and other College Board programs and services.

Test Day and Beyond

COUNTING DOWN TO THE TEST

In the months and weeks leading up to test day, you'll probably spend a good amount of time preparing for the test: brushing up on old skills, developing new ones, going over sample questions and tests, and so on. In the days immediately preceding the test, you might want to consider taking a different approach by focusing on maintaining your physical health and readiness.

Do you exercise, do yoga, sing, or meditate? Carry on with those activities. If you don't exercise regularly and your physical condition permits, go someplace private and swing your arms, kick your legs, and breathe deeply. Jumping can be good, too. If you're alone, sing loudly! During the day, when you're sitting at a table or desk, take some deep, slow breaths. For your brain to function as well as it can, oxygen needs to flow easily and constantly.

Eat well in those preceding days, too. Think about cutting out the refined sugar, such as that found in sodas and many desserts. You won't want to radically change your breakfast habits, but you should also consider that on test day you'll be sitting at a desk and engaging in very little physical activity for the entire morning. Given that, it's probably not a good idea to overload on carbs (say, pancakes) or sugar (which makes up a large proportion of many packaged cold cereals). Consider protein, whether from cheese, fish, soy products, yogurt, nuts and nut butters, or eggs. Whole grains — oatmeal,

PRACTICE AT

khanacademy.org/sat

Resist the temptation to cram hours and hours of test preparation into those last few days before the SAT. Cramming has been shown to be an ineffective study technique and may lead to fatigue and increased anxiety.

brown rice, hot cereal, or hearty bread — can be another good choice. Some people eat dinner leftovers for breakfast. Think about experimenting, trying out some different types of breakfasts several days before the test to see which ones help you stay focused and which ones leave you sluggish. Know that you may feel nervous on test day, too, which can affect your appetite.

Finally, get some sleep. In a TED talk, neuroscientist Jeff Iliff explains that our brains use one-quarter of our energy and that remarkable "cleaning" goes on while we slumber. Most adults and teens know how hard it is to turn off electronics at night. For many, phones, tablets, and computers have become companions, keeping us up-to-date on the latest, well, everything. Using them at night, though, can interfere with sleep. You'll find it an interesting experiment to set a time to turn them off. (Warn your friends of the shutdown; with luck, they'll be willing to make a pact and join you.)

READYING YOURSELF THE DAY BEFORE THE TEST

▶ **Plan how you will get to the test site.** If it's in a large school or office building, be sure to find out which door will be open. If you haven't been in the building before, find out how to get to the room.

▶ **Set two alarms.** Even though alarms rarely fail, it can happen. You'll sleep more easily knowing you have a backup.

▶ **Review the list of things you need to take with you, and pack them all in a bag.**

▶ **Review the test directions once more.**

WHAT TO PACK

▶ **Photo admission ticket** (remember that the photo must resemble you on the day of the exam and comply with the rules posted on www.collegeboard.org/sat)

▶ **Valid photo ID** (driver's license [or other state-issued photo ID], school identification card, valid passport, or student ID form prepared by your school with a photo and the school seal overlapping the photo)

▶ **Several number 2 pencils** with soft erasers (mechanical pencils are not permitted)

▶ **Approved calculator** with fresh batteries, if appropriate (see http://sat.collegeboard.org/register/calculator-policy for more calculator guidance)

▶ **Watch** (one that only tells time; nothing that can be used to record, transmit, receive, or play back audio, photographic, text, or video content)

▶ **Snack** (something quiet, such as raisins or cashews, and hard candies or gum)

▶ **Water** (in a clear bottle, label removed, cap off)

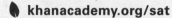

PRACTICE AT

khanacademy.org/sat

It's important to get plenty of sleep during the nights leading up to your SAT. But don't drastically alter your sleep schedule by, for instance, going to sleep much earlier than usual. Stick with a sleep schedule that works for you and allows you to do your best.

WHAT NOT TO PACK

▶ Smartphone or other cell phone

▶ Camera

▶ Recording device of any type

▶ Digital watch that has any capabilities beyond telling time

▶ Timer

If you're seen using any of the items above, they will be held by a test administrator, you will be asked to leave, or you may be denied admission. Obviously, the better choice is to leave them at home.

AVOIDING PROBLEMS ON TEST DAY

You will NOT be allowed to take the test if:

▶ The photo on the admission ticket doesn't look like you or otherwise doesn't comply with the rules posted on www.collegeboard.org/sat (for example, it's too light or too dark, it includes another person, your face is covered)

▶ You're missing either the admission ticket or a valid photo ID

▶ You're late

Please note:

▶ Test center changes are not permitted on test day. You can take the test only at the center where you're registered.

▶ Test-type changes are not guaranteed on test day. (You can only switch from SAT to SAT with Essay at the center if space and materials allow.)

▶ Walk-in (or standby) testing is not permitted.

Using Good Test-Taking Strategies

Let's assume you've arrived at the test center in good time, settled in, reminded yourself that you've prepared well for the SAT, and taken a few deep breaths. Thinking back on all of the time you spent building your knowledge and skills and familiarizing yourself with the test should leave you with feelings of satisfaction and confidence. You're ready! Now you need to make the best use of your time and energy on the test. Below are a few test-taking strategies you might consider. Try these out as you practice and see what works best for you.

▶ Pace yourself by keeping track of the clock — either on the wall or on a watch that's on your desk. Each section of the test has its own amount of time, so, when the test administrator says you can turn to each section,

REMEMBER

You won't be permitted to take the test if you arrive late. Thus, make sure you know exactly how to get to the test site, and plan to arrive early to account for unexpected transportation delays.

glance through a few pages to get a sense of how long you'll have for each chunk of questions. Check yourself one-quarter, one-half, and three-quarters of the way through the allotted time to make sure you're still on pace.

▶ While you need to keep your answer sheet free of stray marks, you're welcome to mark up the test booklet as much as you want. Annotating your test booklet can, if done judiciously, help you recall important facts or work through challenging problems.

▶ Consider skimming the questions in the Reading and the Writing and Language Tests prior to reading each of the passages in order to get a sense of what issues will be important.

▶ After reading each question, imagine the answer you would come up with. Then read the possible answers to find the one closest to your own.

▶ Always read all of the answer choices. You don't want a too-hasty decision to cause you to select the wrong answer to a question.

▶ If you read a question that stumps you, don't dwell on it. Return to the unanswered ones at the end. Make big marks next to questions you decide to skip so you can return to them later.

▶ Remember that there's no penalty for guessing (as there used to be on the SAT), so you should answer all questions before time is up. When you're not sure of an answer, make an educated guess. Draw lines through each of the answer choices you eliminate. Remember, too, that there are only four answer choices (instead of the old five), so cutting down the possibilities by even one substantially increases your odds of choosing correctly.

▶ **Important:** Be sure to check often to make sure that the number of the question you're about to answer matches the number in the test booklet. Erase and adjust if needed.

▶ You very well may finish some sections before time runs out. Review, but do so carefully. You don't want to second-guess yourself and change answers just to change them.

Dealing with Nerves and Distractions

It's not uncommon to feel nervous about the test. Try to consider that adrenaline rush as an aid. It's chemical energy, after all; your body is trying to help. If the energy feels like too much help, shake your arms and hands hard, as if you were shaking off water. While researchers may not understand why this helps, anecdotes from various people, including professional musicians, suggest it has a calming effect.

Also try to keep at the forefront of your mind the idea that you're prepared for this test. Combine that thought with the fact that while this test is

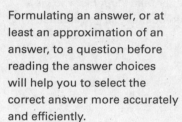

PRACTICE AT
khanacademy.org/sat

Formulating an answer, or at least an approximation of an answer, to a question before reading the answer choices will help you to select the correct answer more accurately and efficiently.

REMEMBER

Unlike on the previous SAT, there's no penalty for guessing on the redesigned SAT. Therefore, never leave a question blank. Eliminate as many answer choices as you can, and make an educated guess from among the remaining choices.

important, it's only one of several factors that colleges consider when they review your application.

Distractions during the test are, well, distracting. You want to put them out of your mind as much as possible. If you're momentarily struggling, a nearby student turning a page, for example, can break your concentration and make you feel like you're falling behind (even if you're not). Remember: You have no idea how well other people are doing on the test, and, anyway, being the fastest doesn't necessarily mean being the most successful. Stay focused on your own effort, and push petty thoughts and doubts away as quickly as they enter your mind. (Also, it should go without saying — but we'll say it anyway — that you should do everything in your power not to be a distraction to others.)

Taking the Test Again?

One more way to quiet your nerves is to remember that you can take the test again. More than half of the students who take the SAT take it twice — once in the spring of their junior year and once in the fall of their senior year. Most students who do so have higher scores on the later test. If you choose this path, make sure you spend time between tests to brush up on areas that you struggled with the first time.

PRACTICE AT

khanacademy.org/sat

It's common and perfectly normal to feel nervous or anxious on test day. Research has shown that, when facing an important event, students who view nervousness as a normal and even positive response by the body perform better than students who view nervousness as detrimental.

CHAPTER 3 RECAP

Getting ready for the SAT involves a lot of time and hard work, but it's also a chance to excel and to stand out to colleges and scholarship search programs. You can make best use of your opportunity by both (1) learning the essential knowledge and skills covered on the test and (2) getting comfortable with the test itself. In sum:

▶ The best practice for the SAT occurs every day as you study hard and acquire important reading, writing, language, and math knowledge and skills. Make use of the information in this book, take stock of how well you do on sample tests and questions, figure out your academic strengths, and work on addressing your weaknesses. Take advantage of the free practice resources on Khan Academy to help you not only learn about the test itself, but also expand your knowledge and skills.

▶ Get familiar with the SAT itself. Understanding the test directions in advance and being comfortable with the format of the various test questions can both save you time and give you added confidence on test day. Taking the PSAT/NMSQT or PSAT 10, using sample questions and tests available from the College Board and Khan Academy, and exploring other resources (such as sat.org/practice and the College Board's social media posts) can also help.

▶ As the time for test day approaches, make sure you're staying as healthy as possible and getting plenty of rest.

▶ Avoid problems on test day by knowing how to get to your test site as well as knowing what to bring and what not to bring with you.

▶ Practice a range of test-taking strategies, such as the ones introduced earlier in this chapter, to find out what works and what doesn't work for you.

▶ Put away those doubts and worries on test day. You're ready! You'll be great! (And if you're still not satisfied with your score, you can consider taking the test again.)

Chapter 4

PSAT/NMSQT®

The PSAT/NMSQT (Preliminary SAT/National Merit Scholarship Qualifying Test) provides an excellent way to preview the SAT. Like the SAT, the redesigned PSAT/NMSQT measures the skills and knowledge that are essential for college and career readiness and success. Taking the PSAT/NMSQT is one of the best ways to practice for the SAT: You'll be asked the same types of questions in the same subject areas that are on the SAT (Reading, Writing and Language, and Math), but at a level appropriate for sophomores and juniors in high school. You'll also get a sense of the time limits for each test. (Note that the Essay is available only on the SAT.) Because the PSAT/NMSQT is aligned with the redesigned SAT, taking the PSAT/NMSQT will not only offer you numerous benefits, including valuable information about your readiness for postsecondary-level work, but it can also enhance your confidence when your SAT test day arrives.

How the PSAT/NMSQT and the SAT Are Linked

The SAT, PSAT/NMSQT and PSAT 10, and PSAT 8/9 are part of an integrated system called the SAT Suite of Assessments. The exams are connected by the same underlying continuum of knowledge and skills that research shows are the most essential for college and career readiness and success. Your test results can be used to monitor your progress over time. The PSAT 8/9 is administered to eighth- and ninth-graders; the PSAT 10, which covers the same content areas as the PSAT/NMSQT, is administered to students in the spring of 10th grade. Schools administer the PSAT/NMSQT during the fall, primarily to high school sophomores and juniors.

The redesigned tests released in 2015–16 are designed to reflect the work students are doing in classrooms across the country and around the globe, and embody the eight key changes described in Chapter 2 and summarized briefly here.

Words in Context: Questions on the Reading and the Writing and Language Tests address word/phrase meaning in context as well as rhetorical word choice, with a focus on words and phrases relevant to a wide range of studies.

Command of Evidence: Questions on the Reading and the Writing and Language Tests require students to demonstrate their ability to interpret and use evidence found in a wide range of passages and informational graphics, such as graphs, tables, and charts.

Essay Analyzing a Source (SAT only): The SAT Essay prompt requires students to read a passage and explain how the author builds an argument to persuade an audience, a task that mirrors college writing assignments. The Essay is an optional component of the SAT (although some school districts and colleges will require it).

Focus on Math that Matters Most: Questions on the Math Test focus on math content that most contributes to readiness for and success in college and career training.

Problems Grounded in Real-World Contexts: Questions are grounded in the real world and are directly related to work performed in college and career.

Analysis in History/Social Studies and in Science: Questions require the application of reading, writing, language, and math skills to answer questions in history, social studies, and science contexts.

U.S. Founding Documents and the Great Global Conversation: Questions that require careful reading of sections of U.S. founding documents, such as the Declaration of Independence and the Bill of Rights, or that have been part of the Great Global Conversation about the nature of civic life.

No Penalty for Wrong Answers: Students earn points for the questions they answer correctly, with no deductions for incorrect answers.

Other Benefits in Addition to Preparing for the SAT

A major reason to take the PSAT/NMSQT is that the score you receive is sent to the National Merit Scholarship Corporation (NMSC). This organization oversees the distribution of almost $50 million in scholarships a year and uses PSAT/NMSQT scores as an initial screen of entrants to their competition. Some students take the test before their junior year, but only the scores from the junior year are submitted to NMSC. Additionally, in 2015, the PSAT/NMSQT began to be used as a tool to broaden access to nearly $180 million a year of additional scholarships from the American Indian Graduate Center and American Indian Graduate Center Scholars (AIGC and AIGCS), Asian & Pacific Islander American Scholarship Fund (APIASF), Hispanic Scholarship Fund (HSF), Jack Kent Cooke Foundation (JKCF), and United Negro College Fund (UNCF).

REMEMBER

There is *not* an essay on the PSAT/NMSQT, PSAT 10, or PSAT 8/9.

REMEMBER

Taking the PSAT/NMSQT will make you eligible to receive scholarships from multiple organizations. Learn more at collegereadiness.collegeboard.org.

Another significant benefit of taking the PSAT/NMSQT (or the PSAT 10) is that you can import your results into Khan Academy to begin to establish a personalized study plan based on exactly what you need to work on next in order to improve your score. With your explicit permission, the College Board will send the question-level results of your exam to Khan Academy, which will use those data to recommend a study plan to set you up for SAT success. Learn more at khanacademy.org/sat.

A third benefit of taking the PSAT/NMSQT (or PSAT 10) is AP Potential™, a free Web-based tool that allows schools to generate rosters of students who are likely to score a 3 or higher on a given AP Exam. Based on research that shows moderate to strong correlations between PSAT/NMSQT scores and AP Exam results, AP Potential is designed to help increase access to AP and to ensure that no student who has the chance of succeeding in AP is overlooked.

A final benefit for signing up to take the PSAT/NMSQT (or the PSAT 10) is that you become eligible to participate in the College Board's Student Search Service, which is a database that colleges, universities, and scholarship programs use to locate and recruit students with particular characteristics. These organizations join the service so they can search for students who might be a good match for their school or scholarship criteria.

When you sign up to participate in Student Search Service, your name, contact information, high school GPA, date of birth, grade level, high school, email address, extracurricular activities, and intended college major are entered into the system. Participating institutions can search for students by desired characteristics, such as "GPA 3.2 or above; choir/band; New Hampshire; botany/biology." Colleges are interested in a diverse student body. Being able to search for students with various interests and activities, hailing from U.S. states or countries overseas, helps colleges assemble a strong and diverse student population that will benefit students and faculty during college and contribute to cohesive, supportive alumni groups in the years following. If your information is made available to them, colleges and universities can invite you to apply for admission to their schools. The same holds true for scholarship programs, which often have very specific criteria relating to geography, family situation, and more.

If you sign up for Student Search Service, any updates you make to your profile (such as changes to your GPA, activities, or planned major) will be reflected in the search database.

Note that joining Student Search Service is your choice. Registering for an exam or an AP course makes the service available to you, but **you have to opt-in by checking the box**. Signing up is the only way your information becomes part of the database. Be assured that the College Board never forwards your scores to any college, university, or scholarship group (except the National Merit Scholarship Corporation) without your permission. Know, too, that the information you give to the College Board will be used only in the ways described

PRACTICE AT
khanacademy.org/sat

If you allow the College Board to send your PSAT/NMSQT or PSAT 10 results to Khan Academy, Khan Academy will use the data to create a personalized study plan for you.

REMEMBER

If you enroll in Student Search Service, participating colleges and scholarship institutions will be able to access your contact information and invite you to apply.

here. Information in the database will not be sold to a private company. Some students report receiving phone calls from companies that claim to have received student scores from the College Board. These are fraudulent and should be disregarded.

How Do I Register and When Will I Learn My Results?

REMEMBER

The *Official Student Guide to the PSAT/NMSQT* and the Khan Academy website are two excellent resources to help you prepare for the PSAT/NMSQT.

When the *Official Student Guide to the PSAT/NMSQT* arrives at your school in September, review the explanation sections and then take the full-length practice test. If any of the questions posed problems for you, return to this book again to review the appropriate chapters to improve your understanding. Use the Khan Academy website to review practice questions and tests. And, of course, keep working in your classes and with your teachers to hone your academic skills.

The PSAT/NMSQT is given in October at high schools both across the country and internationally. Check with your school counselor to register. If you're home-schooled, consult www.collegeboard.org/psat-nmsqt/home-schooled-students for information about registering with a local school. (Students cannot register for the PSAT/NMSQT online.)

The scores for the PSAT/NMSQT are sent to your school in December, whereupon a counselor or test coordinator will give them to you. (Home-schooled students receive their results at home.) Additionally, you'll receive access to an online score report that gives you even more information about your performance.

ARE SCORES SENT TO ANYONE ELSE?

Score results are sent to the National Merit Scholarship Corporation. One of the most important reasons to take the PSAT/NMSQT is to become eligible for scholarship competitions administered by both the NMSC and our other scholarship partners.

In some cases, your scores may be sent to school districts or your state's office of education so that student results can be averaged together and analyzed. This information can help districts and states assess overall student achievement levels and can help administrators who make decisions about curricula and professional development programs for teachers.

WHAT SHOULD I KNOW ABOUT HOW THE TEST IS SCORED?

Every exam in the SAT Suite of Assessments is scored on the same scale, providing a powerful tool for measuring growth. This doesn't mean that a student who scores a 400 on the PSAT 8/9 Math Test is predicted to score a 400 on the PSAT/NMSQT Math Test (or SAT) one or two years later; it does, however, mean that students scoring a 400 on any of the Math Tests are demonstrating similar levels of math achievement regardless of the particular test they took. You'll see in the following descriptions that although the SAT total score is reported on a scale of 400 to 1600, the tests for the PSAT/NMSQT and PSAT 10 and the PSAT 8/9 have somewhat different score ranges. This reflects the fact that the exams assess the same underlying knowledge and skills, but at a level appropriate to the student populations for each exam.

PSAT™ 8/9

In addition to the PSAT/NMSQT, the College Board offers the PSAT 8/9, which is taken in the fall or spring of eighth and/or ninth grade. Scores from the PSAT 8/9 serve as a foundation for interpreting progress as students enter high school. If students stay the course on the areas they're strong in and work harder on their weaker areas, they'll be more likely to be on target for being college and career ready by the time they leave high school. Scores range from 120 to 720 for each of the Math and Evidence-Based Reading and Writing sections.

PSAT/NMSQT and PSAT™ 10

The PSAT/NMSQT and PSAT 10 cover the same content domains, and both serve as a "check-in" on student progress by pinpointing areas for development. Students will take the PSAT/NMSQT in the fall of 10th and 11th grade (though only juniors are eligible for the National Merit Scholarship Program). In addition to delivering the PSAT/NMSQT to 10th-graders in the fall, some schools may also deliver the PSAT 10 in the spring.

Most of the same scores, although using different ranges, are reported for PSAT/NMSQT and PSAT 10 as for the SAT:

A **total** score on the PSAT/NMSQT and PSAT 10 is on a 320 to 1520 scale and is the sum of the scores on the Evidence-Based Reading and Writing section and the Math section.

Section scores are reported on a 160 to 760 scale for both the Evidence-Based Reading and Writing section and the Math section. **Test** scores are reported on a scale of 8 to 38 for each of the three tests: Reading, Writing and Language, and Math.

Cross-test scores are reported on a scale of 8 to 38 and are based on selected questions in the Reading, Writing and Language, and Math Tests that reflect the application of reading, writing, language, and math skills in history/social studies and science contexts.

Seven different subscores, each on a scale of 1 to 15, provide more specific information about how you're doing in a few more specific areas of reading, writing, language, and math.

Two subscores are reported for Writing and Language: Expression of Ideas and Standard English Conventions. The Expression of Ideas subscore

REMEMBER

Scores from the PSAT 8/9 can help you identify areas you're strong in and areas in need of improvement as you enter high school.

☞ **REMEMBER**

The SAT Math Test requires a deeper knowledge of a smaller number of math topics that research has shown are integral to college and career success.

☞ **REMEMBER**

As on the SAT, the PSAT/NMSQT and PSAT 10 won't test you on the meaning of obscure, seldom-used words and phrases presented with little context. Rather, you'll be tested on contextually based words and phrases that often appear in college courses and beyond.

☞ **REMEMBER**

When you're unsure of the answer to a question, eliminate as many answer choices as possible and select from the remaining choices. Never leave a question blank!

is based on questions focusing on topic development, organization, and rhetorically effective use of language. The Standard English Conventions subscore is based on questions focusing on sentence structure, usage, and punctuation.

The Math Test reports three subscores: Heart of Algebra, Problem Solving and Data Analysis, and Passport to Advanced Math. Heart of Algebra focuses on linear equations and inequalities. Problem Solving and Data Analysis focuses on quantitative reasoning, the interpretation and synthesis of data, and solving problems in rich and varied contexts. Passport to Advanced Math focuses on topics central to the ability of students to progress to more advanced mathematics, such as understanding the structure of expressions, reasoning with more complex equations, and interpreting and building functions.

The final two subscores — Words in Context and Command of Evidence — are based on questions in both the Reading and the Writing and Language Tests. The Words in Context questions address word/phrase meaning in context and rhetorical word choice. The Command of Evidence questions ask you to interpret and use evidence found in a wide range of passages and informational graphics, such as graphs, tables, and charts.

As with the SAT, the subscores provide additional insight into your strengths. These results will also allow you and your parents, educators, and counselors to locate specific areas that you need to work on. The scores can also be used to find appropriate AP courses.

As with the SAT, there's no penalty for guessing on the PSAT/NMSQT or PSAT 10. Your scores are derived only from correct answers. Blank answers have no impact on scores.

Score Report

Your PSAT/NMSQT Score Report gives you feedback on your performance, plus other valuable information including:

▶ PSAT/NMSQT scores and score ranges

▶ Percentiles for juniors or sophomores

▶ Selection index used by NMSC for initial entry into their scholarship competitions

▶ Comprehensive question-by-question feedback

▶ Academic skills feedback

▶ Online access to question-and-answer explanations

▶ Basic eligibility criteria and status for National Merit Scholarships

▶ Guidance information to help in college and career planning

What Is the Test Like?

TIMING

Total testing time: 2 hours and 45 minutes

COMPONENTS:

Reading Test: 60 minutes; 47 questions

Writing and Language Test: 35 minutes; 44 questions

Math Test (including a calculator and a no-calculator portion): 70 minutes; 48 questions

Total: 165 minutes (2 hours, 45 minutes); 139 questions

As with the SAT, the PSAT/NMSQT and PSAT 10 are composed of three content-area tests: Reading, Writing and Language, and Math. Sample questions and a practice PSAT/NMSQT are available at collegereadiness.collegeboard.org and in print through schools.

WHAT TO BRING ON TEST DAY

- ▶ Two number 2 pencils with erasers
- ▶ An approved calculator (see the College Board website for details about what's allowed)
- ▶ Current and valid school or government-issued photo for students not testing at their own school and for home-schooled students

WHAT NOT TO BRING

- ▶ Protractors, compasses, rulers
- ▶ Dictionaries or other books
- ▶ Pamphlets or papers of any kind
- ▶ Highlighters and colored pens or pencils
- ▶ Any device that listens, records, copies, or makes photographic images, including cell phones and smart watches

DURING THE TEST, YOU CAN HAVE ON YOUR DESK:

- ▶ A test book
- ▶ An answer sheet
- ▶ Number 2 pencils with soft erasers
- ▶ An approved calculator — only during the designated Math portion

Are You Home-Schooled?

Contact a local school's principal or counselor to make arrangements for the PSAT/NMSQT, PSAT 10, or PSAT 8/9 well in advance of the test dates — preferably over the summer.

TESTING WITH ACCOMMODATIONS

Make arrangements through your school counselor for the accommodations you'll need.

Home-schooled students who are approved for accommodations on test day should notify the school where they are testing and complete the forms by August 27, prior to the October test.

Why Take the PSAT/NMSQT?

▶ Practice for the SAT.

▶ Assess your progress in the knowledge and skills that are essential to college and career readiness and success. A comprehensive score report gives helpful feedback about the areas that you need to work on.

▶ Compare your performance with that of other 10th- and 11th-graders from around the country.

▶ Kick off your practice for the SAT by importing your PSAT/NMSQT results into Khan Academy for a personalized lesson plan.

▶ Qualify for entry into scholarship competitions.

▶ Participate in the Student Search Service.

Preparing for the PSAT/NMSQT

▶ Review the test-taking reminders and tips throughout this book, including ideas about marking up the test booklet, how to make an educated guess, and the usefulness of sleep.

▶ Read Chapter 3, "Read This! Keys to Doing Your Best on the SAT." Many sections in this chapter are relevant to taking the PSAT/NMSQT, including the descriptions of questions in the Reading, Writing and Language, and Math Tests.

▶ Before the test, become familiar with question types and directions by doing practice questions. Directions for the SAT can be found in Chapter 3.

▶ Take the practice test that is included in the *Official Student Guide to the PSAT/NMSQT*. You'll be able to find the correct answers and explanations on the College Board website.

REMEMBER

As you can see here, there are many great reasons for taking the PSAT/NMSQT!

PRACTICE AT

khanacademy.org/sat

Reading and understanding all test directions before test day will save you time and ensure you know exactly what to expect on test day.

▶ Although Khan Academy practice is focused on helping you succeed on the redesigned SAT, you can also use Khan Academy tools for PSAT/NMSQT and PSAT 10 practice because of the close alignment between the assessments.

FINAL NOTE:

The best preparation for the PSAT/NMSQT is to take challenging courses, read widely, write frequently, and develop problem-solving skills both in the classroom and through extracurricular activities. These are the same habits that prepare students for the SAT and the AP Exams as well as for college and career.

Chapter 5

New Scores Mean More Information About Your Learning

One of the important changes of the redesign of the SAT and the PSAT/NMSQT has been a shift in the scales used. The redesigned SAT Suite of Assessments (SAT, PSAT/NMSQT, PSAT 10, and PSAT 8/9) reports a total score, section scores, test scores, cross-test scores, and subscores. These scores are intended to provide insight about your achievement and readiness for college and career.

One of the other principal features of the redesign of the SAT and the PSAT/NMSQT has been a shift in the range of scores provided. Prior to the redesign, the SAT scale ranged from 600 to 2400, representing the combined results on three sections of the test: Critical Reading, Writing, and Mathematics. (The Essay score (SAT only) was combined with the results on the multiple-choice writing questions to produce the Writing section score.) Each section score ranged from 200 to 800. Students became accustomed to the range of numbers, 600 to 2400, which has been the scale since 2005, so the College Board set out to alter it only after determining that such a change would provide several benefits for all.

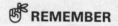 **REMEMBER**

More scores = more information. The scores reported on the redesigned SAT provide detailed information about your achievement and readiness for college and career.

More Scores Illuminate More Insights into Learning

Where the former version of the SAT provided scores for three categories — Critical Reading, Writing, and Mathematics — the redesign provides a wider array of scores. These include a total score; two section scores, for Evidence-Based Reading and Writing and for Math; three test scores; two cross-test scores; and seven subscores on categories within the subjects. Scores for the optional Essay are reported separately.

The **total** score is the most commonly used number associated with the SAT. The total score ranges from 400 to 1600. This score is the sum of the scores on the Evidence-Based Reading and Writing section and the Math section. Of the 154 questions in the entire exam (not counting the Essay), 96 questions are on the Reading and the Writing and Language Tests and 58 questions are on the Math Test.

Section scores for Evidence-Based Reading and Writing and for Math are reported on a scale from 200 to 800. The Evidence-Based Reading and Writing section score is derived in equal measure from the scores on the Reading and the Writing and Language Tests. The Math section score is derived from the score on the Math Test.

Test scores are reported on a scale of 10 to 40 for each of the three required tests: Reading, Writing and Language, and Math.

Cross-test scores — one for Analysis in History/Social Studies and one for Analysis in Science — are reported on a scale of 10 to 40 and are based on selected questions in the Reading, Writing and Language, and Math Tests that reflect the application of reading, writing, language, and math skills in history/social studies and science contexts.

Subscores are reported on a scale of 1 to 15. They provide more detailed information about how you're doing in specific areas of literacy and math.

Two subscores are reported for Writing and Language: Expression of Ideas and Standard English Conventions. The Expression of Ideas subscore is based on questions focusing on topic development, organization, and rhetorically effective use of language. The Standard English Conventions subscore is based on questions focusing on sentence structure, usage, and punctuation.

The Math Test reports three subscores: Heart of Algebra, Problem Solving and Data Analysis, and Passport to Advanced Math. Heart of Algebra focuses on linear equations and inequalities. Problem Solving and Data Analysis focuses on quantitative reasoning, the interpretation and synthesis of data, and solving problems in rich and varied contexts. Passport to Advanced Math focuses on topics central to the ability of students to progress to more advanced mathematics, such as understanding the structure of expressions, reasoning with more complex equations, and interpreting and building functions.

The final two subscores — Words in Context and Command of Evidence — are based on questions in both the Reading and the Writing and Language Tests. The Words in Context questions address word/phrase meaning in context and rhetorical word choice. The Command of Evidence questions ask you to interpret and use evidence found in a wide range of passages and informational graphics, such as graphs, tables, and charts.

The optional Essay yields three **Essay** scores, one each on three dimensions:

▶ **Reading:** How well you demonstrated your understanding of the passage

▶ **Analysis:** How well you analyzed the passage and carried out the task of explaining how the author of the passage builds an argument to persuade an audience

▶ **Writing:** How skillfully you crafted your response

Two scorers read each essay and assign a score of 1 to 4 on each of the three dimensions. The two raters' scores are combined to yield a Reading, Analysis, and Writing score, each on a scale of 2 to 8. These scores aren't combined with each other or with scores on any other part of the SAT.

Concordance

Because the redesigned SAT is a different test than the pre–March 2016 SAT, a numerical score on one test will not be strictly equivalent to the same numerical score on the other. The College Board provides a concordance between the pre–March 2016 SAT and the redesigned SAT that shows how to relate scores on one test to scores on the other. This is important for students who took the pre–March 2016 SAT, as it allows college admission offices to estimate how those students would have scored on the redesigned SAT had they taken it. The concordance allows students who took the pre–March 2016 SAT to keep their college applications complete and up-to-date without having to retake the SAT.

In addition to being used by college admission offices, the concordance is important for K–12 educators and counselors and for students and parents who have been accustomed to thinking in terms of the 600 to 2400 range. For more information, please visit http://sat.org.

REMEMBER

Your Essay scores on the redesigned SAT will be reported separately from your scores on the Math, Reading, and Writing and Language Tests. You'll receive three scores on the Essay — each ranging from 2 to 8 — on three key dimensions.

REMEMBER

A concordance provided by the College Board allows college admission offices to relate scores on the pre–March 2016 SAT to scores on the redesigned SAT.

PART 2

Evidence-Based Reading and Writing

Chapter 6

Command of Evidence

Despite important differences in purpose, topic, format, content, and style, well-done pieces of writing still have a lot in common. Authors of all kinds writing for all sorts of reasons must make use of support — details, examples, reasons, facts, figures, and so on — to help make their ideas compelling, their points clear, and their claims convincing.

Think for a moment about the job of a movie director. It's OK if you don't know the specifics; a general idea will do. Movie directing is in some ways a good parallel to the work that writers do. Directors tell camera operators where to stand, whether to shoot at a distance or up close, and how long to hold a particular shot. Directors also work with actors on how to deliver their lines and what physical actions to use. Music, lighting, costumes, setting, scripts — directors often have input into all of these. Every part of the production must work together and have a clear purpose if the project is to be successful. The same is true for good writing: Every word, every sentence, and every paragraph has a role to play in the overall text. Understanding and being able to explain those roles are parts of skilled reading, and they're among the many important skills that the SAT gives you an opportunity to demonstrate.

The SAT asks you to pay attention to how authors use support in texts that cover a range of subjects and styles. One important way that the SAT does this is by including questions that ask you to identify the part of the text that provides the best evidence (textual support) for the answer to another question. You'll also be asked to make sense of information presented in graphics, such as tables, graphs, and charts, and to draw connections between that information and the information presented in words. You might be asked other sorts of related questions as well, such as how the focus of a piece of writing could be improved (perhaps by deleting irrelevant information) or what role a piece of evidence plays in an author's argument.

Your command of evidence will be tested throughout much of the SAT, including the Reading Test, the Writing and Language Test, and the optional

 **REMEMBER**

You'll frequently be asked to use evidence to create or defend an argument, or to critically assess someone else's argument, in college and in the workforce.

Essay. Command of Evidence questions accompany each Reading and Writing and Language passage and contribute to a Command of Evidence subscore. While your response to the Essay prompt doesn't contribute to this subscore, it will still call on your skill in understanding how an author uses support to make an argument effective.

What Is Meant by Command of Evidence?

The Command of Evidence category includes questions that focus on many of the ways in which authors use support. These include:

▶ Determining the best evidence in a passage (or pair of passages) for the answer to a previous question or the best evidence for a specified conclusion (Reading Test)

▶ Interpreting data presented in informational graphics (such as tables, graphs, and charts) and drawing connections between words and data (Reading Test, Writing and Language Test)

▶ Understanding how the author of an argument uses (or fails to use) evidence to support the claims he or she makes (Reading Test)

▶ Revising a passage to clarify main ideas, strengthen support, or sharpen focus (Writing and Language Test)

REMEMBER

While separate from your Command of Evidence score, the Analysis score on the Essay is largely based on skills related to those required for Command of Evidence questions.

Having a strong Command of Evidence is also central to the Essay. Your Analysis score on the Essay is based in large part on how well you can explain how the author of a passage uses evidence, reasoning, stylistic or persuasive techniques, and/or other means to persuade an audience.

Ten Reading Test questions — two per passage or pair of passages — contribute to the Command of Evidence subscore. Eight Writing and Language Test questions — again, two per passage — also contribute to the subscore. Although not part of the Command of Evidence subscore, the Essay's Analysis score is based heavily on skills related to Command of Evidence questions.

Let's consider the types of questions in a little more detail.

REMEMBER

A total of 18 questions — 10 from the Reading Test and eight from the Writing and Language Test — contribute to the Command of Evidence subscore.

DETERMINING THE BEST EVIDENCE (READING TEST)

Sometimes the Reading Test will ask you a question and then present you with another question that asks for the "best evidence" to support the answer you selected in response to the first question. This is actually simpler than it might seem at first.

You should begin by reading and answering the first question to the best of your ability. This question will often ask you to draw a reasonable conclusion or inference from the passage. As you're reaching that conclusion or inference, you're using textual evidence. Textual evidence can be as simple as a small piece of information, such as a fact or a date, but it can also be more complex, such as the words an author uses that signal his or her point of view on an issue. Textual evidence helps you defend the answer you might give to a teacher asking how you reached a particular interpretation of a text. Consider the following examples:

▶ "I think the author supports clearer labeling on food because . . ."

▶ "The narrator seems to feel sympathy for the main character because . . ."

What would follow "because" in each of these examples is likely to be textual evidence — the "how I know it" part of the statement.

All that the second question in a pair of SAT Reading Test questions is asking you to do, then, is to make explicit what you're already doing when you answer the first question in a pair. Typically, the second question will present you with four snippets from the passage, generally a sentence each, and ask you which one provides the best evidence for the answer to the previous question. All you need to do is figure out which one does the best job of answering the question of "how I know it" — in other words, which one provides the best textual evidence.

It could be that looking at the choices in the second question makes you reconsider your answer to the first one. That can be OK. Maybe rereading particular parts of the passage made something clearer than it had been before or drew your attention to a crucial detail you hadn't considered. While you don't want to second-guess yourself endlessly, sometimes it can be a good idea to rethink an answer based on new information.

You may also see questions that present you with a conclusion already drawn and ask you to determine which of the four answer options provides the best evidence from the passage for that conclusion. You can treat these questions just like the textual evidence questions described earlier, except this time you don't have to draw the conclusion yourself in a separate question.

INTERPRETING DATA IN INFORMATIONAL GRAPHICS (READING TEST, WRITING AND LANGUAGE TEST)

Certain passages in both the Reading Test and the Writing and Language Test are accompanied by one or more informational graphics. These graphics, which are typically tables, graphs, or charts, usually represent numerical data in visual form, such as results from a scientific experiment. On the Reading Test, you may be asked to interpret the information in the graphic, but you may also or instead be asked to draw connections between the graphic and the accompanying passage, such as deciding whether data in the graphic support or weaken a particular conclusion reached by the author of the passage. On the Writing and Language Test, you may be asked to revise a passage to, say, correct an error in the writer's interpretation of a table or to replace a general description with precise figures.

PRACTICE AT

khanacademy.org/sat

When a question refers to a table, graph, or chart, carefully examine the graphic to get a strong understanding of the data being displayed. This may include reading the title, identifying what the x- and y-axes represent, noting the increment values on the axes, and reading any captions or subheadings.

It's important to note that these Reading and Writing and Language questions aren't math questions in disguise. You won't need to add, subtract, multiply, or divide (and you won't have access to a calculator). The questions instead ask you to "read" graphics and draw conclusions, much as you do when you read and interpret a written text.

UNDERSTANDING HOW AN ARGUMENT USES (OR DOESN'T USE) EVIDENCE (READING TEST)

Being able to figure out how an author constructs an argument is an important skill needed for success in college and workforce training programs — and on the SAT. Arguments seek to convince readers (or listeners or viewers) of the rightness of one or more claims, or assertions. To do this, authors of arguments make use of evidence, reasoning, and stylistic and persuasive elements, such as vivid imagery or appeals to emotion, to flesh out and support their claims. A reader convinced by an author's argument may end up changing his or her view on a topic or be persuaded to take a particular action.

Arguments are a consistent part of the Reading Test (as well as the Writing and Language Test and the Essay). Reading Test questions that focus on evidence use may ask you to identify what type of evidence a particular author relies on most heavily (personal anecdotes or survey results, for example) to determine what evidence in the passage supports a particular claim, or to decide whether a new piece of information (such as a research finding) would strengthen or weaken an author's case.

Analyzing an argument, including its use of evidence, is the main focus of the optional Essay, which we'll turn to momentarily.

IMPROVING A PASSAGE'S STRUCTURE, SUPPORT, AND FOCUS (WRITING AND LANGUAGE TEST)

As noted earlier, the Writing and Language Test asks you to revise passages to better incorporate information from graphics into the text. The test asks you to show your command of evidence in other ways as well. You may end up adding or revising a topic sentence to improve the clarity and structure of a passage. You may also add or revise supporting material, such as a description or an example, to make the writer's claim or point more robust. Other questions may ask you to think about whether adding, revising, or removing a particular sentence would improve or blur the focus of a certain paragraph or the passage as a whole. The element that these Writing and Language questions (along with questions about informational graphics) have in common is that they require you to think about how a writer develops a topic through building up claims or points.

PRACTICE AT

khanacademy.org/sat

Questions on the Reading Test that ask about the use of evidence may require you to take a step back from what the author is saying and to focus instead on how the argument is put together.

PRACTICE AT

khanacademy.org/sat

Developing a strong understanding of the writer's overall purpose in a Writing and Language Test passage is critical to answering many Command of Evidence questions. Thus, be sure you're always thinking about the writer's purpose as you read passages on the SAT.

A NOTE ABOUT THE ESSAY

The optional Essay's three scores are not combined with scores on the multiple-choice portion of the SAT and thus don't contribute to the Command of Evidence subscore. However, as we mentioned before, the heart of the task on the Essay is to analyze an argument and to explain how the author builds the argument to persuade an audience through evidence, reasoning, and/or stylistic or persuasive elements (or other elements you identify). The main focus of the Essay — and the foundation for its Analysis score — is, therefore, very much in keeping with the notion of showing off your command of evidence in the broad sense. Receiving a strong Analysis score requires making use of many of the same skills called on by the Command of Evidence questions on the multiple-choice Reading Test and Writing and Language Test.

PRACTICE AT

khanacademy.org/sat

Another reason preparing for and taking the SAT Essay Test is a good idea is that in doing so, you'll also be practicing the skills you need to do well on Command of Evidence questions.

CHAPTER 6 RECAP

The Command of Evidence subscore on the SAT is based on questions from both the Reading Test and the Writing and Language Test. These questions are designed to see whether you understand how authors make use of information and ideas to develop and support their claims and points.

You'll find three types of questions on the **Reading Test** that address command of evidence. They are:

1. **Determining the best evidence:** You'll be asked to figure out which part of a passage offers the strongest support for the answer to another question or for a conclusion that the question provides. These sorts of questions accompany every passage on the test.

2. **Interpreting data presented in informational graphics:** You'll be asked to locate particular information in tables, graphs, charts, and the like; draw conclusions from such data; and/or make connections between the data and the information and ideas in a passage. These sorts of questions accompany select passages on the test, as only some passages on the test include graphics.

3. **Understanding how an argument uses (or doesn't use) evidence:** You'll be asked to think about how an author makes (or fails to make) use of supporting information, such as facts, figures, and quotations, to develop claims. These sorts of questions accompany select passages on the test — those that stake out one or more claims and seek to make those claims convincing through the use of evidence, reasoning, and stylistic and persuasive elements.

You'll find two types of questions on the **Writing and Language Test** that address command of evidence. They are:

1. **Interpreting data presented in informational graphics:** You'll be asked to use data in tables, graphs, charts, and the like when you're revising passages to make the passage more accurate, clear, precise, or convincing. These sorts of questions accompany select passages on the test, as only some passages on the test include graphics.

2. **Improving a passage's structure, support, and focus:** You'll be asked to revise passages to make authors' central ideas sharper; add or revise supporting information, such as facts, figures, and quotations; and add, revise, or delete information that's irrelevant or that just doesn't belong at a particular point in the passage. These sorts of questions accompany nearly every passage on the test.

Although not contributing to the subscore, the optional Essay is very much about command of evidence, as its task centers on analyzing how an author builds an argument to persuade an audience. To do well on the Essay — especially in terms of getting a strong Analysis score — you'll have to consider how the author uses evidence, reasoning, stylistic or persuasive elements, or other techniques to influence readers.

As you approach all of these questions and tasks, you'll want to think like an author. Answering for yourself such questions as "What point is the author trying to make?" and "What support in the passage can I find for my interpretation?" and "How relevant is this information to the passage as a whole?" is critical to getting a strong Command of Evidence subscore on the SAT.

Chapter 7

Words in Context

Relevant Words in Context

You may have already seen references in other parts of this guide to the concept of relevant words and phrases in context. This concept reflects a big shift for the SAT. In the past, the SAT typically tested vocabulary by using questions that offered very little context (often just a sentence or two) and sometimes assessed the meaning of words and phrases that are somewhat obscure and unlikely to be encountered by students in their reading or classroom discussions. In the redesigned SAT, you'll still see a number of questions about the meaning and use of words and phrases, but these questions will all be embedded in multiparagraph passages, and the words and phrases focused on will be ones that are important to readings in many subject areas.

These changes have important implications for how you prepare for the redesigned SAT. Having questions about words and phrases embedded in extended passages means that there'll be more context clues to draw on to determine meaning and to guide you in making choices about which word or phrase to use in a particular writing situation. It also means that the meaning and use of these words and phrases will depend more heavily than before on how a given context shapes word choice. The emphasis of the redesigned SAT's vocabulary questions on words and phrases used fairly frequently in challenging readings in a variety of subjects means that you'll be able to devote your attention to acquiring knowledge of words and phrases that are likely to be of use to you throughout your academic career instead of focusing on vocabulary that you're unlikely to encounter again after taking the test.

Let's consider the kinds of words and phrases that are tested on the redesigned SAT and then briefly examine the sorts of Words in Context questions you'll find on the test.

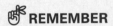 **REMEMBER**

The redesigned SAT won't test you on the meaning of obscure, seldom-used words and phrases presented with little context. Rather, you'll be tested on contextually based words and phrases that often appear in college courses and beyond.

PRACTICE AT

 khanacademy.org/sat

Since the redesigned SAT focuses on academic words and phrases commonly encountered in challenging texts, a good way to prepare is to read texts across a range of subjects and types. As you encounter unfamiliar words or phrases, practice using context clues to determine their meaning.

PRACTICE AT

 khanacademy.org/sat

We do *not* recommend practicing by poring over long lists of obscure, esoteric vocabulary.

High-Utility Academic Words and Phrases

The redesigned SAT focuses on what might be called "high-utility academic words and phrases." This type of vocabulary is the kind that you can find in a wide range of challenging readings across a range of subjects. You may, for example, come across the word "restrain" — one of these high-utility academic words — in a number of different types of texts. You could find it in a novel in which the main character is trying to restrain, or hold in check, his emotions; you could also find it in a social studies text discussing how embargoes can be used to restrain, or limit, trade among nations. (Note, too, how the precise meaning of "restrain" varies to some extent based on the context in which the word appears.)

As the above example suggests, high-utility academic words and phrases are different from other kinds of vocabulary you know and will encounter in school and life. High-utility academic words and phrases aren't necessarily used frequently in casual conversations, so if you already know the common meanings of a word such as "restrain," it's probably because you either learned it by reading a lot or from vocabulary lessons in school. High-utility academic words and phrases are also not the same thing as technical terms. Words and phrases such as "atomic mass," "ductile," and "isotope" may sound like they'd fit into the category of high-utility academic words and phrases. What makes these latter terms different is that they're generally only used in particular types of texts and conversations — in this case, readings about and discussions of science. This doesn't mean that these terms aren't worth knowing — far from it — but it does mean that, in some sense, they are less useful to know than words and phrases that can be found in many different types of readings and thoughtful conversations. Since the SAT can't (and shouldn't) try to test everything, the College Board has chosen to focus on high-utility academic words and phrases because of their great power in unlocking the meaning of complex texts that you're likely to encounter in high school and postsecondary courses.

Words in Context Questions

Questions in the Words in Context category ask you to consider both the meanings and roles of words and phrases as they are used in particular passages. You'll also be asked to think about how to make language use more effective. These questions focus on the following skills:

▶ Interpreting words and phrases in context (Reading Test)

▶ Analyzing word choice rhetorically (Reading Test)

▶ Making effective use of language (Writing and Language Test)

Ten Reading Test questions — two per passage; a mix of questions about word/phrase meanings and rhetorical word choice — contribute to the Words in Context subscore. Eight Writing and Language Test questions — again, two per passage — also contribute to the subscore; these eight questions will cover a range of skills, from making text more precise or concise to maintaining style and tone to combining sentences into a smoother, more effective single sentence.

Let's consider each of these three main types more fully.

INTERPRETING WORDS AND PHRASES IN CONTEXT (READING TEST)

A number of questions on the Reading Test will require you to figure out the precise meaning of a given word or phrase based on how it's used in a particular passage. "Precise" is an important qualifier here, as you'll generally be asked to pick out the most appropriate meaning for a word or phrase with more than one dictionary definition. Remember, we noted earlier that context was more important in vocabulary questions on the redesigned SAT than was previously the case. The extended context — up to and including an entire passage — gives you more clues to meaning, but you'll have to make good use of those clues to decide on which of the offered meanings makes the most sense in a given passage.

Here's an example: Think about the word "intense," which is a pretty good representative of high-utility academic words and phrases. Maybe you associate this word with emotion or attitude, as in "He's an intense person," or perhaps with determination, as in "She did some intense studying in order to do well on the quiz." However, neither of these quite matches how "intense" is used in the following excerpt from a longer passage.

> [...] The coming decades will likely see more intense clustering of jobs, innovation, and productivity in a smaller number of bigger cities and city-regions. Some regions could end up bloated beyond the capacity of their infrastructure, while others struggle, their promise stymied by inadequate human or other resources.
>
> Adapted from Richard Florida, *The Great Reset.* ©2010 by Richard Florida.

In this case, "intense" is more about degree: the clustering of jobs, innovation, and productivity is, according to the author, likely to be denser, or more concentrated in fewer large cities and city-regions, in the coming decades. While prior knowledge of what "intense" often means could be useful here,

PRACTICE AT

khanacademy.org/sat

Often, Reading Test answer choices will each contain one of several possible meanings of the tested word or phrase. Make use of the context clues in the passage to hone in on the precise meaning of the word or phrase as it's used in the passage.

PRACTICE AT

khanacademy.org/sat

A good strategy here is to use the context clues in the paragraph to come up with a word that could replace "intense" while maintaining the intended meaning of the sentence.

63

you'd also have to read and interpret the context in order to determine exactly how the word is being used in this case.

ANALYZING WORD CHOICE RHETORICALLY (READING TEST)

Other Words in Context questions on the Reading Test may ask you to figure out how the author's particular choice of a word, phrase, or pattern of words or phrases influences the meaning, tone, and style of a passage. Sometimes, these questions deal with the connotations, or associations, that certain words and phrases evoke. Consider how you (or an author) might describe someone who wasn't accompanied by other people. Saying that person was "alone" is more or less just pointing out a fact. To say instead that that person was "solitary" offers a stronger sense of isolation. To instead call that person "forlorn" or even "abandoned" goes yet a step further in casting the person's separateness in a particular, negative way. Deciding which word or phrase in a given context offers just the right flavor is something that good authors do all the time; understanding the effects of such word choice on the audience — how it creates mood or tone or shapes meaning — is something that the Reading Test is likely to require you to do.

MAKING EFFECTIVE USE OF LANGUAGE (WRITING AND LANGUAGE TEST)

PRACTICE AT

khanacademy.org/sat

Taking context into consideration is critical when answering questions about the effective use of language. You may, for instance, need to consider the overall tone or style of the passage, or the writer's purpose, when choosing your answer.

While the Reading Test asks you to interpret how authors use words and phrases, the Writing and Language Test calls on you to make those kinds of decisions yourself as you revise passages. Questions about effective language use are varied. Some questions may present you with language that's wordy or redundant, and you'll have to choose a more concise way of conveying the same idea without changing the meaning. Other questions may ask you to choose the most precise way to say something or the most appropriate way to express an idea in a given context (similar to the Reading Test's questions about analyzing word choice). Still other questions may have you pick out the word or phrase that does the best job of maintaining the style or tone of the passage, or of continuing a particular linguistic pattern, such as repeating the same words for emphasis. In these cases, you might have to replace informal language with a more formal expression (or vice versa, depending on the style and tone of the overall passage), or decide which option most effectively continues a pattern already established in the passage (such as the way several sentences in this paragraph began with the idea of "questions"). Yet other questions may require you to combine whole sentences or parts of two or more sentences to make choppy or repetitive sentences flow more smoothly, or to accomplish some other goal (such as placing emphasis on an action rather than on the person performing the action).

It's worth noting here that these language use questions aren't directly about grammar, usage, or mechanics. (Those issues are addressed in other questions on the test.) Instead, these questions try to get you to think about how language should be used to accomplish particular writerly aims, such as being clearer, more precise, or more economical.

CHAPTER 7 RECAP

The Words in Context subscore on the SAT is based on questions from both the Reading Test and the Writing and Language Test. These questions are intended to determine whether you can figure out word and phrase meanings in context and how authors use words and phrases to achieve specific purposes.

There are two types of questions on the **Reading Test** that address words in context. They are:

1. **Interpreting words and phrases in context**: You'll be asked to decide on the precise meaning of particular words and phrases as they're used in context. This will typically involve considering various meanings of words and phrases and picking out the one that most closely matches how the word or phrase is used in the passage. These sorts of questions accompany most passages on the test.

2. **Analyzing word choice rhetorically**: You'll be asked to think about how an author's choice of words and phrases helps shape meaning, tone, and style. These sorts of questions accompany select passages on the test.

You'll find a single main type of question (and several subtypes) on the **Writing and Language Test** that addresses words in context. In questions about effective language use, you'll be asked to revise passages to improve the precision and concision of expression; ensure that the style and/or tone of the passage are appropriate; and combine sentences or parts of sentences to enhance flow or to achieve some other purpose (such as emphasis). These sorts of questions accompany every passage on the test.

While the specific format of Words in Context questions varies within and between the Reading Test and the Writing and Language Test, all of the questions ask you to consider the same kinds of choices about language that good authors routinely make. As you approach each question, you'll want to examine the nuances of word and phrase meanings and connotations as well as the impact that a particular word, phrase, or linguistic pattern is likely to have on the reader.

PRACTICE AT

khanacademy.org/sat

Since the words and phrases you'll be tested on are given within an extended context, you'll have clues to help you determine the correct meaning. Thus, don't be discouraged if you're unfamiliar with some of the tested words or phrases.

REMEMBER

Analyzing word choice is also an integral part of your task on the Essay.

Chapter 8

About the SAT Reading Test

Whatever your postsecondary plans, reading will be a central part of them. Even as other forms of media, such as audiovisual formats, have gained an important and valuable place in education, the written word remains a vital tool in conveying information and ideas. Whether you're taking a course in literature, history, physics, or accounting, your ability to read and understand text — often largely or wholly on your own — will be critical to doing well in the class. The SAT Reading Test is designed to assess how ready you are to read and interpret the very kinds of texts you're likely to encounter in college and career.

The passages (reading selections) on the Reading Test vary in genre, purpose, subject, and complexity in order to assess your skill in comprehending a diverse range of texts like those you'll come across in many different postsecondary courses. The Reading Test will also include a pair of related passages, with some questions asking you to draw connections between the two selections. Some passages will also include one or more informational graphics, such as tables, graphs, and charts, and you'll be expected both to understand those graphics and to link the information contained in them with information found in the passage.

You'll be answering questions that deal with both what's stated and what's implied in these texts — that is, what authors say directly and what they suggest but don't come right out and say explicitly. Some questions deal with the information and ideas in passages, while others focus on structure, purpose, and the craft of writing; still others ask you to draw connections between pairs of related passages or between a passage and an informational graphic or graphics. As a group, these questions require you to use the same sorts of close reading skills you're already using in your high school classes and that are important to have in order to be successful in college courses and workforce training programs.

The rest of this chapter is an overview of the Reading Test. Additional information about the question types can be found in the next three chapters.

 **REMEMBER**

The basic aim of the SAT Reading Test is to determine whether you're able to comprehend the many types of challenging literary and informational texts you're likely to encounter in college and career.

Reading Test Passages

The passages on the Reading Test are as varied as those you're reading now for your high school classes. Some are literary in nature, while others are primarily informational. They differ in purpose as well: Some tell a story, while others share information, explain a process or concept, or try to convince you to accept or do something. They also cover a wide range of subjects. Some passages you may find particularly challenging, while others are more straightforward. In addition, some passages are paired, while others are accompanied by one or more informational graphics.

Here are some of the key features of Reading Test passages.

▶ **Genre:** The Reading Test includes both literary and informational passages. Literary passages are primarily concerned with telling a story, recounting an event or experience, or reflecting on an idea or concept. On the Reading Test, the main literary passage is a fiction selection, although other passages may also have literary elements, such as figurative language or imagery. Informational passages, as the name implies, are mostly concerned with conveying information and ideas.

▶ **Purpose:** As noted above, some Reading Test passages are mainly focused on telling a story, recounting an event or experience, or reflecting on an idea or concept. Other passages present new information and ideas or explain a process or concept. Still other passages are best described as arguments. Their goal is to convince readers to believe something or to take some sort of action through the use of evidence, reasoning, and/or stylistic and persuasive techniques.

▶ **Subject:** The Reading Test includes passages in three major subject areas: U.S. and world literature, history/social studies, and science. Literature passages are selections from classic and more recent works of fiction by authors from the United States and around the world. History/social studies passages include selections from fields such as economics, sociology, and political science. These passages also include selections from U.S. founding documents (e.g., the Declaration of Independence and the Gettysburg Address) and similar texts about civic and political life written by authors from the United States and across the globe. Science passages deal with information, concepts, and experiments in the fields of earth science, biology, chemistry, and physics.

▶ **Complexity:** The reading challenge posed by the passages on the test varies. Some passages are relatively straightforward. They may, for example, have a very clear purpose, present a fairly small amount of information, and use familiar language. Other passages, by contrast, are more complex. They may have multiple levels of meaning (such as a literal and a metaphorical level), require the reader to follow a complicated series of events, and make use of long and involved sentences. (It's important to note here that each adminstration of the Reading Test has a similar range of passage

PRACTICE AT

🖋 **khanacademy.org/sat**

You may find that you're better at reading and interpreting passages from one subject area — history/ social studies, for instance — than from others. It's important, therefore, to practice reading and answering questions about passages from all three subject areas on the SAT (U.S. and world literature, history/social studies, and science). In fact, consider devoting more practice time to the types of passages you're less comfortable reading.

complexity, so you shouldn't worry about getting a test that has nothing but highly complex passages.) Chapter 12 includes examples of low- and high-complexity passages to give you a sense of the spread of difficulty you'll see on the test.

Two other features of passages are important as well.

▶ **Paired passages:** Each version of the Reading Test includes a pair of related informational passages. These passages are on the same topic and interact with one another in some way. They may, for instance, present different perspectives or opinions on the topic, with the first passage taking one position on the subject and the second passage another. In other cases, the two passages may simply contain different information on the same topic. One may be a general overview, for example, while the other zeroes in on one particular element. The set of questions will ask about each passage separately as well as about both passages together. (More on this below.)

▶ **Informational graphics:** Some passages include one or more tables, graphs, charts, and the like that correspond to the topic of the passage. A graphic may, for instance, display the results of an experiment described in the passage. Questions may ask you to locate information in the graphic, draw reasonable conclusions about the data, or make connections between the graphic and the passage. Graphics appear along with one of the history/social studies and one of the science passages.

All of the passages on the Reading Test come from previously published, high-quality sources, so you're getting a chance to read some of the best writing and thinking out there. While you're not likely to forget that you're taking a test while reading the passages, it's our hope that you'll find them interesting and engaging and maybe learn a thing or two from them as well.

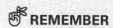
REMEMBER

Two passages on the SAT Reading Test will include one or two informational graphics — tables, charts, graphs, or the like. Related questions will assess your skill in locating and interpreting information and integrating that information with the text.

Reading Test Questions

Now let's shift to the kinds of questions you'll come across on the Reading Test. All of them will be multiple-choice, meaning that you'll be selecting the option that best answers the question. To do this, you'll want to consider what's stated and implied in the passage (or passage pair), along with any additional material (such as a table or graph), and decide which of the four choices makes the most sense. The questions follow something of a natural order. You'll find questions about the passage as a whole — questions about the main idea or point of view, for example — early on in each set, while questions about specific parts of the passage come later. Questions about graphics and questions linking paired passages typically come near the end of the sequence.

The questions are meant to be like those that you'd ask or answer in a lively, serious discussion about a text. Think of the kinds of questions you'd be

REMEMBER

Wrong answer choices are often tempting. You must, therefore, base your answer on a close reading and interpretation of the text and any associated graphics.

REMEMBER

All of the information you need to answer the questions can be found in the passages themselves or in supplementary material such as graphics or footnotes. You won't be tested on your background knowledge of the specific topics covered. In fact, be careful not to apply outside knowledge to the passage or questions, as this may skew your interpretation of the text.

asked to consider in your favorite, most engaging class, and you'll have the general idea of what's in store on the Reading Test. The questions aren't intended to be tricky or trivial, although some will be quite challenging and will require careful reading and thinking. You may find it useful to skim the questions before reading each passage (or passage pair), but this is no substitute for actually reading the passages and grappling with their content. As we said, the questions aren't meant to be tricky, but they *are* designed to determine whether you're reading closely and making reasonable interpretations, so expect to see some answer choices that may seem right or to fit your preconceptions but that don't match up with what an author is saying.

The questions also often reflect the specific sort of passage you're reading. A literature question may ask you to think about plot or character, but a science question won't; instead, it will ask about things such as hypotheses and experimental data. Although these passages are taken from texts on various subjects, the questions don't directly test your background knowledge of the specific topics covered. All of the information you'll need to answer the questions can be found in the passages themselves (or in any supplementary material, such as a graphic or footnotes).

Reading Test questions fall into three general categories: (1) Information and Ideas, (2) Rhetoric, and (3) Synthesis. The questions won't be labeled this way on the test, and it's not crucial that you understand all of the differences. A brief explanation of each category, though, should help you get a sense of what you'll encounter, what knowledge and skills are covered, and how better to prepare for the test.

▶ **Information and Ideas:** These questions focus on a close, careful reading of the passage and on what the author is saying. In these sorts of questions, you'll be asked to locate stated information, make reasonable inferences, and apply what you've read to another, similar situation. You'll also be asked to figure out the best evidence in the text for the answer to another question or the best support for a conclusion offered in the question itself. (This concept was introduced in Chapter 6.) You'll also have to determine the central ideas and themes of passages, summarize important information, and understand relationships (including cause-and-effect, comparison-contrast, and sequence). Other questions will ask you to interpret the meaning of words and phrases as they are used in particular passages. (This concept was introduced in Chapter 7.)

▶ **Rhetoric:** These questions take a different approach, focusing your attention on how an author puts together a text and how the various pieces contribute to the whole text. You'll be asked to think about how an author's word choice shapes meaning, tone, and style. You'll also be asked to consider how the text is structured and what purpose its various parts (such as a particular detail) play. Understanding the author's point of view and purpose is also part of this category, as are questions about the claims, reasons, evidence, and stylistic and persuasive devices (such as appeals to fear or emotion) found in arguments. The common thread tying these questions together is their focus on the author's craft. Instead of thinking about the author's message per se, you'll be asked to think about how the author constructs his or her text to make its message clear, informative, or convincing.

▶ **Synthesis**: Unlike questions in the other two categories, Synthesis questions only accompany certain passages. They come in two basic forms. Some Synthesis questions ask you to draw connections between a pair of passages. For example, a question may ask how the author of the first passage would most likely react to a claim made by the author of the second passage. It might also ask you something more general, such as how the two passages are similar or different in content, form, style, or perspective. Other Synthesis questions ask about an informational graphic. Here, for example, you'll have to find a particular piece of data, figure out which conclusion is the most reasonable given a certain set of results from a study, or integrate information from a table with the information and ideas found in the passage itself.

These categories are discussed more fully in Chapters 9 to 11.

The Reading Test in Overview

Having a general sense of how the Reading Test is put together will help you to prepare for the test and pace yourself during the test itself.

▶ Total Questions: 52

▶ Total Time: 65 minutes (on average, a minute and 15 seconds per question, inclusive of passage reading time)

▶ Number of Passages: Four single passages plus one pair of passages

▶ Passage Length: 500 to 750 words; total of 3,250 words

▶ Passage Subjects: One U.S. and world literature passage, two history/social studies passages (one in social science and one from a U.S. founding document or text in the Great Global Conversation), and two science passages

▶ Passage Complexities: A defined range from grades 9–10 to early postsecondary

▶ Questions per Passage: 10 or 11

▶ Scores: In addition to an overall test score, the questions on the Reading Test contribute to various scores in the following ways:

— Command of Evidence (Chapter 6): 10 questions, two per passage

— Words in Context (Chapter 7): 10 questions, two per passage

REMEMBER

You'll have 65 minutes to answer 52 questions on the Reading Test, or 1 minute and 15 seconds per question on average. However, it is important to keep in mind that you'll spend time reading the four single passages along with one pair of passages.

— Analysis in History/Social Studies: 21 questions (all of the questions on the two history/social studies passages)

— Analysis in Science: 21 questions (all of the questions on the two science passages)

Note: Some Reading Test questions don't contribute to any of these scores (just to the overall test score), and some history/social studies and science questions (such as vocabulary questions) contribute to two of these scores.

Chapter 12 provides sample passages and questions to help you become more familiar with the Reading Test. Chapter 12 also contains explanations for the answers.

CHAPTER 8 RECAP

The SAT Reading Test measures your skill in reading and comprehending texts across a wide range of genres, purposes, subjects, and complexities. The questions on the test are all multiple-choice, mirror those that you'd encounter in a good class discussion, and cover three basic areas: Information and Ideas, Rhetoric, and Synthesis. All of the questions can be answered based on what's stated or implied in the passages (and in any supplementary material provided), and no question tests background knowledge of the topic. Each test includes one passage pair, and two passages (one in history/social studies, one in science) include an informational graphic or graphics.

There's quite a bit to read on the test and also a fair number of questions; the length of the test, however, is balanced by three factors. First, the passages, while often challenging, are like those that you're probably already reading for your high school classes, and they cover many of the same subjects as well. Second, the questions deal with important aspects of the passages rather than trivia, so if you grasp the central ideas and key details of each passage, you're more likely to do well. Finally, enough time is provided (65 minutes) so that you should be able to answer the questions without a lot of rushing as long as you maintain a good, consistent pace and keep track of the clock.

PRACTICE AT

khanacademy.org/sat

Devote ample practice time to reading passages efficiently and strategically, considering the types of things you'll likely be asked in SAT questions. With practice, you'll find that you can read passages more quickly and gain a stronger grasp of the content, structure, and author's purpose.

Chapter 9

Reading: Information and Ideas

As discussed in Chapter 8, questions on the Reading Test can be sorted into one of three categories: (1) Information and Ideas, (2) Rhetoric, and (3) Synthesis. This chapter is the first of three to discuss in more detail what sorts of knowledge and skills are required in these questions. This chapter focuses on the first category, Information and Ideas. Chapter 10 addresses Rhetoric questions, and Chapter 11 talks about Synthesis questions. These three chapters will use some of the sample questions found in Chapter 12, which includes additional examples as well as explanations for the answers to each question.

Information and Ideas: The Author's Message

Information and Ideas questions, as mentioned in Chapter 8, ask you to think carefully about the author's message. To interpret that message, you'll need to consider both what's stated and what's implied in the passage. (To recap: By "stated," we mean the things that the author mentions directly and explicitly, such as facts, figures, and other kinds of main points and key details. "Implied," by contrast, refers to what isn't directly stated but is otherwise strongly suggested and can reasonably be inferred.)

It's now time to examine the specific sorts of questions that make up the Information and Ideas category and what kinds of skills and knowledge these questions expect of you.

Questions in this category are of six main types:

▶ **Reading Closely:** Determining what's stated or implied in a passage and applying what you've learned from it to a new, similar situation

▶ **Citing Textual Evidence:** Deciding which part of a passage best supports either the answer to another question or a given conclusion

▶ **Determining Central Ideas and Themes:** Understanding the main point(s) or theme(s) of a passage

▶ **Summarizing:** Recognizing an effective summary of a passage or of a part of a passage

▶ **Understanding Relationships:** Drawing connections (such as cause-and-effect, comparison-contrast, and sequence) between people, events, ideas, and the like in a passage

▶ **Interpreting Words and Phrases in Context:** Figuring out the precise meaning of a particular word or phrase as it's used in a passage

Let's explore each of these subcategories in turn.

READING CLOSELY

Reading Closely is the most general of the question types on the Reading Test. It includes a broad range of questions that deal with interpreting what an author has said explicitly or implicitly and applying that information to new contexts. You may be asked to locate a point or detail in a passage or to reach a supportable conclusion or inference based on what's been stated directly, or you may be asked to think about how the information and ideas in the passage could be applied to another analogous case or situation.

The questions themselves don't follow an easily recognized pattern, but in each case, you'll have to read attentively and consider what the author is trying to say directly or indirectly. There are also often one or more clues within the question that hint at the kind of work you'll have to do. If the question uses "according to the passage," "states," "indicates," or something similar, it's likely that you should look for something said explicitly in the text. On the other hand, if the question uses "based on the passage," "it can reasonably be inferred," "implies," or the like, you'll probably need to do at least some interpreting of the passage to figure out an implicit message.

CITING TEXTUAL EVIDENCE

Questions in this subcategory call on your skill in determining which portion of the passage provides the best textual evidence for the answer to another question or for a conclusion offered in the question itself. We discussed these questions in some detail in Chapter 6, which covered the Command of Evidence subscore. In that chapter, we talked briefly about the nature of textual evidence (in short, the answer to the question "How do I know it?"), but the Citing Textual Evidence question type comes up frequently, so we should look at an example.

Consider this brief excerpt from a speech by Congresswoman Barbara Jordan, who was discussing the nature and seriousness of the impeachment of a president in the U.S. political process. The sentences that are the focus of the first of two paired questions have been highlighted here for convenience, but they wouldn't be if this were a real test. (The full passage, along with more thorough answer explanations, can be found in Chapter 12.)

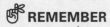 **REMEMBER**

Keywords in the question will often clue you in on whether you're being asked about a detail that was explicitly stated in the passage or about an implicit message that was suggested by the passage. Being aware of this distinction will help you approach questions more effectively.

. . . The North Carolina ratification convention: "No one need be afraid that officers who commit oppression will pass with immunity." **"Prosecutions of impeachments will seldom fail to agitate the passions of the whole community," said Hamilton in the *Federalist Papers*, number 65. "We divide into parties more or less friendly or inimical to the accused." I do not mean political parties in that sense.**

The drawing of political lines goes to the motivation behind impeachment; but impeachment must proceed within the confines of the constitutional term "high crime[s] and misdemeanors." Of the impeachment process, it was Woodrow Wilson who said that "Nothing short of the grossest offenses against the plain law of the land will suffice to give them speed and effectiveness. Indignation so great as to overgrow party interest may secure a conviction; but nothing else can." [. . .]

Adapted from a speech delivered by Congresswoman Barbara Jordan of Texas on July 25, 1974, as a member of the Judiciary Committee of the United States House of Representatives.

In lines 46-50 ("Prosecutions . . . sense"), what is the most likely reason Jordan draws a distinction between two types of "parties"?

A) To counter the suggestion that impeachment is or should be about partisan politics

B) To disagree with Hamilton's claim that impeachment proceedings excite passions

C) To contend that Hamilton was too timid in his support for the concept of impeachment

D) To argue that impeachment cases are decided more on the basis of politics than on justice

The above question isn't our main interest here, but we need to consider it briefly in order to make sense of the second of the two questions. The best answer here is choice A. In the paragraph containing the highlighted sentence, Jordan quotes Alexander Hamilton, who talks about how people "divide into parties" of those who oppose or support impeachment (those who are "more or less friendly or inimical to the accused"). She then goes on to say, "I do not mean political parties in that sense." Here, she draws a distinction between informal groups of people — those simply for and against impeachment, as Hamilton meant — and organized political parties, such as the modern-day Republican and Democratic Parties. The most likely reason Jordan goes to this trouble is because she's worried about being misinterpreted. (This becomes clear elsewhere in the passage, where she indicates that, in her view, impeachment shouldn't be about pure politics but rather about serious violations of the law by a president.)

PRACTICE AT

 **khanacademy.org/sat**

When you're asked to explain why the author of the passage includes a specific statement, carefully consider the context of the statement as well as the author's broader point of view in the passage overall.

But how do we know choice A is the best answer? That's where textual evidence comes in, and it's the basis for the second question in the pair. Before we look at the actual question format, though, consider the following brief quotations from the larger passage. Ask yourself: Which one best supports the answer to the previous question?

> It is wrong, I suggest, it is a misreading of the Constitution for any member here to assert that for a member to vote for an article of impeachment means that that member must be convinced that the President should be removed from office.
>
> The division between the two branches of the legislature, the House and the Senate, assigning to the one the right to accuse and to the other the right to judge—the framers of this Constitution were very astute.
>
> The drawing of political lines goes to the motivation behind impeachment; but impeachment must proceed within the confines of the constitutional term "high crime[s] and misdemeanors."
>
> Congress has a lot to do: appropriations, tax reform, health insurance, campaign finance reform, housing, environmental protection, energy sufficiency, and mass transportation.

The first of the four quotations talks about impeachment, but other than that, it doesn't really have anything clearly to do with the answer to the previous question. The second quotation is about a kind of division, but, again, it has little to do with the matter at hand. The fourth quotation merely offers a list of the many things Jordan feels Congress should be concerning itself with.

That leaves the third quotation. In it, Jordan claims that while a desire to achieve political goals can lead some to want to start impeachment proceedings against a president ("the drawing of political lines goes to the motivation behind impeachment"), the process is too serious for that to be a good basis for such proceedings. Instead, impeachment should only be sought if the president is believed to have committed a serious offense ("must proceed within the confines of the constitutional term 'high crime[s] and misdemeanors'"). This third quotation, then, serves as the best of the four options in terms of textual evidence.

In test format, this Citing Textual Evidence question looks like the following:

> Which choice provides the best evidence for the answer to the previous question?
> A) Lines 13-16 ("It . . . office")
> B) Lines 20-23 ("The division . . . astute")
> C) Lines 51-54 ("The drawing . . . misdemeanors'")
> D) Lines 61-64 ("Congress . . . transportation")

Each of these answer choices refers to one of the quotations presented earlier, only this time passage line numbers stand in for the full quotation. (The words marking the beginning and the end of the quotation are included to make it easier to find the lines in the passage.)

You'll see questions like this throughout the Reading Test, and you should approach each in a similar way: finding the best answer to the first question and then deciding which part of the passage offers the best support for that answer. We mentioned this before, in Chapter 6, but it's worth pointing out again: It's OK to work on both of these questions at once and to reconsider your answer to the first question after you read the second. Sometimes looking at the choices in the second question will help you rethink your original answer to the first question. Just don't overthink it or second-guess yourself too much.

It's possible you'll see variations on the above format as well. One example is when the question itself provides a conclusion (instead of asking you to come up with it on your own in another question) and asks you which choice provides the best support for it. This is fundamentally the same sort of question as the previous Citing Textual Evidence example, only it's a one-part instead of a two-part question.

DETERMINING CENTRAL IDEAS AND THEMES

Some questions on the Reading Test may ask you to figure out what the main points or themes of a passage are. These two concepts are very similar, although many people (and the Reading Test) tend to refer to "theme" instead of "main idea" when talking about the central message of a literary text. In either case, you're typically looking for an overarching statement that succinctly encapsulates a key point the author is trying to make. Main ideas and themes may be stated explicitly or, especially in more challenging texts, only implied. While "theme" questions tend to be only about a passage as a whole, "main idea" questions can be about one or more paragraphs or an entire passage. Generally, words such as "main idea," "main point," "central idea," or "theme" help signal the intent of the question. Because you're looking for the main idea (or theme), you'll want to avoid picking an answer that only refers to a detail or that fails to capture the entire point the author makes.

PRACTICE AT

khanacademy.org/sat

Citing Textual Evidence questions often come as part of a pair, with the answer to the evidence question being related to the answer to an earlier question. You may sometimes find it helpful to revisit your answer to the previous question after reading the answer choices in the evidence question.

PRACTICE AT

khanacademy.org/sat

Keywords such as "main idea" and "theme" clue you in to the fact that you're looking for the answer choice that captures the overarching point the author makes in one or more paragraphs or in the passage as a whole. Be wary of answer choices that focus in on specific details.

SUMMARIZING

When you successfully summarize a text, you've conveyed the most important ideas (generally in the order presented) without adding your own interpretation or including minor details. Although the Reading Test doesn't ask you to create your own summary of a passage or a part of a passage, you may be asked to choose which one of four options offers the best summary, or perhaps to recognize where a proposed summary falls short (maybe because it's inaccurate in some way or includes extraneous details). These sorts of questions generally use some form of the word "summary" as a clue to their purpose.

UNDERSTANDING RELATIONSHIPS

Some questions on the Reading Test may ask you to determine the relationship between people, ideas, events, and the like in passages. These questions tend to fall into one of three types:

▶ **Cause-and-effect:** Understanding how one thing caused another to happen; often signaled by words such as "because" or "since"

▶ **Comparison-contrast:** Understanding how two things are similar and/or different; often signaled by words such as "more" and "less"

▶ **Sequence:** Understanding the order in which things happened; often signaled by words such as "first," "last," "before," and "after"

These sorts of questions can be found with all types of passages. You may, for example, have to determine sequence when figuring out what happened and when in a passage from a novel or which step came first in a science experiment. As noted previously, Understanding Relationships questions will often use words that suggest the kind of relationship you're looking for. This relationship may be directly stated, or you may have to infer it from information in the passage.

INTERPRETING WORDS AND PHRASES IN CONTEXT

We talked about Interpreting Words and Phrases questions in Chapter 7, which dealt with the Words in Context subscore. These questions ask you to determine the precise meaning of a particular word or phrase as it's used in a passage. You'll again be offered four answer options, one of which most closely matches how the author is using the word or phrase. Remember from our previous discussion of "intense" in Chapter 7 that these tested words will often have multiple dictionary definitions, meaning that you can't rely solely on your vocabulary knowledge. Having a broad vocabulary can be helpful, but you'll also have to think about how the word or phrase is being used in a particular case, making this a reading activity.

Although there are some variations, Interpreting Words and Phrases questions typically come in the format of "As used in line *x*, '[word or phrase]' most nearly means," where *x* is a line in the passage and *word or phrase* is

PRACTICE AT
khanacademy.org/sat

As you read the passage, take special note of keywords that signal causes and effects (e.g., "because"), comparisons ("more," "less"), and sequences of events ("first," "after"). You may be asked one or more questions that test your understanding of these relationships.

REMEMBER

On Interpreting Words and Phrases questions, don't rely solely on your vocabulary knowledge. Tested words will often have multiple definitions, so be sure to consider the context in which the word or phrase is being used.

the tested vocabulary. Often, you can try substituting each answer choice into the relevant sentence of the passage to get a better idea of which choice makes the most sense. Note, however, that simply reading the sentence containing the word or phrase isn't always enough; you may need to consider a larger portion of the text — multiple sentences or the surrounding paragraph — or even the passage as a whole to confirm the intended meaning.

CHAPTER 9 RECAP

Information and Ideas questions are, at heart, questions about the message the author is trying to convey. Questions of this type will ask you to read closely, to cite textual evidence, to determine central ideas and themes, to summarize, to understand relationships, and to interpret words and phrases in context. In some cases, the answer can be found word for word (or nearly so) in the passage, but because the Reading Test is also a test of your reasoning skills, you'll often have to do much of the work yourself by making supportable inferences and drawing logical conclusions.

Chapter 10

Reading: Rhetoric

Rhetoric: The Author's Craft

The word "rhetoric" carries several meanings, as you may know — especially if you're involved in speech or debate. One common definition, perhaps the best known today, is "lofty and dishonest language." That meaning is often associated with pronouncements by politicians who are seen as using words to dodge controversy, hide their true position, or prop up a weak argument. The fact that words such as "empty" or "mere" often precede "rhetoric" suggests that the term has a negative connotation for many people.

"Rhetoric," however, has another, broader, more positive meaning, and that is "the study of writing or speaking." Rhetoric in this sense stretches back at least to Aristotle and the ancient Greeks, who helped make rhetoric a formal practice with defined rules and conventions. It's in this second sense that the SAT uses the term. Rhetoric questions on the Reading Test assess how well you understand the choices that authors make in structuring and developing their texts. Paralleling what we did with Information and Ideas in Chapter 9, we'll turn now to the kinds of Rhetoric questions you'll find on the Reading Test.

 **REMEMBER**

Rhetoric questions assess your understanding of how and why the author develops the structure and meaning of the passage. Understanding the author's purpose or point of view is often of central importance to correctly answering Rhetoric questions.

Questions in this category are of five main types:

- **Analyzing word choice:** Understanding how an author selects words, phrases, and language patterns to influence meaning, tone, and style

- **Analyzing text structure:** Describing how an author shapes and organizes a text and how the parts of the passage contribute to the whole text

- **Analyzing point of view:** Understanding the point of view or perspective from which passages are told and how that point of view or perspective affects the content and style of the passage

- **Analyzing purpose:** Determining the main rhetorical aim of a passage or a part of the passage, such as a paragraph

- **Analyzing arguments:** Examining the claims, counterclaims, reasoning, and evidence an author uses in an argument

We'll consider each of these subcategories in the sections that follow.

PRACTICE AT

🌢 **khanacademy.org/sat**

Questions that ask you to analyze word choice aren't assessing your vocabulary knowledge per se. Rather, these questions assess your skill in determining the impact that particular words and phrases have on the meaning, style, and tone of a passage.

PRACTICE AT

🌢 **khanacademy.org/sat**

As you read a passage on the SAT, you'll want to shift back and forth between a focus on the specific content of the passage (the "what") and the structure of the passage (the "how"). Text structure questions require a broader, more abstract understanding of the passage.

ANALYZING WORD CHOICE

Questions about analyzing word choice are — with Information and Ideas questions about interpreting the meaning of words and phrases in context — key elements of the Words in Context subscore, which was discussed in Chapter 7. In contrast to vocabulary questions, Analyzing Word Choice questions focus less on definitions and more on the rhetorical impact that particular words, phrases, and language patterns (such as repetition) have on the meaning, style, and tone of a passage. While there's no standard phrasing to these types of questions, they'll generally call out certain words, phrases, or sentences and ask you to consider the purpose, effect, or impact of this language.

ANALYZING TEXT STRUCTURE

Text structure questions on the Reading Test come in two basic forms. One kind will ask you to characterize in some way the overall structure of the passage. In a few cases, this may be as simple as just recognizing the basic organizing principle of the passage, such as cause-and-effect, sequence, or problem-solution. In most cases, though, such questions will be more complicated and shaped by the content of the individual passage. You may, for example, have to track how the structure shifts over the course of the passage, meaning that the answer will be in two or more parts (as in "the passage begins by doing x and then does y").

Since this last bit was kind of general, let's examine the wording of one such question. The literature passage this question is based on and the explanation for the answer can be found in Chapter 12. Our real interest now is only the format and wording of the question and the approach you'd need to take to respond to it.

> Over the course of the passage, the main focus of the narrative shifts from the
>
> A) reservations a character has about a person he has just met to a growing appreciation that character has of the person's worth.
> B) ambivalence a character feels about his sensitive nature to the character's recognition of the advantages of having profound emotions.
> C) intensity of feeling a character has for another person to the character's concern that that intensity is not reciprocated.
> D) value a character attaches to the wonders of the natural world to a rejection of that sort of beauty in favor of human artistry.

To answer this question (or one like it), you'll have to both think abstractly (moving beyond just understanding the plot to being able to characterize the structure of the passage as an author might) and identify the major change in attitude ("shifts from . . . to") that occurs, in this case, near the end of the passage.

The other kind of text structure question asks about the relationship between an identified part of a passage (such as a phrase or sentence or a particular detail) and the passage as a whole. You may be asked, for example, to recognize that a given detail serves mainly as an example of a particular point the author is trying to make — or that it adds emphasis, foreshadows a later development, calls an assumption into question, or the like. You'll again have to think abstractly, considering not only what the author is saying but also the main contribution that a particular element of the passage makes to furthering the author's overall rhetorical purpose.

ANALYZING POINT OF VIEW

When the Reading Test asks you to consider point of view, it's not usually simply a matter of understanding what's often called "narrative point of view" — whether a passage is told from, say, a first person or a third person omniscient perspective. This can be part of it, but in the world of the Reading Test, "point of view" is a broader term that also includes the idea of the stance or perspective of the author, narrator, or speaker. This is kind of like the attitude (or sometimes the bias) that the author, narrator, or speaker shows toward the subject. In this way, point of view questions are found not just with literary passages but also with informational passages of all sorts.

Point of view questions generally identify themselves by words and phrases such as "perspective" and "point of view." The answer choices frequently offer characterizations of the author, narrator, or speaker. Consider, for instance, the following question from the Barbara Jordan speech we discussed in Chapter 9. (Remember: The passage, additional sample questions, and answer explanations can be found in Chapter 12.)

The stance Jordan takes in the passage is best described as that of

A) an idealist setting forth principles.
B) an advocate seeking a compromise position.
C) an observer striving for neutrality.
D) a scholar researching a historical controversy.

In this case, you have to figure out the stance, or perspective, that Jordan brings to the speech she delivers. To decide on the best answer — which in this instance is choice A — you'll want to both form an overall impression of Jordan and confirm (or modify) that impression based on specific elements of the passage — what Jordan says and how she says it. You might note that Jordan describes her faith in the U.S. Constitution as "whole," "complete," and "total" and that she claims that "the powers relating to impeachment are an essential check in the hands of the body of the legislature against and upon the encroachments of the executive." Her description of her faith in the Constitution strongly suggests idealism, and her claim about impeachment powers can be seen as setting forth a principle. As was the case with Analyzing Text Structure questions, questions about point of view may ask you to note how the perspective from which a passage is told shifts over the course of the text.

ANALYZING PURPOSE

Questions about analyzing purpose are like questions about text structure in that you'll have to think abstractly about the text — not just understanding what the text says but also what the author is trying to achieve. In Analyzing Purpose questions, you'll consider the main purpose or function of the whole passage or of a significant part of the passage, generally one or more paragraphs. The word "purpose" or "function" is often used in such questions, while the answer choices often begin with or include rhetorically focused verbs such as "criticize," "support," "present," or "introduce."

ANALYZING ARGUMENTS

The Reading Test includes passages that are primarily argumentative in nature. Such passages typically include one or more claims, or assertions, that the author attempts to convince the reader to accept through the use of reasoning (analysis), evidence (facts, statistics, expert testimony, case studies, and the like), and stylistic and persuasive elements (vivid imagery, appeals to emotion, and so on). Arguments also sometimes include counterclaims, or assertions made by those whose opinions are different from or opposed to those of the author, which the author may discuss and attempt to pick apart in order to show that his or her own position is stronger. (Confident, fair-minded authors will often take it upon themselves to point out the weaknesses of their own position and the strengths of the positions of others. On the Reading Test, though, you're usually seeing only part of an argument, so counterarguments won't always be present.)

Practically speaking, you probably won't approach Analyzing Arguments questions much differently than you would similar questions about other kinds of passages. A question that asks about the central claim of an argument, for example, is a lot like a question about the main idea or theme of another sort of passage. You'll have to decide on the primary assertion (main point) that the author is making in the argument and distinguish that from secondary assertions (minor points) and details. Analyzing Arguments questions differ from other kinds of Reading Test questions mainly in that they use words and concepts such as "claim," "counterclaim," "reason," and "evidence" to direct your attention to some of the features that distinguish arguments from texts designed to narrate events or experiences, to inform, or to explain.

PRACTICE AT

khanacademy.org/sat

For every SAT passage you read, get in the habit of asking yourself, "Why did the author write this passage?" Or, put differently, "What point or message was the author trying to get across in the passage?" Answering such questions as you read the passage will help you with many of the questions you'll be asked.

PRACTICE AT

khanacademy.org/sat

Keep a sharp eye out for evidence, contrast, and conclusion keywords when reading passages that are argumentative in nature. These keywords will help you to analyze the content and structure of the passage. Evidence use can be signaled by keywords such as "for example" and "because" as well as references to statistics, surveys, and case studies. Contrast keywords include "however," "despite," and "on the contrary." Conclusion keywords include "therefore," "as a result," and "thus."

CHAPTER 10 RECAP

In contrast to Information and Ideas questions, Rhetoric questions on the SAT Reading Test focus on the author's craft rather than on the informational content of passages. When answering Rhetoric questions, you'll think less about the message the author is trying to convey and more about how that message is conveyed and what the author hopes to accomplish. Questions of this sort will ask you to analyze word choice, text structure, point of view, purpose, and arguments. Whatever their specific type, Rhetoric questions will generally be abstract in nature and ask you to step back from the information and ideas in a passage. You'll have a chance to show that you can think as an author would as you trace how particular words, phrases, sentences, and paragraphs interact with an overarching purpose and structure to shape and express the message that the author is trying to share with the audience.

Chapter 11

Reading: Synthesis

Up until now in our discussion of the SAT Reading Test, most of the question types we've examined have focused on taking things (sentences, paragraphs, ideas) apart and examining them closely for their meaning or for their rhetorical purpose or effect. Synthesis questions on the Reading Test, by contrast, focus mainly on putting information and ideas together into a bigger whole to acquire a deeper, broader understanding of a topic. Also in contrast to questions in the Information and Ideas (Chapter 9) and Rhetoric (Chapter 10) categories, Synthesis questions appear only with selected passages — either paired passages or passages with one or more informational graphics.

Questions in this category are of two main types:

▶ **Analyzing multiple texts:** Making connections between topically related informational passages

▶ **Analyzing quantitative information:** Locating data in informational graphics such as tables, graphs, and charts; drawing reasonable conclusions from such graphics; and integrating information displayed graphically with information and ideas in a passage

Each of these categories is discussed in more detail in the following sections.

ANALYZING MULTIPLE TEXTS

Each version of the Reading Test includes one set of two or more topically related informational passages on a subject in either history/social studies or science. We'll call all of these "paired passages" because in most cases there will be two passages in a set — one labeled Passage 1 and the other Passage 2. These pairings are chosen carefully to ensure that the passages are similar enough that meaningful connections can be drawn between the two.

As discussed earlier, the two passages may present opposing positions on the same issue, but it's more likely that the second passage will "respond" to the first in some more general way. The second passage may, for instance, provide a more detailed explanation of an idea that's only touched on in the first passage, or it may offer a practical application of a theoretical concept discussed in the first passage. The two passages will be different enough in content that you should be able to remember who said what if you've read

 **REMEMBER**

Synthesis questions appear only with paired passages or passages that are accompanied by one or more informational graphics. Synthesis questions ask you to draw connections between related passages and to locate data in and draw reasonable conclusions from tables, graphs, and charts, as well as integrate information conveyed in graphics and in words.

REMEMBER

The SAT Reading Test will include one set of topically related passages, or "paired passages," drawn from history/social studies or science. You'll be assessed on your understanding of each passage individually as well as your skill in drawing meaningful connections between the two.

them both carefully, but, as always, you can refer to the test book as often as you like and use notations such as underlines, numbers, and arrows if this will help you keep the two passages straight in your mind.

Here's an example that gives you an idea of how paired passages work.

Passage 1 is adapted from Susan Milius, "A Different Kind of Smart." ©2013 by Science News. Passage 2 is adapted from Bernd Heinrich, *Mind of the Raven: Investigations and Adventures with Wolf-Birds.* ©2007 by Bernd Heinrich.

Passage 1

In 1894, British psychologist C. Lloyd Morgan published what's called Morgan's canon, the principle that suggestions of humanlike mental processes behind an animal's behavior
Line should be rejected if a simpler explanation will do.
5   Still, people seem to maintain certain expectations, especially when it comes to birds and mammals. "We somehow want to prove they are as 'smart' as people," zoologist Sara Shettleworth says. We want a bird that masters a vexing problem to be employing human-
10 style insight.

New Caledonian crows face the high end of these expectations, as possibly the second-best toolmakers on the planet.

Their tools are hooked sticks or strips made from spike-
15 edged leaves, and they use them in the wild to winkle grubs out of crevices. Researcher Russell Gray first saw the process on a cold morning in a mountain forest in New Caledonia, an island chain east of Australia. Over the course of days, he and crow researcher Gavin Hunt had gotten wild crows used to
20 finding meat tidbits in holes in a log. Once the birds were checking the log reliably, the researchers placed a spiky tropical pandanus plant beside the log and hid behind a blind.

A crow arrived. It hopped onto the pandanus plant, grabbed the spiked edge of one of the long straplike leaves and
25 began a series of ripping motions. Instead of just tearing away one long strip, the bird ripped and nipped in a sequence to create a slanting stair-step edge on a leaf segment with a narrow point and a wide base. The process took only seconds. Then the bird dipped the narrow end of its leaf strip into a
30 hole in the log, fished up the meat with the leaf-edge spikes, swallowed its prize and flew off.

"That was my 'oh wow' moment," Gray says. After the crow had vanished, he picked up the tool the bird had left behind. "I had a go, and I couldn't do it," he recalls. Fishing
35 the meat out was tricky. It turned out that Gray was moving the leaf shard too forcefully instead of gently stroking the spines against the treat.

The crow's deft physical manipulation was what inspired Gray and Auckland colleague Alex Taylor to test other wild
40 crows to see if they employed the seemingly insightful string-pulling solutions that some ravens, kea parrots and other brainiac birds are known to employ. Three of four crows passed that test on the first try.

Passage 2

For one month after they left the nest, I led my four young
45 ravens at least once and sometimes several times a day on
thirty-minute walks. During these walks, I wrote down
everything in their environment they pecked at. In the first
sessions, I tried to be teacher. I touched specific objects—
sticks, moss, rocks—and nothing that I touched remained
50 untouched by them. They came to investigate what I had
investigated, leading me to assume that young birds are aided
in learning to identify food from the parents' example. They
also, however, contacted almost everything else that lay
directly in their own paths. They soon became more
55 independent by taking their own routes near mine. Even while
walking along on their own, they pulled at leaves, grass stems,
flowers, bark, pine needles, seeds, cones, clods of earth, and
other objects they encountered. I wrote all this down,
converting it to numbers. After they were thoroughly familiar
60 with the background objects in these woods and started to
ignore them, I seeded the path we would later walk together
with objects they had never before encountered. Some of
these were conspicuous food items: raspberries, dead
meal worm beetles, and cooked corn kernels. Others were
65 conspicuous and inedible: pebbles, glass chips, red
winterberries. Still others were such highly cryptic foods as
encased caddisfly larvae and moth cocoons. The results were
dramatic.

The four young birds on our daily walks contacted all new
70 objects preferentially. They picked them out at a rate of up to
tens of thousands of times greater than background or
previously contacted objects. The main initial criterion for
pecking or picking anything up was its novelty. In subsequent
trials, when the previously novel items were edible, they
75 became preferred and the inedible objects became
"background" items, just like the leaves, grass, and pebbles,
even if they were highly conspicuous. These experiments
showed that ravens' curiosity ensures exposure to all or almost
all items in the environment.

You can probably easily note, even before reading any of the associated test questions, why these two passages might have been chosen for pairing. The two texts share a broad topical similarity — animal intelligence — but if that were all, it probably wouldn't be a very meaningful activity to draw connections between them. Examining more closely, we note that both passages deal with the issue of bird intelligence, although Passage 1 mainly discusses New Caledonian crows while Passage 2 mainly discusses ravens. Delving more deeply still, we can grasp that both passages deal to some extent with the issue of humans' response to and interpretation of animals' signs of intelligence. Passage 1 is explicit about this, noting in the first three paragraphs that people have a tendency to see animals as thinking in humanlike ways even when simpler and perhaps more defensible explanations are possible. Passage 2 isn't as direct in this respect, but the author (the "I" in the passage)

PRACTICE AT

🌱 **khanacademy.org/sat**

Paired passages will be topically related, as are these two passages that broadly deal with bird intelligence. The exact relationship between the two passages, however, may be nuanced.

definitely shows some of that tendency with regard to his ravens (e.g., "These experiments showed that ravens' curiosity ensures exposure to all or almost all items in the environment"). However, the two passages are different enough — at the most basic level, one is about crows and the other is about ravens — that it's fairly easy to keep the information and ideas in each passage separate after you've read both.

The questions you'll find with paired passages are of two general kinds. The first kind consists of questions about either Passage 1 or Passage 2 separately. These come in order — questions about Passage 1, then questions about Passage 2 — and are of the same types that we discussed in Chapters 9 and 10. The second kind consists of the actual Synthesis questions. These questions require you to draw meaningful connections between the two passages. They might ask about the information and ideas in the passages or about the rhetorical strategies used in them, just like questions about single (nonpaired) passages — except in these cases you'll have to draw on an understanding of both texts to answer the questions correctly.

Let's inspect two of the Synthesis questions associated with the paired passages presented earlier. (The questions and a full answer explanation for each can be found in Chapter 12.)

The first question asks you to recognize a relatively straightforward similarity between the animals discussed in the two passages.

> The crows in Passage 1 and the ravens in Passage 2 shared which trait?
>
> A) They modified their behavior in response to changes in their environment.
> B) They formed a strong bond with the humans who were observing them.
> C) They manufactured useful tools for finding and accessing food.
> D) They mimicked the actions they saw performed around them.

To recognize choice A as the best answer, you'll need to note that both the crows described in Passage 1 and the ravens described in Passage 2 changed their behavior due to changes in their environment. As Passage 1 notes, the wild crows began "checking [a] log reliably" after the researchers "had gotten [them] used to finding meat tidbits" in holes in the log. Passage 2, meanwhile, mentions that the ravens "picked . . . out" objects newly introduced by the researcher into their environment "at a rate of up to tens of thousands of times greater than background or previously contacted objects." To answer the question correctly, you'll have to connect specific information found in each passage.

REMEMBER

Sets of questions associated with paired passages will begin with questions that focus on each passage separately and that will be similar in nature to the questions you'll see on nonpaired passages. Next, you'll see Synthesis questions that require you to draw on an understanding of both passages.

The second question we'll consider here is on a point that we touched on when discussing the passages themselves.

> Is the main conclusion presented by the author of Passage 2 consistent with Morgan's canon, as described in Passage 1?
>
> A) Yes, because the conclusion proposes that the ravens' behavior is a product of environmental factors.
> B) Yes, because the conclusion offers a satisfyingly simple explanation of the ravens' behavior.
> C) No, because the conclusion suggests that the ravens exhibit complex behavior patterns.
> D) No, because the conclusion implies that a humanlike quality motivates the ravens' behavior.

Compared to the first question, this one is broader and more abstract and complex. You have to understand (at least) both Morgan's canon, as described in Passage 1, and the main conclusion of Passage 2. We've already hinted at the answer to this question, which is choice D. Passage 1 defines Morgan's canon as "the principle that suggestions of humanlike mental processes behind an animal's behavior should be rejected if a simpler explanation will do." The author of Passage 2, however, indicates his belief that ravens display curiosity — a humanlike trait — and doesn't show any signs of having seriously considered other, simpler possibilities. The main point to remember here is that Synthesis questions aren't always about drawing simple point-A-to-point-B comparisons; some questions will require you to have a solid working knowledge of the subtleties of the passages.

ANALYZING QUANTITATIVE INFORMATION

You'll find one or more informational graphics — tables, graphs, charts, and the like — accompanying one of the history/social studies passages and also one of the science passages on the test. There'll be questions about those graphics as well. These questions fall into three general kinds (although the first two are fairly similar):

▶ Questions that ask you to locate information in one or more informational graphics

▶ Questions that ask you to draw reasonable conclusions from data presented in one or more graphics

▶ Questions that ask you to connect the information displayed in one or more graphics with the information in the accompanying passage

The main difference between the first two types is simply in how explicit the information is. Sometimes we'll ask you to just locate a particular piece of information; in other cases, you'll need to interpret the data to make a reasonable inference. (This difference is analogous to the stated-implied distinction we talked about previously.) The third type of question, on the other

PRACTICE AT

khanacademy.org/sat

Higher difficulty questions associated with paired passages will require you to have a strong understanding of each passage individually and then to draw complex or subtle connections between the two. As you read the second passage in a pair, carefully consider how that passage relates to the first in terms of content, focus, and perspective.

hand, will require you to understand both the passage and the graphic(s) and to integrate the information found in each.

Now we'll briefly examine two different questions involving graphics. The first question is a relatively simple one requiring a straightforward reading of a graphic that accompanies a social science passage on traffic. (As always, the passage, graphic, question, and answer explanation can be found in Chapter 12.)

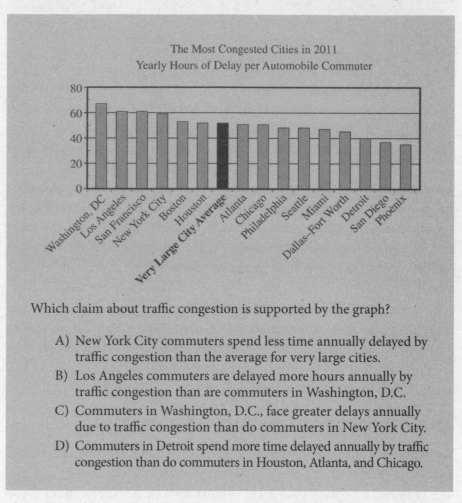

The Most Congested Cities in 2011
Yearly Hours of Delay per Automobile Commuter

Which claim about traffic congestion is supported by the graph?

A) New York City commuters spend less time annually delayed by traffic congestion than the average for very large cities.

B) Los Angeles commuters are delayed more hours annually by traffic congestion than are commuters in Washington, D.C.

C) Commuters in Washington, D.C., face greater delays annually due to traffic congestion than do commuters in New York City.

D) Commuters in Detroit spend more time delayed annually by traffic congestion than do commuters in Houston, Atlanta, and Chicago.

PRACTICE AT

khanacademy.org/sat

Some Analyzing Quantitative Information questions, such as this one, will require you to locate information from a chart, table, or graph or to draw a reasonable conclusion from the data. Carefully analyze the data in the graph — for instance, by reading the title, determining what the axes represent, and understanding the scale or scales used — before selecting your answer.

You can determine the best answer to this question, choice C, by understanding how the graph displays information. As its title indicates, the graph conveys data about the most congested U.S. cities in 2011 in terms of "yearly hours of delay per automobile commuter." A series of U.S. cities is listed on the horizontal (x) axis of the graph, while hours in increments of 20 are marked along the vertical (y) axis. Each light gray bar represents the yearly hours of delay per driver for a given city, with the dark gray bar near the middle representing the average delay for very large cities. Higher bars represent greater yearly delays than lower bars, so automobile commuters in the cities listed toward the left-hand side of the graph experienced longer annual delays than did the automobile commuters in the cities listed toward the right-hand side. Given that, it's a fairly simple matter to answer the question, as Washington, D.C., is to the left of New York City (and all other cities) on the graph.

The second question requires more genuine synthesis, as you'll have to understand both the passage and the graphic to get the question right. Because of this, we'll quote the most relevant bit from the passage and then follow that with the graphic. (In a real testing situation, you'd have to find this portion of the passage on your own. Chapter 12 contains the full passage as well as the question, graphic, and answer explanation.)

[...] Putman works in the lab of Ken Lohmann, who has been studying the magnetic abilities of loggerheads for over 20 years. In his lab at the University of North Carolina, Lohmann places hatchlings in a large water tank surrounded by a large grid of electromagnetic coils. In 1991, he found that the babies started swimming in the opposite direction if he used the coils to reverse the direction of the magnetic field around them. They could use the field as a compass to get their bearing. [...]

Adapted from Ed Yong, "Turtles Use the Earth's Magnetic Field as Global GPS." ©2011 by Kalmbach Publishing Co.

Orientation of Hatchling Loggerheads Tested in Magnetic Fields

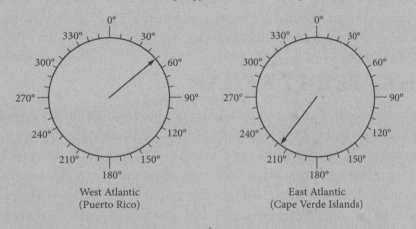

West Atlantic
(Puerto Rico)

East Atlantic
(Cape Verde Islands)

Adapted from Nathan Putman, Courtney Endres, Catherine Lohmann, and Kenneth Lohmann, "Longitude Perception and Bicoordinate Magnetic Maps in Sea Turtles." ©2011 by Elsevier Inc.

Orientation of hatchling loggerheads tested in a magnetic field that simulates a position at the west side of the Atlantic near Puerto Rico (left) and a position at the east side of the Atlantic near the Cape Verde Islands (right). The arrow in each circle indicates the mean direction that the group of hatchlings swam. Data are plotted relative to geographic north (N = 0°).

It can reasonably be inferred from the passage and the graphic that if scientists adjusted the coils to reverse the magnetic field simulating that in the East Atlantic (Cape Verde Islands), the hatchlings would most likely swim in which direction?

A) Northwest
B) Northeast
C) Southeast
D) Southwest

PRACTICE AT

🔥 khanacademy.org/sat

For passages that are accompanied by one or more informational graphics, be sure to carefully read all of the information given, including the title, labels, and captions of all graphics.

PRACTICE AT

khanacademy.org/sat

A more challenging Synthesis question such as this one will require that you integrate a solid understanding of the passage with a strong interpretation of data presented in a chart, table, or graph.

While the first question we examined was just about finding some information in the graphic, this question requires multiple steps involving both the passage and the graphic. We know from the passage that loggerhead turtle hatchlings in a specially constructed tank in Ken Lohmann's lab will start "swimming in the opposite direction" if the direction of the magnetic field around them is reversed. From the graphic and its accompanying caption, we learn, among other things, that geographic north on the diagram is represented by 0 degrees and that loggerhead hatchlings swimming in a magnetic field simulating that of a position in the East Atlantic Ocean near the Cape Verde Islands will normally move in a southwesterly direction (around 218 degrees). Putting these bits of information together, we can reasonably infer that if the magnetic field affecting these "East Atlantic" turtles were reversed, the hatchlings would also reverse direction, swimming in a northeasterly direction. The best answer here, then, is choice B.

As you can tell, questions involving graphics can sometimes get complicated, but the basic set of knowledge and skills you'll apply is the same as you'd use with any other question on the Reading Test. Read carefully, figure out what the author says directly and indirectly, and, when necessary, draw reasonable conclusions supported by textual evidence.

CHAPTER 11 RECAP

The last of the three categories of Reading Test questions, Synthesis, includes just two main types: Analyzing Multiple Texts and Analyzing Quantitative Information. However, as the samples in this chapter (and in Chapter 12) suggest, there's a lot of variety in these sorts of questions, and they can range from relatively simple and straightforward to quite complex. Even when you encounter the more difficult ones, though, you should proceed calmly and thoughtfully. The knowledge and skills these questions call on are fundamentally the same as those needed for any other question on the test. In the end, it's all about reading closely, making use of textual evidence, and drawing supportable conclusions when needed.

Chapters 8 through 11 have covered the content of the SAT Reading Test in quite a bit of detail. The next chapter will present sample passages and questions, along with detailed explanations of how the answer for each question was reached and why the alternatives were not as good a choice in each case. Some of the material in the preceding four chapters will be presented again, but additional passages and questions are included as well.

Chapter 12

Sample Reading Test Questions

In Chapters 8 to 11, you learned about the basic elements of the Reading Test on the redesigned SAT, including the types of passages you will encounter and the types of questions the test will include. In this chapter, you will find five sample passages and associated test questions. Following each question is an explanation for the best answer and some comments about the incorrect answer choices.

These instructions will precede the SAT Reading Test.

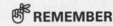
REMEMBER

There will be four single passages and one set of paired passages on the Reading Test. Passages are drawn from U.S. and world literature, history/social studies, and science.

Reading Test

65 MINUTES, 52 QUESTIONS

Turn to Section 1 of your answer sheet to answer the questions in this section.

DIRECTIONS

Each passage or pair of passages below is followed by a number of questions. After reading each passage or pair, choose the best answer to each question based on what is stated or implied in the passage or passages and in any accompanying graphics (such as a table or graph).

SAMPLE 1:

History/Social Studies Passage, Lower Text Complexity

The following passage on commuting is of lower complexity, although some aspects of the passage are more challenging than others (as is generally true of the published materials you read). This passage is accompanied by a graphic.

REMEMBER

The text complexity of the passages will range from lower (grades 9–10) to higher (postsecondary entry).

Questions 1-3 are based on the following passage and supplementary material.

This passage is adapted from Richard Florida, *The Great Reset*. ©2010 by Richard Florida.

In today's idea-driven economy, the cost of time is what really matters. With the constant pressure to innovate, it makes little sense to waste countless collective hours
Line commuting. So, the most efficient and productive regions are
5 those in which people are thinking and working—not sitting in traffic.

The auto-dependent transportation system has reached its limit in most major cities and megaregions. Commuting by car is among the least efficient of all our activities—not to
10 mention among the least enjoyable, according to detailed research by the Nobel Prize–winning economist Daniel Kahneman and his colleagues. Though one might think that the economic crisis beginning in 2007 would have reduced traffic (high unemployment means fewer workers traveling to
15 and from work), the opposite has been true. Average commutes have lengthened, and congestion has gotten worse, if anything. The average commute rose in 2008 to 25.5 minutes, "erasing years of decreases to stand at the level of 2000, as people had to leave home earlier in the morning to
20 pick up friends for their ride to work or to catch a bus or subway train," according to the U.S. Census Bureau, which collects the figures. And those are average figures. Commutes are far longer in the big West Coast cities of Los Angeles and San Francisco and the East Coast cities of New York,
25 Philadelphia, Baltimore, and Washington, D.C. In many of these cities, gridlock has become the norm, not just at rush hour but all day, every day.

The costs are astounding. In Los Angeles, congestion eats up more than 485 million working hours a year; that's seventy
30 hours, or nearly two weeks, of full-time work per commuter. In D.C., the time cost of congestion is sixty-two hours per worker per year. In New York it's forty-four hours. Average it out, and the time cost across America's thirteen biggest city regions is fifty-one hours per worker per year. Across the
35 country, commuting wastes 4.2 billion hours of work time annually—nearly a full workweek for every commuter. The overall cost to the U.S. economy is nearly $90 billion when lost productivity and wasted fuel are taken into account. At the Martin Prosperity Institute, we calculate that every minute
40 shaved off America's commuting time is worth $19.5 billion in value added to the economy. The numbers add up fast: five minutes is worth $97.7 billion; ten minutes, $195 billion; fifteen minutes, $292 billion.

It's ironic that so many people still believe the main
45 remedy for traffic congestion is to build more roads and
highways, which of course only makes the problem worse.
New roads generate higher levels of "induced traffic," that is,
new roads just invite drivers to drive more and lure people
who take mass transit back to their cars. Eventually, we end up
50 with more clogged roads rather than a long-term
improvement in traffic flow.
    The coming decades will likely see more intense clustering
of jobs, innovation, and productivity in a smaller number of
bigger cities and city-regions. Some regions could end up
55 bloated beyond the capacity of their infrastructure, while
others struggle, their promise stymied by inadequate human
or other resources.

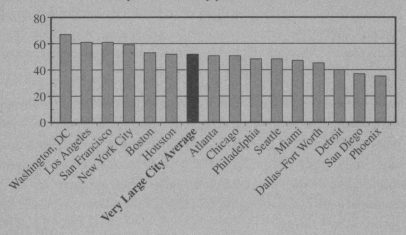

The Most Congested Cities in 2011
Yearly Hours of Delay per Automobile Commuter

Adapted from Adam Werbach, "The American Commuter Spends 38 Hours a Year Stuck in Traffic." ©2013 by The Atlantic.

1

The passage most strongly suggests that researchers at the Martin Prosperity Institute share which assumption?

A) Employees who work from home are more valuable to their employers than employees who commute.

B) Employees whose commutes are shortened will use the time saved to do additional productive work for their employers.

C) Employees can conduct business activities, such as composing memos or joining conference calls, while commuting.

D) Employees who have longer commutes tend to make more money than employees who have shorter commutes.

Content: Rhetoric

Key: B

Objective: Students must reasonably infer an assumption that is implied in the passage.

Explanation: Choice B is the best answer because details in the third paragraph (lines 28-43) strongly suggest that researchers ("we") at the Martin Prosperity Institute assume that shorter commutes will lead to more productive time for workers. The author notes that "across the country, commuting wastes 4.2 billion hours of work time annually" and that "the overall cost to the U.S. economy is nearly $90 billion when lost productivity and wasted fuel are taken into account" (lines 34-38). Given also that those at the institute "calculate that every minute shaved off America's commuting time is worth $19.5 billion in value added to the economy" (lines 39-41), it can reasonably be concluded that some of that added value is from heightened worker productivity.

Choice A is not the best answer because there is no evidence in the passage that researchers at the Martin Prosperity Institute assume that employees who work from home are more valuable to their employers than employees who commute. Although the passage does criticize long commutes, it does not propose working from home as a solution.

Choice C is not the best answer because there is no evidence in the passage that researchers at the Martin Prosperity Institute assume that employees can conduct business activities, such as composing memos or joining conference calls, while commuting. The passage does discuss commuting in some detail, but it does not mention activities that commuters can or should be undertaking while commuting, and it generally portrays commuting time as lost or wasted time.

Choice D is not the best answer because there is no evidence in the passage that researchers at the Martin Prosperity Institute assume that employees who have lengthy commutes tend to make more money than employees who have shorter commutes. The passage does not draw any clear links between the amount of money employees make and the commutes they have.

PRACTICE AT

khanacademy.org/sat

Choice A is tempting, as you might want to draw the inference that people who work from home don't waste time commuting and thus are more valuable to employers. This inference, however, is not supported by the passage, which makes no mention of working from home.

PRACTICE AT

khanacademy.org/sat

On questions that ask for the meaning of a word in context, consider the role the word plays in the context in which it appears. Wrong answer choices will often consist of alternate meanings of the word that do not fit the context.

2

As used in line 52, "intense" most nearly means

A) emotional.
B) concentrated.
C) brilliant.
D) determined.

Content: Information and Ideas

Key: B

Objective: Students must determine the meaning of a word in the context in which it appears.

Explanation: Choice B is the best answer because the context makes clear that the clustering of jobs, innovation, and productivity will be more concentrated in, or more densely packed into, "a smaller number of bigger cities and city-regions" (lines 53-54).

Choice A is not the best answer because although "intense" sometimes means "emotional," it would make no sense in this context to say that the clustering of jobs, innovation, and productivity will be more emotional in "a smaller number of bigger cities and city-regions" (lines 53-54).

Choice C is not the best answer because although "intense" sometimes means "brilliant," it would make no sense in this context to say that the clustering of jobs, innovation, and productivity will be more brilliant in "a smaller number of bigger cities and city-regions" (lines 53-54).

Choice D is not the best answer because although "intense" sometimes means "determined," it would make no sense in this context to say that the clustering of jobs, innovation, and productivity will be more determined in "a smaller number of bigger cities and city-regions" (lines 53-54).

3

Which claim about traffic congestion is supported by the graph?

A) New York City commuters spend less time annually delayed by traffic congestion than the average for very large cities.

B) Los Angeles commuters are delayed more hours annually by traffic congestion than are commuters in Washington, D.C.

C) Commuters in Washington, D.C., face greater delays annually due to traffic congestion than do commuters in New York City.

D) Commuters in Detroit spend more time delayed annually by traffic congestion than do commuters in Houston, Atlanta, and Chicago.

Content: Synthesis

Key: C

Objective: Students must interpret data presented graphically.

Explanation: Choice C is the best answer. Higher bars on the graph represent longer annual commuter delays than lower bars; moreover, the number of hours of annual commuter delay generally decreases as one moves from left to right on the graph. The bar for Washington, D.C., is higher than and to the left of that for New York City, meaning that D.C. automobile commuters experience greater amounts of delay each year.

Choice A is not the best answer because the graph's bar for New York City is higher than and to the left of that for the average for very large cities, meaning that New York City automobile commuters experience greater, not lesser, amounts of delay each year.

PRACTICE AT

🍃 **khanacademy.org/sat**

This question requires you to locate information from a graph and draw a reasonable conclusion from the data. Carefully analyze the data in the graph, including the title, axes labels, and unit increments, before selecting your answer.

Choice B is not the best answer because the graph's bar for Los Angeles is lower than and to the right of that for Washington, D.C., meaning that Los Angeles automobile commuters experience lesser, not greater, amounts of delay each year.

Choice D is not the best answer because the graph's bar for Detroit is lower than and to the right of those for Houston, Atlanta, and Chicago, meaning that Detroit automobile commuters experience lesser, not greater, amounts of delay each year.

SAMPLE 2:

History/Social Studies Passage, Higher Text Complexity

The following passage from a text in the Great Global Conversation is of higher complexity, although some aspects of the passage are less challenging than others (as is generally true of the published materials you read).

PRACTICE AT

khanacademy.org/sat

Some passages, like this one, are preceded by a brief introduction. Be sure to read the introduction as it may provide context that will help you understand the passage.

Questions 4-8 are based on the following passage.

The passage is adapted from a speech delivered by Congresswoman Barbara Jordan of Texas on July 25, 1974. She was a member of the Judiciary Committee of the United States House of Representatives. In the passage, Jordan discusses how and when a United States president may be impeached, or charged with serious offenses while in office. Jordan's speech was delivered in the context of impeachment hearings against then President Richard M. Nixon.

Today, I am an inquisitor. An hyperbole would not be fictional and would not overstate the solemnness that I feel right now. My faith in the Constitution is whole; it is
Line complete; it is total. And I am not going to sit here and be an
5 idle spectator to the diminution, the subversion, the destruction, of the Constitution.
"Who can so properly be the inquisitors for the nation as the representatives of the nation themselves?" "The subjects of its jurisdiction are those offenses which proceed from the
10 misconduct of public men."* And that's what we're talking about. In other words, [the jurisdiction comes] from the abuse or violation of some public trust.
It is wrong, I suggest, it is a misreading of the Constitution for any member here to assert that for a member to vote for an
15 article of impeachment means that that member must be convinced that the President should be removed from office. The Constitution doesn't say that. The powers relating to impeachment are an essential check in the hands of the body of the legislature against and upon the encroachments of the
20 executive. The division between the two branches of the legislature, the House and the Senate, assigning to the one the right to accuse and to the other the right to judge—the framers of this Constitution were very astute. They did not make the accusers and the judges . . . the same person.

25   We know the nature of impeachment. We've been talking
about it a while now. It is chiefly designed for the President
and his high ministers to somehow be called into account. It is
designed to "bridle" the executive if he engages in excesses. "It
is designed as a method of national inquest into the conduct
30 of public men."* The framers confided in the Congress the
power, if need be, to remove the President in order to strike a
delicate balance between a President swollen with power and
grown tyrannical, and preservation of the independence of
the executive.

35   The nature of impeachment: a narrowly channeled
exception to the separation of powers maxim. The Federal
Convention of 1787 said that. It limited impeachment to high
crimes and misdemeanors, and discounted and opposed the
term "maladministration." "It is to be used only for great
40 misdemeanors," so it was said in the North Carolina
ratification convention. And in the Virginia ratification
convention: "We do not trust our liberty to a particular
branch. We need one branch to check the other."

    . . . The North Carolina ratification convention: "No one
45 need be afraid that officers who commit oppression will pass
with immunity." "Prosecutions of impeachments will seldom
fail to agitate the passions of the whole community," said
Hamilton in the *Federalist* Papers, Number 65. "We divide
into parties more or less friendly or inimical to the accused."*
50 I do not mean political parties in that sense.

    The drawing of political lines goes to the motivation
behind impeachment; but impeachment must proceed within
the confines of the constitutional term "high crime[s] and
misdemeanors." Of the impeachment process, it was
55 Woodrow Wilson who said that "Nothing short of the grossest
offenses against the plain law of the land will suffice to give
them speed and effectiveness. Indignation so great as to
overgrow party interest may secure a conviction; but nothing
else can."

60   Common sense would be revolted if we engaged upon this
process for petty reasons. Congress has a lot to do:
appropriations, tax reform, health insurance, campaign
finance reform, housing, environmental protection, energy
sufficiency, mass transportation. Pettiness cannot be allowed
65 to stand in the face of such overwhelming problems. So today
we're not being petty. We're trying to be big, because the task
we have before us is a big one.

---

*Jordan quotes from *Federalist* No. 65, an essay by Alexander Hamilton,
published in 1788, on the powers of the United States Senate, including the
power to decide cases of impeachment against a president of the United States.

4

The stance Jordan takes in the passage is best described as that of

A) an idealist setting forth principles.

B) an advocate seeking a compromise position.

C) an observer striving for neutrality.

D) a scholar researching a historical controversy.

Content: Rhetoric

Key: A

Objective: Students must use information and ideas in the passage to determine the speaker's perspective.

Explanation: Choice A is the best answer. Jordan helps establish her idealism by declaring that she is an "inquisitor" (line 1) and that her "faith in the Constitution is whole; it is complete; it is total" (lines 3-4). At numerous points in the passage, Jordan sets forth principles (e.g., "The powers relating to impeachment are an essential check in the hands of the body of the legislature against and upon the encroachments of the executive," lines 17-20) and refers to important documents that do the same, including the U.S. Constitution and *Federalist* No. 65.

Choice B is not the best answer because although Jordan is advocating a position, there is no evidence in the passage that she is seeking a compromise position. Indeed, she notes that she is "not going to sit here and be an idle spectator to the diminution, the subversion, the destruction, of the Constitution" (lines 4-6), indicating that she is not seeking compromise.

Choice C is not the best answer because Jordan is a participant ("an inquisitor," line 1) in the proceedings, not a mere observer. Indeed, she notes that she is "not going to sit here and be an idle spectator to the diminution, the subversion, the destruction, of the Constitution" (lines 4-6).

Choice D is not the best answer because Jordan is identified as a congresswoman and an "inquisitor" (line 1), not a scholar, and because she is primarily discussing events happening at the moment, not researching an unidentified historical controversy. Although she refers to historical documents and individuals, her main emphasis is on the (then) present impeachment hearings.

5

The main rhetorical effect of the series of three phrases in lines 5-6 (the diminution, the subversion, the destruction) is to

A) convey with increasing intensity the seriousness of the threat Jordan sees to the Constitution.

B) clarify that Jordan believes the Constitution was first weakened, then sabotaged, then broken.

C) indicate that Jordan thinks the Constitution is prone to failure in three distinct ways.

D) propose a three-part agenda for rescuing the Constitution from the current crisis.

Content: Rhetoric

Key: A

Objective: Students must determine the main rhetorical effect of the speaker's choice of words.

Explanation: Choice A is the best answer because the quoted phrases — building from "diminution" to "subversion" to "destruction" — suggest the increasing seriousness of the threat Jordan sees to the Constitution.

Choice B is not the best answer because the passage offers no evidence that the quoted phrases refer to three different events that happened in a strict sequence. It is more reasonable to infer from the passage that Jordan sees "diminution," "subversion," and "destruction" as differing degrees to which the Constitution could be undermined. Moreover, the passage suggests that Jordan sees these three things as products of the same action or series of actions, not as three distinct stages in a process.

Choice C is not the best answer because the passage offers no evidence that the quoted phrases refer to three distinct ways in which the Constitution is prone to failure. It is more reasonable to infer from the passage that Jordan sees "diminution," "subversion," and "destruction" as differing degrees in which the Constitution could be undermined. Moreover, the passage suggests that Jordan sees these three things as products of the same action or series of actions, not as three distinct "ways."

Choice D is not the best answer because the passage offers no evidence that the quoted phrases refer to three unique elements of a proposal to resolve a crisis. It is more reasonable to infer from the passage that Jordan sees "diminution," "subversion," and "destruction" as differing degrees in which the Constitution could be undermined. Moreover, the passage suggests that Jordan sees these three things as products of the same action or series of actions, not as three distinct "parts."

PRACTICE AT

khanacademy.org/sat

What is meant by "rhetorical effect" is the influence or impact that a particular arrangement of words has on the intended meaning of a text.

PRACTICE AT

khanacademy.org/sat

To answer this question, first identify what point the author is trying to get across in the paragraph in which the three phrases appear. Next, consider the effect that the series of three phrases has on the author's intended point.

6

As used in line 35, "channeled" most nearly means

A) worn.

B) sent.

C) constrained.

D) siphoned.

Content: Information and Ideas

Key: C

Objective: Students must determine the meaning of a word in the context in which it appears.

Explanation: Choice C is the best answer because the context makes clear that the kind of "exception" (line 36) Jordan describes should be narrowly constrained, or limited. As lines 37-39 indicate, the Federal Convention of 1787 "limited impeachment to high crimes and misdemeanors, and discounted and opposed the term 'maladministration,'" presumably because the term implied too broad a scope for the exception.

Choice A is not the best answer because while "channeled" sometimes means "worn," it would make no sense in this context to say that the kind of "exception" (line 36) Jordan describes should be narrowly worn.

Choice B is not the best answer because while "channeled" sometimes means "sent," it would make no sense in this context to say that the kind of "exception" (line 36) Jordan describes should be narrowly sent.

Choice D is not the best answer because while "channeled" sometimes means "siphoned," it would make no sense in this context to say that the kind of "exception" (line 36) Jordan describes should be narrowly siphoned.

PRACTICE AT

khanacademy.org/sat

The context clues that indicate the intended meaning of a word may not always be found in the actual sentence in which the word appears. In this question, the strongest clues appear later in the paragraph, when the author states, "It limited impeachment to...," and "It is to be used only for great misdemeanors..."

7

In lines 46-50 ("Prosecutions . . . sense"), what is the most likely reason Jordan draws a distinction between two types of "parties"?

A) To counter the suggestion that impeachment is or should be about partisan politics

B) To disagree with Hamilton's claim that impeachment proceedings excite passions

C) To contend that Hamilton was too timid in his support for the concept of impeachment

D) To argue that impeachment cases are decided more on the basis of politics than on justice

Content: Rhetoric

Key: A

PRACTICE AT

khanacademy.org/sat

As with Question 5, this question depends upon an understanding of the reasoning immediately preceding and following the sentence in which Jordan draws a distinction between types of parties. Be sure, therefore, to consider Jordan's statement in the context in which it appears.

Objective: Students must interpret the speaker's line of reasoning.

Explanation: Choice A is the best answer. Jordan is making a distinction between two types of "parties": the informal associations to which Alexander Hamilton refers and formal, organized political parties such as the modern-day Republican and Democratic parties. Jordan anticipates that listeners to her speech might misinterpret her use of Hamilton's quotation as suggesting that she thinks impeachment is essentially a tool of organized political parties to achieve partisan ends, with one party attacking and another defending the President. Throughout the passage, and notably in the seventh paragraph, Jordan makes clear that she thinks impeachment should be reserved only for the most serious of offenses — ones that should rankle people of any political affiliation.

Choice B is not the best answer because Jordan offers no objection to Hamilton's notion that impeachment proceedings excite passions. Indeed, she quotes Hamilton extensively in a way that indicates that she fundamentally agrees with his view on impeachment. Moreover, she acknowledges that her own speech is impassioned — that she feels a "solemnness" (line 2) and a willingness to indulge in "hyperbole" (line 1).

Choice C is not the best answer because Jordan offers no objection to Hamilton's level of support for the concept of impeachment. Indeed, she quotes Hamilton extensively in a way that indicates that she fundamentally agrees with his view on impeachment.

Choice D is not the best answer because Jordan suggests that she and her fellow members of Congress are "trying to be big" (line 66), or high-minded, rather than decide the present case on the basis of politics. Indeed, throughout the last four paragraphs of the passage (lines 35-67), she elaborates on the principled and just basis on which impeachment should proceed. Moreover, throughout the passage, Jordan is focused on the present impeachment hearings, not on the justice or injustice of impeachments generally.

8

Which choice provides the best evidence for the answer to the previous question?

A) Lines 13-16 ("It . . . office")
B) Lines 20-23 ("The division . . . astute")
C) Lines 51-54 ("The drawing . . . misdemeanors'")
D) Lines 61-64 ("Congress . . . transportation")

Content: Information and Ideas

Key: C

PRACTICE AT

🐧 **khanacademy.org/sat**

Questions 7 and 8 can be viewed as two-part questions since the answer to Question 8 is dependent upon the answer to Question 7. It may be helpful to revisit your answer to the first question after reading the answer choices in the second question.

Objective: Students must determine which portion of the passage provides the best evidence for the answer to question 7.

Explanation: Choice C is the best answer because in lines 51-54, Jordan draws a contrast between political motivations and "high crime[s] and misdemeanors" as the basis for impeachment and argues that impeachment "must proceed within the confines" of the latter concept. These lines thus serve as the best evidence for the answer to the previous question.

Choice A is not the best answer because lines 13-16 only address a misconception that Jordan contends some people have about what a vote for impeachment means. Therefore, these lines do not serve as the best evidence for the answer to the previous question.

Choice B is not the best answer because lines 20-23 only speak to a division of responsibility between the two houses of the U.S. Congress. Therefore, these lines do not serve as the best evidence for the answer to the previous question.

Choice D is not the best answer because lines 61-64 serve mainly to indicate that the U.S. Congress has an extensive and important agenda. Therefore, these lines do not serve as the best evidence for the answer to the previous question.

SAMPLE 3:

Science Passage with Graphic, Lower Text Complexity

The following natural science passage on loggerhead turtles is of lower complexity, although some aspects of the passage are more challenging than others (as is generally true of the published materials you read). This passage is accompanied by a graphic.

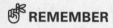
REMEMBER

One science passage on the Reading Test will be accompanied by an informational graphic.

Questions 9-13 are based on the following passage and supplementary material.

This passage is adapted from Ed Yong, "Turtles Use the Earth's Magnetic Field as Global GPS." ©2011 by Kalmbach Publishing Co.

> In 1996, a loggerhead turtle called Adelita swam across 9,000 miles from Mexico to Japan, crossing the entire Pacific on her way. Wallace J. Nichols tracked this epic journey with a
> *Line* satellite tag. But Adelita herself had no such technology at her
> 5 disposal. How did she steer a route across two oceans to find her destination?
>
> Nathan Putman has the answer. By testing hatchling turtles in a special tank, he has found that they can use the Earth's magnetic field as their own Global Positioning System

10 (GPS). By sensing the field, they can work out both their latitude and longitude and head in the right direction.

Putman works in the lab of Ken Lohmann, who has been studying the magnetic abilities of loggerheads for over 20 years. In his lab at the University of North Carolina, Lohmann
15 places hatchlings in a large water tank surrounded by a large grid of electromagnetic coils. In 1991, he found that the babies started swimming in the opposite direction if he used the coils to reverse the direction of the magnetic field around them. They could use the field as a compass to get their bearing.

20 Later, Lohmann showed that they can also use the magnetic field to work out their position. For them, this is literally a matter of life or death. Hatchlings born off the sea coast of Florida spend their early lives in the North Atlantic gyre, a warm current that circles between North America and
25 Africa. If they're swept towards the cold waters outside the gyre, they die. Their magnetic sense keeps them safe.

Using his coil-surrounded tank, Lohmann could mimic the magnetic field at different parts of the Earth's surface. If he simulated the field at the northern edge of the gyre, the
30 hatchlings swam southwards. If he simulated the field at the gyre's southern edge, the turtles swam west-northwest. These experiments showed that the turtles can use their magnetic sense to work out their latitude—their position on a north-south axis. Now, Putnam has shown that they can also
35 determine their longitude—their position on an east-west axis.

He tweaked his magnetic tanks to simulate the fields in two positions with the same latitude at opposite ends of the Atlantic. If the field simulated the west Atlantic near Puerto Rico, the turtles swam northeast. If the field matched that on
40 the east Atlantic near the Cape Verde Islands, the turtles swam southwest. In the wild, both headings would keep them within the safe, warm embrace of the North Atlantic gyre.

Before now, we knew that several animal migrants, from loggerheads to reed warblers to sparrows, had some way of
45 working out longitude, but no one knew how. By keeping the turtles in the same conditions, with only the magnetic fields around them changing, Putman clearly showed that they can use these fields to find their way. In the wild, they might well also use other landmarks like the position of the sea, sun and stars.

50 Putman thinks that the turtles work out their position using two features of the Earth's magnetic field that change over its surface. They can sense the field's inclination, or the angle at which it dips towards the surface. At the poles, this angle is roughly 90 degrees and at the equator, it's roughly
55 zero degrees. They can also sense its intensity, which is strongest near the poles and weakest near the Equator. Different parts of the world have unique combinations of these two variables. Neither corresponds directly to either latitude or longitude, but together, they provide a "magnetic
60 signature" that tells the turtle where it is.

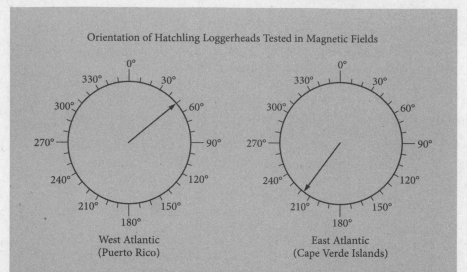

Orientation of Hatchling Loggerheads Tested in Magnetic Fields

West Atlantic
(Puerto Rico)

East Atlantic
(Cape Verde Islands)

Adapted from Nathan Putman, Courtney Endres, Catherine Lohmann, and Kenneth Lohmann, "Longitude Perception and Bicoordinate Magnetic Maps in Sea Turtles." ©2011 by Elsevier Inc.

Orientation of hatchling loggerheads tested in a magnetic field that simulates a position at the west side of the Atlantic near Puerto Rico (left) and a position at the east side of the Atlantic near the Cape Verde Islands (right). The arrow in each circle indicates the mean direction that the group of hatchlings swam. Data are plotted relative to geographic north (N = 0°).

9

The passage most strongly suggests that Adelita used which of the following to navigate her 9,000-mile journey?

A) The current of the North Atlantic gyre

B) Cues from electromagnetic coils designed by Putman and Lohmann

C) The inclination and intensity of Earth's magnetic field

D) A simulated "magnetic signature" configured by Lohmann

Content: Information and Ideas

Key: C

Objective: Students must draw a reasonable inference from the text.

Explanation: Choice C is the best answer. The first paragraph describes the 9,000-mile journey that Adelita made and raises the question, which the rest of the passage tries to answer, of how this loggerhead turtle was able to "steer a route across two oceans to find her destination" (lines 5-6). The answer comes most directly in the last paragraph, which presents Putman's belief that loggerhead turtles "work out their position using two features of the Earth's magnetic field that change over its surface" (lines 50-52): its inclination and its intensity. It is reasonable, therefore, to infer from the passage that this was the method that Adelita used.

Choice A is not the best answer because there is no evidence in the passage that Adelita used the current of the North Atlantic gyre to navigate her 9,000-mile journey. The passage does discuss the North Atlantic gyre but only as the place where loggerhead turtle hatchlings "born off the sea coast of Florida spend their early lives" (lines 22-23).

Choice B is not the best answer because there is no evidence in the passage that Adelita navigated her 9,000-mile journey with the aid of cues from electromagnetic coils designed by Putman and Lohmann. The passage does say that Putman and Lohmann use electromagnetic coils as part of their research on loggerhead turtles, but the coils are part of tanks used in a laboratory to study loggerhead hatchlings (see lines 12-16).

Choice D is not the best answer because there is no evidence in the passage that Adelita navigated her 9,000-mile journey with the aid of a simulated "magnetic signature" configured by Lohmann. The passage does describe how Lohmann and Putman manipulate magnetic fields as part of their research on loggerhead turtle hatchlings (see, for example, lines 14-19), but there is no indication that the two scientists used (or even could use) the kind of equipment necessary for this project outside of laboratory tanks or with Adelita in the wild.

10

Which choice provides the best evidence for the answer to the previous question?

A) Lines 1-3 ("In 1996 . . . way")
B) Lines 27-28 ("Using . . . surface")
C) Lines 48-49 ("In the wild . . . stars")
D) Lines 58-60 ("Neither . . . it is")

Content: Information and Ideas

Key: D

Objective: Students must determine which portion of the passage provides the best support for the answer to question 9.

Explanation: Choice D is the best answer because in lines 58-60, the author indicates that "together, [inclination and intensity] provide a 'magnetic signature' that tells the turtle where it is." Therefore, these lines serve as the best evidence for the answer to the previous question.

Choice A is not the best answer because in lines 1-3, the author establishes that Adelita made a 9,000-mile journey but does not explain how she navigated it. Therefore, these lines do not serve as the best evidence for the answer to the previous question.

Choice B is not the best answer because in lines 27-28, the author indicates that Lohmann is able to "mimic the magnetic field at different parts of the Earth's surface" in his laboratory but does not explain how Adelita navigated her 9,000-mile journey or suggest that Lohmann had any influence over Adelita's trip. Therefore, these lines do not serve as the best evidence for the answer to the previous question.

Choice C is not the best answer because, in lines 48-49, the author notes that loggerhead turtles "in the wild" may make use of "landmarks like the position of the sea, sun and stars" but does not indicate that Adelita used such landmarks to navigate her 9,000-mile journey. Therefore, these lines do not serve as the best evidence for the answer to the previous question.

11

As used in line 3, "tracked" most nearly means

A) searched for.
B) traveled over.
C) followed.
D) hunted.

Content: Information and Ideas

Key: C

Objective: Students must determine the meaning of a word in the context in which it appears.

Explanation: Choice C is the best answer because the context makes clear that Nichols followed Adelita's "epic journey with a satellite tag" (lines 3-4).

Choice A is not the best answer because while "tracked" sometimes means "searched for," it would make little sense in this context to say that Nichols searched for Adelita's "epic journey with a satellite tag" (lines 3-4). It is more reasonable to conclude from the passage that Nichols knew about Adelita and her journey and used a satellite tag to help follow it.

Choice B is not the best answer because while "tracked" sometimes means "traveled over," it would make no sense in this context to say that Nichols traveled over Adelita's "epic journey with a satellite tag" (lines 3-4).

Choice D is not the best answer because while "tracked" sometimes means "hunted," it would make no sense in this context to say that Nichols hunted Adelita's "epic journey with a satellite tag" (lines 3-4).

PRACTICE AT

khanacademy.org/sat

Here's a strategy you may find helpful if you're struggling on a "word in context" question such as Question 11 — substitute each of the answer choices for the given word in the sentence and determine which fits best in the context.

12

Based on the passage, which choice best describes the relationship between Putman's and Lohmann's research?

A) Putman's research contradicts Lohmann's.

B) Putman's research builds on Lohmann's.

C) Lohmann's research confirms Putman's.

D) Lohmann's research corrects Putman's.

Content: Information and Ideas

Key: B

Objective: Students must characterize the relationship between two individuals described in the passage.

Explanation: Choice B is the best answer. Putman "works in the lab of Ken Lohmann, who has been studying the magnetic abilities of loggerheads for over 20 years" (lines 12-14). Lohmann had earlier demonstrated that loggerhead turtles "could use the [magnetic] field as a compass to get their bearing" (line 19) and "use their magnetic sense to work out their latitude—their position on a north-south axis" (lines 32-34). Putman has since ("Now," line 34) built on Lohmann's work by demonstrating that the turtles "can also determine their longitude—their position on an east-west axis" (lines 34-35).

Choice A is not the best answer because the passage does not indicate that Putman's research contradicts Lohmann's. In fact, Putman's work complements Lohmann's. Lohmann had demonstrated that loggerhead turtles "could use the [magnetic] field as a compass to get their bearing" (line 19) and "use their magnetic sense to work out their latitude—their position on a north-south axis" (lines 32-34). Putman has, in turn, demonstrated that the turtles "can also determine their longitude—their position on an east-west axis" (lines 34-35).

Choice C is not the best answer because the research of Lohmann that the passage describes came before that of Putman. Putman "works in the lab of Ken Lohmann, who has been studying the magnetic abilities of loggerheads for over 20 years" (lines 12-14). Lohmann had earlier demonstrated that loggerhead turtles "could use the [magnetic] field as a compass to get their bearing" (line 19) and "use their magnetic sense to work out their latitude—their position on a north-south axis" (lines 32-34). Putman has since ("Now," line 34) built on Lohmann's work by demonstrating that the turtles "can also determine their longitude—their position on an east-west axis" (lines 34-35).

Choice D is not the best answer because the passage does not indicate that Lohmann's research corrects Putman's. First, Lohmann's research that the

PRACTICE AT

khanacademy.org/sat

On Question 12, begin by determining if Putman's and Lohmann's research is complementary or contradictory; doing so will allow you to eliminate two of the four answer choices. Then, research the passage for additional clues that refine the relationship between their research.

passage describes came before that of Putman (see explanation for choice C) and thus could not "correct" Putman's later research. Second, the passage does not indicate that Putman's research contradicts Lohmann's (see explanation for choice A), meaning that there is nothing for Lohmann to "correct" with his own research.

13

The author refers to reed warblers and sparrows (line 44) primarily to

A) contrast the loggerhead turtle's migration patterns with those of other species.

B) provide examples of species that share one of the loggerhead turtle's abilities.

C) suggest that most animal species possess some ability to navigate long distances.

D) illustrate some ways in which the ability to navigate long distances can help a species.

PRACTICE AT

khanacademy.org/sat

Another way to phrase this question is, "Why did the author refer to reed warblers and sparrows?" It's often helpful to paraphrase the question in your own words to ensure you understand what it's asking.

Content: Rhetoric

Key: B

Objective: Students must determine the main rhetorical effect a part of the passage has on the passage as a whole.

Explanation: Choice B is the best answer because the author indicates that reed warblers and sparrows, like loggerhead turtles, had previously been known to have "some way of working out longitude" (lines 44-45).

Choice A is not the best answer because although the author notes that loggerhead turtles, reed warblers, and sparrows are all "animal migrants" (line 43), he offers no specifics about the migration patterns of reed warblers and sparrows, and the only connection he draws among the three animals is their recognized ability of somehow "working out longitude" (line 45).

Choice C is not the best answer because the author only mentions three "animal migrants" by name (loggerhead turtles, reed warblers, and sparrows) and indicates that "several" such migrants had previously been known to have "some way of working out longitude" (lines 43-45). He makes no claim in the passage that most animal species have some long-distance navigation ability.

Choice D is not the best answer because although the author indicates that reed warblers and sparrows, like loggerhead turtles, are "animal migrants" (line 43), he offers no specifics about how the ability to navigate long distances might help reed warblers and sparrows (nor, for that matter, much information about how this ability might help loggerhead turtles).

SAMPLE 4:

U.S. and World Literature Passage, Higher Text Complexity

The following passage from a literary text is of higher complexity, although some aspects of the passage are less challenging than others (as is generally true of the published materials you read).

Questions 14-18 are based on the following passage.

This passage is adapted from Edith Wharton, *Ethan Frome,* originally published in 1911. Mattie Silver is Ethan's household employee.

Mattie Silver had lived under Ethan's roof for a year, and from early morning till they met at supper he had frequent chances of seeing her; but no moments in her company
Line were comparable to those when, her arm in his, and her
5 light step flying to keep time with his long stride, they walked back through the night to the farm. He had taken to the girl from the first day, when he had driven over to the Flats to meet her, and she had smiled and waved to him from the train, crying out, "You must be Ethan!" as she
10 jumped down with her bundles, while he reflected, looking over her slight person: "She don't look much on housework, but she ain't a fretter, anyhow." But it was not only that the coming to his house of a bit of hopeful young life was like the lighting of a fire on a cold hearth. The girl was more
15 than the bright serviceable creature he had thought her. She had an eye to see and an ear to hear: he could show her things and tell her things, and taste the bliss of feeling that all he imparted left long reverberations and echoes he could wake at will.
20   It was during their night walks back to the farm that he felt most intensely the sweetness of this communion. He had always been more sensitive than the people about him to the appeal of natural beauty. His unfinished studies had given form to this sensibility and even in his unhappiest moments
25 field and sky spoke to him with a deep and powerful persuasion. But hitherto the emotion had remained in him as a silent ache, veiling with sadness the beauty that evoked it. He did not even know whether any one else in the world felt as he did, or whether he was the sole victim of this mournful
30 privilege. Then he learned that one other spirit had trembled with the same touch of wonder: that at his side, living under his roof and eating his bread, was a creature to whom he could say: "That's Orion down yonder; the big fellow to the right is Aldebaran, and the bunch of little ones—like bees swarming—
35 they're the Pleiades . . ." or whom he could hold entranced before a ledge of granite thrusting up through the fern while he unrolled the huge panorama of the ice age, and the long dim stretches of succeeding time. The fact that admiration for his learning mingled with Mattie's wonder at what he taught

40 was not the least part of his pleasure. And there were other
sensations, less definable but more exquisite, which drew them
together with a shock of silent joy: the cold red of sunset
behind winter hills, the flight of cloud-flocks over slopes of
golden stubble, or the intensely blue shadows of hemlocks on
45 sunlit snow. When she said to him once: "It looks just as if it
was painted!" it seemed to Ethan that the art of definition
could go no farther, and that words had at last been found to
utter his secret soul. . . .

    As he stood in the darkness outside the church these
50 memories came back with the poignancy of vanished
things. Watching Mattie whirl down the floor from hand
to hand he wondered how he could ever have thought that
his dull talk interested her. To him, who was never gay but
in her presence, her gaiety seemed plain proof of
55 indifference. The face she lifted to her dancers was the
same which, when she saw him, always looked like a
window that has caught the sunset. He even noticed two or
three gestures which, in his fatuity, he had thought she
kept for him: a way of throwing her head back when she
60 was amused, as if to taste her laugh before she let it out,
and a trick of sinking her lids slowly when anything
charmed or moved her.

PRACTICE AT

🌱 khanacademy.org/sat

Keywords and phrases throughout
the final paragraph signal a shift
in the focus of the narrative. For
instance, "…these memories
came back with the poignancy
of vanished things," signals a
temporal shift, and words such as
"dull," "indifference," and "fatuity"
point to a change in the main
character's feelings.

PRACTICE AT

🌱 khanacademy.org/sat

This question, like many
questions from the rhetoric
category, asks you to think about
the passage on a broader level.
Thus, when reading passages on
the SAT, pay as much attention to
the structure and purpose of the
passage (the "how" and "why")
as you do to the content of the
passage (the "what").

14

Over the course of the passage, the main focus of the narrative shifts
from the

A) reservations a character has about a person he has just met to a growing
appreciation that character has of the person's worth.

B) ambivalence a character feels about his sensitive nature to the
character's recognition of the advantages of having profound emotions.

C) intensity of feeling a character has for another person to the character's
concern that that intensity is not reciprocated.

D) value a character attaches to the wonders of the natural world to a
rejection of that sort of beauty in favor of human artistry.

Content: Rhetoric

Key: C

Objective: Students must describe the overall structure of a text.

Explanation: Choice C is the best answer. The first paragraph traces the
inception of Ethan's feelings for Mattie: Ethan "had taken to the girl from
the first day" (lines 6-7) and saw her arrival as "like the lighting of a fire
on a cold hearth" (line 14). The second paragraph (lines 20-48) focuses on
"their night walks back to the farm" (line 20) and Ethan's elation in perceiv-
ing that "one other spirit . . . trembled with the same touch of wonder" that
characterized his own (lines 30-31). In other words, the main focus of the

first two paragraphs is the intensity of feeling one character, Ethan, has for another, Mattie. The last paragraph shifts the focus of the passage to Ethan's change in perception; he sees Mattie in a social setting interacting with other men, wonders "how he could ever have thought that his dull talk interested her" (lines 52-53), interprets her seeming happiness as "plain proof of indifference" toward him (lines 54-55), and sees betrayal in the "two or three gestures which, in his fatuity, he had thought she kept for him" (lines 57-59).

Choice A is not the best answer because while Ethan acknowledges that Mattie "don't look much on housework" (line 11), the first paragraph also notes that Ethan "had taken to the girl from the first day" (lines 6-7); therefore, there is no support for the notion that Ethan's "reservations" about Mattie lasted for any length of time or ever constituted the main focus of the narrative.

Choice B is not the best answer because while Ethan does exhibit ambivalence about his sensitive nature, seeing it as a "mournful privilege" (lines 29-30), the main focus of the narrative does not shift to his recognition of the advantages of having profound emotions. Indeed, in the last paragraph, Ethan's profound emotions give him only grief, as he sees Mattie seemingly rejecting him.

Choice D is not the best answer because while the second paragraph (lines 20-48) does discuss in depth the value Ethan attaches to natural beauty, nothing in the passage signifies that he has rejected natural beauty in favor of human artistry. The closest the passage comes to this is in lines 45-46, in which Mattie is said to have likened a natural scene to a painting, an assertion with which Ethan agrees.

15

In the context of the passage, the author's use of the phrase "her light step flying to keep time with his long stride" (lines 4-5) is primarily meant to convey the idea that

A) Ethan and Mattie share a powerful enthusiasm.

B) Mattie strives to match the speed at which Ethan works.

C) Mattie and Ethan playfully compete with each other.

D) Ethan walks at a pace that frustrates Mattie.

Content: Rhetoric

Key: A

Objective: Students must determine the main rhetorical effect of the author's choice of words.

Explanation: Choice A is the best answer. The author uses the phrase mainly to introduce a topic discussed at length in the second paragraph (lines 20-48) — namely, the growing connection Ethan sees himself form-ing with Mattie over the course of many evening walks during which they share similar feelings for the wonders of the natural world. In the context of the passage, the phrase evokes an image of two people walking eagerly and in harmony.

Choice B is not the best answer because while the phrase literally conveys Mattie's attempts to keep up with Ethan's pace, the phrase relates to times of leisure during which Ethan and Mattie walked arm-in-arm (see lines 1-4) rather than times of work. Moreover, the phrase is used primarily in a figu-rative way to suggest shared enthusiasm (see explanation for choice A).

Choice C is not the best answer because while the phrase literally describes Mattie's attempts to keep up with Ethan's pace, the context makes clear that Mattie and Ethan are not in competition with each other; instead, they are enjoying times of leisure during which the two walk arm-in-arm (see lines 1-4). Moreover, the phrase is used primarily in a figurative way to suggest shared enthusiasm (see explanation for choice A).

Choice D is not the best answer because while the phrase could in isolation be read as conveying some frustration on the part of Mattie, who had to expend extra effort to keep up with Ethan's pace, the context makes clear that Mattie is not annoyed with Ethan but is instead enjoying times of leisure during which the two walk arm-in-arm (see lines 1-4). The phrase is used primarily to suggest shared enthusiasm (see explanation for choice A).

PRACTICE AT
khanacademy.org/sat

Choice C may seem tempting, as the relationship between Ethan and Mattie is described in the passage as containing an aspect of playfulness. The idea that Mattie and Ethan playfully compete with one another is not, however, the intended purpose of the phrase referred to in the question.

16

The description in the first paragraph indicates that what Ethan values most about Mattie is her

A) fitness for farm labor.
B) vivacious youth.
C) receptive nature.
D) freedom from worry.

Content: Information and Ideas

Key: C

Objective: Students must characterize the relationship between two individ-uals in the passage.

Explanation: Choice C is the best answer. Lines 8-14 mention many of Mattie's traits: she is friendly ("smiled and waved"), eager ("jumped down with her bundles"), easygoing ("she ain't a fretter"), and energetic ("like the lighting of a fire on a cold hearth"). However, the trait that appeals the most to Ethan, as suggested by it being mentioned last in the paragraph, is her openness to the world around her: "She had an eye to see and an ear to hear: he could show her things and tell her things, and taste the bliss of feeling that all he imparted left long reverberations and echoes he could wake at will" (lines 15-19).

Choice A is not the best answer because the passage suggests that Ethan does not actually view Mattie as particularly well suited to farm labor. When first seeing Mattie, Ethan thinks to himself, after "looking over her slight person," that "she don't look much on housework" (lines 10-11).

Choice B is not the best answer because the passage suggests that Mattie's youth is not what Ethan values most about Mattie. Although the passage does note that "the coming to his house of a bit of hopeful young life was like the lighting of a fire on a cold hearth" (line 12-14), the narrator goes on to note that "the girl was more than the bright serviceable creature [Ethan] had thought her" (lines 14-15), indicating that Ethan values something more in Mattie than simply her vivacity.

Choice D is not the best answer because although Ethan acknowledges that Mattie "ain't a fretter" (line 12), there is no evidence that Mattie's freedom from worry is what Ethan values the most about Mattie. The first paragraph lists several positive traits that Mattie has, with the most emphasis being placed on her openness to the world around her (see explanation for choice C).

PRACTICE AT

khanacademy.org/sat

What makes this question particularly challenging is that there is quite a bit of support for choice B in the first paragraph of the passage. Choice C, however, is the best answer because the first paragraph ends with a strong emphasis on Mattie's receptive nature, underscored by the keyword "But" in line 12.

17

Which choice provides the best evidence for the answer to the previous question?
A) Lines 1-6 ("Mattie . . . farm")
B) Lines 6-12 ("He had . . . anyhow")
C) Lines 12-14 ("But it . . . hearth")
D) Lines 15-19 ("She had . . . will")

Content: Information and Ideas

Key: D

Objective: Students must determine which portion of the passage provides the best evidence for the answer to the previous question.

Explanation: Choice D is the best answer. Lines 15-19 explain that Mattie "had an eye to see and an ear to hear: [Ethan] could show her things and tell her things, and taste the bliss of feeling that all he imparted left long reverberations and echoes he could wake at will." In other words, Mattie is open, or receptive, to ideas and experiences, and the placement of this point at the end of the list of traits Ethan admires ("But it was not only . . .") suggests that her openness is most important to him. Therefore, these lines serve as the best evidence for the answer to the previous question.

PRACTICE AT

khanacademy.org/sat

Questions 16 and 17 form an interrelated question pair. The thought process that led you to the answer for Question 16 will help you select the answer for Question 17.

Choice A is not the best answer because lines 1-6 only describe Ethan and Mattie's living situation and indicate that Ethan enjoys walking with her in the evenings. They do not indicate which quality of Mattie's Ethan values the most. Therefore, these lines do not serve as the best evidence for the answer to the previous question.

Choice B is not the best answer because lines 6-12 only indicate Ethan's first impression of Mattie. Mattie comes across as generally friendly and enthusiastic in their first encounter, but it is not these qualities that Ethan values the most. Therefore, these lines do not serve as the best evidence for the answer to the previous question.

Choice C is not the best answer because lines 12-14 only convey that there was something special about Mattie beyond her friendliness and enthusiasm. They do not indicate what Ethan values the most about Mattie. Therefore, these lines do not serve as the best evidence for the answer to the previous question.

PRACTICE AT

🖌 **khanacademy.org/sat**

The clues that can help you answer this question can be found in the lines immediately preceding the lines referenced in the question. When asked why the author includes a particular detail, always consider the context in which the detail appears.

18

The author includes the descriptions of the sunset, the clouds, and the hemlock shadows (lines 42-45) primarily to

A) suggest the peacefulness of the natural world.
B) emphasize the acuteness of two characters' sensations.
C) foreshadow the declining fortunes of two characters.
D) offer a sense of how fleeting time can be.

Content: Rhetoric

Key: B

Objective: Students must analyze the relationship between a particular part of a text and the whole text.

Explanation: Choice B is the best answer. Lines 40-45 indicate that "there were other sensations, less definable but more exquisite, which drew [Ethan and Mattie] together with a shock of silent joy: the cold red of sunset behind winter hills, the flight of cloud-flocks over slopes of golden stubble, or the intensely blue shadows of hemlocks on sunlit snow." In the context of the second paragraph (lines 20-48), which focuses on the connection Ethan and Mattie establish through their shared interest in and sensitivity to nature, the descriptions primarily serve to emphasize the acuteness, or intensity, of the characters' sensations. According to the passage, Ethan and Mattie do not merely appreciate nature or see it as pretty or calm; rather, they experience a powerful "shock of silent joy" when in the presence of natural beauty.

Choice A is not the best answer because there is no indication that the descriptions are included primarily to emphasize the peacefulness of the natural world. Some readers may see "the cold red of sunset behind winter hills, the flight of cloud-flocks over slopes of golden stubble, or the intensely blue shadows of hemlocks on sunlit snow" (lines 42-45) as evoking a peaceful, harmonious scene. However, Ethan and Mattie do not merely appreciate nature or see it as pretty or calm; rather, they experience a powerful "shock of silent joy" (line 42) when in the presence of natural beauty.

Choice C is not the best answer because there is no evidence in the passage that the descriptions are included primarily to foreshadow Ethan's and Mattie's declining fortunes. In fact, there is no evidence in the passage of decline for either character apart from the agitation that Ethan experiences over his relationship with Mattie.

Choice D is not the best answer because there is no evidence in the passage that the descriptions are included primarily to offer a sense of time as fleeting. In fact, the speed at which time passes plays no particular role in the passage.

SAMPLE 5:

Science Passage Pair, Medium Text Complexity

The following pair of passages from a life science text is of medium complexity: it represents the middle range of language difficulty and cognitive demand of passages that you'll find on the Reading Test.

REMEMBER

You will see one set of paired passages on the SAT Reading Test.

Questions 19-23 are based on the following passages.

Passage 1 is adapted from Susan Milius, "A Different Kind of Smart." ©2013 by Science News. Passage 2 is adapted from Bernd Heinrich, *Mind of the Raven: Investigations and Adventures with Wolf-Birds.* ©2007 by Bernd Heinrich.

Passage 1

In 1894, British psychologist C. Lloyd Morgan published what's called Morgan's canon, the principle that suggestions of humanlike mental processes behind an animal's behavior
Line should be rejected if a simpler explanation will do.
5   Still, people seem to maintain certain expectations, especially when it comes to birds and mammals. "We somehow want to prove they are as 'smart' as people," zoologist Sara Shettleworth says. We want a bird that masters a vexing problem to be employing human-
10 style insight.
New Caledonian crows face the high end of these expectations, as possibly the second-best toolmakers on the planet.
Their tools are hooked sticks or strips made from spike-
15 edged leaves, and they use them in the wild to winkle grubs out of crevices. Researcher Russell Gray first saw the process on a cold morning in a mountain forest in New Caledonia, an

island chain east of Australia. Over the course of days, he and
crow researcher Gavin Hunt had gotten wild crows used to
20 finding meat tidbits in holes in a log. Once the birds were
checking the log reliably, the researchers placed a spiky
tropical pandanus plant beside the log and hid behind a blind.

A crow arrived. It hopped onto the pandanus plant,
grabbed the spiked edge of one of the long straplike leaves and
25 began a series of ripping motions. Instead of just tearing away
one long strip, the bird ripped and nipped in a sequence to
create a slanting stair-step edge on a leaf segment with a
narrow point and a wide base. The process took only seconds.
Then the bird dipped the narrow end of its leaf strip into a
30 hole in the log, fished up the meat with the leaf-edge spikes,
swallowed its prize and flew off.

"That was my 'oh wow' moment," Gray says. After the
crow had vanished, he picked up the tool the bird had left
behind. "I had a go, and I couldn't do it," he recalls. Fishing
35 the meat out was tricky. It turned out that Gray was moving
the leaf shard too forcefully instead of gently stroking the
spines against the treat.

The crow's deft physical manipulation was what inspired
Gray and Auckland colleague Alex Taylor to test other wild
40 crows to see if they employed the seemingly insightful string-
pulling solutions that some ravens, kea parrots and other
brainiac birds are known to employ. Three of four crows
passed that test on the first try.

Passage 2

For one month after they left the nest, I led my four young
45 ravens at least once and sometimes several times a day on
thirty-minute walks. During these walks, I wrote down
everything in their environment they pecked at. In the first
sessions, I tried to be teacher. I touched specific objects—
sticks, moss, rocks—and nothing that I touched remained
50 untouched by them. They came to investigate what I had
investigated, leading me to assume that young birds are aided
in learning to identify food from the parents' example. They
also, however, contacted almost everything else that lay
directly in their own paths. They soon became more
55 independent by taking their own routes near mine. Even while
walking along on their own, they pulled at leaves, grass stems,
flowers, bark, pine needles, seeds, cones, clods of earth, and
other objects they encountered. I wrote all this down,
converting it to numbers. After they were thoroughly familiar
60 with the background objects in these woods and started to
ignore them, I seeded the path we would later walk together
with objects they had never before encountered. Some of
these were conspicuous food items: raspberries, dead
meal worm beetles, and cooked corn kernels. Others were
65 conspicuous and inedible: pebbles, glass chips, red
winterberries. Still others were such highly cryptic foods as
encased caddisfly larvae and moth cocoons. The results were
dramatic.

The four young birds on our daily walks contacted all new
70 objects preferentially. They picked them out at a rate of up to
tens of thousands of times greater than background or
previously contacted objects. The main initial criterion for
pecking or picking anything up was its novelty. In subsequent
trials, when the previously novel items were edible, they
75 became preferred and the inedible objects became
"background" items, just like the leaves, grass, and pebbles,
even if they were highly conspicuous. These experiments
showed that ravens' curiosity ensures exposure to all or almost
all items in the environment.

19

Within Passage 1, the main purpose of the first two paragraphs (lines 1-10)
is to

A) offer historical background in order to question the uniqueness of two
researchers' findings.

B) offer interpretive context in order to frame the discussion of an
experiment and its results.

C) introduce a scientific principle in order to show how an experiment's
outcomes validated that principle.

D) present seemingly contradictory stances in order to show how they can
be reconciled empirically.

Content: Rhetoric

Key: B

Objective: Students must determine the main purpose of two paragraphs in
relation to the passage as a whole.

Explanation: Choice B is the best answer. Passage 1 opens with an explanation of Morgan's canon and continues with a discussion of people's expectations regarding animal intelligence. Taken together, the first two paragraphs
indicate that despite cautions to the contrary, people still tend to look for
humanlike levels of intelligence in many animals, including birds. These two
paragraphs provide a framework in which to assess the work of Gray and
Hunt, presented in the rest of the passage. The passage's characterization
of the experiment Gray and Hunt conduct, in which they observe a crow's
tool-making ability and to which Gray responds by trying and failing to
mimic the bird's behavior ("I had a go, and I couldn't do it," line 34), suggests
that Shettleworth, quoted in the second paragraph, is at least partially correct in her assessment that "we somehow want to prove [birds] are as 'smart'
as people" (lines 6-7).

Choice A is not the best answer because while the reference to Morgan's canon in the first paragraph offers a sort of historical background (given that the canon was published in 1894), the second paragraph describes people's continuing expectations regarding animal intelligence. Furthermore, the fact that Gray and Hunt may share with other people the tendency to look for humanlike intelligence in many animals does not by itself establish that the main purpose of the first two paragraphs is to question the uniqueness of Gray and Hunt's findings.

Choice C is not the best answer because while the reference to Morgan's canon in the first paragraph does introduce a scientific principle, the discussion in the second paragraph of people's expectations regarding animal intelligence, as well as the passage's characterization of Gray and Hunt's experiment and how the researchers interpret the results, primarily suggest that people tend to violate the canon by attributing humanlike levels of intelligence to many animals.

Choice D is not the best answer because although the first two paragraphs do present different perspectives, they are not seemingly or genuinely contradictory. The second paragraph, particularly the quotation from Shettleworth, serves mainly to qualify (not contradict) the position staked out in the first paragraph by suggesting that while Morgan's canon is probably a sound principle, people still tend to project humanlike levels of intelligence onto many animals. Moreover, the experiment depicted in the rest of the passage primarily bears out Shettleworth's claim that "We somehow want to prove [birds] are as 'smart' as people" (lines 6-7) and thus does not reconcile the perspectives found in the opening paragraphs.

PRACTICE AT

🖊 **khanacademy.org/sat**

In contrast to Question 19, which requires a broader understanding of the passage, Question 20 asks about a specific detail. On this type of question, it may help to locate and reread the relevant detail in the passage before selecting your answer.

20

According to the experiment described in Passage 2, whether the author's ravens continued to show interest in a formerly new object was dictated primarily by whether that object was

A) edible.

B) plentiful.

C) conspicuous.

D) natural.

Content: Information and Ideas/Understanding relationships

Key: A

Objective: Students must identify an explicitly stated relationship between events.

Explanation: Choice A is the best answer. The last paragraph of Passage 2 presents the results of an experiment in which the author scattered unfamiliar objects in the path of some ravens. According to the passage, the birds initially "contacted all new objects preferentially" but in "subsequent trials" only preferred those "previously novel items" that "were edible" (line 69-74).

Choice B is not the best answer because the ravens studied by the author only preferred those "previously novel items" that "were edible," whereas "the inedible objects became 'background' items, just like the leaves, grass, and pebbles" (lines 74-76). In other words, plentiful items did not continue to interest the ravens unless the items were edible.

Choice C is not the best answer because the ravens studied by the author only preferred those "previously novel items" that "were edible," whereas "the inedible objects became 'background' items, just like the leaves, grass, and pebbles, even if they were highly conspicuous" (lines 74-77). In other words, conspicuous items did not continue to interest the ravens unless the items were edible.

Choice D is not the best answer because the ravens studied by the author only preferred those "previously novel items" that "were edible," whereas "the inedible objects became 'background' items, just like the leaves, grass, and pebbles" (lines 74-76). In other words, natural items did not continue to interest the ravens unless the items were edible.

21

The crows in Passage 1 and the ravens in Passage 2 shared which trait?

A) They modified their behavior in response to changes in their environment.
B) They formed a strong bond with the humans who were observing them.
C) They manufactured useful tools for finding and accessing food.
D) They mimicked the actions they saw performed around them.

Content: Synthesis/Analyzing multiple texts

Key: A

Objective: Students must synthesize information and ideas from paired texts.

Explanation: Choice A is the best answer. Both bird species studied modified their behavior in response to changes in their environment. The researchers described in Passage 1 "had gotten wild crows used to finding meat tidbits in holes in a log" (lines 19-20). In other words, the researchers had repeatedly placed meat in the log — that is, changed the crows' environment — and the birds had responded by modifying their behavior, a point reinforced in line 21, which notes that the birds began "checking the log reliably." The ravens in Passage 2 act in analogous fashion, responding to the introduction of new objects in their environment by "pick[ing] them out at a rate of up to

PRACTICE AT

🔵 **khanacademy.org/sat**

The incorrect answers to Question 21 are traits that may have been possessed by either the crows in Passage 1 or the ravens in Passage 2. Only choice A describes a trait that the birds from both passages exhibited.

tens of thousands of times greater than background or previously contacted objects" (lines 70-72).

Choice B is not the best answer because while there is some evidence that the ravens described in Passage 2 formed a bond with the author, going on walks with him and possibly viewing him as their "teacher," there is no evidence that a similar bond formed between the researchers described in Passage 1 and the crows they studied. Indeed, these researchers "hid behind a blind" (line 22) in an effort to avoid contact with their subjects.

Choice C is not the best answer because while crows' tool-making ability is the central focus of the experiment described in Passage 1, there is no evidence that the ravens in Passage 2 did anything similar. Passage 1 does mention that "some ravens" use "seemingly insightful string-pulling solutions" (lines 40-41), but nothing in Passage 2 suggests that the ravens in that particular study had or displayed tool-making abilities.

Choice D is not the best answer because while there is some evidence that the ravens described in Passage 2 mimicked human behavior, going on walks with the author and possibly viewing him as their "teacher," there is no evidence that the crows in Passage 1 did any mimicking. Passage 1, in fact, suggests that the ability of the crow to produce the meat-fishing tool was innate rather than a skill it had acquired from either humans or other birds.

22

One difference between the experiments described in the two passages is that unlike the researchers discussed in Passage 1, the author of Passage 2

A) presented the birds with a problem to solve.
B) intentionally made the birds aware of his presence.
C) consciously manipulated the birds' surroundings.
D) tested the birds' tool-using abilities.

Content: Synthesis/Analyzing multiple texts

Key: B

Objective: Students must synthesize information and ideas from paired texts.

Explanation: Choice B is the best answer. The researchers described in Passage 1 "hid behind a blind" (line 22) to avoid being seen by the crow. The author of Passage 2, on the other hand, made no attempt to conceal his presence; in fact, as he describes it, he "led" the ravens in his study on "walks" (lines 44-46), during which he "touched specific objects" (line 48) and then watched to see whether the birds touched the same objects. The author of Passage 2 notes that the ravens "soon became more independent" (line 54-55), going their own way rather than continuing to follow the author.

PRACTICE AT

khanacademy.org/sat

This question asks you to identify something the author of Passage 2 did that the researchers discussed in Passage 1 did not do. Thus, the correct answer must fulfill both of these criteria. If an answer choice fulfills only one of two criteria, eliminate it!

From this, it is clear that the author of Passage 2, unlike the researchers described in Passage 1, intentionally made the birds aware of his presence.

Choice A is not the best answer because while a case could be made that the author of Passage 2 gave the ravens a problem to solve (Which new objects are best to touch?), the researchers described in Passage 1 presented the crows with a problem as well: how to extract meat from a log. Thus, presenting birds with a problem to solve was not a difference between the experiments.

Choice C is not the best answer because both the researchers described in Passage 1 and the author of Passage 2 consciously manipulated the birds' surroundings. The crow researchers placed meat pieces in a log and a pandanus plant behind the log (see lines 18-22). The author of Passage 2 put unfamiliar objects on a path for the ravens to find (see lines 61-62). Thus, conscious manipulation of the birds' surroundings was not a difference between the experiments.

Choice D is not the best answer because there is no evidence that the author of Passage 2 tested the ravens' tool-using abilities. The passage instead indicates that the author recorded observations about the birds' interactions with objects naturally occurring in and artificially introduced into the environment.

23

Is the main conclusion presented by the author of Passage 2 consistent with Morgan's canon, as described in Passage 1?

A) Yes, because the conclusion proposes that the ravens' behavior is a product of environmental factors.

B) Yes, because the conclusion offers a satisfyingly simple explanation of the ravens' behavior.

C) No, because the conclusion suggests that the ravens exhibit complex behavior patterns.

D) No, because the conclusion implies that a humanlike quality motivates the ravens' behavior.

Content: Synthesis/Analyzing Multiple Texts

Key: D

Objective: Students must synthesize information and ideas from paired texts.

Explanation: Choice D is the best answer. According to Passage 1, Morgan's canon is "the principle that suggestions of humanlike mental processes behind an animal's behavior should be rejected if a simpler explanation will do" (lines 2-4). The main conclusion drawn by the author of Passage 2 is that "ravens' curiosity ensures exposure to all or almost all items in the

PRACTICE AT

khanacademy.org/sat

Break this challenging question down into a series of logical steps. First, identify the main conclusion of Passage 2 and refresh your memory of Morgan's canon. Next, determine if the conclusion in Passage 2 is consistent with Morgan's canon, and eliminate two answer choices accordingly. Lastly, examine the differences between the remaining two choices and select the one that is supported by the passages.

environment" (lines 78-79). In referring to the ravens' behavior as reflecting "curiosity," a human trait, the author of Passage 2 would seem to be ascribing a humanlike mental process to an animal's behavior without explicitly considering alternate explanations.

Choice A is not the best answer because the main conclusion drawn by the author of Passage 2 is that "ravens' curiosity ensures exposure to all or almost all items in the environment" (lines 78-79). In referring to the ravens' behavior as reflecting "curiosity," a human trait, the author of Passage 2 would seem to be ascribing a humanlike mental process to an animal's behavior without explicitly considering alternate explanations. Morgan's canon holds that such suggestions should be rejected unless a "simpler explanation" cannot be found (line 4); therefore, the conclusion the author of Passage 2 reaches is not consistent with Morgan's canon. Moreover, by ascribing the ravens' behavior to "curiosity," the author of Passage 2 seems to reject environmental factors as the cause.

Choice B is not the best answer because the main conclusion drawn by the author of Passage 2 is that "ravens' curiosity ensures exposure to all or almost all items in the environment" (lines 78-79). In referring to the ravens' behavior as reflecting "curiosity," a human trait, the author of Passage 2 would seem to be ascribing a humanlike mental process to an animal's behavior without explicitly considering alternate explanations. Morgan's canon holds that such suggestions should be rejected unless a "simpler explanation" cannot be found (line 4); therefore, the conclusion the author of Passage 2 reaches cannot be the type of "simpler explanation" Morgan was alluding to.

Choice C is not the best answer because while the main conclusion drawn by the author of Passage 2 is not consistent with Morgan's canon (see explanation for choice D), nothing about how the canon is described in Passage 1 precludes the possibility that animals can exhibit complex behavior patterns. The canon merely rejects the idea that humanlike mental processes should quickly or easily be attributed to animals.

Chapter 13

About the SAT Writing and Language Test

Writing will be central to your postsecondary education, whether your plans involve college or some form of workforce training. Along with speaking and creating media, writing is a critical communication tool — one that you'll use continually in a variety of ways both informal and formal. You may use notes, journaling, or the like to record information, to aid memory, and to clarify thoughts and feelings for yourself; you may also create essays, poems, reports, and so on to share information and ideas with others in a more structured, fully developed way.

In the latter cases, you'll probably take each piece of writing through a variety of steps, from planning to polishing. Your writing process may differ from that of others, and your own process may change depending on the nature of the writing task, purpose, and audience (not to mention how much time you have), but revising your writing to improve the content and editing your writing to ensure that you've followed the conventions of standard written English are likely to be key parts of most projects. The SAT Writing and Language Test is designed to emulate these two tasks, assessing how well you can revise and edit a range of texts to improve the expression of ideas and to correct errors in sentence structure, usage, and punctuation.

The passages on the Writing and Language Test vary in purpose, subject, and complexity. Some passages (and possibly questions) will also include one or more informational graphics, such as tables, graphs, and charts, and you'll be expected to use the information in these graphics to inform decisions about revising and editing the associated passage.

Unlike passages on the Reading Test (discussed in Chapter 8), passages on the Writing and Language Test are written specifically for the test; that way, we can more easily introduce "errors" — our general term for the various rhetorical and mechanical problems we assess on the test.

 **REMEMBER**

On the SAT Writing and Language Test, you'll be placed in the role of someone revising and editing the work of another writer.

You'll encounter the passages and questions in side-by-side columns, with each passage (spread over multiple pages) in the left-hand column and associated questions in the right-hand column. Question numbers embedded in the passages, along with other forms of annotation (especially underlining), let you know what part of the passage is being tested at any given point; in some cases, questions may ask about a passage as a whole.

You'll be asked questions that deal with the expression of ideas in a passage — specifically, questions about development, organization, and effective language use. You'll also be given questions that require you to apply your knowledge of the conventions of standard written English to the passage — specifically, to recognize and correct errors in sentence structure, usage, and punctuation. All of the questions are based in multiparagraph passages, so each question has an extended context and no question requires the rote recall of language "rules." As a group, the questions call on the same sorts of revising and editing skills that you're using already in your high school classes and that are important to have in order to be ready for and to succeed in college and workforce training programs.

The rest of this chapter offers a general description of the Writing and Language Test. The following two chapters go into more detail about the question types that are included on the test.

Writing and Language Test Format

Before we delve into the passages and questions, let's review the test format. Understanding how things work will help you get a quick start on test day and allow you to focus your full attention on answering the questions.

A sample of the Writing and Language Test format appears on the next page. Each passage will be headed by a title in boldface type. The passage itself will be spread across multiple pages (so, unless you're on the last question set on the test, don't assume that you've reached the end of a given passage until you see the title of the next one). The passage is positioned in the left-hand column of each page, and the questions related to the portion of the passage on that page appear in order in the right-hand column.

Most questions are "anchored" to a particular location in the passage via a boxed question number in the passage. Sometimes this boxed number will stand alone; in these cases, the associated question will tell you what to do, such as consider adding a sentence at that point. At other times, this boxed number will be followed by underlined text; for these questions, you'll have to consider which of four answer options results either in the most rhetorically effective expression in the context of the passage or in an expression that is correct in terms of standard written English sentence structure, usage, or punctuation.

PRACTICE AT

khanacademy.org/sat

Getting a strong score on the Writing and Language Test is not about rote recall of language rules or knowing all about grammar. You'll instead need to consider context — often at the paragraph or passage level — when choosing your answer.

REMEMBER

In many cases, a boxed question number as well as underlining specify the part of the passage that a particular question refers to.

REMEMBER

Some questions with an underlined portion may not include directions. For these questions, assume that your task is to select the answer that's the most effective or correct.

Questions 1-11 are based on the following passage.

A Life in Traffic

A subway system is expanded to provide service to a growing suburb. A bike-sharing program is adopted to encourage nonmotorized transportation. **1** To alleviate rush hour traffic jams in a congested downtown area, stoplight timing is coordinated. When any one of these changes **2** occur, it is likely the result of careful analysis conducted by transportation planners.

The work of transportation planners generally includes evaluating current transportation needs,

---

1

Which choice best maintains the sentence pattern already established in the paragraph?

A) NO CHANGE

B) Coordinating stoplight timing can help alleviate rush hour traffic jams in a congested downtown area.

C) Stoplight timing is coordinated to alleviate rush hour traffic jams in a congested downtown area.

D) In a congested downtown area, stoplight timing is coordinated to alleviate rush hour traffic jams.

2

A) NO CHANGE

B) occur, they are

C) occurs, they are

D) occurs, it is

While some questions with an underlined portion include a question-specific direction (as in question 1 above), others don't (as in question 2 above). When there are no additional directions, assume that you're to choose the option that's the most rhetorically effective in context or that results in a conventionally correct expression. If a question includes a "NO CHANGE" option — it'll always be the first answer choice — pick it if you think the original version presented in the passage is the best option; otherwise, pick one of the three alternatives.

You may come across some other forms of passage annotation as well. If the paragraphs in a passage or the sentences in a paragraph are numbered, one or more questions will refer to those numbers. You may be asked, for example, to consider where a particular sentence should be placed (e.g., "after sentence 3"). You may also, on occasion, be advised that a particular question asks about the passage as a whole. In that case, you'll have to apply your understanding of the entire passage when answering the question.

REMEMBER

Some questions include a "NO CHANGE" option; choose this answer if you think the original text presented in the passage is the best choice.

Writing and Language Test Passages

The passages on the Writing and Language Test are varied in order to better assess whether you can apply your revising and editing knowledge and skills in a wide range of contexts important for college and career. Passages differ in purpose: Some primarily serve to relate events or experiences narratively, while others serve mainly to convey information, explain a process or idea, or argue for a particular way of thinking or acting. Passages also represent numerous different subject areas. In addition, passages vary in complexity, with some being relatively straightforward and others being highly challenging.

Let's consider some of the key features of Writing and Language Test passages.

▶ **Purpose:** As previously mentioned, some Writing and Language Test passages are focused on narrating experiences in a storylike way. Though there is no fiction passage on the Writing and Language Test (as there is on the Reading Test), a nonfiction narrative, such as one recounting a historical event or relating the steps in a scientific investigation, is found on each test. Other passages on the test serve mainly to inform, to explain, or to argue in support of a claim.

REMEMBER

Passage purpose, subject matter, and complexity will vary in order to provide a broad assessment of your revising and editing skills.

▶ **Subject:** Writing and Language Test passages cover a variety of subject areas, including career-related topics, the humanities, history/social studies, and science. Passages on career-related topics aren't workplace documents, such as memos or reports; instead, they're general-interest pieces on trends, issues, and debates in common career pathways, such as health care and information technology. Humanities passages focus on the arts and letters and include texts on fine art, film, music, literature, and the like. History/social studies passages include texts on topics in history as well as in the social sciences, such as anthropology, archaeology, economics, and psychology. Science passages cover both foundational scientific concepts as well as recent advances in fields such as Earth science, biology, chemistry, astronomy, and physics.

▶ **Complexity:** The reading challenge posed by the passages on the test varies. Some passages are relatively straightforward. They may, for example, have a very clear purpose, present a fairly small amount of information, and use familiar language. Other passages, by contrast, are more complex. They may have a more subtle purpose, require the reader to follow a complicated series of events, and make use of long and involved sentences. (It's important to note that each Writing and Language Test has a similar range of passage complexity, so you shouldn't worry about taking a test that has nothing but highly challenging passages.)

One additional feature of passages is also important to note here.

PRACTICE AT

🌱 **khanacademy.org/sat**

When you answer questions on the Writing and Language Test that relate to informational graphics, you'll be using skills similar to those you'll use on Data Analysis questions on the SAT Math Test and Synthesis questions on the SAT Reading Test.

▶ **Informational graphics:** Passages (and occasionally questions) on the Writing and Language Test may include one or more tables, graphs, or charts that relate to the topic of the passage. A graphic may, for example, provide additional statistical support for a point made in the passage. Questions may ask you, for example, to use information from the graphic(s) to correct a factual error in the passage or to replace the passage's vague description with a more precise one using specific quantities.

All of the passages on the Writing and Language Test are high-quality, well-edited pieces of writing developed specifically for the test. They convey interesting information, explore intriguing ideas, and offer new insights. Although the primary purpose of the passages is to help assess your revising and editing skills, it's our hope that you find the passages engaging and worth reading.

Writing and Language Test Questions

Now that we've talked about the passages, it's time to turn to the questions on the Writing and Language Test. All of the questions are multiple-choice, which means that you'll pick the best of four answer options for each question. The questions are also all centered in multiparagraph passages, so you won't be tested on isolated rhetorical or grammar, usage, and mechanics knowledge and/or skills. Because all questions are passage based, you'll want to consider the passage context carefully before answering each question. Sometimes focusing only on the sentence that a particular question refers to is enough to get that question right, but in other cases you'll have to think about the entire paragraph or the passage as a whole to get a good feel for the best response. Questions are sequenced in order of appearance, meaning that questions addressing the first paragraph come before those addressing the second paragraph, and so on. Any questions about the passage as a whole come last in a set. You'll encounter questions about informational graphics in the most logical spots in the order.

The questions on the test are designed to reflect as closely as possible the kinds of revising and editing decisions that writers and editors make. Think about a piece of writing that you've written and then gone back to improve. When you reread what you'd written, what came to mind? Maybe you realized that a particular point you were making didn't have enough support, so you added some. Maybe you recognized that you'd forgotten to put in a transition between two ideas, so you clarified the connection. Or maybe you saw that a subject and verb didn't agree, so you corrected the problem. Although you're not working with your own writing on the Writing and Language Test, the thinking process you'll use as you revise and edit the pieces on the test is similar.

The questions also often reflect the demands of the specific sort of passage you're working with. In some passages (particularly those with graphics), data are important, so you're likely to be working to improve the accuracy, clarity, and precision of the writer's descriptions of those data. In other passages (particularly in narratives), sequence will be central, so a question about the logical order and flow of information and ideas is likely to show up. Although these passages are grounded in particular subject areas, the questions don't test your background knowledge of the specific topics covered. The passages and any supplementary material, such as tables or graphs, will provide all of the information about a given topic that you'll need to make revision and editing decisions.

Writing and Language questions can be sorted into two general categories: (1) Expression of Ideas and (2) Standard English Conventions. The questions won't have those labels on them, but usually it'll be pretty easy to tell the difference. A brief discussion of each category should help you get a sense of what's on the test, what knowledge and skills you're likely to make use of, and how to focus your preparation for the test.

1. **Expression of Ideas:** These questions focus on the rhetorical elements of passages. To put it another way, Expression of Ideas questions deal

REMEMBER

All questions on the Writing and Language Test are multiple-choice with four answer options.

REMEMBER

All questions are passage based, so consider each question in the context of the passage before selecting your answer.

REMEMBER

You won't need any background knowledge of the topic covered in a passage; all the information you need to answer the questions will be in the passage and in any supplementary material, such as a table or graph.

131

☞ **REMEMBER**

Expression of Ideas questions ask you to assess and improve the substance and quality of passage text, while Standard English Conventions questions require you to recognize and correct errors in grammar, usage, and punctuation.

with improving the substance and quality of the writer's message. You'll be asked to revise passages to improve the development of the topic, the organization of information and ideas, and the effectiveness of the language use. Development questions, which include questions about main ideas (such as topic sentences and thesis statements), supporting details, focus, and quantitative information in tables, graphs, charts, and so on, were discussed briefly in Chapter 6's overview of the Command of Evidence subscore. Organization questions focus on logical sequence and placement of information and ideas as well as effective introductions, conclusions, and transitions. Effective Language Use questions ask you to improve precision and concision (e.g., eliminating wordiness), consider style and tone (e.g., making sure that the tone is consistent throughout the passage), and combine sentences to improve flow and to achieve particular rhetorical effects (such as emphasis on one point over another). These sorts of questions were briefly discussed in Chapter 7's overview of the Words in Context subscore.

2. **Standard English Conventions:** These questions focus on correcting grammar, usage, and mechanics problems in passages. More specifically, these questions ask you to recognize and correct errors in sentence structure (such as run-on or incomplete sentences), usage (such as lack of subject-verb or pronoun-antecedent agreement), and punctuation (such as missing or unnecessary commas).

These categories are discussed in more detail in Chapters 14 and 15.

The Writing and Language Test in Overview

Some of the basic elements of the Writing and Language Test are listed below. Familiarizing yourself with this overview may help you prepare for the test and pace yourself on test day.

▶ Total Questions: 44

▶ Total Time: 35 minutes (on average, slightly under a minute per question, inclusive of passage reading time)

▶ Number of Passages: Four

▶ Passage Length: 400 to 450 words; total of 1,700 words

▶ Passage Subjects: One passage on a career-related topic and one passage each in the humanities, history/social studies, and science

▶ Passage Writing Modes: One nonfiction narrative, one to two informative/ explanatory texts, and one to two arguments

▶ Passage Complexities: A defined range from grades 9–10 to early postsecondary

▶ Questions per Passage: 11

▶ In addition to an overall test score, the questions on the Writing and Language Test contribute to various scores in the following ways:

— Expression of Ideas: 24 questions, six per passage

— Standard English Conventions: 20 questions, five per passage

— Command of Evidence (Chapter 6): Eight questions, two per passage

— Words in Context (Chapter 7): Eight questions, two per passage

— Analysis in History/Social Studies: Six questions (all of the Expression of Ideas questions on the history/social studies passage)

— Analysis in Science: Six questions (all of the Expression of Ideas questions on the science passage)

Note: Some Writing and Language questions contribute to multiple scores.

Chapter 16 provides sample passages and questions to help you become more familiar with the Writing and Language Test. Chapter 16 also contains explanations for the answers.

CHAPTER 13 RECAP

The SAT Writing and Language Test measures your knowledge and skills in revising and editing texts widely varied in purpose, subject, and complexity. The questions on the test are multiple-choice and passage based; represent the kinds of choices writers and editors routinely have to make; reflect differences in the content and nature of the passages; and cover two basic areas: Expression of Ideas and Standard English Conventions. Questions don't test topic-specific background knowledge; all of the information about each topic needed to answer the questions is included in the passages themselves. Some passages and/or questions on the test include one or more informational graphics.

The Writing and Language Test offers a significant but fair challenge to college- and career-ready students. Since the questions are fairly "natural" in the sense that they mimic common revision and editing issues and are based in extended pieces of high-quality writing, you won't have to worry about applying obscure conventions or dealing with highly artificial or brief passages that provide little context for an answer. On the other hand, you *will* have to pay attention to the context as you answer the questions. Sometimes you'll have to "read around" a given place in the passage — looking both before it and after it — or you'll have to think about the whole passage to see how the larger text influences the answer to a particular question. Sometimes, too, what would seem like the best answer in many situations — such as adopting a formal tone — is a weaker choice in a given case, such as in a highly informal essay. The questions themselves will also often state the goal to be accomplished, such as adding support or shifting emphasis. Paying careful attention to the contextual clues provided in the questions themselves and by the passages will go a long way toward ensuring that you do your best on the Writing and Language Test.

Chapter 14

Writing and Language: Expression of Ideas

As we mentioned in Chapter 13, questions on the SAT Writing and Language Test fall into two broad categories: (1) Expression of Ideas and (2) Standard English Conventions. Here in Chapter 14, we'll go into more detail about the first of these two categories, using some of the sample Writing and Language questions also found in Chapter 16. That chapter contains additional samples as well as explanations for the answer to each question. Chapter 15 covers Standard English Conventions.

Expression of Ideas: The Art of Writing

In Chapter 13, we noted that Expression of Ideas was the Writing and Language category focused on refining the substance and quality of the writer's message. Specifically, Expression of Ideas questions focus on development, organization, and language use in relation to the writer's purpose. Collectively, these questions address the rhetorical aspects of the passages on the test. You may recall that in Chapter 10, we defined "rhetoric" as, roughly, the study of the art of writing (and speaking) and the application of that art in practice. When you answer the rhetorically oriented Expression of Ideas questions, you're using your knowledge of and skill in writing to make each passage clearer, sharper, richer, and more engaging.

Expression of Ideas includes a wide range of rhetorical question types. Within Development, Organization, and Effective Language Use are a number of specific testing points that we'll explain in turn. Broken down, the Expression of Ideas category consists of these elements:

- ▶ **Development:** Refining the content of a passage to achieve the writer's purpose, including:
  - *Proposition:* Adding, revising, or retaining (leaving unchanged) thesis statements, topic sentences, claims, and the like — the "main ideas" of a passage or paragraph
  - *Support:* Adding, revising, or retaining material that supports a passage's points or claims

— *Focus:* Adding, revising, retaining, or deleting material on the basis of relevance to the purpose (e.g., deleting an irrelevant sentence)

— *Quantitative information:* Using data from informational graphics (tables, graphs, charts, and the like) to enhance the accuracy, precision, and overall effectiveness of a passage

▶ **Organization:** Improving the structure of a passage to enhance logic and cohesion, including:

— *Logical sequence:* Ensuring that material is presented in a passage in the most logical place and order

— *Introductions, conclusions, and transitions:* Improving the openings and closings of paragraphs and passages and the connections between and among information and ideas in a passage

▶ **Effective Language Use:** Revising text to improve written expression and to achieve the writer's purpose, including:

— *Precision:* Making word choice more exact or appropriate for the context

— *Concision:* Making word choice more economical and eliminating wordiness and redundancy

— *Style and tone:* Making word choice consistent with the overall style and tone of a passage or accomplishing some particular rhetorical goal

— *Syntax:* Combining sentences to improve the flow of language or to accomplish some particular rhetorical goal

In the following sections, we'll examine the contents of each of these subcategories in turn.

DEVELOPMENT

Development questions on the Writing and Language Test get to the heart of the substance of the passage. They're the questions that focus most directly on the content of the writer's message. (Note, though, that you won't need background knowledge of the passage's topic to answer the questions; all the information you'll need will be in the passage itself.) When you answer a Development question, you'll be looking for ways to enhance the writer's message by clarifying the main points, working with supporting details, sharpening the focus, and — in some passages — using data from informational graphics such as tables, graphs, and charts to make the passage more accurate, more precise, and generally more effective. Let's go into a little more detail on each of these points.

Proposition

Proposition questions require you to think about the "big ideas" in the passage and how they can be refined to better clarify and structure the writer's message. The forms these big ideas take vary from passage to passage, but there are several common types: *Thesis statements* express the main idea of the overall passage. *Topic sentences* are used to help structure and clarify the focus of paragraphs. These often (but not always) come at the beginning of a paragraph and serve to preview (and limit) what's to come. *Claims* and *counterclaims* are features specific to arguments. A claim is an assertion that the writer is trying to convey, such as the writer's position on a debate or issue, while a counterclaim is someone else's assertion that differs from, and sometimes opposes, the assertion the writer is making. (You might think of claims and counterclaims this way: In the formula "While many people believe *x*, *y* is actually the case," *y* is the writer's claim and *x* is the counterclaim the writer is arguing against.)

Writing and Language Test questions won't always use words and phrases such as "claim" or "topic sentence," but it's helpful to use them here to get a sense of the focus of the Proposition questions. Proposition questions will typically ask you to add or revise topic sentences, thesis statements, and so on in order to clarify and sharpen the writer's points or to leave them as is if the original version presented in the passage is better than any of the alternatives offered.

Support

Support questions are basically the flip side of Proposition questions. When you answer a Support question, you'll be thinking about how best to flesh out and make more effective or convincing the writer's big ideas. Support comes in many forms, but among the most common are descriptive details, facts, figures, and examples. The questions will typically use a word such as "support" and indicate what idea in the passage the writer wants to develop. You'll be asked to add or revise supporting material in order to strengthen a writer's points or to leave supporting material unchanged if the original version in the passage is the best way to accomplish the writer's goal.

Focus

Focus questions are mainly about relevance in relation to the writer's purpose. Purpose is a key consideration here because while some questions will ask you to remove information or an idea that's clearly irrelevant to the topic, the harder questions of this type will offer a detail that's loosely but not sufficiently tied to the point that the writer is making or that goes off on an interesting but ultimately unhelpful tangent. Focus questions are often about recognizing and deleting material that's irrelevant or only vaguely connected to the writer's aim, and these types of questions will often identify a sentence and ask you whether it should be kept or deleted. Focus questions, however, can also be about adding or retaining relevant information and ideas, so you shouldn't assume that every time you see a Focus question the answer will be to remove something. For these types of questions, it's especially important to consider the larger context of a particular paragraph or of the passage as a

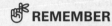
REMEMBER

Proposition questions focus on the "big ideas" in the passage and ask you, for instance, to add or revise thesis statements or topic sentences in order to clarify the writer's points.

REMEMBER

Whereas Proposition questions focus on the big ideas, Support questions get into the details of how the writer backs up the big ideas with evidence, examples, and the like.

REMEMBER

Some Focus questions may ask you to determine what information is irrelevant or insufficiently connected to the writer's purpose. Other Focus questions may ask you to determine what information should be added or retained.

whole; without an understanding of the goal the writer is trying to achieve, it's very difficult to make informed decisions about relevance.

Quantitative Information

We talked at length in the discussion of the Reading Test about comprehension questions related to informational graphics. Although the Writing and Language Test also includes a number of such graphics, the focus of questions about them is significantly different. On both tests, you'll have to read and interpret informational graphics, but on the Writing and Language Test you'll have to integrate text and graphics in a more direct way than on the Reading Test. Let's cruise through an example from a passage on traffic congestion. (As with the other samples in this chapter, the full passage text, question, and answer explanation can be found in Chapter 16.)

[. . .] Transportation planners perform critical work within the broader field of urban and regional planning. As of 2010, there were approximately 40,300 urban and regional planners employed in the United States. The United States Bureau of Labor Statistics forecasts steady job growth in this field, **11** projecting that 16 percent of new jobs in all occupations will be related to urban and regional planning. Population growth and concerns about environmental sustainability are expected to spur the need for transportation planning professionals.

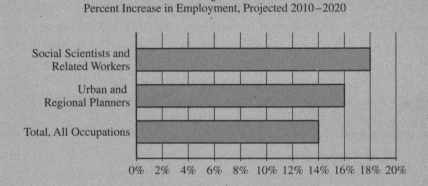

Urban and Regional Planners
Percent Increase in Employment, Projected 2010–2020

11. Which choice completes the sentence with accurate data based on the graph?

A) NO CHANGE

B) warning, however, that job growth in urban and regional planning will slow to 14 percent by 2020.

C) predicting that employment of urban and regional planners will increase 16 percent between 2010 and 2020.

D) indicating that 14 to 18 percent of urban and regional planning positions will remain unfilled.

To answer this question, you need to understand both the passage and the accompanying graph. The question directs you to the underlined portion of the passage excerpt above and asks you to complete the sentence with accurate data from the graphic. (Unless told otherwise by a question, you should assume that the graphic itself is accurate, so you don't need to worry about whether you're working with "true" information.)

The basic logic of the question is similar to that of other questions on the test that include a "NO CHANGE" option: If you think the original version in the passage is the best, select choice A; if you think that one of the other choices better meets the goal set out in the question, pick that one instead.

REMEMBER

Pick choice A, "NO CHANGE," if you think the original version presented in the passage provides the most accurate description of data from the graph.

In this case, the original version doesn't accurately capture what's in the graph. The graph's title lets us know that the bars represent projected increases in employment between 2010 and 2020. (These increases are "projected" because at the time the graph was put together, actual data on those years weren't available.) The original version (choice A) is inaccurate because the graph indicates that employment in "all occupations" is expected to increase 14 percent between 2010 and 2020, not that 16 percent of new jobs in all occupations during that period will be related to urban and regional planning. So we have to look at the other choices for a better option. Choice C proves to be the best answer because the middle bar in the graph indicates that the employment of urban and regional planners is expected to increase 16 percent over the indicated time period. As is true on the Reading Test, you won't have to use math skills to answer a question such as this; you'll just be "reading" the graphic and locating and interpreting the data.

While many Quantitative Information questions will be like this one, you may come across other styles. For instance, you may be asked to replace a general description with a more precise one based on numerical data. (To take a simple example, the preceding passage might simply have said that there's expected to be "a great deal of growth in the employment of urban and regional planners," and you would replace that vague assertion with the fact that growth is expected to be 16 percent.) You may also be told that the writer is considering adding a particular graphic to the passage and asked to decide whether doing so would help make a particular point. In any case, you'll need to have a good understanding of the graphic and be able to draw a meaningful connection between the graphic and the passage.

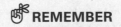

REMEMBER

Quantitative Information questions may come in a few different forms, but all of them require you to establish a meaningful connection between graphic(s) and passage.

ORGANIZATION

Questions about organization ask you to consider whether the placement or sequence of material in a passage could be made more logical or whether the openings and closings of a passage and its paragraphs and the transitions tying information and ideas together could be improved. We'll now examine each of these types.

⚘ **REMEMBER**

Logical Sequence questions generally ask you to determine the best placement for a given sentence within a paragraph or passage.

PRACTICE AT

🌱 **khanacademy.org/sat**

Context is critical for Development and Organization questions. Always consider the tested element in context as well as how the element relates to the writer's purpose.

PRACTICE AT

🌱 **khanacademy.org/sat**

Be on the lookout for specific words or phrases such as "for instance," "however," and "thus." These keywords signal the logical relationship between information and ideas in the passage and play an important role in some Organization questions.

Logical Sequence

If you're recounting an event, you'll typically want to present things in the order in which they happened, and if you're presenting new information or ideas, you'll want to follow a sequence that makes things easy for the reader to understand. Logical Sequence questions address these sorts of issues. One common question of this type directs you to consider the numbered sentences in a paragraph and to decide whether one of those sentences is out of place. In this situation, you'll identify the best placement for the given sentence within the paragraph in terms of logic and cohesion. If you think the sentence is OK in its present location, you'll choose an option such as "where it is now" (similar to the "NO CHANGE" choice found in many other questions); otherwise, you'll pick one of the alternative placements, which are generally phrased in terms of "before" or "after" another numbered sentence (e.g., "before sentence 1," "after sentence 3"). Other questions may ask you to find the most logical place for a sentence within the passage as a whole or to add at a logical point a new sentence that's not already in the passage; other variations are possible as well. The basic approach is the same in every case: After reading and considering the passage, figure out which order or placement makes the passage the most logical and cohesive.

Introductions, Conclusions, and Transitions

Introductions, conclusions, and transitions are, in a sense, the connective tissue that holds a text together. They help orient the reader, generate interest, serve as reminders of the purpose and point of a text, and build conceptual bridges between information and ideas. Questions about introductions, conclusions, and transitions on the Writing and Language Test ask you to think about how to make the reader's movement through a passage smoother and more meaningful. You may, for instance, be asked to add or revise the opening or closing of a passage or paragraph or to incorporate or replace a word, phrase, or sentence in order to create or clarify the logical link within or between sentences and paragraphs. Again, you often have a "NO CHANGE" option, which you should select if you think the original version found in the passage is better than any of the offered alternatives. Once more, context is critical: You'll need to read more than just the tested sentence to know what relationship the writer is trying to establish between and among ideas.

A note on transitions: Many questions about transitions focus on those critical words and phrases that signal the logical relationship of information and ideas within and between sentences. If you see "for instance" in a text, you know that you're getting what the writer hopes is a clarifying example of a general point; if you see "however," you know that the writer is trying to tell you that something is actually the case despite what might seem to be the case. Becoming comfortable with the function of common transition words and phrases such as "by contrast," "additionally," "in spite of that," "thus," and the like will be of great value in answering questions about transitions. Still (there's another one of those words!), not all transitions can be reduced to a single word or phrase, so some questions on the Writing and Language Test may ask you to add or revise (or retain) a full-sentence transition between sentences or paragraphs.

EFFECTIVE LANGUAGE USE

A whole category of questions, discussed in more detail in the next chapter, deals with applying the conventions of standard written English. Effective Language Use questions, by contrast, focus on using language to accomplish particular rhetorical goals. Questions in this subcategory deal with improving the precision and economy of expression, making sure that the style and tone of a passage are appropriate and consistent, putting sentences together to make ideas flow more smoothly, and other specified aims. In the following discussion, we'll examine the ways in which Effective Language Use is tested on the SAT.

Precision

Vague language is usually sorta bad. Put more, er, precisely, vague language is imprecise and often fails to make clear the point the writer is trying to convey or, worse, confuses the reader by using language that just isn't appropriate to a particular situation. Precision questions on the Writing and Language Test generally require you to replace vague language with something more specific or to recognize that a particular word or phrase doesn't make sense in a given context.

If you're familiar with the 1987 movie *The Princess Bride*, you probably remember the scene where Inigo Montoya tells Vizzini, who has a fondness for using the word "inconceivable" in inappropriate ways, that "I do not think it means what you think it means." Many Precision questions are much like this. When answering them, you'll have to consider whether a particular word or phrase in the passage means what is intended in the context in which it appears or whether another word or phrase should be used instead.

Here's an example, taken from a humanities passage about painter Dong Kingman (available in full in Chapter 16).

 **REMEMBER**

If a word or phrase in the passage is vague or not appropriate for the given context, you may be asked to replace the word or phrase with the best alternative.

[…] As Kingman developed as a painter, his works were often compared to paintings by Chinese landscape artists dating back to CE 960, a time when a strong tradition of landscape painting emerged in Chinese art. Kingman, however, **16** vacated from that tradition in a number of ways, most notably in that he chose to focus not on natural landscapes, such as mountains and rivers, but on cities. […]

16. A) NO CHANGE
    B) evacuated
    C) departed
    D) retired

 **PRACTICE AT**

khanacademy.org/sat

While all four of the answer choices have to do with the concept of "moving away from" or "leaving," only one of them is appropriate in the context of this sentence.

All four of the tested words have something to do with "leaving," but only one of them makes good contextual sense. It's not "vacated" — the version already in the passage — because while you might vacate, or leave, a place, you wouldn't "vacate" from a tradition. Similar problems occur if you try to use "evacuated" or "retired" in that context. Only "departed" (choice C) has both the correct general sense and says what it means to say. We're confident that Inigo would approve.

While many Precision questions take this approach, other forms are possible. For example, you may simply be presented with language that is vague or otherwise unclear and asked to sharpen it by using more specific, precise phrasing.

Concision

Sometimes language can be repetitive, duplicative, and say the same thing more than once. Concision questions will ask you to recognize such cases — like the one in the preceding sentence — and to eliminate wordy or redundant language. Sometimes this repetitiveness will be in the underlined portion of the passage itself, but other times you'll have to recognize that the writer made the same point elsewhere in a sentence or passage and that the underlined portion should be deleted for the sake of economy. You'll want to avoid automatically picking the shortest answer in every case, though, because there's such a thing as being too concise, and sometimes a particular phrasing is just too "telegraphic" to be clear or to include all the necessary information.

Style and Tone

Sometimes a writer will lose track of the "voice" he or she is trying to establish in a piece of writing and use language that's "super casual" or that "embodies a stultifying degree of ponderousness" that's not in keeping with the level of formality (or informality) established in the rest of the passage. One common type of Style and Tone question on the Writing and Language Test asks you to recognize such cases and to revise the passage as needed to better maintain a consistent tone. To answer such questions, you'll need to have a clear sense of the writer's voice and be able to identify language that fits in with that voice. Across the test, passages exhibit a range of tones, meaning that sometimes a very casual or a highly formal choice may, in fact, be the right one in context.

This question type addresses more than just tone, however. A question may specify a particular stylistic effect that the writer wants to create and ask you to determine which choice best achieves that goal. One such approach involves stylistic patterns. Maybe the writer has used a series of sentence fragments (incomplete sentences) for emphasis, and you'll be expected to recognize that only one of the four answer choices maintains that pattern. You might instinctively want a complete sentence since we're often told that fragments are "wrong," but in this case the goal specified in the question should override that instinct. Fragments aren't the only kind of pattern that a writer might establish to create a particular effect. Perhaps the writer wants to set up a series of short, descriptive sentences ("The wind blew. The trees waved. The leaves spun."), and only one of the four options ("The onlookers shivered.") extends that pattern. We've said it before, but it's true here again: The context provided by the passage (and often a goal named in the question itself) should guide you as you select your answer to such questions.

Syntax

"Syntax" is a fancy term for the arrangement of words into phrases, clauses, and sentences. While there are grammatical "rules" (really, standard practices or conventions, as we'll see in the next chapter) for syntax that most well-edited writing usually follows, what we're talking about here is the arrangement of words to achieve specific rhetorical purposes or effects. Syntax questions will ask you to consider how two (or sometimes more) sentences can be combined — blended together — to improve flow and cohesion or to achieve some other end, such as placing emphasis on a particular element. In some cases, you'll be combining two (or sometimes more) full sentences; in others, you'll identify the choice that creates the best link between sentences. You won't be changing the meaning of the original text, just connecting ideas to achieve a particular writerly goal.

The following example will give you a good sense of the format. (The full passage, along with this and other questions and their answer explanations, can, again, be found in Chapter 16.)

> [. . .] During his career, Kingman exhibited his work
>
> **21** internationally. He garnered much acclaim. [. . .]
>
> 21. Which choice most effectively combines the sentences at the underlined portion?
>   A) internationally, and Kingman also garnered
>   B) internationally; from exhibiting, he garnered
>   C) internationally but garnered
>   D) internationally, garnering

There's nothing grammatically wrong with having two separate sentences here, but the writing is rather choppy, and a good writer or editor might reasonably want to combine the two sentences to create a clearer, more fluid single thought. The best answer here is choice D, which — importantly, without changing the original meaning — creates a logical, smooth connection between the two ideas (Kingman exhibited his work and Kingman earned recognition). Note how choice C is also grammatical but creates an illogical proposition: Despite exhibiting his work internationally, Kingman garnered

 **REMEMBER**

On Style and Tone questions, you'll want to factor in what the writer is trying to accomplish in the passage when choosing your answer.

REMEMBER

On Syntax questions, you'll be asked how two or more sentences can be combined to improve flow or cohesion or to achieve another rhetorical goal.

REMEMBER

The best answer to a Syntax question will improve flow or cohesion (or achieve some other rhetorical goal) without altering the meaning of the original sentences.

acclaim. Note also how choices A and B really don't do anything to improve the sentence flow. Choice A creates two partially redundant independent clauses (". . . Kingman exhibited . . . and Kingman also garnered . . .") and doesn't make clear that the exhibitions were what won Kingman the acclaim. Choice B does draw that connection but, in a clunky way, repeats the idea of exhibiting (". . . Kingman exhibited . . .; from exhibiting . . ."). When you answer Syntax questions, you'll have to think less about what works from a technical, grammatical standpoint and more about what creates the most effective connections between and among phrases, clauses, and ideas.

CHAPTER 14 RECAP

The Expression of Ideas category of Writing and Language Test questions focuses on the rhetorical aspects of writing. In answering these questions, you'll have to revise passages as a writer or editor would, considering the issues of how best to develop the topic and the points the writer is attempting to convey; how to organize information and ideas to create a logical, smooth progression; and how to use language purposefully to achieve particular results. These questions will often specify a goal that the writer is seeking to achieve, and you should use this information, along with a full understanding of the passage and its intended purpose, to make the best choice in each case.

Chapter 15

Writing and Language: Standard English Conventions

The preceding chapter focused on Expression of Ideas, the rhetorical part of the Writing and Language Test. In Expression of Ideas questions, you'll recall, the emphasis was on development, organization, and effective language use, with questions asking you to revise passages in order to achieve particular writerly purposes, such as adding support, clarifying the relationship between and among sentences and ideas, and eliminating unnecessary repetition. In this chapter, we turn to the other part of the Writing and Language Test: Standard English Conventions. Before delving in, though, we should briefly consider what we mean by "conventions" and why they're important (and not just picky "rules" that we have to learn and follow).

Standard English Conventions: The Craft of Language

"Conventions" is just another way of referring to standard practices and expectations that we follow in all sorts of areas of our lives, not just in language. We rely on conventions in most of life: driving in the correct lane, waiting our turn to pay at the store, making room for people on the sidewalk or in an elevator, and so much more. Conventions aren't just about etiquette; they're the customs we use and rely on throughout the culture in order to make our dealings with other people function more smoothly.

Language conventions are much like conventions in other parts of our lives. Language conventions offer a standard (typical, broadly agreed-upon) way to construct written expression in a manner that meets people's expectations and thereby helps ensure that our spoken and, especially, our written utterances are received and understood. To take a simple but important example, we commonly agree that in most cases a "sentence" in writing consists of a more or less complete thought, that a sentence will have certain parts (at least a subject and a verb), that the start of a new sentence should be signaled by a capital letter, and that the end of a sentence should be indicated with punctuation (a period, question mark, or exclamation point).

Of course, people violate conventions all the time. When the violation is against the law, there are generally clear and obvious penalties. But what's the "penalty" if you break a language convention?

Sometimes there's none at all. It could be that your reader or listener fully understands what you mean and can essentially skip over the irregularity. Sometimes you may even intentionally deviate from a convention to achieve a particular purpose. You may remember our discussion of sentence fragments in Chapter 14. A sentence fragment breaks convention by lacking key elements of a typical sentence but, in certain cases, can be very effective in creating emphasis, reflecting surprise or shock, or the like.

In most cases, though, following language conventions proves highly useful. When a writer observes them, the reader's attention can be focused on the message being sent. When a writer fails to observe them, the reader is likely to be distracted, annoyed, or confused.

REMEMBER

Observing standard English conventions is about more than ticking off items on a long list of grammar, punctuation, and usage rules; rather, it's closely tied to the meaning a writer wishes to convey.

It should be clear from the preceding discussion that observing language conventions is about more than just following rules for rules' sake. Part of the craft of using language skillfully is following conventions. Conventions aren't truly separate from the meaning that you as a writer are trying to convey; they're part and parcel of it, a critical means by which you ensure that the message you intend to convey is the same as what the reader understands.

As is the case for Expression of Ideas, Standard English Conventions on the Writing and Language Test is an overarching category that includes three subcategories, each of which contains several testing points. Standard English Conventions questions require you to edit passages for sentence structure, usage, and punctuation. (Spelling and capitalization aren't directly tested.) In list form, the conventions category looks like this:

▶ **Sentence Structure:** Recognizing and correcting sentence formation problems and inappropriate shifts in sentence construction, including:

— *Sentence boundaries:* Recognizing and correcting grammatically incomplete sentences that aren't rhetorically effective (like the "good" — clearly deliberate — sentence fragments we spoke of earlier)

— *Subordination and coordination:* Recognizing and correcting problems in how major parts of sentences are related

— *Parallel structure:* Recognizing and correcting problems with parallelism

— *Modifier placement:* Recognizing and correcting problems with modifier placement, including dangling and misplaced modifiers

— *Inappropriate shifts in verb tense, mood, and voice* (e.g., changing inappropriately from past to present tense)

— *Inappropriate shifts in pronoun person and number* (e.g., changing inappropriately from second person "you" to third person "one")

▶ **Conventions of Usage:** Observing standard usage practices, including:

— *Pronoun clarity:* Recognizing and correcting ambiguous or vague pronouns (pronouns with more than one possible antecedent or no clear antecedent at all)

— *Possessive determiners:* Distinguishing between and among possessive determiners ("its," "your," "their"), contractions ("it's," "you're," "they're"), and adverbs ("there")

— *Agreement:* Ensuring grammatical agreement between subject and verb, between pronoun and antecedent, and between nouns

— *Frequently confused words:* Distinguishing between and among words that are commonly mistaken for one another (e.g., "affect" and "effect")

— *Logical comparison:* Recognizing and correcting cases in which unlike terms are compared

— *Conventional expression:* Recognizing and correcting cases in which, for no good rhetorical reason, language fails to follow conventional practice

▶ **Conventions of Punctuation:** Observing standard punctuation practices, including:

— *End-of-sentence punctuation:* Using the correct form of ending punctuation (period, question mark, or exclamation point) when the context makes the writer's intent clear

— *Within-sentence punctuation:* Correctly using and recognizing and correcting misuses of colons, semicolons, and dashes

— *Possessive nouns and pronouns:* Recognizing and correcting inappropriate uses of possessive nouns and pronouns and deciding between plural and possessive forms

— *Items in a series:* Using commas and sometimes semicolons to separate lists of items

— *Nonrestrictive and parenthetical elements:* Using punctuation to set off nonessential sentence elements and recognizing and correcting cases in which punctuation is wrongly used to set off essential sentence elements

— *Unnecessary punctuation:* Recognizing and eliminating unneeded punctuation

PRACTICE AT
khanacademy.org/sat

As you can see, there are a lot of English conventions that may be tested on the SAT. Spend ample time practicing standard English conventions, especially those that you know you tend to struggle with. Check out khanacademy.org/sat for help.

Three general observations are in order before we discuss the three subcategories in some detail. First, while many Expression of Ideas questions specify what to consider as you answer them, many Standard English Conventions questions don't. You'll most often be presented with an underlined portion of the passage and four choices, generally consisting of a "NO CHANGE" option and three alternatives. Choose "NO CHANGE" if you find no conventions problem; otherwise, choose the alternative that follows the conventions of standard written English. Each question tests one concept or at most two closely related concepts, so you should find it pretty easy to figure out what's being assessed. (Plus, in real life, you're not always told what to look out for when you're editing a piece of writing.)

Second, the main purpose of this chapter is to familiarize you with what's tested in the Standard English Conventions questions on the Writing and Language Test. While you may learn a thing or two about those conventions from reading this chapter, it's beyond the chapter's scope to teach the knowledge and skills you'll need to do well on the test. If a particular concept touched on in this chapter is unclear, take a look at the sample questions in Chapter 16 — each question identifies what's being tested — or consult other sources, such as your teachers, textbooks, or high-quality print and digital reference materials. As always, Khan Academy provides an outstanding resource for SAT readiness at khanacademy.org/sat.

Finally, while you may be used to thinking of language conventions as absolute rules, in reality linguists, educators, writers, and authors of style manuals debate quite a few of these issues. For example, while many books and experts advise using a comma before a coordinating conjunction in a list of three or more items (*x*, *y*, and *z*), others suggest that it's often not necessary (*x*, *y* and *z*). Although the Writing and Language Test includes questions about items in a series, we don't directly test this particular comma usage. In general terms, the test stays away from assessing what's sometimes called "contested usage" — those issues that experts disagree about. There's no definitive list of what we don't test — indeed, that list changes over time as some issues get settled and new ones crop up — but if good reference books disagree on a particular point, it's likely that we don't test the matter directly.

In the following sections, we'll describe the general features of each of the three conventions subcategories and touch on the specific knowledge and skills addressed in each. To keep things manageable, we won't go into detail on each possible testable issue.

SENTENCE STRUCTURE

In Chapter 14, we introduced the concept of syntax, defining it as the arrangement of words into phrases, clauses, and sentences. Syntax in the Effective Language Use questions is about finding the most effective arrangement of words to accomplish a specific rhetorical purpose. Sentence

PRACTICE AT

khanacademy.org/sat

For more practice with the standard English conventions tested on the SAT, visit Khan Academy at khanacademy.org/sat.

Structure questions, in contrast, address syntax from a conventions perspective. You'll have to recognize and correct problems in how sentences are formed as well as identify and fix cases in which constructions shift inappropriately within or between sentences. For discussion purposes, let's divide this subcategory into two basic groupings: sentence formation and inappropriate shifts in construction.

Sentence Formation

Questions about sentence formation try to determine whether you can recognize and correct fundamental (but not always simple) problems with how sentences are constructed. Some of these questions may ask you to identify and fix (rhetorically ineffective) sentence fragments (incomplete sentences), run-ons (independent clauses fused together without punctuation or conjunction), and comma splices (independent clauses joined by only a comma).

Other questions will ask you to identify and fix problems in how the various phrases and clauses within a sentence are related. Sometimes the problem will be the coordination or subordination of clauses, as when a coordinating conjunction such as "and" or "but" is used when the logic of the sentence calls for a subordinating conjunction such as "although" or "because." In other cases, the problem will be a lack of parallel structure — a failure to treat grammatically similar structures in a series in the same way. The sentence "She likes running, swimming, and to go on hikes," for example, exhibits flawed parallelism because the pattern of gerunds ("running," "swimming") is broken by an infinitive phrase ("to go on hikes"). In yet other instances, a sentence will include a dangling or misplaced modifier — a word, phrase, or clause that doesn't modify what it's supposed to. For example, the sentence "Even after paying for costly repairs, the car still broke down" has a dangling modifier because presumably a person, not the car, paid for the repairs.

Inappropriate Shifts in Construction

Sometimes sentence structure problems emerge because of a failure to be consistent either within or between sentences. If a writer has been using past tense and for no clear reason suddenly (and often illogically) switches to using present tense, an inappropriate shift in construction has occurred. On the Writing and Language Test, such problematic shifts can happen with either verbs or pronouns. A question about verb shifts may ask you to edit an inappropriate shift from, say, past to present tense, indicative to conditional mood, or active to passive voice. A question about pronoun shifts may ask you to recognize and correct an inappropriate shift from, for example, a second person to a third person pronoun (such as from "you" to "one") or from a singular to a plural pronoun. Of course, not all shifts are inappropriate; some are, in fact, quite necessary. If a writer has been describing his or her present feelings and then flashes back to the events that led to those feelings, a shift from present to past tense is perfectly warranted. It's when

PRACTICE AT

khanacademy.org/sat

When a sentence includes a series of items, each item must possess parallel structure. For instance, the sentence "She likes running, swimming, and hiking" exhibits basic but sound parallelism.

PRACTICE AT

khanacademy.org/sat

The Writing and Language Test may include questions on consistent verb tense, mood, voice, and pronoun person and number.

these shifts happen inappropriately, or for no clear reason, that they become fodder for questions on the Writing and Language Test.

CONVENTIONS OF USAGE

"Usage" is a technical term used to describe a range of language practices that are widely accepted and understood by people speaking and writing the same language within a particular culture or community. Particular "rules" for speaking and writing solidify over time (often over many generations) and become the standard by which formal speech and writing are judged. Often these "rules" develop without conscious thought. You'd be hard-pressed to find a rational reason for why native speakers of English would recognize the phrase "A big red balloon" as standard but "A red big balloon" as nonstandard, but nearly all would immediately notice the difference (and probably consider the second an error). It's a little circular, but usage conventions are, ultimately, conventions regarding how particular groups of people customarily use language.

On the Writing and Language Test, the subcategory Conventions of Usage calls on a variety of skills associated with common practices in English writing. We'll treat each of these briefly now.

Pronoun Clarity

In well-written and well-edited writing, all pronouns have a clear and appropriate antecedent, or noun to which they refer. Because writers generally know their subjects better than their audiences do, however, sometimes vague or ambiguous pronouns creep in. These are pronouns that have no clear and appropriate antecedent or that have potentially more than one antecedent. To cite one example: In the sentence "Michael gave Steven his book," the pronoun "his" is ambiguous. Does the writer mean that Michael gave Steven one of Michael's own books or that Michael returned Steven's own book to him? It's not possible to know from the sentence alone. Even if the surrounding text made the intended antecedent clear, it's still not good practice to leave vague or ambiguous pronouns in a text. The Writing and Language Test will sometimes present you with such problematic pronouns and ask you to correct the situation (in many cases by replacing a vague or ambiguous pronoun with a noun).

Possessive Determiners

The bane of many writers' and editors' existence is remembering the differences between "its" and "it's"; "your" and "you're"; and "their," "they're," and "there." That so many people — even good writers and editors — have trouble keeping these words straight is probably due of a number of factors. "Its" and "it's," for instance, sound the same and have similar spellings; that "its" lacks the apostrophe generally used to signal possession is no help either. Still, these words do have different functions, many people will recognize when they're confused with one another, and questions about them

PRACTICE AT

khanacademy.org/sat

If you have trouble using homophones like "its" and "it's" or "their" and "they're" correctly, pay close attention to these words in your everyday writing in school. Becoming more familiar with the proper use of these words will be good practice for the Writing and Language Test (and will serve you well throughout your life!).

are likely to appear on the Writing and Language Test. It's worth the time and effort, therefore, to learn how to use these words in a conventional way if you struggle with them.

Agreement

The Writing and Language Test includes questions that cover a range of agreement issues. A question may ask you to recognize and correct problems in agreement between subject and verb, between pronoun and antecedent, and between nouns. You most likely already understand the conventions for subject-verb and pronoun-antecedent agreement, but the concept of noun agreement may be less familiar. In essence, for related nouns to agree they must have the same number — singular noun with singular noun and plural noun with plural noun. The sentence "Alfredo and Julia became a doctor after many years of study" contains a problem with noun agreement because the compound subject "Alfredo and Julia" is plural but "doctor" is singular. A better version of the sentence would be "Alfredo and Julia became doctors after many years of study."

Frequently Confused Words

The Writing and Language Test may include questions asking you to distinguish between and among frequently confused words — words that have similar or identical sounds and/or similar spellings but that have different meanings and are used in different ways. The "its"/"it's" distinction we discussed earlier is really just a special (and particularly troublesome) case of the more general problem of frequently confused words. "Affect" and "effect" is a commonly cited pair of such words because they often show up in writing. In most cases, "affect" should be used as a verb and "effect" as a noun, but even good writers sometimes mistake one for the other due to the words' similarity in sound and spelling. (We said "most cases" because psychologists sometimes use "affect" as a noun to refer to mood and because "effect" is — infrequently — used as a verb, as in "to effect a change.") If you feel that you often get words such as these mixed up, consider consulting one of the many lists of frequently confused words available in language handbooks and on the Internet.

Logical Comparison

Problems with illogical comparisons arise when unlike or dissimilar things are treated as equivalent. For example, the sentence "The cost of living in the city differs from the suburb" contains an illogical comparison because instead of comparing the cost of living in the city and in the suburb — two similar concepts — the sentence actually compares a concept (cost of living) with a location (suburb). One easy way to correct the error is to add the phrase "that in," as in "The cost of living in the city differs from that in the suburb." Another approach would be to make "suburb" possessive: "The cost of living in the city differs from the suburb's [cost of living]." Questions on the Writing and Language Test may require you to identify and fix such comparison problems.

PRACTICE AT

khanacademy.org/sat

There are many words that sound and are spelled similarly but that have different meanings and uses. Practice identifying the correct uses of these words. Examples include:

affect / effect
accept / except
than / then

PRACTICE AT

khanacademy.org/sat

When a sentence compares two or more things, check to make sure that the items being compared are parallel in nature.

Conventional Expression

Conventional Expression questions don't fit neatly into one of the usage types listed earlier, but like them they focus on recognizing and correcting instances in which word choice doesn't conform to the practices of standard written English.

CONVENTIONS OF PUNCTUATION

PRACTICE AT

khanacademy.org/sat

Conventions of Punctuation questions ask you to correct problematic punctuation or to add punctuation to clarify a sentence's meaning.

A number of questions on the Writing and Language Test concern the use and misuse of various forms of punctuation, including end punctuation (periods, question marks, and exclamation points), commas, semicolons, colons, and dashes, to signal various relationships within and between sentences. In many cases, you'll be expected to recognize and correct problematic punctuation; in some cases, you'll be asked to add punctuation to clarify and enhance meaning. There are a number of particular types of Conventions of Punctuation questions, which we'll touch on briefly in the sections that follow.

End-of-Sentence Punctuation

End punctuation — periods, question marks, and exclamation points — is, of course, used to mark the conclusion of sentences and to offer some clue as to their nature (a question mark signaling a question, and the like). By now, you've doubtless mastered the use of such punctuation in most situations, so questions on the Writing and Language Test are limited to challenging cases. One such case is the indirect question — a question that's embedded in a declarative sentence and that takes a period instead of a question mark. "He asked whether I could come along" is an example of an indirect question. While it could easily be rewritten as a typical question, in its present form the question is phrased more like a statement and should be concluded with a period.

Within-Sentence Punctuation

On the Writing and Language Test, questions about the appropriate use of colons, semicolons, and dashes to signal sharp breaks in thought come under the heading of Within-Sentence Punctuation. You may be asked to recognize when one of these forms of punctuation is misused and to correct the situation, or you may be expected to use one of these forms properly to establish a particular relationship among words and ideas. The best answer to a particular question of this latter sort may involve using a semicolon to connect two closely related independent clauses or a colon to introduce a list or an idea that builds on one previously introduced in the sentence.

Possessive Nouns and Pronouns

In Writing and Language Test questions about possessive nouns and pronouns, you may be asked to recognize and correct cases in which the incorrect form of a possessive noun or pronoun is used, such as when a singular possessive is used when the context calls for a plural possessive. You may also have to edit instances in which a possessive form is incorrectly used in place of a plural form and vice versa.

Items in a Series

Series that contain more than two elements typically require some form of punctuation to separate the elements. In most cases, commas are used as separators, but in more complex situations (particularly when one or more of the elements has its own commas), semicolons may be used instead. On the Writing and Language Test, you may find questions asking you to add or remove commas (and sometimes semicolons) to eliminate ambiguity and to reflect conventional practice. In all cases, the passage context will make clear how many items there are in the series. (As noted earlier, the Writing and Language Test doesn't directly test whether a comma should be placed immediately before the coordinating conjunction in a series of three or more elements.)

Nonrestrictive and Parenthetical Elements

Some questions on the Writing and Language Test may ask you to recognize whether a given part of a sentence is essential or nonessential to the meaning of the sentence and to make punctuation decisions accordingly. Essential (restrictive) sentence elements are critical to the sentence's meaning and aren't set off with punctuation, whereas nonessential (nonrestrictive, parenthetical) sentence elements are set off from the rest of the sentence with commas, dashes, or parentheses. On the Writing and Language Test, you may have to remove punctuation from essential elements, add punctuation to nonessential elements, or correct instances in which nonessential elements are set off with mismatched punctuation (a comma and a dash, for example).

Unnecessary Punctuation

While just the right amount of punctuation can improve the clarity and effectiveness of writing, too much punctuation can slow the reader down and introduce confusion. Some questions on the Writing and Language Test will assess whether you can recognize and remove such extraneous punctuation. Sometimes this stray punctuation will clearly disrupt the meaning and flow of a sentence, as when a comma appears between an adjective and the noun it modifies, but other instances will be trickier to root out because they occur where there seem to be natural "pauses" in a sentence, such as between a subject and a predicate. It's true that writers have some freedom in how much punctuation to use and where, so the Writing and Language Test will only test unnecessary punctuation when it clearly falls beyond what is considered typical in well-edited writing (that is, where the punctuation actually interferes with the meaning).

CHAPTER 15 RECAP

The Standard English Conventions questions on the SAT Writing and Language Test deal with a wide range of sentence structure, usage, and punctuation issues. To answer them correctly, you'll have to apply your knowledge of language conventions and your editing skills to a variety of multiparagraph passages. While the questions on the test deal with matters of standard practice, they focus on more than just correcting surface errors and following "rules" for rules' sake. Instead, Standard English Conventions questions address issues of substance that affect the meaning and communicative power and persuasiveness of text, and answering them correctly goes a long way toward demonstrating that you're ready for the kinds of writing tasks that you'll be expected to undertake in your postsecondary courses of study.

Chapter 16

Sample Writing and Language Test Questions

In Chapters 13 to 15, you learned about the basic elements of the Writing and Language Test on the redesigned SAT, including the types of passages you will encounter and the types of questions the test will include. In this chapter, you will find two sample passages and associated test questions. Following each question is an explanation of the best answer and some comments about the incorrect answer choices.

These instructions will precede the SAT Writing and Language Test.

PRACTICE AT

khanacademy.org/sat

Carefully read the test directions now so that you won't have to spend much time on them on test day.

Writing and Language Test

35 MINUTES, 44 QUESTIONS

Turn to Section 2 of your answer sheet to answer the questions in this section.

DIRECTIONS

Each passage below is accompanied by a number of questions. For some questions, you will consider how the passage might be revised to improve the expression of ideas. For other questions, you will consider how the passage might be edited to correct errors in sentence structure, usage, or punctuation. A passage or a question may be accompanied by one or more graphics (such as a table or graph) that you will consider as you make revising and editing decisions.

Some questions will direct you to an underlined portion of a passage. Other questions will direct you to a location in a passage or ask you to think about the passage as a whole.

After reading each passage, choose the answer to each question that most effectively improves the quality of writing in the passage or that makes the passage conform to the conventions of standard written English. Many questions include a "NO CHANGE" option. Choose that option if you think the best choice is to leave the relevant portion of the passage as it is.

SAMPLE 1

Careers Passage with Graphic

REMEMBER

Note how the words, phrases, and sentences tested on the Writing and Language Test are embedded within a fairly lengthy passage (400–450 words). This is because many of the questions require you to consider paragraph- or passage-level context when choosing your answer.

PRACTICE AT

khanacademy.org/sat

Read the passage as a whole carefully, identifying things such as the writer's purpose, the organization of the passage, and the writer's style and tone, much as you would on the Reading Test.

Questions 1–11 are based on the following passage and supplementary material.

A Life in Traffic

A subway system is expanded to provide service to a growing suburb. A bike-sharing program is adopted to encourage nonmotorized transportation. **1** To alleviate rush hour traffic jams in a congested downtown area, stoplight timing is coordinated. When any one of these changes **2** occur, it is likely the result of careful analysis conducted by transportation planners.

The work of transportation planners generally includes evaluating current transportation needs, assessing the effectiveness of existing facilities, and improving those facilities or **3** they design new ones. Most transportation planners work in or near cities, **4** but some are employed in rural areas. Say, for example, a large factory is built on the outskirts of a small town. Traffic to and from that location would increase at the beginning and end of work shifts. The transportation **5** planner's job, might involve conducting a traffic count to determine the daily number of vehicles traveling on the road to the new factory. If analysis of the traffic count indicates that there is more traffic than the **6** current road as it is designed at this time can efficiently accommodate, the transportation planner might recommend widening the road to add another lane.

Transportation planners work closely with a number of community stakeholders, such as government officials and other interested organizations and individuals. **7** Next, representatives from the local public health department might provide input in designing a network of trails and sidewalks to encourage people to walk more. **8** According to the American Heart Association, walking provides numerous benefits related to health and well-being. Members of the Chamber of Commerce might share suggestions about designing transportation and parking facilities to support local businesses.

9 People who pursue careers in transportation planning have a wide variety of educational backgrounds. A two-year degree in transportation technology may be sufficient for some entry-level jobs in the field. Most jobs, however, require at least a bachelor's degree; majors of transportation planners are **10** varied, including fields such as urban studies, civil engineering, geography, or transportation and logistics management. For many positions in the field, a master's degree is required.

Transportation planners perform critical work within the broader field of urban and regional planning. As of 2010, there were approximately 40,300 urban and regional planners employed in the United States. The United States Bureau of Labor Statistics forecasts steady job growth in this field, **11** projecting that 16 percent of new jobs in all occupations will be related to urban and regional planning. Population growth and concerns about environmental sustainability are expected to spur the need for transportation planning professionals.

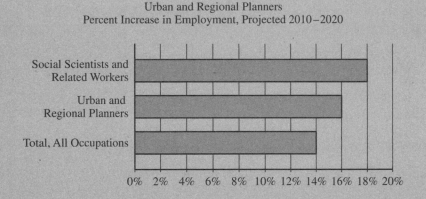

Urban and Regional Planners
Percent Increase in Employment, Projected 2010–2020

Adapted from United States Bureau of Labor Statistics, Employment Projections program. "All occupations" includes all occupations in the United States economy.

1

Which choice best maintains the sentence pattern already established in the paragraph?

A) NO CHANGE

B) Coordinating stoplight timing can help alleviate rush hour traffic jams in a congested downtown area.

C) Stoplight timing is coordinated to alleviate rush hour traffic jams in a congested downtown area.

D) In a congested downtown area, stoplight timing is coordinated to alleviate rush hour traffic jams.

PRACTICE AT

🌱 **khanacademy.org/sat**

To answer this question correctly, you'll want to read the two preceding sentences, determine the pattern that's been established, and choose the answer that's most consistent with that pattern.

Content: Language Use

Key: C

Objective: Students must revise text to ensure consistency of style within a series of sentences.

Explanation: Choice C is the best answer because it most closely maintains the sentence pattern established by the two preceding sentences, which begin with noun and passive verb phrases ("A subway system is expanded," "A bike-sharing program is adopted").

Choice A is not the best answer because it does not maintain the sentence pattern established by the two preceding sentences. Rather, it begins the sentence with an infinitive phrase.

Choice B is not the best answer because it does not maintain the sentence pattern established by the two preceding sentences. Rather, it begins the sentence with a gerund phrase.

Choice D is not the best answer because it does not maintain the sentence pattern established by the two preceding sentences. Rather, it places a prepositional phrase, "in a congested downtown area," at the beginning of the sentence.

🖐 REMEMBER

When a question has no additional directions, such as Question 2, assume that you're to choose the option that's the most effective or correct.

PRACTICE AT

🌱 khanacademy.org/sat

This question tests your understanding of both subject-verb agreement and pronoun-antecedent agreement. The key to this question is correctly identifying the subject of the sentence; is it "any one" or "changes"?

2

A) NO CHANGE
B) occur, they are
C) occurs, they are
D) occurs, it is

Content: Conventions of Usage

Key: D

Objective: Students must maintain grammatical agreement between pronoun and antecedent and between subject and verb.

Explanation: Choice D is the best answer because it maintains agreement between the pronoun ("it") and the antecedent ("any one") and between the subject ("any one") and the verb ("occurs").

Choice A is not the best answer because the plural verb "occur" does not agree with the singular subject "any one."

Choice B is not the best answer because the plural verb "occur" does not agree with the singular subject "any one" and because the plural pronoun "they" does not agree with the singular antecedent "any one."

Choice C is not the best answer because the plural pronoun "they" does not agree with the singular antecedent "any one."

3

   A) NO CHANGE
   B) to design
   C) designing
   D) design

Content: Sentence Structure

Key: C

Objective: Students must maintain parallel structure.

Explanation: Choice C is the best answer because "designing" maintains parallelism with "evaluating," "assessing," and "improving."

Choice A is not the best answer because "they design" does not maintain parallelism with "evaluating," "assessing," and "improving."

Choice B is not the best answer because "to design" does not maintain parallelism with "evaluating," "assessing," and "improving."

Choice D is not the best answer because "design" does not maintain parallelism with "evaluating," "assessing," and "improving."

4

Which choice results in the most effective transition to the information that follows in the paragraph?

   A) NO CHANGE
   B) where job opportunities are more plentiful.
   C) and the majority are employed by government agencies.
   D) DELETE the underlined portion and end the sentence with a period.

Content: Organization

Key: A

Objective: Students must determine the most effective transition between ideas.

Explanation: Choice A is the best answer because it effectively signals the shift in the paragraph to the example of the work a transportation planner might perform if he or she were employed in a rural area and asked to consider the effects of a new factory built "on the outskirts of a small town."

Choice B is not the best answer because noting that job opportunities are more plentiful in cities does not effectively signal the shift in the paragraph to the example of the work a transportation planner might perform if he or she were employed in a rural area.

Choice C is not the best answer because noting that most transportation planners work for government agencies does not effectively signal the shift

PRACTICE AT

khanacademy.org/sat

Don't assume that the best answer will always involve a change to the text in the passage. Sometimes the passage text as originally presented is the best option, in which case you'll choose choice A, "NO CHANGE."

159

in the paragraph to the example of the work a transportation planner might perform if he or she were employed in a rural area.

Choice D is not the best answer because the proposed deletion would create a jarring shift from the statement "Most transportation planners work in or near cities" to the example of the work a transportation planner might perform if he or she were employed in a rural area.

PRACTICE AT

khanacademy.org/sat

As on Question 2, this question tests two topics — here, possessive nouns and unnecessary punctuation. Be sure the answer you choose is the best option overall. Some answer choices may correct one problem but not the other or may correct one problem but introduce an alternate error.

5

A) NO CHANGE
B) planner's job
C) planners job,
D) planners job

Content: Conventions of Punctuation

Key: B

Objective: Students must recognize and correct inappropriate uses of possessive nouns and pronouns as well as differentiate between possessive and plural forms. Students must also recognize and correct cases in which unnecessary punctuation appears in a sentence.

Explanation: Choice B is the best answer because it correctly uses an apostrophe to indicate possession and does not introduce any unnecessary punctuation.

Choice A is not the best answer because while it correctly indicates the possessive relationship between "transportation planner" and "job," it introduces an unnecessary comma after the word "job."

Choice C is not the best answer because it does not indicate the possessive relationship between "transportation planner" and "job," and because it introduces an unnecessary comma after the word "job."

Choice D is not the best answer because it does not indicate the possessive relationship between "transportation planner" and "job."

REMEMBER

Economy of expression, or conveying meaning as concisely as possible, may be tested on some questions.

6

A) NO CHANGE
B) current design of the road right now
C) road as it is now currently designed
D) current design of the road

Content: Effective Language Use

Key: D

Objective: Students must improve the economy of expression.

Explanation: Choice D is the best answer because it offers a clear and concise wording without redundancy or wordiness.

Choice A is not the best answer because "current" is redundant with "at this time" and because "as it is designed" is unnecessarily wordy.

Choice B is not the best answer because "current" is redundant with "right now."

Choice C is not the best answer because "now" is redundant with "currently."

7

A) NO CHANGE
B) For instance,
C) Furthermore,
D) Similarly,

Content: Organization

Key: B

Objective: Students must determine the most logical transitional word or phrase.

Explanation: Choice B is the best answer because the transitional phrase "For instance" logically indicates that what follows provides an example related to the previous sentence. "Representatives from the local public health department" is an example of the kinds of people with whom transportation planners work.

Choice A is not the best answer because the transitional word "Next" indicates sequence, which is not logical given that what follows provides an example related to the previous sentence.

Choice C is not the best answer because the transitional word "Furthermore" indicates addition, which is not logical given that what follows provides an example related to the previous sentence.

Choice D is not the best answer because the transitional word "Similarly" indicates comparison or likeness, which is not logical given that what follows provides an example related to the previous sentence.

8

The writer is considering deleting the underlined sentence. Should the sentence be kept or deleted?

A) Kept, because it provides supporting evidence about the benefits of walking.
B) Kept, because it provides an additional example of a community stakeholder with whom transportation planners work.
C) Deleted, because it blurs the paragraph's focus on the community stakeholders with whom transportation planners work.
D) Deleted, because it doesn't provide specific examples of what the numerous benefits of walking are.

Content: Development

Key: C

PRACTICE AT

khanacademy.org/sat

If a question asks you to choose the most appropriate transitional word or phrase at the beginning of a sentence, carefully consider how that sentence relates to the previous sentence. Does it function as a contradiction, an example, a comparison?

Objective: Students must delete information that blurs the focus of the paragraph and weakens cohesion.

PRACTICE AT

khanacademy.org/sat

Information should be kept only if it's clearly relevant and effectively connected to the writer's purpose.

Explanation: Choice C is the best answer because it identifies the best reason the underlined sentence should not be kept. At this point in the passage and paragraph, a general statement about the benefits of walking only serves to interrupt the discussion of the community stakeholders with whom transportation planners work.

Choice A is not the best answer because the underlined sentence should not be kept. Although the sentence theoretically provides supporting evidence about the benefits of walking, the passage has not made a claim that needs to be supported in this way, and including such a statement only serves to interrupt the discussion of the community stakeholders with whom transportation planners work.

Choice B is not the best answer because the underlined sentence should not be kept. Although the American Heart Association could theoretically be an example of "other interested organizations" with which transportation planners work, the sentence does not suggest that this is the case. Instead, the association is merely the source for the general statement about the benefits of walking, a statement that only serves to interrupt the discussion of the actual community stakeholders with whom transportation planners work.

Choice D is not the best answer because although the underlined sentence should be deleted, it is not because the sentence lacks specific examples of the numerous benefits of walking. Adding such examples would only serve to blur the focus of the paragraph further with general factual information, as the paragraph's main purpose is to discuss the community stakeholders with whom transportation planners work.

9

A) NO CHANGE
B) People, who pursue careers in transportation planning,
C) People who pursue careers, in transportation planning,
D) People who pursue careers in transportation planning,

Content: Conventions of Punctuation

Key: A

Objective: Students must distinguish between restrictive/essential and nonrestrictive/nonessential sentence elements and avoid unneeded punctuation.

Explanation: Choice A is the best answer because "who pursue careers in transportation planning" is, in context, a restrictive clause that should not be set off with punctuation. "Who pursue careers in transportation planning" is essential information defining who the "people" are.

Choice B is not the best answer because it incorrectly sets off the restrictive clause "who pursue careers in transportation planning" with commas as though the clause were nonrestrictive or not essential to defining who the "people" are.

Choice C is not the best answer because it incorrectly sets off the essential sentence element "in transportation planning" with commas as though the phrase were not essential to the meaning of the sentence. "In transportation planning" is essential information defining what the "careers" are.

Choice D is not the best answer because it introduces an unnecessary comma after the word "planning," incorrectly setting off the subject of the sentence ("people who pursue careers in transportation planning") from the predicate ("have a wide variety of educational backgrounds").

10

A) NO CHANGE
B) varied, and including
C) varied and which include
D) varied, which include

Content: Sentence Structure

Key: A

Objective: Students must recognize and correct problems in coordination and subordination in sentences.

Explanation: Choice A is the best answer because it effectively uses a comma and "including" to set off the list of varied fields in which transportation planners major.

Choice B is not the best answer because "and including" results in an ungrammatical sentence.

Choice C is not the best answer because "and which include" results in an ungrammatical sentence.

Choice D is not the best answer because it is unclear from this construction to what exactly the relative pronoun "which" refers.

11

Which choice completes the sentence with accurate data based on the graph?

A) NO CHANGE
B) warning, however, that job growth in urban and regional planning will slow to 14 percent by 2020.
C) predicting that employment of urban and regional planners will increase 16 percent between 2010 and 2020.
D) indicating that 14 to 18 percent of urban and regional planning positions will remain unfilled.

Content: Development

Key: C

Objective: Students must evaluate text based on data presented graphically.

PRACTICE AT

khanacademy.org/sat

When examining the underlined portion of the passage being tested, it may be helpful to think about how (if at all) the underlined portion can be improved *before* you look at the answer choices. Doing so may help you more quickly and accurately choose your answer.

PRACTICE AT

khanacademy.org/sat

In Question 11, you must integrate information from the text with data presented in the graph. Make sure that the data cited is both accurate and aligns with the content of the sentence.

163

Explanation: Choice C is the best answer because it completes the sentence with an accurate interpretation of data in the graph. The graph displays projections of how much growth in employment there is expected to be between 2010 and 2020 for "social scientists and related workers," for "urban and regional planners," and in "all occupations" in the U.S. economy. According to the graph, the employment of urban and regional planners is expected to increase 16 percent between 2010 and 2020.

Choice A is not the best answer because the data in the graph do not support the claim that 16 percent of new jobs in all occupations will be related to urban and regional planning.

Choice B is not the best answer because the data in the graph do not support the claim that job growth in urban and regional planning will slow to 14 percent by 2020.

Choice D is not the best answer because the data in the graph do not support the claim that 14 to 18 percent of urban and regional planning positions will remain unfilled.

SAMPLE 2

Humanities Passage

Questions 12–22 are based on the following passage.

Dong Kingman: Painter of Cities

A 1954 documentary about renowned watercolor painter Dong Kingman shows the artist sitting on a stool on Mott Street in New York City's Chinatown. A crowd of admiring spectators **12** watched as Kingman squeezes dollops of paint from several tubes into a tin watercolor **13** box, from just a few primary colors, Kingman creates dozens of beautiful hues as he layers the translucent paint onto the paper on his easel. Each stroke of the brush and dab of the sponge transforms thinly sketched outlines into buildings, shop signs, and streetlamps. The street scene Kingman begins composing in this short film is very much in keeping with the urban landscapes for which he is best known.

[1] Kingman was keenly interested in landscape painting from an early age. [2] In Hong Kong, where Kingman completed his schooling, teachers at that time customarily assigned students a formal "school name." [3] His interest was so keen, in fact, that he was

named after it. [4] The young boy who had been Dong Moy Shu became Dong Kingman. [5] The name Kingman was selected for its two **14** parts, "king" and "man"; Cantonese for "scenery" and "composition." [6] As Kingman developed as a painter, his works were often compared to **15** paintings by Chinese landscape artists dating back to CE 960, a time when a strong tradition of landscape painting emerged in Chinese art. [7] Kingman, however, **16** vacated from that tradition in a number of ways, most notably in that he chose to focus not on natural landscapes, such as mountains and rivers, but on cities. **17**

18 His fine brushwork conveys detailed street-level activity: a peanut vendor pushing his cart on the sidewalk, a pigeon pecking for crumbs around a fire **19** hydrant, an old man tending to a baby outside a doorway. His broader brush strokes and sponge-painted shapes create majestic city skylines, with skyscrapers towering in the background, bridges connecting neighborhoods on either side of a river, and **20** delicately painted creatures, such as a tiny, barely visible cat prowling in the bushes of a park. To art critics and fans alike, these city scenes represent the innovative spirit of twentieth-century urban Modernism.

During his career, Kingman exhibited his work **21** internationally. He garnered much acclaim. In 1936, a critic described one of Kingman's solo exhibits as "twenty of the freshest, most satisfying watercolors that have been seen hereabouts in many a day." **22**

12

A) NO CHANGE
B) had watched
C) would watch
D) watches

Content: Sentence Structure

Key: D

Objective: Students must recognize and correct inappropriate shifts in verb tense and mood.

PRACTICE AT

🌱 khanacademy.org/sat

When a question asks you to choose the tense and mood of a verb, look for consistency with the surrounding text to help determine your answer. Note that while no shift is warranted here, sometimes shifts are necessary.

Explanation: Choice D is the best answer because the simple present tense verb "watches" is consistent with the tense of the verbs in the rest of the sentence and paragraph.

Choice A is not the best answer because "watched" creates an inappropriate shift to the past tense.

Choice B is not the best answer because "had watched" creates an inappropriate shift to the past perfect tense.

Choice C is not the best answer because "would watch" creates an inappropriate shift that suggests a habitual or hypothetical aspect when other verbs in the sentence and paragraph indicate that a specific, actual instance is being narrated.

13

A) NO CHANGE
B) box. From just a few primary colors,
C) box from just a few primary colors,
D) box, from just a few primary colors

Content: Sentence Structure

Key: B

Objective: Students must create two grammatically complete and standard sentences.

Explanation: Choice B is the best answer because it provides punctuation that creates two grammatically complete and standard sentences.

Choice A is not the best answer because it results in a comma splice as well as some confusion about what the prepositional phrase "from just a few primary colors" modifies.

Choice C is not the best answer because it results in a run-on sentence as well as some confusion about what the prepositional phrase "from just a few primary colors" modifies.

Choice D is not the best answer because it results in a comma splice.

14

A) NO CHANGE
B) parts: "king" and "man,"
C) parts "king" and "man";
D) parts; "king" and "man"

Content: Conventions of Punctuation

Key: B

PRACTICE AT

🌱 **khanacademy.org/sat**

A colon is used to signal a break in a sentence; what follows the colon further defines the concept that precedes the colon. A semicolon connects two closely related independent clauses.

Objective: Students must both signal a strong within-sentence break and set off nonessential elements of the sentence.

Explanation: Choice B is the best answer because the colon after "parts" effectively signals that what follows in the sentence further defines what the "two parts" of Kingman's name are and because the comma after "man" properly indicates that "'king' and 'man'" and "Cantonese for 'scenery' and 'composition'" are nonrestrictive appositives.

Choice A is not the best answer because the semicolon after "man" incorrectly joins an independent clause and a phrase. Moreover, the comma after "parts" is arguably a weak form of punctuation to be signaling the strong break in the sentence indicated here.

Choice C is not the best answer because the semicolon after "man" incorrectly joins an independent clause and a phrase and because the absence of appropriate punctuation after "parts" fails to indicate that "two parts" and "'king' and 'man'" are nonrestrictive appositives.

Choice D is not the best answer because the semicolon after "parts" incorrectly joins an independent clause and two phrases and because the absence of appropriate punctuation after "man" fails to indicate that "'king' and 'man'" and "Cantonese for 'scenery' and 'composition'" are nonrestrictive appositives.

15

A) NO CHANGE
B) Chinese landscape artists
C) painters of Chinese landscapes
D) artists

Content: Conventions of Usage

Key: A

Objective: Students must ensure that like terms are being compared.

Explanation: Choice A is the best answer because it creates a comparison between like terms: "works" by Kingman and "paintings by Chinese landscape artists."

Choice B is not the best answer because it creates a comparison between unlike terms: "works" by Kingman and "Chinese landscape artists."

Choice C is not the best answer because it creates a comparison between unlike terms: "works" by Kingman and "painters of Chinese landscapes."

Choice D is not the best answer because it creates a comparison between unlike terms: "works" by Kingman and "artists."

PRACTICE AT

khanacademy.org/sat

Comparisons must be logical; that is, the items compared must be of a parallel nature. What are Kingman's "works" most logically compared to in sentence 6 of the passage?

REMEMBER

Question 16 is very similar to a Words in Context question from the SAT Reading Test. You're asked to determine the most appropriate word given the context of the sentence.

16

A) NO CHANGE
B) evacuated
C) departed
D) retired

Content: Effective Language Use

Key: C

Objective: Students must determine the most contextually appropriate word.

Explanation: Choice C is the best answer because "departed" is the most contextually appropriate way to indicate that Kingman had deviated from the tradition of Chinese landscape painting in a number of ways.

Choice A is not the best answer because while "vacated" does offer some sense of "leaving," it would be awkward and unconventional to say that a person was vacating from a tradition in a number of ways.

Choice B is not the best answer because while "evacuated" does offer some sense of "leaving," it would be awkward and unconventional to say that a person was evacuating from a tradition in a number of ways.

Choice D is not the best answer because while "retired" does offer some sense of "leaving," it would be awkward and unconventional to say that a person was retiring from a tradition in a number of ways

17

To make this paragraph most logical, sentence 3 should be placed

A) where it is now.
B) before sentence 1.
C) after sentence 1.
D) after sentence 4.

Content: Organization

Key: C

Objective: Students must improve the cohesion of a paragraph.

Explanation: Choice C is the best answer because placing sentence 3 after sentence 1 makes the paragraph most cohesive. Sentence 3 refers to Kingman's "interest" being "so keen," a continuation of the idea in sentence 1, which says that "Kingman was keenly interested in landscape painting from an early age."

Choice A is not the best answer because leaving sentence 3 where it is now creates a sequence of sentences that lacks sufficient cohesion. Keeping sentence 3 in its current location disrupts the link between sentence 2 (which describes

PRACTICE AT

khanacademy.org/sat

Consider the overall meaning of the paragraph when deciding the most logical placement of sentence 3. Also, look for words or concepts found in sentence 3 in other sentences in the paragraph, as these may signal a continuation of ideas.

the concept of "school names" in Hong Kong) and sentence 4 (which reveals that Dong Kingman was the school name of Dong Moy Shu).

Choice B is not the best answer because placing sentence 3 before sentence 1 creates a sequence of sentences that lacks sufficient cohesion. Putting sentence 3 at the beginning of the paragraph would offer a poor introduction to the paragraph, in large part because sentence 3 builds directly on a point made in sentence 1.

Choice D is not the best answer because placing sentence 3 after sentence 4 creates a sequence of sentences that lacks sufficient cohesion. Putting sentence 3 after sentence 4 would disrupt the link between sentence 4 (which mentions that Dong Moy Shu was given the school name Dong Kingman) and sentence 5 (which explains what the two parts composing the name Kingman mean in Cantonese).

18

Which choice most effectively establishes the main topic of the paragraph?

A) Kingman is considered a pioneer of the California Style school of painting.

B) Although cities were his main subject, Kingman did occasionally paint natural landscapes.

C) In his urban landscapes, Kingman captures the vibrancy of crowded cities.

D) In 1929 Kingman moved to Oakland, California, where he attended the Fox Art School.

Content: Development

Key: C

Objective: Students must determine which sentence best signals the main topic of a paragraph.

Explanation: Choice C is the best answer because it clearly establishes the main topic of the paragraph: Kingman's urban landscapes.

Choice A is not the best answer because it would begin the paragraph with a loosely related detail about Kingman's painting style and would not clearly establish the main topic of the paragraph.

Choice B is not the best answer because it would suggest that the main topic of the paragraph is the natural landscapes Kingman occasionally painted, which is incorrect given the focus of the rest of the sentences in the paragraph.

Choice D is not the best answer because it would begin the paragraph with a loosely related detail about Kingman's life and would not clearly establish the main topic of the paragraph.

19

A) NO CHANGE
B) hydrant—
C) hydrant:
D) hydrant

Content: Conventions of Punctuation

Key: A

Objective: Students must effectively separate items in a series.

Explanation: Choice A is the best answer because a comma after the word "hydrant" separates the phrase "a pigeon pecking for crumbs around a fire hydrant" from the phrase "an old man tending to a baby outside a doorway." A comma is also consistent with the punctuation choice made to separate the first two phrases in the asyndetic series following the colon in the sentence.

Choice B is not the best answer because a dash is not a conventional choice for punctuating items in a series.

Choice C is not the best answer because although a colon can be used to introduce a series, it is not a conventional choice for separating items within a series.

Choice D is not the best answer because it fuses together two items in the series. Separating the phrases "a pigeon pecking for crumbs around a fire hydrant" and "an old man tending to a baby outside a doorway" requires punctuation (and could also involve a coordinating conjunction).

20

PRACTICE AT

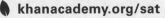
khanacademy.org/sat

Consider which answer choice best continues the theme of "majestic city skylines" established by the first two examples in the sentence.

The writer wants to complete the sentence with a third example of a detail Kingman uses to create his majestic city skylines. Which choice best accomplishes this goal?

A) NO CHANGE
B) exquisitely lettered street and storefront signs.
C) other details that help define Kingman's urban landscapes.
D) enormous ships docking at busy urban ports.

Content: Development

Key: D

Objective: Students must revise supporting information to accomplish a writing goal.

Explanation: Choice D is the best answer because the phrase "enormous ships docking at busy urban ports" effectively continues the sentence's series of details ("skyscrapers towering in the background" and "bridges connecting neighborhoods") conveying the majesty of city skylines as depicted by Kingman.

Choice A is not the best answer because the phrase "delicately painted creatures, such as a tiny, barely visible cat prowling in the bushes of a park" does not convey a sense of the majesty of city skylines as depicted by Kingman and thus does not effectively continue the sentence's series of details ("skyscrapers towering in the background" and "bridges connecting neighborhoods").

Choice B is not the best answer because the phrase "exquisitely lettered street and storefront signs" does not convey a sense of the majesty of city skylines as depicted by Kingman and thus does not effectively continue the sentence's series of details ("skyscrapers towering in the background" and "bridges connecting neighborhoods").

Choice C is not the best answer because the phrase "other details that help define Kingman's urban landscapes" is too vague and general to constitute a third example that conveys a sense of the majesty of city skylines as depicted by Kingman and thus does not effectively continue the sentence's series of details ("skyscrapers towering in the background" and "bridges connecting neighborhoods").

21

Which choice most effectively combines the sentences at the underlined portion?

A) internationally, and Kingman also garnered
B) internationally; from exhibiting, he garnered
C) internationally but garnered
D) internationally, garnering

PRACTICE AT

khanacademy.org/sat

You'll want to choose the answer that combines the sentences in the most efficient manner possible without altering the original meaning.

Content: Effective Language Use

Key: D

Objective: Students must combine sentences effectively.

Explanation: Choice D is the best answer because it combines the sentences logically and efficiently, with the original second sentence becoming a participial phrase describing Kingman.

Choice A is not the best answer because it creates a wordy and awkward construction and because it fails to link the acclaim Kingman received with the exhibition of his work.

Choice B is not the best answer because it creates a repetitive and awkward construction.

Choice C is not the best answer because "but" suggests contrast or exception, neither of which makes sense in the context of the sentence.

22

The writer wants to conclude the passage with a sentence that emphasizes an enduring legacy of Kingman's work. Which choice would best accomplish this goal?

A) Although Kingman's work might not be as famous as that of some other watercolor painters, such as Georgia O'Keeffe and Edward Hopper, it is well regarded by many people.

B) Since Kingman's death in 2000, museums across the United States and in China have continued to ensure that his now-iconic landscapes remain available for the public to enjoy.

C) The urban landscapes depicted in Kingman's body of work are a testament to aptness of the name chosen for Kingman when he was just a boy.

D) Kingman's work was but one example of a long-lasting tradition refreshed by an innovative artist with a new perspective.

Content: Organization

Key: B

Objective: Students must determine the most effective ending of a text given a particular writing goal.

Explanation: Choice B is the best answer because it concludes the passage with a sentence that emphasizes the enduring legacy of Kingman's work by indicating that museums continue to make Kingman's iconic paintings accessible to the public.

Choice A is not the best answer because it concludes the passage with a sentence that acknowledges that the works of other painters are more famous than Kingman's (which downplays, rather than emphasizes, the enduring legacy of Kingman's work) and offers only a general assertion that Kingman's work is "well regarded by many people."

Choice C is not the best answer because instead of referring to the enduring legacy of Kingman's work, it concludes the passage with a sentence that recalls a detail the passage provides about Kingman's early life.

Choice D is not the best answer because it concludes the passage with a sentence that is too vague and general to emphasize effectively an enduring legacy of Kingman's work. It is not clear what the idea of refreshing a long-lasting tradition is intended to mean or how (or even whether) this represents an enduring legacy. Moreover, referring to Kingman's work as "but one example" downplays the significance of any potential legacy that might be suggested.

Chapter 17

About the SAT Essay

No part of the SAT has been more deeply affected by the redesign than the Essay. Nearly everything about the Essay has changed, from the format and length of the test to how it's scored to the fact that the test is now optional. To do well on the new Essay, you'll have to have a good sense of what the test will ask of you as well as the reading, analysis, and writing skills required to compose a response to the Essay prompt. This chapter is intended primarily to get you more familiar with the redesigned Essay. After we discuss the test in general, we'll turn to some sample prompts as well as examples of student papers and what scores they would receive. Before that, though, we'll quickly examine how the Essay has changed with the SAT redesign.

Key Changes to the SAT Essay

Even though you're planning to take the redesigned SAT Essay after March 2016, it may be helpful to know what the test was like prior to spring 2016 to get some sense of how significantly different the redesigned Essay is. The following table lists those key changes, which the rest of this chapter will delve into in more detail.

DIFFERENCES BETWEEN THE ORIGINAL SAT ESSAY AND THE REDESIGNED SAT ESSAY

REMEMBER

As illustrated in this table, the redesigned SAT Essay is very different from the original SAT Essay.

Feature	Original SAT Essay (unavailable after January 2016)	Redesigned SAT Essay (available beginning March 2016)
Required or optional	Required	Optional
Position within the SAT test	At the beginning of the SAT test, before any of the multiple-choice sections	At the end of the SAT test, after both multiple-choice sections have been given
Test length	25 minutes	50 minutes
Number of prompts (questions) and responses (answers)	1 each	1 each
Nature of prompt	Take a position on an issue	Analyze an argument
Prompt varies?	Yes; general format stays the same; reading and prompt change from test to test	No; general format stays the same; reading changes from test to test; prompt is virtually the same every time
Reading included	Brief (80–100 words) passage designed mainly to get students thinking about an issue	Extended (650–750 words) passage designed to be the main focus of the task
Support to be used	Reasoning and examples taken from students' own reading, studies, experiences, or observations	Reasoning and textual evidence from the included reading
Scores	One holistic Essay score (2–12), combined with the score on the multiple-choice writing portion to get a Writing score on a 200–800 scale	Three analytic Essay scores (2–8 each): Reading, Analysis, and Writing; scores not combined with each other or with any other scores on the test

REMEMBER

If you choose to take the Essay, you'll receive three scores on your response. These scores won't be combined with each other or with any other scores on the test.

Important Features of the Redesigned SAT Essay

Now that you have a general sense of the redesigned SAT Essay, let's consider each of the important features more closely.

OPTIONAL TEST

Unlike the original Essay, the Essay on the redesigned SAT is optional for students. This means that — unless you're required to take the test by your school or some other institution — you need to make an informed, personal choice about whether to take the Essay Test. You should figure out whether one or more of the postsecondary institutions that you're applying to require Essay scores; if so, your decision is pretty simple. If that's not the case and you're not otherwise required to take the Essay, you'll have to make up your own mind about it.

We recommend that you seriously consider taking the Essay. The task the Essay asks you to complete — analyzing how an argument works — is an interesting and engaging one. The Essay also gives you an excellent opportunity to demonstrate your reading, analysis, and writing skills — skills critical to readiness for and success in college and career — and the scores you'll get back will give you insight into your strengths in these areas as well as indications of any skills that may still need work.

POSITION WITHIN THE SAT TEST

The Essay is administered after the multiple-choice sections of the SAT. This makes it easier to give the test to some students and not to others, since the Essay is no longer required.

TEST LENGTH

The SAT Essay is 50 minutes in length. This is longer than in the past, in large part because we want to make sure you have enough time to read and analyze the passage. This passage is about the same length as the longest passage you'll see on the SAT Reading Test, and you'll need to spend a fair amount of time reading, selectively rereading, analyzing, and drawing evidence from it in order to do well on the Essay Test.

You may find it reassuring to know that the College Board decided to allot 50 minutes for the test only after careful study and review. This process included examining papers from thousands of students who took the Essay as part of our research. From this process, we learned that 50 minutes provided enough time for most students to complete the Essay task without rushing. Although you'll still have to pace yourself and pay attention to the time available, you should have enough time to do your best work on the Essay.

NUMBER OF PROMPTS AND RESPONSES

The Essay includes only one prompt, or question. You'll produce a single essay in response to that prompt.

THE ESSAY TASK

The SAT Essay asks you to analyze a provided argument in order to explain how the author builds his or her argument to persuade an audience. This is a *very* different task from the one used in the previous Essay. While the redesigned Essay prompt will present you with an issue to consider — this time,

 **REMEMBER**

The Essay is optional for students. If your school or the postsecondary institutions you're applying to don't require Essay scores, you'll have to make an informed, personal decision as to whether to take the Essay.

 **REMEMBER**

You'll have 50 minutes to complete the Essay task. While you'll want to pace yourself, this should be enough time for you to produce your best work, especially if you've practiced with some sample passages.

REMEMBER

The Essay *won't* ask you to take a stance on an issue. Rather, your task will be to analyze an argument presented in a passage in order to explain how the author builds the argument to persuade his or her audience.

REMEMBER

The Essay task will be the same in every test. What will change is the reading selection you'll be asked to analyze. Familiarizing yourself with the Essay prompt ahead of time, and understanding exactly what your task is, will save you time on test day and will likely result in your writing a stronger essay.

REMEMBER

The three scores you'll receive reflect the three main criteria your Essay will be evaluated on. As you practice for the Essay, focus on each of these three areas and try to assess honestly your performance in each.

in the form of a lengthy argumentative passage — you will *not* be asked to take a stance on that issue. (In fact, if all you do is express your own feelings on the issue, you won't receive a strong score on the test's Analysis dimension because you didn't demonstrate that you understood the nature of the assigned task.) As you can probably guess from what we've said so far, the support you provide for your analysis won't come primarily from your own prior knowledge, opinions, or experiences. Instead, you'll be drawing on information and ideas found in the accompanying reading passage and using those to develop your analysis. In other words, you'll be making extensive use of textual evidence to flesh out your response to the question of how the author builds his or her argument in the passage to persuade an audience.

The redesigned SAT uses virtually the same prompt in every single test given to students. The reading selection and a sentence describing that selection change each time the test is given, but you'll always know what you're going to be asked to write about. This has huge advantages for you over how most essay tests are administered. You'll be able to focus your preparation on developing important reading, analysis, and writing knowledge and skills instead of on trying to guess what question we'll ask, and on test day you can get right to work instead of spending a lot of valuable time trying to form an opinion on a topic you may not have even thought much about.

We'll come back to that prompt after a brief discussion of how the new Essay is evaluated.

SCORES

When you take the Essay, you'll receive three scores:

▶ **Reading:** How well you demonstrated your understanding of the passage

▶ **Analysis:** How well you analyzed the passage and carried out the task of explaining how the author of builds his or her argument to persuade an audience

▶ **Writing:** How skillfully you crafted your response

Each score will be on a 2–8 scale, the combined result of two raters scoring each dimension independently on a 1–4 scale. These three scores aren't combined with each other or with scores on any other part of the test.

Why the changes? For one thing, the fact that the Essay is now optional meant that we could no longer combine scores on multiple-choice writing questions with the Essay scores, since some students will elect not to take the Essay. For another, we believed that the richness and depth of the new Essay task meant that we could — and needed to — offer you (and the institutions you send your scores to) more and better information about your performance than we did with the original Essay. By evaluating your performance into three main areas, we're able to better pinpoint your strengths and weaknesses. Perhaps your response shows that you understood the passage very well and were able to produce a clear and cohesive essay but that you struggled some with the analysis task. If we combined that into one score, it might be indistinguishable from the score of a student who did very well in analysis and in demonstrating reading comprehension but less well in putting his or her thoughts into words. By giving you three separate scores, we make it easier for you to know where you did well and where you might have struggled. This, in turn, will help you find ways to improve specific shortcomings.

More details about how the Essay is scored, along with the complete scoring rubric, appear later in this chapter.

THE ESSAY PROMPT IN DETAIL

Now let's examine the prompt for the redesigned Essay. And we do mean *the* prompt because, as we noted above, the prompt is nearly identical on every single administration of the SAT.

Let's now examine some of the most important elements in this prompt.

> As you read the passage below, consider how [the author] uses
>
> - evidence, such as facts or examples, to support claims.
> - reasoning to develop ideas and to connect claims and evidence.
> - stylistic or persuasive elements, such as word choice or appeals to emotion, to add power to the ideas expressed.

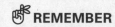 **REMEMBER**

The prompt provided here will be nearly identical to the prompt you'll see on test day. Thus, read it carefully now and make sure you understand what it's asking you to do.

> Write an essay in which you explain how [the author] builds an argument to persuade [his/her] audience that [author's claim]. In your essay, analyze how [the author] uses one or more of the features listed above (or features of your own choice) to strengthen the logic and persuasiveness of [his/her] argument. Be sure that your analysis focuses on the most relevant features of the passage.
>
> Your essay should not explain whether you agree with [the author's] claims, but rather explain how the author builds an argument to persuade [his/her] audience.

The Passage

Your response to the Essay prompt will be firmly rooted in a reading selection of between 650 and 750 words — about the length of one of the longer passages on the Reading Test. All of your work on the Essay will center on your ability to understand, analyze, and explain your analysis of this passage. While the passage will come from any one of a wide range of high-quality sources and will differ on each administration of the test, all Essay passages

REMEMBER

The Essay's reading selection
will change with each test
administration, but it will always
take the form of an argument of
about 650–750 words in length
written for a broad audience.
You won't need to bring in
any specialized background
knowledge; everything you need
to write a strong essay will be in
the passage.

REMEMBER

The primary focus of your essay
should *not* be on what the
author says. Rather, your essay
should focus on how the author
develops an argument that is
persuasive and powerful.

REMEMBER

Evidence, reasoning, and stylistic
and persuasive elements are
three main ways authors can
develop their arguments. A
strong SAT Essay will analyze the
author's use of one or more of
these components.

take the form of an argument written for a broad audience. By this we mean that the form of the writing will always be argumentative (i.e., the author will always be making a claim, or assertion, and trying to convince an audience to agree with that claim) and that the subject will be generally accessible to a wide readership. You won't see a highly technical argument on a specialized subject that requires background knowledge. All of the relevant information needed to understand the topic will be included in the passage itself.

Building an Argument to Persuade an Audience

By asking you to focus on how the author of the passage "builds an argument to persuade an audience," the Essay prompt is pushing you into what may be called rhetorical analysis. We discussed the concept of rhetoric a bit in Chapter 10, but the main point here is that your analysis is focused on matters related to the art and craft of writing, and not, strictly speaking, the informational content of the passage. In this rhetorical analysis, you're paying attention to how the author uses particular techniques and elements to make his or her writing more convincing, persuasive, and powerful; your discussion should focus on what the author does, why he or she does it, and what effect this is likely to have on readers. You'll definitely want to capture some of the main ideas and key details of the passage in your analysis, but your main task is *not* to summarize that information but rather to assess its contribution to the argument.

Evidence, Reasoning, and Stylistic and Persuasive Elements . . . and Other Things

The Essay directions advise you to think about how the author uses evidence, reasoning, and stylistic and persuasive elements to develop his or her argument. These are cornerstones to much argumentative writing, so we should examine briefly what we mean by each of these.

Evidence is information and ideas that the author uses to support a claim. Evidence takes many forms, and the forms vary depending on the kind of argument the author is writing and the nature of the point the author is trying to make. Evidence can come in the form of facts, statistics, quotations from (other) experts, the results of experiments or other research, examples, and the like. The author of any given passage may use some of these or rely on other kinds of sources entirely. It'll be up to you to figure out what constitutes evidence in a particular passage and how the author uses it to support his or her claims.

Your analysis of an author's use of evidence can take many forms, depending on the particular passage in question. You may end up pointing out that the author relies (perhaps too much) on one kind of evidence or another — or on little or no evidence at all, likely weakening the argument's effectiveness. You may instead or in addition point to specific cases in which the author's choice of evidence was particularly effective in supporting a claim or point. Other approaches are possible as well.

Reasoning is the connective tissue that holds an argument together. It's the "thinking" — the logic, the analysis — that develops the argument and ties the claim and evidence together. Reasoning plays a stronger role in some texts than in others. Some authors are very careful about making their thought processes clear so that readers can follow and critique them. In other cases, texts rely less heavily on logic.

Your analysis of an author's use of reasoning can take a number of different approaches. You may decide to discuss how the author uses (or fails to use) clear, logical reasoning to draw a connection between a claim and the evidence supporting that claim. You may also or instead choose to evaluate the impact that particular aspects of the author's reasoning (e.g., unstated assumptions) have on how convincing the argument is. Other approaches are possible as well.

Stylistic and persuasive elements are rhetorical techniques that an author might bring to bear in order to enhance the power of his or her argument. An author could make use of appeals, such as to the audience's fears or sense of honor, or employ particularly vivid descriptive language to create a mood of anticipation or anxiety, or use one or more of any number of other such devices. There's no definitive list of these techniques, and you don't have to know them all by heart or by name to be able to get strong scores on the Essay. The key thing here is to be on the lookout for ways in which the author attempts to influence the audience, sometimes by using something other than a strictly logical, rational approach.

Your analysis of the author's use of stylistic and persuasive elements can follow a number of paths. You may point out instances in which the author uses such devices and evaluate their role or their effectiveness in convincing an audience to action. You may also or in addition analyze and evaluate the varying extent to which logic and emotion contribute to the persuasiveness of the text. Other approaches are possible as well.

We've listed some examples of how evidence, reasoning, and stylistic and persuasive elements might be analyzed in a passage, but these are by no means the only ways. For some passages, evidence may be less important than reasoning and/or stylistic and persuasive elements, so it makes sense to devote less attention to evidence in such a case. Indeed, successful responses do *not* need to cover each of these three categories. In fact, it's generally better to focus your essay on a few points that are well made than attempt to check off a long list of rhetorical elements. You can also choose to discuss some aspect of the passage that doesn't fit neatly into one of the three categories but that plays an important part in how the author builds the argument.

PRACTICE AT

khanacademy.org/sat

Your analysis does *not* have to focus exclusively on how the author's use of evidence, reasoning, and stylistic and persuasive elements makes the argument stronger or more persuasive. Instead, you may choose to point out ways in which the author's use (or lack of use) of one or more of these elements weakens the effectiveness of the argument.

REMEMBER

Your Essay does *not* have to address the author's use of all three components discussed here (evidence, reasoning, and stylistic and persuasive elements) in order to earn high scores. An essay that provides strong analysis of fewer but well-chosen points will likely score better than an essay that provides little analysis of a long list of points.

The Most Relevant Aspects of the Passage

As the preceding discussion suggests, your analysis should be selective. That is, you should focus your attention on those features of the passage that you feel make the biggest contribution to the persuasive power of the passage. While 50 minutes is a fair amount of time, it's not enough to write about everything that's going on in the passage. Pick and choose what you analyze.

Not Explaining Whether You Agree with the Author's Claims

Remember that when we talked about the concept of "building an argument to persuade an audience," we noted that your main purpose in the Essay is rhetorical. That is, you should focus your analysis on how the author attempts to persuade an audience through such techniques as citing evidence, using reasoning, and employing various stylistic and persuasive techniques. Your main goal is *not* to show why or whether you agree or disagree with the points the author makes.

This can be hard. We all have opinions and the urge to share them. You've also probably done a lot of writing in which you've argued for one position or another. What's more, it can be tough to stay emotionally detached if you read something that you either strongly agree or strongly disagree with. Nevertheless, such detachment is something we all have to demonstrate at times, and it's a skill that postsecondary instructors will expect you to be able to make use of routinely. It's also an important general reading skill. If you make your own judgments too early while reading, you're likely to miss something that the author says and maybe even distort the text's message to fit your own preconceptions. Being able to differentiate your own views from those of others is a critical academic and life skill, and it's something that the SAT Essay will — indirectly — call on you to do.

It's a slightly different case, though, when you feel that the passage on the Essay isn't particularly effective or persuasive. Here, you're on somewhat safer ground, as you're still thinking and analyzing rhetorically — still focusing on the art and craft of writing, only this time on one or more ways that you feel the author is failing to make a strong point. It's okay to fault the author in this sense, but be sure to make clear what you think the author's intent probably was. You could point out, for instance, that the author's description seems too idealized to be truly believable or that the author gives too much attention to anecdotes instead of solid evidence, but you should still devote your main effort to what the author *does* do and what the author *intends* to accomplish (even if he or she sometimes misses the mark).

SAT Essay Scoring Rubric

Reproduced in this section is the rubric that two scorers will use to assess your essay. Each scorer will assign a score of 1–4 in each of three categories: Reading, Analysis, and Writing. These scores will be added together to give you a 2–8 score on each of the three dimensions. Recall that these scores aren't combined with each other or with other scores on the SAT.

👉 **REMEMBER**

While it's tempting to state your opinion on the topic discussed in the Essay passage, remember that this is *not* your task. Your task is to analyze how the author attempts to persuade an audience through the use of evidence, reasoning, and stylistic and persuasive elements and/or other features you identify.

👉 **REMEMBER**

Your essay will be scored by two raters, each of whom will assign a score of 1–4 in the categories of Reading, Analysis, and Writing. The two raters' scores for each dimension will be added together. Thus, you'lll receive three scores on your essay, each ranging from 2–8.

Score	Reading	Analysis	Writing
4 Advanced	The response demonstrates thorough comprehension of the source text. The response shows an understanding of the text's central idea(s) and of most important details and how they interrelate, demonstrating a comprehensive understanding of the text. The response is free of errors of fact or interpretation with regard to the text. The response makes skillful use of textual evidence (quotations, paraphrases, or both), demonstrating a complete understanding of the source text.	The response offers an insightful analysis of the source text and demonstrates a sophisticated understanding of the analytical task. The response offers a thorough, well-considered evaluation of the author's use of evidence, reasoning, and/or stylistic and persuasive elements, and/or feature(s) of the student's own choosing. The response contains relevant, sufficient, and strategically chosen support for claim(s) or point(s) made. The response focuses consistently on those features of the text that are most relevant to addressing the task.	The response is cohesive and demonstrates a highly effective use and command of language. The response includes a precise central claim. The response includes a skillful introduction and conclusion. The response demonstrates a deliberate and highly effective progression of ideas both within paragraphs and throughout the essay. The response has wide variety in sentence structures. The response demonstrates a consistent use of precise word choice. The response maintains a formal style and objective tone. The response shows a strong command of the conventions of standard written English and is free or virtually free of errors.
3 Proficient	The response demonstrates effective comprehension of the source text. The response shows an understanding of the text's central idea(s) and important details. The response is free of substantive errors of fact and interpretation with regard to the text. The response makes appropriate use of textual evidence (quotations, paraphrases, or both), demonstrating an understanding of the source text.	The response offers an effective analysis of the source text and demonstrates an understanding of the analytical task. The response competently evaluates the author's use of evidence, reasoning, and/or stylistic and persuasive elements, and/or feature(s) of the student's own choosing. The response contains relevant and sufficient support for claim(s) or point(s) made. The response focuses primarily on those features of the text that are most relevant to addressing the task.	The response is mostly cohesive and demonstrates effective use and control of language. The response includes a central claim or implicit controlling idea. The response includes an effective introduction and conclusion. The response demonstrates a clear progression of ideas both within paragraphs and throughout the essay. The response has variety in sentence structures. The response demonstrates some precise word choice. The response maintains a formal style and objective tone. The response shows a good control of the conventions of standard written English and is free of significant errors that detract from the quality of writing.

(continued)

Score	Reading	Analysis	Writing
2 Partial	The response demonstrates some comprehension of the source text. The response shows an understanding of the text's central idea(s) but not of important details. The response may contain errors of fact and/or interpretation with regard to the text. The response makes limited and/or haphazard use of textual evidence (quotations, paraphrases, or both), demonstrating some understanding of the source text.	The response offers limited analysis of the source text and demonstrates only partial understanding of the analytical task. The response identifies and attempts to describe the author's use of evidence, reasoning, and/or stylistic and persuasive elements, and/or feature(s) of the student's own choosing, but merely asserts rather than explains their importance. Or one or more aspects of the response's analysis are unwarranted based on the text. The response contains little or no support for claim(s) or point(s) made. The response may lack a clear focus on those features of the text that are most relevant to addressing the task.	The response demonstrates little or no cohesion and limited skill in the use and control of language. The response may lack a clear central claim or controlling idea or may deviate from the claim or idea over the course of the response. The response may include an ineffective introduction and/or conclusion. The response may demonstrate some progression of ideas within paragraphs but not throughout the response. The response has limited variety in sentence structures; sentence structures may be repetitive. The response demonstrates general or vague word choice; word choice may be repetitive. The response may deviate noticeably from a formal style and objective tone. The response shows a limited control of the conventions of standard written English and contains errors that detract from the quality of writing and may impede understanding.
1 Inadequate	The response demonstrates little or no comprehension of the source text. The response fails to show an understanding of the text's central idea(s) and may include only details without reference to central idea(s). The response may contain numerous errors of fact and/or interpretation with regard to the text. The response makes little or no use of textual evidence (quotations, paraphrases, or both), demonstrating little or no understanding of the source text.	The response offers little or no analysis or ineffective analysis of the source text and demonstrates little or no understanding of the analytic task. The response identifies without explanation some aspects of the author's use of evidence, reasoning, and/or stylistic and persuasive elements, and/or feature(s) of the student's choosing. Or numerous aspects of the response's analysis are unwarranted based on the text. The response contains little or no support for claim(s) or point(s) made, or support is largely irrelevant. The response may not focus on features of the text that are relevant to addressing the task. Or the response offers no discernible analysis (e.g., is largely or exclusively summary).	The response demonstrates little or no cohesion and inadequate skill in the use and control of language. The response may lack a clear central claim or controlling idea. The response lacks a recognizable introduction and conclusion. The response does not have a discernible progression of ideas. The response lacks variety in sentence structures; sentence structures may be repetitive. The response demonstrates general and vague word choice; word choice may be poor or inaccurate. The response may lack a formal style and objective tone. The response shows a weak control of the conventions of standard written English and may contain numerous errors that undermine the quality of writing.

We've provided two samples that illustrate the sorts of reading passages you can expect to find on the Essay. After you read each passage, you can review samples of the essays that actual students wrote in response to that reading passage.

Each student response has received a separate score for each of the three dimensions assessed: Reading, Analysis, and Writing. The scores are presented directly preceding each sample essay and in order, meaning that a "1/2/1" would refer to a score of 1 in Reading, 2 in Analysis, and 1 in Writing. Scores for the samples were assigned on a 1–4 scale according to the scoring rubric. It's important to note that although these samples are representative of student achievement, neither set comprehensively illustrates the many ways in which students can earn a particular score on a particular dimension.

Although all of the sample essays were handwritten by students, they're shown typed here for ease of reading. Each essay has been transcribed exactly as the student wrote it, without alterations to spelling, punctuation, or paragraph breaks.

PRACTICE AT

🔥 **khanacademy.org/sat**

Take some time to read the sample passages and student essays below. As you read each student essay, consider how well the student does in each of the three scoring dimensions (Reading, Analysis, and Writing), using the scoring rubric as a guide. Compare your assessment of each essay to the assessment provided.

Sample Passage 1:

As you read the passage below, consider how Peter S. Goodman uses

- evidence, such as facts or examples, to support claims.
- reasoning to develop ideas and to connect claims and evidence.
- stylistic or persuasive elements, such as word choice or appeals to emotion, to add power to the ideas expressed.

PRACTICE AT

🔥 **khanacademy.org/sat**

As you read the passage, be on the lookout for the author's use of these three elements (evidence, reasoning, and stylistic and persuasive elements). You may find it helpful to take brief notes in the margins.

Adapted from Peter S. Goodman, "Foreign News at a Crisis Point." ©2013 by TheHuffingtonPost.com, Inc. Originally published September 25, 2013. Peter Goodman is the executive business and global news editor at TheHuffingtonPost.com.

1   Back in 2003, American Journalism Review produced a census of foreign correspondents then employed by newspapers based in the United States, and found 307 full-time people. When AJR repeated the exercise in the summer of 2011, the count had dropped to 234. And even that number was significantly inflated by the inclusion of contract writers who had replaced full-time staffers.

2   In the intervening eight years, 20 American news organizations had entirely eliminated their foreign bureaus.

3   The same AJR survey zeroed in on a representative sampling of American papers from across the country and found that the space devoted to foreign news had shrunk by 53 percent over the previous quarter-century.

4   All of this decline was playing out at a time when the U.S. was embroiled
in two overseas wars, with hundreds of thousands of Americans
deployed in Iraq and Afghanistan. It was happening as domestic politics
grappled with the merits and consequences of a global war on terror, as a
Great Recession was blamed in part on global imbalances in savings, and
as world leaders debated a global trade treaty and pacts aimed at
addressing climate change. It unfolded as American workers heard
increasingly that their wages and job security were under assault by
competition from counterparts on the other side of oceans.

5   In short, news of the world is becoming palpably more relevant to the
day-to-day experiences of American readers, and it is rapidly
disappearing.

6   Yet the same forces that have assailed print media, eroding foreign news
along the way, may be fashioning a useful response. Several nonprofit
outlets have popped up to finance foreign reporting, and a for-profit
outfit, GlobalPost, has dispatched a team of 18 senior correspondents
into the field, supplemented by dozens of stringers and freelancers. . . .

7   We are intent on forging fresh platforms for user-generated content:
testimonials, snapshots and video clips from readers documenting
issues in need of attention. Too often these sorts of efforts wind up
feeling marginal or even patronizing: "Dear peasant, here's your chance
to speak to the pros about what's happening in your tiny little corner of
the world." We see user-generated content as a genuine reporting tool,
one that operates on the premise that we can only be in so many places
at once. Crowd-sourcing is a fundamental advantage of the web, so
why not embrace it as a means of piecing together a broader and more
textured understanding of events?

8   We all know the power of Twitter, Facebook and other forms of social
media to connect readers in one place with images and impressions
from situations unfolding far away. We know the force of social media
during the Arab Spring, as activists convened and reacted to changing
circumstances. . . . Facts and insights reside on social media, waiting to
be harvested by the digitally literate contemporary correspondent.

9   And yet those of us who have been engaged in foreign reporting for
many years will confess to unease over many of the developments
unfolding online, even as we recognize the trends are as unstoppable as
globalization or the weather. Too often it seems as if professional
foreign correspondents, the people paid to use their expertise while
serving as informational filters, are being replaced by citizen
journalists who function largely as funnels, pouring insight along with
speculation, propaganda and other white noise into the mix.

10   We can celebrate the democratization of media, the breakdown of
monopolies, the rise of innovative means of telling stories, and the
inclusion of a diversity of voices, and still ask whether the results are
making us better informed. Indeed, we have a professional responsibility
to continually ask that question while seeking to engineer new models
that can channel the web in the interest of better informing readers. . . .

11 We need to embrace the present and gear for the future. These are days in which newsrooms simply must be entrepreneurial and creative in pursuit of new means of reporting and paying for it. That makes this a particularly interesting time to be doing the work, but it also requires forthright attention to a central demand: We need to put back what the Internet has taken away. We need to turn the void into something fresh and compelling. We need to re-examine and update how we gather information and how we engage readers, while retaining the core values of serious-minded journalism.

12 This will not be easy. . . . But the alternative—accepting ignorance and parochialism—is simply not an option.

Write an essay in which you explain how Peter S. Goodman builds an argument to persuade his audience that news organizations should increase the amount of professional foreign news coverage provided to people in the United States. In your essay, analyze how Goodman uses one or more of the features listed in the box above (or features of your own choice) to strengthen the logic and persuasiveness of his argument. Be sure that your analysis focuses on the most relevant features of the passage.

PRACTICE AT

khanacademy.org/sat

If you decide to practice for the SAT Essay, select a passage to use for your analysis. Take several minutes to brainstorm some of the points you may choose to focus on. Next, create an outline in which you decide on the structure and progression of your essay. An outline will help ensure your essay is well organized and cohesive. This strategy may also be useful on test day.

Sample Student Essays

STUDENT SAMPLE 1— SCORES: 1/1/1

In the Article, "Foreign News at a Crisis Point" by Peter S. Goodman ©2013 by TheHuffingtonPost.com, the author builds up an argument to persuade his audience. He provided information about American Journalism Review to let people in the community know how it started.

"we need to embrace the present and gear for the future." This means that the author wants to find new ways of communicating with the community now, that will help later on in the future. This is important because the author wants better media to transmit to the public. "We all know the Power of Twitter, Facebook, and other forms of Social media to connect leaders in one Place with images and [unfinished]

Sample 1 Scoring Explanation: This response scored a 1/1/1.

Reading—1: This response demonstrates little comprehension of Goodman's text. Although the inclusion of two quotations from the text (*"we need to embrace the present . . ."*; *"We all know the power of Twitter, Facebook . . ."*) suggests that the writer has read the passage, the writer does not provide any actual indication of an understanding of the text. The writer fails to show a clear understanding of Goodman's central claim, saying vaguely that *the author wants better media to transmit to the public.* The response is further limited by vague references to details from the passage that are largely unconnected to the passage's central idea, such as when the writer states that Goodman *provided information about American Journalism Review to let people in the community know how it started.* Overall, this response demonstrates inadequate reading comprehension.

Analysis—1: This response demonstrates little understanding of the analytical task. The writer makes few attempts to analyze the source text. What attempts are offered either repeat the prompt without elaboration (*the author builds up an argument to persuade his audience*) or merely paraphrase the text in a general way (*This means that the author wants to find new ways of communicating*). The brief response consists mostly of quotations taken from the passage, with very few of the writer's own ideas included. Overall, this response demonstrates inadequate analysis.

Writing—1: This response demonstrates little cohesion and inadequate skill in the use and control of language. While the writer does include a very basic central claim (*the author builds up an argument to persuade his audience*), the response does not have a discernible progression of ideas. Much of the brief response is comprised of quotations from Goodman's text, and the language that is the writer's own is repetitive and vague. For example, the writer states that Goodman shares information with his readers to *let people in the community know how it started*, with no clear indication of what "it" refers to. Overall, this response demonstrates inadequate writing.

STUDENT SAMPLE 2 — SCORES: 2/1/2

In the article "Foreign News At a Crisis Point", Peter S. Goodman argues that the news orginizations should increase the amount of Foreign news coverage offered to the Americans.

Peter S. Goodman offers many explanations of why the American public needs more profetional Foreign news covarage. He appeals to our emotions when he states that it's seen very often that when news orginization ask for a review by a reader/viewer they might end up to feel marginal. Goodman gives an idea to fix that problem and says, "Crowd-Sourcing is a fundimental advantage of the web, so why not emdrace it as means of piecing together a broader and more textual understanding of events?" He talks about this because he believes that the news should add what the people want to hear and not what the reportors want to talk about.

He also states a fact from the American Journalism Review, the AJR sampled many news papers from across the country and they observed that the space of which belonged to foreign news had shrunk by 53% over the previous quarter-century. Goodman took this into consideration and noticed that the decline was talking place around the time in which America was in the middle of two wars overseas. It was also around the time the government viewed the consequences and merits of global war on terrorism.

Peter S. Goodman offered many reason for which Foreign news should be in creased so the American public could view it and they all have great support and add relavence to the viewer.

Sample 2 Scoring Explanation: This response scored a 2/1/2.

Reading—2: This response demonstrates some comprehension of Goodman's text. The writer shows an understanding of Goodman's central idea, stating that *news orginizations should increase the amount of Foreign news coverage offered to the Americans.* While the writer includes some details from the source text (*it's seen very often that when news orginization ask for a review by a reader/viewer they might end up to feel marginal*); *Goodman . . . noticed that the decline was talking place around the time in which America was in the middle of two wars overseas*), these details are, for the most part, unconnected to the central idea. The use of textual evidence is limited, and therefore it is unclear whether the writer understands how important details relate to the central idea. Further, the writer demonstrates some evidence of having misinterpreted the argument, stating that Goodman *talks about this because he believes that the news should add what the people want to hear and not what the reportors want to talk about.* Overall, the response demonstrates partially successful reading comprehension.

Analysis—1: This response demonstrates very little understanding of the analytical task. The writer does identify an argumentative strategy in Goodman's text when the writer says Goodman *appeals to our emotions*; however, the writer does not analyze this moment further or provide elaboration about how the example appeals to the audience's emotions. Instead, the writer reverts to summary and writes that *Goodman gives an idea to fix that problem.* Throughout the rest of the response, the writer only describes Goodman's use of evidence by summarizing parts of the text rather than providing analysis. Overall, this response demonstrates inadequate analysis.

Writing—2: This response demonstrates limited cohesion and writing skill. The writer includes a central claim, but the introductory paragraph is not effective. Individual paragraphs display some progression of ideas, but there is little to connect ideas between paragraphs or in the response as a whole. The writer's word choice is general, and sentence structures follow a simple, repetitive subject-verb structure (*Peter S. Goodman offers*; *He appeals*; *Goodman gives*; *He talks*). Some language errors (*emdrace*; *talking place*) detract from the quality of writing throughout the essay but do not seriously impede understanding. Overall, this response demonstrates partially successful writing.

STUDENT SAMPLE 3: — SCORES: 3/2/3

Peter Goodman's purpose in writing "Foreign News at a Crisis Point" was to persuade his audience that the news should include more information about the world as a whole. Goodmans argument becomes powerful through the use of pathos, using evidence, and also embracing reasoning.

Goodman is extremely persuasive in his argument when he brings pathos into effect. He uses pathos to appeal to the emotions of the readers. He plays out the hard times of the U.S. by saying "American workers heard increasingly that their ways and job security were under assault" and "hundreds of thousands of Americans deployed in Iraq and Afghanistan." This information is used to show the reader why the

PRACTICE AT

khanacademy.org/sat

Unlike the previous two responses, this response utilizes a clearer organizational structure. The introductory paragraph summarizes Goodman's primary claim and previews the persuasive elements that will be discussed later in the response.

news coverage in foreign countries is diminishing. Goodman wants the reader to know that he understands why coverage is focusing more on the United States but not that its a good thing.

Goodman uses evidence to support his claims that coverage of foreign news is dwindling. Goodman says "20 American news organizations had entirely eliminated their foreign bureaus." He also explains "in the summer of 2011, the count (of full time foreign correspondents) had dropped to 234." This factual information is used so that Goodman can prove that he knows what he's talking about. These facts prove that Goodman had researched the information and persuades readers to believe Goodman's argument.

Goodman also uses reasoning to show readers that there can always be improvement. He says, "these are days in which newsrooms simply must be entreprenuial and creative in pursuit of new means of reporting and paying for it." Goodman uses the argument that we have to take matters into our own hands to prepare and change the future. Goodmans advice to change now internet focused journalism is comes from a strong skill of reasoning.

Goodman uses pathos evidence and reasoning to persuade readers that foreign news coverage needs to be increased. He plays on the reader's emotions by talking about issues that matter to them. He provides facts to show that his argument is valid. He also uses reasoning to come up with a solution to the issue. Goodman uses these features to successfully make a persuasive argument about the amount of professional foreign news coverage provided to Americans.

Sample 3 Scoring Explanation: This response scored a 3/2/3.

Reading—3: This response demonstrates effective comprehension of the source text in terms of both the central idea and important details. The writer accurately paraphrases the central claim of Goodman's text (*Peter Goodman's purpose in writing "Foreign News at a Crisis Point" was to persuade his audience that the news should include more information about* *the world as a whole*). The writer also makes use of appropriate textual evidence to demonstrate an understanding of key details (*He plays out the hard times of the U.S. by saying "American workers heard increasingly that their ways and job security were under assault" and "hundreds of thousands of Americans deployed in Iraq and Afghanistan"; Goodman uses evidence to support his claims that coverage of foreign news is dwindling. Goodman says "20 American news organizations had entirely eliminated their foreign bureaus"*). The response is free of errors of fact or interpretation. Overall, this response demonstrates proficient reading comprehension.

Analysis—2: This response demonstrates a limited understanding of the analytical task and offers an incomplete analysis of how Goodman builds his argument. The writer identifies some important pieces of evidence in Goodman's text and attempts to describe their use (*This factual information is used so that Goodman can prove that he knows what he's talking about. These facts prove that Goodman had researched the information and persuades readers to believe Goodman's argument*), but the writer's reliance on assertions leads only to limited analysis. For example, in the third body paragraph, which discusses Goodman's use of reasoning, the writer merely paraphrases a selected quotation from the text (*He says, "these are days in which newsrooms simply must be entreprenuial and creative in pursuit of new means of reporting and paying for it." Goodman uses the argument that we have to take matters into our own hands to prepare and change the future*) and then asserts circularly that Goodman's advice *comes from a strong skill of reasoning.* Overall, this response demonstrates partially successful analysis.

Writing—3: The writer demonstrates effective use and command of language in this response, and the response as a whole is cohesive. The response includes a precise central claim (*Goodmans argument becomes powerful through the use of pathos, using evidence, and also embracing reasoning*). The brief but focused introduction establishes the framework for the writer's organizational structure, which the writer follows faithfully in the body of the response, progressing from idea to idea and ending with a competent conclusion that summarizes the response. The response displays variety in sentence structure (*He uses pathos to appeal to the emotion of the readers; coverage of foreign news is dwindling; Goodman uses these features to successfully make a persuasive argument about the amount of professional foreign news coverage provided to Americans*) and generally good control of the conventions of standard written English. Overall, this response demonstrates proficient writing.

STUDENT SAMPLE 4 — SCORES: 3/3/3

Logic, reason, and rhetoric create a strong persuasive argument. Peter S. Goodman utilizes these tools in his article "Foreign News At a Crisis Point". Goodman presents a cause and effect argument as well, by presenting the facts and revealing their consequences. What truly persuades his audience is his use of logic, reasen, and rhetoric. These occur in forms of examples, explanations and conclusions, and persuasive and rhetorical statements.

Goodman's use of logic occurs throughout his article, but is most prevelant in the beginning. Examples and statistical presentations initially draw interest from readers. Goodman begins with a census from year 2003 and year 2011 that reveals the major decline of foreign correspondents employed by newspapers based in the United States. The numbers themselves raise a concern in the audiences mind, but may not capture their attention. Goodman then presents more apalling examples, including the sharp decrease of space devoted to foreign news over a quarter century, in order to further capture the reader's attention and raise concern. The connection between the decline in foreign news and increased American involvement overseas heightens curiosity for the reader. Goodman employs logic, basic reasoning and evidence presentation in order to raise concern, curiosity, and questions from the reader.

Goodman's use of reason is present throughout the entire article. After Goodman's presentation of his statistics and facts, he raises more concern about how to increase these statistics and factual numbers. Goodman uses reason to recognize that it would be more "genuine" and better informing for readers to hear of first hand experiences. The reader of his article begins to wonder how Goodman plans to increase the amount of professional foreign news coverage for Americans, and Goodman utilizes reason to draw a simple solution. Social media sites provide an outlet for individuals to have a voice "electronically" speaking. Goodman uses reason to reveal to the reader that first-hand knowledge is best and social media sites provide easy access, so why not create an outlet for people who know more to say more? Goodman also utilizes reason to present the problem of inaccurate information on social media sites. He further builds and enhances his argument when he states that there must be a way to "engage readers, while retaining the core values of journalism." Goodman also uses reason to evoke agreement within the reader's mind when he draws simple conclusions and presents simple solutions. Reason allows Goodman to construct upon his solid foundation of evidence that creates his argument.

Rhetoric seals the deal in Goodman's argument. After presenting the facts using logic, and making connections using reason, Goodman utilizes rhetoric to place the cherry on the top of his argument. Rhetoric is crucial in an argument because it determines how the reader feels after reading an article. Goodman utilizes rhetoric after he presents the fundamental advantage of crowd-sourcing on the web, when he asks a rhetorical question. Goodman presents obvious and exciting information that seems more than reasonable, and asks whether this great idea should be practiced or not. A rhetorical question is meant to evoke either disagreement or agreement of the author's purpose. In this case, Goodman's use of rhetoric evokes agreement from the reader. In his final stanza, after presenting all methods of reform, Goodman utilizes rhetoric to once again state the obvious. Goodman presents his solutions, then asks if it is better to stay ignorant and parochial; the answer to his statement is obvious, and causes the reader to agree with him.

Great persuasive essays utilize the tools of persuasion. Goodman began his argument with logic, combined in reason, and finalized with rhetoric. A flow of examples to connections, to solutions, and consequences propels the reader into agreement with the author. Goodman solidifies his argument and builds his argument with logic, reason, and rhetoric, allowing for a reader to be in more agreement and satisfaction of his argument.

Sample 4 Scoring Explanation: This response scored a 3/3/3.

Reading—3: This response demonstrates effective comprehension of the source text. Although the central idea is never explicitly stated in the introduction, the writer accurately captures the main focus of Goodman's argument: his *concern* for *the major decline of foreign correspondents employed by newspapers based in the United States.* The writer also accurately paraphrases (*Goodman begins with a census from year 2003 and year 2011*) and directly quotes important details from the source text, demonstrating effective comprehension. In the second body paragraph, for example, the writer demonstrates understanding of Goodman's discussion of the benefits and drawbacks of social media, effectively tracing Goodman's argument from the value of *first-hand knowledge* to *the problem of inaccurate information on social media sites.* Overall, this response demonstrates proficient reading comprehension.

Analysis—3: This response demonstrates an understanding of the analytical task and offers an effective analysis of the source text. The writer discusses how various elements of the text are used to build Goodman's argument and how they contribute to the text's persuasiveness. For example, the writer discusses Goodman's use of statistical evidence as well as Goodman's use of reasoning in the analysis of the social media argument (*He further builds and enhances his argument when he states that there must be a way to "engage readers, while retaining the core values of journalism"*). The writer then discusses how Goodman makes effective use of rhetoric toward the end of paragraph 7 of the passage by posing a rhetorical question (*Goodman utilizes rhetoric after he presents the fundamental advantage of crowd-sourcing on the web, when he asks a rhetorical question*). Although the response occasionally relies upon assertions about the elements of persuasive arguments (*Goodman's use of logic occurs throughout his article; Goodman employs logic, basic reasoning and evidence presentation in order to raise concern, curiosity, and questions from the reader; Reason allows Goodman to construct upon his solid foundation of evidence; Rhetoric seals the deal*), the writer provides effective support in other places (for example in the discussion of Goodman's use of rhetoric in the third body paragraph). Overall, this response demonstrates proficient analysis.

Writing—3: This response is generally cohesive and demonstrates effective use of language. The writer provides an effective introduction that lays out in broad strokes the ways in which Goodman builds his argument (*What truly persuades his audience is his use of logic, reasen, and rhetoric. These occur in forms of examples, explanations and conclusions, and persuasive and rhetorical statements*). The response also includes a summarizing conclusion. The three body paragraphs are structured around the three features the writer has chosen to focus on: *logic, reason,* and *rhetoric.* Within each paragraph, there is a clear progression of ideas, though there are few transitions between paragraphs. Although the response sometimes demonstrates awkwardness and repetitive phrasing (*Goodman's use of reason; Goodman uses reason; Goodman also uses reason*), the writer's word choice is generally effective. The response demonstrates some variety in sentence structure and also maintains a formal style and objective tone. Overall, this response demonstrates proficient writing.

STUDENT SAMPLE 5 — SCORES: 3/3/4

Peter S. Goodman builds a solid argument for the growing need for foreign news coverage and utilizes concrete evidence, logical reasoning and persuasive appeals to not only expose the paucity of international news feeds, but also convince his audience that it is crucial that news organizations increase the amount of foreign news coverage provided to Americans.

Goodman begins by clearly laying out the raw statistics from a census produced by the American Journalism Review to show the dramatic decline of foreign correspondents and bureaus that had been "entirely eliminated" by American news organizations over the past decayed. In an attempt to point out the incredulous absurdity of these facts, Goodman goes on to discuss the context of the decrease in foreign coverage by providing examples of real world events that affected all Americans. Goodman uses this irony—that in the wake of pivotal global changes like war, global trade treaties and the war on terror, the foreign coverage in the U.S. was diminishing rather than growing—to try to show the American audience that this argument is very much relevant to their everyday lives. He hones in on examples that resonate with many Americans, like the threat to their wages and job security posed by international counterparts, in order to grab the reader's attention and connect his claims to their "day-to-day experiences". This also serves as a way to persuade leaders of the increasing importance of the need for a stronger stream of foreign news coverage by appealing to the audience's emotions and insinuating that they are missing out on critical information that pertains directly to their lives.

Goodman employs stylistic elements through his careful choice of words that strengthen the argument and make a more powerful impression on the reader. He alludes to the "forces" that have destructively "eroded foreign news", but also remains intent on solving this issue by boldly "forging fresh platforms" that will relay a wider range of news to the American people. He appeals to the individual, always referencing the practical need for "user-generated" content available to all people.

Goldman closes his argument by condemning ignorance and calling for action in an exigency.

[unfinished]

PRACTICE AT

🌢 **khanacademy.org/sat**

Keep track of pacing during the Essay to ensure you can complete your response in the allotted time. An unfinished essay will not allow you to demonstrate your full reading, analysis, and writing abilities and may lower your score.

Scoring Explanation Sample 5: This response scored a 3/3/4.

Reading—3: This response demonstrates effective comprehension of the source text, citing both the central idea and important details in Goodman's piece. The writer accurately paraphrases the central claim of Goodman's text (*Goodman builds a solid argument for the growing need for foreign news coverage . . . [to] convince his audience that it is crucial that news organizations increase the amount of foreign news coverage provided to Americans*). The writer also demonstrates an understanding of the details of Goodman's text: Goodman's use of *raw statistics*; *the context* for *the decrease in foreign coverage*; that Goodman *condemn[s] ignorance and call[s] for action*. The response is also free of errors of fact or interpretation. Overall, this response demonstrates proficient reading comprehension.

Analysis—3: The response demonstrates an understanding of the analytical task and offers an effective analysis of the source text. The writer discusses how various elements of the text are used to build Goodman's argument and how they contribute to the text's persuasiveness: *Goodman begins by clearly laying out the raw statistics . . . to show the dramatic decline of foreign correspondents and bureaus*; *Goodman uses this irony—that in the wake of pivotal global changes like war, global trade treaties and the war on terror, the foreign coverage . . . was diminishing rather than growing—to try to show . . . that this argument is very much relevant to their everyday lives.* The writer then discusses how Goodman *employs stylistic elements* to further the argument, competently selecting textual evidence of the author's strong, deliberate language, namely *the "forces" that have destructively "eroded foreign news."* Had the writer elaborated more on this discussion, perhaps by explaining how these words *make a powerful impression on the reader*, this response might have moved from a competent evaluation into a more advanced analysis. Overall, this response demonstrates proficient analysis.

Writing—4: This response is cohesive and demonstrates highly effective use and control of language. The writer presents a generally skillful, concise introduction, which is also the response's central claim: *Peter S. Goodman builds a solid argument for the growing need for foreign news coverage and* utilizes concrete evidence, logical reasoning and persuasive appeals to not only expose the paucity of international news feeds, but also convince his audience that it is crucial that news organizations increase the amount of foreign news coverage provided to Americans. The writer employs precise word choice throughout the response (*dramatic decline, discuss the context of the decrease, uses this irony, hones in on examples, make a more powerful impression on the reader, appeals to the individual, always referencing the practical need*). Although the writer was not able to finish the response, the two existing body paragraphs are tightly focused and deliberately structured to advance the writer's analysis of Goodman's use of *concrete evidence* and *stylistic elements* (mainly *choice of words* and *persuasive appeals*). The response maintains a formal style and objective tone and contains clear transitions (*Goodman begins by clearly laying out; Goldman* [sic] *closes his argument*) to guide the reader. Overall, this response demonstrates advanced writing skill.

STUDENT SAMPLE 6 — SCORES: 4/3/3

Over the years what is going on in the outside world has started to affect us more. Whether it is a war that is going to effect us physically or even an oil disaster that will effect us economically. However, this news is not always covered. The U.S. news focuses more on what is going on in our own country then outside of it we are not well informed to the world around us. Peter S. Goodman uses many different types of evidence to support his claims and persuade his audience that news organizations should increase the amount of professional foreign news coverage provided to Americans.

Within the first three paragraphs of this article the author offers many statistical evidence. He throws out numbers. As a reader this appeals to a logical thinking audience. Also, many people will start to believe that this author is a credible source. He appears to know what he is talking about. Peter S. Goodman appears to have done some research on this topic and proves this within his first three paragraphs. The author uses the numbers "307" and "234" in the first paragraph. He wanted to illustrate to this audience the decreasing amount of foreign correspondents that are employed by news companies within the U.S. Right away goodman shows the audience the subject of the article. He establishes his purpose. He wants to call for a change. The author never comes out and says this in the first paragraph, but he subtely hints at it. Next he shows how many news organizations no longer have "foreign bureaus." Again he throws out a number, "53 percent" to show how much foreign news has decreased within the United States. All these facts are to support his claim that foreign news has shrunk within the United States over the years. He feels as if this should change so people are better informed. Peter S. Goodman then shifts from using statistical evidence to historical evidence.

Peter S. Goodman talks about things that are going on in the world around us today. He brings up many issues that have just recently occured. As a reader I now start to question whether I know what these issues are all about. Did I ever hear about them or even read about them? These are all questions the author has put into the readers' mind. First, he starts off with the war in Iraq and Afghanistan which almost every reader would know about. There are issues that many of them had to deal with personality. Some of their family members may be serving overseas. The author makes a personal connection with the audience. They know the feeling of not knowing exactly what is going on overseas. They constantly question what is happening and whether their loved ones are safe. The author then claims that world news has started to have an affect on our day to day lives in the US. He illustrates how our wages and economy depend on what is going on outside of the United States. Peter S. Goodman transitions from histerical evidence to things that we use for news such as social media to make a connection to his audience.

The author starts to talk about how we now rely on social media for our world news. He again backs up his claim that we need more "professional" foreign coverage in the United States. He explains how common people are providing the news. This may make for "speculation, propaganda, and other white noise into the mix." These people are not professional writers. Also, most of them are not neutral on an issue. He shows that common people are bias. They all have an opinion and share it. Instead of saying what is actually going on; they may say what they think is going on. The author uses the example of bias saying there was not new organization reporting on this. All of our news came from social media. People talk these accounts as truth. They do not realize that they are not filtered. He compares "professional foreign correspondents" to "informational filters" while he compares "citizen journalists" to "funnels". Professional reporters that would investigate foreign issues would only report back what they know is true. Only facts would be included. However, every day people that are writing on the web would say anything and everything they could think of. He uses this comparison to show his audience the different ways they are given information. He wants to show them that right now they are depending on opinions when in fact they should be depending on facts. The author goes from how people are obtaining their information to how he thinks people should obtain their information.

Peter S. Goodman uses his last few paragraphs to state his claims once again. He renforces the idea that we need to take back "what the Internet has taken away." He supports this earlier in his article when he [shows] how we do not also receive the full story when we rely on day to day people to report the world news. The author wants to journalists to change the way they write. He believes that they will be much more successful in providing information to the public. They need to "engage" their readers. The author's last few paragraphs are used to restate his claims that he supported with evidence through out his article.

The author uses many different types of evidence to back up his claims. He shows that he has researched his topic by providing statistical evidence that agrees with his opinions. He shows the decrease in the amount of foreign correspondents with this evidence. Then he shifts to historical evidence. This evidence is used to show how much the world around us has an impact on our society. Then he transitions to how we obtain information today. He shows we do not always receive the full story. He uses this to claim how we should gain our information. The author believes in more foreign correspondents. Throughout "Foreign News At a Crisis Point" Peter S. Goodman uses evidence to portray why we need to increase the amount of foreign news we receive instead the United States. In using the evidence he shows how and why the world around us constantly has an impact on us; this is why it is so important that the United States citizens have an accurate description of issues and situations that are developing in foreign nations.

Scoring Explanation Sample 6: This response scored a 4/3/3.

Reading—4: This response demonstrates thorough comprehension of the source text and illustrates an understanding of the interrelation between the central idea and the important details of Goodman's article. The writer paraphrases Goodman's central claim (*news organizations should increase the amount of professional foreign news coverage provided to Americans*) and then accurately describes the statistical evidence that undergirds that claim (the decrease of foreign correspondents as well as the decrease of foreign bureaus). The writer goes on to discuss how Goodman ties the central claim to important details such as *the war in Iraq and Afghanistan* and the reliance on *social media for our world news*, thereby showing an understanding of these details. The response is free of errors of fact or interpretation. Overall, this response demonstrates advanced reading comprehension.

Analysis—3: This response demonstrates good understanding of the analytical task and offers an effective analysis of the source text. The writer effectively analyzes how Goodman uses various elements of his text to build a persuasive argument. For example, the writer discusses two statistical pieces of evidence at the beginning of Goodman's argument (*The author uses the numbers "307" and "234" . . . to illustrate . . . the decreasing amount of foreign correspondents*; *he throws out a number, "53 percent" to show how much foreign news has decreased*). The writer then discusses how Goodman shifts from *statistical evidence to historical evidence* to further his argument. Although the example then given is not historical but current, the writer competently evaluates the effect of this element of Goodman's text (*he starts off with the war in Iraq and Afghanistan which almost every reader would*

know about. . . . The author makes a personal connection with the audience).
Finally, the writer makes good analytical use of textual evidence, saying that
Goodman *compares "professional foreign correspondents" to "informational
filters" while he compares "citizen journalists" to "funnels."* The writer then
explains what using this comparison illustrates ("filters" present *facts*, while
"funnels" convey *anything and everything they could think of*) for Goodman's
audience. Overall, this response demonstrates proficient analysis.

Writing—3: The response demonstrates effective use and command of language and as a whole is cohesive. The response includes a precise central
claim (*Goodman uses many different types of evidence to support his claims
and persuade his audience that news organizations should increase the
amount of professional foreign news coverage*). The effective introduction
provides context for the analysis that follows and the conclusion effectively
encapsulates that analysis. In addition, the writer progresses smoothly from
idea to idea within and between paragraphs. Although the response displays
a consistently formal and objective tone and good control of the conventions
of standard written English, the writer sometimes relies on choppy sentence
structure and awkward or repetitive phrasing (*. . . the author offers many
statistical evidence. He throws out numbers; He shows that common people are
bias. They all have an opinion and share it*). Overall, this response demonstrates proficient writing.

STUDENT SAMPLE 7 — SCORES: 4/3/3

Media presentation from across the globe is vital to the upkeep and
maintenance of our society. How this information is obtained and
presented, if presented at all, is a different story, however. Goodman
builds an argument to persuade his audience that news organizations
should increase the amount of professional foreign news coverage to
the Americas through the presentation of statistics, connections to
social media as well as using specific diction to establish his argument.

Goodman uses statistics and facts, as presented by the AJR, in order to
show the loss of foreign correspondents reporting to the U.S. in order
to persuade his audience that there is a need for more professional
coverage. He begins his essay with the statistic saying that the level of
professional foreign correspondents dropped from 307 full-time
people to 234. This conveys that the number of people providing
legitimate and credible information to news services in the U.S. is

going down, thus alluding to the overall decrease in foreign Media. Goodman uses this to build his argument by envoking his audience to think that they may not be getting all the true media and facts presented. He uses the statistic of the shrinking correspondents to establish the fact that if this number is continually decreasing, there may be in the future a lack of unbiased media presentation, asking his audience to consider the importance of foreign news coverage.

Goodman connects to the vast implications of bias presented via social media to further build his argument. Reporters "know the power of Twitter, Facebook and other forms of social media" and, as they continue to rise in popularity in the distribution of media, are enabling the genesis of "citizen journalists who function largely as funnels . . . pouring white noise into the mix". Goodman further builds his argument here in order to persuade his audience by showing how with the rise of social media, more biased and superfluous information can be projected and wrongly viewed.

Goodman says this to evoke a concern within his audience about the truth in media. Blatantly put, Goodman accounts for that if you want unbiased foreign media people must turn from social media such as Twitter and Facebook and turn toward professional foreign media presentation. Presenting this idea of a possible falacy within social media greatly establishes his purpose as well as affirms his audience on weather they agree with him or not.

Also, Goodman uses specific diction to further establish his argument to persuade his audience. Goodman uses personal prounouns such as "we" to show that he personally is a part of the media presentation community, not only establishing his credibility on the subject, but also aiding in his persuasion of his audience by allowing them to think he is an expert in the field. Through his word choice, Goodman further establishes his argument by ascribing the need for more foreign reporter not as a burden but as a challenge. This adds in the persuasion of his audience by showing them that this is a real problem and that there are people rising up to it, and so should they.

Goodman's use of up-to-date references as well as connections to social media, use of statistics, and diction establish his argument of the need for more foreign reporters as well as persuading his audience of the need to do so.

Scoring Explanation Sample 7: This response scored a 4/3/3.

Reading—4: This response demonstrates thorough comprehension of the source text and shows an understanding of the relationship between the central idea and the important details in Goodman's piece. The writer includes the central claim of Goodman's text (*news organizations should increase the amount of professional foreign news coverage to the Americas*) and even paraphrases the claim in broader terms (*Media presentation from across the globe is vital to the upkeep and maintenance of our society*). The writer also exhibits an understanding of the details in Goodman's text (*He begins his essay with the statistic saying that the level of professional foreign correspondents dropped from 307 full-time people to 234; if you want unbiased foreign media people must turn from social media such as Twitter and Facebook and turn toward professional foreign media presentation*). The response is also free of errors of fact or interpretation. Overall, this response demonstrates advanced reading comprehension.

Analysis—3: This response demonstrates good understanding of the analytical task by offering an effective analysis of the source text. Focusing on the most relevant features of Goodman's argument, the writer thoroughly discusses, for example, the use of Goodman's opening statistic (the drop from 307 full-time foreign correspondents to 234), how it *conveys that the number of people providing legitimate and credible information to news services . . . is going down*, and how, therefore, *Goodman [is] . . . envoking his audience to think that they may not be getting all the true . . . facts*. The writer then follows up the point by saying that Goodman is *asking his audience to consider the importance of foreign news coverage*. The writer also competently selects relevant textual evidence from Goodman's argument about the dangers of social media, citing the evocative quotation *"citizen journalists who function largely as funnels . . . pouring white noise into the mix."* Additionally, the writer analyzes the diction in Goodman's text by discussing the author's deliberate choice of *personal pronouns such as "we"* to establish *credibility on the subject*. Overall, this response demonstrates proficient analysis.

Writing—3: This response demonstrates cohesion as well as effective use and command of language. The response includes a precise central claim (*Goodman builds an argument to persuade his audience that news organizations should increase the amount of professional foreign news coverage to the Americas through the presentation of statistics, connections to social media as well as using specific diction to establish his argument*). The focused introduction establishes context for the writer's analysis and provides the framework for the response's organizational structure. The writer then follows that framework faithfully in the body of the response, progressing clearly from idea to idea. The response displays variety in sentence structure and some precise word choice (*vital to the upkeep and maintenance of our society, vast implications of bias, superfluous information*), although the writer sometimes uses infelicitous phrasing and vocabulary (*envoking his audience to think*; *a possible falacy within social media greatly establishes his purpose*). Overall, this response demonstrates proficient writing.

Sample Passage 2:

As you read the passage below, consider how Adam B. Summers uses

- evidence, such as facts or examples, to support claims.

- reasoning to develop ideas and to connect claims and evidence.

- stylistic or persuasive elements, such as word choice or appeals to emotion, to add power to the ideas expressed.

Adapted from Adam B. Summers, "Bag Ban Bad for Freedom and Environment." ©2013 by The San Diego Union-Tribune, LLC. Originally published June 13, 2013.

1 Californians dodged yet another nanny-state regulation recently when the state Senate narrowly voted down a bill to ban plastic bags statewide, but the reprieve might only be temporary. Not content to tell us how much our toilets can flush or what type of light bulb to use to brighten our homes, some politicians and environmentalists are now focused on deciding for us what kind of container we can use to carry our groceries.

2 The bill . . . would have prohibited grocery stores and convenience stores with at least $2 million in gross annual sales and 10,000 square feet of retail space from providing single-use plastic or paper bags, although stores would have been allowed to sell recycled paper bags for an unspecified amount. The bill fell just three votes short of passage in the Senate . . . and Sen. Alex Padilla, D-Los Angeles, who sponsored the measure, has indicated that he would like to bring it up again, so expect this fight to be recycled rather than trashed.

3 While public debate over plastic bag bans often devolves into emotional pleas to save the planet or preserve marine life (and, believe me, I love sea turtles as much as the next guy), a little reason and perspective is in order.

4   According to the U.S. Environmental Protection Agency, plastic bags, sacks, and wraps of all kinds (not just grocery bags) make up only about 1.6 percent of all municipal solid waste materials. High-density polyethylene (HDPE) bags, which are the most common kind of plastic grocery bags, make up just 0.3 percent of this total.

5   The claims that plastic bags are worse for the environment than paper bags or cotton reusable bags are dubious at best. In fact, compared to paper bags, plastic grocery bags produce fewer greenhouse gas emissions, require 70 percent less energy to make, generate 80 percent less waste, and utilize less than 4 percent of the amount of water needed to manufacture them. This makes sense because plastic bags are lighter and take up less space than paper bags.

6   Reusable bags come with their own set of problems. They, too, have a larger carbon footprint than plastic bags. Even more disconcerting are the findings of several studies that plastic bag bans lead to increased health problems due to food contamination from bacteria that remain in the reusable bags. A November 2012 statistical analysis by University of Pennsylvania law professor Jonathan Klick and George Mason University law professor and economist Joshua D. Wright found that San Francisco's plastic bag ban in 2007 resulted in a subsequent spike in hospital emergency room visits due to E. coli, salmonella, and campylobacter-related intestinal infectious diseases. The authors conclude that the ban even accounts for several additional deaths in the city each year from such infections.

7   The description of plastic grocery bags as "single-use" bags is another misnomer. The vast majority of people use them more than once, whether for lining trash bins or picking up after their dogs. (And still other bags are recycled.) Since banning plastic bags also means preventing their additional uses as trash bags and pooper scoopers, one unintended consequence of the plastic bag ban would likely be an increase in plastic bag purchases for these other purposes. This is just what happened in Ireland in 2002 when a 15 Euro cent ($0.20) tax imposed on plastic shopping bags led to a 77 percent increase in the sale of plastic trash can liner bags.

8   And then there are the economic costs. The plastic bag ban would threaten the roughly 2,000 California jobs in the plastic bag manufacturing and recycling industry, although, as noted in the Irish example above, they might be able to weather the storm if they can successfully switch to producing other types of plastic bags. In addition, taxpayers will have to pony up for the added bureaucracy, and the higher regulatory costs foisted upon bag manufacturers and retailers will ultimately be borne by consumers in the form of price increases.

9   Notwithstanding the aforementioned reasons why plastic bags are not, in fact, evil incarnate, environmentalists have every right to try to convince people to adopt certain beliefs or lifestyles, but they do not have the right to use government force to compel people to live the way they think best. In a free society, we are able to live our lives as we please, so long as we do not infringe upon the rights of others. That includes the right to make such fundamental decisions as "Paper or plastic?"

Write an essay in which you explain how Adam B. Summers builds an argument to persuade his audience that plastic shopping bags should not be banned. In your essay, analyze how Summers uses one or more of the features listed in the box above (or features of your own choice) to strengthen the logic and persuasiveness of his argument. Be sure that your analysis focuses on the most relevant features of the passage.

Your essay should not explain whether you agree with Summers's claims, but rather explain how Summers builds an argument to persuade his audience.

Sample Student Essays:

STUDENT SAMPLE 1 — SCORES: 2/1/1

Adams B. Summers argues what the damages of a proposed plastic bag ban would do if the legislation gets passed. Summers presents his argument well, and his use of fact/examples, reasoning to devolope ideas, and persuasive word choice build his argument. He uses examples/facts, such as plastic bags only make up 1.6 percent of all solid waste. His excellent word choice that appeals to your mind such as him saying the politician hopes to bring up the bill again to essentially "recycle rather than trash it". He uses reasoning that makes sense to a reader stating how many jobs may be potentially lost due to the bill and how much waste is really caused by plastic bags v. paper.

Scoring Explanation Sample 1: This response scored a 2/1/1.

Reading—2: This response demonstrates some comprehension of Summers's text. The writer indicates an understanding of the main idea of Summers's argument (*Summers argues what the damages of a proposed plastic bag ban would do if the legislation gets passed*). The writer also selects some important details from the text (*plastic bags only make up 1.6 percent of all solid waste*; *many jobs may be potentially lost due to the bill*). However, the writer does not expand on the significance of these details in relation to the main ideas of Summers's text. The response makes limited and haphazard use of textual evidence with little or no interpretation. Overall, this response demonstrates partially successful reading comprehension.

Analysis—1: This response demonstrates little understanding of the analytical task. Although the writer identifies some argumentative elements in Summers's text (*his use of fact/examples, reasoning to devolope ideas, and persuasive word* *choice*), the writer does not explain how these elements build Summers's argument. Instead, the writer only identifies these aspects of the text and names an example of each, with no further analysis (*He uses examples/facts, such as plastic bags only make up 1.6 percent of all solid waste*). There are two moments in which the writer attempts to analyze Summers's use of word choice and reasoning (*His excellent word choice that appeals to your mind* and *He uses reasoning that makes sense to a reader*). There is not enough textual evidence given to support these claims, however. For example, the writer does not analyze Summers's use of specific words and instead falls back into summary of the passage. Overall, this response demonstrates inadequate analysis.

Writing—1: This response demonstrates little cohesion and limited skill in the use of language. The response is only one brief paragraph and lacks a recognizable introduction and conclusion. Although there is a central claim, taken directly from the prompt (*Summers presents his argument well, and his use of fact/examples, reasoning to devolope ideas, and persuasive word choice build his argument*), there is no discernible progression of ideas in the response. Furthermore, sentence structures are repetitive. Due to the brief nature of the response, there is not enough evidence of writing ability to merit a score higher than 1. Overall, this response demonstrates inadequate writing.

STUDENT SAMPLE 2 — SCORES: 3/1/2

Adam B. Summers brings up several good points as to why plastic shoping bags should not be banned. He explains how the EPA says all plastic bags only make up 1.6 percent of all waste, and plastic shoping bags only contribute 0.3 percent to all the waste. The bags hardly make up any waste and require less energy to make compared to paper or cotton bags. Plastic bags produce fewer greenhouse gasses, 80 percent less waste and less water to make them over paper or cotton reusable bags. Reusable bags also have a higher risk of giving a consumer food poising because of bacteria left in them and then the bags are used again.

Plastic bags are also called "single use" bags, but that is not true because people re-use them for garabge bags. By cutting of plastic shoping bags people would by more garabge bags wich are plastic so it would defeat the purpose. eliminating plastic bags would also cause the people who make them and dispose them lose their jobs too. Enviornmentalist can try to convince people paper is better than plastic but people should also look at it from the other prespective, and choose, "Paper or Plastic?".

Scoring Explanation Sample 2: This response scored a 3/1/2.

Reading—3: This response demonstrates effective comprehension of Summers's text. The writer provides appropriate textual evidence (in this case, paraphrases) to articulate both the central idea (*plastic shoping bags should not be banned*) and important details from the passage (*all plastic bags only make up 1.6 percent of all waste, and plastic shoping bags only contribute 0.3 percent to all the waste; Plastic bags produce fewer greenhouse gasses, 80 percent less waste and less water to make them over paper or cotton reusable bags*). The writer also demonstrates a proficient understanding of the entirety of Summers's text by incorporating details from various points throughout Summers's argument (*Plastic bags are also called "single use" bags, but that is not true because people re-use them for garbge bags; eliminating plastic bags would also cause the people who make them and dispose them lose their jobs too*). The response, which is essentially summary, is free of substantive errors of fact and interpretation. Overall, this response demonstrates proficient reading comprehension.

Analysis—1: This response demonstrates no understanding of the analytic task, as it is exclusively summary and offers no discernible analysis of Summers's text. The writer fails to identify aspects of evidence, reasoning, or stylistic and persuasive elements that Summers uses to build his argument and instead only provides a general statement on the quality of the passage (*Adam B. Summers brings up several good points as to why plastic shoping bags should not be banned*). Overall, this response demonstrates inadequate analysis.

Writing—2: This response demonstrates limited cohesion and writing skill. The response includes an ineffective introduction and conclusion based on the brief, general central claim that opens the response (*Adam B. Summers brings up several good points as to why plastic shoping bags should not be banned*) and the concluding sentence of the response (*Enviornmentalist can try to convince people paper is better than plastic but people should also look at it from the other prespective, and choose, "Paper or Plastic?"*). There is no real organization of ideas within paragraphs, and there are no transitions between the two paragraphs that indicate how the ideas in one relate to the other. Although there is some limited progression of ideas over the course of the response, there is little progression of ideas within paragraphs. There are numerous errors that detract from the quality of writing, and the response at times exhibits limited control of language and vague word choice (*By cutting of plastic shoping bags people would by more garabge bags wich are plastic so it would defeat the purpose*). Overall, this response demonstrates partially successful writing.

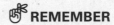 **REMEMBER**

Your response on the Essay should not simply be a summary of the argument presented in the passage. A critical part of your task is to analyze how the author builds an argument using evidence, reasoning, and stylistic or persuasive elements.

STUDENT SAMPLE 3 — SCORES: 3/2/2

In Adam B Summers' essay he gives valid reasons why plastic bags should not be banned. His essay is persuasive in many ways such as focusing on the effect on the earth and also job cutting. He also gives alternative ways to use a plastic bag. Summers gives examples on how banning plastic bags can lead to worse human damage.

Summers states that a plastic bag is easy to make without using much of anything. Knowing that making a plastic bag takes up to 70% more energy and can also help our earth because it doesn't produce green house gases. Saying this part persuades the earth lovers and it persuades them to side with the no bag ban because it's not as harmful as the reusible bags.

Reusible bags are more harmful than anyone could think and when Summers put in the facts that people die from food born illnesses it catches the doctors and people who care about the well being of others his essay persuades them to not only use the plastic bags but to use cation when using reusible bags because of the illnesses and deaths.

There are many ways to use a plastic bag not just for groceries and when Adam Summers states this it focuses on the renew and reusers where can use plastic bags in the home and daily life. Also being a cheaper alternative. Summers states that if the banning of plastic bags will cost the jobs of 2000 people which to the companies and workers this is a valid argument if they want to keep their jobs.

Summers provides multiple ways to persuade some one and any one with different beliefs. This build many persusive arguments and cause and effects fact based conclusions.

Scoring Explanation Sample 3: This response scored a 3/2/2.

Reading—3: This response demonstrates effective comprehension of Summers's text. The writer accurately paraphrases the central idea (*plastic bags should not be banned*) and important details from the passage — for instance, the environmental impacts of plastic vs. reusable bags (*Knowing that making a plastic bag takes up to 70% more energy and can also help our earth because it doesn't produce green house gases*) and the impact of the bag ban on jobs (*Summers states that if the banning of plastic bags will cost the jobs of 2000 people*). The writer summarizes all of the major points in Summers's argument with no substantive errors of fact or interpretation. Overall, this response demonstrates proficient reading comprehension.

Analysis—2: This response offers a limited analysis of Summers's text, indicating only partial understanding of the analytical task. Although the writer attempts to explain how Summers's use of evidence builds his argument, the writer only asserts the importance of this evidence and its effect on the audience. For example, the fact that plastic bags take 70 percent less energy to make *persuades the earth lovers . . . to side with the no bag ban because it's not as harmful as the reusible bags*. The writer then asserts that this evidence helps build Summers's argument but does not explain how or why. This pattern of assertion without explanation continues in the subsequent paragraph about the health consequences of reusable bags (*when Summers put in the facts that people die from food born illnesses it catches the doctors and people who care about the well being of others . . .* [and] *persuades them to not only use the plastic bags but to use cation when using reusible bags*) and in the paragraph about job cuts (*to the companies and workers this is a valid argument if they want to keep their jobs*). Overall, the response demonstrates partially successful analysis.

Writing—2: This response demonstrates limited cohesion and writing skill. The response does contain a central claim (Summers *gives valid reasons why plastic bags should not be banned*). It also contains an introduction and conclusion; however, they are mostly ineffective due to imprecise word choice (*Summers provides multiple ways to persuade some one and any one with different beliefs. This build many persusive arguments and cause and effects fact based conclusions*). Although each body paragraph is loosely centered on one of three aspects of Summers's argument (ecological, health, and unemployment consequences of the plastic bag ban), there is limited variety in sentence structures and vague word choice throughout the response (*Summers gives examples on how banning plastic bags can lead to worse human damage; when Adam Summers states this it focuses on the renew and reusers where can use plastic bags in the home and daily life. Also being a cheaper alternative*). Language and writing errors, such as syntactically awkward sentences, run-on sentences, and sentence fragments, detract from the quality of writing and impede understanding. Overall, this response demonstrates partially successful writing.

STUDENT SAMPLE 4 — SCORES: 3/3/3

The style and features an author use can help persuade the audience if clearly used. Adam B. Summers in the essay "Bag ban bad for freedom and environment" uses factual evidence, word choice, and emotion to build his argument. In doing this, Summers successfully persuades his audience into believing "Paper or Plastic" is a personal right.

When using factual evidence, Summers further persuades his reader. Readers are often attracted to facts because they are hard evidence to proving a point. Summers touches upon how plastic bag waste makes up only 0.3 percent out of the 1.6 percent of all munciple solid waste products. By providing this fact Summers shows the low numbered statistics which persuade the reader. The reader sees the small numbers and is immediately taking the authors side. Another use of factual evidence is when Summers discusses Ireland's problem since they've banned the use of plastic bags. By adding in the effects this had on another country, the audience realizes the same situation could happen in California, causing the reader to further his mind to Summer's ideas.

The word choice Summers uses helps lure his readers into his argument. In the first paragraph, Summers uses words such as "dodged", "narrowly", and "down". The usage of words makes the reader feel as if he is in the actual voting process of the bill, taking the rocky road in state government only to get voted down. From the start, Summers makes the audience feel involved which intrigues the reader further. In the second to last paragraph, Summers plays with the phrases "weather the storm" and "pony up" to represent the possibilities to come if a bill banning plastic bags is passed. By telling the reader to "get ready", he puts a negative feeling to the future of the bill and persuades the reader into thinking that the future may not be something they like.

Summers also adds in personal emotion to make the reader feel connected to the author. He writes "I love sea turtles as much as the next guy" to show that he is human too and cares about nature. The claim would touch many readers who are in the same position as Summers;

they love nature but think the banning of plastic bags is unreasonable. Summers connects to all readers in his audience when he further helps [unfinished]

Student Sample 4: This response scored a 3/3/3.

Reading—3: This response demonstrates effective comprehension of the source text by exhibiting proficient understanding of both the central idea and important details in Summers's text. The writer accurately paraphrases the central idea of the passage (*Summers successfully persuades his audience into believing "Paper or Plastic" is a personal right*). The writer also both paraphrases and directly quotes important details from the text (*Summers plays with the phrases "weather the storm" and "pony up" to represent the possibilities to come if a bill banning plastic bags is passed; Summers touches upon how plastic bag waste makes up only 0.3 percent out of the 1.6 percent of all munciple solid waste products*). Although the response is incomplete, as it ends midsentence, there are enough details provided from the text to indicate that the writer adequately understands the entirety of Summers's argument. The response is also free of substantive errors of fact and interpretation. Overall, this response demonstrates proficient reading comprehension.

Analysis—3: This response offers an effective analysis of Summers's argument and demonstrates proficient understanding of the analytical task. The writer identifies three persuasive elements—*factual evidence, word choice, and emotion*—and competently evaluates how these aspects of Summers's text contribute to building his argument. Moreover, the writer explains, with sufficient support, what effects these persuasive elements have on Summers's audience. One example of this type of analysis occurs in the paragraph that analyzes Summers's use of factual evidence, particularly *Ireland's problem since they've banned the use of plastic bags. By adding in the effects this had on another country, the audience realizes the same situation could happen in California, causing the reader to further his mind to Summer's ideas.* Effective analysis continues in the paragraph that analyzes Summers's word choice (*By telling the reader to "get ready", he puts a negative feeling to the future of the bill and persuades the reader into thinking that the future may not be something they like*). Although these moments of analysis are effective, the response lacks the thoroughness and insight seen in responses scoring higher. Overall, this response demonstrates proficient analysis.

Writing—3: The response is mostly cohesive and demonstrates effective use and control of language. The introduction is brief but effectively provides a clear central claim (*Adam B. Summers in the essay "Bag ban bad for freedom and environment" uses factual evidence, word choice, and emotion to build* *his argument*). The rest of the response is organized according to this three-pronged structure, with each body paragraph remaining on topic. A clear progression of ideas is demonstrated both within paragraphs and throughout the response. The writer integrates quotations and examples from the source text to connect ideas and paragraphs logically. There is a variety of sentence structures (*He writes "I love sea turtles as much as the next guy" to show that he is human too and cares about nature. The claim would touch many readers who are in the same position as Summers; they love nature but think the banning of plastic bags is unreasonable*). There also are some examples of precise word choice (*helps lure his readers into his argument; taking the rocky road in state government only to get voted down; makes the audience feel involved which intrigues the reader further*). Although the response has no conclusion, this does not preclude the response from demonstrating proficient writing overall.

STUDENT SAMPLE 5 — SCORES: 3/3/4

In the wake of environmental concerns in the United States, a bill in California which would ban plastic bags for groceries failed to make it through the state Senate by a small margin. In his article "Bag ban bad for freedom and environment" (2013), Adam Summers asserts that the plastic bag ban would be harmful for consumers and the environment. He conveys this through citing statistics, appealing to the audience's emotions and sense of self-interests, and utilizing sarcastic diction. The intended audience for this article is primarily readers who support the proposed bag ban and intend to help it pass.

The author's statistics cited throughout the article reinforce his argument and provide a solid base. In the fourth paragraph he mentions the most common plastic grocery bags, which "make up just 0.3 percent of solid municipal waste materials. The author also cites the "77 percent increase in the sale of plastic trash can liner bags" as a result of a similar ban in Ireland. These statistics appeal to the reader's logic and ensure that they can follow a logical path to support the author and oppose the ban. The statistics provide solid evidence that are enhanced by the numbers and cannot be easily argued against.

The author's patriotic asides in the first and final paragraphs appeal to the audience's emotions and self-interests. In the first paragraph, the author talks of the rights the government has impeded and talks of a regulation of "what kind of container we can use to carry our groceries." In the final paragraph, the author talks of the fundamental rights to decide "paper or plastic." This causes the readers to feel violated by the government and want to look out for his rights. When the regulations start to harm the individuals themselves, then they are more likely to take measures to oppose the bill.

The author's sarcastic tone throughout the article conveys the conception that those people supporting this bill are misinformed and incorrect. In the sixth paragraph, the author says "The claims that plastic bags are worse for the environment than paper bags or cotton reusable bags are dubious at best." He also leads the reader to infer that supporters of the bill believe plastic bags are "evil incarnate" and "use government force to compel people to live the way they think best." In the first paragraph, the author talks of how "Californians dodged yet another nanny-state regulation." This sarcastic tone causes the audience to lost faith in these Environmentalists. It also causes the reader to question the motives of the bill and its supporters.

Through citing statistics, appealing to self interest and emotions, and utilizing sarcastic diction, Adam Summers conveys his beliefs that California should not pass a law banning plastic grocery bags.

Scoring Explanation Sample 5: This response scored a 3/3/4.

Reading—3: This response demonstrates effective comprehension of the source text, with the writer showing an understanding of both the central idea (*the plastic bag ban would be harmful for consumers and the environment*) and important details of the passage (*the most common plastic grocery bags, which "make up just 0.3 percent" of solid municipal waste; government . . . regulation of "what kind of container we can use to carry our groceries"*). Throughout the response, the writer conveys an understanding of the text with appropriate use of both quotations and paraphrases. There are also no errors of fact or interpretation. Overall, this response demonstrates proficient reading comprehension.

Analysis—3: This response demonstrates an understanding of the analytical task by offering an effective analysis of the source text. The writer centers the analysis on how Summers conveys his argument through *citing statistics, appealing to the audience's emotions and sense of self-interest, and utilizing sarcastic diction*. In each of these areas, the writer competently discusses the effect of Summers's argumentative strategies. For example, in the first body paragraph, the writer cites some of the statistical evidence in the source text and points out that *these statistics appeal to the reader's logic and ensure that they can follow a logical path to support the author and oppose the ban*. Further, the writer states that the statistics *cannot be easily argued against*. The analysis continues in the second body paragraph, in which the writer evaluates Summers's *patriotic asides* and the fact that they cause the reader to *feel violated by the government and want to look out for his rights*. The response is consistently focused on analyzing the effect of various argumentative strategies on the audience, and the writer chooses relevant support for the analysis. Overall, this response demonstrates proficient analysis.

Writing—4: This response demonstrates a highly effective use of language in this cohesive essay. The body paragraphs closely follow the central claim (*Adam Summers asserts that the plastic bag ban would be harmful . . . through citing statistics, appealing to the audience's emotions and sense of self-interests, and utilizing sarcastic diction*) presented in the introduction. There are some slight organizational mistakes that lead to a somewhat clumsy progression of ideas. For example, the last sentence of the introductory paragraph, although informative, does not enhance the introduction in any way or provide a smooth segue into the following paragraphs. However, these organizational mistakes are balanced by a consistent variety of sentence structures and precise word choice (*wake of environmental concerns, take measures to oppose the bill*) and language errors do not impede understanding. Overall, this response demonstrates advanced writing.

STUDENT SAMPLE 6 — SCORES: 4/4/4

In Adam B. Summers' "Bag ban bad for freedom and environment" editorial for the San Diego Union-Tribune, he argues against the possible laws hindering Californians from using plastic bags at grocery stores. He believes they would do more harm than good, and that "a little reason and perspective is in order." By the end of this piece the reader will likely find themselves nodding in agreement with what Summers has to say, and this isn't just because he's right. Summers, like any good writer, employs tactical reasoning and persuasive devices to plead with the audience to take his side. In this article, he demonstrates many such devices.

"Plastic bags . . . make up only about 1.6 percent of all municipal solid waste materials," Summers ventures, his first utilization of a cold, hard fact. The truth in the numbers is undeniable, and he cites his sources promptly, making the statement that much more authentic. Knowledge is often viewed as power, and with information as direct as a statistic, Summers is handing that power to the reader – the power to agree with him. Not only does Summers spread the facts with numbers, he also does so with trends. He talks about the price increase in Ireland, and the documented health hazards of reusable bags. He uses the truth, backed by reliable sources, to infiltrate the readers' independent mind. His thoroughness in this regard carefully builds his argument against this piece of legislation, and this is just one of the many ways he spreads his opposition.

Additionally, Summers appeals to the ethnical and emotional side of individuals. With key phrases like "taxpayers will have to pony up" and "borne by consumers," Summers activates the nature of a human to act in their own self-interest. While one might view this as selfish, Summers reassures the reader that they are not alone in feeling this way, further contributing to his argument. With his statement that he "love[s] sea turtles as much as the next guy," Summers adds acceptance to those who don't care to act with regard for the environment. By putting himself beside the reader as a typical consumer, he equals them, and makes himself more likeable in the process. Appealing to environmentalists, too, Summers qualifies that they "have every right to try to convince people to adopt certain beliefs or lifestyles, but they do not have the right to use government force . . ." A statement such as this is an attempt to get readers of either persuasion on his side, and his ingenius qualification only adds to the strength of his argument. An article focusing on the choice between "paper or plastic," and how that choice might be taken away certainly seems fairly standard, but by adjusting his diction (i.e. using well known phrases, selecting words with strong connotations), Summers creates something out of the ordinary. It is with word choice such as "recycled rather than trashed" that the author reveals the legislations intent to stir up a repeat bill. Because the issue at hand is one of waste and environmental protection, his humorous diction provides a link between he and the audience, revealing not only an opportunity to laugh, but also reinforcement of the concept that Summers is trustworthy and just like everyone else. Negative words with specifically poor connotations also aid Summers in his persuasive struggle. "Reprieve," "dubious," "bureaucracy," and "evil incarnate" all depict a disparaging tone of annoyance and anger, surely helping Summers to spread his message.

It is through many rhetorical devices that Summers sells his argument. Powerful diction, qualification, ethos, pathos, logos, and informative facts all contribute to an exceptionally well-written argument. It is his utilization of these practices and more that make this article worthy of recognition. Once one reads the piece, they'll be nodding along in accordance with Summers, and it isn't for no reason.

Scoring Explanation Sample 6: This response scored a 4/4/4.

Reading—4: This response demonstrates thorough comprehension of the source text. The writer provides a brief summary of Summers's main point in the introductory paragraph (*he argues against the possible laws hindering Californians from using plastic bags at grocery stores*) and throughout the response uses a mixture of direct quotations and paraphrases to show an understanding of the central idea and important details from the source text interrelate (*He talks about the price increase in Ireland, and the documented health hazards of reusable bags; the legislations intent to stir up a repeat bill*). Further, the writer demonstrates an understanding of how the central idea and important details interrelate by consistently relating details to the main argument of the source text. The response is free from errors of fact or interpretation. Overall, this response demonstrates advanced reading comprehension.

Analysis—4: This response demonstrates a sophisticated understanding of the analytical task by offering an insightful analysis of Summers's employment of *tactical reasoning and persuasive devices to plead with the audience to take his side*. The writer puts forth a thorough evaluation of Summers's use of evidence, reasoning, and stylistic and persuasive elements by continually analyzing even the smallest features of Summers's piece. For example, when citing a fact that Summers provides (*"Plastic bags . . . make up only about 1.6 percent of all municipal solid waste materials"*), the writer focuses on *the truth in the numbers* as well as Summers's deliberate choice to share the fact's source and the effect doing so has on Summers's argument. The writer continues the analysis by broadening the focus to a brief but sophisticated discussion of knowledge as power and the persuasive approach of *handing that power to the reader*. This type of well-considered evaluation continues throughout the response, during which the writer touches on Summers's appeals *to the ethical and emotional side of individuals* and Summers's use of diction to create *something out of the ordinary*. The response is focused on relevant and strategically chosen features of the source text in support of the writer's analysis. Overall, this essay demonstrates advanced analysis.

Writing—4: This response demonstrates highly effective command of language and cohesion. The response is organized around the writer's claim that readers *will likely find themselves nodding in agreement with what Summers has to say, and this isn't just because he's right* but also because of his use of *tactical reasoning and persuasive devices*. The response is highly organized and demonstrates a deliberate progression of ideas, with the writer seamlessly transitioning from point to point. Sentence structures are varied and often sophisticated (*While one might view this as selfish, Summers reassures the reader that they are not alone in feeling this way, further contributing to his argument*). Word choice is precise without tonal missteps (*tactical reasoning; his ingenius qualification only adds to the strength of his argument; disparaging tone of annoyance and anger*). The response shows a strong command of the conventions of standard written English and is virtually free of errors. Minor conventions errors (*Summers adds acceptance to those who don't care to act; and it isn't for no reason*) do not detract from the quality of the writing. Overall, this response demonstrates advanced writing ability.

STUDENT SAMPLE 7 — SCORES: 4/4/4

"Paper or plastic?" This is often a question we are asked at our weekly and/or bi-weekly trip to the supermarket to purchase groceries to keep our family fed. Adam B. Summers has created a highly plausible argument that may change your answer next time you go grocery

PRACTICE AT

🌱 khanacademy.org/sat

Your response doesn't have to be an exhaustive analysis of the passage. Focusing your essay on a few key points, with ample textual evidence and analysis, can yield a strong score.

shopping. He has developed valid claims that are backed up with crucial evidence and has been able to properly persuade the reader by appealing to logos and other rhetorical strategies.

Summers uses his words and research to reason with the reader and explain to them why plastic bags really are the correct choice. A vast majority of people are misled about all of the waste that plastic bags cause when Summers writes, ". . . plastic bags, sacks, and wraps of all kinds (not just grocery bags) make up only about 1.6 percent of all municipal solid waste materials." This number is definitely lower that we all assume, going into this passage, and we are left surprised. Using reusable bags is a solution that others have come up with to attempt to create less waste, however Summers delivers an appealing argument. ". . . plastic bag bans lead to increased health problems due to food contamination from bacteria that remain in the reusable bags." This excerpt creates another claim that leaves the reader wondering if reusable bags are really worth it. These past two claims are connected well because they both draw the reader back to the idea of using plastic bags. Another claim by Summers, ". . . one unintended consequence of the plastic bag would likely be an increase in plastic bag purchases for these other purposes." These "other purposes" can be for lining trash bins, picking up after your dog on a walk, collecting kitty litter, and many more things we use plastic bags for. When the author brings in all of these additional uses of the plastic bag, we see the significance of the plastic bag and how much money we save by reusing them. A final claim by Summers, "The plastic bag ban would threaten the roughly 2,000 California jobs in the plastic bag manufacturing and recycling industry . . ." Now the reader almost feels guilty because they do not want to take away jobs of others and the fact that some people even depend on shoppers using plastic bags. These two final claims are well connected because the author stressed the economic benefits of using plastic bags. Not only are these bags saving you money, but they also are keeping some people in work. These four ideas are successfully connected and convince the reader to use plastic bags over paper bags and other types of reusable bags.

Evidence is a key component of this passage and Summers is sure to include this when presenting us with key facts. He references important agencies such as the U.S. Environmental Protection Agency and includes a professor from the University of Pennsylvania, Jonathan Klick and a professor from George Mason University, Joshua D. Wright. The inclusion of this agency and these professors make the work of Summers credible and believable because us readers are confident of what we are being told is correct and true. Evidence he also uses are facts such as, ". . . plastic grocery bags produce fewer greenhouse gas emissions, require 70 percent less energy to make, generate 80 percent less waste." These facts back up Summers' claims that plastic bags are the better choice. Without evidence, his passage would not mean a thing to us readers and we would never be able to believe what he has said.

Persuasive elements are what make this passage successful. Summers has excellent ideas and credible evince, but his use of persuasion are what capture the reader. He appeals to logos when stating all of his claims about how using plastic bags can save you money and keep you from getting sick, but he also appeals to pathos because this passage described how plastic bags amount to less waste than most of us think and he wants to help us make the Earth a better place to live. Throwing examples at us, ". . . San Francisco's plastic bag ban in 2007 resulted in a subsequent spike in hospital emercgency room visits due to E. Coli, salmonella, . . ." persuade the reader as well. With rhetorical strategies and direct examples, Summers is clearly able to persuade the reader to choose plastic next time.

So what will you choose next time you're shopping for groceries with your family? Summers has made the choice obvious with his persuasive and effective passage. He has been able to develop several ideas and backed them up with evidence that us readers can trust. After reading this passage, there seems to be no other choice than plastic.

Scoring Explanation Sample 7: This response scored a 4/4/4.

Reading—4: This response demonstrates thorough comprehension of the source text. The writer shows an understanding of Summers's *highly plausible argument* and the important specifics that add detail to one of Summers's central claims: that *plastic bags really are the correct choice.* The writer accurately paraphrases ideas from Summers's text throughout the essay (*These "other purposes" can be for lining trash bins, picking up after your dog on a walk, collecting kitty litter, and many more things we use plastic bags for*), and the writer skillfully incorporates direct quotations within the response (*people are misled about all of the waste that plastic bags cause when Summers writes, ". . . plastic bags, sacks and wraps of all kinds"*). The writer also understands how the details in Summers's text interrelate to convey the main point of the piece (*valid claims that are backed up with crucial evidence; Summers uses his words and research to reason with the reader; These past two claims are connected well because they both draw the reader back to the idea; Summers has . . . credible evince, but his use of persuasion are what capture the reader*). The response is free from errors of fact or interpretation. Overall, this response demonstrates advanced reading comprehension.

Analysis—4: This response demonstrates a sophisticated understanding of the analytical task by offering an insightful analysis of the source text. Rather than relying on assertions as analysis, the writer thoroughly evaluates how Summers uses *words and research to reason with the reader,* how *evidence is a key component,* and how *persuasive elements . . . make this passage successful.* The writer is able to fully discuss each of these aspects of Summers's piece, using relevant examples from the source text as support for the writer's analysis. For example, the writer uses Summers's claim that *"The plastic bag ban would threaten the roughly 2,000 California jobs in the plastic bag manufacturing and recycling industry"* to discuss the guilt the writer perceives the reader feels in reaction to this claim. The writer also explains how Summers uses this claim in conjunction with discussion of alternate uses for plastic bags to stress *the economic benefits of using plastic bags.* The writer consistently focuses on the features of Summers's text that are most relevant and offers well-considered evaluations throughout the response. Overall, this response demonstrates advanced analysis.

Writing—4: This response demonstrates highly effective command of language and cohesion. Beginning with the skillful introduction, the writer constructs a response that demonstrates a deliberate and highly effective progression of ideas, starting with an examination of Summers's claims and evidence and ending with emphasis on the use of persuasive elements. This skillful control over organization occurs at the body paragraph level as well, as the writer connects pieces of evidence from different parts of the source text within each paragraph. The writer's word choice is precise (*a highly plausible argument, a key component, the inclusion of this agency*), and sentence structures are varied and sophisticated. This response demonstrates a strong command of written English and is virtually free of errors. Overall, this response demonstrates advanced writing.

PART 3

Math

Chapter 18

About the SAT Math Test

Focus on Math That Matters Most

A group of select mathematics skills and abilities contributes the most to readiness for a college education and career training. These skills and abilities are used extensively in a wide range of college majors and careers. The three areas of focus for math in the redesigned SAT are:

- Heart of Algebra

- Problem Solving and Data Analysis

- Passport to Advanced Math

Heart of Algebra focuses on linear equations and systems of linear equations that are found in many fields of study. These questions ask you to create equations that represent a situation and solve equations and systems of equations as well as to make connections between different representations of linear relationships.

Problem Solving and Data Analysis includes using ratios, percentages, and proportional reasoning to solve problems in real-world situations, including science, social science, and career contexts. It also includes describing relationships shown graphically and analyzing statistical data. This group of skills is really about being quantitatively literate and demonstrating a command of the math that resonates throughout college courses, career training programs, and everyday life.

These two areas of math provide a powerful foundation for the math you will do in the future.

Passport to Advanced Math is the third area of focus in the redesigned SAT Math Test, and once again, it is the math that is used in a wide variety of careers and college work. The problems in this area focus on the math you will need to pursue further study in a discipline such as science and for career opportunities in the STEM fields of science, technology, engineering, and math. The Passport to Advanced Math area requires familiarity with

REMEMBER

Questions on the SAT Math Test are distributed among these three topics with 19 Heart of Algebra questions, 17 Problem Solving and Data Analysis questions, and 16 Passport to Advanced Math questions. The remaining six questions test your understanding of additional topics in math such as area, volume, circles, triangles, and trigonometry.

more-complex equations or functions, which will prepare you for calculus and advanced courses in statistics. There is also a brief section on **Additional Topics in Math**, including geometry, trigonometry, radian measure, and the arithmetic of complex numbers.

The redesigned SAT Math Test also contains questions that focus on several other areas that are important for a wide range of college courses and careers. Some of these problems focus on key concepts from geometry, including applications of volume, surface area, area, and coordinate geometry; similarity, which is another instance of proportional reasoning; and properties of lines, angles, triangles and other polygons, and circles. There are also problems that focus on the fundamental ideas of trigonometry and radian measure, which are essential for study in STEM fields. Finally, there are problems involving the arithmetic of complex numbers, another concept needed for more-advanced study in math and the STEM fields.

Rigor

Throughout the redesigned SAT Math Test, questions require conceptual understanding, procedural skill and fluency, and application of mathematics in college and career contexts. These three aspects appear in relatively equal amounts on each SAT test.

Conceptual understanding and procedural skill and fluency are complementary skills. Together, they lead to a thorough understanding of mathematical ideas and methods for solving problems. Questions on the SAT Math portions test these skills in various ways because the ability to use mathematical ideas and methods flexibly is characteristic of an understanding of math that can be applied to a wide variety of settings.

An essential idea in the relationship between fluency and conceptual understanding is observing structure. Recognizing structure allows you to understand mathematical relationships in a coherent manner that allows you both to apply these relationships more widely and to extend these relationships in useful ways. Many of the examples and sample questions in the following chapters are more simply and deeply understood (and more quickly solved!) if you observe structure in the mathematics of the problem.

Problems Grounded in Real-World Contexts

The Math Test features multistep problems with applications in science, social science, career scenarios, and other real-life contexts. In some cases, you will be presented with a scenario and then asked several questions about it. You learn specific math skills in your math classes, and these skills are applied in your science and social studies classes. When you use your mathematical skills outside of the math classroom, you are preparing for the redesigned SAT.

The Makeup of the SAT Math Test

CALCULATOR AND NO-CALCULATOR PORTIONS

There are calculator and no-calculator portions on the SAT Math Test (as is also often true of Advanced Placement® assessments). A calculator is a tool, and the ability to determine when to use it is a skill that you are expected to have. In the calculator portion, many questions do not require a calculator and many questions can be completed faster by hand without using a calculator. In general, the questions in the calculator portion are more complex than those in the no-calculator portion. Questions in the no-calculator portion are intended to reward your ability to do problems efficiently and accurately.

You should bring a calculator to use on the math section of the SAT. A scientific or graphing calculator is recommended, and familiarity with your calculator may provide an advantage on some questions. Every question on the SAT can be solved without a calculator; however, strategically deciding when to use a calculator will reduce the time required to complete the test. Using a calculator can also help you avoid missing a question because of computation errors.

MULTIPLE-CHOICE AND GRIDDED-RESPONSE QUESTIONS

About 80% of the questions on the Math Test are multiple-choice. Each multiple-choice question consists of a question followed by four options. There is only one correct answer and there is no penalty for selecting an incorrect answer. (The pre–March 2016 SAT had a one-quarter-point penalty for an incorrect answer.) Therefore, you should provide an answer to every question on the test.

The other questions on the Math Test are gridded-response questions (also called student-produced response questions), and these questions make up about 20% of the test. The answer to each gridded-response question is a number (fraction, decimal, or positive integer) that you will enter on the answer sheet into a grid like the one shown on the next page. Like all questions on the SAT, there is no penalty for answering a gridded-response question incorrectly.

Examples of filled-in answer grids are shown on the next page. Note that you may also enter a fraction line or a decimal point. Further details on how to grid your answers are provided in Chapter 24.

REMEMBER

You are permitted to use a calculator on one portion of the SAT Math Test, so be sure to bring a calculator with you to the test. However, many questions don't require a calculator and can actually be solved more quickly without one, so use careful judgment in deciding when to use it.

PRACTICE AT

khanacademy.org/sat

Make sure that you're very familiar with and comfortable using the calculator you bring with you on test day. Practice using the calculator you'll use on the test throughout your test preparation.

PRACTICE AT

khanacademy.org/sat

We know we've stressed this many times already, but it's worth repeating: There is no penalty for selecting an incorrect answer on the SAT, so never leave a question blank! On questions that you're not sure how to solve, eliminate as many answer choices as you can, and then guess from among the remaining choices.

REMEMBER

On gridded-response questions, you must fill in the circles that correspond to your answer. You won't receive credit if you write your answer only in the boxes at the top of the grid.

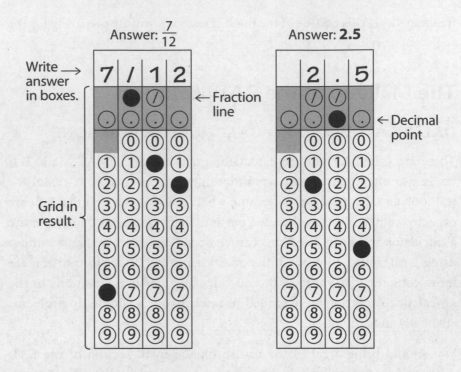

Answer: $\frac{7}{12}$

Write answer in boxes.

← Fraction line

Grid in result.

Answer: **2.5**

← Decimal point

PRACTICE AT

khanacademy.org/sat

Make sure to get lots of practice using the facts and formulas provided in the Reference section in the Math Test directions. Practicing with these facts and formulas will ensure you can use them accurately and efficiently.

MATHEMATICS REFERENCE INFORMATION

The Math Test includes the reference information shown below. You may find these facts and formulas helpful as you answer some of the test questions, but make sure you have plenty of practice with this information beforehand. To do well, you have to be comfortable working with these facts and formulas. If you have lots of practice using these facts and formulas before the test, you will be a lot more relaxed when you use them during the test.

REFERENCE

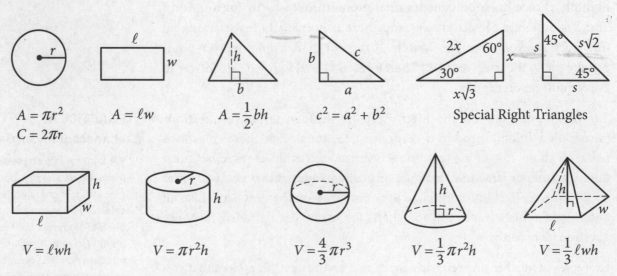

$A = \pi r^2$
$C = 2\pi r$

$A = \ell w$

$A = \frac{1}{2}bh$

$c^2 = a^2 + b^2$

Special Right Triangles

$V = \ell wh$

$V = \pi r^2 h$

$V = \frac{4}{3}\pi r^3$

$V = \frac{1}{3}\pi r^2 h$

$V = \frac{1}{3}\ell wh$

The number of degrees of arc in a circle is 360.

The number of radians of arc in a circle is 2π.

The sum of the measures in degrees of the angles of a triangle is 180.

Test Summary

The following table summarizes the key content dimensions of the SAT Math Test.

SAT Math Test Content Specifications

Time Allotted	80 minutes	
Calculator Portion (38 questions)	55 minutes	
No-Calculator Portion (20 questions)	25 minutes	

	Number	Percentage of Test
Total Questions	**58 questions**	**100%**
Multiple-Choice (MC, 4 options)	45 questions	78%
Student-Produced Response (SPR—grid-in)	13 questions	22%

Contribution of Questions to Subscores

Heart of Algebra	19 questions	33%

Analyzing and fluently solving linear equations and systems of linear equations

Creating linear equations and inequalities to represent relationships between quantities and to solve problems

Understanding and using the relationship between linear equations and inequalities and their graphs to solve problems

Problem Solving and Data Analysis	17 questions	29%

Creating and analyzing relationships using ratios, proportional relationships, percentages, and units

Representing and analyzing quantitative data

Finding and applying probabilities in context

Passport to Advanced Math	16 questions	28%

Identifying and creating equivalent algebraic expressions

Creating, analyzing, and fluently solving quadratic and other nonlinear equations

Creating, using, and graphing exponential, quadratic, and other nonlinear functions

PRACTICE AT

◖ khanacademy.org/sat

Take plenty of time to familiarize yourself with this table. Knowing exactly what the Math Test consists of, including the number of questions and time allotted as well as the distribution of question categories, will help you to feel confident and prepared on test day.

PRACTICE AT

🌱 **khanacademy.org/sat**

As you progress through your test practice, assess which math skills you're strongest in and which you have the greatest room for improvement in. Allocate your study time appropriately, and make use of the many resources available to you on the Khan Academy website (khanacademy.org/sat).

Additional Topics in Math*	6 questions	10%

Solving problems related to area and volume

Applying definitions and theorems related to lines, angles, triangles, and circles

Working with right triangles, the unit circle, and trigonometric functions

Contribution of Questions to Cross-Test Scores		
Analysis in Science	8 questions	14%
Analysis in History/Social Studies	8 questions	14%

*Questions under Additional Topics in Math contribute to the total Math Test score but do not contribute to a subscore within the Math Test.

As indicated in the content specifications previously, the Math Test has two portions. One is a 55-minute portion — 38 questions for which you are allowed to use a calculator to solve the problems. The other is a 25-minute portion — 20 questions for which you are not allowed to use a calculator. The blueprint for each portion is shown below.

Calculator Portion

	Number of Questions	% of Test
Total Questions	**38**	**100%**
Multiple-Choice (MC)	30	79%
Student-Produced Response (SPR—grid-in)	8	21%
Content Categories	**38**	**100%**
Heart of Algebra	11	29%
Problem Solving and Data Analysis	17	45%
Passport to Advanced Math	7	18%
Additional Topics in Math	3	8%
Time Allocated	**55 minutes**	

No-Calculator Portion

	Number of Questions	% of Test
Total Questions	20	100%
Multiple-Choice (MC)	15	75%
Student-Produced Response (SPR—grid-in)	5	25%
Content Categories	20	100%
Heart of Algebra	8	40%
Passport to Advanced Math	9	45%
Additional Topics in Math	3	15%
Time Allocated	**25 minutes**	

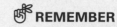

REMEMBER

Don't be intimidated by the fact that you aren't permitted to use a calculator on one of the SAT Math portions. Questions in the no-calculator portion are more conceptual in nature and don't require a calculator to be solved.

Chapter 19

Heart of Algebra

Heart of Algebra focuses on the mastery of linear equations, systems of linear equations, and linear functions. The ability to analyze and create linear equations, inequalities, and functions is essential for success in college and careers, as is the ability to solve linear equations and systems fluently. The questions in Heart of Algebra include both multiple-choice questions and student-produced response questions. On some questions, the use of a calculator is not permitted; on other questions, the use of a calculator is allowed.

The questions in Heart of Algebra vary significantly in form and appearance. They may be straightforward fluency exercises or pose challenges of strategy or understanding, such as interpreting the relationship between graphical and algebraic representations or solving as a process of reasoning. You will be required to demonstrate both procedural skill and a deep understanding of concepts.

Let's explore the content and skills assessed by Heart of Algebra questions.

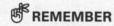 **REMEMBER**

The SAT Math Test requires you to demonstrate a deep understanding of several core algebra topics, namely linear equations, systems of linear equations, and linear functions. These topics are fundamental to the learning and work often required in college and career.

Linear Equations, Linear Inequalities, and Linear Functions in Context

When you use algebra to analyze and solve a problem in real life, a key step is to represent the context of the problem algebraically. To do this, you may need to define one or more variables that represent quantities in the context. Then you need to write one or more expressions, equations, inequalities, or functions that represent the relationships described in the context. For example, once you write an equation that represents the context, you solve the equation. Then you interpret the solution to the equation in terms of the context. Questions on the SAT Math Test may assess your ability to accomplish any or all of these steps.

EXAMPLE 1

In 2014, County X had 783 miles of paved roads. Starting in 2015, the county has been building 8 miles of new paved roads each year. At this rate, how many miles of paved road will County X have in 2030? (Assume that no paved roads go out of service.)

PRACTICE AT

khanacademy.org/sat

Many Heart of Algebra questions such as this one will require you to accomplish the following steps:

1. Define one or more variables that represent quantities in the question.

2. Write one or more equations, expressions, inequalities, or functions that represent the relationships described in the question.

3. Solve the equation, and interpret the solution in terms of what the question is asking.

Ample practice with each of these steps will help you develop your math skills and knowledge.

The first step in answering this question is to decide what variable or variables you need to define. The question is asking how the number of miles of paved road in County X depends on the year. This can be represented using n, the number of years after 2014. Then, since the question says that County X had 783 miles of paved road in 2014 and is building 8 miles of new paved roads each year, the expression $783 + 8n$ gives the number of miles of paved roads in County X in year n. The year 2030 is $2030 - 2014 = 16$ years after 2014; thus, the year 2030 corresponds to $n = 16$. Hence, to find the number of miles of paved roads in County X in 2030, substitute 16 for n in the expression $783 + 8n$, giving $783 + 8(16) = 783 + 128 = 911$. Therefore, at the given rate of building, County X will have 911 miles of paved roads in 2030.

There are different questions that can be asked about the same context.

EXAMPLE 2

In 2014, County X had 783 miles of paved roads. Starting in 2015, the county has been building 8 miles of new paved roads each year. At this rate, if n is the number of years after 2014, which of the following functions f gives the number of miles of paved road there will be in County X? (Assume that no paved roads go out of service.)

A) $f(n) = 8 + 783n$

B) $f(n) = 2{,}014 + 783n$

C) $f(n) = 783 + 8n$

D) $f(n) = 2{,}014 + 8n$

REMEMBER

There are several different ways you can be tested on the same underlying algebra concepts. Practicing a variety of questions, with different contexts, is a good way to ensure you'll be ready for the questions you'll come across on the SAT.

This question already defines the variable and asks you to create a function that describes the context. The discussion in Example 1 shows that the correct answer is choice C.

EXAMPLE 3

In 2014, County X had 783 miles of paved roads. Starting in 2015, the county has been building 8 miles of new paved roads each year. At this rate, in which year will County X first have at least 1,000 miles of paved roads? (Assume that no paved roads go out of service.)

In this question, you must solve an inequality. As in Example 1, let n be the number of years after 2014. Then the expression $783 + 8n$ gives the number of miles of paved roads in County X. The question is asking when there will first be at least 1,000 miles of paved roads in County X. This condition can be represented by the inequality $783 + 8n \geq 1,000$. To find the year in which there will first be at least 1,000 miles of paved roads, you solve this inequality for n. Subtracting 783 from each side of $783 + 8n \geq 1,000$ gives $8n \geq 217$. Then dividing each side of $8n \geq 217$ gives $n \geq 27.125$. Note that an important part of relating the inequality $783 + 8n \geq 1,000$ back to the context is to notice that n is counting calendar years and so it must be an integer. The least value of n that satisfies $783 + 8n \geq 1,000$ is 27.125, but the year $2014 + 27.125 = 2041.125$ does not make sense as an answer, and in 2041, there would be only $783 + 8(27) = 999$ miles of paved roads in the county. Therefore, the variable n needs to be rounded up to the next integer, and so the least possible value of n is 28. Therefore, the year that County X will first have at least 1,000 miles of paved roads is 28 years after 2014, or 2042.

In Example 1, once the variable n was defined, you needed to find an expression that represents the number of miles of paved road in terms of n. In other questions, creating the correct expression, equation, or function may require a more insightful understanding of the context.

PRACTICE AT

khanacademy.org/sat

Solving an equation or inequality is often only part of the problem-solving process. You must also interpret the solution in the context of the question, so be sure to remind yourself of the question's context and the meaning of the variables you solved for before selecting your answer.

EXAMPLE 4

To edit a manuscript, Miguel charges $50 for the first 2 hours and $20 per hour after the first 2 hours. Which of the following expresses the amount in dollars, C, Miguel charges if it takes him x hours to edit a manuscript, where $x > 2$?

A) $C = 20x$

B) $C = 20x + 10$

C) $C = 20x + 50$

D) $C = 20x + 90$

The question defines the variables C and x and asks you to express C in terms of x. To create the correct expression, you must note that since the $50 that Miguel charges pays for his first 2 hours of editing, he charges $20 per hour only *after* the first 2 hours. Thus, if it takes x hours for Miguel to edit a manuscript, he charges $50 for the first 2 hours and $20 per hour for the remaining time, which is $x - 2$ hours. Thus, his total charge, C, can be written as $C = 50 + 20(x - 2)$. This does not match any of the choices. But when the right-hand side of $C = 50 + 20(x - 2)$ is expanded, you get $C = 50 + 20x - 40$, or $C = 20x + 10$, which is choice B.

As with Examples 1 to 3, there are different questions that could be asked about this context. For example, you could be asked to find how long it took Miguel to edit a manuscript if he charged $370.

PRACTICE AT

khanacademy.org/sat

When the solution you arrive at doesn't match any of the answer choices, consider if expanding, simplifying, or rearranging your solution will cause it to match an answer choice. Often, this extra step is needed to arrive at the correct answer.

Absolute Value

Absolute value expressions, inequalities, and equations are included in Heart of Algebra. (Graphs of absolute value equations and functions are in Passport to Advanced Math.) One definition of absolute value is

$$|x| = \begin{cases} x, \text{ if } x \geq 0 \\ -x, \text{ if } x < 0 \end{cases}$$

The absolute value of any real number is nonnegative. An important consequence of this definition is that $|-x| = |x|$ for any real number x. Another important consequence of this definition is that if a and b are any two real numbers, then $|a - b|$ is equal to the distance between a and b on the number line.

EXAMPLE 5

> The stratosphere is the layer of the Earth's atmosphere that is more than 10 kilometers (km) and less than 50 km above the Earth's surface. Which of the following inequalities describes all possible heights x, in km, above the Earth's surface that are in the stratosphere?
>
> A) $|x + 10| < 50$
> B) $|x - 10| < 50$
> C) $|x + 30| < 20$
> D) $|x - 30| < 20$

The question states that the stratosphere is the layer of the Earth's atmosphere that is greater than 10 km and less than 50 km above the Earth's surface. Thus, the possible heights x, in km, above the Earth's surface that are in the stratosphere are given by the inequality $10 < x < 50$. To answer the question, you need to find an absolute value inequality that is equivalent to $10 < x < 50$.

The inequality $10 < x < 50$ describes the open interval $(10, 50)$. To describe an interval with an absolute value inequality, use the midpoint and the size of the interval. The midpoint of $(10, 50)$ is $\dfrac{10 + 50}{2} = 30$. Then observe that the interval $(10, 50)$ consists of all points that are within 20 of the midpoint. That is, $(10, 50)$ consists of x, whose distance from 30 on the number line is less than 20. The distance between x and 30 on the number line is $|x - 30|$. Therefore, the possible values of x are described by $|x - 30| < 20$, which is choice D.

Systems of Linear Equations and Inequalities in Context

You may need to define more than one variable and create more than one equation or inequality to represent a context and answer a question. There are questions on the SAT Math Test that require you to create and solve a system of equations or create a system of inequalities.

EXAMPLE 6

> Maizah bought a pair of pants and a briefcase at a department store. The sum of the prices before sales tax was $130.00. There was no sales tax on the pants and a 9% sales tax on the briefcase. The total Maizah paid, including the sales tax, was $136.75. What was the price, in dollars, of the pants?

To answer the question, you first need to define the variables. The question discusses the prices of a pair of pants and a briefcase and asks you to find the price of the pants. So it is appropriate to let P be the price of the pants, in dollars, and to let B be the price of the briefcase, in dollars. Since the sum of the prices before sales tax was $130.00, the equation $P + B = 130$ is true. A sales tax of 9% was added to the price of the briefcase. Since 9% is equal to 0.09, the price of the briefcase with tax was $B + 0.09B = 1.09B$. There was no sales tax on the pants, and the total Maizah paid, including tax, was $136.75, so the equation $P + 1.09B = 136.75$ holds.

Now, you need to solve the system

$$P + B = 130$$
$$P + 1.09B = 136.75$$

Subtracting the sides of the first equation from the corresponding sides of the second equation gives you $(P + 1.09B) - (P + B) = 136.75 - 130$, which simplifies to $0.09B = 6.75$. Now you can divide each side of $0.09B = 6.75$ by 0.09. This gives you $B = \dfrac{6.75}{0.09} = 75$. This is the value of B, the price, in dollars, of the briefcase. The question asks for the price, in dollars, of the pants, which is P. You can substitute 75 for B in the equation $P + B = 130$, which gives you $P + 75 = 130$, or $P = 130 - 75 = 55$, so the pants cost $55.

(Note that this example has no choices. It is a student-produced response question. On the SAT, you would grid your answer in the spaces provided on the answer sheet.)

PRACTICE AT

khanacademy.org/sat

You can use either of two approaches — combination or substitution — when solving a system of linear equations. One may get you to the answer more quickly than the other, depending on the equations you're working with and what you're solving for. Practice using both to give you greater flexibility on test day.

REMEMBER

While this question may seem complex, as it involves numerous steps, solving it requires a strong understanding of the same underlying principles outlined above: defining variables, creating equations to represent relationships, solving equations, and interpreting the solution.

EXAMPLE 7

Each morning, John jogs at 6 miles per hour and rides a bike at 12 miles per hour. His goal is to jog and ride his bike a total of at least 9 miles in less than 1 hour. If John jogs j miles and rides his bike b miles, which of the following systems of inequalities represents John's goal?

A) $\dfrac{j}{6} + \dfrac{b}{12} < 1$
$j + b \geq 9$

B) $\dfrac{j}{6} + \dfrac{b}{12} \geq 1$
$j + b < 9$

C) $6j + 12b \geq 9$
$j + b < 1$

D) $6j + 12b < 1$
$j + b \geq 9$

PRACTICE AT

khanacademy.org/sat

In Example 7, the answer choices each contain two parts. Use this to your advantage by tackling one part at a time and eliminating answers that don't work.

PRACTICE AT

khanacademy.org/sat

You should be able to quickly rearrange three-part equations such as the rate equation (rate = distance / time) for any of the three parts. Example 7 requires you to solve the equation for time.

John jogs j miles and rides his bike b miles; his goal to jog and ride his bike a total of at least 9 miles is represented by the inequality $j + b \geq 9$. This eliminates choices B and C.

Since rate × time = distance, it follows that time is equal to distance divided by rate. John jogs j miles at 6 miles per hour, so the time he jogs is equal to $\dfrac{j \text{ miles}}{6 \text{ miles/hour}} = \dfrac{j}{6}$ hours. Similarly, since John rides his bike b miles at 12 miles per hour, the time he rides his bike is $\dfrac{b}{12}$ hours. Thus, John's goal to complete his jog and his bike ride in less than 1 hour can be represented by the inequality $\dfrac{j}{6} + \dfrac{b}{12} = < 1$. The system $j + b \geq 9$ and $\dfrac{j}{6} + \dfrac{b}{12} < 1$ is choice A.

Fluency in Solving Linear Equations, Linear Inequalities, and Systems of Linear Equations

Creating linear equations, linear inequalities, and systems of linear equations that represent a context is a key skill for success in college and careers. It is also essential to be able to fluently solve linear equations, linear inequalities, and systems of linear equations. Some of the questions in the Heart of Algebra section of the SAT Math Test present equations, inequalities, or systems without a context and directly assess your fluency in solving them.

Some fluency questions allow the use of a calculator; other questions do not permit the use of a calculator and test your ability to solve equations, inequalities, and systems of equations by hand. Even for questions where a calculator is allowed, you may be able to answer the question more quickly without using a calculator, such as in Example 9. Part of what the SAT Math Test assesses is your ability to decide when using a calculator to answer a question is appropriate. Example 8 is an example of a question that could appear on either the calculator or no-calculator portion of the Math Test.

EXAMPLE 8

$$3\left(\frac{1}{2} - y\right) = \frac{3}{5} + 15y$$

What is the solution to the equation above?

Expanding the left-hand side of the equation gives $\frac{3}{2} - 3y = \frac{3}{5} + 15y$, which can be rewritten as $18y = \frac{3}{2} - \frac{3}{5}$. Multiplying each side of $18y = \frac{3}{2} - \frac{3}{5}$ by 10, the least common multiple of 2 and 5, clears the denominators: $180y = \frac{30}{2} - \frac{30}{5} = 15 - 6 = 9$. Therefore, $y = \frac{9}{180} = \frac{1}{20}$.

EXAMPLE 9

$$-2(3x - 2.4) = -3(3x - 2.4)$$

What is the solution to the equation above?

You could solve this in the same way as Example 8, by multiplying everything out and simplifying. But the structure of the equation reveals that −2 times a quantity, $3x - 2.4$, is equal to −3 times the same quantity. This is only possible if the quantity $3x - 2.4$ is equal to zero. Thus, $3x - 2.4 = 0$, or $3x = 2.4$. Therefore, the solution is $x = 0.8$.

EXAMPLE 10

$$-2x = 4y + 6$$
$$2(2y + 3) = 3x - 5$$

What is the solution (x, y) to the system of equations above?

This is an example of a system you can solve quickly by substitution. Since $-2x = 4y + 6$, it follows that $-x = 2y + 3$. Now you can substitute $-x$ for $2y + 3$ in the second equation. This gives you $2(-x) = 3x - 5$, which simplifies to $5x = 5$, or $x = 1$. Substituting 1 for x in the first equation gives you $-2 = 4y + 6$, which simplifies to $4y = -8$, or $y = -2$. Therefore, the solution to the system is $(1, -2)$.

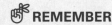
REMEMBER

While a calculator is permitted on one portion of the SAT Math Test, it's important to not over-rely on a calculator. Some questions, such as Example 9, can be solved more efficiently without using a calculator. Your ability to choose when to use and when not to use a calculator is one of the things the SAT Math Test assesses, so be sure to practice this in your studies.

PRACTICE AT

khanacademy.org/sat

In Example 6, the combination approach yields an efficient solution to the question. In Example 10, substitution turns out to be a fast approach. These examples illustrate the benefits of knowing both approaches and thinking critically about which approach may be faster on a given question.

In the preceding examples, you have found a unique solution to linear equations and to systems of two linear equations in two variables. But not all such equations and systems have solutions, and some have infinitely many solutions. Some questions on the SAT Math Test assess your ability to determine whether an equation or a system has one solution, no solutions, or infinitely many solutions.

The Relationships among Linear Equations, Lines in the Coordinate Plane, and the Contexts They Describe

A system of two linear equations in two variables can be solved by graphing the lines in the coordinate plane. For example, you can graph the system of equations in Example 10 in the *xy*-plane:

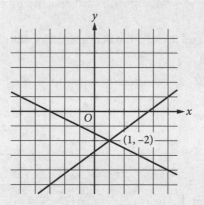

The point of intersection gives the solution to the system.

If the equations in a system of two linear equations in two variables are graphed, each graph will be a line. There are three possibilities:

1. The lines intersect in one point. In this case, the system has a unique solution.

2. The lines are parallel. In this case, the system has no solution.

3. The lines are identical. In this case, every point on the line is a solution, and so the system has infinitely many solutions.

By putting the equations in the system into slope-intercept form, the second and third cases can be identified. If the lines have the same slope and different *y*-intercepts, they are parallel; if both the slope and the *y*-intercept are the same, the lines are identical.

How are the second and third cases represented algebraically? Examples 11 and 12 concern this question.

PRACTICE AT

khanacademy.org/sat

Graphing systems of two linear equations is another effective approach to solving them. Practice arranging linear equations into $y = mx + b$ form and graphing them in the coordinate plane.

EXAMPLE 11

$$2y + 6x = 3$$
$$y + 3x = 2$$

How many solutions (x, y) are there to the system of equations above?

A) Zero

B) One

C) Two

D) More than two

If you multiply each side of $y + 3x = 2$ by 2, you get $2y + 6x = 4$. Then subtracting each side of $2y + 6x = 3$ from the corresponding side of $2y + 6x = 4$ gives $0 = 1$. This is a false statement. Therefore, the system has zero solutions (x, y).

Alternatively, you could graph the two equations. The graphs are parallel lines, so there are no points of intersection.

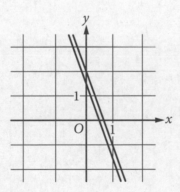

REMEMBER

When the graphs of a system of two linear equations are parallel lines, as in Example 11, the system has zero solutions. If the question states that a system of two linear equations has an infinite number of solutions, as in Example 12, the equations must be equivalent.

EXAMPLE 12

$$3s - 2t = a$$
$$-15s + bt = -7$$

In the system of equations above, a and b are constants. If the system has infinitely many solutions, what is the value of a?

If a system of two linear equations in two variables has infinitely many solutions, the two equations in the system must be equivalent. Since the two equations are presented in the same form, the second equation must be equal to the first equation multiplied by a constant. Since the coefficient of s in the second equation is -5 times the coefficient of s in the first equation, multiply each side of the first equation by -5. This gives you the system

$$-15s + 10t = -5a$$
$$-15s + bt = -7$$

Since these two equations are equivalent and have the same coefficient of s, the coefficients of t and the constants on the right-hand side must also be the same. Thus, $b = 10$ and $-5a = -7$. Therefore, the value of a is $\dfrac{7}{5}$.

There will also be questions on the SAT Math Test that assess your knowledge of the relationship between the algebraic and the geometric representations of a line, that is, between an equation of a line and its graph. The key concepts are:

▶ If the slopes of line ℓ and line k are each defined (that is, if neither line is a vertical line), then

— Line ℓ and line k are parallel if and only if they have the same slope.

— Line ℓ and line k are perpendicular if and only if the product of their slopes is -1.

EXAMPLE 13

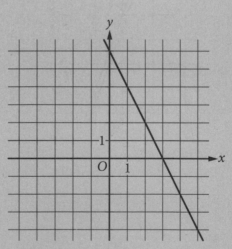

The graph of line k is shown in the xy-plane above. Which of the following is an equation of a line that is perpendicular to line k?

A) $y = -2x + 1$

B) $y = -\dfrac{1}{2}x + 2$

C) $y = \dfrac{1}{2}x + 3$

D) $y = 2x + 4$

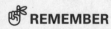 **REMEMBER**

The SAT Math Test will further assess your understanding of linear equations by, for instance, asking you to select a linear equation that describes a given graph, select a graph that describes a given linear equation, or determine how a graph may be impacted by a change in its equation.

Note that the graph of line k passes through the points $(0, 6)$ and $(3, 0)$. Thus, the slope of line k is $\frac{0-6}{3-0} = -2$. Since the product of the slopes of perpendicular lines is -1, a line that is perpendicular to line k will have slope $\frac{1}{2}$. All the choices are in slope-intercept form, and so the coefficient of x is the slope of the line represented by the equation. Therefore, choice C, $y = \frac{1}{2}x + 3$, is an equation of a line with slope $\frac{1}{2}$, and thus this line is perpendicular to line k.

PRACTICE AT

khanacademy.org/sat

Example 13 requires a strong understanding of slope as well as the ability to calculate slope: slope = rise / run = change in y / change in x. Parallel lines have slopes that are equal. Perpendicular lines have slopes whose product is -1.

As we've noted, some contexts can be described with a linear equation. The graph of a linear equation is a line. A line has geometric properties such as its slope and its y-intercept. These geometric properties can often be interpreted in terms of the context. The SAT Math Test has questions that assess your ability to make these interpretations. For example, look back at the contexts in Examples 1 to 3. You created a linear function, $f(n) = 783 + 8n$, that describes the number of miles of paved road County X will have n years after 2014. This equation can be graphed in the coordinate plane, with n on the horizontal axis and $f(n)$ on the vertical axis. This graph is a line with slope 8 and vertical intercept 783. The slope, 8, gives the number of miles of new paved roads added each year, and the vertical intercept gives the number of miles of paved roads in 2014, the year that corresponds to $n = 0$.

EXAMPLE 14

A voter registration drive was held in Town Y. The number of voters, V, registered T days after the drive began can be estimated by the equation $V = 3,450 + 65T$. What is the best interpretation of the number 65 in this equation?

A) The number of registered voters at the beginning of the registration drive

B) The number of registered voters at the end of the registration drive

C) The total number of voters registered during the drive

D) The number of voters registered each day during the drive

The correct answer is choice D. For each day that passes, it is the next day of the registration drive, and so T increases by 1. When T increases by 1, the value of $V = 3,450 + 65T$ increases by 65. That is, the number of voters registered increased by 65 for each day of the drive. Therefore, 65 is the number of voters registered each day during the drive.

You should note that choice A describes the number 3,450, and the numbers described by choices B and C can be found only if you know how many days the registration drive lasted; this information is not given in the question.

Mastery of linear equations, systems of linear equations, and linear functions is built upon key skills such as analyzing rates and ratios. Several key skills are discussed in the next domain, Problem Solving and Data Analysis.

Chapter 20

Problem Solving and Data Analysis

The Problem Solving and Data Analysis section of the SAT Math Test assesses your ability to use your math understanding and skills to solve problems set in the real world. Problem Solving and Data Analysis questions test your ability to create a representation of a problem, consider the units involved, pay attention to the meaning of quantities, know and use different properties of mathematical operations and representations, and apply key principles of statistics. Special focus in this domain will be given to mathematical models. You may be asked to create and use a model and to understand the distinction between the model predictions and data collected. Models are a representation of real life. They help us to explain or interpret the behavior of certain components of a system and to predict future results that are as yet unobserved or unmeasured.

The questions involve quantitative reasoning about ratios, rates, and proportional relationships and may require understanding and applying unit rates. Many of the problems are set in academic and career settings and draw from science, including the social sciences.

Some questions present information about the relationship between two variables in a graph, scatterplot, table, or another form and ask you to analyze and draw conclusions about the given information. The questions assess your understanding of the key properties of, and the differences between, linear, quadratic, and exponential relationships and how these properties apply to the corresponding real-life contexts. An important example is understanding the difference between simple interest and compound interest.

Problem Solving and Data Analysis also includes questions that assess your understanding of essential concepts in statistics. You may be asked to analyze univariate data presented in bar graphs, histograms, line graphs, and box-and-whisker plots, or bivariate data presented in scatterplots and two-way tables. This includes computing and interpreting measures of center, interpreting measures of spread, describing overall patterns, and recognizing the effects of outliers on measures of center. These questions may test your understanding of the conceptual meaning of standard deviation (although you will not be asked to calculate a standard deviation).

Other questions may ask you to estimate the probability of a simple or compound event, employing different approaches, rules, or probability models. Special attention is given to the notion of conditional probability, which is tested using two-way tables or other contexts.

Some questions require the ability to draw conclusions about an entire population from a random sample of that population and how variability affects those conclusions. The questions may test your understanding of randomization-based inference and the conceptual meaning of the margin of error (although you will not be asked to calculate a margin of error) when the mean or the proportion of a population is estimated using sample data. You may be presented with a description of a study and asked to explain what types of conclusions can be drawn with regard to relationships between variables involved and to what population can the study findings be appropriately generalized.

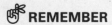
REMEMBER

Problem Solving and Data Analysis comprise 17 of the 58 questions (29%) on the Math Test.

The questions in Problem Solving and Data Analysis include both multiple-choice questions and student-produced response questions. The use of a calculator is allowed for all questions in this domain.

Problem Solving and Data Analysis is one of the three SAT Math Test sub-scores, reported on a scale of 1 to 15.

Let's explore the content and skills assessed by Problem Solving and Data Analysis questions.

Ratio, Proportion, Units, and Percentage

Ratio and proportion is one of the major ideas in mathematics. Introduced well before high school, ratio and proportion is a theme throughout mathematics, in applications, in careers, in college mathematics courses, and beyond.

EXAMPLE 1

On Thursday, 240 adults and children attended a show. The ratio of adults to children was 5 to 1. How many children attended the show?

A) 40
B) 48
C) 192
D) 200

Because the ratio of adults to children was 5 to 1, there were 5 adults for every 1 child. In fractions, $\frac{5}{6}$ of the 240 who attended were adults and $\frac{1}{6}$ were children. Therefore, $\frac{1}{6} \times 240 = 40$ children attended the show, which is choice A.

Ratios on the SAT may be expressed in the form 3 to 1, 3:1, $\frac{3}{1}$, or simply 3.

PRACTICE

khanacademy.

A ratio represents a rela between quantities, not the actual quantities themselves. Fractions are an especially effective way to represent and work with ratios.

EXAMPLE 2

On an architect's drawing of the floor plan for a house, 1 inch represents 3 feet. If a room is represented on the floor plan by a rectangle that has sides of lengths 3.5 inches and 5 inches, what is the actual floor area of the room in square feet?

A) 17.5
B) 51.0
C) 52.5
D) 157.5

Because 1 inch represents 3 feet, the actual dimensions of the room are $3 \times 3.5 = 10.5$ feet and $3 \times 5 = 15$ feet. Therefore, the floor area of the room is $10.5 \times 15 = 157.5$ square feet, which is choice D.

Another classic example of ratio is the length of a shadow. At a given location and time of day, it might be true that a fence post that is 4 feet high casts a shadow that is 6 feet long. This ratio of the height of the object to the length of the shadow, 4 to 6 or $\frac{2}{3}$, remains the same for any object at the same location and time. So, for example, a person who is 6 feet tall would cast a shadow that is $\frac{3}{2} \times 6 = 9$ feet long. In this situation, in which one variable quantity is always a fixed constant times another variable quantity, the two quantities are said to be directly proportional.

Variables x and y are said to be directly proportional if $y = kx$, where k is a nonzero constant. The constant k is called the constant of proportionality.

In the preceding example, you would say the length of an object's shadow is directly proportional to the height of the object, with constant of proportionality $\frac{3}{2}$. So if you let L be the length of the shadow and H be the height of the object, then $L = \frac{3}{2}H$.

Notice that both L and H are lengths, so the constant of proportion, $\frac{L}{H} = \frac{3}{2}$, has no units. In contrast, let's consider Example 2 again. On the scale drawing, 1 inch represents 3 feet. The length of an actual measurement is directly proportional to its length on the scale drawing. But to find the constant of proportionality, you need to keep track of units: $\frac{3 \text{ feet}}{1 \text{ inch}} = \frac{36 \text{ inches}}{1 \text{ inch}} = 36.$

Hence, if S is a length on the scale drawing that corresponds to an actual length of A, then $A = 36S$.

Many of the questions on the SAT Math Test require you to pay attention to units. Some questions in Problem Solving and Data Analysis require you to convert units either between the English system and the metric system or within those systems.

EXAMPLE 3

Scientists estimate that the Pacific Plate, one of Earth's tectonic plates, has moved about 1,060 kilometers in the past 10.3 million years. What was the average speed of the Pacific Plate during that time period, in centimeters per year?

A) 1.03
B) 10.3
C) 103
D) 1,030

PRACTICE AT

khanacademy.org/sat

Pay close attention to units, and convert units if required by the question. Writing out the unit conversion as a series of multiplication steps, as seen here, will help ensure accuracy. Intermediate units should cancel (as do the kilometers and meters in Example 3), leaving you with the desired unit (centimeters per year).

Since 1 kilometer = 1,000 meters and 1 meter = 100 centimeters, you get

$$\frac{1,060 \text{ kilometers}}{10,300,000 \text{ years}} \times \frac{1,000 \text{ meters}}{1 \text{ kilometer}} \times \frac{100 \text{ centimeters}}{1 \text{ meter}} = 10.3 \text{ centimeters}$$

per year.

Therefore, the correct answer is choice B.

Questions may require you to move between unit rates and total amounts.

EXAMPLE 4

County Y consists of two districts. One district has an area of 30 square miles and a population density of 370 people per square mile, and the other district has an area of 50 square miles and a population density of 290 people per square mile. What is the population density, in people per square mile, for all of County Y?

REMEMBER

13 of the 58 questions on the Math Test, or 22%, are student-produced response questions in which you will grid your answers in the spaces provided on the answer sheet.

(Note that this example has no choices. It is a student-produced response question. On an SAT, you would grid your answer in the spaces provided on the answer sheet.)

The first district has an area of 30 square miles and a population density of 370 people per square mile, so its total population is

30 square miles $\times$ 370 $\dfrac{\text{people}}{\text{square mile}}$ = 11,100 people. The other district has an

area of 50 square miles and a population density of 290 people per square mile,

so its total population is 50 square miles $\times$ 290 $\dfrac{\text{people}}{\text{square mile}}$ = 14,500 people.

Thus, County Y has total population 11,100 + 14,500 = 25,600 people and total area 30 + 50 = 80 square miles. Therefore, the population density of County Y is $\frac{25,600}{80}$ = 320 people per square mile.

Problem Solving and Data Analysis also includes questions involving percentages, which are a type of proportion. These questions may involve the concepts of percentage increase and percentage decrease.

EXAMPLE 5

A furniture store buys its furniture from a wholesaler. For a particular table, the store usually charges its cost from the wholesaler plus 75%. During a sale, the store charged the wholesale cost plus 15%. If the sale price of the table was $299, what is the usual price for the table?

A) $359
B) $455
C) $479
D) $524

The sale price of the table was $299. This is equal to the cost from the wholesaler plus 15%. Thus, $299 = 1.15(wholesale cost), and the cost from the wholesaler is $\frac{\$299}{1.15}$ = $260. Therefore, the usual price the store charges for the table is 1.75 × $260 = $455, which is choice B.

Interpreting Relationships Presented in Scatterplots, Graphs, Tables, and Equations

The behavior of a variable and the relationship between two variables in a real-world context may be explored by considering data presented in tables and graphs.

The relationship between two variables may be modeled by a function or equation. The function or equation may be found by examining ordered pairs of data values and by analyzing how the variables are related to one another in the real world. The model may allow very accurate predictions, as for example models used in physical sciences, or may only describe a trend, with considerable variability between the actual and predicted values, as for example models used in behavioral and social sciences.

Questions on the SAT Math Test assess your ability to understand and analyze the relationships between two variables, the properties of the functions used to model these relationships, and the conditions under which a model is considered to be good, acceptable, or inappropriate. The questions in Problem Solving and Data Analysis focus on linear, quadratic, and exponential relationships.

PRACTICE AT

khanacademy.org/sat

Percent is a type of proportion that means "per 100." 20%, for instance, means 20 out of (or per) 100. Percent increase or decrease is calculated by finding the difference between two quantities, then dividing the difference by the original quantity and multiplying by 100.

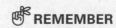

REMEMBER

The ability to interpret and synthesize data from charts, graphs, and tables is a widely applicable skill in college and in many careers and thus is tested on the SAT Math Test.

EXAMPLE 6

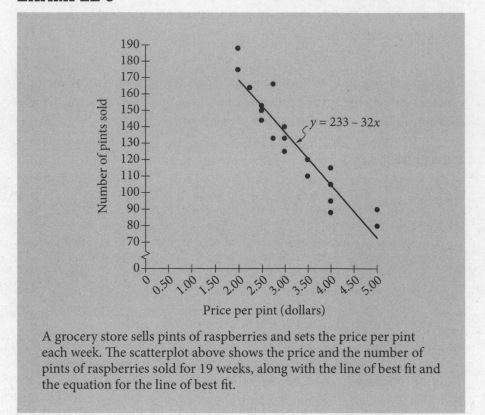

A grocery store sells pints of raspberries and sets the price per pint each week. The scatterplot above shows the price and the number of pints of raspberries sold for 19 weeks, along with the line of best fit and the equation for the line of best fit.

There are several different questions that could be asked about this context.

A. According to the line of best fit, how many pints of raspberries would the grocery store expect to sell in a week when the price of raspberries is $4.50 per pint?

Because the line of best fit has equation $y = 233 - 32x$, where x is the price, in dollars, for a pint of raspberries and y is the number of pints of raspberries sold, the number of pints the store would be expected to sell in a week where the price of raspberries is $4.50 per pint is $233 - 32(4.50) = 89$ pints.

B. For how many of the 19 weeks shown was the number of pints of raspberries sold greater than the amount predicted by the line of best fit?

For a given week, the number of pints of raspberries sold is greater than the amount predicted by the line of best fit if and only if the point representing that week lies above the line of best fit. Of the 19 points, 8 lie above the line of best fit, so there were 8 weeks in which the number of pints sold was greater than what was predicted by the line of best fit.

C. What is the best interpretation of the meaning of the slope of the line of best fit?

On the SAT, this question would be followed by multiple-choice answer options. The slope of the line of best fit is -32. This means that the correct answer would state that for each dollar that the price of a pint of raspberries increases, the store expects to sell 32 fewer pints of raspberries.

D. What is the best interpretation of the meaning of the y-intercept of the line of best fit?

On the SAT, this question would be followed by multiple-choice answer options.

In this context, the y-intercept does not represent a likely scenario, so it cannot be accurately interpreted in terms of this context. According to the model, the y-intercept means that if the store sold raspberries for $0 per pint — that is, if the store gave raspberries away — 233 people would be expected to accept the free raspberries. However, it is not realistic that the store would give away raspberries, and if they did, it is likely that far more people would accept the free raspberries.

The fact that the y-intercept indicates that 233 people would accept free raspberries is one limitation of the model. Another limitation is that for a price of $7.50 per pint or above, the model predicts that a negative number of people would buy raspberries, which is impossible. In general, you should be cautious about applying a model for values outside of the given data. In this example, you should only be confident in the prediction of sales for prices between $2 and $5.

Giving a line of best fit, as in this example, assumes that the relationship between the variables is best modeled by a linear function, but that is not always true. On the SAT, you may see data that are best modeled by a linear, quadratic, or exponential model.

(**Note:** Questions interpreting the slope and intercepts of a line of best fit, such as in **C** and **D**, may be classified as part of the Heart of Algebra section and contribute to the Heart of Algebra subscore.)

EXAMPLE 7

Time (hours)	Number of bacteria
0	1×10^3
1	4×10^3
2	1.6×10^4
3	6.4×10^4

The table above gives the initial number (at time $t = 0$) of bacteria placed in a growth medium and the number of bacteria in the growth medium over 3 hours. Which of the following functions models the number of bacteria, $N(t)$, after t hours?

A) $N(t) = 4,000t$
B) $N(t) = 1,000 + 3,000t$
C) $N(t) = 1,000(4^{-t})$
D) $N(t) = 1,000(4^t)$

PRACTICE AT

khanacademy.org/sat

To determine if a model is linear or exponential, examine the change in the quantity between successive time periods. If the difference in quantity is constant, the model is linear. If the ratio in the quantity is constant (for instance, 4 times greater than the preceding time period), then the model is exponential.

The given choices are linear and exponential models. If a quantity is increasing linearly with time, then the *difference* in the quantity between successive time periods is constant. If a quantity is increasing exponentially with time, then the *ratio* in the quantity between successive time periods is constant. According to the table, after each hour, the number of bacteria in the culture is 4 times as great as it was the preceding hour: $\frac{4 \times 10^3}{1 \times 10^3} = \frac{1.6 \times 10^4}{4 \times 10^3} = \frac{6.4 \times 10^4}{1.6 \times 10^4} = 4$.

That is, for each increase of 1 in t, the value of $N(t)$ is multiplied by 4. At $t = 0$, which corresponds to the time when the culture was placed in the medium, there were 10^3 bacteria. This is modeled by the exponential function $N(t) = 1,000(4^t)$, which has value 1,000 at $t = 0$ and increases by a factor of 4 for each increase of 1 in the value of t. Choice D is the correct answer.

The SAT Math Test may have questions on simple and compound interest, which are important examples of linear and exponential growth, respectively.

EXAMPLE 8

A bank has opened a new branch and, as part of a promotion, the bank branch is offering $1,000 certificates of deposit at simple interest of 4% per year. The bank is selling certificates with terms of 1, 2, 3, or 4 years. Which of the following functions gives the total amount, A, in dollars, a customer will receive when a certificate with a term of k years is finally paid?

A) $A = 1,000(1.04k)$
B) $A = 1,000(1 + 0.04k)$
C) $A = 1,000(1.04)^k$
D) $A = 1,000(1 + 0.04^k)$

For 4% simple interest, 4% of the original deposit is added to the original deposit for each year the deposit was held. That is, if the certificate has a term of k years, $4k\%$ is added to the original deposit to get the final amount. Because $4k\%$ is $0.04k$, the final amount paid to the customer is $A = 1,000 + 1,000(0.04k) = 1,000(1 + 0.04k)$. Choice B is the correct answer.

The general formula for simple interest is $A = P(1 + rt)$, where P is the original deposit, called the principal; r is the annual interest rate expressed as a decimal; and t is the length the deposit is held. In Example 8, $P = \$1,000$, $r = 0.04$, and $t = k$ years; so A, in dollars, is given by $A = 1,000[1 + (0.04)k]$.

In contrast, compound interest is an example of exponential growth.

EXAMPLE 9

A bank has opened a new branch and, as part of a promotion, the bank branch is offering $1,000 certificates of deposit at an interest rate of 4% per year, compounded semiannually. The bank is selling certificates with terms of 1, 2, 3, or 4 years. Which of the following functions gives the total amount, A, in dollars, a customer will receive when a certificate with a term of k years is finally paid?

A) $A = 1,000(1 + 0.04k)$

B) $A = 1,000(1 + 0.08k)$

C) $A = 1,000(1.04)^k$

D) $A = 1,000(1.02)^{2k}$

The interest is compounded semiannually, that is, twice a year. At the end of the first half year, 2% of the original deposit is added to the value of the certificate (4% annual interest multiplied by the time period, which is $\frac{1}{2}$ year, gives 2% interest). When the interest is added, the value, in dollars, of the certificate is now $1,000 + 1,000(0.02) = 1,000(1.02)$. Since the interest is reinvested (compounded), the new principal at the beginning of the second half year is $1,000(1.02)$. At the end of the second half year, 2% of $1,000(1.02)$ is added to the value of the certificate; the value, in dollars, of the certificate is now $1,000(1.02) + 1,000(1.02)(0.02)$, which is equal to $1,000(1.02)(1.02) = 1,000(1.02)^2$. In general, after n compounding periods, the amount, A, in dollars, is $A = 1,000(1.02)^n$.

When the certificate is paid after k years, the value of the certificate will have been multiplied by the factor (1.02) a total of $2k$ times. Therefore, the total amount, A, in dollars, a customer will receive when a certificate with a term of k years is finally paid is $A = 1,000(1.02^{2k})$. Choice D is the correct answer.

The general formula for compound interest is $A = P\left(1 + \dfrac{r}{n}\right)^{nt}$, where P is the principal, r is the annual interest rate expressed as a decimal, t is the number of years the deposit is held, and n is the number of times the interest is compounded per year. In Example 9, $P = \$1,000$, $r = 0.04$, $t = k$, and $n = 2$; so A, in dollars, is given by $A = 1,000\left(1 + \dfrac{0.04}{2}\right)^{2k} = 1,000(1.02)^{2k}$.

Note: Although the stated interest rate is 4% per year in Example 9, the value of the account increases by more than 4% in a year, namely 4.04% per year. (You may have seen banks offer an account in this way, for example, 5.00% annual interest rate, 5.13% effective annual yield.) If you take calculus, you will often see a situation in which a stated rate of change differs from the change over an interval. But on the SAT, other than compound interest,

PRACTICE AT

khanacademy.org/sat

Know the formulas for simple and compound interest.

Simple interest: $A = P(1 + rt)$

Compound interest: $A = P(1 + r/n)^{nt}$

A is the total amount, P is the principal, r is the interest rate expressed as a decimal, t is the time period, and n is the number of times the interest is compounded per year.

the stated rate of change is always equal to the actual rate of change. For example, if a question says that the height of a plant increases by 10% each month, it means that $\dfrac{\text{height of the plant now}}{\text{height of the plant a month ago}} = 1.1$ (or if a question says that the population of a city is decreasing by 3% per year, it means that $\dfrac{\text{population of the city now}}{\text{population of the city a year ago}} = 0.97$. Then, if the question asks by what percentage the height of the plant will increase in 2 months, you can write

$$\dfrac{\text{height of the plant in 2 months}}{\text{height of the plant now}} = \dfrac{\text{height of the plant in 2 months}}{\text{height of the plant in 1 month}}$$

$$+ \dfrac{\text{height of the plant in 1 month}}{\text{height of the plant now}}$$

$$= 1.1 \times 1.1 = 1.21$$

Therefore, the answer is that the height of the plant increases by 21% in 2 months.

An SAT Math Test question may ask you to interpret a graph that shows the relationship between two variables.

EXAMPLE 10

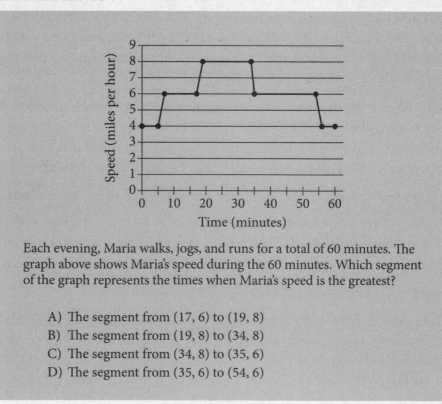

Each evening, Maria walks, jogs, and runs for a total of 60 minutes. The graph above shows Maria's speed during the 60 minutes. Which segment of the graph represents the times when Maria's speed is the greatest?

    A) The segment from (17, 6) to (19, 8)
    B) The segment from (19, 8) to (34, 8)
    C) The segment from (34, 8) to (35, 6)
    D) The segment from (35, 6) to (54, 6)

The correct answer is choice B. Because the vertical coordinate represents Maria's speed, the part of the graph with the greatest vertical coordinate represents the times when Maria's speed is the greatest. This is the highest part of the graph, the segment from (19, 8) to (34, 8), when Maria runs at 8 miles per hour (mph). Choice A represents the time during which Maria's speed is increasing from 6 to 8 mph; choice C represents the time during which Maria's speed is decreasing from 8 to 6 mph; and choice D represents the longest period of Maria moving at the same speed, not the times when Maria's speed is the greatest.

More Data and Statistics

Some questions on the SAT Math Test will assess your ability to understand and analyze data presented in a table, bar graph, histogram, line graph, or other display.

EXAMPLE 11

A store is deciding whether to install a new security system to prevent shoplifting. The security manager of the store estimates that 10,000 customers enter the store each week, 24 of whom will attempt to shoplift. The manager estimates the results of the new security system in detecting shoplifters would be as shown in the table below.

	Alarm sounds	Alarm does not sound	Total
Customer attempts to shoplift	21	3	24
Customer does not attempt to shoplift	35	9,941	9,976
Total	56	9,944	10,000

According to the manager's estimates, if the alarm sounds for a customer, what is the probability that the customer did *not* attempt to shoplift?

A) 0.03%
B) 0.35%
C) 0.56%
D) 62.5%

PRACTICE AT

khanacademy.org/sat

Probability is the measure of how likely an event is. When calculating the probability of an event, use the following formula:

probability = number of favorable (or desired) outcomes / total number of possible outcomes

According to the manager's estimates, the alarm will sound for 56 customers. Of these 56 customers, 35 did *not* attempt to shoplift. Therefore, if the alarm sounds, the probability that the customer did *not* attempt to shoplift is $\frac{35}{56} = \frac{5}{8} = 62.5\%$. The correct answer is choice D.

Example 11 is an example of a conditional probability.

You may be asked to answer questions that involve a measure of center for a data set: the average (arithmetic mean) or the median. A question may ask you to draw conclusions about one or more of these measures of center even if the exact values cannot be calculated. To recall briefly:

The mean of a set of numerical values is the sum of all the values divided by the number of values in the set.

The median of a set of numerical values is the middle value when the values are listed in increasing (or decreasing) order. If the set has an even number of values, then the median is the average of the two middle values.

EXAMPLE 12

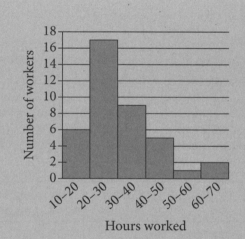

The histogram above summarizes the number of hours worked last week by the 40 employees of a landscaping company. In the histogram, the first bar represents all workers who worked at least 10 hours but less than 20 hours; the second represents all workers who worked at least 20 hours but less than 30 hours; and so on. Which of the following could be the median and mean number of hours worked for the 40 employees?

A) Median = 22, Mean = 23
B) Median = 24, Mean = 22
C) Median = 26, Mean = 32
D) Median = 32, Mean = 30

(**Note:** On the SAT, all histograms have the same type of boundary condition. That is, the values represented by a bar include the left endpoint but do not include the right endpoint.)

If the number of hours the 40 employees worked is listed in increasing order, the median will be the average of the 20th and the 21st numbers on the list. The first 6 numbers on the list will be workers represented by the first bar; hence, each of the first 6 numbers will be at least 10 but less than 20. The next 17 numbers, that is, the 7th through the 23rd numbers on the list, will be workers represented by the second bar; hence, each of the next 17 numbers will be at least 20 but less than 30. Thus, the 20th and the 21st numbers on the list will be at least 20 but less than 30. Therefore, any of the median values in choices A, B, or C are possible, but the median value in choice D is not.

Now let's find the possible values of the mean. Each of the 6 employees represented by the first bar worked at least 10 hours but less than 20 hours. Thus, the total number of hours worked by these 6 employees is at least 60. Similarly, the total number of hours worked by the 17 employees represented by the second bar is at least 340; the total number of hours worked by the 9 employees represented by the third bar is at least 270; the total number of hours worked by the 5 employees represented by the fourth bar is at least 200; the total number of hours worked by the 1 employee represented by the fifth bar is at least 50; and the total number of hours worked by the 2 employees represented by the sixth bar is at least 120. Adding all these hours up shows that the total number of hours worked by all 40 employees is at least $60 + 340 + 270 + 200 + 50 + 120 = 1,040$. Therefore, the mean number of hours worked by all 40 employees is at least $\frac{1,040}{40} = 26$. Therefore, only the values of the average given in choices C and D are possible. Because only choice C has possible values for both the median and the mean, it is the correct answer.

A data set may have a few values that are much larger or smaller than the rest of the values in the set. These values are called *outliers*. An outlier may represent an important piece of data. For example, if a data set consists of rates of a certain illness in various cities, a data point with a very high value could indicate a serious health issue to be investigated.

In general, outliers affect the mean but not the median. Therefore, outliers that are larger than the rest of the points in the data set tend to make the mean greater than the median, and outliers that are smaller than the rest of the points in the data set tend to make the mean less than the median. The most evident graphical display used to identify outliers is the box plot.

The mean and the median are different ways to describe the center of a data set. Another key characteristic of a data set is the amount of variation, or spread, in the data. One measure of spread is the *standard deviation*, which is a measure of how far away the points in the data set are from the average value. On the SAT Math Test, you will *not* be asked to compute the standard deviation of a data set, but you do need to understand that a larger standard deviation corresponds to a data set whose values are more spread out from the mean value.

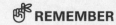 **REMEMBER**

You will not be asked to calculate the standard deviation of a set of data on the SAT Math Test, but you will be expected to demonstrate an understanding of what standard deviation measures.

EXAMPLE 13

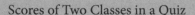

Scores of Two Classes in a Quiz

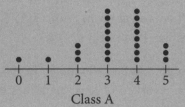

Class A

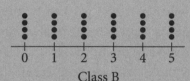

Class B

The dot plots above summarize the scores that two classes, each with 24 students, at Central High School achieved on a current events quiz. Which of the following correctly compares the standard deviation of the scores in each of the classes?

A) The standard deviation of the scores in Class A is smaller.
B) The standard deviation of the scores in Class B is smaller.
C) The standard deviation of the scores in Class A and Class B is the same.
D) The relationship cannot be determined from the information given.

In Class A, the large majority of scores are 3 and 4, with only a few scores of 0, 1, 2, and 5; the average score is between 3 and 4. In Class B, the scores are evenly spread out across all possible scores, with many scores not close to the average score, which is 2.5. Because the scores in Class A are more closely clustered around the mean, the standard deviation of the scores in Class A is smaller. The correct answer is choice A.

A *population parameter* is a numerical value that describes a characteristic of a population. For example, the percentage of registered voters who would vote for a certain candidate is a parameter describing the population of registered voters in an election. Or the average income of a household for a city is a parameter describing the population of households in that city. An essential purpose of statistics is to estimate a population parameter based on a sample from the population. A common example is election polling, where researchers will interview a random sample of registered voters in an election to estimate the outcome of an election. The precision of the estimate depends on the variability of the data and the sample size. For example, if household incomes in a city vary widely or the sample is small, the estimate that comes from a sample may differ considerably from the actual value for the population (the parameter).

For example, suppose you want to estimate the average amount of time each week that the students at a high school spend on the Internet.

Suppose the high school has 1,200 students. It would be time consuming to ask all 1,200 students, but you can ask a sample of students. Suppose you have time to ask 80 students. Which 80 students? In order to have a sample that is representative of the population, students who will participate in the study should be selected *at random*. That is, each student must have the same chance to be selected. Randomization is essential in protecting against bias and helps to calculate the sampling error reliably. This can be done in different ways. You could write each student's name on a slip of paper, put all the slips in a bowl, mix up the slips, and then draw 80 names from the bowl. In practice, a computer is often used to select a random sample.

If you do not select a random sample, it may introduce bias. For example, if you found 80 students from those attending a game of the school's football team, those people would be more likely to be interested in sports, and in turn, an interest in sports might affect the average amount of time the students spend on the Internet. The result would be that the average time those 80 students spend on the Internet might not be an accurate estimate of the average amount of time *all* students at the school spend on the Internet.

Suppose you select 80 students at random from the 1,200 students at the high school. You ask them how much time they spend on the Internet each week, and you find that the average time is 14 hours. You also find that 6 of the 80 students spend less than 2 hours each week on the Internet. How can these results be used to make a generalization about the entire population of 1,200 students?

Because the sample was selected at random, the average of 14 hours is the most reasonable estimate for average time on the Internet for all 1,200 students. Also, we can use the sample to estimate how many students spend less than 2 hours on the Internet each week. In the sample, that number is 6 out of 80, or 7.5%. Applying this percentage to the entire population of 1,200 students, we estimate that 90 students at the school spend less than 2 hours per week on the Internet.

But this is not all. An essential part of statistics is accounting for the variability of the estimate. The estimates above are reasonable, but they are unlikely to be exactly correct. Statistical analysis can also describe how far from the estimates the actual values are likely to be. To describe the precision of an estimate, statisticians use *margins of error*. On the SAT, you will not be expected to compute a margin of error, but you should understand how different factors affect the margin of error and how to interpret a given margin of error in the context.

If the example above were an SAT question, you might be told that the estimate of an average of 14 hours per week on the Internet from the random sample of 80 students has a margin of error of 1.2 hours. This means that in

REMEMBER

You will not need to calculate margins of error on the SAT Math Test, but you should understand what these concepts mean and be able to interpret them in context.

random samples of size 80, the actual average will likely be within 1.2 hours of the true average.

There are some key points to note.

1. The size of the margin of error is affected by two factors: the variability in the data and the sample size. The larger the standard deviation, the larger the margin of error; the smaller the standard deviation, the smaller the margin of error. Increasing the size of the random sample provides more information and reduces the margin of error.

2. The margin of error applies to the estimated value of the parameter for the entire population, *not* for the value of the variable for particular individuals. In the example, the interval from 12.8 to 15.2 hours includes *the true average* amount of time on the Internet for all students at the school.

EXAMPLE 14

A quality control researcher at an electronics company is testing the life of the company's batteries in a certain camera. The researcher selects 100 batteries at random from the daily output of the batteries and finds that the life of the batteries has a mean of 342 pictures with an associated margin of error of 18 pictures. Which of the following is the best conclusion based on these data?

A) All the batteries produced by the company that day have a life between 324 and 360 pictures.

B) All the batteries ever produced by the company have a life between 324 and 360 pictures.

C) It is plausible that the true average life of batteries produced by the company that day is between 324 and 360 pictures.

D) It is plausible that the true average life of all the batteries ever produced by the company is between 324 and 360 pictures.

PRACTICE AT

khanacademy.org/sat

When a margin of error is provided, determine the value to which the margin of error applies. The margin of error concerns the average value of a population and does not apply to values of individual objects in the population.

The correct answer is choice C. Choices A and B are incorrect because the margin of error gives information about the true *average* life of all batteries produced by the company that day, not about the life of any individual battery. Choice D is incorrect because the sample of batteries was taken from the population of all of the batteries produced by the company on that day. The population of all batteries the company ever produced may have a different average life because of changes in the formulation of the batteries, wear on machinery, improvements in production processes, and many other factors.

The statistics examples discussed so far are largely based on investigations intended to estimate some characteristic of a population: the amount of time students spend on the Internet, the life of a battery, and the percentage of registered voters who plan to vote for a candidate. Another primary focus of statistics is to investigate relationships between variables and to draw conclusions about cause and effect. For example, does a new type of physical therapy help people recover from knee surgery faster? For such a study, some people who have had knee surgery will be randomly assigned to the new therapy, while other people who have had knee surgery will be randomly assigned to the usual therapy. The medical results of these patients can be compared. The key questions from a statistical viewpoint are:

▶ Can the results appropriately be generalized from the sample of patients in the study to the entire population of people who are recovering from knee surgery?

▶ Do the results allow one to appropriately conclude that the new therapy *caused* any difference in the results for the two groups of patients?

The answers depend on the use of random sampling and random assignment of individuals into groups of different conditions.

▶ If the sample of all subjects in a study were selected at random from the entire population in question, the results can appropriately be generalized to the entire population because random sampling ensures that each individual has the same chance to be selected for the sample.

▶ If the subjects in the sample were randomly assigned to treatments, it may be appropriate to make conclusions about cause and effect because the treatment groups will be roughly equivalent at the beginning of the experiment other than the treatment they receive.

This can be summarized in the following table.

	Subjects Selected at Random	Subjects Not Selected at Random
Subjects randomly assigned to treatments	Results can be appropriately generalized to the entire population. Conclusions about cause and effect can appropriately be drawn.	Results *cannot* be appropriately generalized to the entire population. Conclusions about cause and effect can appropriately be drawn.
Subjects not randomly assigned to treatments	Results can be appropriately generalized to the entire population. Conclusions about cause and effect *cannot* appropriately be drawn.	Results *cannot* be appropriately generalized to the entire population. Conclusions about cause and effect *cannot* appropriately be drawn.

The previous example discussed treatments in a medical experiment. The word *treatment* refers to any factor that is deliberately varied in an experiment.

PRACTICE AT

khanacademy.org/sat

In order for results of a study to be generalized to the entire population, and for a cause-and-effect relationship to be established, both random sampling and random assignment of individuals to treatments is needed.

EXAMPLE 15

A community center offers a Spanish course. This year, all students in the course were offered additional audio lessons they could take at home. The students who took these additional audio lessons did better in the course than students who didn't take the additional audio lessons. Which of the following is an appropriate conclusion?

A) Taking additional audio lessons will cause an improvement for any student who takes any foreign language course.

B) Taking additional audio lessons will cause an improvement for any student who takes a Spanish course.

C) Taking additional audio lessons was the cause of the improvement for the students at the community center who took the Spanish course.

D) No conclusion about cause and effect can be made regarding students at the community center who took the additional audio lessons at home and their performance in the Spanish course.

PRACTICE AT

khanacademy.org/sat

Be wary of conclusions that claim a cause-and-effect relationship or that generalize a conclusion to a broader population. Before accepting a conclusion, assess whether or not the subjects were selected at random from the broader population and whether or not subjects were randomly assigned treatments.

The correct answer is choice D. The better results of these students may have been a result of being more motivated, as shown in their willingness to do extra work, and not the additional audio lessons. Choice A is incorrect because no conclusion about cause and effect is possible without random assignment to treatments and because the sample was only students taking a Spanish course, so no conclusion can be appropriately made about students taking all foreign language courses. Choice B is incorrect because no conclusion about cause and effect is possible without random assignment to treatments and because the students taking a Spanish course at the community center is not a random sample of all students who take a Spanish course. Choice C is incorrect because the students taking the Spanish course at the community center were not randomly assigned to use the additional audio lessons or not use the additional audio lessons.

Chapter 21

Passport to Advanced Math

Passport to Advanced Math questions include topics that are especially important for students to master *before* studying advanced math. Chief among these topics is the understanding of the structure of expressions and the ability to analyze, manipulate, and rewrite these expressions. This section also includes reasoning with more complex equations and interpreting and building functions. Passport to Advanced Math is one of the three subscores in the SAT Math Test that are reported on a scale of 1 to 15. Questions in this section may be part of the Science subscore or part of the History and Social Studies subscore.

As you saw in Chapter 19, the questions in Heart of Algebra focus on the mastery of linear equations, systems of linear equations, and linear functions. In contrast, the questions in Passport to Advanced Math focus on the ability to work with and analyze more complex equations. The questions may require you to demonstrate procedural skill in adding, subtracting, and multiplying polynomials and in dividing a polynomial by a linear expression. You may be required to work with expressions involving exponentials, integer and rational powers, radicals, or fractions with a variable in the denominator. The questions may ask you to solve a quadratic equation, a radical equation, a rational equation, or a system consisting of a linear equation and a nonlinear equation. You may be required to manipulate an equation in several variables to isolate a quantity of interest.

Some questions in Passport to Advanced Math will ask you to build a quadratic or exponential function or an equation that describes a context or to interpret the function or solution to the equation in terms of the context.

Throughout the section, your ability to recognize structure is assessed. Expressions and equations that appear complex may use repeated terms or repeated expressions. By noticing these patterns, the complexity of a problem can be quickly simplified. Structure may be used to factor or otherwise rewrite an expression, to solve a quadratic or other equation, or to draw conclusions about the context represented by an expression, equation, or function. You may be asked to identify or derive the form of an expression or function that reveals information about the expression or function or the context it represents.

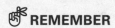 **REMEMBER**

16 of the 58 questions (28%) on the SAT Math Test are Passport to Advanced Math questions.

263

Passport to Advanced Math questions also assess your understanding of functions and their graphs. A question may require you to demonstrate your understanding of function notation, including interpreting an expression where the argument of a function is an expression rather than a variable. The questions may assess your knowledge of the domain and range of a function and your understanding of how the algebraic properties of a function relate to the geometric characteristics of its graph.

The questions in this section include both multiple-choice questions and student-produced response questions. On some questions, the use of a calculator is not permitted; on other questions, the use of a calculator is allowed. On questions where the use of a calculator is permitted, you must decide whether using your calculator is an effective strategy.

Let's consider the content and skills assessed by Passport to Advanced Math questions.

Operations with Polynomials and Rewriting Expressions

Questions on the SAT Math Test may assess your ability to add, subtract, and multiply polynomials.

EXAMPLE 1

$$(x^2 + bx - 2)(x + 3) = x^3 + 6x^2 + 7x - 6$$

In the equation above, b is a constant. If the equation is true for all values of x, what is the value of b?

A) 2
B) 3
C) 7
D) 9

To find the value of b, expand the left-hand side of the equation and then collect like terms so that the left-hand side is in the same form as the right-hand side.

$$(x^2 + bx - 2)(x + 3) = (x^3 + bx^2 - 2x) + (3x^2 + 3bx - 6)$$
$$= x^3 + (3 + b)x^2 + (3b - 2)x - 6$$

 **REMEMBER**

Passport to Advanced Math questions build on the knowledge and skills tested on Heart of Algebra questions. Develop proficiency with Heart of Algebra questions before tackling Passport to Advanced Math questions.

Since the two polynomials are equal for all values of x, the coefficient of matching powers of x should be the same. Therefore, $x^3 + (3 + b)x^2 + (3b - 2)x - 6$ and $x^3 + 6x^2 + 7x - 6$ reveals that $3 + b = 6$ and $3b - 2 = 7$. Solving either of these equations gives $b = 3$, which is choice B.

Questions may also ask you to use structure to rewrite expressions. The expression may be of a particular type, such as a difference of squares, or it may require insightful analysis.

EXAMPLE 2

Which of the following is equivalent to $16s^4 - 4t^2$?

A) $4(s^2 - t)(4s^2 + t)$
B) $4(4s^2 - t)(s^2 + t)$
C) $4(2s^2 - t)(2s^2 + t)$
D) $(8s^2 - 2t)(8s^2 + 2t)$

This example appears complex at first, but it is very similar to the equation $x^2 - y^2$ and this factors as $(x - y)(x + y)$. The expression $16s^4 - 4t^2$ is also the difference of two squares: $16s^4 - 4t^2 = (4s^2)^2 - (2t)^2$. Therefore, it can be factored as $(4s^2)^2 - (2t)^2 = (4s^2 - 2t)(4s^2 + 2t)$. This expression can be rewritten as $(4s^2 - 2t)(4s^2 + 2t) = 2(2s^2 - t)(2)(2s^2 + t) = 4(2s^2 - t)(2s^2 + t)$, which is choice C.

EXAMPLE 3

$$y^5 - 2y^4 - cxy + 6x$$

In the polynomial above, c is a constant. If the polynomial is divisible by $y - 2$, what is the value of c?

If the expression is divisible by $y - 2$, then the expression $y - 2$ can be factored from the larger expression. Since $y^5 - 2y^4 = (y - 2)y^4$, you have $y^5 - 2y^4 - cxy + 6x = (y - 2)(y^4) - cxy + 6x$. If this entire expression is divisible by $y - 2$, then $-cxy + 6x$ must be divisible by $y - 2$. Thus, $-cxy + 6x = (y - 2)(-cx) = -cxy + 2cx$. Therefore, $2c = 6$, and the value of c is 3.

Quadratic Functions and Equations

Questions in Passport to Advanced Math may require you to build a quadratic function or an equation to represent a context.

EXAMPLE 4

A car is traveling at x feet per second. The driver sees a red light ahead, and after 1.5 seconds reaction time, the driver applies the brake. After the brake is applied, the car takes $\frac{x}{24}$ seconds to stop, during which time the average speed of the car is $\frac{x}{2}$ feet per second. If the car travels 165 feet from the time the driver saw the red light to the time it comes to a complete stop, which of the following expressions can be used to find the value of x?

A) $x^2 + 48x - 3{,}960$

B) $x^2 + 48x - 7{,}920$

C) $x^2 + 72x - 3{,}960$

D) $x^2 + 72x - 7{,}920$

PRACTICE AT

khanacademy.org/sat

Example 4 requires careful translation of a word problem into an algebraic equation. It pays to be deliberate and methodical when translating word problems into equations on the SAT.

During the 1.5-second reaction time, the car is still traveling at x feet per second, so it travels a total of $1.5x$ feet. The average speed of the car during the $\frac{x}{24}$-second braking interval is $\frac{x}{2}$ feet per second, so over this interval, the car travels $\left(\frac{x}{2}\right)\left(\frac{x}{24}\right) = \frac{x^2}{48}$ feet. Since the total distance the car travels from the time the driver saw the red light to the time it comes to a complete stop is 165 feet, you have the equation $\frac{x^2}{48} + 1.5x = 165$. This quadratic equation can be rewritten in standard form by subtracting 165 from each side and then multiplying each side by 48, giving $x^2 + 72x - 7{,}920$, which is choice D.

Some questions on the SAT Math Test will ask you to solve a quadratic equation. You must determine the appropriate procedure: factoring, completing the square, the quadratic formula, use of a calculator (if permitted), or use of structure. You should also know the following facts in addition to the formulas in the directions:

▶ The sum of the solutions of $x^2 + bx + c = 0$ is $-b$.

▶ The product of the solutions of $x^2 + bx + c = 0$ is c.

Each of the facts can be seen from the factored form of a quadratic. If r and s are the solutions of $x^2 + bx + c = 0$, then $x^2 + bx + c = (x - r)(x - s)$. Thus, $b = -(r + s)$ and $c = (-r)(-s)$.

REMEMBER

The SAT Math Test may ask you to solve a quadratic equation. Be prepared to use the appropriate method. Practice using the various methods (below) until you are comfortable with all of them.

1. Factoring
2. Completing the square
3. Quadratic formula
4. Using a calculator (if permitted)

EXAMPLE 5

What are the solutions x of $x^2 - 3 = x$?

A) $\dfrac{-1 \pm \sqrt{11}}{2}$

B) $\dfrac{-1 \pm \sqrt{13}}{2}$

C) $\dfrac{1 \pm \sqrt{11}}{2}$

D) $\dfrac{1 \pm \sqrt{13}}{2}$

The equation can be solved by using the quadratic formula or by completing the square. Let's use the quadratic formula. First, subtract x from each side of $x^2 - 3 = x$ to put it in standard form: $x^2 - x - 3 = 0$. The quadratic formula states the solutions x of the equation $ax^2 + bx + c = 0$ are $\dfrac{-b \pm \sqrt{b^2 - 4ac}}{2a}$. For the equation $x^2 - x - 3 = 0$, you have $a = 1$, $b = -1$, and $c = -3$. Substituting these formulas into the quadratic formula gives $x = \dfrac{-(-1) \pm \sqrt{(-1)^2 - 4(1)(-3)}}{2(1)} = \dfrac{1 \pm \sqrt{1 - (-12)}}{2} = \dfrac{1 \pm \sqrt{13}}{2}$, which is choice D.

PRACTICE AT

khanacademy.org/sat

The quadratic formula states that the solutions x of the equation $ax^2 + bx + c = 0$ are $x = \dfrac{-b \pm \sqrt{b^2 - 4ac}}{2a}$.

EXAMPLE 6

If $x > 0$ and $2x^2 + 3x - 2 = 0$, what is the value of x?

The left-hand side of the equation can be factored: $2x^2 + 3x - 2 = (2x - 1)(x + 2) = 0$. Therefore, either $2x - 1 = 0$, which gives $x = \dfrac{1}{2}$, or $x + 2 = 0$, which gives $x = -2$. Since $x > 0$, the value of x is $\dfrac{1}{2}$.

REMEMBER

Pay close attention to all of the details in the question. In Example 6, x can equal $\dfrac{1}{2}$ or -2, but since the question states that $x > 0$, the value of x must be $\dfrac{1}{2}$.

EXAMPLE 7

What is the sum of the solutions of $(2x - 1)^2 = (x + 2)^2$?

If a and b are real numbers and $a^2 = b^2$, then either $a = b$ or $a = -b$. Since $(2x - 1)^2 = (x + 2)^2$, either $2x - 1 = x + 2$ or $2x - 1 = -(x + 2)$. In the first case, $x = 3$, and in the second case, $3x = -1$, or $x = -\dfrac{1}{3}$. Therefore, the sum of the solutions x of $(2x - 1)^2 = (x + 2)^2$ is $3 + \left(-\dfrac{1}{3}\right) = \left(\dfrac{8}{3}\right)$.

Exponential Functions, Equations, and Expressions and Radicals

We examined exponential functions in Examples 7 and 8 of Chapter 20. Some questions in Passport to Advanced Math ask you to build a function that models a given context. As discussed in Chapter 20, exponential functions model situations in which a quantity is multiplied by a constant factor for each time period. An exponential function can be increasing with time, in which case it models exponential growth, or it can be decreasing with time, in which case it models exponential decay.

EXAMPLE 8

A researcher estimates that the population of a city is declining at an annual rate of 0.6%. If the current population of the city is 80,000, which of the following expressions appropriately models the population of the city t years from now according to the researcher's estimate?

A) $80,000(1 - 0.006)^t$

B) $80,000(1 - 0.006^t)$

C) $80,000 - 1.006^t$

D) $80,000(0.006^t)$

PRACTICE AT

🌱 **khanacademy.org/sat**

A quantity that grows or decays by a fixed percent at regular intervals is said to possess exponential growth or decay.

Exponential growth is represented by the function $y = a(1 + r)^t$, while exponential decay is represented by the function $y = a(1 - r)^t$, where y is the new population, a is the initial population, r is the rate of growth or decay, and t is the number of time intervals that have elapsed.

According to the researcher's estimate, the population is decreasing by 0.6% each year. Since 0.6% is equal to 0.006, after the first year, the population is $80,000 - 0.006(80,000) = 80,000(1 - 0.006)$. After the second year, the population is $80,000(1 - 0.006) - 0.006(80,000)(1 - 0.006) = 80,000(1 - 0.006)^2$. Similarly, after t years, the population will be $80,000(1 - 0.006)^t$ according to the researcher's estimate. This is choice A.

Another well-known example of exponential decay is the decay of a radioactive isotope. One example is iodine-131, a radioactive isotope used in some medical treatments. The decay of iodine-131 emits beta and gamma radiation, and it decays to xenon-131. The half-life of iodine-131 is 8.02 days; that is, after 8.02 days, half of the iodine-131 in a sample will have decayed to xenon-131. Suppose a sample of A milligrams of iodine-131 decays for d days. Every 8.02 days, the quantity of iodine-131 is multiplied by $\frac{1}{2}$, or 2^{-1}. In d days, a total of $\frac{d}{8.02}$ different 8.02-day periods will have passed, and so the original quantity will have been multiplied by 2^{-1} a total of $\frac{d}{8.02}$ times. Therefore, the amount, in milligrams, of iodine-131 remaining in the sample will be $A(2^{-1})^{\frac{d}{8.02}} = A\left(2^{-\frac{d}{8.02}}\right)$. In the preceding discussion, we used the identity $\frac{1}{2} - 2^{-1}$. Questions on the SAT Math Test may require you to apply this and other laws of exponents and the relationship between powers and radicals.

EXAMPLE 9

Which of the following is equivalent to $\left(\dfrac{1}{\sqrt{x}}\right)^{n}$?

A) $x^{\frac{n}{2}}$

B) $x^{-\frac{n}{2}}$

C) $x^{n+\frac{1}{2}}$

D) $x^{n-\frac{1}{2}}$

The square root $\sqrt{x}$ is equal to $x^{\frac{1}{2}}$. Thus, $\dfrac{1}{\sqrt{x}} = x^{-\frac{1}{2}}$, and $\left(\dfrac{1}{\sqrt{x}}\right)^{n} = \left(x^{-\frac{1}{2}}\right)^{n} = x^{-\frac{n}{2}}$. Choice B is the correct answer.

An SAT Math Test question may also ask you to solve a radical equation. In solving radical equations, you may square both sides of an equation. Since squaring is *not* a reversible operation, you may end up with an extraneous root, that is, a root to the simplified equation that is *not* a root to the original equation. Thus, when solving a radical equation, you should check any solution you get in the original equation.

PRACTICE AT

khanacademy.org/sat

Practice your exponent rules. Know, for instance, that $\sqrt{x} = x^{\frac{1}{2}}$ and that $\dfrac{1}{\sqrt{x}} = x^{-\frac{1}{2}}$.

EXAMPLE 10

$$x - 12 = \sqrt{x + 44}$$

What is the solution set for the above equation?

A) $\{5\}$

B) $\{20\}$

C) $\{-5, 20\}$

D) $\{5, 20\}$

Squaring each side of $x - 12 = \sqrt{x + 44}$ gives

$$(x - 12)^2 = (\sqrt{x + 44})^2 = x + 44$$
$$x^2 - 24x + 144 = x + 44$$
$$x^2 - 25x + 100 = 0$$
$$(x - 5)(x - 20) = 0$$

The solutions to the quadratic are $x = 5$ and $x = 20$. However, since the first step was to square each side of the given equation, which is not a reversible operation, you need to check $x = 5$ and $x = 20$ in the original equation. Substituting 5 for x gives

$$5 - 12 = \sqrt{5 + 44}$$
$$-7 = \sqrt{49}$$

PRACTICE AT

khanacademy.org/sat

A good strategy to use when solving radical equations is to square both sides of the equation. When doing so, however, be sure to check the solutions in the original equation, as you may end up with a root that is not a solution to the original equation.

This is not a true statement (since $\sqrt{49}$ represents only the positive square root, 7), so $x = 5$ is *not* a solution to $x - 12 = \sqrt{x + 44}$. Substituting 20 for x gives

$$20 - 12 = \sqrt{20 + 44}$$
$$8 = \sqrt{64}$$

This is a true statement, so $x = 20$ is a solution to $x - 12 = \sqrt{x + 44}$. Therefore, the solution set is $\{20\}$, which is choice B.

Dividing Polynomials by a Linear Expression and Solving Rational Equations

Questions on the SAT Math Test may assess your ability to work with rational expressions, including fractions with a variable in the denominator. This may include long division of a polynomial by a linear expression or finding the solution to a rational equation.

EXAMPLE 11

> When $6x^2 - 5x + 4$ is divided by $3x + 2$, the result is $2x - 3 + \dfrac{R}{(3x + 2)}$, where R is a constant. What is the value of R?

Performing the long division gives

$$
\begin{array}{r}
2x - 3 \\
3x + 2 \overline{)6x^2 - 5x + 4} \\
\underline{6x^2 + 4x} \\
-9x + 4 \\
\underline{-9x - 6} \\
10
\end{array}
$$

Therefore, the remainder is 10.

If $ax + b$ is a factor of the polynomial $P(x)$, then $P(x)$ can be written as

$$P(x) = (ax + b)Q(x)$$

for some polynomial $Q(x)$. It follows that the solution to $ax + b = 0$, namely, $x = -\dfrac{b}{a}$, is a solution to $P(x) = 0$. More generally, if the number r is the remainder when $P(x)$ is divided by $ax + b$, you have

$$P(x) = (ax + b)Q(x) + r$$

It follows that for $x = -\dfrac{b}{a}$, the value of $P\left(-\dfrac{b}{a}\right) = (0)(Q(x)) + r = r$. This is another way to solve Example 11. The solution of $3x + 2 = 0$ is $x = -\dfrac{2}{3}$, so the remainder when $6x^2 - 5x + 4$ is divided by $3x + 2$ is the value of $6x^2 - 5x + 4$ when $-\dfrac{2}{3}$ is substituted for x: Remainder: $6\left(-\dfrac{2}{3}\right)^2 - 5\left(-\dfrac{2}{3}\right) + 4 = \dfrac{8}{3} + \dfrac{10}{3} + 4 = 10$.

EXAMPLE 12

$$\frac{3}{t+1} = \frac{2}{t+3} + \frac{1}{4}$$

If t is a solution to the equation above and $t > 0$, what is the value of t?

The first step in solving this equation is to clear the variable out of the denominators by multiplying each side by $(t + 1)(t + 3)$. This gives $3(t + 3) = 2(t + 1) + \frac{1}{4}(t + 1)(t + 3)$. Now multiply each side by 4 to get rid of the fraction: $12(t + 3) = 8(t + 1) + (t + 1)(t + 3)$. Expanding all the products and moving all the terms to the right-hand side gives $0 = t^2 - 25$. Therefore, the solutions to the equation are $t = 5$ and $t = -5$. Since $t > 0$, the value of t is 5.

PRACTICE AT

khanacademy.org/sat

When solving for a variable in an equation involving fractions, a good first step is to clear the variable out of the denominators of the fractions.

Systems of Equations

Questions on the SAT Math Test may ask you to solve a system of equations in two variables in which one equation is linear and the other equation is quadratic or another nonlinear equation.

EXAMPLE 13

$$3x + y = -3$$
$$(x + 1)^2 - 4(x + 1) - 6 = y$$

If (x, y) is a solution of the system of equations above and $y > 0$, what is the value of y?

The structure of the second equation suggests that $(x + 1)$ is a factor of the first equation. Subtracting $3x$ from each side of the first equation gives you $y = -3 - 3x$, which can be rewritten as $y = -3(x + 1)$. Substituting $-3(x + 1)$ for y in the second equation gives you $(x + 1)^2 - 4(x + 1) - 6 = -3(x + 1)$, which can be rewritten as $(x + 1)^2 - (x + 1) - 6 = 0$. The structure of this equation suggests that $x + 1$ can be treated as a variable. Factoring gives you $((x + 1) - 3)((x + 1) + 2) = 0$, or $(x - 2)(x + 3) = 0$. Thus, either $x = 2$, which gives $y = -3 - 3(2) = -9$; or $x = -3$, which gives $y = -3 - 3(-3) = 6$. Therefore, the solutions to the system are $(2, -9)$ and $(-3, 6)$. Since the question states that $y > 0$, the value of y is 6.

PRACTICE AT

khanacademy.org/sat

The first step to solving this example is substitution, an approach you may use on Heart of Algebra questions. The other key was noticing that $(x + 1)$ can be treated as a variable.

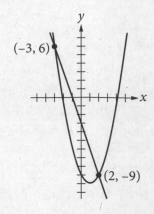

The solutions of the system are given by the intersection points of the two graphs. Questions on the SAT Math Test may assess this or other relationships between algebraic and graphical representations of functions.

Relationships Between Algebraic and Graphical Representations of Functions

A function $f(x)$ has a graph in the xy-plane, which is the graph of the equation $y = f(x)$ (or, equivalently, consists of all ordered pairs $(x, f(x))$). Some questions in Passport to Advanced Math assess your ability to relate properties of the function f to properties of its graph, and vice versa. You may be required to apply some of the following relationships:

▶ **Intercepts.** The x-intercepts of the graph of f correspond to values of x such that $f(x) = 0$; if the function f has no zeros, its graph has no x-intercepts, and vice versa. The y-intercept of the graph of f corresponds to the value of $f(0)$. If $x = 0$ is not in the domain of f, the graph of f has no y-intercept, and vice versa.

▶ **Domain and range.** The domain of f is the set of all x for which $f(x)$ is defined. The range of f is the set of all y with $y = f(x)$ for some value of x in the domain. The domain and range can be found from the graph of f as the set of all x-coordinates and y-coordinates, respectively, of points on the graph.

▶ **Maximum and minimum values.** The maximum and minimum values of f can be found by locating the highest and the lowest points on the graph, respectively. For example, suppose P is the highest point on the graph of f. Then the y-coordinate of P is the maximum value of f, and the x-coordinate of P is where f takes on its maximum value.

▶ **Increasing and decreasing.** The graph of f shows the intervals over which the function f is increasing and decreasing.

▶ **End behavior.** The graph of f can indicate if $f(x)$ increases or decreases without limit as x gets very large and positive or very large and negative.

▶ **Asymptotes.** If the values of f approach a fixed value, say K, as x gets very large and positive or very large and negative, the graph of f has a horizontal asymptote at $y = K$. If f is a rational function whose denominator is zero and numerator is nonzero at $x = a$, then the graph of f has a vertical asymptote at $x = a$.

▶ **Symmetry.** If the graph of f is symmetric about the y-axis, then f is an even function, that is, $f(-x) = f(x)$ for all x in the domain of f. If the graph of f is symmetric about the origin, then f is an odd function, that is, $f(-x) = -f(x)$ for all x in the domain of f.

▶ **Transformations.** For a graph of a function f, a change of the form $f(x) + a$ will result in a vertical shift of a units and a change of the form $f(x + a)$ will result in a horizontal shift of a units.

Note: The SAT Math Test uses the following conventions about graphs in the xy-plane *unless* a particular question clearly states or shows a different convention:

▶ The axes are perpendicular.

▶ Scales on the axes are linear scales.

▶ The size of the units on the two axes *cannot* be assumed to be equal unless the question states they are equal or you are given enough information to conclude they are equal.

▶ The values on the horizontal axis increase as you move to the right.

▶ The values on the vertical axis increase as you move up.

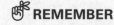 **REMEMBER**

Don't assume the size of the units on the two axes are equal unless the question states they are equal or you can conclude they are equal from the information given.

EXAMPLE 14

The graph of which of the following functions in the xy-plane has x-intercepts at -4 and 5?

A) $f(x) = (x + 4)(x - 5)$

B) $g(x) = (x - 4)(x + 5)$

C) $h(x) = (x - 4)^2 + 5$

D) $k(x) = (x + 5)^2 - 4$

The x-intercepts of the graph of a function correspond to the zeros of the function. If a function has x-intercepts at -4 and 5, then the values of the function at -4 and 5 are each 0. The function in choice A is in factored form,

PRACTICE AT

🌱 **khanacademy.org/sat**

Another way to think of this question is to ask yourself, "Which answer choice represents a function that has values of zero when $x = -4$ and $x = +5$?"

which shows that $f(x) = 0$ if and only if $x + 4 = 0$ or $x - 5 = 0$, that is, if $x = -4$ or $x = 5$. Therefore, $f(x) = (x + 4)(x - 5)$ has x-intercepts at -4 and 5.

The graph in the xy-plane of each of the functions in the previous example is a parabola. Using the defining equations, you can tell that the graph of g has x-intercepts at 4 and -5; the graph of h has its vertex at $(4, 5)$; and the graph of k has its vertex at $(-5, -4)$.

EXAMPLE 15

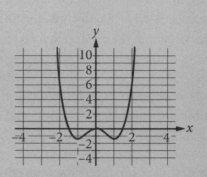

The function $f(x) = x^4 - 2.4x^2$ is graphed in the xy-plane as shown above. If k is a constant such that the equation $f(x) = k$ has 4 solutions, which of the following could be the value of k?

A) 1
B) 0
C) −1
D) −2

Choice C is correct. The equation $f(x) = k$ will have 4 solutions if and only if the graph of the horizontal line with equation $y = k$ intersects the graph of f at 4 points. The graph shows that of the given choices, only for choice C, −1, does the graph of $y = -1$ intersect the graph of f at 4 points.

Function Notation

The SAT Math Test assesses your understanding of function notation. You must be able to evaluate a function given the rule that defines it, and if the function describes a context, you may need to interpret the value of the function in the context. A question may ask you to interpret a function when an expression, such as $2x$ or $x + 1$, is used as the argument instead of the variable x, or a question may ask you to evaluate the composition of two functions.

EXAMPLE 16

If $g(x) = 2x + 1$ and $f(x) = g(x) + 4$, what is $f(2)$?

PRACTICE AT
khanacademy.org/sat

What may seem at first to be a complex question boils down to straightforward substitution.

You are given $f(x) = g(x) + 4$ and therefore $f(2) = g(2) + 4$. To determine the value of $g(2)$, use the function $g(x) = 2x + 1$. Thus, $g(2) = 2(2) + 1$, and $g(2) = 5$. Substituting $g(2)$ gives $f(2) = 5 + 4$, or $f(2) = 9$.

Analyzing More Complex Equations in Context

Equations and functions that describe a real-life context can be complex. Often it is not possible to analyze them as completely as you can analyze a linear equation or function. You still can acquire key information about the context by analyzing the equation or function that describes it. Questions on the Passport to Advanced Math section may ask you to use an equation describing a context to determine how a change in one quantity affects another quantity. You may also be asked to manipulate an equation to isolate a quantity of interest on one side of the equation. You may be asked to produce or identify a form of an equation that reveals new information about the context it represents or about the graphical representation of the equation.

EXAMPLE 17

If an object of mass m is moving at speed v, the object's kinetic energy KE is given by the equation $KE = \frac{1}{2}mv^2$. If the mass of the object is halved and its speed is doubled, how does the kinetic energy change?

A) The kinetic energy is halved.
B) The kinetic energy is unchanged.
C) The kinetic energy is doubled.
D) The kinetic energy is quadrupled (multiplied by a factor of 4).

PRACTICE AT
khanacademy.org/sat

Another way to check your answer here is to pick simple numbers for mass and speed and examine the impact on kinetic energy when those values are altered as indicated by the question. If mass and speed both equal 1, kinetic energy is $\frac{1}{2}$.

When mass is halved, to $\frac{1}{2}$, and speed is doubled, to 2, the new kinetic energy is 1. Since 1 is twice the value of $\frac{1}{2}$, we know that kinetic energy is doubled.

Choice C is correct. If the mass of the object is halved, the new mass is $\frac{m}{2}$. If the speed of the object is doubled, its new speed is $2v$. Therefore, the new kinetic energy is $\frac{1}{2}\left(\frac{m}{2}\right)(2v)^2 = \frac{1}{2}\left(\frac{m}{2}\right)(4v^2) = mv^2$. This is double the kinetic energy of the original object, which was $\frac{1}{2}mv^2$.

EXAMPLE 18

A gas in a container will escape through holes of microscopic size, as long as the holes are larger than the gas molecules. This process is called effusion. If a gas of molar mass M_1 effuses at a rate of r_1 and a gas of molar mass M_2 effuses at a rate of r_2, then the following relationship holds.

$$\frac{r_1}{r_2} = \sqrt{\frac{M_2}{M_1}}$$

This is known as Graham's law. Which of the following correctly expresses M_2 in terms of M_1, r_1, and r_2?

A) $M_2 = M_1 \dfrac{r_1^2}{r_2^2}$

B) $M_2 = M_1 \dfrac{r_2^2}{r_1^2}$

C) $M_2 = \sqrt{M_1} \dfrac{r_1}{r_2}$

D) $M_2 = \sqrt{M_1} \dfrac{r_2}{r_1}$

PRACTICE AT

khanacademy.org/sat

Always start by identifying exactly what the question asks. In this case, you are being asked to isolate the variable M_2. Squaring both sides of the equation is a great first step as it allows you to eliminate the radical sign.

Squaring each side of $\dfrac{r_1}{r_2} = \sqrt{\dfrac{M_2}{M_1}}$ gives $\left(\dfrac{r_1}{r_2}\right)^2 = \left(\sqrt{\dfrac{M_2}{M_1}}\right)^2$, which can be rewritten as $\dfrac{M_2}{M_1} = \dfrac{r_1^2}{r_2^2}$. Multiplying each side of $\dfrac{M_2}{M_1} = \dfrac{r_1^2}{r_2^2}$ by M_1 gives $M_2 = M_1 \dfrac{r_1^2}{r_2^2}$, which is choice A.

EXAMPLE 19

A store manager estimates that if a video game is sold at a price of p dollars, the store will have weekly revenue, in dollars, of $r(p) = -4p^2 + 200p$ from the sale of the video game. Which of the following equivalent forms of $r(p)$ shows, as constants or coefficients, the maximum possible weekly revenue and the price that results in the maximum revenue?

A) $r(p) = 200p - 4p^2$
B) $r(p) = -2(2p^2 - 100p)$
C) $r(p) = -4(p^2 - 50p)$
D) $r(p) = -4(p - 25)^2 + 2,500$

PRACTICE AT

khanacademy.org/sat

The fact that the coefficient of the squared term is negative for this function indicates that the graph of r in the coordinate plane is a parabola that opens downward. Thus, the maximum value of revenue corresponds to the vertex of the parabola.

Choice D is correct. The graph of r in the coordinate plane is a parabola that opens downward. The maximum value of revenue corresponds to the vertex of the parabola. Since the square of any real number is always nonnegative, the form $r(p) = -4(p - 25)^2 + 2,500$ shows that the vertex of the parabola is $(25, 2,500)$; that is, the maximum must occur where $-4(p - 25)^2$ is 0, which is $p = 25$, and this maximum is $r(25) = 2,500$. Thus, the maximum possible weekly revenue and the price that results in the maximum revenue occur as constants in the form $r(p) = -4(p - 25)^2 + 2,500$.

Chapter 22

Additional Topics in Math

In addition to the questions in Heart of Algebra, Problem Solving and Data Analysis, and Passport to Advanced Math, the SAT Math Test includes several questions that are drawn from areas of geometry, trigonometry, and the arithmetic of complex numbers. They include both multiple-choice and student-produced response questions. On some questions, the use of a calculator is not permitted; on others, the use of a calculator is allowed.

Let's explore the content and skills assessed by these questions.

Geometry

The SAT Math Test includes questions that assess your understanding of the key concepts in the geometry of lines, angles, triangles, circles, and other geometric objects. Other questions may also ask you to find the area, surface area, or volume of an abstract figure or a real-life object. You do not need to memorize a large collection of formulas. Many of the geometry formulas are provided in the Reference Information at the beginning of each section of the SAT Math Test, and less commonly used formulas required to answer a question are given with the question.

To answer geometry questions on the SAT Math Test, you should recall the geometry definitions learned prior to high school and know the essential concepts extended while learning geometry in high school. You should also be familiar with basic geometric notation.

Here are some of the areas that may be the focus of some questions on the SAT Math Test.

▶ Lines and angles

   — Lengths and midpoints

   — Vertical angles

   — Straight angles and the sum of the angles about a point

REMEMBER

6 of the 58 questions (approximately 10%) on the SAT Math Test will be drawn from Additional Topics in Math, which includes geometry, trigonometry, and the arithmetic of complex numbers.

REMEMBER

You do not need to memorize a large collection of geometry formulas. Many geometry formulas are provided on the SAT Math Test in the Reference section of the directions.

— Properties of parallel lines and the angles formed when parallel lines are cut by a transversal

— Properties of perpendicular lines

▶ Triangles and other polygons

— Right triangles and the Pythagorean theorem

— Properties of equilateral and isosceles triangles

— Properties of 30°-60°-90° triangles and 45°-45°-90° triangles

— Congruent triangles and other congruent figures

— Similar triangles and other similar figures

— The triangle inequality

— Squares, rectangles, parallelograms, trapezoids, and other quadrilaterals

— Regular polygons

▶ Circles

— Radius, diameter, and circumference

— Measure of central angles and inscribed angles

— Arc length and area of sectors

— Tangents and chords

PRACTICE AT

khanacademy.org/sat

The triangle inequality theorem states that for any triangle, the length of any side of the triangle must be less than the sum of the other two sides of the triangle and greater than the difference of the other two sides.

You should be familiar with the geometric notation for points and lines, line segments, angles and their measures, and lengths.

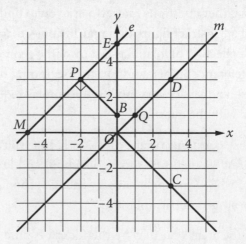

In the figure above, the xy-plane has origin O. The values of x on the horizontal x-axis increase as you move to the right, and the values of y on the vertical y-axis increase as you move up. Line e contains point P, which has coordinates $(-2, 3)$, and point E, which has coordinates $(0, 5)$. Line m passes through the origin O $(0, 0)$ and the point Q $(1, 1)$.

Lines e and m are parallel — they never meet. This is written $e \parallel m$.

You will also need to know the following notation:

▶ $\overleftrightarrow{PE}$: the line containing the points P and E (this is the same as line e)

▶ $\overline{PE}$ or segment PE: the line segment with endpoints P and E

▶ PE: the length of segment PE (you can write $PE = 2\sqrt{2}$)

▶ $\overrightarrow{PE}$: the ray starting at point P and extending indefinitely in the direction of E

▶ $\overrightarrow{EP}$: the ray starting at point E and extending indefinitely in the direction of P

▶ $\angle DOC$: the angle formed by $\overrightarrow{OD}$ and $\overrightarrow{OC}$

▶ $m\angle DOC$: the measure of $\angle DOC$ (you can write $m\angle DOC = 90°$)

▶ $\triangle PEB$: the triangle with vertices P, E, and B

▶ $BPMO$: the quadrilateral with vertices B, P, M, and O

▶ $\overline{BP} \perp \overline{PM}$: segment BP is perpendicular to segment PM (you should also recognize that the small square within $\angle BPM$ means this angle is a right angle)

PRACTICE AT

🌰 **khanacademy.org/sat**

Familiarize yourself with these notations in order to avoid confusion on test day.

EXAMPLE 1

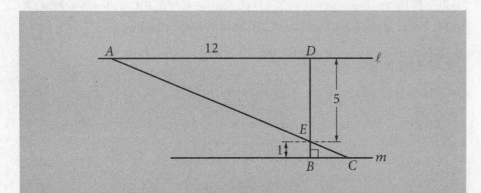

In the figure above, line ℓ is parallel to line m, segment BD is perpendicular to line m, and segment AC and segment BD intersect at E. What is the length of segment AC?

Since segment AC and segment BD intersect at E, $\angle AED$ and $\angle CEB$ are vertical angles, and so the measure of $\angle AED$ is equal to the measure of $\angle CEB$. Since line ℓ is parallel to line m, $\angle BCE$ and $\angle DAE$ are alternate interior angles of parallel lines cut by a transversal, and so the measure of $\angle BCE$ is equal to the measure of $\angle DAE$. By the angle-angle theorem, $\triangle AED$ is similar to $\triangle CEB$, with vertices A, E, and D corresponding to vertices C, E, and B, respectively.

PRACTICE AT

🌱 **khanacademy.org/sat**

A shortcut here is remembering that 5, 12, 13 is a Pythagorean triple (5 and 12 are the lengths of the sides of the right triangle, and 13 is the length of the hypotenuse). Another common Pythagorean triple is 3, 4, 5.

PRACTICE AT

🌱 **khanacademy.org/sat**

Note how Example 1 requires the knowledge and application of numerous fundamental geometry concepts. Develop mastery of the fundamental concepts and practice applying them on test-like questions.

Also, $\triangle AED$ is a right triangle, so by the Pythagorean theorem, $AE = \sqrt{AD^2 + DE^2} = \sqrt{12^2 + 5^2} = \sqrt{169} = 13$. Since $\triangle AED$ is similar to $\triangle CEB$, the ratios of the lengths of corresponding sides of the two triangles are in the same proportion, which is $\dfrac{ED}{EB} = \dfrac{5}{1} = 5$. Thus, $\dfrac{AE}{EC} = \dfrac{13}{EC} = 5$, and so $EC = \dfrac{13}{5}$. Therefore, $AC = AE + EC = 13 + \dfrac{13}{5} = \dfrac{78}{5}$.

Note some of the key concepts that were used in Example 1:

▶ Vertical angles have the same measure.

▶ When parallel lines are cut by a transversal, the alternate interior angles have the same measure.

▶ If two angles of a triangle are congruent to (have the same measure as) two angles of another triangle, the two triangles are similar.

▶ The Pythagorean theorem.

▶ If two triangles are similar, then all ratios of lengths of corresponding sides are equal.

▶ If point E lies on line segment AC, then $AC = AE + EC$.

Note that if two triangles or other polygons are similar or congruent, the order in which the vertices are named does *not* necessarily indicate how the vertices correspond in the similarity or congruence. Thus, it was stated explicitly in Example 1 that "$\triangle AED$ is similar to $\triangle CEB$, with vertices A, E, and D corresponding to vertices C, E, and B, respectively."

EXAMPLE 2

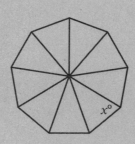

In the figure above, a regular polygon with 9 sides has been divided into 9 congruent isosceles triangles by line segments drawn from the center of the polygon to its vertices. What is the value of x?

The sum of the measures of the angles around a point is 360°. Since the 9 triangles are congruent, the measures of each of the 9 angles are the same. Thus, the measure of each angle is $\dfrac{360°}{9} = 40°$. In any triangle, the sum of the measures of the interior angles is 180°. So in each triangle, the sum of the measures of the remaining two angles is 180° − 40° = 140°. Since each triangle is isosceles, the measure of each of these two angles is the same. Therefore, the measure of each of these angles is $\frac{140°}{2}$ = 70°. Hence, the value of x is 70.

Note some of the key concepts that were used in Example 2:

▸ The sum of the measures of the angles about a point is 360°.

▸ Corresponding angles of congruent triangles have the same measure.

▸ The sum of the measure of the interior angles of any triangle is 180°.

▸ In an isosceles triangle, the angles opposite the sides of equal length are of equal measure.

EXAMPLE 3

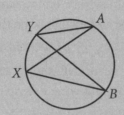

In the figure above, ∠AXB and ∠AYB are inscribed in the circle. Which of the following statements is true?

    A) The measure of ∠AXB is greater than the measure of ∠AYB.

    B) The measure of ∠AXB is less than the measure of ∠AYB.

    C) The measure of ∠AXB is equal to the measure of ∠AYB.

    D) There is not enough information to determine the relationship between the measure of ∠AXB and the measure of ∠AYB.

Choice C is correct. Let the measure of arc $\overset{\frown}{AB}$ be $d°$. Since ∠AXB is inscribed in the circle and intercepts arc $\overset{\frown}{AB}$, the measure of ∠AXB is equal to half the measure of arc $\overset{\frown}{AB}$. Thus, the measure of ∠AXB is $\frac{d°}{2}$. Similarly, since ∠AYB is also inscribed in the circle and intercepts arc $\overset{\frown}{AB}$, the measure of ∠AYB is also $\frac{d°}{2}$. Therefore, the measure of ∠AXB is equal to the measure of ∠AYB.

Note the key concept that was used in Example 3:

▸ The measure of an angle inscribed in a circle is equal to half the measure of its intercepted arc.

You also should know this related concept:

▸ The measure of a central angle in a circle is equal to the measure of its intercepted arc.

PRACTICE AT

khanacademy.org/sat

At first glance, it may appear as though there is not enough information to determine the relationship between the two angle measures. One key to this question is identifying what is the same about the two angle measures. In this case, both angles intercept arc $\overset{\frown}{AB}$.

You should also be familiar with notation for arcs and circles on the SAT:

▶ A circle may be named by the point at its center. So, the center of a circle M would be point M.

▶ An arc named with only its two endpoints, such as $\overset{\frown}{AB}$, will always refer to a minor arc. A minor arc has a measure that is less than 180°.

▶ An arc may also be named with three points: the two endpoints and a third point that the arc passes through. So, $\overset{\frown}{ACB}$ has endpoints at A and B and passes through point C. Three points may be used to name a minor arc or an arc that has a measure of 180° or more.

REMEMBER

Figures are drawn to scale on the SAT Math Test unless explicitly stated otherwise. If a question states that a figure is not drawn to scale, be careful not to make unwarranted assumptions about the figure.

In general, figures that accompany questions on the SAT Math Test are intended to provide information that is useful in answering the question. They are drawn as accurately as possible EXCEPT in a particular question when it is stated that the figure is not drawn to scale. In general, even in figures not drawn to scale, the relative positions of points and angles may be assumed to be in the order shown. Also, line segments that extend through points and appear to lie on the same line may be assumed to be on the same line. A point that appears to lie on a line or curve may be assumed to lie on the line or curve.

The text "Note: Figure not drawn to scale." is included with the figure when degree measures may not be accurately shown and specific lengths may not be drawn proportionally. The following example illustrates what information can and cannot be assumed from a figure not drawn to scale.

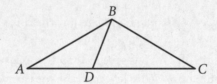

Note: Figure not drawn to scale.

A question may refer to a triangle such as *ABC* above. Although the note indicates that the figure is not drawn to scale, you may assume the following from the figure:

▶ *ABD* and *DBC* are triangles.

▶ *D* is between *A* and *C*.

▶ *A*, *D*, and *C* are points on a line.

▶ The length of $\overline{AD}$ is less than the length of $\overline{AC}$.

▶ The measure of angle *ABD* is less than the measure of angle *ABC*.

You may *not* assume the following from the figure:

▶ The length of $\overline{AD}$ is less than the length of $\overline{DC}$.

▶ The measures of angles *BAD* and *DBA* are equal.

▶ The measure of angle *DBC* is greater than the measure of angle *ABD*.

▶ Angle *DBC* is a right angle.

EXAMPLE 4

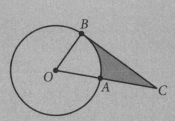

In the figure above, O is the center of the circle, segment BC is tangent to the circle at B, and A lies on segment OC. If $OB = AC = 6$, what is the area of the shaded region?

A) $18\sqrt{3} - 3\pi$

B) $18\sqrt{3} - 6\pi$

C) $36\sqrt{3} - 3\pi$

D) $36\sqrt{3} - 6\pi$

Since segment BC is tangent to the circle at B, it follows that $\overline{BC} \perp \overline{OB}$, and so triangle OBC is a right triangle with its right angle at B. Since $OB = 6$ and OB and OA are both radii of the circle, $OA = OB = 6$, and $OC = OA + AC = 12$. Thus, triangle OBC is a right triangle with the length of the hypotenuse ($OC = 12$) twice the length of one of its legs ($OB = 6$). It follows that triangle OBC is a 30°-60°-90° triangle with its 30° angle at C and its 60° angle at O. The area of the shaded region is the area of triangle OBC minus the area of the sector bounded by radii OA and OB.

In the 30°-60°-90° triangle OBC, the length of side OB, which is opposite the 30° angle, is 6. Thus, the length of side BC, which is opposite the 60° angle, is $6\sqrt{3}$. Hence, the area of triangle OBC is $\frac{1}{2}(6)(6\sqrt{3}) = 18\sqrt{3}$. Since the sector bounded by radii OA and OB has central angle 60°, the area of this sector is $\frac{60}{360} = \frac{1}{6}$ of the area of the circle. Since the circle has radius 6, its area is $\pi(6)^2 = 36\pi$, and so the area of the sector is $\frac{1}{6}(36\pi) = 6\pi$. Therefore, the area of the shaded region is $18\sqrt{3} - 6\pi$, which is choice B.

Note some of the key concepts that were used in Example 4:

▶ A tangent to a circle is perpendicular to the radius of the circle drawn to the point of tangency.

▶ Properties of 30°-60°-90° triangles.

▶ Area of a circle.

▶ The area of a sector with central angle $x°$ is equal to $\frac{x}{360}$, the area of the entire circle.

PRACTICE AT

🌱 **khanacademy.org/sat**

On complex multistep questions such as Example 4, start by identifying the task (finding the area of the shaded region) and considering the intermediate steps that you'll need to solve for (the area of triangle OBC and the area of sector OBA) in order to get to the final answer. Breaking up this question into a series of smaller questions will make it more manageable.

PRACTICE AT

🌱 **khanacademy.org/sat**

Arc length, area of a sector, and central angle are all proportional to each other in a circle. This proportionality is written as:

arc length / circumference = central angle / 360 degrees = area of a sector / area of a circle

EXAMPLE 5

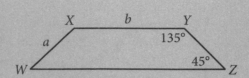

Trapezoid *WXYZ* is shown above. How much greater is the area of this trapezoid than the area of a parallelogram with side lengths *a* and *b* and base angles of measure 45° and 135°?

A) $\frac{1}{2}a^2$

B) $\sqrt{2}\,a^2$

C) $\frac{1}{2}ab$

D) $\sqrt{2}\,ab$

PRACTICE AT

🍂 **khanacademy.org/sat**

Note how drawing the parallelogram within trapezoid *WXYZ* makes it much easier to compare the areas of the two shapes, minimizing the amount of calculation needed to arrive at the solution. Be on the lookout for time-saving shortcuts such as this one.

In the figure, draw a line segment from *Y* to the point *P* on side *WZ* of the trapezoid such that ∠*YPW* has measure 135°, as shown in the figure below.

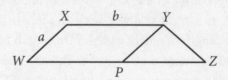

Since in trapezoid *WXYZ* side *XY* is parallel to side *WZ*, it follows that *WXYP* is a parallelogram with side lengths *a* and *b* and base angles of measure 45° and 135°. Thus, the area of the trapezoid is greater than a parallelogram with side lengths *a* and *b* and base angles of measure 45° and 135° by the area of triangle *PYZ*. Since ∠*YPW* has measure 135°, it follows that ∠*YPZ* has measure 45°. Hence, triangle *PYZ* is a 45°-45°-90° triangle with legs of length *a*. Therefore, its area is $\frac{1}{2}a^2$, which is choice A.

Note some of the key concepts that were used in Example 5:

▸ Properties of trapezoids and parallelograms

▸ Area of a 45°-45°-90° triangle

Some questions on the SAT Math Test may ask you to find the area, surface area, or volume of an object, possibly in a real-life context.

EXAMPLE 6

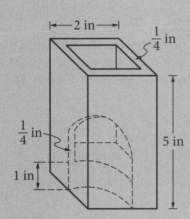

Note: Figure not drawn to scale.

A glass vase is in the shape of a rectangular prism with a square base. The figure above shows the vase with a portion cut out. The external dimensions of the vase are height 5 inches (in), with a square base of side length 2 inches. The vase has a solid base of height 1 inch, and the sides are each $\frac{1}{4}$ inch thick. Which of the following is the volume, in cubic inches, of the glass used in the vase?

A) 6

B) 8

C) 9

D) 11

The volume of the glass used in the vase can be calculated by subtracting the inside volume of the vase from the outside volume of the vase. Both the inside and outside volumes are from different-sized rectangular prisms. The outside dimensions of the prism are 5 inches by 2 inches by 2 inches, so its volume, including the glass, is $5 \times 2 \times 2 = 20$ cubic inches. For the inside volume of the vase, since it has a solid base of height 1 inch, the height of the prism removed is $5 - 1 = 4$ inches. In addition, each side of the vase is $\frac{1}{4}$ inch thick, so each side length of the inside volume is $2 - \frac{1}{4} - \frac{1}{4} = \frac{3}{2}$ inches. Thus, the inside volume of the vase removed is $4 \times \frac{3}{2} \times \frac{3}{2} = 9$ cubic inches. Therefore, the volume of the glass used in the vase is $20 - 9 = 11$ cubic inches, which is choice D.

Coordinate Geometry

Questions on the SAT Math Test may ask you to use the coordinate plane and equations of lines and circles to describe figures. You may be asked to create the equation of a circle given the figure or use the structure of a given equation to determine a property of a figure in the coordinate plane. You

PRACTICE AT

khanacademy.org/sat

Pay close attention to detail on a question such as Example 6. You must take into account the fact that the vase has a solid base of height 1 inch when subtracting the inside volume of the vase from the outside volume of the vase.

MATH

PRACTICE AT

 khanacademy.org/sat

You should know that the graph of $(x - a)^2 + (y - b)^2 = r^2$ in the xy-plane is a circle with center (a, b) and radius r.

should know that the graph of $(x - a)^2 + (y - b)^2 = r^2$ in the xy-plane is a circle with center (a, b) and radius r.

EXAMPLE 7

$$x^2 + (y + 1)^2 = 4$$

The graph of the equation above in the xy-plane is a circle. If the center of this circle is translated 1 unit up and the radius is increased by 1, which of the following is an equation of the resulting circle?

A) $x^2 + y^2 = 5$
B) $x^2 + y^2 = 9$
C) $x^2 + (y + 2)^2 = 5$
D) $x^2 + (y + 2)^2 = 9$

The graph of the equation $x^2 + (y + 1)^2 = 4$ in the xy-plane is a circle with center $(0, -1)$ and radius $\sqrt{4} = 2$. If the center is translated 1 unit up, the center of the new circle will be $(0, 0)$. If the radius is increased by 1, the radius of the new circle will be 3. Therefore, an equation of the new circle in the xy-plane is $x^2 + y^2 = 3^2 = 9$, so choice B is correct.

EXAMPLE 8

$$x^2 + 8x + y^2 - 6y = 24$$

The graph of the equation above in the xy-plane is a circle. What is the radius of the circle?

The given equation is not in the standard form $(x - a)^2 + (y - b)^2 = r^2$. You can put it in standard form by completing the square. Since the coefficient of x is 8 and the coefficient of y is -6, you can write the equation in terms of $(x + 4)^2$ and $(y - 3)^2$ as follows:

$$x^2 + 8x + y^2 - 6y = 24$$

$$(x^2 + 8x + 16) - 16 + (y^2 - 6y + 9) - 9 = 24$$

$$(x + 4)^2 - 16 + (y - 3)^2 - 9 = 24$$

$$(x + 4)^2 + (y - 3)^2 = 24 + 16 + 9 = 49 = 7^2$$

Therefore, the radius of the circle is 7. (Also, the center of the circle is $(-4, 3)$.)

Trigonometry and Radians

Questions on the SAT Math Test may ask you to apply the definitions of right triangle trigonometry. You should also know the definition of radian measure; you may also need to convert between angle measure in degrees and radians.

You may need to evaluate trigonometric functions at benchmark angle measures such as $0, \frac{\pi}{6}, \frac{\pi}{4}, \frac{\pi}{3}$, and $\frac{\pi}{2}$ radians (which are equal to the angle measures $0°$, $30°$, $45°$, $60°$, and $90°$, respectively). You will *not* be asked for values of trigonometric functions that require a calculator.

For an acute angle, the trigonometric functions sine, cosine, and tangent can be defined using right triangles. (Note that the functions are often abbreviated as sin, cos, and tan, respectively.)

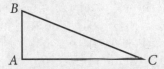

For $\angle C$ in the right triangle above:

▶ $\sin(\angle C) = \dfrac{AB}{BC} = \dfrac{\text{length of leg opposite } \angle C}{\text{length of hypotenuse}}$

▶ $\cos(\angle C) = \dfrac{AC}{BC} = \dfrac{\text{length of leg adjacent to } \angle C}{\text{length of hypotenuse}}$

▶ $\tan(\angle C) = \dfrac{AB}{AC} = \dfrac{\text{length of leg opposite } \angle C}{\text{length of leg adjacent to } \angle C} = \dfrac{\sin(\angle C)}{\cos(\angle C)}$,

The functions will often be written as sin C, cos C, and tan C, respectively.

Note that the trigonometric functions are actually functions of the *measures* of an angle, not the angle itself. Thus, if the measure of $\angle C$ is, say, $30°$, you can write $\sin(30°)$, $\cos(30°)$, and $\tan(30°)$, respectively.

Also note that $\sin B = \dfrac{\text{length of leg opposite } \angle B}{\text{length of hypotenuse}} = \dfrac{AC}{BC} = \cos C$. This is the complementary angle relationship: $\sin(x°) = \cos(90° - x°)$.

EXAMPLE 9

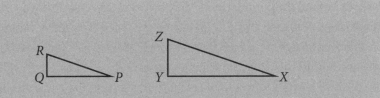

In the figure above, right triangle PQR is similar to right triangle XYZ, with vertices P, Q, and R corresponding to vertices X, Y, and Z, respectively. If $\cos R = 0.263$ what is the value of $\cos Z$?

By the definition of cosine, $\cos R = \dfrac{RQ}{RP}$ and $\cos Z = \dfrac{ZY}{ZX}$. Since triangle PQR is similar to triangle XYZ, with vertices P, Q, and R corresponding to vertices X, Y, and Z, respectively, the ratios $\dfrac{RQ}{RP}$ and $\dfrac{ZY}{ZX}$ are equal. Therefore, since $\cos R = \dfrac{RQ}{RP} = 0.263$, it follows that $\cos Z = \dfrac{ZY}{ZX} = 0.263$.

Note that this is why, to find the values of the trigonometric functions of, say, $d°$, you can use *any* right triangle with an acute angle of measure $d°$ and then take the appropriate ratio of lengths of sides.

Note that since an acute angle of a right triangle has measure between 0° and 90°, exclusive, right triangles can be used only to find values of trigonometric functions for angles with measures between 0° and 90°, exclusive. The definitions of sine, cosine, and tangent can be extended to all values. This is done using radian measure and the unit circle.

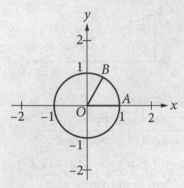

The circle above has radius 1 and is centered at the origin, O. An angle in the coordinate plane is said to be in standard position if it meets these two conditions: (1) its vertex lies at the origin and (2) one of its sides lies along the positive x-axis. Since angle AOB above, formed by segments OA and OB, meets both these conditions, it is said to be in *standard position*. As segment OB, also called the *terminal side* of angle AOB, rotates counterclockwise about the circle, while OA is anchored along the x-axis, the *radian* measure of angle AOB is defined to be the length s of the arc that angle AOB intercepts on the unit circle. In turn, $m\angle AOB$ is s radians.

When an acute angle AOB is in standard position within the unit circle, the x-coordinate of point B is $\cos(\angle AOB)$, and the y-coordinate of point B is $\sin(\angle AOB)$. When $\angle AOB$ is greater than 90 degrees (or $\dfrac{\pi}{4 \text{ radians}}$), and point B extends beyond the boundaries of the positive x-axis and positive y-axis, the values of $\cos(\angle AOB)$ and $\sin(\angle AOB)$ can be expressed as negative values depending on the coordinates of point B. For any angle AOB, place angle AOB in standard position within the circle of radius 1 centered at the origin, with side OA along the positive x-axis and terminal side OB intersecting the circle at point B. Then the cosine of angle AOB is the x-coordinate of B, and the sine of angle AOB is the y-coordinate of B. The tangent of angle AOB is the cosine of angle AOB divided by the sine of angle AOB.

An angle with a full rotation about point O has measure 360°. This angle intercepts the full circumference of the circle, which has length 2π. Thus,

PRACTICE AT

khanacademy.org/sat

To convert from degrees to radians, multiply the number of degrees by 2π / 360 degrees. To convert from radians to degrees, multiply the number of radians by 360 degrees / 2π.

$\dfrac{\text{measure of an angle in radians}}{\text{measure of an angle in degrees}} = \dfrac{2\pi}{360°}$. It follows that

$$\text{measure of an angle in radians} = \dfrac{2\pi}{360°} \times \text{measure of an angle in degrees and}$$

$$\text{measure of an angle in degrees} = \dfrac{360°}{2\pi} \times \text{measure of an angle in radians.}$$

Also note that since a rotation of 2π about point O brings you back to the same point on the unit circle, $\sin(s + 2\pi) = \sin(s)$, $\cos(s + 2\pi) = \cos(s)$, and $\tan(s + 2\pi) = \tan(s)$, for any radian measure s.

Let angle DEF be a central angle in a circle of radius r, as shown in the following figure.

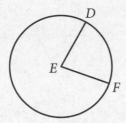

A circle of radius r is similar to a circle of radius 1, with constant of proportionality equal to r. Thus, the length s of the arc intercepted by angle DEF is r times the length of the arc that would be intercepted by an angle of the same measure in a circle of radius 1. Therefore, in the figure above, $s = r \times$ (radian measure of angle DEF), or $\angle DEF = \dfrac{s}{r}$.

EXAMPLE 10

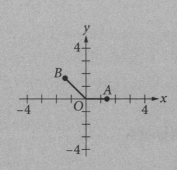

In the figure above, the coordinates of point B are $(-\sqrt{2}, \sqrt{2})$. What is the measure, in radians, of angle AOB?

A) $\dfrac{\pi}{4}$

B) $\dfrac{\pi}{2}$

C) $\dfrac{3\pi}{4}$

D) $\dfrac{5\pi}{4}$

Let *C* be the point $(-\sqrt{2}, 0)$. Then triangle *BOC*, shown in the figure below, is a right triangle with both legs of length $\sqrt{2}$.

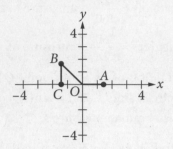

Hence, triangle *BOC* is a 45°-45°-90° triangle. Thus, angle *COB* has measure 45°, and angle *AOB* has measure 180° − 45° = 135°. Therefore, the measure of angle *AOB* in radians is $135° \times \dfrac{2\pi}{360°} = \dfrac{3\pi}{4}$, which is choice C.

EXAMPLE 11

$$\sin(x) = \cos(K - x)$$

In the equation above, the angle measures are in radians and *K* is a constant. Which of the following could be the value of *K*?

A) 0

B) $\dfrac{\pi}{4}$

C) $\dfrac{\pi}{2}$

D) π

The complementary angle relationship for sine and cosine implies that the equation $\sin(x) = \cos(K - x)$ holds if *K* = 90°. Since $90° = \dfrac{2\pi}{360°} \times 90° = \dfrac{\pi}{2}$ radians, the value of *K* could be $\dfrac{\pi}{2}$, which is choice C.

Complex Numbers

The SAT Math Test may have questions on the arithmetic of complex numbers.

The square of any real number is nonnegative. The number *i* is defined to be the solution to the equation $x^2 = -1$. That is, $i^2 = -1$, or $i = \sqrt{-1}$. Note that $i^3 = i^2(i) = -i$ and $i^4 = i^2(i^2) = -1(-1) = 1$.

A complex number is a number of the form $a + bi$, where a and b are real numbers and $i = \sqrt{-1}$. This is called the standard form of a complex number. The number a is called the real part of $a + bi$, and the number bi is called the imaginary part of $a + bi$.

Addition and subtraction of complex numbers are performed by adding their real and complex parts. For example,

▶ $(-3 - 2i) + (4 - i) = (-3 + 4) + (-2i + (-i)) = 1 - 3i$

▶ $(-3 - 2i) - (4 - i) = (-3 - 4) + (-2i - (-i)) = -7 - i$

Multiplication of complex numbers is performed similarly to multiplication of binomials, using the fact that $i^2 = -1$. For example,

$$
\begin{aligned}
(-3 - 2i)(4 - i) &= (-3)(4) + (-3)(-i) + (-2i)(4) + (-2i)(-i) \\
&= -12 + 3i - 8i + (-2)(-1)i^2 \\
&= -12 - 5i + 2i^2 \\
&= -12 - 5i + 2(-1) \\
&= -14 - 5i
\end{aligned}
$$

The complex number $a - bi$ is called the conjugate of $a + bi$. The product of $a + bi$ and $a - bi$ is $a^2 - bi + bi - b^2i^2$; this reduces to $a^2 + b^2$, a real number. The fact that the product of a complex number and its conjugate is a real number can be used to perform division of complex numbers.

$$
\begin{aligned}
\frac{-3 - 2i}{4 - i} &= \frac{-3 - 2i}{4 - i} \times \frac{4 + i}{4 + i} \\
&= \frac{(-3 - 2i)(4 + i)}{(4 - i)(4 + i)} \\
&= \frac{-12 - 3i - 8i - 2i^2}{4^2 - i^2} \\
&= \frac{-10 - 11i}{17} \\
&= -\frac{10}{17} - \frac{11}{17}i
\end{aligned}
$$

EXAMPLE 12

Which of the following is equal to $\dfrac{1 + i}{1 - i}$?

A) i

B) $2i$

C) $-1 + i$

D) $1 + i$

REMEMBER

If you have little experience working with complex numbers, practice adding, subtracting, multiplying, and dividing complex numbers until you are comfortable doing so. You may see complex numbers on the SAT Math Test.

Multiply both the numerator and denominator of $\frac{1+i}{1-i}$ by $1+i$ to get rid of i from the denominator.

$$\frac{1+i}{1-i} = \frac{1+i}{1-i} \times \frac{1+i}{1+i}$$

$$= \frac{(1+i)(1+i)}{(1-i)(1+i)}$$

$$= \frac{1+2i+i^2}{1^2-i^2}$$

$$= \frac{1+2i-1}{1-(-1)}$$

$$= \frac{2i}{2}$$

$$= i$$

Choice A is the correct answer.

Chapter 23

Sample Math Questions: Multiple-Choice

In the previous chapters, you learned about the four areas covered by the SAT Math Test. On the test, questions from the areas are mixed together, requiring you to solve different types of problems as you progress. In each portion, calculator and no calculator, you will first see multiple-choice questions and then student-produced response questions. This chapter will illustrate sample multiple-choice questions. These sample questions are divided into calculator and no-calculator portions just as they would be on the actual test.

Test-Taking Strategies

While taking the SAT Math Test, you may find that some questions are more difficult than others. Do not spend too much time on any one question. If you cannot answer a question in a reasonable amount of time, skip it and return to it after completing the rest of the section. It is important to practice this strategy because you do not want to waste time skipping around to find "easy" questions. Mark each question that you do not answer in your booklet so that you can easily go back to it later. In general, the multiple-choice and student-produced response sections are ordered with the easier questions first and the harder questions last, so keep in mind that the questions near the end of the test may take more time than the those at the beginning of the test.

Read each question carefully, making sure to pay attention to units and other key words and to understand exactly what information the question

 REMEMBER

It is important not to spend too much time on any question. You will have on average a little less than a minute and a half per question on the calculator portion and a minute and fifteen seconds per question on the no-calculator portion. If you can't solve a question in a reasonable amount of time, skip it (remembering to mark it in your booklet) and return to it later.

 **REMEMBER**

In general, the multiple-choice and student-produced response questions are ordered with the easier ones first and the harder ones last, so the later questions may take more time to solve than those at the beginning.

is asking for. You may find it helpful to underline key information in the problem, to draw figures to visualize the information given, or to mark key information on graphs and diagrams provided in the booklet.

When working through the test, remember to check your answer sheet to make sure you are filling in your answer on the correct row for the question you are answering. If your strategy involves skipping questions, it can be easy to get off track, so pay careful attention to your answer sheet.

On the calculator portion, keep in mind that using a calculator may not always be an advantage. Some questions are designed to be solved more quickly with manual calculations, so using a calculator may take more time. When using a calculator, always consider the reasonableness of an answer — this is the best way to catch mistakes that may have occurred when inputting your numbers.

Remember, there is no penalty for guessing on the SAT. Make your best guess for each question. Do not leave any questions blank on your answer sheet. For a question in which you are unsure of the correct answer, eliminating the answers that you know are wrong will give you a better chance of guessing the correct answer from the remaining choices.

On the no-calculator portion of the test, you have 25 minutes to answer 20 questions. This allows you an average of about 1 minute 15 seconds per question. Keep in mind that you should spend less time on easier questions so that you have more time available to spend on the more difficult ones.

Directions

The directions below precede the no-calculator portion of the SAT Math Test. The directions for the calculator portion follow on the next page. The same references provided in the calculator portion of the SAT Math Test are also provided in the no-calculator portion of the test.

PRACTICE AT

◗ **khanacademy.org/sat**

Familiarize yourself with all test directions now so that you don't have to waste precious time on test day reading the directions.

Math Test – No Calculator
25 MINUTES, 20 QUESTIONS

Turn to Section 3 of your answer sheet to answer the questions in this section.

DIRECTIONS

For questions 1-15, solve each problem, choose the best answer from the choices provided, and fill in the corresponding circle on your answer sheet. **For questions 16-20**, solve the problem and enter your answer in the grid on the answer sheet. Please refer to the directions before question 16 on how to enter your answers in the grid. You may use any available space in your test booklet for scratch work.

NOTES

1. The use of a calculator **is not permitted**.

2. All variables and expressions used represent real numbers unless otherwise indicated.

3. Figures provided in this test are drawn to scale unless otherwise indicated.

4. All figures lie in a plane unless otherwise indicated.

5. Unless otherwise indicated, the domain of a given function f is the set of all real numbers x for which $f(x)$ is a real number.

REFERENCE

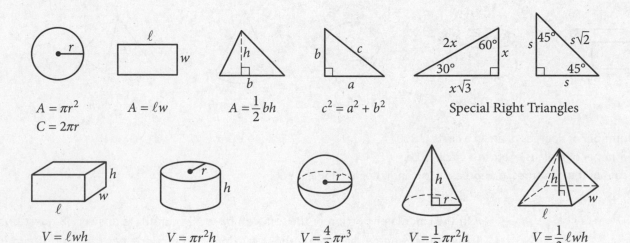

$A = \pi r^2$
$C = 2\pi r$

$A = \ell w$

$A = \frac{1}{2}bh$

$c^2 = a^2 + b^2$

Special Right Triangles

$V = \ell wh$

$V = \pi r^2 h$

$V = \frac{4}{3}\pi r^3$

$V = \frac{1}{3}\pi r^2 h$

$V = \frac{1}{3}\ell wh$

The number of degrees of arc in a circle is 360.

The number of radians of arc in a circle is 2π.

The sum of the measures in degrees of the angles of a triangle is 180.

Math Test – Calculator

55 MINUTES, 38 QUESTIONS

Turn to Section 4 of your answer sheet to answer the questions in this section.

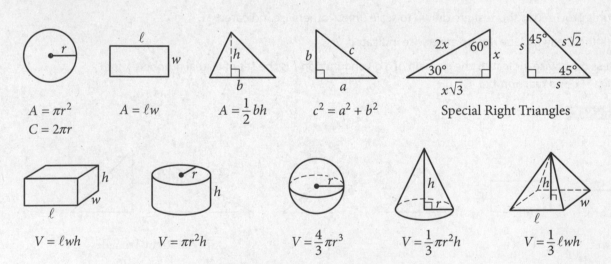
On the calculator portion of the test, you have 55 minutes to answer 38 questions. This allows you an average of about 1 minute 26 seconds per question. Keep in mind that you should spend less time on easier questions so that you have more time to spend on the more difficult ones.

Sample Questions:
Multiple Choice — Calculator

1

The recommended daily calcium intake for a 20-year-old is 1,000 milligrams (mg). One cup of milk contains 299 mg of calcium and one cup of juice contains 261 mg of calcium. Which of the following inequalities represents the possible number of cups of milk, m, and cups of juice, j, a 20-year-old could drink in a day to meet or exceed the recommended daily calcium intake from these drinks alone?

A) $299m + 261j \geq 1,000$

B) $299m + 261j > 1,000$

C) $\dfrac{299}{m} + \dfrac{261}{j} \geq 1,000$

D) $\dfrac{299}{m} + \dfrac{261}{j} > 1,000$

Content: Heart of Algebra

Key: A

Objective: You must identify the correct mathematical notation for an inequality to represent a real-world situation.

Explanation: Choice A is correct. Multiplying the number of cups of milk by the amount of calcium each cup contains and multiplying the number of cups of juice by the amount of calcium each cup contains gives the total amount of calcium from each source. You must then find the sum of these two numbers to find the total amount of calcium. Because the question asks for the calcium from these two sources to meet or exceed the recommended daily intake, the sum of these two products must be greater than or equal to 1,000.

Choice B is incorrect and may result from a misunderstanding of the meaning of inequality symbols as they relate to real-life situations. This answer does not allow for the daily intake to meet the recommended daily amount.

Choice C is incorrect and may result from a misunderstanding of proportional relationships. Here the wrong operation is applied, with the total amount of calcium per cup divided by the number of cups of each type of drink. These values should be multiplied.

Choice D is incorrect and may result from a combination of mistakes. The inequality symbol used allows the option to exceed, but not to meet, the recommended daily value, and the wrong operation may have been applied when calculating the total amount of calcium intake from each drink.

PRACTICE AT

khanacademy.org/sat

On questions involving inequalities, pay close attention to whether or not the correct answer should include an equal sign.

2

A research assistant randomly selected 75 undergraduate students from the list of all students enrolled in the psychology-degree program at a large university. She asked each of the 75 students, "How many minutes per day do you typically spend reading?" The mean reading time in the sample was 89 minutes, and the margin of error for this estimate was 4.28 minutes. Another research assistant intends to replicate the survey and will attempt to get a smaller margin of error. Which of the following samples will most likely result in a smaller margin of error for the estimated mean time students in the psychology-degree program read per day?

A) 40 randomly selected undergraduate psychology-degree program students

B) 40 randomly selected undergraduate students from all degree programs at the college

C) 300 randomly selected undergraduate psychology-degree program students

D) 300 randomly selected undergraduate students from all degree programs at the college

Content: Problem Solving and Data Analysis

Key: C

Objective: You must first read and understand the statistics calculated from the survey. Then, you must apply your knowledge about the relationship between sample size and subject selection on margin of error.

Explanation: Choice C is correct. Increasing the sample size while randomly selecting participants from the original population of interest will most likely result in a decrease in the margin of error.

Choice A is incorrect and may result from a misunderstanding of the importance of sample size to a margin of error. The margin of error is likely to increase with a smaller sample size.

Choice B is incorrect and may result from a misunderstanding of the importance of sample size and participant selection to a margin of error. The margin of error is likely to increase due to the smaller sample size. Also, a sample of undergraduate students from all degree programs at the college is a different population than the original survey; therefore, the impact to the mean and margin of error cannot be predicted.

Choice D is incorrect. A sample of undergraduate students from all degree programs at the college is a different population than the original survey and therefore the impact to the mean and margin of error cannot be predicted.

PRACTICE AT

khanacademy.org/sat

As discussed in Chapter 20, margin of error is affected by two factors: the variability in the data and the sample size. Increasing the size of the random sample provides more information and reduces the margin of error.

3

A company's manager estimated that the cost C, in dollars, of producing n items is $C = 7n + 350$. The company sells each item for $12. The company makes a profit when the total income from selling a quantity of items is greater than the total cost of producing that quantity of items. Which of the following inequalities gives all possible values of n for which the manager estimates that the company will make a profit?

A) $n < 70$

B) $n < 84$

C) $n > 70$

D) $n > 84$

Content: Heart of Algebra

Key: C

Objective: You must interpret an expression or equation that models a real-world situation and be able to interpret the whole expression (or specific parts) in terms of its context.

Explanation: Choice C is correct. One way to find the correct answer is to create an inequality. The income from sales of n items is $12n$. For the company to profit, $12n$ must be greater than the cost of producing n items; therefore, the inequality $12n > 7n + 350$ can be used to model the context. Solving this inequality yields $n > 70$.

Choice A is incorrect and may result from a misunderstanding of the properties of inequalities. You may have found the number of items of the break-even point as 70 and used the incorrect notation to express the answer, or you may have incorrectly modeled the scenario when setting up an inequality to solve.

Choice B is incorrect and may result from a misunderstanding of how the cost equation models the scenario. If you use the cost of $12 as the number of items n and evaluate the expression $7n$, you will find the value of 84. Misunderstanding how the inequality relates to the scenario might lead you to think n should be less than this value.

Choice D is incorrect and may result from a misunderstanding of how the cost equation models the scenario. If you use the cost of $12 as the number of items n and evaluate the expression $7n$, you will find the value of 84. Misunderstanding how the inequality relates to the scenario might lead you to think n should be greater than this value.

PRACTICE AT

khanacademy.org/sat

Remember to solve an inequality just as you would an equation, with one important exception. When multiplying or dividing both sides of an inequality by a negative number, you must reverse the direction of the inequality:

If $-2x > 6$, then $x < -3$.

4

At a primate reserve, the mean age of all the male primates is 15 years, and the mean age of all female primates is 19 years. Which of the following must be true about the mean age m of the combined group of male and female primates at the primate reserve?

A) $m = 17$

B) $m > 17$

C) $m < 17$

D) $15 < m < 19$

Content: Problem Solving and Data Analysis

Key: D

Objective: You must evaluate the means for two separate populations in order to determine the constraints on the mean for the combined population.

Explanation: Choice D is correct. You must reason that because the mean of the males is lower than that of the females, the combined mean cannot be greater than or equal to that of the females, while also reasoning that because the mean of the females is greater than that of the males, the combined mean cannot be less than or equal to the mean of the males. Therefore, the combined mean must be between the two separate means.

Choice A is incorrect and results from finding the mean of the two means. This answer makes an unjustified assumption that there are an equal number of male and female primates.

Choice B is incorrect and results from finding the mean of the two means and misapplying an inequality to the scenario. This answer makes an unjustified assumption that there are more females than males.

Choice C is incorrect and results from finding the mean of the two means and misapplying an inequality to the scenario. This answer makes an unjustified assumption that there are more males than females.

PRACTICE AT

khanacademy.org/sat

Question 4 does not require extensive calculation, or really any calculation at all. Rather, it relies upon a solid understanding of mean along with careful reasoning. On the SAT, it pays to reason critically about the question before diving into calculations.

PRACTICE AT

khanacademy.org/sat

When deciding what conclusions are supported by the data from a study or survey, ask yourself:

1. Was the sample of subjects in the study selected at random from the entire population in question? If so, the results can be generalized to the entire population in question. However, check to make sure that the conclusion is referring to the same population as that in the study.

2. Were the subjects randomly assigned to treatments? If so, conclusions about cause and effect can be drawn.

5

A researcher wanted to know if there is an association between exercise and sleep for the population of 16-year-olds in the United States. She obtained survey responses from a random sample of 2,000 United States 16-year-olds and found convincing evidence of a positive association between exercise and sleep. Which of the following conclusions is well supported by the data?

A) There is a positive association between exercise and sleep for 16-year-olds in the United States.

B) There is a positive association between exercise and sleep for 16-year-olds in the world.

C) Using exercise and sleep as defined by the study, an increase in sleep is caused by an increase of exercise for 16-year-olds in the United States.

D) Using exercise and sleep as defined by the study, an increase in sleep is caused by an increase of exercise for 16-year-olds in the world.

Content: Problem Solving and Data Analysis

Key: A

Objective: You must use information from a research study to evaluate whether the results can be generalized to the study population and whether a cause-and-effect relationship exists. To conclude a cause-and-effect relationship like the ones described in choices C and D, there must be a random assignment of participants to groups receiving different treatments. To conclude that the relationship applies to a population, participants must be randomly selected from that population.

Explanation: Choice A is correct. A relationship in the data can only be generalized to the population that the sample was drawn from.

Choice B is incorrect. A relationship in the data can only be generalized to the population that the sample was drawn from. The sample was from high school students in the United States, not from high school students in the entire world.

Choice C is incorrect. Evidence for a cause-and-effect relationship can only be established when participants are randomly assigned to groups who receive different treatments.

Choice D is incorrect. Evidence for a cause-and-effect relationship can only be established when participants are randomly assigned to groups who receive different treatments. Also, a relationship in the data can only be generalized to the population that the sample was drawn from. The sample was from high school students in the United States, not from high school students in the entire world.

6

A biology class at Central High School predicted that a local population of animals will double in size every 12 years. The population at the beginning of 2014 was estimated to be 50 animals. If P represents the population n years after 2014, then which of the following equations represents the class's model of the population over time?

A) $P = 12 + 50n$

B) $P = 50 + 12n$

C) $P = 50(2)^{12n}$

D) $P = 50(2)^{\frac{n}{12}}$

Content: Passport to Advanced Math

Key: D

Objective: You must identify the correct mathematical notation for an exponential relationship that represents a real-world situation.

Explanation: Choice D is correct. You first recognize that a population that doubles in size over equal time periods is increasing at an exponential rate. In a doubling scenario, an exponential growth model can be written in the form $y = a(2)^{\frac{n}{b}}$, where a is the initial population (that is, the population when $n = 0$) and b is the number of years it takes for the population to double in size. In this case, the initial population is 50, the number of animals at the

PRACTICE AT

 **khanacademy.org/sat**

A good strategy for checking your answer on Question 6 is to pick a number for n and test the answer choices. If $n = 12$, for instance, P should equal 100 (since after 12 years, the initial population of 50 should double to 100). Only choice D yields a value of 100 when you plug in 12 for n.

beginning of 2014. Therefore, $a = 50$. The text explains that the population will double in size every 12 years. Therefore, $b = 12$.

Choice A is incorrect and may result from a misunderstanding of exponential equations or of the context. This linear model indicates that the initial population is 12 animals and the population is increasing by 50 animals each year. However, this is not the case.

Choice B is incorrect and may result from a misunderstanding of exponential equations or of the scenario. This linear model indicates that the initial population is 50 animals and the population is increasing by 12 animals each year. However, this is not the case.

Choice C is incorrect. This exponential model indicates that the initial population is 50 animals and is doubling. However, the exponent $12n$ indicates that the population is doubling 12 times per year, not every 12 years. This is not the case.

REMEMBER

When a question explicitly states that a figure is *not* drawn to scale, avoid making unwarranted assumptions. Rely instead on your knowledge of mathematical properties and theorems.

7

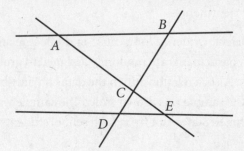

Note: Figure not drawn to scale.

In the figure above, $\triangle ABC \sim \triangle EDC$. Which of the following must be true?

A) $\overline{AE} \parallel \overline{BD}$
B) $\overline{AE} \perp \overline{BD}$
C) $\overline{AB} \parallel \overline{DE}$
D) $\overline{AB} \perp \overline{DE}$

Content: Additional Topics in Math

Key: C

Objective: You must use spatial reasoning and geometric logic to deduce which relationship is true based on the given information. You must also use mathematical notation to express the relationship between the line segments.

Explanation: Choice C is correct. Given that $\triangle ABC$ is similar to $\triangle EDC$, you can determine that the corresponding $\angle BAC$ is congruent to $\angle CED$. The converse of the alternate interior angle theorem tells us that $\overline{AB} \parallel \overline{DE}$. (You can also use the fact that $\angle ABC$ and $\angle CDE$ are congruent to make a similar argument.)

Choice A is incorrect and may result from multiple misconceptions. You may have misidentified the segments as perpendicular and used the wrong notation to express this statement.

Choice B is incorrect and may result from using only the diagram and not considering the given information. The line segments appear to be perpendicular, but need not be, given the information provided.

Choice D is incorrect and may result from misunderstanding either the notation or the vocabulary of parallel and perpendicular lines. You may have incorrectly identified or notated parallel lines as perpendicular.

8

The function f is defined by $f(x) = 2x^3 + 3x^2 + cx + 8$ where c is a constant. In the xy-plane, the graph of f intersects the x-axis at the three points $(-4, 0)$, $\left(\frac{1}{2}, 0\right)$, and $(p, 0)$. What is the value of c?

A) -18

B) -2

C) 2

D) 10

Content: Passport to Advanced Math

Key: A

Objective: You could tackle this problem in many different ways, but the focus is on your understanding of the zeros of a polynomial function and how they are used to construct algebraic representations of polynomials.

Explanation: Choice A is correct. The given zeros can be used to set up an equation to solve for c. Substituting -4 for x and 0 for y yields $-4c = 72$, or $c = -18$. Alternatively, since -4, $\frac{1}{2}$, and p are zeros of the polynomial function, it follows that $f(x) = (2x - 1)(x + 4)(x - p)$. Were this polynomial multiplied out, the constant term would be $(-1)(4)(-9) = 4p$. (We can grasp this without performing the full expansion.) Since it is given that this value is 8, it goes that $4p = 8$ or, rather, $p = 2$. Substituting 2 for p in the polynomial function yields $f(x) = (2x - 1)(x + 4)(x - 2)$, and after multiplying the factors, one finds that the coefficient of the x term, or the value of c, is -18.

Choice B is incorrect. This value may be the result of solving for $p(p = 2)$ and then misunderstanding the relationship between the constants p and c in the equation.

Choice C is incorrect. This is the value of p, not c. Finding the value of p is an intermediate step to finding the value of c, but the value of p is not the final answer.

Choice D is incorrect. This value could be the result of an arithmetic error. Using the value of $p(p = 2)$ and the other zeros, $f(x)$ can be factored as $f(x) = (2x - 1)(x + 4)(x - 2)$. If the x terms in the product were erroneously found to be $14x$ and $-4x$, then combining like terms could result in this incorrect answer.

PRACTICE AT

khanacademy.org/sat

When a question states that the graph of a function intersects the x-axis at specific points, this means that the dependent variable ($f(x)$) equals zero for the specified values of the independent variable (x). Applying this concept leads to the solution on Question 8.

SAMPLE QUESTION SET

Samples 9 to 11 refer to the following information:

The first metacarpal bone is located in the hand. The scatterplot below shows the relationship between the length of the first metacarpal bone and the height of 9 people. The line of best fit is also shown.

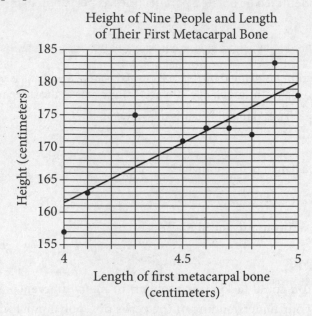

Height of Nine People and Length of Their First Metacarpal Bone

---

9

How many of the 9 people have an actual height that differs by more than 3 centimeters from the height predicted by the line of best fit?

A) 2

B) 4

C) 6

D) 9

Content: Problem Solving and Data Analysis

Key: B

Objective: You must read and interpret information from a data display.

Explanation: Choice B is correct. The people who have first metacarpal bones of length 4.0, 4.3, 4.8, and 4.9 centimeters have heights that differ by more than 3 centimeters from the height predicted by the line of best fit.

Choice A is incorrect. There are 2 people whose actual heights are more than 3 centimeters above the height predicted by the line of best fit. However, there are also 2 people whose actual heights are farther than 3 centimeters below the line of best fit.

Choice C is incorrect. There are 6 data points in which the absolute value between the actual height and the height predicted by the line of best fit is greater than 1 centimeter.

PRACTICE AT

🌱 **khanacademy.org/sat**

Pay close attention to axis labels as well as to the size of the units on the two axes.

Choice D is incorrect. The data on the graph represent 9 different people; however, the absolute value of the difference between actual height and predicted height is not greater than 3 for all of the people.

10

Which of the following is the best interpretation of the slope of the line of best fit in the context of this problem?

A) The predicted height increase in centimeters for one centimeter increase in the first metacarpal bone

B) The predicted first metacarpal bone increase in centimeters for every centimeter increase in height

C) The predicted height in centimeters of a person with a first metacarpal bone length of 0 centimeters

D) The predicted first metacarpal bone length in centimeters for a person with a height of 0 centimeters

Content: Heart of Algebra

Key: A

Objective: You must interpret the meaning of the slope of the line of best fit in the context provided.

Explanation: Choice A is correct. The slope is the change in the vertical distance divided by the change in the horizontal distance between any two points on a line. In this context, the change in the vertical distance is the change in the predicted height of a person, and the change in the horizontal distance is the change in the length of his or her first metacarpal bone. The unit rate, or slope, is the increase in predicted height for each increase of one centimeter of the first metacarpal bone.

Choice B is incorrect. If you selected this answer, you may have interpreted slope incorrectly as run over rise.

Choice C is incorrect. If you selected this answer, you may have mistaken slope for the y-intercept.

Choice D is incorrect. If you selected this answer, you may have mistaken slope for the x-intercept.

PRACTICE AT
khanacademy.org/sat

Throughout the SAT Math Test, you will be asked to apply your knowledge of math principles and properties, such as slope, to specific contexts, such as the line of best fit in the scatterplot above. To do so requires that you possess a strong understanding of these math concepts.

11

Based on the line of best fit, what is the predicted height for someone with a first metacarpal bone that has a length of 4.45 centimeters?

A) 168 centimeters

B) 169 centimeters

C) 170 centimeters

D) 171 centimeters

Content: Problem Solving and Data Analysis

Key: C

PRACTICE AT

🌱 **khanacademy.org/sat**

The answer choices on Question 11 are very close together. Thus, be very precise when examining the scatterplot to find the *y*-value that corresponds to an *x*-value of 4.45 on the line of best fit.

Objective: You must use the line of best fit to make a prediction. You must also demonstrate fluency in reading graphs and decimal numbers.

Explanation: Choice C is correct. First, notice that the scale of the *x*-axis is 0.1, and therefore the *x*-value of 4.45 is halfway between the unmarked value of 4.4 and the marked value of 4.5. Then, find the *y*-value on the line of best fit that corresponds with an *x*-value of 4.45, which is 170.

Choice A is incorrect. If you mistakenly find the point on the line between the *x*-values of 4.3 and 4.4, you will likely find a predicted metacarpal bone length of 168 centimeters.

Choice B is incorrect. If you mistakenly find the point on the line that corresponds to an *x*-value of 4.4 centimeters, you will likely find a predicted height of approximately 169 centimeters.

Choice D is incorrect. If you mistakenly find the point on the line that corresponds with an *x*-value of 4.5 centimeters, you will likely find a predicted height of approximately 171 centimeters. You might also choose this option if you mistakenly use the data point that has an *x*-value closest to 4.45 centimeters.

Sample Questions: Multiple Choice — No Calculator

12

Line ℓ is graphed in the *xy*-plane below.

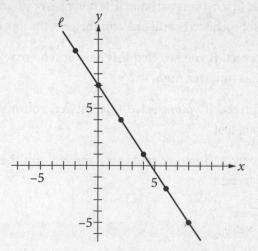

If line ℓ is translated up 5 units and right 7 units, then what is the slope of the new line?

A) $-\dfrac{2}{5}$

B) $-\dfrac{3}{2}$

C) $-\dfrac{8}{9}$

D) $-\dfrac{11}{14}$

Content: Heart of Algebra

Key: B

Objective: You must make a connection between the graphical form of a relationship and a numerical description of a key feature.

Explanation: Choice B is correct. The slope of a line can be determined by finding the difference in the y-coordinates divided by the difference in the x-coordinates for any two points on the line. Using the points indicated, the slope of line ℓ is $-\frac{3}{2}$. Translating line ℓ moves all the points on the line the same distance in the same direction, and the image will be a line parallel to ℓ. Therefore, the slope of the image is also $-\frac{3}{2}$.

Choice A is incorrect. This value may result from a combination of errors. You may have erroneously determined the slope of the new line by adding 5 to the numerator and adding 7 to the denominator in the slope of line ℓ and gotten the result $(-3 + 5)/(-2 + 7)$.

Choice C is incorrect. This value may result from a combination of errors. You may have erroneously determined the slope of the new line by subtracting 5 from the numerator and subtracting 7 from the denominator in the slope of line ℓ.

Choice D is incorrect and may result from adding $\frac{5}{7}$ to the slope of line ℓ.

PRACTICE AT

khanacademy.org/sat

Your first instinct on this question may be to identify two coordinates on line ℓ, shift each of them over 5 and up 7, and then calculate the slope using the change in y over the change in x. While this will yield the correct answer, realizing that a line that is translated is simply shifted on the coordinate plane but retains its original slope will save time and reduce the chance for error. Always think critically about a question before diving into your calculations.

13

The mean number of students per classroom, y, at Central High School can be estimated using the equation $y = 0.8636x + 27.227$, where x represents the number of years since 2004 and $x \leq 10$. Which of the following statements is the best interpretation of the number 0.8636 in the context of this problem?

A) The estimated mean number of students per classroom in 2004

B) The estimated mean number of students per classroom in 2014

C) The estimated yearly decrease in the mean number of students per classroom

D) The estimated yearly increase in the mean number of students per classroom

Content: Heart of Algebra

Key: D

Objective: You must interpret the slope of an equation in relation to the real-world situation it models. Also, when the models are created from data, you must recognize that these models only estimate the independent variable, y, for a given value of x.

Explanation: Choice D is correct. When an equation is written in the form $y = mx + b$, the coefficient of the x-term (in this case 0.8636) is the slope. The slope of this linear equation gives the amount that the mean number of students per classroom (represented by y) changes per year (represented by x).

Choice A is incorrect and may result from a misunderstanding of slope and y-intercept. The y-intercept of the equation represents the estimated mean number of students per classroom in 2004.

Choice B is incorrect and may result from a misunderstanding of the limitations of the model. You may have seen that $x \leq 10$ and erroneously used this statement to determine that the model finds the mean number of students in 2014.

Choice C is incorrect and may result from a misunderstanding of slope. You may have recognized that slope models the rate of change but thought that a slope of less than 1 indicates a decreasing function.

14

If $\dfrac{2}{a-1} = \dfrac{4}{y}$, and $y \neq 0$ where $a \neq 1$, what is y in terms of a?

A) $y = 2a - 2$

B) $y = 2a - 4$

C) $y = 2a - \dfrac{1}{2}$

D) $y = \dfrac{1}{2}a + 1$

Content: Passport to Advanced Math

Key: A

Objective: You must complete operations with multiple terms and manipulate an equation to isolate the variable of interest.

Explanation: Choice A is correct. Multiplying both sides of the equation by the denominators of the rational expressions in the equation gives $2y = 4a - 4$. You should then divide both sides by 2 to isolate the y variable, yielding the equation $y = 2a - 2$.

Choice B is incorrect. This equation may be the result of not dividing both terms by 2 when isolating y in the equation $2y = 4a - 4$.

Choice C is incorrect. This equation may result from not distributing the 4 when multiplying 4 and $(a - 1)$.

Choice D is incorrect. This equation may result from solving $2y = 4a - 4$ for a, yielding $a = \dfrac{1}{2}y + 1$. A misunderstanding of the meaning of variables may have resulted in switching the variables to match the answer choice.

15

Which of the following is equal to $(14 - 2i)(7 + 12i)$? (Note: $i = \sqrt{-1}$)

A) 74

B) 122

C) $74 + 154i$

D) $122 + 154i$

Content: Additional Topics in Math

Key: D

Objective: You must apply the distributive property on two complex binomials and then simplify the result.

Explanation: Choice D is correct. Applying the distributive property to multiply the binomials yields the expression $98 + 168i - 14i - 24i^2$. The note in the question reminds you that $i = \sqrt{-1}$, therefore, $i^2 = -1$. Substituting this value into the expression gives you $98 + 168i - 14i - (-24)$, and combining like terms results in $122 + 154i$.

Choice A is incorrect and may result from a combination of errors. You may not have correctly distributed when multiplying the binomials, multiplying only the first terms together and the second terms together. You may also have used the incorrect equality $i^2 = 1$.

Choice B is incorrect and may result from a combination of errors. You may not have correctly distributed when multiplying the binomials, multiplying only the first terms together and the second terms together.

Choice C is incorrect and results from misapplying the statement $i = \sqrt{-1}$.

PRACTICE AT

khanacademy.org/sat

Multiply complex numbers in the same way you would multiply binomials (by "FOIL"ing).

Remember that $i = \sqrt{-1}$ and that $i^2 = -1$.

16

The graph of $y = (2x - 4)(x - 4)$ is a parabola in the xy-plane. In which of the following equivalent equations do the x- and y-coordinates of the vertex of the parabola appear as constants or coefficients?

A) $y = 2x^2 - 12x + 16$
B) $y = 2x(x - 6) + 16$
C) $y = 2(x - 3)^2 + (-2)$
D) $y = (x - 2)(2x - 8)$

Content: Passport to Advanced Math

Key: C

Objective: You must be able to see structure in expressions and equations and create a new form of an expression that reveals a specific property.

Explanation: Choice C is correct. The equation $y = (2x - 4)(x - 4)$ can be written in vertex form, $y = a(x - h)^2 + k$, to display the vertex, (h, k), of the parabola. To put the equation in vertex form, first multiply: $(2x - 4)(x - 4) = 2x^2 - 8x - 4x + 16$. Then, add like terms, $2x^2 - 8x - 4x + 16 = 2x^2 - 12x + 16$. The next step is completing the square.

$y = 2x^2 - 12x + 16$	
$y = 2(x^2 - 6x) + 16$	Isolate the x^2 term by factoring
$y = 2(x^2 - 6x + 9 - 9) + 16$	Make a perfect square in the parentheses
$y = 2(x^2 - 6x + 9) - 18 + 16$	Move the extra term out of the parentheses
$y = 2(x - 3)^2 - 18 + 16$	Factor inside the parentheses
$y = 2(x - 3)^2 - 2$	Simplify the remaining terms

Therefore, the coordinates of the vertex, (3, −2), are both revealed only in choice C. Since you are told that all of the equations are equivalent, simply knowing the form that displays the coordinates of the vertex will save all of these steps — this is known as "seeing structure in the expression or equation."

Choice A is incorrect; it displays the y-value of the y-intercept of the graph (0, 16) as a constant.

Choice B is incorrect; it displays the y-value of the y-intercept of the graph (0, 16) as a constant.

Choice D is incorrect; it displays the x-value of one of the x-intercepts of the graph (2, 0) as a constant.

17

If $a^{-\frac{1}{2}} = x$, where $a > 0$ and $x > 0$, which of the following equations gives a in terms of x?

A) $a = \dfrac{1}{\sqrt{x}}$

B) $a = \dfrac{1}{x^2}$

C) $a = \sqrt{x}$

D) $a = -x^2$

Content: Passport to Advanced Math

Key: B

Objective: You must demonstrate fluency with the properties of exponents. You must be able to relate fractional exponents to radicals as well as demonstrate an understanding of negative exponents.

Explanation: Choice B is correct. There are multiple ways to approach this problem, but all require an understanding of the properties of exponents. You may rewrite the equation as $\dfrac{1}{\sqrt{a}} = x$ and then proceed to solve for a, first by squaring both sides, which gives $\dfrac{1}{a} = x^2$, and then by multiplying both sides by a to find $1 = ax^2$. Finally, dividing both sides by x^2 isolates the desired variable.

Choice A is incorrect and may result from a misunderstanding of the properties of exponents. You may understand that a negative exponent can be translated to a fraction but misapply the fractional exponent.

Choice C is incorrect and may result from a misunderstanding of the properties of exponents. You may recognize that an exponent of $\frac{1}{2}$ is the same as the square root but misapply this information.

Choice D is incorrect and may result from a misunderstanding of the properties of exponents. You may recognize that raising a to the power of $\frac{1}{2}$ is the same as taking the square root of a and, therefore, that a can be isolated by squaring both sides. However, you may not have understood how the negative exponent affects the base of the exponent.

18

If $y = x^3 + 2x + 5$ and $z = x^2 + 7x + 1$, what is $2y + z$ in terms of x?

A) $3x^3 + 11x + 11$

B) $2x^3 + x^2 + 9x + 6$

C) $2x^3 + x^2 + 11x + 11$

D) $2x^3 + 2x^2 + 18x + 12$

Content: Passport to Advanced Math

Key: C

Objective: You must substitute polynomials into an expression and then simplify the resulting expression by combining like terms.

Explanation: Choice C is correct. Substituting the expressions equivalent to y and z into $2y + z$ results in the expression $2(x^3 + 2x + 5) + x^2 + 7x + 1$. You must apply the distributive property to multiply $x^3 + 2x + 5$ by 2 and then combine the like terms in the expression.

Choice A is incorrect and may result if you correctly found $2y$ in terms of x but did not pay careful attention to exponents when adding the expression for $2y$ to the expression for z. As a result, you may have combined the x^3 and x^2 terms.

Choice B is incorrect and may result if you failed to distribute the 2 when multiplying $2(x^3 + 2x + 5)$.

Choice D is incorrect and may result from finding $2(y + z)$ instead of $2y + z$.

PRACTICE AT

khanacademy.org/sat

Don't worry if you missed this question, there are several ways to make a careless mistake. Always be methodical when doing calculations or simplifying expressions, and use your test booklet to perform the steps in finding your answer.

19

Which of the following is equal to $\sin\left(\frac{\pi}{5}\right)$?

A) $-\cos\left(\frac{\pi}{5}\right)$

B) $-\sin\left(\frac{\pi}{5}\right)$

C) $\cos\left(\frac{3\pi}{10}\right)$

D) $\sin\left(\frac{7\pi}{10}\right)$

Content: Additional Topics in Math

Key: C

Objective: You must understand radian measure and have a conceptual understanding of trigonometric relationships.

311

Explanation: Choice C is correct. Sine and cosine are related by the equation $\sin(x) = \cos\left(\frac{\pi}{2} - x\right)$. Therefore, $\sin\left(\frac{\pi}{5}\right) = \cos\left(\frac{\pi}{2} - \frac{\pi}{5}\right)$, which reduces to $\cos\left(\frac{3\pi}{10}\right)$.

Choice A is incorrect and may result from a misunderstanding about trigonometric relationships. You may have thought that cosine is the inverse function of sine and therefore reasoned that the negative of the cosine of an angle is equivalent to the sine of that angle.

Choice B is incorrect and may result from a misunderstanding of the unit circle and how it relates to trigonometric expressions. You may have thought that, on a coordinate grid, the negative sign only changes the orientation of the triangle formed, not the value of the trigonometric expression.

Choice D is incorrect. You may have confused the relationship between sine and cosine and erroneously added $\frac{\pi}{2}$ to the given angle measure instead of subtracting the angle measure from $\frac{\pi}{2}$.

20

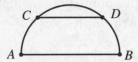

The semicircle above has a radius of r inches, and chord $\overline{CD}$ is parallel to the diameter $\overline{AB}$. If the length of $\overline{CD}$ is $\frac{2}{3}$ of the length of $\overline{AB}$, what is the distance between the chord and the diameter in terms of r?

A) $\frac{1}{3}\pi r$

B) $\frac{2}{3}\pi r$

C) $\frac{\sqrt{2}}{2}r$

D) $\frac{\sqrt{5}}{3}r$

Content: Additional Topics in Math

Key: D

Objective: This problem requires you to make use of properties of circles and parallel lines in an abstract setting. You will have to draw an additional line in order to find the relationship between the distance of the chord from the diameter and the radius of the semicircle. This question provides an opportunity for using different approaches to find the distance required: one can use either the Pythagorean theorem or the trigonometric ratios.

PRACTICE AT

khanacademy.org/sat

Question 20 is a particularly challenging question, one that may require additional time to solve. Be careful, however, not to spend too much time on a question. If you're unable to solve a question in a reasonable amount of time at first, flag it in your test booklet and return to it after you have attempted the rest of the questions in the section.

Explanation: Choice D is correct. Let the semicircle have center O. The diameter $\overline{AB}$ has length $2r$. Because chord $\overline{CD}$ is $\frac{2}{3}$ of the length of the diameter, $CD = \frac{2}{3}(2r) = \frac{4}{3}r$. It follows that $\frac{1}{2}CD = \frac{1}{2}\left(\frac{4}{3}\right)r$ or $\frac{2}{3}r$. To find the distance, x, between $\overline{AB}$ and $\overline{CD}$, draw a right triangle connecting center O, the midpoint of chord $\overline{CD}$, and point C. The Pythagorean theorem can then be set up as follows: $r^2 = x^2 + \left(\frac{2}{3}r\right)^2$. Simplifying the right-hand side of the equation yields $r^2 = x^2 + \frac{4}{9}r^2$. Subtracting $\frac{4}{9}r^2$ from both sides of the equation yields $\frac{5}{9}r^2 = x^2$. Finally, taking the square root of both sides of the equation will reveal $\frac{\sqrt{5}}{3}r = x$.

Choice A is incorrect. If you selected this answer, you may have tried to use the circumference formula to determine the distance rather than making use of the radius of the circle to create a triangle.

Choice B is incorrect. If you selected this answer, you may have tried to use the circumference formula to determine the distance rather than making use of the radius of the circle to create a triangle.

Choice C is incorrect. If you selected this answer, you may have made a triangle within the circle, using a radius to connect the chord and the diameter, but then may have mistaken the triangle for a 45-45-90 triangle and tried to use this relationship to determine the distance.

PRACTICE AT

khanacademy.org/sat

Advanced geometry questions may require you to draw shapes, such as triangles, within a given shape in order to arrive at the solution.

Chapter 24

Sample Math Questions: Student-Produced Response

In this chapter, you will see examples of student-produced response math questions. This type of question appears in both the calculator and the no-calculator portions of the test. Student-produced response questions can come from any of the four areas covered by the SAT Math Test.

Student-Produced Response Strategies

Student-produced response questions do not have answer choices to select from. You must solve the problem and grid your answer on the answer sheet. There is a space to write your answer, and there are circles below to fill in for your answer. Use your written answer to make sure you fill in the correct circles. The filled-in circles are what determine how your answer is scored. You will not receive credit if you only write in your answer without filling in the circles.

Each grid has four columns. If your answer does not fill all four columns, leave the unneeded spaces blank. You may start your answer in any column as long as there is space to fill in the complete answer.

You should use many of the same test-taking strategies you used on the multiple-choice questions as for student-produced response questions, but here are a few additional tips to consider: First, remember that your answer must be able to fit in the grid on the answer sheet. If you solve the question and you found an answer that is negative or is greater than 9999, you should try to solve the problem a different way to find the correct answer. On some questions, your answer may include a dollar sign, a percent sign, or a degree symbol. You should not include these symbols in your answer, and as a reminder, the question will instruct you not to grid them.

When filling in fractions or decimals, keep a few things in mind. Answers cannot be mixed numbers. You must give your answer as an improper

REMEMBER

You must fill in the circles on the answer sheet in order to receive credit. You will not receive credit if you only write in your answer but don't fill in the circles.

 **REMEMBER**

Answers cannot be mixed numbers. Give your answer as an improper fraction or as the equivalent decimal form. Thus, for instance, do *not* submit $3\frac{1}{2}$ as your answer. Instead, submit either $\frac{7}{2}$ or 3.5.

 **REMEMBER**

You do not need to reduce fractions to their lowest terms as long as the fraction fits in the grid. You can save time and prevent calculation errors by giving your answer as an unreduced fraction.

 **REMEMBER**

Carefully read the directions for the student-produced response questions now so you won't have to spend precious time doing so on test day.

fraction or as the equivalent decimal form. If your answer is a decimal with more digits than will fit in the grid, you must fill the entire grid with the most accurate value possible, either rounding the number or truncating it. Do not include a leading zero when gridding in decimals. For example, if your answer is $\frac{2}{3}$, you can grid 2/3, .666, or .667; however, 0.6, .66, and 0.67 would all be considered incorrect. Do not round up when truncating a number unless the decimal should be rounded up. For example, if the answer is $\frac{1}{3}$, .333 is an acceptable answer, but .334 is not. It is also not necessary to reduce fractions to their lowest terms as long as the fraction fits in the grid. If your answer is $\frac{6}{18}$, you do not need to reduce it to $\frac{1}{3}$. Giving your answer as an unreduced fraction (if it fits in the grid) can save you time and prevent simple calculation mistakes.

Make sure to read the question carefully and answer what is being asked. If the question asks for the number of thousands and the correct answer is 2 thousands, grid in 2 as the answer, not 2000. If the question asks for your answer to be rounded to the nearest tenth or hundredth, only a correctly rounded answer will be accepted.

Some student-produced response questions may have more than one correct answer. You only need to provide one answer. Do not attempt to grid in more than one answer. You should not spend your time looking for additional answers. Just like multiple-choice questions, there is no penalty for guessing on student-produced response questions. If you are not sure of the correct answer, make an educated guess. Try not to leave questions unanswered.

The actual test directions for the student-produced response questions appear on the next page.

DIRECTIONS

For questions 31–38, solve the problem and enter your answer in the grid, as described below, on the answer sheet.

1. Although not required, it is suggested that you write your answer in the boxes at the top of the columns to help you fill in the circles accurately. You will receive credit only if the circles are filled in correctly.

2. Mark no more than one circle in any column.

3. No question has a negative answer.

4. Some problems may have more than one correct answer. In such cases, grid only one answer.

5. **Mixed numbers** such as $3\frac{1}{2}$ must be gridded as 3.5 or 7/2. (If [3][1][/][2] is entered into the grid, it will be interpreted as $\frac{31}{2}$, not $3\frac{1}{2}$.)

6. **Decimal answers:** If you obtain a decimal answer with more digits than the grid can accommodate, it may be either rounded or truncated, but it must fill the entire grid.

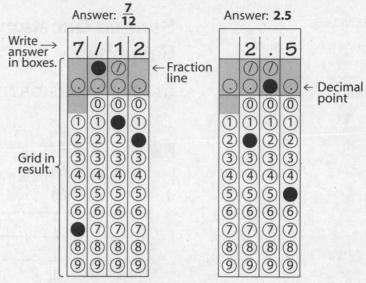

Answer: $\frac{7}{12}$ Answer: **2.5**

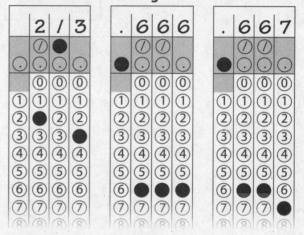

Acceptable ways to grid $\frac{2}{3}$ are:

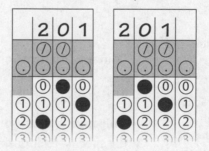

Answer: **201** – either position is correct

NOTE: You may start your answers in any column, space permitting. Columns you don't need to use should be left blank.

Sample Questions: Student-Produced Response

CALCULATOR PORTION

1

The table below classifies 103 elements as metal, metalloid, or nonmetal and as solid, liquid, or gas at standard temperature and pressure.

	Solids	Liquids	Gases	Total
Metals	77	1	0	78
Metalloids	7	0	0	7
Nonmetals	6	1	11	18
Total	90	2	11	103

What fraction of all solids and liquids in the table are metalloids?

PRACTICE AT

🌿 **khanacademy.org/sat**

The denominator of the fraction will be the total number of solids and liquids, while the numerator will be the number of liquids and solids that are metalloids. Carefully retrieve that information from the table, and remember to shade in the circles that correspond to the answer.

Content: Problem Solving and Data Analysis

Key: $.076, \dfrac{7}{92}$

Objective: You must read information from a two-way table and determine the specific relationship between two categorical variables.

Explanation: There are 7 metalloids that are solid or liquid, and there are 92 total solids and liquids. Therefore, the fraction of solids and liquids that are metalloids is $\dfrac{7}{92}$.

2

A typical image taken of the surface of Mars by a camera is 11.2 gigabits in size. A tracking station on Earth can receive data from the spacecraft at a data rate of 3 megabits per second for a maximum of 11 hours each day. If 1 gigabit equals 1,024 megabits, what is the maximum number of typical images that the tracking station could receive from the camera each day?

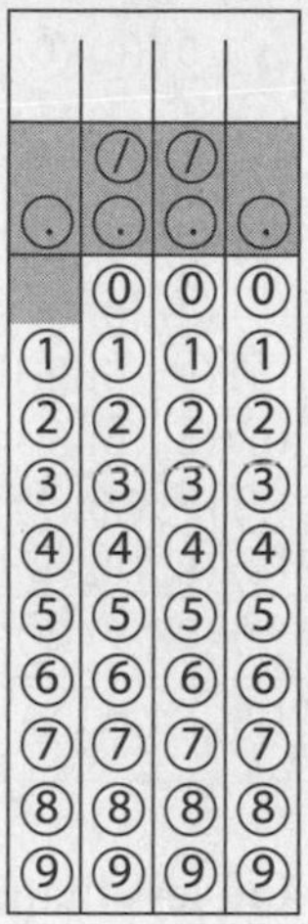

Content: Problem Solving and Data Analysis

Key: 10

Objective: In this problem, students must use the unit rate (data-transmission rate) and the conversion between gigabits and megabits as well as conversions in units of time. Unit analysis is critical to solving the problem correctly, and the problem represents a typical calculation that would be done when working with electronic files and data-transmission rates.

Explanation: The tracking station can receive 118,800 megabits each day $\left(\dfrac{3 \text{ megabits}}{1 \text{ second}} \times \dfrac{60 \text{ seconds}}{1 \text{ minute}} \times \dfrac{60 \text{ minutes}}{1 \text{ hour}} \times 11 \text{ hours}\right)$, which is about 116 gigabits each day $\left(\dfrac{118,800}{1,024}\right)$. If each image is 11.2 gigabits, then the number of images that can be received each day is $\dfrac{116}{11.2} \approx 10.4$. Since the question asks for the maximum number of typical images, rounding the answer down to 10 is appropriate because the tracking station will not receive a completed 11th image in one day.

PRACTICE AT

khanacademy.org/sat

Unit analysis and conversion is an important skill on the SAT Math Test and features prominently on this question. It may help to write out the conversion, including the units, as illustrated here.

PRACTICE AT

khanacademy.org/sat

Consider whether rounding up or down is appropriate based on the question. Here, rounding 10.4 down to 10 is required to receive credit on this question since the question specifically asks for the maximum number of images that the tracking station can receive each day.

3

If $-\dfrac{9}{5} < -3t + 1 < -\dfrac{7}{4}$, what is one possible value of $9t - 3$?

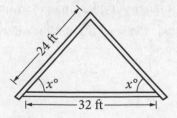

PRACTICE AT

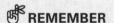

khanacademy.org/sat

When you multiply an inequality by a negative number, remember to reverse the inequality signs.

REMEMBER

When entering your answer to this question, do not enter your answer as a mixed fraction. Rather, enter your answer as a decimal or an improper fraction.

Content: Heart of Algebra

Key: Any value greater than $\dfrac{21}{4}$ and less than $\dfrac{27}{5}$

Objective: You should recognize the structure of the inequality to form a strategy to solve the inequality.

Explanation: Using the structure of the inequality to solve, you could note that the relationship between $-3t + 1$ and $9t - 3$ is that the latter is -3 multiplied by the former. Multiplying all parts of the inequality by -3 reverses the inequality signs, resulting in $\dfrac{27}{5} > 9t - 3 > \dfrac{21}{4}$ or rather $\dfrac{21}{4} < 9t - 3 < \dfrac{27}{5}$ when written with increasing values from left to right. Any value that is greater than $\dfrac{21}{4}$ and less than $\dfrac{27}{5}$ is correct.

4

An architect drew the sketch below while designing a house roof. The dimensions shown are for the interior of the triangle.

Note: Figure not drawn to scale.

What is the value of cos x?

Content: Additional Topics in Math

Key: $\dfrac{2}{3}, \dfrac{4}{6}, \dfrac{8}{12}$, .666, .667

Objective: You must make use of properties of triangles to solve a problem.

Explanation: Because the triangle is isosceles, constructing a perpendicular from the top vertex to the opposite side will bisect the base and create two smaller right triangles. In a right triangle, the cosine of an acute angle is equal to the length of the side adjacent to the angle divided by the length of the hypotenuse. This gives $\cos x = \dfrac{16}{24}$, which can be simplified to $\cos x = \dfrac{2}{3}$. Note that $\dfrac{16}{24}$ cannot be entered into the answer grid, so this fraction must be reduced. Acceptable answers to grid are 2/3, 4/6, 6/9, 8/12, .666, and .667.

SAMPLE QUESTION SET

Questions 5 and 6 refer to the following information:

An international bank issues its Traveler credit cards worldwide. When a customer makes a purchase using a Traveler card in a currency different from the customer's home currency, the bank converts the purchase price at the daily foreign exchange rate and then charges a 4% fee on the converted cost.

Sara lives in the United States and is on vacation in India. She used her Traveler card for a purchase that cost 602 rupees (Indian currency). The bank posted a charge of $9.88 to her account that included a 4% fee.

PRACTICE AT

khanacademy.org/sat

The cosine of an acute angle is equal to the length of the side adjacent to the angle divided by the length of the hypotenuse. Learn to solve for sine, cosine, and tangent of an acute angle; this may be tested on the SAT.

5

What foreign exchange rate, in Indian rupees per one U.S. dollar, did the bank use for Sara's charge? Round your answer to the nearest whole number.

Content: Problem Solving and Data Analysis

Key: 63

Objective: You must use the information in the problem to set up a ratio that will allow you to find the exchange rate.

Explanation: $9.88 represents the conversion of 602 rupees plus a 4% fee on the converted cost. To calculate the original cost of the item in dollars, x, find $1.04x = 9.88$, $x = 9.5$. Since the original cost is $9.50, to calculate the exchange rate r, in Indian rupees per one U.S. dollar: 9.50 dollars $\times \dfrac{r \text{ rupees}}{1 \text{ dollar}}$ = 602 rupees; solving for r yields approximately 63 rupees.

PRACTICE AT

🌱 **khanacademy.org/sat**

It is helpful to divide this question into two steps. First, calculate the original cost of Sara's purchase in dollars. Then, set up a ratio to find the exchange rate, keeping track of your units.

6

A bank in India sells a prepaid credit card worth 7500 rupees. Sara can buy the prepaid card using dollars at the daily exchange rate with no fee, but she will lose any money left unspent on the prepaid card. What is the least number of the 7500 rupees on the prepaid card Sara must spend for the prepaid card to be cheaper than charging all her purchases on the Traveler card? Round your answer to the nearest whole number of rupees.

Content: Problem Solving and Data Analysis

Key: 7212

Objective: You must set up an inequality to solve a multistep problem.

Explanation: Let d dollars be the cost of the 7500-rupee prepaid card. This implies that the exchange rate on this particular day is $\dfrac{d}{7500}$ dollars per rupee. Suppose Sara's total purchases on the prepaid card were r rupees. The value of r rupees in dollars is $\left(\dfrac{d}{7500}\right) r$ dollars. If Sara spent the r rupees on the Traveler card instead, she would be charged $1.04 \left(\dfrac{d}{7500}\right) r$ dollars. To answer the question about how many rupees Sara must spend in order to make the Traveler card a cheaper option (in dollars) for spending the r rupees, you must set up the inequality $1.04 \left(\dfrac{d}{7500}\right) r \geq d$. Rewriting both sides reveals $1.04 \left(\dfrac{r}{7500}\right) d \geq (1)d$, from which you can infer $1.04\left(\dfrac{r}{7500}\right) \geq 1$. Dividing both sides by 1.04 and multiplying both sides by 7500 finally yields $r \geq 7{,}212$. Hence the least number of rupees Sara must spend for the prepaid card to be cheaper than the Traveler card is 7212.

PRACTICE AT

khanacademy.org/sat

Another helpful way to think about this question is to keep in mind the fact that Sara will pay 7500 rupees for the prepaid card, regardless of how much money she leaves unspent. For the prepaid card to be cheaper than using the Traveler card, the Traveler card must end up costing Sara more than 7500 rupees. You can set up an inequality to calculate the least amount of purchases Sara needs to make using the Traveler card to exceed 7500 rupees. This value, when rounded to the nearest whole number, yields the correct answer.

Student-Produced Response Sample Questions

NO-CALCULATOR PORTION

7

If $a^2 + 14a = 51$ and $a > 0$, what is the value of $a + 7$?

Content: Passport to Advanced Math

Key: 10

Objective: You must use your knowledge of quadratic equations to determine the best way to efficiently solve this problem.

Explanation: There is more than one way to solve this problem. You can apply standard techniques by rewriting the equation $a^2 + 14a = 51$ as $a^2 + 14a - 51 = 0$ and then factoring. Since the coefficient of a is 14 and the constant term is -51, factoring requires writing 51 as the product of two numbers that differ by 14. This is $51 = (3)(17)$, which gives the factorization $(a + 17)(a - 3) = 0$. The possible values of a are -17 and 3. Since it is given that $a > 0$, it must be true that $a = 3$. Thus, the value of $a + 7$ is $3 + 7 = 10$.

You could also use the quadratic formula to find the possible values of a.

A third way to solve this problem is to recognize that adding 49 to both sides of the equation yields $a^2 + 14a + 49 = 51 + 49$, or rather $(a + 7)^2 = 100$, which has a perfect square on each side. Since $a > 0$, the solution to $a + 7 = 10$ is evident.

8

If $\dfrac{1}{2}x + \dfrac{1}{3}y = 4$, what is the value of $3x + 2y$?

Content: Heart of Algebra

Key: 24

Objective: You must use the structure of the equation to efficiently solve the problem.

Explanation: Using the structure of the equation allows you to quickly solve the problem if you see that multiplying both sides of the equation by 6 clears the fractions and yields $3x + 2y = 24$.

9

What is one possible solution to the equation $\dfrac{24}{x+1} - \dfrac{12}{x-1} = 1$?

Content: Passport to Advanced Math

Key: 5, 7

Objective: You should seek the best solution method for solving rational equations before beginning. Searching for structure and common denominators will prove very useful at the onset and will help prevent complex computations that do not lead to a solution.

Explanation: In this problem, multiplying both sides of the equation by the common denominator $(x + 1)(x - 1)$ yields $24(x - 1) - 12(x + 1) = (x + 1)$ $(x - 1)$. Multiplication and simplification then yields $12x - 36 = x^2 - 1$, or $x^2 - 12x + 35 = 0$. Factoring the quadratic gives $(x - 5)(x - 7) = 0$, so the solutions occur at $x = 5$ and $x = 7$, both of which should be checked in the original equation to ensure they are not extraneous. In this case, both values are solutions, and either is a correct answer.

PRACTICE AT

khanacademy.org/sat

Eliminating fractions is often a good first step when asked to solve a rational equation. To eliminate the fractions in this equation, multiply both sides of the equation by the common denominator, which is $(x + 1)(x - 1)$.

10

$$x^2 + y^2 - 6x + 8y = 144$$

The equation of a circle in the xy-plane is shown above. What is the *diameter* of the circle?

Content: Additional Topics in Math

Key: 26

Objective: You must determine a circle property given the equation of the circle.

Explanation: Completing the square yields the equation $(x - 3)^2 + (y + 4)^2 = 169$, the standard form of an equation of the circle. Understanding this form results in the equation $r^2 = 169$, which when solved for r gives the value of the radius as 13. Diameter is twice the value of the radius; therefore, the diameter is 26.

Four Official Practice Tests with Answer Explanations

Introduction

TIME TO PRACTICE

The remainder of this book is composed of four full SAT practice tests, with answer sheets and answer explanations included. These practice tests and explanations were written by the College Board's Assessment Design and Development team using the same processes and review standards used when writing the actual SAT. Everything from the layout of the page to the construction of the questions accurately reflects what you'll see on test day.

The practice tests will provide the most valuable insight into your performance on the actual SAT when completed in a single sitting. As such, we urge you not to leaf through these tests for question practice, but instead to take them under conditions similar to those of a real test. If you are looking for additional questions, you can find them in the Practice section of collegereadiness.collegeboard.org.

TIPS FOR TAKING THE PRACTICE TESTS

You'll get the most out of the practice tests if you take them under conditions that are as close as possible to those of the real test:

▶ Leave yourself 3 hours to complete each sample test and an additional 50 minutes to complete the SAT Essay.

▶ Sit at a desk or table cleared of any other papers or books. Items such as dictionaries, books, or notes won't be allowed when you take the actual SAT.

▶ For the math questions that allow calculators, use the calculator that you plan to use on test day.

▶ Set a timer or use a watch or clock to time yourself on each section.

▶ Tear out or make a copy of the practice test answer sheet located immediately after each practice test and fill it in just as you will on the day of the actual test.

HOW TO SCORE YOUR PRACTICE TESTS

For more information on how to score your practice tests, go to sat.org/scoring. As you learned in Chapter 5, your SAT results will include a number of scores that provide additional information about your achievement and readiness for college and career. The College Board has also produced a free app that will allow you to immediately score your answer sheet by taking a picture of it. This app will take much of the manual labor out of scoring a paper-and-pencil test, and we hope it will encourage you to engage in productive practice. You can find more information on the app as well as how to score your tests without the app at sat.org/scoring.

CONNECTION TO KHAN ACADEMY

Through the College Board practice app, you'll be able to automatically score your practice tests and send those results to Khan Academy to power your personalized practice. Then, when you log on to its website (khanacademy.org/sat), Khan Academy will recommend specific lessons and resources to target the skills that will most improve your score on the SAT. Since the SAT is a measure of college and career readiness, this practice will also better prepare you for success beyond the SAT.

CollegeBoard

SAT® Practice Test #1

IMPORTANT REMINDERS

 1

A No. 2 pencil is required for the test. Do not use a mechanical pencil or pen.

 2

Sharing any questions with anyone is a violation of Test Security and Fairness policies and may result in your scores being canceled.

This cover is representative of what you'll see on test day.

THIS TEST BOOK MUST NOT BE TAKEN FROM THE ROOM. UNAUTHORIZED REPRODUCTION OR USE OF ANY PART OF THIS TEST BOOK IS PROHIBITED.

Test begins on the next page.

Reading Test

65 MINUTES, 52 QUESTIONS

Turn to Section 1 of your answer sheet to answer the questions in this section.

Each passage or pair of passages below is followed by a number of questions. After reading each passage or pair, choose the best answer to each question based on what is stated or implied in the passage or passages and in any accompanying graphics (such as a table or graph).

Questions 1-10 are based on the following passage.

This passage is from Lydia Minatoya, *The Strangeness of Beauty*. ©1999 by Lydia Minatoya. The setting is Japan in 1920. Chie and her daughter Naomi are members of the House of Fuji, a noble family.

Akira came directly, breaking all tradition. Was that it? Had he followed form—had he asked his mother to speak to his father to approach a
Line go-between—would Chie have been more receptive?
5   He came on a winter's eve. He pounded on the door while a cold rain beat on the shuttered veranda, so at first Chie thought him only the wind. The maid knew better. Chie heard her soft scuttling footsteps, the creak of the door. Then the maid brought a
10 calling card to the drawing room, for Chie.

Chie was reluctant to go to her guest; perhaps she was feeling too cozy. She and Naomi were reading at a low table set atop a charcoal brazier. A thick quilt spread over the sides of the table so their legs were
15 tucked inside with the heat.

"Who is it at this hour, in this weather?" Chie questioned as she picked the name card off the maid's lacquer tray.

"Shinoda, Akira. Kobe Dental College," she read.
20   Naomi recognized the name. Chie heard a soft intake of air.

"I think you should go," said Naomi.

Akira was waiting in the entry. He was in his early twenties, slim and serious, wearing the black
25 military-style uniform of a student. As he bowed—his hands hanging straight down, a black cap in one, a yellow oil-paper umbrella in the other—Chie glanced beyond him. In the glistening surface of the courtyard's rain-drenched paving
30 stones, she saw his reflection like a dark double.

"Madame," said Akira, "forgive my disruption, but I come with a matter of urgency."

His voice was soft, refined. He straightened and stole a deferential peek at her face.
35   In the dim light his eyes shone with sincerity. Chie felt herself starting to like him.

"Come inside, get out of this nasty night. Surely your business can wait for a moment or two."

"I don't want to trouble you. Normally I would
40 approach you more properly but I've received word of a position. I've an opportunity to go to America, as dentist for Seattle's Japanese community."

"Congratulations," Chie said with amusement. "That is an opportunity, I'm sure. But how am I
45 involved?"

Even noting Naomi's breathless reaction to the name card, Chie had no idea. Akira's message, delivered like a formal speech, filled her with maternal amusement. You know how children speak
50 so earnestly, so hurriedly, so endearingly about things that have no importance in an adult's mind? That's how she viewed him, as a child.

CONTINUE

It was how she viewed Naomi. Even though
Naomi was eighteen and training endlessly in the arts
55 needed to make a good marriage, Chie had made no
effort to find her a husband.

Akira blushed.

"Depending on your response, I may stay in
Japan. I've come to ask for Naomi's hand."
60 Suddenly Chie felt the dampness of the night.

"Does Naomi know anything of your . . .
ambitions?"

"We have an understanding. Please don't judge
my candidacy by the unseemliness of this proposal. I
65 ask directly because the use of a go-between takes
much time. Either method comes down to the same
thing: a matter of parental approval. If you give your
consent, I become Naomi's yoshi.* We'll live in the
House of Fuji. Without your consent, I must go to
70 America, to secure a new home for my bride."

Eager to make his point, he'd been looking her full
in the face. Abruptly, his voice turned gentle. "I see
I've startled you. My humble apologies. I'll take no
more of your evening. My address is on my card. If
75 you don't wish to contact me, I'll reapproach you in
two weeks' time. Until then, good night."

He bowed and left. Taking her ease, with effortless
grace, like a cat making off with a fish.

"Mother?" Chie heard Naomi's low voice and
80 turned from the door. "He has asked you?"

The sight of Naomi's clear eyes, her dark brows
gave Chie strength. Maybe his hopes were
preposterous.

"Where did you meet such a fellow? Imagine! He
85 thinks he can marry the Fuji heir and take her to
America all in the snap of his fingers!"

Chie waited for Naomi's ripe laughter.

Naomi was silent. She stood a full half minute
looking straight into Chie's eyes. Finally, she spoke.
90 "I met him at my literary meeting."

Naomi turned to go back into the house, then
stopped.

"Mother."

"Yes?"
95 "I mean to have him."

* a man who marries a woman of higher status and takes her
family's name

1

Which choice best describes what happens in the
passage?

A) One character argues with another character
who intrudes on her home.

B) One character receives a surprising request from
another character.

C) One character reminisces about choices she has
made over the years.

D) One character criticizes another character for
pursuing an unexpected course of action.

2

Which choice best describes the developmental
pattern of the passage?

A) A careful analysis of a traditional practice

B) A detailed depiction of a meaningful encounter

C) A definitive response to a series of questions

D) A cheerful recounting of an amusing anecdote

3

As used in line 1 and line 65, "directly" most
nearly means

A) frankly.

B) confidently.

C) without mediation.

D) with precision.

4

Which reaction does Akira most fear from Chie?

A) She will consider his proposal inappropriate.

B) She will mistake his earnestness for immaturity.

C) She will consider his unscheduled visit an
imposition.

D) She will underestimate the sincerity of his
emotions.

CONTINUE

5

Which choice provides the best evidence for the answer to the previous question?

A) Line 33 ("His voice . . . refined")

B) Lines 49-51 ("You . . . mind")

C) Lines 63-64 ("Please . . . proposal")

D) Lines 71-72 ("Eager . . . face")

6

In the passage, Akira addresses Chie with

A) affection but not genuine love.

B) objectivity but not complete impartiality.

C) amusement but not mocking disparagement.

D) respect but not utter deference.

7

The main purpose of the first paragraph is to

A) describe a culture.

B) criticize a tradition.

C) question a suggestion.

D) analyze a reaction.

8

As used in line 2, "form" most nearly means

A) appearance.

B) custom.

C) structure.

D) nature.

9

Why does Akira say his meeting with Chie is "a matter of urgency" (line 32)?

A) He fears that his own parents will disapprove of Naomi.

B) He worries that Naomi will reject him and marry someone else.

C) He has been offered an attractive job in another country.

D) He knows that Chie is unaware of his feelings for Naomi.

10

Which choice provides the best evidence for the answer to the previous question?

A) Line 39 ("I don't . . . you")

B) Lines 39-42 ("Normally . . . community")

C) Lines 58-59 ("Depending . . . Japan")

D) Lines 72-73 ("I see . . . you")

CONTINUE ➡

Questions 11-21 are based on the following passage and supplementary material.

This passage is adapted from Francis J. Flynn and Gabrielle S. Adams, "Money Can't Buy Love: Asymmetric Beliefs about Gift Price and Feelings of Appreciation." ©2008 by Elsevier Inc.

Every day, millions of shoppers hit the stores in full force—both online and on foot—searching frantically for the perfect gift. Last year, Americans
Line spent over $30 billion at retail stores in the month of
5 December alone. Aside from purchasing holiday gifts, most people regularly buy presents for other occasions throughout the year, including weddings, birthdays, anniversaries, graduations, and baby showers. This frequent experience of gift-giving can
10 engender ambivalent feelings in gift-givers. Many relish the opportunity to buy presents because gift-giving offers a powerful means to build stronger bonds with one's closest peers. At the same time, many dread the thought of buying gifts; they worry
15 that their purchases will disappoint rather than delight the intended recipients.

Anthropologists describe gift-giving as a positive social process, serving various political, religious, and psychological functions. Economists, however, offer
20 a less favorable view. According to Waldfogel (1993), gift-giving represents an objective waste of resources. People buy gifts that recipients would not choose to buy on their own, or at least not spend as much money to purchase (a phenomenon referred to as
25 "the deadweight loss of Christmas"). To wit, givers are likely to spend $100 to purchase a gift that receivers would spend only $80 to buy themselves. This "deadweight loss" suggests that gift-givers are not very good at predicting what gifts others will
30 appreciate. That in itself is not surprising to social psychologists. Research has found that people often struggle to take account of others' perspectives— their insights are subject to egocentrism, social projection, and multiple attribution errors.

35 What is surprising is that gift-givers have considerable experience acting as both gift-givers and gift-recipients, but nevertheless tend to overspend each time they set out to purchase a meaningful gift. In the present research, we propose a unique
40 psychological explanation for this overspending problem—i.e., that gift-givers equate how much they spend with how much recipients will appreciate the gift (the more expensive the gift, the stronger a gift-recipient's feelings of appreciation). Although a
45 link between gift price and feelings of appreciation might seem intuitive to gift-givers, such an assumption may be unfounded. Indeed, we propose that gift-recipients will be less inclined to base their feelings of appreciation on the magnitude of a gift
50 than givers assume.

Why do gift-givers assume that gift price is closely linked to gift-recipients' feelings of appreciation? Perhaps givers believe that bigger (i.e., more expensive) gifts convey stronger signals of
55 thoughtfulness and consideration. According to Camerer (1988) and others, gift-giving represents a symbolic ritual, whereby gift-givers attempt to signal their positive attitudes toward the intended recipient and their willingness to invest resources in a future
60 relationship. In this sense, gift-givers may be motivated to spend more money on a gift in order to send a "stronger signal" to their intended recipient. As for gift-recipients, they may not construe smaller and larger gifts as representing smaller and larger
65 signals of thoughtfulness and consideration.

The notion of gift-givers and gift-recipients being unable to account for the other party's perspective seems puzzling because people slip in and out of these roles every day, and, in some cases, multiple
70 times in the course of the same day. Yet, despite the extensive experience that people have as both givers and receivers, they often struggle to transfer information gained from one role (e.g., as a giver) and apply it in another, complementary role (e.g., as
75 a receiver). In theoretical terms, people fail to utilize information about their own preferences and experiences in order to produce more efficient outcomes in their exchange relations. In practical terms, people spend hundreds of dollars each year on
80 gifts, but somehow never learn to calibrate their gift expenditures according to personal insight.

CONTINUE

Givers' Perceived and Recipients'
Actual Gift Appreciations

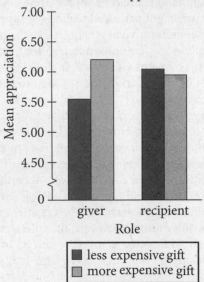

11

The authors most likely use the examples in lines 1-9 of the passage ("Every . . . showers") to highlight the

A) regularity with which people shop for gifts.

B) recent increase in the amount of money spent on gifts.

C) anxiety gift shopping causes for consumers.

D) number of special occasions involving gift-giving.

12

In line 10, the word "ambivalent" most nearly means

A) unrealistic.

B) conflicted.

C) apprehensive.

D) supportive.

13

The authors indicate that people value gift-giving because they feel it

A) functions as a form of self-expression.

B) is an inexpensive way to show appreciation.

C) requires the gift-recipient to reciprocate.

D) can serve to strengthen a relationship.

14

Which choice provides the best evidence for the answer to the previous question?

A) Lines 10-13 ("Many . . . peers")

B) Lines 22-23 ("People . . . own")

C) Lines 31-32 ("Research . . . perspectives")

D) Lines 44-47 ("Although . . . unfounded")

15

The "social psychologists" mentioned in paragraph 2 (lines 17-34) would likely describe the "deadweight loss" phenomenon as

A) predictable.

B) questionable.

C) disturbing.

D) unprecedented.

16

The passage indicates that the assumption made by gift-givers in lines 41-44 may be

A) insincere.

B) unreasonable.

C) incorrect.

D) substantiated.

CONTINUE

17

Which choice provides the best evidence for the answer to the previous question?

A) Lines 53-55 ("Perhaps . . . consideration")

B) Lines 55-60 ("According . . . relationship")

C) Lines 63-65 ("As . . . consideration")

D) Lines 75-78 ("In . . . relations")

18

As it is used in line 54, "convey" most nearly means

A) transport.

B) counteract.

C) exchange.

D) communicate.

19

The authors refer to work by Camerer and others (line 56) in order to

A) offer an explanation.

B) introduce an argument.

C) question a motive.

D) support a conclusion.

20

The graph following the passage offers evidence that gift-givers base their predictions of how much a gift will be appreciated on

A) the appreciation level of the gift-recipients.

B) the monetary value of the gift.

C) their own desires for the gifts they purchase.

D) their relationship with the gift-recipients.

21

The authors would likely attribute the differences in gift-giver and recipient mean appreciation as represented in the graph to

A) an inability to shift perspective.

B) an increasingly materialistic culture.

C) a growing opposition to gift-giving.

D) a misunderstanding of intentions.

CONTINUE

Questions 22-31 are based on the following passage and supplementary material.

This passage is adapted from J. D. Watson and F. H. C. Crick, "Genetical Implications of the Structure of Deoxyribonucleic Acid." ©1953 by Nature Publishing Group. Watson and Crick deduced the structure of DNA using evidence from Rosalind Franklin and R. G. Gosling's X-ray crystallography diagrams of DNA and from Erwin Chargaff's data on the base composition of DNA.

The chemical formula of deoxyribonucleic acid (DNA) is now well established. The molecule is a very long chain, the backbone of which consists of a
Line regular alternation of sugar and phosphate groups.
5 To each sugar is attached a nitrogenous base, which can be of four different types. Two of the possible bases—adenine and guanine—are purines, and the other two—thymine and cytosine—are pyrimidines. So far as is known, the sequence of bases along the
10 chain is irregular. The monomer unit, consisting of phosphate, sugar and base, is known as a nucleotide.

The first feature of our structure which is of biological interest is that it consists not of one chain, but of two. These two chains are both coiled around
15 a common fiber axis. It has often been assumed that since there was only one chain in the chemical formula there would only be one in the structural unit. However, the density, taken with the X-ray evidence, suggests very strongly that there are two.
20 The other biologically important feature is the manner in which the two chains are held together. This is done by hydrogen bonds between the bases. The bases are joined together in pairs, a single base from one chain being hydrogen-bonded to a single
25 base from the other. The important point is that only certain pairs of bases will fit into the structure. One member of a pair must be a purine and the other a pyrimidine in order to bridge between the two chains. If a pair consisted of two purines, for
30 example, there would not be room for it.

We believe that the bases will be present almost entirely in their most probable forms. If this is true, the conditions for forming hydrogen bonds are more restrictive, and the only pairs of bases possible are:
35 adenine with thymine, and guanine with cytosine. Adenine, for example, can occur on either chain; but when it does, its partner on the other chain must always be thymine.

The phosphate-sugar backbone of our model is
40 completely regular, but any sequence of the pairs of bases can fit into the structure. It follows that in a

long molecule many different permutations are possible, and it therefore seems likely that the precise sequence of bases is the code which carries the
45 genetical information. If the actual order of the bases on one of the pair of chains were given, one could write down the exact order of the bases on the other one, because of the specific pairing. Thus one chain is, as it were, the complement of the other, and it is
50 this feature which suggests how the deoxyribonucleic acid molecule might duplicate itself.

The table shows, for various organisms, the percentage of each of the four types of nitrogenous bases in that organism's DNA.

Base Composition of DNA				
Organism	Percentage of base in organism's DNA			
	adenine (%)	guanine (%)	cytosine (%)	thymine (%)
Maize	26.8	22.8	23.2	27.2
Octopus	33.2	17.6	17.6	31.6
Chicken	28.0	22.0	21.6	28.4
Rat	28.6	21.4	20.5	28.4
Human	29.3	20.7	20.0	30.0
Grasshopper	29.3	20.5	20.7	29.3
Sea urchin	32.8	17.7	17.3	32.1
Wheat	27.3	22.7	22.8	27.1
Yeast	31.3	18.7	17.1	32.9
E. coli	24.7	26.0	25.7	23.6

Adapted from Manju Bansal, "DNA Structure: Revisiting the Watson-Crick Double Helix." ©2003 by Current Science Association, Bangalore.

CONTINUE ▶

22

The authors use the word "backbone" in lines 3 and 39 to indicate that

A) only very long chains of DNA can be taken from an organism with a spinal column.

B) the main structure of a chain in a DNA molecule is composed of repeating units.

C) a chain in a DNA molecule consists entirely of phosphate groups or of sugars.

D) nitrogenous bases form the main structural unit of DNA.

23

A student claims that nitrogenous bases pair randomly with one another. Which of the following statements in the passage contradicts the student's claim?

A) Lines 5-6 ("To each . . . types")

B) Lines 9-10 ("So far . . . irregular")

C) Lines 23-25 ("The bases . . . other")

D) Lines 27-29 ("One member . . . chains")

24

In the second paragraph (lines 12-19), what do the authors claim to be a feature of biological interest?

A) The chemical formula of DNA

B) The common fiber axis

C) The X-ray evidence

D) DNA consisting of two chains

25

The authors' main purpose of including the information about X-ray evidence and density is to

A) establish that DNA is the molecule that carries the genetic information.

B) present an alternate hypothesis about the composition of a nucleotide.

C) provide support for the authors' claim about the number of chains in a molecule of DNA.

D) confirm the relationship between the density of DNA and the known chemical formula of DNA.

26

Based on the passage, the authors' statement "If a pair consisted of two purines, for example, there would not be room for it" (lines 29-30) implies that a pair

A) of purines would be larger than the space between a sugar and a phosphate group.

B) of purines would be larger than a pair consisting of a purine and a pyrimidine.

C) of pyrimidines would be larger than a pair of purines.

D) consisting of a purine and a pyrimidine would be larger than a pair of pyrimidines.

27

The authors' use of the words "exact," "specific," and "complement" in lines 47-49 in the final paragraph functions mainly to

A) confirm that the nucleotide sequences are known for most molecules of DNA.

B) counter the claim that the sequences of bases along a chain can occur in any order.

C) support the claim that the phosphate-sugar backbone of the authors' model is completely regular.

D) emphasize how one chain of DNA may serve as a template to be copied during DNA replication.

CONTINUE ▶

28

Based on the table and passage, which choice gives the correct percentages of the purines in yeast DNA?

A) 17.1% and 18.7%

B) 17.1% and 32.9%

C) 18.7% and 31.3%

D) 31.3% and 32.9%

29

Do the data in the table support the authors' proposed pairing of bases in DNA?

A) Yes, because for each given organism, the percentage of adenine is closest to the percentage of thymine, and the percentage of guanine is closest to the percentage of cytosine.

B) Yes, because for each given organism, the percentage of adenine is closest to the percentage of guanine, and the percentage of cytosine is closest to the percentage of thymine.

C) No, because for each given organism, the percentage of adenine is closest to the percentage of thymine, and the percentage of guanine is closest to the percentage of cytosine.

D) No, because for each given organism, the percentage of adenine is closest to the percentage of guanine, and the percentage of cytosine is closest to the percentage of thymine.

30

According to the table, which of the following pairs of base percentages in sea urchin DNA provides evidence in support of the answer to the previous question?

A) 17.3% and 17.7%

B) 17.3% and 32.1%

C) 17.3% and 32.8%

D) 17.7% and 32.8%

31

Based on the table, is the percentage of adenine in each organism's DNA the same or does it vary, and which statement made by the authors is most consistent with that data?

A) The same; "Two of . . . pyrimidines" (lines 6-8)

B) The same; "The important . . . structure" (lines 25-26)

C) It varies; "Adenine . . . thymine" (lines 36-38)

D) It varies; "It follows . . . information" (lines 41-45)

CONTINUE

Questions 32-41 are based on the following passage.

This passage is adapted from Virginia Woolf, *Three Guineas*. ©1938 by Harcourt, Inc. Here, Woolf considers the situation of women in English society.

Close at hand is a bridge over the River Thames, an admirable vantage ground for us to make a survey. The river flows beneath; barges pass, laden
Line with timber, bursting with corn; there on one side are
5 the domes and spires of the city; on the other, Westminster and the Houses of Parliament. It is a place to stand on by the hour, dreaming. But not now. Now we are pressed for time. Now we are here to consider facts; now we must fix our eyes upon the
10 procession—the procession of the sons of educated men.

There they go, our brothers who have been educated at public schools and universities, mounting those steps, passing in and out of those
15 doors, ascending those pulpits, preaching, teaching, administering justice, practising medicine, transacting business, making money. It is a solemn sight always—a procession, like a caravanserai crossing a desert. . . . But now, for the past twenty
20 years or so, it is no longer a sight merely, a photograph, or fresco scrawled upon the walls of time, at which we can look with merely an esthetic appreciation. For there, trapesing along at the tail end of the procession, we go ourselves. And that
25 makes a difference. We who have looked so long at the pageant in books, or from a curtained window watched educated men leaving the house at about nine-thirty to go to an office, returning to the house at about six-thirty from an office, need look passively
30 no longer. We too can leave the house, can mount those steps, pass in and out of those doors, . . . make money, administer justice. . . . We who now agitate these humble pens may in another century or two speak from a pulpit. Nobody will dare contradict us
35 then; we shall be the mouthpieces of the divine spirit—a solemn thought, is it not? Who can say whether, as time goes on, we may not dress in military uniform, with gold lace on our breasts, swords at our sides, and something like the old
40 family coal-scuttle on our heads, save that that venerable object was never decorated with plumes of white horsehair. You laugh—indeed the shadow of the private house still makes those dresses look a little queer. We have worn private clothes so
45 long. . . . But we have not come here to laugh, or to talk of fashions—men's and women's. We are here, on the bridge, to ask ourselves certain questions. And they are very important questions; and we have very little time in which to answer them. The
50 questions that we have to ask and to answer about that procession during this moment of transition are so important that they may well change the lives of all men and women for ever. For we have to ask ourselves, here and now, do we wish to join that
55 procession, or don't we? On what terms shall we join that procession? Above all, where is it leading us, the procession of educated men? The moment is short; it may last five years; ten years, or perhaps only a matter of a few months longer. . . . But, you will
60 object, you have no time to think; you have your battles to fight, your rent to pay, your bazaars to organize. That excuse shall not serve you, Madam. As you know from your own experience, and there are facts that prove it, the daughters of educated men
65 have always done their thinking from hand to mouth; not under green lamps at study tables in the cloisters of secluded colleges. They have thought while they stirred the pot, while they rocked the cradle. It was thus that they won us the right to our
70 brand-new sixpence. It falls to us now to go on thinking; how are we to spend that sixpence? Think we must. Let us think in offices; in omnibuses; while we are standing in the crowd watching Coronations and Lord Mayor's Shows; let us think . . . in the
75 gallery of the House of Commons; in the Law Courts; let us think at baptisms and marriages and funerals. Let us never cease from thinking—what is this "civilization" in which we find ourselves? What are these ceremonies and why should we take part in
80 them? What are these professions and why should we make money out of them? Where in short is it leading us, the procession of the sons of educated men?

32

The main purpose of the passage is to

A) emphasize the value of a tradition.

B) stress the urgency of an issue.

C) highlight the severity of social divisions.

D) question the feasibility of an undertaking.

CONTINUE ▶

33

The central claim of the passage is that

A) educated women face a decision about how to engage with existing institutions.

B) women can have positions of influence in English society only if they give up some of their traditional roles.

C) the male monopoly on power in English society has had grave and continuing effects.

D) the entry of educated women into positions of power traditionally held by men will transform those positions.

34

Woolf uses the word "we" throughout the passage mainly to

A) reflect the growing friendliness among a group of people.

B) advance the need for candor among a group of people.

C) establish a sense of solidarity among a group of people.

D) reinforce the need for respect among a group of people.

35

According to the passage, Woolf chooses the setting of the bridge because it

A) is conducive to a mood of fanciful reflection.

B) provides a good view of the procession of the sons of educated men.

C) is within sight of historic episodes to which she alludes.

D) is symbolic of the legacy of past and present sons of educated men.

36

Woolf indicates that the procession she describes in the passage

A) has come to have more practical influence in recent years.

B) has become a celebrated feature of English public life.

C) includes all of the richest and most powerful men in England.

D) has become less exclusionary in its membership in recent years.

37

Which choice provides the best evidence for the answer to the previous question?

A) Lines 12-17 ("There . . . money")

B) Lines 17-19 ("It . . . desert")

C) Lines 23-24 ("For . . . ourselves")

D) Lines 30-34 ("We . . . pulpit")

CONTINUE

38

Woolf characterizes the questions in lines 53-57 ("For we . . . men") as both

A) controversial and threatening.

B) weighty and unanswerable.

C) momentous and pressing.

D) provocative and mysterious.

39

Which choice provides the best evidence for the answer to the previous question?

A) Lines 46-47 ("We . . . questions")

B) Lines 48-49 ("And . . . them")

C) Line 57 ("The moment . . . short")

D) Line 62 ("That . . . Madam")

40

Which choice most closely captures the meaning of the figurative "sixpence" referred to in lines 70 and 71?

A) Tolerance

B) Knowledge

C) Opportunity

D) Perspective

41

The range of places and occasions listed in lines 72-76 ("Let us . . . funerals") mainly serves to emphasize how

A) novel the challenge faced by women is.

B) pervasive the need for critical reflection is.

C) complex the political and social issues of the day are.

D) enjoyable the career possibilities for women are.

CONTINUE

Questions 42-52 are based on the following passages.

Passage 1 is adapted from Michael Slezak, "Space Mining: the Next Gold Rush?" ©2013 by New Scientist. Passage 2 is from the editors of *New Scientist*, "Taming the Final Frontier." ©2013 by New Scientist.

Passage 1

Follow the money and you will end up in space. That's the message from a first-of-its-kind forum on mining beyond Earth.

Convened in Sydney by the Australian Centre for Space Engineering Research, the event brought together mining companies, robotics experts, lunar scientists, and government agencies that are all working to make space mining a reality.

The forum comes hot on the heels of the 2012 unveiling of two private asteroid-mining firms. Planetary Resources of Washington says it will launch its first prospecting telescopes in two years, while Deep Space Industries of Virginia hopes to be harvesting metals from asteroids by 2020. Another commercial venture that sprung up in 2012, Golden Spike of Colorado, will be offering trips to the moon, including to potential lunar miners.

Within a few decades, these firms may be meeting earthly demands for precious metals, such as platinum and gold, and the rare earth elements vital for personal electronics, such as yttrium and lanthanum. But like the gold rush pioneers who transformed the western United States, the first space miners won't just enrich themselves. They also hope to build an off-planet economy free of any bonds with Earth, in which the materials extracted and processed from the moon and asteroids are delivered for space-based projects.

In this scenario, water mined from other worlds could become the most desired commodity. "In the desert, what's worth more: a kilogram of gold or a kilogram of water?" asks Kris Zacny of HoneyBee Robotics in New York. "Gold is useless. Water will let you live."

Water ice from the moon's poles could be sent to astronauts on the International Space Station for drinking or as a radiation shield. Splitting water into oxygen and hydrogen makes spacecraft fuel, so ice-rich asteroids could become interplanetary refuelling stations.

Companies are eyeing the iron, silicon, and aluminium in lunar soil and asteroids, which could be used in 3D printers to make spare parts or machinery. Others want to turn space dirt into concrete for landing pads, shelters, and roads.

Passage 2

The motivation for deep-space travel is shifting from discovery to economics. The past year has seen a flurry of proposals aimed at bringing celestial riches down to Earth. No doubt this will make a few billionaires even wealthier, but we all stand to gain: the mineral bounty and spin-off technologies could enrich us all.

But before the miners start firing up their rockets, we should pause for thought. At first glance, space mining seems to sidestep most environmental concerns: there is (probably!) no life on asteroids, and thus no habitats to trash. But its consequences —both here on Earth and in space—merit careful consideration.

Part of this is about principles. Some will argue that space's "magnificent desolation" is not ours to despoil, just as they argue that our own planet's poles should remain pristine. Others will suggest that glutting ourselves on space's riches is not an acceptable alternative to developing more sustainable ways of earthly life.

History suggests that those will be hard lines to hold, and it may be difficult to persuade the public that such barren environments are worth preserving. After all, they exist in vast abundance, and even fewer people will experience them than have walked through Antarctica's icy landscapes.

There's also the emerging off-world economy to consider. The resources that are valuable in orbit and beyond may be very different to those we prize on Earth. Questions of their stewardship have barely been broached—and the relevant legal and regulatory framework is fragmentary, to put it mildly.

Space miners, like their earthly counterparts, are often reluctant to engage with such questions. One speaker at last week's space-mining forum in Sydney, Australia, concluded with a plea that regulation should be avoided. But miners have much to gain from a broad agreement on the for-profit exploitation of space. Without consensus, claims will be disputed, investments risky, and the gains made insecure. It is in all of our long-term interests to seek one out.

CONTINUE

42

In lines 9-17, the author of Passage 1 mentions several companies primarily to

A) note the technological advances that make space mining possible.

B) provide evidence of the growing interest in space mining.

C) emphasize the large profits to be made from space mining.

D) highlight the diverse ways to carry out space mining operations.

43

The author of Passage 1 indicates that space mining could have which positive effect?

A) It could yield materials important to Earth's economy.

B) It could raise the value of some precious metals on Earth.

C) It could create unanticipated technological innovations.

D) It could change scientists' understanding of space resources.

44

Which choice provides the best evidence for the answer to the previous question?

A) Lines 18-22 ("Within . . . lanthanum")

B) Lines 24-28 ("They . . . projects")

C) Lines 29-30 ("In this . . . commodity")

D) Lines 41-44 ("Companies . . . machinery")

45

As used in line 19, "demands" most nearly means

A) offers.

B) claims.

C) inquiries.

D) desires.

46

What function does the discussion of water in lines 35-40 serve in Passage 1?

A) It continues an extended comparison that begins in the previous paragraph.

B) It provides an unexpected answer to a question raised in the previous paragraph.

C) It offers hypothetical examples supporting a claim made in the previous paragraph.

D) It examines possible outcomes of a proposal put forth in the previous paragraph.

47

The central claim of Passage 2 is that space mining has positive potential but

A) it will end up encouraging humanity's reckless treatment of the environment.

B) its effects should be thoughtfully considered before it becomes a reality.

C) such potential may not include replenishing key resources that are disappearing on Earth.

D) experts disagree about the commercial viability of the discoveries it could yield.

48

As used in line 68, "hold" most nearly means

A) maintain.

B) grip.

C) restrain.

D) withstand.

CONTINUE

49

Which statement best describes the relationship between the passages?

A) Passage 2 refutes the central claim advanced in Passage 1.

B) Passage 2 illustrates the phenomenon described in more general terms in Passage 1.

C) Passage 2 argues against the practicality of the proposals put forth in Passage 1.

D) Passage 2 expresses reservations about developments discussed in Passage 1.

50

The author of Passage 2 would most likely respond to the discussion of the future of space mining in lines 18-28, Passage 1, by claiming that such a future

A) is inconsistent with the sustainable use of space resources.

B) will be difficult to bring about in the absence of regulations.

C) cannot be attained without technologies that do not yet exist.

D) seems certain to affect Earth's economy in a negative way.

51

Which choice provides the best evidence for the answer to the previous question?

A) Lines 60-63 ("Some . . . pristine")

B) Lines 74-76 ("The resources . . . Earth")

C) Lines 81-83 ("One . . . avoided")

D) Lines 85-87 ("Without . . . insecure")

52

Which point about the resources that will be highly valued in space is implicit in Passage 1 and explicit in Passage 2?

A) They may be different resources from those that are valuable on Earth.

B) They will be valuable only if they can be harvested cheaply.

C) They are likely to be primarily precious metals and rare earth elements.

D) They may increase in value as those same resources become rare on Earth.

STOP

If you finish before time is called, you may check your work on this section only.
Do not turn to any other section.

No Test Material On This Page

Writing and Language Test

35 MINUTES, 44 QUESTIONS

Turn to Section 2 of your answer sheet to answer the questions in this section.

Each passage below is accompanied by a number of questions. For some questions, you will consider how the passage might be revised to improve the expression of ideas. For other questions, you will consider how the passage might be edited to correct errors in sentence structure, usage, or punctuation. A passage or a question may be accompanied by one or more graphics (such as a table or graph) that you will consider as you make revising and editing decisions.

Some questions will direct you to an underlined portion of a passage. Other questions will direct you to a location in a passage or ask you to think about the passage as a whole.

After reading each passage, choose the answer to each question that most effectively improves the quality of writing in the passage or that makes the passage conform to the conventions of standard written English. Many questions include a "NO CHANGE" option. Choose that option if you think the best choice is to leave the relevant portion of the passage as it is.

Questions 1-11 are based on the following passage.

Whey to Go

Greek yogurt—a strained form of cultured yogurt—has grown enormously in popularity in the United States since it was first introduced in the country in the late 1980s.

From 2011 to 2012 alone, sales of Greek yogurt in the US increased by 50 percent. The resulting increase in Greek yogurt production has forced those involved in the business to address the detrimental effects that the yogurt-making process may be having on the environment. Fortunately, farmers and others in the

Unauthorized copying or reuse of any part of this page is illegal.

CONTINUE

350

Greek yogurt business have found many methods of controlling and eliminating most environmental threats. Given these solutions as well as the many health benefits of the food, the advantages of Greek yogurt **1** outdo the potential drawbacks of its production.

[1] The main environmental problem caused by the production of Greek yogurt is the creation of acid whey as a by-product. [2] Because it requires up to four times more milk to make than conventional yogurt does, Greek yogurt produces larger amounts of acid whey, which is difficult to dispose of. [3] To address the problem of disposal, farmers have found a number of uses for acid whey. [4] They can add it to livestock feed as a protein **2** supplement, and people can make their own Greek-style yogurt at home by straining regular yogurt. [5] If it is improperly introduced into the environment, acid-whey runoff **3** can pollute waterways, depleting the oxygen content of streams and rivers as it decomposes. [6] Yogurt manufacturers, food **4** scientists; and government officials are also working together to develop additional solutions for reusing whey. **5**

1
A) NO CHANGE
B) defeat
C) outperform
D) outweigh

2
Which choice provides the most relevant detail?
A) NO CHANGE
B) supplement and convert it into gas to use as fuel in electricity production.
C) supplement, while sweet whey is more desirable as a food additive for humans.
D) supplement, which provides an important element of their diet.

3
A) NO CHANGE
B) can pollute waterway's,
C) could have polluted waterways,
D) has polluted waterway's,

4
A) NO CHANGE
B) scientists: and
C) scientists, and
D) scientists, and,

5
To make this paragraph most logical, sentence 5 should be placed
A) where it is now.
B) after sentence 1.
C) after sentence 2.
D) after sentence 3.

CONTINUE

[6] Though these conservation methods can be costly and time-consuming, they are well worth the effort. Nutritionists consider Greek yogurt to be a healthy food: it is an excellent source of calcium and protein, serves [7] to be a digestive aid, and [8] it contains few calories in its unsweetened low- and non-fat forms. Greek yogurt is slightly lower in sugar and carbohydrates than conventional yogurt is. [9] Also, because it is more concentrated, Greek yogurt contains slightly more protein per serving, thereby helping people stay

6

The writer is considering deleting the underlined sentence. Should the writer do this?

A) Yes, because it does not provide a transition from the previous paragraph.

B) Yes, because it fails to support the main argument of the passage as introduced in the first paragraph.

C) No, because it continues the explanation of how acid whey can be disposed of safely.

D) No, because it sets up the argument in the paragraph for the benefits of Greek yogurt.

7

A) NO CHANGE

B) as

C) like

D) for

8

A) NO CHANGE

B) containing

C) contains

D) will contain

9

A) NO CHANGE

B) In other words,

C) Therefore,

D) For instance,

CONTINUE

10 satiated for longer periods of time. These health benefits have prompted Greek yogurt's recent surge in popularity. In fact, Greek yogurt can be found in an increasing number of products such as snack food and frozen desserts. Because consumers reap the nutritional benefits of Greek yogurt and support those who make and sell **11** it, therefore farmers and businesses should continue finding safe and effective methods of producing the food.

10

A) NO CHANGE
B) fulfilled
C) complacent
D) sufficient

11

A) NO CHANGE
B) it, farmers
C) it, so farmers
D) it: farmers

CONTINUE

Questions 12-22 are based on the following passage and supplementary material.

Dark Snow

Most of Greenland's interior is covered by a thick layer of ice and compressed snow known as the Greenland Ice Sheet. The size of the ice sheet fluctuates seasonally: in summer, average daily high temperatures in Greenland can rise to slightly above 50 degrees Fahrenheit, partially melting the ice; in the winter, the sheet thickens as additional snow falls, and average daily low temperatures can drop **12** to as low as 20 degrees.

12

Which choice most accurately and effectively represents the information in the graph?

A) NO CHANGE

B) to 12 degrees Fahrenheit.

C) to their lowest point on December 13.

D) to 10 degrees Fahrenheit and stay there for months.

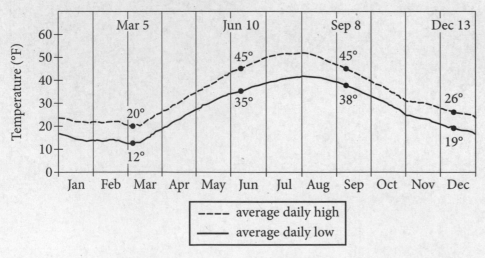

Average Daily High and Low Temperatures Recorded at Nuuk Weather Station, Greenland (1961—1990)

Adapted from WMO. ©2014 by World Meteorological Organization.

Unauthorized copying or reuse of any part of this page is illegal.

CONTINUE

354

Typically, the ice sheet begins to show evidence of thawing in late [13] summer. This follows several weeks of higher temperatures. [14] For example, in the summer of 2012, virtually the entire Greenland Ice Sheet underwent thawing at or near its surface by mid-July, the earliest date on record. Most scientists looking for the causes of the Great Melt of 2012 have focused exclusively on rising temperatures. The summer of 2012 was the warmest in 170 years, records show. But Jason [15] Box, an associate professor of geology at Ohio State believes that another factor added to the early [16] thaw; the "dark snow" problem.

13

Which choice most effectively combines the two sentences at the underlined portion?

A) summer, following

B) summer, and this thawing follows

C) summer, and such thawing follows

D) summer and this evidence follows

14

A) NO CHANGE

B) However,

C) As such,

D) Moreover,

15

A) NO CHANGE

B) Box an associate professor of geology at Ohio State,

C) Box, an associate professor of geology at Ohio State,

D) Box, an associate professor of geology, at Ohio State

16

A) NO CHANGE

B) thaw; and it was

C) thaw:

D) thaw: being

CONTINUE

According to Box, a leading Greenland expert, tundra fires in 2012 from as far away as North America produced great amounts of soot, some **17** of it drifted over Greenland in giant plumes of smoke and then **18** fell as particles onto the ice sheet. Scientists have long known that soot particles facilitate melting by darkening snow and ice, limiting **19** it's ability to reflect the Sun's rays. As Box explains, "Soot is an extremely powerful light absorber. It settles over the ice and captures the Sun's heat." The result is a self-reinforcing cycle. As the ice melts, the land and water under the ice become exposed, and since land and water are darker than snow, the surface absorbs even more heat, which **20** is related to the rising temperatures.

17

A) NO CHANGE
B) soot
C) of which
D) DELETE the underlined portion.

18

A) NO CHANGE
B) falls
C) will fall
D) had fallen

19

A) NO CHANGE
B) its
C) there
D) their

20

Which choice best completes the description of a self-reinforcing cycle?

A) NO CHANGE
B) raises the surface temperature.
C) begins to cool at a certain point.
D) leads to additional melting.

CONTINUE

[1] Box's research is important because the fires of 2012 may not be a one-time phenomenon. [2] According to scientists, rising Arctic temperatures are making northern latitudes greener and thus more fire prone. [3] The pattern Box observed in 2012 may repeat **21** itself again, with harmful effects on the Arctic ecosystem. [4] Box is currently organizing an expedition to gather this crucial information. [5] The next step for Box and his team is to travel to Greenland to perform direct sampling of the ice in order to determine just how much the soot is contributing to the melting of the ice sheet. [6] Members of the public will be able to track his team's progress—and even help fund the expedition—through a website Box has created. **22**

21

A) NO CHANGE
B) itself,
C) itself, with damage and
D) itself possibly,

22

To make this paragraph most logical, sentence 4 should be placed

A) where it is now.
B) after sentence 1.
C) after sentence 2.
D) after sentence 5.

CONTINUE

Questions 23-33 are based on the following passage.

Coworking: A Creative Solution

When I left my office job as a website developer at a small company for a position that allowed me to work full-time from home, I thought I had it made: I gleefully traded in my suits and dress shoes for sweatpants and slippers, my frantic early-morning bagged lunch packing for a leisurely midday trip to my refrigerator. The novelty of this comfortable work-from-home life, however, [23] soon got worn off quickly. Within a month, I found myself feeling isolated despite having frequent email and instant messaging contact with my colleagues. Having become frustrated trying to solve difficult problems, [24] no colleagues were nearby to share ideas. It was during this time that I read an article [25] into coworking spaces.

23

A) NO CHANGE
B) was promptly worn
C) promptly wore
D) wore

24

A) NO CHANGE
B) colleagues were important for sharing ideas.
C) ideas couldn't be shared with colleagues.
D) I missed having colleagues nearby to consult.

25

A) NO CHANGE
B) about
C) upon
D) for

CONTINUE

The article, published by *Forbes* magazine, explained that coworking spaces are designated locations that, for a fee, individuals can use to conduct their work. The spaces are usually stocked with standard office **26** equipment, such as photocopiers, printers, and fax machines. **27** In these locations, however, the spaces often include small meeting areas and larger rooms for hosting presentations. **28** The cost of launching a new coworking business in the United States is estimated to be approximately $58,000.

26

A) NO CHANGE

B) equipment, such as:

C) equipment such as:

D) equipment, such as,

27

A) NO CHANGE

B) In addition to equipment,

C) For these reasons,

D) Likewise,

28

The writer is considering deleting the underlined sentence. Should the sentence be kept or deleted?

A) Kept, because it provides a detail that supports the main topic of the paragraph.

B) Kept, because it sets up the main topic of the paragraph that follows.

C) Deleted, because it blurs the paragraph's main focus with a loosely related detail.

D) Deleted, because it repeats information that has been provided in an earlier paragraph.

CONTINUE

What most caught my interest, though, was a quotation from someone who described coworking spaces as "melting pots of creativity." The article refers to a 2012 survey in which **29** <u>64 percent of respondents noted that coworking spaces prevented them from completing tasks in a given time.</u> The article goes on to suggest that the most valuable resources provided by coworking spaces are actually the people **30** <u>whom use</u> them.

29

At this point, the writer wants to add specific information that supports the main topic of the paragraph.

Perceived Effect of Coworking on Business Skills

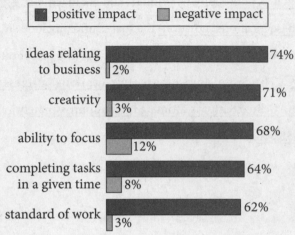

Adapted from "The 3rd Global Coworking Survey." ©2013 by Deskmag.

Which choice most effectively completes the sentence with relevant and accurate information based on the graph above?

A) NO CHANGE

B) 71 percent of respondents indicated that using a coworking space increased their creativity.

C) respondents credited coworking spaces with giving them 74 percent of their ideas relating to business.

D) respondents revealed that their ability to focus on their work improved by 12 percent in a coworking space.

30

A) NO CHANGE

B) whom uses

C) who uses

D) who use

CONTINUE ➤

[1] Thus, even though I already had all the equipment I needed in my home office, I decided to try using a coworking space in my city. [2] Because I was specifically interested in coworking's reported benefits related to creativity, I chose a facility that offered a bright, open work area where I wouldn't be isolated. [3] Throughout the morning, more people appeared. [4] Periods of quiet, during which everyone worked independently, were broken up occasionally with lively conversation. **31**

I liked the experience so much that I now go to the coworking space a few times a week. Over time, I've gotten to know several of my coworking **32** colleagues: another website developer, a graphic designer, a freelance writer, and several mobile app coders. Even those of us who work in disparate fields are able to **33** share advice and help each other brainstorm. In fact, it's the diversity of their talents and experiences that makes my coworking colleagues so valuable.

31

The writer wants to add the following sentence to the paragraph.

> After filling out a simple registration form and taking a quick tour of the facility, I took a seat at a table and got right to work on my laptop.

The best placement for the sentence is immediately

A) before sentence 1.

B) after sentence 1.

C) after sentence 2.

D) after sentence 3.

32

A) NO CHANGE

B) colleagues;

C) colleagues,

D) colleagues

33

A) NO CHANGE

B) give some wisdom

C) proclaim our opinions

D) opine

CONTINUE

Questions 34-44 are based on the following passage.

The Consolations of Philosophy

Long viewed by many as the stereotypical useless major, philosophy is now being seen by many students and prospective employers as in fact a very useful and practical major, offering students a host of transferable skills with relevance to the modern workplace. 34 In broad terms, philosophy is the study of meaning and the values underlying thought and behavior. But 35 more pragmatically, the discipline encourages students to analyze complex material, question conventional beliefs, and express thoughts in a concise manner.

Because philosophy 36 teaching students not what to think but how to think, the age-old discipline offers consistently useful tools for academic and professional achievement. 37 A 1994 survey concluded that only 18 percent of American colleges required at least one philosophy course. 38 Therefore, between 1992 and 1996, more than 400 independent philosophy departments were eliminated from institutions.

34

A) NO CHANGE
B) For example,
C) In contrast,
D) Nevertheless,

35

A) NO CHANGE
B) speaking in a more pragmatic way,
C) speaking in a way more pragmatically,
D) in a more pragmatic-speaking way,

36

A) NO CHANGE
B) teaches
C) to teach
D) and teaching

37

Which choice most effectively sets up the information that follows?

A) Consequently, philosophy students have been receiving an increasing number of job offers.
B) Therefore, because of the evidence, colleges increased their offerings in philosophy.
C) Notwithstanding the attractiveness of this course of study, students have resisted majoring in philosophy.
D) However, despite its many utilitarian benefits, colleges have not always supported the study of philosophy.

38

A) NO CHANGE
B) Thus,
C) Moreover,
D) However,

CONTINUE

More recently, colleges have recognized the practicality and increasing popularity of studying philosophy and have markedly increased the number of philosophy programs offered. By 2008 there were 817 programs, up from 765 a decade before. In addition, the number of four-year graduates in philosophy has grown 46 percent in a decade. Also, studies have found that those students who major in philosophy often do better than students from other majors in both verbal reasoning and analytical **39** writing. These results can be measured by standardized test scores. On the Graduate Record Examination (GRE), for example, students intending to study philosophy in graduate school **40** has scored higher than students in all but four other majors.

These days, many **41** student's majoring in philosophy have no intention of becoming philosophers; instead they plan to apply those skills to other disciplines. Law and business specifically benefit from the complicated theoretical issues raised in the study of philosophy, but philosophy can be just as useful in engineering or any field requiring complex analytic skills. **42** That these skills are transferable across professions

---

39

Which choice most effectively combines the sentences at the underlined portion?

A) writing as

B) writing, and these results can be

C) writing, which can also be

D) writing when the results are

40

A) NO CHANGE

B) have scored

C) scores

D) scoring

41

A) NO CHANGE

B) students majoring

C) students major

D) student's majors

42

At this point, the writer is considering adding the following sentence.

> The ancient Greek philosopher Plato, for example, wrote many of his works in the form of dialogues.

Should the writer make this addition here?

A) Yes, because it reinforces the passage's main point about the employability of philosophy majors.

B) Yes, because it acknowledges a common counterargument to the passage's central claim.

C) No, because it blurs the paragraph's focus by introducing a new idea that goes unexplained.

D) No, because it undermines the passage's claim about the employability of philosophy majors.

CONTINUE

43 which makes them especially beneficial to twenty-first-century students. Because today's students can expect to hold multiple jobs—some of which may not even exist yet—during **44** our lifetime, studying philosophy allows them to be flexible and adaptable. High demand, advanced exam scores, and varied professional skills all argue for maintaining and enhancing philosophy courses and majors within academic institutions.

43

A) NO CHANGE
B) that
C) and
D) DELETE the underlined portion.

44

A) NO CHANGE
B) one's
C) his or her
D) their

STOP

If you finish before time is called, you may check your work on this section only.
Do not turn to any other section.

No Test Material On This Page

Math Test – No Calculator

25 MINUTES, 20 QUESTIONS

Turn to Section 3 of your answer sheet to answer the questions in this section.

DIRECTIONS

For questions 1-15, solve each problem, choose the best answer from the choices provided, and fill in the corresponding circle on your answer sheet. **For questions 16-20**, solve the problem and enter your answer in the grid on the answer sheet. Please refer to the directions before question 16 on how to enter your answers in the grid. You may use any available space in your test booklet for scratch work.

NOTES

1. The use of a calculator **is not permitted**.

2. All variables and expressions used represent real numbers unless otherwise indicated.

3. Figures provided in this test are drawn to scale unless otherwise indicated.

4. All figures lie in a plane unless otherwise indicated.

5. Unless otherwise indicated, the domain of a given function f is the set of all real numbers x for which $f(x)$ is a real number.

REFERENCE

    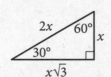

$A = \pi r^2$
$C = 2\pi r$

$A = \ell w$

$A = \frac{1}{2} bh$

$c^2 = a^2 + b^2$

Special Right Triangles

$V = \ell w h$

$V = \pi r^2 h$

$V = \frac{4}{3} \pi r^3$

$V = \frac{1}{3} \pi r^2 h$

$V = \frac{1}{3} \ell w h$

The number of degrees of arc in a circle is 360.
The number of radians of arc in a circle is 2π.
The sum of the measures in degrees of the angles of a triangle is 180.

CONTINUE ▶

1

If $\dfrac{x-1}{3} = k$ and $k = 3$, what is the value of x ?

A)   2

B)   4

C)   9

D)   10

2

For $i = \sqrt{-1}$, what is the sum $(7 + 3i) + (-8 + 9i)$?

A) $-1 + 12i$

B) $-1 - 6i$

C) $15 + 12i$

D) $15 - 6i$

3

On Saturday afternoon, Armand sent m text messages each hour for 5 hours, and Tyrone sent p text messages each hour for 4 hours. Which of the following represents the total number of messages sent by Armand and Tyrone on Saturday afternoon?

A) $9mp$

B) $20mp$

C) $5m + 4p$

D) $4m + 5p$

4

Kathy is a repair technician for a phone company. Each week, she receives a batch of phones that need repairs. The number of phones that she has left to fix at the end of each day can be estimated with the equation $P = 108 - 23d$, where P is the number of phones left and d is the number of days she has worked that week. What is the meaning of the value 108 in this equation?

A) Kathy will complete the repairs within 108 days.

B) Kathy starts each week with 108 phones to fix.

C) Kathy repairs phones at a rate of 108 per hour.

D) Kathy repairs phones at a rate of 108 per day.

CONTINUE

5

$$(x^2y - 3y^2 + 5xy^2) - (-x^2y + 3xy^2 - 3y^2)$$

Which of the following is equivalent to the expression above?

A) $4x^2y^2$

B) $8xy^2 - 6y^2$

C) $2x^2y + 2xy^2$

D) $2x^2y + 8xy^2 - 6y^2$

6

$$h = 3a + 28.6$$

A pediatrician uses the model above to estimate the height h of a boy, in inches, in terms of the boy's age a, in years, between the ages of 2 and 5. Based on the model, what is the estimated increase, in inches, of a boy's height each year?

A) 3

B) 5.7

C) 9.5

D) 14.3

7

$$m = \frac{\left(\dfrac{r}{1,200}\right)\left(1 + \dfrac{r}{1,200}\right)^N}{\left(1 + \dfrac{r}{1,200}\right)^N - 1} P$$

The formula above gives the monthly payment m needed to pay off a loan of P dollars at r percent annual interest over N months. Which of the following gives P in terms of m, r, and N ?

A) $P = \dfrac{\left(\dfrac{r}{1,200}\right)\left(1 + \dfrac{r}{1,200}\right)^N}{\left(1 + \dfrac{r}{1,200}\right)^N - 1} m$

B) $P = \dfrac{\left(1 + \dfrac{r}{1,200}\right)^N - 1}{\left(\dfrac{r}{1,200}\right)\left(1 + \dfrac{r}{1,200}\right)^N} m$

C) $P = \left(\dfrac{r}{1,200}\right) m$

D) $P = \left(\dfrac{1,200}{r}\right) m$

CONTINUE

8

If $\dfrac{a}{b} = 2$, what is the value of $\dfrac{4b}{a}$?

A) 0

B) 1

C) 2

D) 4

9

$$3x + 4y = -23$$
$$2y - x = -19$$

What is the solution (x, y) to the system of equations above?

A) $(-5, -2)$

B) $(3, -8)$

C) $(4, -6)$

D) $(9, -6)$

10

$$g(x) = ax^2 + 24$$

For the function g defined above, a is a constant and $g(4) = 8$. What is the value of $g(-4)$?

A) 8

B) 0

C) −1

D) −8

11

$$b = 2.35 + 0.25x$$
$$c = 1.75 + 0.40x$$

In the equations above, b and c represent the price per pound, in dollars, of beef and chicken, respectively, x weeks after July 1 during last summer. What was the price per pound of beef when it was equal to the price per pound of chicken?

A) $2.60

B) $2.85

C) $2.95

D) $3.35

12

A line in the xy-plane passes through the origin and has a slope of $\dfrac{1}{7}$. Which of the following points lies on the line?

A) $(0, 7)$

B) $(1, 7)$

C) $(7, 7)$

D) $(14, 2)$

CONTINUE

13

If $x > 3$, which of the following is equivalent

to $\dfrac{1}{\dfrac{1}{x+2} + \dfrac{1}{x+3}}$?

A) $\dfrac{2x+5}{x^2+5x+6}$

B) $\dfrac{x^2+5x+6}{2x+5}$

C) $2x+5$

D) x^2+5x+6

14

If $3x - y = 12$, what is the value of $\dfrac{8^x}{2^y}$?

A) 2^{12}

B) 4^4

C) 8^2

D) The value cannot be determined from the information given.

15

If $(ax + 2)(bx + 7) = 15x^2 + cx + 14$ for all values of x, and $a + b = 8$, what are the two possible values for c ?

A) 3 and 5

B) 6 and 35

C) 10 and 21

D) 31 and 41

CONTINUE

DIRECTIONS

For questions 16–20, solve the problem and enter your answer in the grid, as described below, on the answer sheet.

1. Although not required, it is suggested that you write your answer in the boxes at the top of the columns to help you fill in the circles accurately. You will receive credit only if the circles are filled in correctly.

2. Mark no more than one circle in any column.

3. No question has a negative answer.

4. Some problems may have more than one correct answer. In such cases, grid only one answer.

5. **Mixed numbers** such as $3\frac{1}{2}$ must be gridded as 3.5 or 7/2. (If [3 1 / 2] is entered into the grid, it will be interpreted as $\frac{31}{2}$, not $3\frac{1}{2}$.)

6. **Decimal answers:** If you obtain a decimal answer with more digits than the grid can accommodate, it may be either rounded or truncated, but it must fill the entire grid.

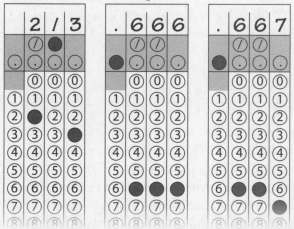

Answer: $\frac{7}{12}$ Answer: 2.5

Acceptable ways to grid $\frac{2}{3}$ are:

Answer: 201 – either position is correct

NOTE: You may start your answers in any column, space permitting. Columns you don't need to use should be left blank.

CONTINUE ➤

16

If $t > 0$ and $t^2 - 4 = 0$, what is the value of t ?

17

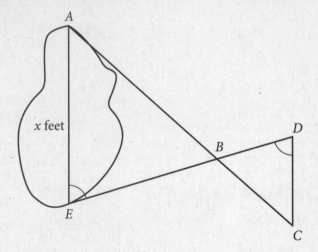

A summer camp counselor wants to find a length, x, in feet, across a lake as represented in the sketch above. The lengths represented by AB, EB, BD, and CD on the sketch were determined to be 1800 feet, 1400 feet, 700 feet, and 800 feet, respectively. Segments AC and DE intersect at B, and $\angle AEB$ and $\angle CDB$ have the same measure. What is the value of x ?

18

$$x + y = -9$$
$$x + 2y = -25$$

According to the system of equations above, what is the value of x ?

19

In a right triangle, one angle measures $x°$, where $\sin x° = \dfrac{4}{5}$. What is $\cos(90° - x°)$?

20

If $a = 5\sqrt{2}$ and $2a = \sqrt{2x}$, what is the value of x ?

STOP

If you finish before time is called, you may check your work on this section only.
Do not turn to any other section.

No Test Material On This Page

Math Test – Calculator

55 MINUTES, 38 QUESTIONS

Turn to Section 4 of your answer sheet to answer the questions in this section.

DIRECTIONS

For questions 1-30, solve each problem, choose the best answer from the choices provided, and fill in the corresponding circle on your answer sheet. **For questions 31-38**, solve the problem and enter your answer in the grid on the answer sheet. Please refer to the directions before question 31 on how to enter your answers in the grid. You may use any available space in your test booklet for scratch work.

NOTES

1. The use of a calculator **is permitted**.

2. All variables and expressions used represent real numbers unless otherwise indicated.

3. Figures provided in this test are drawn to scale unless otherwise indicated.

4. All figures lie in a plane unless otherwise indicated.

5. Unless otherwise indicated, the domain of a given function f is the set of all real numbers x for which $f(x)$ is a real number.

REFERENCE

    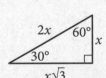

$A = \pi r^2$
$C = 2\pi r$

$A = \ell w$

$A = \dfrac{1}{2}bh$

$c^2 = a^2 + b^2$

Special Right Triangles

$V = \ell wh$

$V = \pi r^2 h$

$V = \dfrac{4}{3}\pi r^3$

$V = \dfrac{1}{3}\pi r^2 h$

$V = \dfrac{1}{3}\ell wh$

The number of degrees of arc in a circle is 360.

The number of radians of arc in a circle is 2π.

The sum of the measures in degrees of the angles of a triangle is 180.

CONTINUE

1

John runs at different speeds as part of his training program. The graph shows his target heart rate at different times during his workout. On which interval is the target heart rate strictly increasing then strictly decreasing?

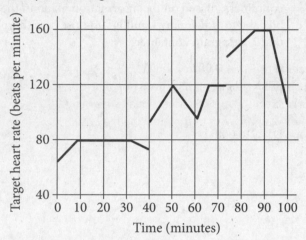

A) Between 0 and 30 minutes

B) Between 40 and 60 minutes

C) Between 50 and 65 minutes

D) Between 70 and 90 minutes

2

If $y = kx$, where k is a constant, and $y = 24$ when $x = 6$, what is the value of y when $x = 5$?

A) 6

B) 15

C) 20

D) 23

3

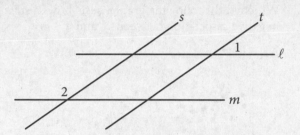

In the figure above, lines ℓ and m are parallel and lines s and t are parallel. If the measure of $\angle 1$ is 35°, what is the measure of $\angle 2$?

A) 35°

B) 55°

C) 70°

D) 145°

4

If $16 + 4x$ is 10 more than 14, what is the value of $8x$?

A) 2

B) 6

C) 16

D) 80

CONTINUE

5

Which of the following graphs best shows a strong negative association between d and t ?

A)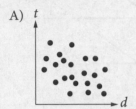

B)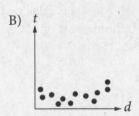

C)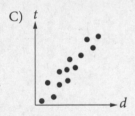

D)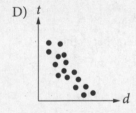

6

1 decagram = 10 grams

1,000 milligrams = 1 gram

A hospital stores one type of medicine in 2-decagram containers. Based on the information given in the box above, how many 1-milligram doses are there in one 2-decagram container?

A)   0.002

B)   200

C)   2,000

D)   20,000

CONTINUE

7

Rooftop Solar Panel
Installations in Five Cities

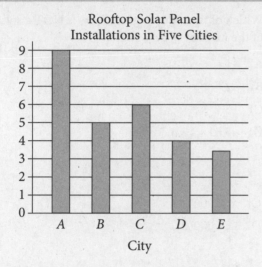

City

The number of rooftops with solar panel installations in 5 cities is shown in the graph above. If the total number of installations is 27,500, what is an appropriate label for the vertical axis of the graph?

A) Number of installations (in tens)

B) Number of installations (in hundreds)

C) Number of installations (in thousands)

D) Number of installations (in tens of thousands)

8

For what value of n is $|n - 1| + 1$ equal to 0 ?

A)   0

B)   1

C)   2

D)   There is no such value of n.

CONTINUE

Questions 9 and 10 refer to the following information.

$$a = 1,052 + 1.08t$$

The speed of a sound wave in air depends on the air temperature. The formula above shows the relationship between a, the speed of a sound wave, in feet per second, and t, the air temperature, in degrees Fahrenheit (°F).

9

Which of the following expresses the air temperature in terms of the speed of a sound wave?

A) $t = \dfrac{a - 1,052}{1.08}$

B) $t = \dfrac{a + 1,052}{1.08}$

C) $t = \dfrac{1,052 - a}{1.08}$

D) $t = \dfrac{1.08}{a + 1,052}$

10

At which of the following air temperatures will the speed of a sound wave be closest to 1,000 feet per second?

A) −46°F

B) −48°F

C) −49°F

D) −50°F

11

Which of the following numbers is NOT a solution of the inequality $3x - 5 \geq 4x - 3$?

A) −1

B) −2

C) −3

D) −5

12

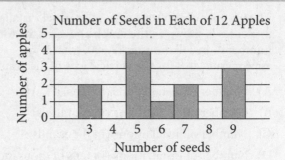

Number of Seeds in Each of 12 Apples

Based on the histogram above, of the following, which is closest to the average (arithmetic mean) number of seeds per apple?

A) 4

B) 5

C) 6

D) 7

CONTINUE

13

		Course			
		Algebra I	Geometry	Algebra II	Total
Gender	Female	35	53	62	150
	Male	44	59	57	160
	Total	79	112	119	310

A group of tenth-grade students responded to a survey that asked which math course they were currently enrolled in. The survey data were broken down as shown in the table above. Which of the following categories accounts for approximately 19 percent of all the survey respondents?

A) Females taking Geometry

B) Females taking Algebra II

C) Males taking Geometry

D) Males taking Algebra I

14

Lengths of Fish (in inches)						
8	9	9	9	10	10	11
11	12	12	12	12	13	13
13	14	14	15	15	16	24

The table above lists the lengths, to the nearest inch, of a random sample of 21 brown bullhead fish. The outlier measurement of 24 inches is an error. Of the mean, median, and range of the values listed, which will change the most if the 24-inch measurement is removed from the data?

A) Mean

B) Median

C) Range

D) They will all change by the same amount.

CONTINUE

Questions 15 and 16 refer to the following information.

Total Cost of Renting a Boat by the Hour

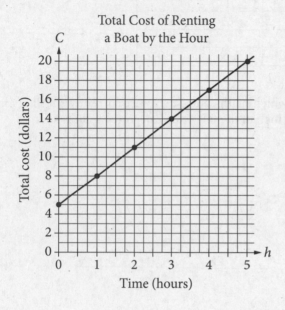

The graph above displays the total cost C, in dollars, of renting a boat for h hours.

15

What does the C-intercept represent in the graph?

A) The initial cost of renting the boat
B) The total number of boats rented
C) The total number of hours the boat is rented
D) The increase in cost to rent the boat for each additional hour

16

Which of the following represents the relationship between h and C ?

A) $C = 5h$

B) $C = \dfrac{3}{4}h + 5$

C) $C = 3h + 5$

D) $h = 3C$

17

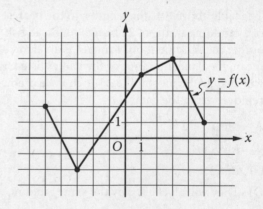

The complete graph of the function f is shown in the xy-plane above. For what value of x is the value of $f(x)$ at its minimum?

A) -5
B) -3
C) -2
D) 3

CONTINUE

18

$$y < -x + a$$
$$y > x + b$$

In the xy-plane, if $(0,0)$ is a solution to the system of inequalities above, which of the following relationships between a and b must be true?

A) $a > b$

B) $b > a$

C) $|a| > |b|$

D) $a = -b$

19

A food truck sells salads for $6.50 each and drinks for $2.00 each. The food truck's revenue from selling a total of 209 salads and drinks in one day was $836.50. How many salads were sold that day?

A) 77

B) 93

C) 99

D) 105

CONTINUE

20

Alma bought a laptop computer at a store that gave a 20 percent discount off its original price. The total amount she paid to the cashier was p dollars, including an 8 percent sales tax on the discounted price. Which of the following represents the original price of the computer in terms of p ?

A) $0.88p$

B) $\dfrac{p}{0.88}$

C) $(0.8)(1.08)p$

D) $\dfrac{p}{(0.8)(1.08)}$

21

Dreams Recalled during One Week

	None	1 to 4	5 or more	Total
Group X	15	28	57	100
Group Y	21	11	68	100
Total	36	39	125	200

The data in the table above were produced by a sleep researcher studying the number of dreams people recall when asked to record their dreams for one week. Group X consisted of 100 people who observed early bedtimes, and Group Y consisted of 100 people who observed later bedtimes. If a person is chosen at random from those who recalled at least 1 dream, what is the probability that the person belonged to Group Y ?

A) $\dfrac{68}{100}$

B) $\dfrac{79}{100}$

C) $\dfrac{79}{164}$

D) $\dfrac{164}{200}$

CONTINUE

Questions 22 and 23 refer to the following information.

Annual Budgets for Different Programs in Kansas, 2007 to 2010

Program	Year			
	2007	2008	2009	2010
Agriculture/natural resources	373,904	358,708	485,807	488,106
Education	2,164,607	2,413,984	2,274,514	3,008,036
General government	14,347,325	12,554,845	10,392,107	14,716,155
Highways and transportation	1,468,482	1,665,636	1,539,480	1,773,893
Human resources	4,051,050	4,099,067	4,618,444	5,921,379
Public safety	263,463	398,326	355,935	464,233

The table above lists the annual budget, in thousands of dollars, for each of six different state programs in Kansas from 2007 to 2010.

22

Which of the following best approximates the average rate of change in the annual budget for agriculture/natural resources in Kansas from 2008 to 2010 ?

A) $50,000,000 per year

B) $65,000,000 per year

C) $75,000,000 per year

D) $130,000,000 per year

23

Of the following, which program's ratio of its 2007 budget to its 2010 budget is closest to the human resources program's ratio of its 2007 budget to its 2010 budget?

A) Agriculture/natural resources

B) Education

C) Highways and transportation

D) Public safety

CONTINUE

24

Which of the following is an equation of a circle in the xy-plane with center $(0, 4)$ and a radius with endpoint $\left(\dfrac{4}{3}, 5\right)$?

A) $x^2 + (y - 4)^2 = \dfrac{25}{9}$

B) $x^2 + (y + 4)^2 = \dfrac{25}{9}$

C) $x^2 + (y - 4)^2 = \dfrac{5}{3}$

D) $x^2 + (y + 4)^2 = \dfrac{3}{5}$

25

$$h = -4.9t^2 + 25t$$

The equation above expresses the approximate height h, in meters, of a ball t seconds after it is launched vertically upward from the ground with an initial velocity of 25 meters per second. After approximately how many seconds will the ball hit the ground?

A) 3.5

B) 4.0

C) 4.5

D) 5.0

26

Katarina is a botanist studying the production of pears by two types of pear trees. She noticed that Type A trees produced 20 percent more pears than Type B trees did. Based on Katarina's observation, if the Type A trees produced 144 pears, how many pears did the Type B trees produce?

A) 115

B) 120

C) 124

D) 173

27

A square field measures 10 meters by 10 meters. Ten students each mark off a randomly selected region of the field; each region is square and has side lengths of 1 meter, and no two regions overlap. The students count the earthworms contained in the soil to a depth of 5 centimeters beneath the ground's surface in each region. The results are shown in the table below.

Region	Number of earthworms	Region	Number of earthworms
A	107	F	141
B	147	G	150
C	146	H	154
D	135	I	176
E	149	J	166

Which of the following is a reasonable approximation of the number of earthworms to a depth of 5 centimeters beneath the ground's surface in the entire field?

A) 150

B) 1,500

C) 15,000

D) 150,000

CONTINUE

28

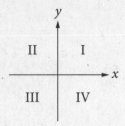

If the system of inequalities $y \geq 2x + 1$ and

$y > \dfrac{1}{2}x - 1$ is graphed in the xy-plane above, which

quadrant contains no solutions to the system?

A) Quadrant II

B) Quadrant III

C) Quadrant IV

D) There are solutions in all four quadrants.

29

For a polynomial $p(x)$, the value of $p(3)$ is -2. Which of the following must be true about $p(x)$?

A) $x - 5$ is a factor of $p(x)$.

B) $x - 2$ is a factor of $p(x)$.

C) $x + 2$ is a factor of $p(x)$.

D) The remainder when $p(x)$ is divided by $x - 3$ is -2.

30

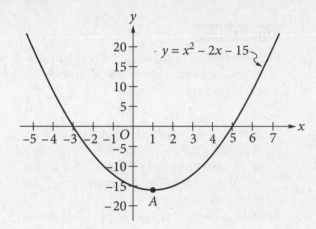

Which of the following is an equivalent form of the equation of the graph shown in the xy-plane above, from which the coordinates of vertex A can be identified as constants in the equation?

A) $y = (x + 3)(x - 5)$

B) $y = (x - 3)(x + 5)$

C) $y = x(x - 2) - 15$

D) $y = (x - 1)^2 - 16$

CONTINUE

DIRECTIONS

For questions 31–38, solve the problem and enter your answer in the grid, as described below, on the answer sheet.

1. Although not required, it is suggested that you write your answer in the boxes at the top of the columns to help you fill in the circles accurately. You will receive credit only if the circles are filled in correctly.

2. Mark no more than one circle in any column.

3. No question has a negative answer.

4. Some problems may have more than one correct answer. In such cases, grid only one answer.

5. **Mixed numbers** such as $3\frac{1}{2}$ must be gridded as 3.5 or 7/2. (If [3|1|/|2] is entered into the grid, it will be interpreted as $\frac{31}{2}$, not $3\frac{1}{2}$.)

6. **Decimal answers:** If you obtain a decimal answer with more digits than the grid can accommodate, it may be either rounded or truncated, but it must fill the entire grid.

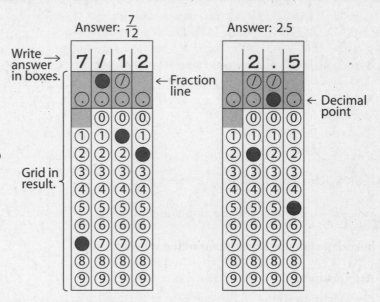

Answer: $\frac{7}{12}$

Write answer in boxes. → Fraction line

Grid in result.

Answer: 2.5

← Decimal point

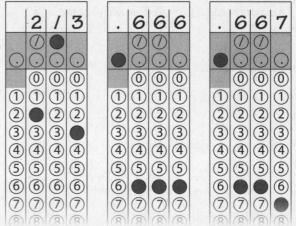

Acceptable ways to grid $\frac{2}{3}$ are:

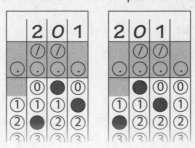

Answer: 201 – either position is correct

NOTE: You may start your answers in any column, space permitting. Columns you don't need to use should be left blank.

CONTINUE ▶

31

Wyatt can husk at least 12 dozen ears of corn per hour and at most 18 dozen ears of corn per hour. Based on this information, what is a possible amount of time, in hours, that it could take Wyatt to husk 72 dozen ears of corn?

32

The posted weight limit for a covered wooden bridge in Pennsylvania is 6000 pounds. A delivery truck that is carrying x identical boxes each weighing 14 pounds will pass over the bridge. If the combined weight of the empty delivery truck and its driver is 4500 pounds, what is the maximum possible value for x that will keep the combined weight of the truck, driver, and boxes below the bridge's posted weight limit?

33

Number of Portable Media Players
Sold Worldwide Each Year from 2006 to 2011

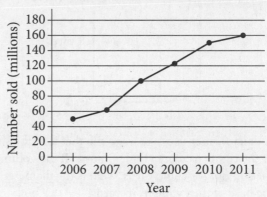

According to the line graph above, the number of portable media players sold in 2008 is what fraction of the number sold in 2011 ?

34

A local television station sells time slots for programs in 30-minute intervals. If the station operates 24 hours per day, every day of the week, what is the total number of 30-minute time slots the station can sell for Tuesday and Wednesday?

CONTINUE

35

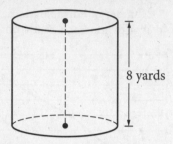

8 yards

A dairy farmer uses a storage silo that is in the shape of the right circular cylinder above. If the volume of the silo is 72π cubic yards, what is the <u>diameter</u> of the base of the cylinder, in yards?

36

$$h(x) = \frac{1}{(x-5)^2 + 4(x-5) + 4}$$

For what value of x is the function h above undefined?

Questions 37 and 38 refer to the following information.

Jessica opened a bank account that earns 2 percent interest compounded annually. Her initial deposit was $100, and she uses the expression $\$100(x)^t$ to find the value of the account after t years.

37

What is the value of x in the expression?

38

Jessica's friend Tyshaun found an account that earns 2.5 percent interest compounded annually. Tyshaun made an initial deposit of $100 into this account at the same time Jessica made a deposit of $100 into her account. After 10 years, how much more money will Tyshaun's initial deposit have earned than Jessica's initial deposit? (Round your answer to the nearest cent and ignore the dollar sign when gridding your response.)

STOP

If you finish before time is called, you may check your work on this section only.

Do not turn to any other section.

No Test Material On This Page

YOUR NAME (PRINT) ....

LAST   FIRST   MI

TEST CENTER ....

NUMBER   NAME OF TEST CENTER   ROOM NUMBER

The SAT

GENERAL DIRECTIONS

– You may work on only one section at a time.
– If you finish a section before time is called, check your work on that section. You may NOT turn to any other section.

MARKING ANSWERS

– Be sure to mark your answer sheet properly.

COMPLETE MARK ● EXAMPLES OF INCOMPLETE MARKS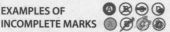

– You must use a No. 2 pencil.
– Carefully mark only one answer for each question.
– Make sure you fill the entire circle darkly and completely.
– Do not make any stray marks on your answer sheet.
– If you erase, do so completely. Incomplete erasures may be scored as intended answers.
– Use only the answer spaces that correspond to the question numbers.

USING YOUR TEST BOOK

– You may use the test book for scratch work, but you will not receive credit for anything that you write in your test book.
– After time has been called, you may not transfer answers from your test book to your answer sheet or fill in circles.
– You may not fold or remove pages or portions of a page from this book, or take the book or answer sheet from the testing room.

SCORING

– For each correct answer, you receive one point.
– You do not lose points for wrong answers; therefore, you should try to answer every question even if you are not sure of the correct answer.

5KSA09

Ideas contained in passages for this test, some of which are excerpted or adapted from published material, do not necessarily represent the opinions of the College Board.

DO NOT OPEN THIS BOOK UNTIL THE SUPERVISOR TELLS YOU TO DO SO.

SAT® Practice Essay #1

 ESSAY BOOK

DIRECTIONS

The essay gives you an opportunity to show how effectively you can read and comprehend a passage and write an essay analyzing the passage. In your essay, you should demonstrate that you have read the passage carefully, present a clear and logical analysis, and use language precisely.

Your essay must be written on the lines provided in your answer booklet; except for the Planning Page of the answer booklet, you will receive no other paper on which to write. You will have enough space if you write on every line, avoid wide margins, and keep your handwriting to a reasonable size. Remember that people who are not familiar with your handwriting will read what you write. Try to write or print so that what you are writing is legible to those readers.

You have 50 minutes to read the passage and write an essay in response to the prompt provided inside this booklet.

REMINDERS

— Do not write your essay in this booklet. Only what you write on the lined pages of your answer booklet will be evaluated.

— An off-topic essay will not be evaluated.

Follow this link for more information on scoring your practice test: **www.sat.org/scoring**

This cover is representative of what you'll see on test day.

THIS TEST BOOKLET MUST NOT BE TAKEN FROM THE ROOM. UNAUTHORIZED REPRODUCTION OR USE OF ANY PART OF THIS TEST BOOKLET IS PROHIBITED.

As you read the passage below, consider how Jimmy Carter uses

- evidence, such as facts or examples, to support claims.
- reasoning to develop ideas and to connect claims and evidence.
- stylistic or persuasive elements, such as word choice or appeals to emotion, to add power to the ideas expressed.

Adapted from former US President Jimmy Carter, Foreword to *Arctic National Wildlife Refuge: Seasons of Life and Land, A Photographic Journey* by Subhankar Banerjee. ©2003 by Subhankar Banerjee.

1   The Arctic National Wildlife Refuge stands alone as America's last truly great wilderness. This magnificent area is as vast as it is wild, from the windswept coastal plain where polar bears and caribou give birth, to the towering Brooks Range where Dall sheep cling to cliffs and wolves howl in the midnight sun.

2   More than a decade ago, [my wife] Rosalynn and I had the fortunate opportunity to camp and hike in these regions of the Arctic Refuge. During bright July days, we walked along ancient caribou trails and studied the brilliant mosaic of wildflowers, mosses, and lichens that hugged the tundra. There was a timeless quality about this great land. As the never-setting sun circled above the horizon, we watched muskox, those shaggy survivors of the Ice Age, lumber along braided rivers that meander toward the Beaufort Sea.

3   One of the most unforgettable and humbling experiences of our lives occurred on the coastal plain. We had hoped to see caribou during our trip, but to our amazement, we witnessed the migration of tens of thousands of caribou with their newborn calves. In a matter of a few minutes, the sweep of tundra before us became flooded with life, with the sounds of grunting animals and clicking hooves filling the air. The dramatic procession of the Porcupine caribou herd was a once-in-a-lifetime wildlife spectacle. We understand firsthand why some have described this special birthplace as "America's Serengeti."

4   Standing on the coastal plain, I was saddened to think of the tragedy that might occur if this great wilderness was consumed by a web of roads and pipelines, drilling rigs and industrial facilities. Such proposed developments would forever destroy the wilderness character of America's only Arctic Refuge and disturb countless numbers of animals that depend on this northernmost terrestrial ecosystem.

5   The extraordinary wilderness and wildlife values of the Arctic Refuge have long been recognized by both Republican and Democratic presidents. In 1960, President Dwight D. Eisenhower established the original 8.9 million-acre Arctic National Wildlife Range to preserve its unique wildlife, wilderness, and recreational values. Twenty years later, I signed the Alaska National Interest Lands Conservation Act, monumental legislation that safeguarded more than 100 million acres of national parks, refuges, and forests in Alaska. This law specifically created the Arctic National Wildlife Refuge, doubled the size of the former range, and restricted development in areas that are clearly incompatible with oil exploration.

6   Since I left office, there have been repeated proposals to open the Arctic Refuge coastal plain to oil drilling. Those attempts have failed because of tremendous opposition by the American people, including the Gwich'in Athabascan Indians of Alaska and Canada, indigenous people whose culture has depended on the Porcupine caribou herd for thousands of years. Having visited many aboriginal peoples around the world, I can empathize with the Gwich'ins' struggle to safeguard one of their precious human rights.

7   We must look beyond the alleged benefits of a short-term economic gain and focus on what is really at stake. At best, the Arctic Refuge might provide 1 to 2 percent of the oil our country consumes each day. We can easily conserve more than that amount by driving more fuel-efficient vehicles. Instead of tearing open the heart of our greatest refuge, we should use our resources more wisely.

8   There are few places on earth as wild and free as the Arctic Refuge. It is a symbol of our national heritage, a remnant of frontier America that our first settlers once called wilderness. Little of that precious wilderness remains.

9   It will be a grand triumph for America if we can preserve the Arctic Refuge in its pure, untrammeled state. To leave this extraordinary land alone would be the greatest gift we could pass on to future generations.

Write an essay in which you explain how Jimmy Carter builds an argument to persuade his audience that the Arctic National Wildlife Refuge should not be developed for industry. In your essay, analyze how Carter uses one or more of the features listed in the box above (or features of your own choice) to strengthen the logic and persuasiveness of his argument. Be sure that your analysis focuses on the most relevant features of the passage.

Your essay should not explain whether you agree with Carter's claims, but rather explain how Carter builds an argument to persuade his audience.

YOUR NAME (PRINT) ....
LAST FIRST MI

TEST CENTER ....
NUMBER NAME OF TEST CENTER ROOM NUMBER

This page represents the back cover of the Practice Essay.

5LS05E

Ideas contained in the passage for this test, which is excerpted or adapted from published material, do not necessarily represent the opinions of the College Board.

DO NOT OPEN THIS BOOK UNTIL THE SUPERVISOR TELLS YOU TO DO SO.

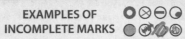

CollegeBoard

SAT PRACTICE ANSWER SHEET

| COMPLETE MARK ● | EXAMPLES OF INCOMPLETE MARKS | It is recommended that you use a No. 2 pencil. It is very important that you fill in the entire circle darkly and completely. If you change your response, erase as completely as possible. Incomplete marks or erasures may affect your score. |

■ TEST NUMBER   ■ SECTION 1

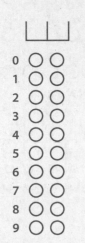

ENTER TEST NUMBER

For instance, for Practice Test #1, fill in the circle for 0 in the **first column** and for 1 in the **second column**.

0 ○ ○
1 ○ ○
2 ○ ○
3 ○ ○
4 ○ ○
5 ○ ○
6 ○ ○
7 ○ ○
8 ○ ○
9 ○ ○

	A B C D		A B C D		A B C D		A B C D
1	○○○○	14	○○○○	27	○○○○	40	○○○○
2	○○○○	15	○○○○	28	○○○○	41	○○○○
3	○○○○	16	○○○○	29	○○○○	42	○○○○
4	○○○○	17	○○○○	30	○○○○	43	○○○○
5	○○○○	18	○○○○	31	○○○○	44	○○○○
6	○○○○	19	○○○○	32	○○○○	45	○○○○
7	○○○○	20	○○○○	33	○○○○	46	○○○○
8	○○○○	21	○○○○	34	○○○○	47	○○○○
9	○○○○	22	○○○○	35	○○○○	48	○○○○
10	○○○○	23	○○○○	36	○○○○	49	○○○○
11	○○○○	24	○○○○	37	○○○○	50	○○○○
12	○○○○	25	○○○○	38	○○○○	51	○○○○
13	○○○○	26	○○○○	39	○○○○	52	○○○○

Download the College Board SAT Practice app to instantly score this test.
Learn more at sat.org/scoring.

● ● ● ● ●   ● ●

 **CollegeBoard**

SAT PRACTICE ANSWER SHEET

COMPLETE MARK ● EXAMPLES OF INCOMPLETE MARKS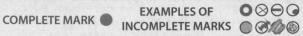

It is recommended that you use a No. 2 pencil. It is very important that you fill in the entire circle darkly and completely. If you change your response, erase as completely as possible. Incomplete marks or erasures may affect your score.

■ **SECTION 2**

	A B C D		A B C D		A B C D		A B C D		A B C D
1	○○○○	10	○○○○	19	○○○○	28	○○○○	37	○○○○
2	○○○○	11	○○○○	20	○○○○	29	○○○○	38	○○○○
3	○○○○	12	○○○○	21	○○○○	30	○○○○	39	○○○○
4	○○○○	13	○○○○	22	○○○○	31	○○○○	40	○○○○
5	○○○○	14	○○○○	23	○○○○	32	○○○○	41	○○○○
6	○○○○	15	○○○○	24	○○○○	33	○○○○	42	○○○○
7	○○○○	16	○○○○	25	○○○○	34	○○○○	43	○○○○
8	○○○○	17	○○○○	26	○○○○	35	○○○○	44	○○○○
9	○○○○	18	○○○○	27	○○○○	36	○○○○		

 If you're scoring with our mobile app we recommend that you cut these pages out of the back of this book. The scoring does best with a flat page.

● ● ● ● ●   ●   ●

CollegeBoard

SAT PRACTICE ANSWER SHEET

COMPLETE MARK ●   EXAMPLES OF INCOMPLETE MARKS ⊘⊗⊖◔ ◓◉⊗◍

It is recommended that you use a No. 2 pencil. It is very important that you fill in the entire circle darkly and completely. If you change your response, erase as completely as possible. Incomplete marks or erasures may affect your score.

■ SECTION 3

	A B C D		A B C D		A B C D		A B C D		A B C D
1	○ ○ ○ ○	4	○ ○ ○ ○	7	○ ○ ○ ○	10	○ ○ ○ ○	13	○ ○ ○ ○
2	○ ○ ○ ○	5	○ ○ ○ ○	8	○ ○ ○ ○	11	○ ○ ○ ○	14	○ ○ ○ ○
3	○ ○ ○ ○	6	○ ○ ○ ○	9	○ ○ ○ ○	12	○ ○ ○ ○	15	○ ○ ○ ○

Only answers that are gridded will be scored. You will not receive credit for anything written in the boxes.

16	17	18	19	20
/ ○ ○	/ ○ ○	/ ○ ○	/ ○ ○	/ ○ ○
. ○ ○ ○ ○	. ○ ○ ○ ○	. ○ ○ ○ ○	. ○ ○ ○ ○	. ○ ○ ○ ○
0 ○ ○ ○ ○	0 ○ ○ ○ ○	0 ○ ○ ○ ○	0 ○ ○ ○ ○	0 ○ ○ ○ ○
1 ○ ○ ○ ○	1 ○ ○ ○ ○	1 ○ ○ ○ ○	1 ○ ○ ○ ○	1 ○ ○ ○ ○
2 ○ ○ ○ ○	2 ○ ○ ○ ○	2 ○ ○ ○ ○	2 ○ ○ ○ ○	2 ○ ○ ○ ○
3 ○ ○ ○ ○	3 ○ ○ ○ ○	3 ○ ○ ○ ○	3 ○ ○ ○ ○	3 ○ ○ ○ ○
4 ○ ○ ○ ○	4 ○ ○ ○ ○	4 ○ ○ ○ ○	4 ○ ○ ○ ○	4 ○ ○ ○ ○
5 ○ ○ ○ ○	5 ○ ○ ○ ○	5 ○ ○ ○ ○	5 ○ ○ ○ ○	5 ○ ○ ○ ○
6 ○ ○ ○ ○	6 ○ ○ ○ ○	6 ○ ○ ○ ○	6 ○ ○ ○ ○	6 ○ ○ ○ ○
7 ○ ○ ○ ○	7 ○ ○ ○ ○	7 ○ ○ ○ ○	7 ○ ○ ○ ○	7 ○ ○ ○ ○
8 ○ ○ ○ ○	8 ○ ○ ○ ○	8 ○ ○ ○ ○	8 ○ ○ ○ ○	8 ○ ○ ○ ○
9 ○ ○ ○ ○	9 ○ ○ ○ ○	9 ○ ○ ○ ○	9 ○ ○ ○ ○	9 ○ ○ ○ ○

NO CALCULATOR ALLOWED

Did you know that you can print out these test sheets from the web? Learn more at sat.org/scoring.

● ● ● ● ●   ●   ●

 **CollegeBoard**

■ SECTION 4

	A B C D		A B C D		A B C D		A B C D		A B C D
1	○ ○ ○ ○	7	○ ○ ○ ○	13	○ ○ ○ ○	19	○ ○ ○ ○	25	○ ○ ○ ○
2	○ ○ ○ ○	8	○ ○ ○ ○	14	○ ○ ○ ○	20	○ ○ ○ ○	26	○ ○ ○ ○
3	○ ○ ○ ○	9	○ ○ ○ ○	15	○ ○ ○ ○	21	○ ○ ○ ○	27	○ ○ ○ ○
4	○ ○ ○ ○	10	○ ○ ○ ○	16	○ ○ ○ ○	22	○ ○ ○ ○	28	○ ○ ○ ○
5	○ ○ ○ ○	11	○ ○ ○ ○	17	○ ○ ○ ○	23	○ ○ ○ ○	29	○ ○ ○ ○
6	○ ○ ○ ○	12	○ ○ ○ ○	18	○ ○ ○ ○	24	○ ○ ○ ○	30	○ ○ ○ ○

CALCULATOR ALLOWED

 If you're using our mobile app keep in mind that bad lighting and even shadows cast over the answer sheet can affect your score. Be sure to scan this in a well-lit area for best results.

● ● ● ● ●   ●   ●

CollegeBoard

■ **SECTION 4 (Continued)**

Only answers that are gridded will be scored. You will not receive credit for anything written in the boxes.

31   32   33   34   35

Only answers that are gridded will be scored. You will not receive credit for anything written in the boxes.

36   37   38

CALCULATOR ALLOWED

PLANNING PAGE You may plan your essay in the unlined planning space below, but use only the lined pages following this one to write your essay. Any work on this planning page will not be scored.

Use pages 7 through 10 for your ESSAY ⟶

FOR PLANNING ONLY

Use pages 7 through 10 for your ESSAY ⟶

Page 6

401

You may continue on the next page.

You may continue on the next page.

SERIAL #

STOP.

Answer Explanations

SAT Practice Test #1

Section 1: Reading Test

QUESTION 1.

Choice B is the best answer. In the passage, a young man (Akira) asks a mother (Chie) for permission to marry her daughter (Naomi). The request was certainly surprising to the mother, as can be seen from line 47, which states that prior to Akira's question Chie "had no idea" the request was coming.

Choice A is incorrect because the passage depicts two characters engaged in a civil conversation, with Chie being impressed with Akira's "sincerity" and finding herself "starting to like him." Choice C is incorrect because the passage is focused on the idea of Akira's and Naomi's present lives and possible futures. Choice D is incorrect because the interactions between Chie and Akira are polite, not critical; for example, Chie views Akira with "amusement," not animosity.

QUESTION 2.

Choice B is the best answer. The passage centers on a night when a young man tries to get approval to marry a woman's daughter. The passage includes detailed descriptions of setting (a "winter's eve" and a "cold rain," lines 5-6); character (Akira's "soft, refined" voice, line 33; Akira's eyes "sh[ining] with sincerity," line 35); and plot ("Naomi was silent. She stood a full half minute looking straight into Chie's eyes. Finally, she spoke," lines 88-89).

Choice A is incorrect because the passage focuses on a nontraditional marriage proposal. Choice C is incorrect because the passage concludes without resolution to the question of whether Akira and Naomi will receive permission to marry. Choice D is incorrect because the passage repeatedly makes clear that for Chie, her encounter with Akira is momentous and unsettling, as when Akira acknowledges in line 73 that he has "startled" her.

QUESTION 3.

Choice C is the best answer. Akira "came directly, breaking all tradition," (line 1) when he approached Chie and asked to marry her daughter, and he "ask[ed] directly," without "a go-between" (line 65) or "mediation," because doing otherwise would have taken too much time.

Choices A, B, and D are incorrect because in these contexts, "directly" does not mean in a frank, confident, or precise manner.

QUESTION 4.

Choice A is the best answer. Akira is very concerned Chie will find his marriage proposal inappropriate because he did not follow traditional protocol and use a "go-between" (line 65). This is clear in lines 63-64, when Akira says to Chie "Please don't judge my candidacy by the unseemliness of this proposal."

Choice B is incorrect because there is no evidence in the passage that Akira worries that Chie will mistake his earnestness for immaturity. Choice C is incorrect because while Akira recognizes that his unscheduled visit is a nuisance, his larger concern is that Chie will reject him due to the inappropriateness of his proposal. Choice D is incorrect because there is no evidence in the passage that Akira worries Chie will underestimate the sincerity of his emotions.

QUESTION 5.

Choice C is the best answer. In lines 63-64, Akira says to Chie, "Please don't judge my candidacy by the unseemliness of this proposal." This reveals Akira's concern that Chie may say no to the proposal simply because Akira did not follow traditional practices.

Choices A, B, and D do not provide the best evidence for the answer to the previous question. Choice A is incorrect because line 33 merely describes Akira's voice as "soft, refined." Choice B is incorrect because lines 49-51 reflect Chie's perspective, not Akira's. Choice D is incorrect because lines 71-72 indicate only that Akira was speaking in an eager and forthright matter.

QUESTION 6.

Choice D is the best answer because Akira clearly treats Chie with respect, including "bow[ing]" (line 26) to her, calling her "Madame" (line 31), and looking at her with "a deferential peek" (line 34). Akira does not offer Chie utter deference, though, as he asks to marry Naomi after he concedes that he is not following protocol and admits to being a "disruption" (line 31).

Choice A is incorrect because while Akira conveys respect to Chie, there is no evidence in the passage that he feels affection for her. Choice B is incorrect because neither objectivity nor impartiality accurately describes how Akira addresses Chie. Choice C is incorrect because Akira conveys respect to Chie and takes the conversation seriously.

QUESTION 7.

Choice D is the best answer. The first paragraph (lines 1-4) reflects on how Akira approached Chie to ask for her daughter's hand in marriage. In these lines, the narrator is wondering whether Chie would have been more likely to say yes to Akira's proposal if Akira had followed tradition: "Akira came directly, breaking all tradition. Was that it? Had he followed form—had he asked his mother to speak to his father to approach a go-between—would Chie have been more receptive?" Thus, the main purpose of the first paragraph is to examine why Chie reacted a certain way to Akira's proposal.

Choice A is incorrect because the first paragraph describes only one aspect of Japanese culture (marriage proposals) but not the culture as a whole. Choice B is incorrect because the first paragraph implies a criticism of Akira's individual marriage proposal but not the entire tradition of Japanese marriage proposals. Choice C is incorrect because the narrator does not question a suggestion.

QUESTION 8.

Choice B is the best answer. In line 1, the narrator suggests that Akira's direct approach broke "all tradition." The narrator then wonders if Akira had "followed form," or the tradition expected of him, would Chie have been more receptive to his proposal. In this context, following "form" thus means following a certain tradition or custom.

Choices A, C, and D are incorrect because in this context "form" does not mean the way something looks (appearance), the way it is built (structure), or its essence (nature).

QUESTION 9.

Choice C is the best answer. Akira states that his unexpected meeting with Chie occurred only because of a "matter of urgency," which he explains as "an opportunity to go to America, as dentist for Seattle's Japanese community" (lines 41-42). Akira decides to directly speak to Chie because Chie's response to his marriage proposal affects whether Akira accepts the job offer.

Choice A is incorrect because there is no evidence in the passage that Akira is worried his parents will not approve of Naomi. Choice B is incorrect because Akira has "an understanding" with Naomi (line 63). Choice D is incorrect; while Akira may know that Chie is unaware of his feelings for Naomi, this is not what he is referring to when he mentions "a matter of urgency."

QUESTION 10.

Choice B is the best answer. In lines 39-42, Akira clarifies that the "matter of urgency" is that he has "an opportunity to go to America, as dentist for Seattle's Japanese community." Akira needs Chie's answer to his marriage proposal so he can decide whether to accept the job in Seattle.

Choices A, C, and D do not provide the best evidence for the answer to the previous question. Choice A is incorrect because in line 39 Akira apologizes for interrupting Chie's quiet evening. Choice C is incorrect because lines 58-59 address the seriousness of Akira's request, not its urgency. Choice D is incorrect because line 73 shows only that Akira's proposal has "startled" Chie and does not explain why his request is time-sensitive.

QUESTION 11.

Choice A is the best answer. Lines 1-9 include examples of how many people shop ("millions of shoppers"), how much money they spend ("over $30 billion at retail stores in the month of December alone"), and the many occasions that lead to shopping for gifts ("including weddings, birthdays, anniversaries, graduations, and baby showers."). Combined, these examples show how frequently people in the US shop for gifts.

Choice B is incorrect because even though the authors mention that "$30 billion" had been spent in retail stores in one month, that figure is never discussed as an increase (or a decrease). Choice C is incorrect because lines 1-9 provide a context for the amount of shopping that occurs in the US, but the anxiety (or "dread") it might cause is not introduced until later in the passage. Choice D is incorrect because lines 1-9 do more than highlight the number of different occasions that lead to gift-giving.

QUESTION 12.

Choice B is the best answer. Lines 9-10 state "This frequent experience of gift-giving can engender ambivalent feelings in gift-givers." In the subsequent sentences, those "ambivalent" feelings are further exemplified as conflicted feelings, as shopping is said to be something that "[m]any relish" (lines 10-11) and "many dread" (line 14).

Choices A, C, and D are incorrect because in this context, "ambivalent" does not mean feelings that are unrealistic, apprehensive, or supportive.

QUESTION 13.

Choice D is the best answer. In lines 10-13, the authors clearly state that some people believe gift-giving can help a relationship because it "offers a powerful means to build stronger bonds with one's closest peers."

Choice A is incorrect because even though the authors state that some shoppers make their choices based on "egocentrism," (line 33) there is no evidence in the passage that people view shopping as a form of self-expression. Choice B is incorrect because the passage implies that shopping is an expensive habit. Choice C is incorrect because the passage states that most people have purchased and received gifts, but it never implies that people are *required* to reciprocate the gift-giving process.

QUESTION 14.

Choice A is the best answer. In lines 10-13, the authors suggest that people value gift-giving because it may strengthen their relationships with others: "Many relish the opportunity to buy presents because gift-giving offers a powerful means to build stronger bonds with one's closest peers."

Choices B, C, and D do not provide the best evidence for the answer to the previous question. Choice B is incorrect because lines 22-23 discuss how people often buy gifts that the recipients would not purchase. Choice C is incorrect because lines 31-32 explain how gift-givers often fail to consider the recipients' preferences. Choice D is incorrect because lines 44-47 suggest that the cost of a gift may not correlate to a recipient's appreciation of it.

QUESTION 15.

Choice A is the best answer. The "deadweight loss" mentioned in the second paragraph is the significant monetary difference between what a gift-giver would pay for something and what a gift-recipient would pay for the same item. That difference would be predictable to social psychologists, whose research "has found that people often struggle to take account of others' perspectives—their insights are subject to egocentrism, social projection, and multiple attribution errors" (lines 31-34).

Choices B, C, and D are all incorrect because lines 31-34 make clear that social psychologists would expect a disconnect between gift-givers and gift-recipients, not that they would question it, be disturbed by it, or find it surprising or unprecedented.

QUESTION 16.

Choice C is the best answer. Lines 41-44 suggest that gift-givers assume a correlation between the cost of a gift and how well-received it will be: ". . . gift-givers equate how much they spend with how much recipients will appreciate the gift (the more expensive the gift, the stronger a gift-recipient's feelings of appreciation)." However, the authors suggest this assumption may be incorrect or "unfounded" (line 47), as gift-recipients "may not construe smaller and larger gifts as representing smaller and larger signals of thoughtfulness and consideration" (lines 63-65).

Choices A, B, and D are all incorrect because the passage neither states nor implies that the gift-givers' assumption is insincere, unreasonable, or substantiated.

QUESTION 17.

Choice C is the best answer. Lines 63-65 suggest that the assumption made by gift-givers in lines 41-44 may be incorrect. The gift-givers assume that recipients will have a greater appreciation for costly gifts than for less costly gifts, but the authors suggest this relationship may be incorrect, as gift-recipients "may not construe smaller and larger gifts as representing smaller and larger signals of thoughtfulness and consideration" (lines 63-65).

Choices A and D are incorrect because lines 53-55 and 75-78 address the question of "why" gift-givers make specific assumptions rather than addressing the validity of these assumptions. Choice B is incorrect because lines 55-60 focus on the reasons people give gifts to others.

QUESTION 18.

Choice D is the best answer. Lines 53-55 state that "Perhaps givers believe that bigger (i.e., more expensive) gifts convey stronger signals of thoughtfulness and consideration." In this context, saying that more expensive gifts "convey" stronger signals means the gifts send, or communicate, stronger signals to the recipients.

Choices A, B, and C are incorrect because in this context, to "convey" something does not mean to transport it (physically move something), counteract it (act in opposition to something), or exchange it (trade one thing for another).

QUESTION 19.

Choice A is the best answer. The paragraph examines how gift-givers believe expensive gifts are more thoughtful than less expensive gifts and will be more valued by recipients. The work of Camerer and others offers an explanation for the gift-givers' reasoning: "gift-givers attempt to signal their positive attitudes toward the intended recipient and their willingness to invest resources in a future relationship" (lines 57-60).

Choices B, C, and D are incorrect because the theory articulated by Camerer and others is used to explain an idea put forward by the authors ("givers believe that bigger . . . gifts convey stronger signals"), not to introduce an argument, question a motive, or support a conclusion.

QUESTION 20.

Choice B is the best answer. The graph clearly shows that gift-givers believe that a "more valuable" gift will be more appreciated than a "less valuable gift." According to the graph, gift-givers believe the monetary value of a gift will determine whether that gift is well received or not.

Choice A is incorrect because the graph does not suggest that gift-givers are aware of gift-recipients' appreciation levels. Choices C and D are incorrect because neither the gift-givers' desire for the gifts they purchase nor the gift-givers' relationship with the gift-recipients is addressed in the graph.

410

QUESTION 21.

Choice A is the best answer. Lines 69-75 explain that while people are often both gift-givers and gift-receivers, they struggle to apply information they learned as a gift-giver to a time when they were a gift-receiver: "Yet, despite the extensive experience that people have as both givers and receivers, they often struggle to transfer information gained from one role (e.g., as a giver) and apply it in another, complementary role (e.g., as a receiver)." The authors suggest that the disconnect between how much appreciation a gift-giver thinks a gift merits and how much appreciation a gift-recipient displays for the gift may be caused by both individuals' inability to comprehend the other's perspective.

Choices B and C are incorrect because neither the passage nor the graph addresses the idea that society has become more materialistic or that there is a growing opposition to gift-giving. Choice D is incorrect because the passage emphasizes that gift-givers and gift-recipients fail to understand each other's perspective, but it offers no evidence that the disconnect results only from a failure to understand the other's intentions.

QUESTION 22.

Choice B is the best answer. Lines 2-4 of the passage describe DNA as "a very long chain, the backbone of which consists of a regular alternation of sugar and phosphate groups." The backbone of DNA, in other words, is the main structure of a chain made up of repeating units of sugar and phosphate.

Choice A is incorrect because the passage describes DNA on the molecular level only and never mentions the spinal column of organisms. Choice C is incorrect because the passage describes the backbone of the molecule as having "a regular alternation" of sugar and phosphate, not one or the other. Choice D is incorrect because the nitrogenous bases are not the main structural unit of DNA; rather, they are attached only to the repeating units of sugar.

QUESTION 23.

Choice D is the best answer. The authors explain that hydrogen bonds join together pairs of nitrogenous bases, and that these bases have a specific structure that leads to the pairing: "One member of a pair must be a purine and the other a pyrimidine in order to bridge between the two chains" (lines 27-29). Given the specific chemical properties of a nitrogenous base, it would be inaccurate to call the process random.

Choice A is incorrect because lines 5-6 describe how nitrogenous bases attach to sugar but not how those bases pair with one another. Choice B is incorrect because lines 9-10 do not contradict the student's claim. Choice C is incorrect because lines 23-25 describe how the two molecules' chains are linked, not what the specific pairing between nitrogenous bases is.

QUESTION 24.

Choice D is the best answer. In lines 12-14 the authors state: "the first feature of our structure which is of biological interest is that it consists not of one chain, but of two."

Choices A and B are incorrect because lines 12-14 explicitly state that it is the two chains of DNA that are of "biological interest," not the chemical formula of DNA, nor the common fiber axis those two chains are wrapped around. Choice C is incorrect because, while the X-ray evidence did help Watson and Crick to discover that DNA consists of two chains, it was not claimed to be the feature of biological interest.

QUESTION 25.

Choice C is the best answer. In lines 12-14 the authors claim that DNA molecules appear to be comprised of two chains, even though "it has often been assumed . . . there would be only one" (lines 15-17). The authors support this claim with evidence compiled from an X-ray: "the density, taken with the X-ray evidence, suggests very strongly that there are two [chains]" (lines 18-19).

Choices A, B, and D are incorrect because the authors mention density and X-ray evidence to support a claim, not to establish that DNA carries genetic information, present a hypothesis about the composition of a nucleotide, or confirm a relationship between the density and chemical formula of DNA.

QUESTION 26.

Choice B is the best answer. The authors explain that "only certain pairs of bases will fit into the structure" (lines 25-26) of the DNA molecule. These pairs must contain "a purine and the other a pyrimidine in order to bridge between the two chains" (lines 27-29), which implies that any other pairing would not "fit into the structure" of the DNA molecule. Therefore, a pair of purines would be larger than the required purine/pyrimidine pair and would not fit into the structure of the DNA molecule.

Choice A is incorrect because this section is not discussing the distance between a sugar and phosphate group. Choice C is incorrect because the passage never makes clear the size of the pyrimidines or purines in relation to each other, only in relation to the space needed to bond the chains of the DNA molecule. Choice D is incorrect because the lines do not make an implication about the size of a pair of pyrimidines in relation to the size of a pair consisting of a purine and a pyrimidine.

QUESTION 27.

Choice D is the best answer. The authors explain how the DNA molecule contains a "precise sequence of bases" (lines 43-44), and that the authors can use the order of bases on one chain to determine the order of bases on the other chain: "If the actual order of the bases on one of the pair of chains were given, one could write down the exact order of the bases on the other one, because of the specific pairing. Thus one chain is, as it were, the complement of the other, and it is this feature which suggests how the deoxyribonucleic acid molecule might duplicate itself" (lines 45-51). The authors use the words "exact," "specific," and "complement" in these lines to suggest that the base pairings along a DNA chain is understood and predictable, and may explain how DNA "duplicate[s] itself" (line 51).

Choice A is incorrect because the passage does not suggest that most nucleotide sequences are known. Choice B is incorrect because these lines are not discussing the random nature of the base sequence along one chain of DNA. Choice C is incorrect because the authors are describing the bases attached only to the sugar, not to the sugar-phosphate backbone.

QUESTION 28.

Choice C is the best answer. Lines 6-7 state that "Two of the possible bases—adenine and guanine—are purines," and on the table the percentages of adenine and guanine in yeast DNA are listed as 31.3% and 18.7% respectively.

Choices A, B, and D are incorrect because they do not state the percentages of both purines, adenine and guanine, in yeast DNA.

QUESTION 29.

Choice A is the best answer. The authors state: "We believe that the bases will be present almost entirely in their most probable forms. If this is true, the conditions for forming hydrogen bonds are more restrictive, and the only pairs of bases possible are: adenine with thymine, and guanine with cytosine" (lines 31-35). The table shows that the pairs adenine/thymine and guanine/cytosine have notably similar percentages in DNA for all organisms listed.

Choice B is incorrect. Although the choice of "Yes" is correct, the explanation for that choice misrepresents the data in the table. Choices C and D are incorrect because the table does support the authors' proposed pairing of nitrogenous bases in DNA molecules.

QUESTION 30.

Choice A is the best answer because it gives the percentage of cytosine (17.3%) in sea urchin DNA and the percentage of guanine (17.7%) in sea urchin DNA. Their near similar pairing supports the authors' proposal that possible pairings of nitrogenous bases are "adenine with thymine, and guanine with cytosine" (line 35).

Choices B, C, and D do not provide the best evidence for the answer to the previous question. Choice B (cytosine and thymine), Choice C (cytosine and adenine), and Choice D (guanine and adenine) are incorrect because they show pairings of nitrogenous bases that do not compose a similar percentage of the bases in sea urchin DNA.

QUESTION 31.

Choice D is the best answer. The table clearly shows that the percentage of adenine in each organism's DNA is different, ranging from 24.7% in *E.coli* to 33.2% in the octopus. That such a variability would exist is predicted in lines 41-43, which states that "in a long molecule many different permutations are possible."

Choices A and B are incorrect because the table shows that the percentage of adenine varies between 24.7% and 33.2% in different organisms. Choice C is incorrect because lines 36-38 state that adenine pairs with thymine but does not mention the variability of the base composition of DNA.

QUESTION 32.

Choice B is the best answer. In this passage, Woolf asks women a series of questions. Woolf wants women to consider joining "the procession of educated men" (lines 56-57) by becoming members of the workforce. Woolf stresses that this issue is urgent, as women "have very little time in which to answer [these questions]" (lines 48-49).

Choice A is incorrect because Woolf argues against the tradition of only "the sons of educated men" (lines 82-83) joining the workforce. Choice C is incorrect because Woolf is not highlighting the severity of social divisions as much as she is explaining how those divisions might be reduced (with women joining the workforce). Choice D is incorrect because Woolf does not question the feasibility of changing the workforce dynamic.

QUESTION 33.

Choice A is the best answer. Throughout the passage, Woolf advocates for more women to engage with existing institutions by joining the workforce: "We too can leave the house, can mount those steps [to an office], pass in and out of those doors, . . . make money, administer justice . . ." (lines 30-32). Woolf tells educated women that they are at a "moment of transition" (line 51) where they must consider their future role in the workforce.

Choice B is incorrect because even though Woolf mentions women's traditional roles (lines 68-69: "while they stirred the pot, while they rocked the cradle"), she does not suggest that women will have to give up these traditional roles to gain positions of influence. Choice C is incorrect because though Woolf wonders how "the procession of the sons of educated men" impacts women's roles, she does not argue that this male-dominated society has had grave and continuing effects. Choice D is incorrect because while Woolf suggests educated women can hold positions currently held by men, she does not suggest that women's entry into positions of power will change those positions.

QUESTION 34.

Choice C is the best answer. Woolf uses the word "we" to refer to herself and educated women in English society, the "daughters of educated men" (line 64). Woolf wants these women to consider participating in a changing workforce: "For there, trapesing along at the tail end of the procession [to and from work], we go ourselves" (lines 23-24). In using the word "we" throughout the passage, Woolf establishes a sense of solidarity among educated women.

Choice A is incorrect because Woolf does not use "we" to reflect on whether people in a group are friendly to one another; she is concerned with generating solidarity among women. Choice B is incorrect because though Woolf admits women have predominantly "done their thinking" within traditional female roles (lines 64-69), she does not use "we" to advocate for more candor among women. Choice D is incorrect because Woolf does not use "we" to emphasize a need for people in a group to respect one other; rather, she wants to establish a sense of solidarity among women.

QUESTION 35.

Choice B is the best answer. Woolf argues that the "bridge over the River Thames, [has] an admirable vantage ground for us to make a survey" (lines 1-3). The phrase "make a survey" means to carefully examine an event or activity. Woolf wants educated women to "fix [their] eyes upon the procession—the procession of the sons of educated men" (lines 9-11) walking to work.

Choice A is incorrect because while Woolf states the bridge "is a place to stand on by the hour dreaming," she states that she is using the bridge "to consider the facts" (lines 6-9). Woolf is not using the bridge for fanciful reflection; she is analyzing "the procession of the sons of educated men" (lines 10-11). Choice C is incorrect because Woolf does not compare the bridge to historic episodes. Choice D is incorrect because Woolf does not suggest that the bridge is a symbol of a male-dominated past, but rather that it serves as a good place to watch men proceed to work.

QUESTION 36.

Choice D is the best answer. Woolf writes that the men who conduct the affairs of the nation (lines 15-17: "ascending those pulpits, preaching, teaching, administering justice, practising medicine, transacting business, making money") are the same men who go to and from work in a "procession" (line 10). Woolf notes that women are joining this procession, an act that suggests the workforce has become less exclusionary: "For there, trapesing along at the tail end of the procession, we go ourselves" (lines 23-24).

Choice A is incorrect because the procession is described as "a solemn sight always" (lines 17-18), which indicates that it has always been influential. Choice B is incorrect because the passage does not indicate that this procession has become a celebrated feature of English life. Choice C is incorrect because the passage states only that the procession is made up of "the sons of educated men" (lines 10-11).

QUESTION 37.

Choice C is the best answer, as lines 23-24 suggest that the workforce has become less exclusionary. In these lines Woolf describes how women are joining the male-dominated procession that travels to and from the work place: "For there, trapesing along at the tail end of the procession, we go ourselves."

Choices A, B, and D are incorrect because they do not provide the best evidence for the answer to the previous question. Choice A is incorrect because lines 12-17 describe the positions predominantly held by men. Choice B is incorrect because lines 17-19 use a metaphor to describe how the procession physically looks. Choice D is incorrect because lines 30-34 hypothesize about future jobs for women.

QUESTION 38.

Choice C is the best answer. Woolf characterizes the questions she asks in lines 53-57 as significant ("so important that they may well change the lives of all men and women for ever," lines 52-53) and urgent ("we have very little time in which to answer them," lines 48-49). Therefore, Woolf considers the questions posed in lines 53-57 as both momentous (significant) and pressing (urgent).

Choice A is incorrect because Woolf characterizes the questions as urgent and important, not as something that would cause controversy or fear. Choice B is incorrect because though Woolf considers the questions to be weighty (or "important"), she implies that they can be answered. Choice D is incorrect because Woolf does not imply that the questions are mysterious.

QUESTION 39.

Choice B is the best answer. The answer to the previous question shows how Woolf characterizes the questions posed in lines 53-57 as momentous and pressing. In lines 48-49, Woolf describes these questions as "important," or momentous, and states that women "have very little time in which to answer them," which shows their urgency.

Choices A, C, and D do not provide the best evidence for the answer to the previous question. Choices A and D are incorrect because lines 46-47 and line 62 suggest that women need to think about these questions and not offer trivial objections to them. Choice C is incorrect because line 57 characterizes only the need for urgency and does not mention the significance of the questions.

QUESTION 40.

Choice C is the best answer. Woolf writes that women "have thought" while performing traditional roles such as cooking and caring for children (lines 67-69). Woolf argues that this "thought" has shifted women's roles in society and earned them a "brand-new sixpence" that they need to learn how to "spend" (lines 70-71). The "sixpence" mentioned in these lines is not a literal coin. Woolf is using the "sixpence" as a metaphor, as she is suggesting women take advantage of the opportunity to join the male-dominated workforce.

Choices A, B, and D are incorrect because in this context, "sixpence" does not refer to tolerance, knowledge, or perspective.

QUESTION 41.

Choice B is the best answer. In lines 72-76, Woolf repeats the phrase "let us think" to emphasize how important it is for women to critically reflect on their role in society. Woolf states this reflection can occur at any time: "Let us think in offices; in omnibuses; while we are standing in the crowd watching Coronations and Lord Mayor's Shows; let us think . . . in the gallery of the House of Commons; in the Law Courts; let us think at baptisms and marriages and funerals."

Choices A, C, and D are incorrect because in lines 72-76 Woolf is not emphasizing the novelty of the challenge faced by women, the complexity of social and political issues, or the enjoyable aspect of women's career possibilities.

QUESTION 42.

Choice B is the best answer. The author of Passage 1 identifies specific companies such as the "Planetary Resources of Washington," "Deep Space Industries of Virginia," and "Golden Spike of Colorado" to support his earlier assertion that there are many interested groups "working to make space mining a reality" (line 8).

Choices A, C, and D are incorrect because the author of Passage 1 does not mention these companies to profile the technological advances in space mining, the profit margins from space mining, or the diverse approaches to space mining.

QUESTION 43.

Choice A is the best answer. The author of Passage 1 explicitly states that one benefit to space mining is access to precious metals and earth elements: "within a few decades, [space mining] may be meeting earthly demands for precious metals, such as platinum and gold, and the rare earth elements vital for personal electronics, such as yttrium and lanthanum" (lines 18-22).

Choice B is incorrect because Passage 1 does not suggest that precious metals extracted from space may make metals more valuable on Earth. Choice C and Choice D are incorrect because Passage 1 never mentions how space mining could create unanticipated technological innovations or change scientists' understanding of space resources.

QUESTION 44.

Choice A is the best answer. Lines 18-22 suggest that space mining may help meet "earthly demands for precious metals . . . and the rare earth elements vital for personal electronics." In this statement, the author is stating materials ("metals," "earth elements") that may be gathered as a result of space mining, and that these materials may be important to Earth's economy.

Choices B, C, and D do not provide the best evidence for the answer to the previous question. Choice B is incorrect because lines 24-28 focus on an "off-planet economy" but never address positive effects of space mining. Choice C is incorrect because lines 29-30 suggest the relative value of water found in space. Choice D is incorrect because lines 41-44 state that space mining companies hope to find specific resources in lunar soil and asteroids but do not address how these resources are important to Earth's economy.

QUESTION 45.

Choice D is the best answer. The author suggests in lines 19-22 that space mining may meet "earthly demands for precious metals, such as platinum and gold, and the rare earth elements vital for personal electronics." In this sentence, "earthly demands" suggests that people want, or desire, these precious metals and rare earth elements.

Choices A, B, and C are incorrect because in this context "demands" does not mean offers, claims, or inquiries.

QUESTION 46.

Choice C is the best answer. Lines 29-30 introduce the idea that water mined in space may be very valuable: "water mined from other worlds could become the most desired commodity." Lines 35-40 support this assertion by suggesting how mined space water could be used "for drinking or as a radiation shield" (lines 36-37) or to make "spacecraft fuel" (line 38).

Choice A is incorrect because the comparison in the previous paragraph (the relative value of gold and water to someone in the desert) is not expanded upon in lines 35-40. Choice B is incorrect because the question asked in the previous paragraph is also answered in that paragraph. Choice D is incorrect because no specific proposals are made in the previous paragraph; rather, an assertion is made and a question is posed.

QUESTION 47.

Choice B is the best answer. The author of Passage 2 recognizes that space mining may prove beneficial to humanity, stating that "we all stand to gain: the mineral bounty and spin-off technologies could enrich us all" (lines 50-52). The author also repeatedly mentions that space mining should be carefully considered before it is implemented: "But before the miners start firing up their rockets, we should pause for thought" (lines 53-54); "But [space mining's] consequences—both here on Earth and in space—merit careful consideration" (lines 57-59).

Choice A is incorrect because the author of Passage 2 concedes that "space mining seems to sidestep most environmental concerns" (lines 55-56) but does not imply that space mining will recklessly harm the environment, either on Earth or in space. Choice C is incorrect because the author of Passage 2 does not address any key resources that may be disappearing on Earth. Choice D is incorrect because the author of Passage 2 admits that "resources that are valuable in orbit and beyond may be very different to those we prize on Earth" (lines 74-76) but does not mention any disagreement about the commercial viabilities of space mining discoveries.

QUESTION 48.

Choice A is the best answer. In lines 60-66, the author presents some environmental arguments against space mining: "[space] is not ours to despoil" and we should not "[glut] ourselves on space's riches." The author then suggests that these environmental arguments will be hard to "hold," or maintain, when faced with the possible monetary rewards of space mining: "History suggests that those will be hard lines to hold . . ." (line 68).

Choices B, C, and D are incorrect because in this context, "hold" does not mean grip, restrain, or withstand.

QUESTION 49.

Choice D is the best answer. The author of Passage 1 is excited about the possibilities of space mining and how it can yield valuable materials, such as metals and elements (lines 19-20 and lines 41-42), water ice (line 35), and space dirt (line 44). The author of Passage 2, on the other hand, recognizes the possible benefits of space mining but also states that space mining should be thoughtfully considered before being implemented. Therefore, the author of Passage 2 expresses some concerns about a concept discussed in Passage 1.

Choice A is incorrect because the author of Passage 2 does not refute the central claim of Passage 1; both authors agree there are possible benefits to space mining. Choice B is incorrect because the author of Passage 1 does not describe space mining in more general terms than does the author of Passage 2. Choice C is incorrect because the author of Passage 2 is not suggesting that the space mining proposals stated in Passage 1 are impractical.

QUESTION 50.

Choice B is the best answer. In lines 18-28, the author of Passage 1 describes many of the possible economic benefits of space mining, including the building of "an off-planet economy" (line 25). The author of Passage 2 warns that there may be ramifications to implementing space mining and building an "emerging off-world economy" (line 73) without regulation: "But miners have much to gain from a broad agreement on the for-profit exploitation of space. Without consensus, claims will be disputed, investments risky, and the gains made insecure" (lines 83-87).

Choices A, C, and D are incorrect because the author of Passage 2 does not suggest that the benefits to space mining mentioned in lines 18-28 of Passage 1 are unsustainable, unachievable, or will negatively affect Earth's economy. Rather, the author recognizes the benefits of space mining but advocates for the development of regulation procedures.

QUESTION 51.

Choice D is the best answer. In lines 85-87, the author of Passage 2 states that the future of space mining will prove difficult without regulations because "claims will be disputed, investments risky, and the gains made insecure."

Choices A, B, and C are incorrect because they do not provide the best evidence for the answer to the previous question. Choice A is incorrect because lines 60-63 present some environmental concerns toward space mining. Choice B is incorrect because lines 74-76 focus on how space mining may discover valuable resources that are different from the ones found on Earth. Choice C is incorrect because lines 81-83 simply describe one person's objections to the regulation of the space mining industry.

QUESTION 52.

Choice A is the best answer because both Passage 1 and Passage 2 indicate a belief that the resources most valued in space may differ from those most valued on our planet. Passage 2 says this explicitly in lines 74-76: "The resources that are valuable in orbit and beyond may be very different to those we prize on Earth." Meanwhile Passage 1 suggests that water mined from space may be more valuable than metals or other earth elements when creating an "off-plant economy" (lines 25-30).

Choice B is incorrect because neither passage discusses, either implicitly or explicitly, the need for space mining to be inexpensive. Choice C is incorrect because Passage 2 does not specifically identify precious metals or rare earth elements but instead focuses on theoretical problems with space mining. Choice D is incorrect because diminishing resources on Earth is not discussed in Passage 2.

Section 2: Writing and Language Test

QUESTION 1.

Choice D is the best answer because "outweigh" is the only choice that appropriately reflects the relationship the sentence sets up between "advantages" and "drawbacks."

Choices A, B, and C are incorrect because each implies a competitive relationship that is inappropriate in this context.

QUESTION 2.

Choice B is the best answer because it offers a second action that farmers can undertake to address the problem of acid whey disposal, thus supporting the claim made in the previous sentence ("To address the problem of disposal, farmers have found a *number of uses* for acid whey").

Choices A, C, and D are incorrect because they do not offer examples of how farmers could make use of acid whey.

QUESTION 3.

Choice A is the best answer because it results in a sentence that is grammatically correct and coherent. In choice A, "waterways," the correct plural form of "waterway," conveys the idea that acid whey could impact multiple bodies of water. Additionally, the compound verb "can pollute" suggests that acid whey presents an ongoing, potential problem.

Choices B and D are incorrect because both use the possessive form of "waterway." Choice C is incorrect because it creates an unnecessary shift in verb tense. The present tense verb "can pollute" should be used instead, as it is consistent with the other verbs in the paragraph.

QUESTION 4.

Choice C is the best answer because it utilizes proper punctuation for items listed in a series. In this case those items are nouns: "Yogurt manufacturers, food scientists, and government officials."

Choices A and B are incorrect because both fail to recognize that the items are a part of a series. Since a comma is used after "manufacturers," a semicolon or colon should not be used after "scientists." Choice D is incorrect because the comma after "and" is unnecessary and deviates from grammatical conventions for presenting items in a series.

QUESTION 5.

Choice C is the best answer because sentence 5 logically links sentence 2, which explains why Greek yogurt production yields large amounts of acid whey, and sentence 3, which mentions the need to dispose of acid whey properly.

Choices A, B, and D are incorrect because each would result in an illogical progression of sentences for this paragraph. If sentence 5 were left where it is or placed after sentence 3, it would appear illogically after the discussion of "the problem of disposal." If sentence 5 were placed after sentence 1, it would illogically discuss "acid-whey runoff" before the mention of acid whey being "difficult to dispose of."

QUESTION 6.

Choice D is the best answer because the paragraph includes several benefits of consuming Greek yogurt, particularly in regard to nutrition and satisfying hunger, to support the sentence's claim that the conservation efforts are "well worth the effort." This transition echoes the passage's earlier claim that "the advantages of Greek yogurt outweigh the potential drawbacks of its production."

Choices A, B, and C are incorrect because they inaccurately describe the sentence in question.

QUESTION 7.

Choice B is the best answer because it provides a grammatically standard preposition that connects the verb "serves" and noun "digestive aid" and accurately depicts their relationship.

Choice A is incorrect because the infinitive form "to be" yields a grammatically incorrect verb construction: "serves to be." Choices C and D are incorrect because both present options that deviate from standard English usage.

QUESTION 8.

Choice C is the best answer because it presents a verb tense that is consistent in the context of the sentence. The choice is also free of the redundant "it."

Choice A is incorrect because the subject "it" creates a redundancy. Choices B and D are incorrect because they present verb tenses that are inconsistent in the context of the sentence.

QUESTION 9.

Choice A is the best answer because it properly introduces an additional health benefit in a series of sentences that list health benefits. "Also" is the logical and coherent choice to communicate an addition.

Choices B, C, and D are incorrect because none of the transitions they offer logically fits the content that precedes or follows the proposed choice.

QUESTION 10.

Choice A is the best answer because "satiated" is the only choice that communicates effectively that Greek yogurt will satisfy hunger for a longer period of time.

Choices B, C, and D are incorrect because each is improper usage in this context. A person can be "fulfilled" spiritually or in other ways, but a person who has eaten until he or she is no longer hungry cannot be described as fulfilled. Neither can he or she be described as being "complacent" or "sufficient."

QUESTION 11.

Choice B is the best answer because it provides a syntactically coherent and grammatically correct sentence.

Choices A and C are incorrect because the adverbial conjunctions "therefore" and "so," respectively, are unnecessary following "Because." Choice D is incorrect because it results in a grammatically incomplete sentence (the part of the sentence before the colon must be an independent clause).

QUESTION 12.

Choice B is the best answer because the graph clearly indicates that, on March 5, average low temperatures are at their lowest point: 12 degrees Fahrenheit.

Choice A is incorrect because the phrase "as low as" suggests that the temperature falls no lower than 20 degrees Fahrenheit, but the chart shows that in January, February, and March, the temperature frequently falls below that point. Choices C and D are incorrect because the information each provides is inconsistent with the information on the chart.

QUESTION 13.

Choice A is the best answer because it concisely combines the two sentences while maintaining the original meaning.

Choices B, C, and D are incorrect because each is unnecessarily wordy, thus undermining one purpose of combining two sentences: to make the phrasing more concise.

QUESTION 14.

Choice B is the best answer because it provides a conjunctive adverb that accurately represents the relationship between the two sentences. "However" signals an exception to a case stated in the preceding sentence.

Choices A, C, and D are incorrect because each provides a transition that does not accurately represent the relationship between the two sentences, and as a result each compromises the logical coherence of these sentences.

QUESTION 15.

Choice C is the best answer because it provides commas to offset the non-restrictive modifying clause "an associate professor of geology at Ohio State."

Choices A, B, and D are incorrect because each provides punctuation that does not adequately separate the nonrestrictive modifying clause about Jason Box from the main clause.

QUESTION 16.

Choice C is the best answer because the colon signals that the other factor that contributed to the early thaw is about to be provided.

Choice A is incorrect because it results in a sentence that deviates from grammatical standards: a semicolon should be used to separate two independent clauses, but in choice A the second clause only has a subject, not a verb. Choice B is incorrect because it is unnecessarily wordy. Choice D is incorrect because "being" is unnecessary and creates an incoherent clause.

QUESTION 17.

Choice C is the best answer because it provides the correct preposition ("of") and relative pronoun ("which") that together create a dependent clause following the comma.

Choices A, B, and D are incorrect because each results in a comma splice. Two independent clauses cannot be joined with only a comma.

QUESTION 18.

Choice A is the best answer because the verb tense is consistent with the preceding past tense verbs in the sentence, specifically "produced" and "drifted."

Choices B, C, and D are incorrect because each utilizes a verb tense that is not consistent with the preceding past tense verbs in the sentence.

QUESTION 19.

Choice D is the best answer because "their" is the possessive form of a plural noun. In this case, the noun is plural: "snow and ice."

Choices A and B are incorrect because the possessive pronoun must refer to a plural noun, "snow and ice," rather than a singular noun. Choice C is incorrect because "there" would result in an incoherent sentence.

QUESTION 20.

Choice D is the best answer. The preceding sentences in the paragraph have established that a darker surface of soot-covered snow leads to more melting because this darker surface absorbs heat, whereas a whiter surface, free of soot, would deflect heat. As the passage points out, exposed land and water are also dark and cannot deflect heat the way ice and snow can. Only choice D reflects the self-reinforcing cycle that the preceding sentences already imply.

Choices A, B, and C are incorrect because the information each provides fails to support the previous claim that the "result" of the soot "is a self-reinforcing cycle."

QUESTION 21.

Choice B is the best answer because it is free of redundancies.

Choices A, C, and D are incorrect because each of the three presents a redundancy: Choice A uses "repeat" and "again"; Choice C uses "damage" and "harmful effects"; and Choice D uses "may" and "possibly."

QUESTION 22.

Choice D is the best answer because sentence 5 describes the information Box seeks: "to determine just how much the soot is contributing to the melting of the ice sheet." Unless sentence 4 comes after sentence 5, readers will not know what the phrase "this crucial information" in sentence 4 refers to.

Choices A, B, and C are incorrect because each results in an illogical sentence progression. None of the sentences that would precede sentence 4 provides details that could be referred to as "this crucial information."

QUESTION 23.

Choice D is the best answer because it is free of redundancies and offers the correct form of the verb "wear" in this context.

Choices A, B, and C are incorrect because all three contain a redundancy. Considering that "quickly" is a fixed part of the sentence, choice A's "soon" and choice B and C's "promptly" all result in redundancies. Choices A and B are also incorrect because each uses an incorrect form of the verb.

QUESTION 24.

Choice D is the best answer because it is the only choice that provides a grammatically standard and coherent sentence. The participial phrase "Having become frustrated. . ." functions as an adjective modifying "I," the writer.

Choices A, B, and C are incorrect because each results in a dangling modifier. The participial phrase "Having become frustrated . . ." does not refer to choice A's "no colleagues," choice B's "colleagues," or choice C's "ideas." As such, all three choices yield incoherent and grammatically incorrect sentences.

QUESTION 25.

Choice B is the best answer because it provides the correct preposition in this context, "about."

Choices A, C, and D are incorrect because each provides a preposition that deviates from correct usage. One might read an article "about" coworking spaces but not an article "into," "upon," or "for" coworking spaces.

QUESTION 26.

Choice A is the best answer because it provides the correct punctuation for the dependent clause that begins with the phrase "such as."

Choices B, C, and D are incorrect because each presents punctuation that deviates from the standard way of punctuating the phrase "such as." When "such as" is a part of a nonrestrictive clause, as it is here, only one comma is needed to separate it from the main independent clause.

QUESTION 27.

Choice B is the best answer because it provides a transitional phrase, "In addition to equipment," that accurately represents the relationship between the two sentences connected by the transitional phrase. Together, the sentences describe the key features of coworking spaces, focusing on what the spaces offer (equipment and meeting rooms).

Choices A, C, and D are incorrect because each provides a transition that does not accurately represent the relationship between the two sentences.

QUESTION 28.

Choice C is the best answer because the sentence is a distraction from the paragraph's focus. Nothing in the paragraph suggests that the cost of setting up a coworking business is relevant here.

Choices A and D are incorrect because neither accurately represents the information in the paragraph. Choice B is incorrect because it does not accurately represent the information in the next paragraph.

QUESTION 29.

Choice B is the best answer because it logically follows the writer's preceding statement about creativity and accurately represents the information in the graph.

Choices A, C, and D are incorrect because they present inaccurate and unsupported interpretations of the information in the graph. In addition, none of these choices provides directly relevant support for the main topic of the paragraph.

QUESTION 30.

Choice D is the best answer because it provides a relative pronoun and verb that create a standard and coherent sentence. The relative pronoun "who" refers to the subject "the people," and the plural verb "use" corresponds grammatically with the plural noun "people."

Choices A and B are incorrect because "whom" is the relative pronoun used to represent an object. The noun "people" is a subject performing an action (using the coworking space). Choices B and C are also incorrect because they display a form of the verb "to use" that does not correspond to the plural noun "people."

QUESTION 31.

Choice C is the best answer because the proposed sentence offers a necessary and logical transition between sentence 2, which introduces the facility the writer chose, and sentence 3, which tells what happened at the facility "Throughout the morning."

Choices A, B, and D are incorrect because each would result in an illogical progression of sentences.

QUESTION 32.

Choice A is the best answer because the punctuation it provides results in a grammatically standard and coherent sentence. When an independent clause is followed by a list, a colon is used to link the two.

Choice B is incorrect because the punctuation creates a fragment (a semicolon should be used to link two independent clauses). Choice C is incorrect because its use of the comma creates a series in which "several of my coworking colleagues" are distinguished from the "website developer" and others, although the logic of the sentence would suggest that they are the same. Choice D is incorrect because it lacks the punctuation necessary to link the independent clause and the list.

QUESTION 33.

Choice A is the best answer because it provides a phrase that is consistent with standard English usage and also maintains the tone and style of the passage.

Choice B is incorrect because "give some wisdom" deviates from standard English usage and presents a somewhat colloquial phrase in a text that is generally free of colloquialisms. Choices C and D are incorrect because both are inconsistent with the tone of the passage as well as its purpose. The focus of the paragraph is on sharing, not on proclaiming opinions.

QUESTION 34.

Choice A is the best answer because it offers a phrase that introduces a basic definition of philosophy and thereby fits the sentence.

Choices B, C, and D are incorrect because each offers a transition that does not suit the purpose of the sentence.

QUESTION 35.

Choice A is the best answer because it offers the most succinct comparison between the basic definition of philosophy and the fact that students can gain specific, practical skills from the study of philosophy. There is no need to include the participle "speaking" in this sentence, as it is clear from context that the writer is offering a different perspective.

Choices B, C, and D are incorrect because they provide options that are unnecessarily wordy.

QUESTION 36.

Choice B is the best answer because it provides a verb that creates a grammatically complete, standard, and coherent sentence.

Choices A, C, and D are incorrect because each results in a grammatically incomplete and incoherent sentence.

QUESTION 37.

Choice D is the best answer because it most effectively sets up the information in the following sentences, which state that (according to information from the 1990s) "only 18 percent of American colleges required at least one philosophy course," and "more than 400 independent philosophy departments were eliminated" from colleges. These details are most logically linked to the claim that "colleges have not always supported the study of philosophy."

Choices A, B, and C are incorrect because none of these effectively sets up the information that follows, which is about colleges' failure to support the study of philosophy.

QUESTION 38.

Choice C is the best answer because it provides a transition that logically connects the information in the previous sentence to the information in this one. Both sentences provide evidence of colleges' lack of support of philosophy programs, so the adverb "Moreover," which means "In addition," accurately captures the relationship between the two sentences.

Choices A, B, and D are incorrect because each presents a transition that does not accurately depict or support the relationship between the two sentences. The second sentence is not a result of the first ("Therefore," "Thus"), and the sentences do not provide a contrast ("However").

QUESTION 39.

Choice A is the best answer because it succinctly expresses the idea that "students who major in philosophy often do better . . . as measured by standardized test scores."

Choices B and D are incorrect because they introduce a redundancy and a vague term, "results." The first part of the sentence mentions a research finding or conclusion but does not directly address any "results," so it is confusing to refer to "these results" and indicate that they "can be" or "are measured by standardized test scores." The best way to express the idea is simply to say that some students "often do better" than some other students "in both verbal reasoning and analytical writing as measured by standardized test scores." Choice C is incorrect because there is no indication that multiple criteria are used to evaluate students' "verbal reasoning and analytical writing": test scores and something else. Only test scores are mentioned.

QUESTION 40.

Choice B is the best answer because it provides subject-verb agreement and thus creates a grammatically correct and coherent sentence.

Choice A is incorrect because the verb "has scored" does not correspond with the plural subject "students." Similarly, Choice C is incorrect because the verb "scores" would correspond with a singular subject, but not the plural subject present in this sentence. Choice D is incorrect because it results in a grammatically incomplete and incoherent sentence.

QUESTION 41.

Choice B is the best answer because it provides a coherent and grammatically standard sentence.

Choices A and D are incorrect because both present "students" in the possessive form, whereas the sentence establishes "students" as the subject ("many students . . . have"). Choice C is incorrect because the verb form it proposes results in an incomplete and incoherent sentence.

QUESTION 42.

Choice C is the best answer because it accurately depicts how inserting this sentence would affect the overall paragraph. The fact that Plato used the dialogue form has little relevance to the preceding claim about the usefulness of a philosophy background.

Choices A and B are incorrect because the proposed sentence interrupts the progression of reasoning in the paragraph. Choice D is incorrect because, as with Choice A, Plato's works have nothing to do with "the employability of philosophy majors."

QUESTION 43.

Choice D is the best answer because it creates a complete and coherent sentence.

Choices A, B, and C are incorrect because each inserts an unnecessary relative pronoun or conjunction, resulting in a sentence without a main verb.

QUESTION 44.

Choice D is the best answer because it provides a possessive pronoun that is consistent with the sentence's plural subject "students," thus creating a grammatically sound sentence.

Choices A, B, and C are incorrect because each proposes a possessive pronoun that is inconsistent with the plural noun "students," the established subject of the sentence.

Section 3: Math Test — No Calculator

QUESTION 1.

Choice D is correct. Since $k = 3$, one can substitute 3 for k in the equation $\frac{x-1}{3} = k$, which gives $\frac{x-1}{3} = 3$. Multiplying both sides of $\frac{x-1}{3} = 3$ by 3 gives $x - 1 = 9$ and then adding 1 to both sides of $x - 1 = 9$ gives $x = 10$.

Choices A, B, and C are incorrect because the result of subtracting 1 from the value and dividing by 3 is not the given value of k, which is 3.

QUESTION 2.

Choice A is correct. To calculate $(7 + 3i) + (-8 + 9i)$, add the real parts of each complex number, $7 + (-8) = -1$, and then add the imaginary parts, $3i + 9i = 12i$. The result is $-1 + 12i$.

Choices B, C, and D are incorrect and likely result from common errors that arise when adding complex numbers. For example, choice B is the result of adding $3i$ and $-9i$, and choice C is the result of adding 7 and 8.

QUESTION 3.

Choice C is correct. The total number of messages sent by Armand is the 5 hours he spent texting multiplied by his rate of texting: m texts/hour $\times$ 5 hours $= 5m$ texts. Similarly, the total number of messages sent by Tyrone is the 4 hours he spent texting multiplied by his rate of texting: p texts/hour $\times$ 4 hours $= 4p$ texts. The total number of messages sent by Armand and Tyrone is the sum of the total number of messages sent by Armand and the total number of messages sent by Tyrone: $5m + 4p$.

Choice A is incorrect and arises from adding the coefficients and multiplying the variables of $5m$ and $4p$. Choice B is incorrect and is the result of multiplying $5m$ and $4p$. The total number of messages sent by Armand and Tyrone should be the sum of $5m$ and $4p$, not the product of these terms. Choice D is incorrect because it multiplies Armand's number of hours spent texting by Tyrone's rate of texting, and vice versa. This mix-up results in an expression that does not equal the total number of messages sent by Armand and Tyrone.

QUESTION 4.

Choice B is correct. The value 108 in the equation is the value of P in $P = 108 - 23d$ when $d = 0$. When $d = 0$, Kathy has worked 0 days that week. In other words, 108 is the number of phones left before Kathy has started work for the week. Therefore, the meaning of the value 108 in the equation is that Kathy starts each week with 108 phones to fix because she has worked 0 days and has 108 phones left to fix.

Choice A is incorrect because Kathy will complete the repairs when $P = 0$. Since $P = 108 - 23d$, this will occur when $0 = 108 - 23d$ or when $d = \frac{108}{23}$, not when $d = 108$. Therefore, the value 108 in the equation does not represent the number of days it will take Kathy to complete the repairs. Choices C and D are incorrect because the number 23 in $P = 108 - 23P = 108$ indicates that the number of phones left will decrease by 23 for each increase in the value of d by 1; in other words, that Kathy is repairing phones at a rate of 23 per day, not 108 per hour (choice C) or 108 per day (choice D).

QUESTION 5.

Choice C is correct. Only like terms, with the same variables and exponents, can be combined to determine the answer as shown here:

$$(x^2y - 3y^2 + 5xy^2) - (-x^2y + 3xy^2 - 3y^2)$$
$$= (x^2y - (-x^2y)) + (-3y^2 - (-3y^2)) + (5xy^2 - 3xy^2)$$
$$= 2x^2y + 0 + 2xy^2$$
$$= 2x^2y + 2xy^2$$

Choices A, B, and D are incorrect and are the result of common calculation errors or of incorrectly combining like and unlike terms.

QUESTION 6.

Choice A is correct. In the equation $h = 3a + 28.6$, if a, the age of the boy, increases by 1, then h becomes $h = 3(a + 1) + 28.6 = 3a + 3 + 28.6 = (3a + 28.6) + 3$. Therefore, the model estimates that the boy's height increases by 3 inches each year.

Alternatively: The height, h, is a linear function of the age, a, of the boy. The coefficient 3 can be interpreted as the rate of change of the function; in this case, the rate of change can be described as a change of 3 inches in height for every additional year in age.

Choices B, C, and D are incorrect and are likely to result from common errors in calculating the value of h or in calculating the difference between the values of h for different values of a.

QUESTION 7.

Choice B is correct. Since the right-hand side of the equation is P times the

expression $\dfrac{\left(\dfrac{r}{1,200}\right)\left(1+\dfrac{r}{1,200}\right)^{N}}{\left(1+\dfrac{r}{1,200}\right)^{N}-1}$, multiplying both sides of the equation by

the reciprocal of this expression results in $\dfrac{\left(1+\dfrac{r}{1,200}\right)^{N}-1}{\left(\dfrac{r}{1,200}\right)\left(1+\dfrac{r}{1,200}\right)^{N}}\,m=P.$

Choices A, C, and D are incorrect and are likely the result of conceptual or computation errors while trying to solve for P.

QUESTION 8.

Choice C is correct. Since $\dfrac{a}{b}=2$, it follows that $\dfrac{b}{a}=\dfrac{1}{2}$. Multiplying both sides of the equation by 4 gives $4\left(\dfrac{b}{a}\right)=\dfrac{4b}{a}=2$.

Choice A is incorrect because if $\dfrac{4b}{a}=0$, then $\dfrac{a}{b}$ would be undefined. Choice B is incorrect because if $\dfrac{4b}{a}=1$, then $\dfrac{a}{b}=4$. Choice D is incorrect because if $\dfrac{4b}{a}=4$, then $\dfrac{a}{b}=1$.

QUESTION 9.

Choice B is correct. Adding x and 19 to both sides of $2y-x=-19$ gives $x=2y+19$. Then, substituting $2y+19$ for x in $3x+4y=-23$ gives $3(2y+19)+4y=-23$. This last equation is equivalent to $10y+57=-23$. Solving $10y+57=-23$ gives $y=-8$. Finally, substituting -8 for y in $2y-x=-19$ gives $2(-8)-x=-19$, or $x=3$. Therefore, the solution (x,y) to the given system of equations is $(3,-8)$.

Choices A, C, and D are incorrect because when the given values of x and y are substituted in $2y-x=-19$, the value of the left side of the equation does not equal -19.

QUESTION 10.

Choice A is correct. Since g is an even function, $g(-4)=g(4)=8$.

Alternatively: First find the value of a, and then find $g(-4)$. Since $g(4)=8$, substituting 4 for x and 8 for $g(x)$ gives $8=a(4)^{2}+24=16a+24$. Solving this last equation gives $a = -1$. Thus $g(x) = -x^2 + 24$, from which it follows that $g(-4) = -(-4)^2 + 24$; $g(-4) = -16 + 24$; and $g(-4) = 8$.

Choices B, C, and D are incorrect because g is a function and there can only be one value of $g(-4)$.

QUESTION 11.

Choice D is correct. To determine the price per pound of beef when it was equal to the price per pound of chicken, determine the value of x (the number of weeks after July 1) when the two prices were equal. The prices were equal when $b = c$; that is, when $2.35 + 0.25x = 1.75 + 0.40x$. This last equation is equivalent to $0.60 = 0.15x$, and so $x = \dfrac{0.60}{0.15} = 4$. Then to determine b, the price per pound of beef, substitute 4 for x in $b = 2.35 + 0.25x$, which gives $b = 2.35 + 0.25(4) = 3.35$ dollars per pound.

Choice A is incorrect. It results from using the value 1, not 4, for x in $b = 2.35 + 0.25x$. Choice B is incorrect. It results from using the value 2, not 4, for x in $b = 2.35 + 0.25x$. Choice C is incorrect. It results from using the value 3, not 4, for x in $c = 1.75 + 0.40x$.

QUESTION 12.

Choice D is correct. Determine the equation of the line to find the relationship between the x- and y-coordinates of points on the line. All lines through the origin are of the form $y = mx$, so the equation is $y = \dfrac{1}{7}x$. A point lies on the line if and only if its y-coordinate is $\dfrac{1}{7}$ of its x-coordinate. Of the given choices, only choice D, $(14, 2)$, satisfies this condition: $2 = \dfrac{1}{7}(14)$.

Choice A is incorrect because the line determined by the origin $(0, 0)$ and $(0, 7)$ is the vertical line with equation $x = 0$; that is, the y-axis. The slope of the y-axis is undefined, not $\dfrac{1}{7}$. Therefore, the point $(0, 7)$ does not lie on the line that passes the origin and has slope $\dfrac{1}{7}$. Choices B and C are incorrect because neither of the ordered pairs has a y-coordinate that is $\dfrac{1}{7}$ the value of the x-coordinate.

QUESTION 13.

Choice B is correct. To rewrite $\dfrac{1}{\dfrac{1}{x+2} + \dfrac{1}{x+3}}$, multiply by $\dfrac{(x+2)(x+3)}{(x+2)(x+3)}$.

This results in the expression $\dfrac{(x+2)(x+3)}{(x+3) + (x+2)}$, which is equivalent to the expression in choice B.

Choices A, C, and D are incorrect and could be the result of common algebraic errors that arise while manipulating a complex fraction.

QUESTION 14.

Choice A is correct. One approach is to express $\dfrac{8^x}{2^y}$ so that the numerator and denominator are expressed with the same base. Since 2 and 8 are both powers of 2, substituting 2^3 for 8 in the numerator of $\dfrac{8^x}{2^y}$ gives $\dfrac{(2^3)^x}{2^y}$, which can be rewritten as $\dfrac{2^{3x}}{2^y}$. Since the numerator and denominator of $\dfrac{2^{3x}}{2^y}$ have a common base, this expression can be rewritten as 2^{3x-y}. It is given that $3x - y = 12$, so one can substitute 12 for the exponent, $3x - y$, giving that the expression $\dfrac{8^x}{2^y}$ is equal to 2^{12}.

Choices B and C are incorrect because they are not equal to 2^{12}. Choice D is incorrect because the value of $\dfrac{8^x}{2^y}$ can be determined.

QUESTION 15.

Choice D is correct. One can find the possible values of a and b in $(ax + 2)(bx + 7)$ by using the given equation $a + b = 8$ and finding another equation that relates the variables a and b. Since $(ax + 2)(bx + 7) = 15x^2 + cx + 14$, one can expand the left side of the equation to obtain $abx^2 + 7ax + 2bx + 14 = 15x^2 + cx + 14$. Since ab is the coefficient of x^2 on the left side of the equation and 15 is the coefficient of x^2 on the right side of the equation, it must be true that $ab = 15$. Since $a + b = 8$, it follows that $b = 8 - a$. Thus, $ab = 15$ can be rewritten as $a(8 - a) = 15$, which in turn can be rewritten as $a^2 - 8a + 15 = 0$. Factoring gives $(a - 3)(a - 5) = 0$. Thus, either $a = 3$ and $b = 5$, or $a = 5$ and $b = 3$. If $a = 3$ and $b = 5$, then $(ax + 2)(bx + 7) = (3x + 2)(5x + 7) = 15x^2 + 31x + 14$. Thus, one of the possible values of c is 31. If $a = 5$ and $b = 3$, then $(ax + 2)(bx + 7) = (5x + 2)(3x + 7) = 15x^2 + 41x + 14$. Thus, another possible value for c is 41. Therefore, the two possible values for c are 31 and 41.

Choice A is incorrect; the numbers 3 and 5 are possible values for a and b, but not possible values for c. Choice B is incorrect; if $a = 5$ and $b = 3$, then 6 and 35 are the coefficients of x when the expression $(5x + 2)(3x + 7)$ is expanded as $15x^2 + 35x + 6x + 14$. However, when the coefficients of x are 6 and 35, the value of c is 41 and not 6 and 35. Choice C is incorrect; if $a = 3$ and $b = 5$, then 10 and 21 are the coefficients of x when the expression $(3x + 2)(5x + 7)$ is expanded as $15x^2 + 21x + 10x + 14$. However, when the coefficients of x are 10 and 21, the value of c is 31 and not 10 and 21.

QUESTION 16.

The correct answer is 2. To solve for t, factor the left side of $t^2 - 4 = 0$, giving $(t - 2)(t + 2) = 0$. Therefore, either $t - 2 = 0$ or $t + 2 = 0$. If $t - 2 = 0$, then $t = 2$, and if $t + 2 = 0$, then $t = -2$. Since it is given that $t > 0$, the value of t must be 2.

Another way to solve for t is to add 4 to both sides of $t^2 - 4 = 0$, giving $t^2 = 4$. Then, taking the square root of the left and the right side of the equation gives $t = \pm\sqrt{4} = \pm 2$. Since it is given that $t > 0$, the value of t must be 2.

QUESTION 17.

The correct answer is 1600. It is given that $\angle AEB$ and $\angle CDB$ have the same measure. Since $\angle ABE$ and $\angle CBD$ are vertical angles, they have the same measure. Therefore, triangle EAB is similar to triangle DCB because the triangles have two pairs of congruent corresponding angles (angle-angle criterion for similarity of triangles). Since the triangles are similar, the corresponding sides are in the same proportion; thus $\frac{CD}{x} = \frac{BD}{EB}$. Substituting the given values of 800 for CD, 700 for BD, and 1400 for EB in $\frac{CD}{x} = \frac{BD}{EB}$ gives $\frac{800}{x} = \frac{700}{1400}$. Therefore, $x = \frac{(800)(1400)}{700} = 1600$.

QUESTION 18.

The correct answer is 7. Subtracting the left and right sides of $x + y = -9$ from the corresponding sides of $x + 2y = -25$ gives $(x + 2y) - (x + y) = -25 - (-9)$, which is equivalent to $y = -16$. Substituting -16 for y in $x + y = -9$ gives $x + (-16) = -9$, which is equivalent to $x = -9 - (-16) = 7$.

QUESTION 19.

The correct answer is $\frac{4}{5}$ or 0.8. By the complementary angle relationship for sine and cosine, $\sin(x°) = \cos(90° - x°)$. Therefore, $\cos(90° - x°) = \frac{4}{5}$. Either the fraction $\frac{4}{5}$ or its decimal equivalent, 0.8, may be gridded as the correct answer.

Alternatively, one can construct a right triangle that has an angle of measure $x°$ such that $\sin(x°) = \frac{4}{5}$, as shown in the figure below, where $\sin(x°)$ is equal to the ratio of the opposite side to the hypotenuse, or $\frac{4}{5}$.

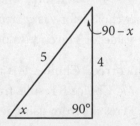

Since two of the angles of the triangle are of measure $x°$ and $90°$, the third angle must have the measure $180° - 90° - x° = 90° - x°$. From the figure, $\cos(90° - x°)$, which is equal to the ratio of the adjacent side to the hypotenuse, is also $\frac{4}{5}$.

QUESTION 20.

The correct answer is 100. Since $a = 5\sqrt{2}$, one can substitute $5\sqrt{2}$ for a in $2a = \sqrt{2}x$, giving $10\sqrt{2} = \sqrt{2}x$. Squaring each side of $10\sqrt{2} = \sqrt{2}x$ gives $(10\sqrt{2})^2 = (\sqrt{2}x)^2$, which simplifies to $(10)^2(\sqrt{2})^2 = (\sqrt{2}x)^2$, or $200 = 2x$. This gives $x = 100$. Checking $x = 100$ in the original equation gives $2(5\sqrt{2}) = \sqrt{(2)(100)}$, which is true since $2(5\sqrt{2}) = 10\sqrt{2}$ and $\sqrt{(2)(100)} = (\sqrt{2})(\sqrt{100}) = 10\sqrt{2}$.

Section 4: Math Test — Calculator

QUESTION 1.

Choice B is correct. On the graph, a line segment with a positive slope represents an interval over which the target heart rate is strictly increasing as time passes. A horizontal line segment represents an interval over which there is no change in the target heart rate as time passes, and a line segment with a negative slope represents an interval over which the target heart rate is strictly decreasing as time passes. Over the interval between 40 and 60 minutes, the graph consists of a line segment with a positive slope followed by a line segment with a negative slope, with no horizontal line segment in between, indicating that the target heart rate is strictly increasing then strictly decreasing.

Choice A is incorrect because the graph over the interval between 0 and 30 minutes contains a horizontal line segment, indicating a period in which there was no change in the target heart rate. Choice C is incorrect because the graph over the interval between 50 and 65 minutes consists of a line segment with a negative slope followed by a line segment with a positive slope, indicating that the target heart rate is strictly decreasing then strictly increasing. Choice D is incorrect because the graph over the interval between 70 and 90 minutes contains horizontal line segments and no segment with a negative slope.

QUESTION 2.

Choice C is correct. Substituting 6 for x and 24 for y in $y = kx$ gives $24 = (k)(6)$, which gives $k = 4$. Hence, $y = 4x$. Therefore, when $x = 5$, the value of y is $(4)(5) = 20$. None of the other choices for y is correct because y is a function of x, and so there is only one y-value for a given x-value.

Choices A, B, and D are incorrect. Choice A is the result of using 6 for y and 5 for x when solving for k. Choice B results from using a value of 3 for k when solving for y. Choice D results from using $y = k + x$ instead of $y = kx$.

QUESTION 3.

Choice D is correct. Consider the measures of $\angle 3$ and $\angle 4$ in the figure below.

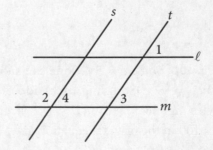

The measure of ∠3 is equal to the measure of ∠1 because they are corresponding angles for the parallel lines ℓ and m intersected by the transversal line t. Similarly, the measure of ∠3 is equal to the measure of ∠4 because they are corresponding angles for the parallel lines s and t intersected by the transversal line m. Since the measure of ∠1 is 35°, the measures of ∠3 and ∠4 are also 35°. Since ∠4 and ∠2 are supplementary, the sum of the measures of these two angles is 180°. Therefore, the measure of ∠2 is $180° − 35° = 145°$.

Choice A is incorrect because 35° is the measure of ∠1, and ∠1 is not congruent to ∠2. Choice B is incorrect because it is the measure of the complementary angle of ∠1, and ∠1 and ∠2 are not complementary angles. Choice C is incorrect because it is double the measure of ∠1.

QUESTION 4.

Choice C is correct. The description "$16 + 4x$ is 10 more than 14" can be written as the equation $16 + 4x = 10 + 14$, which is equivalent to $16 + 4x = 24$. Subtracting 16 from each side of $16 + 4x = 24$ gives $4x = 8$. Since $8x$ is 2 times $4x$, multiplying both sides of $4x = 8$ by 2 gives $8x = 16$. Therefore, the value of $8x$ is 16.

Choice A is incorrect because it is the value of x, not $8x$. Choices B and D are incorrect; those choices may be a result of errors in rewriting $16 + 4x = 10 + 14$. For example, choice D could be the result of subtracting 16 from the left side of the equation and adding 16 to the right side of $16 + 4x = 10 + 14$, giving $4x = 40$ and $8x = 80$.

QUESTION 5.

Choice D is correct. A graph with a strong negative association between d and t would have the points on the graph closely aligned with a line that has a negative slope. The more closely the points on a graph are aligned with a line, the stronger the association between d and t, and a negative slope indicates a negative association. Of the four graphs, the points on graph D are most closely aligned with a line with a negative slope. Therefore, the graph in choice D has the strongest negative association between d and t.

Choice A is incorrect because the points are more scattered than the points in choice D, indicating a weak negative association between d and t. Choice B is incorrect because the points are aligned to either a curve or possibly a line with a small positive slope. Choice C is incorrect because the points are aligned to a line with a positive slope, indicating a positive association between d and t.

QUESTION 6.

Choice D is correct. Since there are 10 grams in 1 decagram, there are $2 \times 10 = 20$ grams in 2 decagrams. Since there are 1,000 milligrams in 1 gram, there are $20 \times 1,000 = 20,000$ milligrams in 20 grams. Therefore, 20,000 1-milligram doses of the medicine can be stored in a 2-decagram container.

Choice A is incorrect; 0.002 is the number of grams in 2 milligrams. Choice B is incorrect; it could result from multiplying by 1,000 and dividing by 10 instead of multiplying by both 1,000 and 10 when converting from decagrams to milligrams. Choice C is incorrect; 2,000 is the number of milligrams in 2 grams, not the number of milligrams in 2 decagrams.

QUESTION 7.

Choice C is correct. Let x represent the number of installations that each unit on the y-axis represents. Then $9x$, $5x$, $6x$, $4x$, and $3.5x$ are the number of rooftops with solar panel installations in cities A, B, C, D, and E, respectively. Since the total number of rooftops is 27,500, it follows that $9x + 5x + 6x + 4x + 3.5x = 27,500$, which simplifies to $27.5x = 27,500$. Thus, $x = 1,000$. Therefore, an appropriate label for the y-axis is "Number of installations (in thousands)."

Choices A, B, and D are incorrect and may result from errors when setting up and calculating the units for the y-axis.

QUESTION 8.

Choice D is correct. If the value of $|n - 1| + 1$ is equal to 0, then $|n - 1| + 1 = 0$. Subtracting 1 from both sides of this equation gives $|n - 1| = -1$. The expression $|n - 1|$ on the left side of the equation is the absolute value of $n - 1$, and the absolute value can never be a negative number. Thus $|n - 1| = -1$ has no solution. Therefore, there are no values for n for which the value of $|n - 1| + 1$ is equal to 0.

Choice A is incorrect because $|0 - 1| + 1 = 1 + 1 = 2$, not 0. Choice B is incorrect because $|1 - 1| + 1 = 0 + 1 = 1$, not 0. Choice C is incorrect because $|2 - 1| + 1 = 1 + 1 = 2$, not 0.

QUESTION 9.

Choice A is correct. Subtracting 1,052 from both sides of the equation $a = 1,052 + 1.08t$ gives $a - 1,052 = 1.08t$. Then dividing both sides of $a - 1,052 = 1.08t$ by 1.08 gives $t = \dfrac{a - 1,052}{1.08}$.

Choices B, C, and D are incorrect and could arise from errors in rewriting $a = 1,052 + 1.08t$. For example, choice B could result if 1,052 is added to the left side of $a = 1,052 + 1.08t$ and subtracted from the right side, and then both sides are divided by 1.08.

QUESTION 10.

Choice B is correct. Substituting 1,000 for a in the equation $a = 1,052 + 1.08t$ gives $1,000 = 1,052 + 1.08t$, and thus $t = \dfrac{-52}{1.08} \approx -48.15$. Of the choices given, $-48°F$ is closest to $-48.15°F$. Since the equation $a = 1,052 + 1.08t$ is linear, it follows that of the choices given, $-48°F$ is the air temperature when the speed of a sound wave is closest to 1,000 feet per second.

Choices A, C, and D are incorrect, and might arise from errors in calculating $\dfrac{-52}{1.08}$ or in rounding the result to the nearest integer. For example, choice C could be the result of rounding -48.15 to -49 instead of -48.

QUESTION 11.

Choice A is correct. Subtracting $3x$ and adding 3 to both sides of $3x - 5 \geq 4x - 3$ gives $-2 \geq x$. Therefore, x is a solution to $3x - 5 \geq 4x - 3$ if and only if x is less than or equal to -2 and x is NOT a solution to $3x - 5 \geq 4x - 3$ if and only if x is greater than -2. Of the choices given, only -1 is greater than -2 and, therefore, cannot be a value of x.

Choices B, C, and D are incorrect because each is a value of x that is less than or equal to -2 and, therefore, could be a solution to the inequality.

QUESTION 12.

Choice C is correct. The average number of seeds per apple is the total number of seeds in the 12 apples divided by the number of apples, which is 12. On the graph, the horizontal axis is the number of seeds per apple and the height of each bar is the number of apples with the corresponding number of seeds. The first bar on the left indicates that 2 apples have 3 seeds each, the second bar indicates that 4 apples have 5 seeds each, the third bar indicates that 1 apple has 6 seeds, the fourth bar indicates that 2 apples have 7 seeds each, and the fifth bar indicates that 3 apples have 9 seeds each. Thus, the total number of seeds for the 12 apples is $(2 \times 3) + (4 \times 5) + (1 \times 6) + (2 \times 7) + (3 \times 9) = 73$, and the average number of seeds per apple is $\dfrac{73}{12} = 6.08$. Of the choices given, 6 is closest to 6.08.

Choice A is incorrect; it is the number of apples represented by the tallest bar but is not the average number of seeds for the 12 apples. Choice B is incorrect; it is the number of seeds per apple corresponding to the tallest bar, but is not the average number of seeds for the 12 apples. Choice D is incorrect; a student might choose this by correctly calculating the average number of seeds, 6.08, but incorrectly rounding up to 7.

QUESTION 13.

Choice C is correct. From the table, there was a total of 310 survey respondents, and 19% of all survey respondents is equivalent to $\frac{19}{100} \times 310 = 58.9$ respondents. Of the choices given, 59, the number of males taking geometry, is closest to 58.9 respondents.

Choices A, B, and D are incorrect because the number of males taking geometry is closer to 58.9 than the number of respondents in each of these categories.

QUESTION 14.

Choice C is correct. The range of the 21 fish is $24 - 8 = 16$ inches, and the range of the 20 fish after the 24-inch measurement is removed is $16 - 8 = 8$ inches. The change in range, 8 inches, is much greater than the change in the mean or median.

Choice A is incorrect. Let m be the mean of the lengths, in inches, of the 21 fish. Then the sum of the lengths, in inches, of the 21 fish is $21m$. After the 24-inch measurement is removed, the sum of the lengths, in inches, of the remaining 20 fish is $21m - 24$, and the mean length, in inches, of these 20 fish is $\frac{21m - 24}{20}$, which is a change of $\frac{24 - m}{20}$ inches. Since m must be between the smallest and largest measurements of the 21 fish, it follows that $8 < m < 24$, from which it can be seen that the change in the mean, in inches, is between $\frac{24 - 24}{20} = 0$ and $\frac{24 - 8}{20} = \frac{4}{5}$, and so must be less than the change in the range, 8 inches. Choice B is incorrect because the median length of the 21 fish is the length of the 11th fish, 12 inches. After removing the 24-inch measurement, the median of the remaining 20 lengths is the average of the 10th and 11th fish, which would be unchanged at 12 inches. Choice D is incorrect because the changes in the mean, median, and range of the measurements are different.

QUESTION 15.

Choice A is correct. The total cost C of renting a boat is the sum of the initial cost to rent the boat plus the product of the cost per hour and the number of hours, h, that the boat is rented. The C-intercept is the point on the C-axis where h, the number of hours the boat is rented, is 0. Therefore, the C-intercept is the initial cost of renting the boat.

Choice B is incorrect because the graph represents the cost of renting only one boat. Choice C is incorrect because the total number of hours of rental is represented by h-values, each of which corresponds to the first coordinate of a point on the graph. Choice D is incorrect because the increase in cost for each additional hour is given by the slope of the line, not by the C-intercept.

QUESTION 16.

Choice C is correct. The relationship between h and C is represented by any equation of the given line. The C-intercept of the line is 5. Since the points $(0, 5)$ and $(1, 8)$ lie on the line, the slope of the line is $\frac{8-5}{1-0}=\frac{3}{1}=3$. Therefore, the relationship between h and C can be represented by $C = 3h + 5$, the slope-intercept equation of the line.

Choices A and D are incorrect because each uses the wrong values for both the slope and intercept. Choice B is incorrect; this choice would result from computing the slope by counting the number of grid lines instead of using the values represented by the axes.

QUESTION 17.

Choice B is correct. The minimum value of the function corresponds to the y-coordinate of the point on the graph that is the lowest along the vertical or y-axis. Since the grid lines are spaced 1 unit apart on each axis, the lowest point along the y-axis has coordinates $(-3, -2)$. Therefore, the value of x at the minimum of $f(x)$ is -3.

Choice A is incorrect; -5 is the smallest value for an x-coordinate of a point on the graph of f, not the lowest point on the graph of f. Choice C is incorrect; it is the minimum value of f, not the value of x that corresponds to the minimum of f. Choice D is incorrect; it is the value of x at the maximum value of f, not at the minimum value of f.

QUESTION 18.

Choice A is correct. Since $(0, 0)$ is a solution to the system of inequalities, substituting 0 for x and 0 for y in the given system must result in two true inequalities. After this substitution, $y < -x + a$ becomes $0 < a$, and $y > x + b$ becomes $0 > b$. Hence, a is positive and b is negative. Therefore, $a > b$.

Choice B is incorrect because $b > a$ cannot be true if b is negative and a is positive. Choice C is incorrect because it is possible to find an example where $(0, 0)$ is a solution to the system, but $|a| < |b|$; for example, if $a = 6$ and $b = -7$. Choice D is incorrect because the equation $a = -b$ could be true, but doesn't have to be true; for example, if $a = 1$ and $b = -2$.

QUESTION 19.

Choice B is correct. To determine the number of salads sold, write and solve a system of two equations. Let x equal the number of salads sold and let y equal the number of drinks sold. Since the number of salads plus the number of drinks sold equals 209, the equation $x + y = 209$ must hold. Since each salad cost \$6.50, each soda cost \$2.00, and the total revenue was \$836.50, the equation $6.50x + 2.00y = 836.50$ must also hold. The equation $x + y = 209$ is equivalent to $2x + 2y = 418$, and subtracting each side of $2x + 2y = 418$ from the respective side of $6.50x + 2.00y = 836.50$ gives $4.5x = 418.50$. Therefore, the number of salads sold, x, was $x = \dfrac{418.50}{4.50} = 93$.

Choices A, C, and D are incorrect and could result from errors in writing the equations and solving the system of equations. For example, choice C could have been obtained by dividing the total revenue, \$836.50, by the total price of a salad and a soda, \$8.50, and then rounding up.

QUESTION 20.

Choice D is correct. Let x be the original price of the computer, in dollars. The discounted price is 20 percent off the original price, so $x - 0.2x = 0.8x$ is the discounted price, in dollars. The tax is 8 percent of the discounted price, so $0.08(0.8x)$ is the tax on the purchase, in dollars. The price p, in dollars, that Alma paid the cashiers is the sum of the discounted price and the tax: $p = 0.8x + (0.08)(0.8x)$ which can be rewritten as $p = 1.08(0.8x)$. Therefore, the original price, x, of the computer, in dollars, can be written as $\dfrac{p}{(0.8)(1.08)}$ in terms of p.

Choices A, B, and C are incorrect; each choice either switches the roles of the original price and the amount Alma paid, or incorrectly combines the results of the discount and the tax as $0.8 + 0.08 = 0.88$ instead of as $(0.8)(1.08)$.

QUESTION 21.

Choice C is correct. The probability that a person from Group Y who recalled at least 1 dream was chosen from the group of all people who recalled at least 1 dream is equal to the number of people in Group Y who recalled at least 1 dream divided by the total number of people in the two groups who recalled at least 1 dream. The number of people in Group Y who recalled at least 1 dream is the sum of the 11 people in Group Y who recalled 1 to 4 dreams and the 68 people in Group Y who recalled 5 or more dreams: $11 + 68 = 79$. The total number of people who recalled at least 1 dream is the sum of the 79 people in Group Y who recalled at least 1 dream, the 28 people in Group X who recalled 1 to 4 dreams, and the 57 people in Group X who recalled 5 or more dreams: $79 + 28 + 57 = 164$. Therefore, the probability is $\dfrac{79}{164}$.

Choice A is incorrect; it is the number of people in Group Y who recalled 5 or more dreams divided by the total number of people in Group Y. Choice B is incorrect; it uses the total number of people in Group Y as the denominator of the probability. Choice D is incorrect; it is the total number of people in the two groups who recalled at least 1 dream divided by the total number of people in the two groups.

QUESTION 22.

Choice B is correct. The average rate of change in the annual budget for agriculture/natural resources from 2008 to 2010 is the total change from to 2008 to 2010 divided by the number of years, which is 2. The total change in the annual budget for agriculture/natural resources from 2008 to 2010 is $488,106 - 358,708 = 129,398$, in thousands of dollars, so the average change in the annual budget for agriculture/natural resources from 2008 to 2010 is $\frac{\$129,398,000}{2} = \$64,699,000$ per year. Of the options given, this average rate of change is closest to \$65,000,000 per year.

Choices A and C are incorrect; they could result from errors in setting up or calculating the average rate of change. Choice D is incorrect; \$130,000,000 is the approximate total change from 2008 to 2010, not the average change from 2008 to 2010.

QUESTION 23.

Choice B is correct. The human resources budget in 2007 was 4,051,050 thousand dollars, and the human resources budget in 2010 was 5,921,379 thousand dollars. Therefore, the ratio of the 2007 budget to the 2010 budget is slightly greater than $\frac{4}{6} = \frac{2}{3}$. Similar estimates for agriculture/natural resources give a ratio of the 2007 budget to the 2010 budget of slightly greater than $\frac{3}{4}$; for education, a ratio of slightly greater than $\frac{2}{3}$; for highways and transportation, a ratio of slightly less than $\frac{5}{6}$; and for public safety, a ratio of slightly greater than $\frac{5}{9}$. Therefore, of the given choices, education's ratio of the 2007 budget to the 2010 budget is closest to that of human resources.

Choices A, C, and D are incorrect because the 2007 budget to 2010 budget ratio for each of these programs in these choices is further from the corresponding ratio for human resources than the ratio for education.

QUESTION 24.

Choice A is correct. The equation of a circle can be written as $(x - h)^2 + (y - k)^2 = r^2$ where (h, k) are the coordinates of the center of the circle and r is the radius of the circle. Since the coordinates of the center of the circle are $(0, 4)$, the equation is $x^2 + (y - 4)^2 = r^2$, where r is the radius. The radius of the circle is the distance from the center, $(0, 4)$, to the given endpoint of a radius, $\left(\frac{4}{3}, 5\right)$. By the distance formula, $r^2 = \left(\frac{4}{3} - 0\right)^2 + (5 - 4)^2 = \frac{25}{9}$. Therefore, an equation of the given circle is $x^2 + (y - 4)^2 = \frac{25}{9}$.

Choice B is incorrect; it results from the incorrect equation $(x + h)^2 + (y + k)^2 = r^2$. Choice C is incorrect; it results from using r instead of r^2 in the equation for the circle. Choice D is incorrect; it results from using the incorrect equation $(x + h)^2 + (y + k)^2 = \frac{1}{r}$.

QUESTION 25.

Choice D is correct. When the ball hits the ground, its height is 0 meters. Substituting 0 for h in $h = -4.9t^2 + 25t$ gives $0 = -4.9t^2 + 25t$, which can be rewritten as $0 = t(-4.9t + 25)$. Thus, the possible values of t are $t = 0$ and $t = \frac{25}{4.9} \approx 5.1$. The time $t = 0$ seconds corresponds to the time the ball is launched from the ground, and the time $t \approx 5.1$ seconds corresponds to the time after launch that the ball hits the ground. Of the given choices, 5.0 seconds is closest to 5.1 seconds, so the ball returns to the ground approximately 5.0 seconds after it is launched.

Choice A, B, and C are incorrect and could arise from conceptual or computation errors while solving $0 = -4.9t^2 + 25t$ for t.

QUESTION 26.

Choice B is correct. Let x represent the number of pears produced by the Type B trees. Then the Type A trees produce 20 percent more pears than x, which is $x + 0.20x = 1.20x$ pears. Since Type A trees produce 144 pears, the equation $1.20x = 144$ holds. Thus $x = \frac{144}{1.20} = 120$. Therefore, the Type B trees produced 120 pears.

Choice A is incorrect because while 144 is reduced by approximately 20 percent, increasing 115 by 20 percent gives 138, not 144. Choice C is incorrect; it results from subtracting 20 from the number of pears produced by the Type A trees. Choice D is incorrect; it results from adding 20 percent of the number of pears produced by Type A trees to the number of pears produced by Type A trees.

QUESTION 27.

Choice C is correct. The area of the field is 100 square meters. Each 1-meter-by-1-meter square has an area of 1 square meter. Thus, on average, the earthworm counts to a depth of 5 centimeters for each of the regions investigated by the students should be about $\frac{1}{100}$ of the total number of earthworms to a depth of 5 centimeters in the entire field. Since the counts for the smaller regions are from 107 to 176, the estimate for the entire field should be between 10,700 and 17,600. Therefore, of the given choices, 15,000 is a reasonable estimate for the number of earthworms to a depth of 5 centimeters in the entire field.

Choice A is incorrect; 150 is the approximate number of earthworms in 1 square meter. Choice B is incorrect; it results from using 10 square meters as the area of the field. Choice D is incorrect; it results from using 1,000 square meters as the area of the field.

QUESTION 28.

Choice C is correct. To determine which quadrant does not contain any solutions to the system of inequalities, graph the inequalities. Graph the inequality $y \geq 2x + 1$ by drawing a line through the y-intercept $(0, 1)$ and the point $(1, 3)$, and graph the inequality $y > \frac{1}{2}x - 1$ by drawing a dashed line through the y-intercept $(0, -1)$ and the point $(2, 0)$, as shown in the figure below.

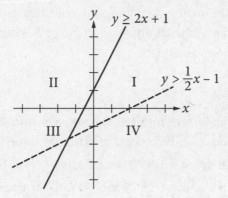

The solution to the system of inequalities is the intersection of the shaded regions above the graphs of both lines. It can be seen that the solutions only include points in quadrants I, II, and III and do not include any points in quadrant IV.

Choices A and B are incorrect because quadrants II and III contain solutions to the system of inequalities, as shown in the figure above. Choice D is incorrect because there are no solutions in quadrant IV.

QUESTION 29.

Choice D is correct. If the polynomial $p(x)$ is divided by $x - 3$, the result can be written as $\frac{p(x)}{x - 3} = q(x) + \frac{r}{x - 3}$, where $q(x)$ is a polynomial and r is the remainder. Since $x - 3$ is a degree 1 polynomial, the remainder is a real number. Hence, $p(x)$ can be written as $p(x) = (x - 3)q(x) + r$, where r is a real number. It is given that $p(3) = -2$ so it must be true that $-2 = p(3) = (3 - 3)q(3) + r = (0)q(3) + r = r$. Therefore, the remainder when $p(x)$ is divided by $x - 3$ is -2.

Choice A is incorrect because $p(3) = -2$ does <u>not</u> imply that $p(5) = 0$. Choices B and C are incorrect because the remainder -2 or its negative, 2, need not be a root of $p(x)$.

QUESTION 30.

Choice D is correct. Any quadratic function q can be written in the form $q(x) = a(x - h)^2 + k$, where a, h, and k are constants and (h, k) is the vertex of the parabola when q is graphed in the coordinate plane. (Depending on the sign of a, the constant k must be the minimum or maximum value of q, and h is the value of x for which $a(x - h)^2 = 0$ and $q(x)$ has value k.) This form can be reached by completing the square in the expression that defines q. The given equation is $y = x^2 - 2x - 15$, and since the coefficient of x is -2, the equation can be written in terms of $(x - 1)^2 = x^2 - 2x + 1$ as follows: $y = x^2 - 2x - 15 = (x^2 - 2x + 1) - 16 = (x - 1)^2 - 16$. From this form of the equation, the coefficients of the vertex can be read as $(1, -16)$.

Choices A and C are incorrect because the coordinates of the vertex A do not appear as constants in these equations. Choice B is incorrect because it is not equivalent to the given equation.

QUESTION 31.

The correct answer is any number between 4 and 6, inclusive. Since Wyatt can husk at least 12 dozen ears of corn per hour, it will take him no more than $\frac{72}{12} = 6$ hours to husk 72 dozen ears of corn. On the other hand, since Wyatt can husk at most 18 dozen ears of corn per hour, it will take him at least $\frac{72}{18} = 4$ hours to husk 72 dozen ears of corn. Therefore, the possible times it could take Wyatt to husk 72 dozen ears of corn are 4 hours to 6 hours, inclusive. Any number between 4 and 6, inclusive, can be gridded as the correct answer.

QUESTION 32.

The correct answer is 107. Since the weight of the empty truck and its driver is 4500 pounds and each box weighs 14 pounds, the weight, in pounds, of the delivery truck, its driver, and x boxes is $4500 + 14x$. This weight is below the bridge's posted weight limit of 6000 pounds if $4500 + 14x < 6000$. That inequality is equivalent to $14x \leq 1500$ or $x < \frac{1500}{14} = 107\frac{1}{7}$. Since the number of packages must be an integer, the maximum possible value for x that will keep the combined weight of the truck, its driver, and the x identical boxes below the bridge's posted weight limit is 107.

QUESTION 33.

The correct answer is $\frac{5}{8}$ or .625. Based on the line graph, the number of portable media players sold in 2008 was 100 million, and the number of portable media players sold in 2011 was 160 million. Therefore, the number of portable media players sold in 2008 is $\frac{100 \text{ million}}{160 \text{ million}}$ of the portable media players sold in 2011. This fraction reduces to $\frac{5}{8}$. Either $\frac{5}{8}$ or its decimal equivalent, .625, may be gridded as the correct answer.

QUESTION 34.

The correct answer is 96. Since each day has a total of 24 hours of time slots available for the station to sell, there is a total of 48 hours of time slots available to sell on Tuesday and Wednesday. Each time slot is a 30-minute interval, which is equal to a $\frac{1}{2}$-hour interval. Therefore, there are a total of $\dfrac{48 \text{ hours}}{\frac{1}{2} \text{ hours/time slot}} = 96$ time slots of 30 minutes for the station to sell on Tuesday and Wednesday.

QUESTION 35.

The correct answer is 6. The volume of a cylinder is $\pi r^2 h$, where r is the radius of the base of the cylinder and h is the height of the cylinder. Since the storage silo is a cylinder with volume 72π cubic yards and height 8 yards, it is true that $72\pi = \pi r^2(8)$, where r is the radius of the base of the cylinder, in yards. Dividing both sides of $72\pi = \pi r^2(8)$ by 8π gives $r^2 = 9$, and so the radius of base of the cylinder is 3 yards. Therefore, the <u>diameter</u> of the base of the cylinder is 6 yards.

QUESTION 36.

The correct answer is 3. The function $h(x)$ is undefined when the denominator of $\dfrac{1}{(x-5)^2 + 4(x-5) + 4}$ is equal to zero. The expression $(x-5)^2 + 4(x-5) + 4$ is a perfect square: $(x-5)^2 + 4(x-5) + 4 = ((x-5)+2)^2$, which can be rewritten as $(x-3)^2$. The expression $(x-3)^2$ is equal to zero if and only if $x = 3$. Therefore, the value of x for which $h(x)$ is undefined is 3.

QUESTION 37.

The correct answer is 1.02. The initial deposit earns 2 percent interest compounded annually. Thus at the end of 1 year, the new value of the account is the initial deposit of \$100 plus 2 percent of the initial deposit: $\$100 + \dfrac{2}{100}(\$100) = \$100(1.02)$. Since the interest is compounded annually, the value at the end of each succeeding year is the sum of the previous year's value plus 2 percent of the previous year's value. This is again equivalent to multiplying the previous year's value by 1.02. Thus, after 2 years, the value will be $\$100(1.02)(1.02) = \$100(1.02)^2$; after 3 years, the value will be $\$100(1.02)^3$; and after t years, the value will be $\$100(1.02)^t$. Therefore, in the formula for the value for Jessica's account after t years, $\$100(x)^t$, the value of x must be 1.02.

QUESTION 38.

The correct answer is 6.11. Jessica made an initial deposit of \$100 into her account. The interest on her account is 2 percent compounded annually, so after 10 years, the value of her initial deposit has been multiplied 10 times by the factor $1 + 0.02 = 1.02$. Hence, after 10 years, Jessica's deposit is worth $\$100(1.02)^{10} = \$121.899$ to the nearest tenth of a cent. Tyshaun made an initial deposit of \$100 into his account. The interest on his account is 2.5 percent compounded annually, so after 10 years, the value of his initial deposit has been multiplied 10 times by the factor $1 + 0.025 = 1.025$. Hence, after 10 years, Tyshaun's deposit is worth $\$100(1.025)^{10} = \$128.008$ to the nearest tenth of a cent. Hence, Jessica's initial deposit earned $\$21.899$ and Tyshaun's initial deposit earned $\$28.008$. Therefore, to the nearest cent, Tyshaun's initial deposit earned $\$6.11$ more than Jessica's initial deposit.

CollegeBoard

SAT® Practice Test #2

IMPORTANT REMINDERS

 1

A No. 2 pencil is required for the test.
Do not use a mechanical pencil or pen.

 2

Sharing any questions with anyone
is a violation of Test Security
and Fairness policies and may result
in your scores being canceled.

This cover is representative of what you'll see on test day.

THIS TEST BOOK MUST NOT BE TAKEN FROM THE ROOM. UNAUTHORIZED
REPRODUCTION OR USE OF ANY PART OF THIS TEST BOOK IS PROHIBITED.

Test begins on the next page.

Reading Test

65 MINUTES, 52 QUESTIONS

Turn to Section 1 of your answer sheet to answer the questions in this section.

DIRECTIONS

Each passage or pair of passages below is followed by a number of questions. After reading each passage or pair, choose the best answer to each question based on what is stated or implied in the passage or passages and in any accompanying graphics (such as a table or graph).

Questions 1-10 are based on the following passage.

This passage is from Charlotte Brontë, *The Professor*, originally published in 1857.

No man likes to acknowledge that he has made a mistake in the choice of his profession, and every man, worthy of the name, will row long against wind
Line and tide before he allows himself to cry out, "I am
5 baffled!" and submits to be floated passively back to land. From the first week of my residence in X—— I felt my occupation irksome. The thing itself—the work of copying and translating business-letters—was a dry and tedious task enough, but had that been
10 all, I should long have borne with the nuisance; I am not of an impatient nature, and influenced by the double desire of getting my living and justifying to myself and others the resolution I had taken to become a tradesman, I should have endured in
15 silence the rust and cramp of my best faculties; I should not have whispered, even inwardly, that I longed for liberty; I should have pent in every sigh by which my heart might have ventured to intimate its distress under the closeness, smoke, monotony, and
20 joyless tumult of Bigben Close, and its panting desire for freer and fresher scenes; I should have set up the image of Duty, the fetish of Perseverance, in my small bedroom at Mrs. King's lodgings, and they two should have been my household gods, from which

25 my darling, my cherished-in-secret, Imagination, the tender and the mighty, should never, either by softness or strength, have severed me. But this was not all; the antipathy which had sprung up between myself and my employer striking deeper root and
30 spreading denser shade daily, excluded me from every glimpse of the sunshine of life; and I began to feel like a plant growing in humid darkness out of the slimy walls of a well.
Antipathy is the only word which can express the
35 feeling Edward Crimsworth had for me—a feeling, in a great measure, involuntary, and which was liable to be excited by every, the most trifling movement, look, or word of mine. My southern accent annoyed him; the degree of education evinced in my language
40 irritated him; my punctuality, industry, and accuracy, fixed his dislike, and gave it the high flavour and poignant relish of envy; he feared that I too should one day make a successful tradesman. Had I been in anything inferior to him, he would not
45 have hated me so thoroughly, but I knew all that he knew, and, what was worse, he suspected that I kept the padlock of silence on mental wealth in which he was no sharer. If he could have once placed me in a ridiculous or mortifying position, he would have
50 forgiven me much, but I was guarded by three faculties—Caution, Tact, Observation; and prowling and prying as was Edward's malignity, it could never baffle the lynx-eyes of these, my natural sentinels. Day by day did his malice watch my tact, hoping it
55 would sleep, and prepared to steal snake-like on its slumber; but tact, if it be genuine, never sleeps.

CONTINUE

I had received my first quarter's wages, and was returning to my lodgings, possessed heart and soul with the pleasant feeling that the master who had
60 paid me grudged every penny of that hard-earned pittance—(I had long ceased to regard Mr. Crimsworth as my brother—he was a hard, grinding master; he wished to be an inexorable tyrant: that was all). Thoughts, not varied but strong,
65 occupied my mind; two voices spoke within me; again and again they uttered the same monotonous phrases. One said: "William, your life is intolerable." The other: "What can you do to alter it?" I walked fast, for it was a cold, frosty night in January; as I
70 approached my lodgings, I turned from a general view of my affairs to the particular speculation as to whether my fire would be out; looking towards the window of my sitting-room, I saw no cheering red gleam.

1

Which choice best summarizes the passage?

A) A character describes his dislike for his new job and considers the reasons why.

B) Two characters employed in the same office become increasingly competitive.

C) A young man regrets privately a choice that he defends publicly.

D) A new employee experiences optimism, then frustration, and finally despair.

2

The main purpose of the opening sentence of the passage is to

A) establish the narrator's perspective on a controversy.

B) provide context useful in understanding the narrator's emotional state.

C) offer a symbolic representation of Edward Crimsworth's plight.

D) contrast the narrator's good intentions with his malicious conduct.

3

During the course of the first paragraph, the narrator's focus shifts from

A) recollection of past confidence to acknowledgment of present self-doubt.

B) reflection on his expectations of life as a tradesman to his desire for another job.

C) generalization about job dissatisfaction to the specifics of his own situation.

D) evaluation of factors making him unhappy to identification of alternatives.

4

The references to "shade" and "darkness" at the end of the first paragraph mainly have which effect?

A) They evoke the narrator's sense of dismay.

B) They reflect the narrator's sinister thoughts.

C) They capture the narrator's fear of confinement.

D) They reveal the narrator's longing for rest.

5

The passage indicates that Edward Crimsworth's behavior was mainly caused by his

A) impatience with the narrator's high spirits.

B) scorn of the narrator's humble background.

C) indignation at the narrator's rash actions.

D) jealousy of the narrator's apparent superiority.

6

The passage indicates that when the narrator began working for Edward Crimsworth, he viewed Crimsworth as a

A) harmless rival.

B) sympathetic ally.

C) perceptive judge.

D) demanding mentor.

CONTINUE

7

Which choice provides the best evidence for the answer to the previous question?

A) Lines 28-31 ("the antipathy . . . life")

B) Lines 38-40 ("My southern . . . irritated him")

C) Lines 54-56 ("Day . . . slumber")

D) Lines 61-62 ("I had . . . brother")

8

At the end of the second paragraph, the comparisons of abstract qualities to a lynx and a snake mainly have the effect of

A) contrasting two hypothetical courses of action.

B) conveying the ferocity of a resolution.

C) suggesting the likelihood of an altercation.

D) illustrating the nature of an adversarial relationship.

9

The passage indicates that, after a long day of work, the narrator sometimes found his living quarters to be

A) treacherous.

B) dreary.

C) predictable.

D) intolerable.

10

Which choice provides the best evidence for the answer to the previous question?

A) Lines 17-21 ("I should . . . scenes")

B) Lines 21-23 ("I should . . . lodgings")

C) Lines 64-67 ("Thoughts . . . phrases")

D) Lines 68-74 ("I walked . . . gleam")

CONTINUE

Questions 11-21 are based on the following passage and supplementary material.

This passage is adapted from Iain King, "Can Economics Be Ethical?" ©2013 by Prospect Publishing.

Recent debates about the economy have rediscovered the question, "is that right?", where "right" means more than just profits or efficiency.
Some argue that because the free markets allow
5 for personal choice, they are already ethical. Others have accepted the ethical critique and embraced corporate social responsibility. But before we can label any market outcome as "immoral," or sneer at economists who try to put a price on being ethical,
10 we need to be clear on what we are talking about.

There are different views on where ethics should apply when someone makes an economic decision. Consider Adam Smith, widely regarded as the founder of modern economics. He was a moral
15 philosopher who believed sympathy for others was the basis for ethics (we would call it empathy nowadays). But one of his key insights in *The Wealth of Nations* was that acting on this empathy could be counter-productive—he observed people becoming
20 better off when they put their own empathy aside, and interacted in a self-interested way. Smith justifies selfish behavior by the outcome. Whenever planners use cost-benefit analysis to justify a new railway line, or someone retrains to boost his or her earning
25 power, or a shopper buys one to get one free, they are using the same approach: empathizing with someone, and seeking an outcome that makes that person as well off as possible—although the person they are empathizing with may be themselves in the
30 future.

Instead of judging consequences, Aristotle said ethics was about having the right character—displaying virtues like courage and honesty. It is a view put into practice whenever
35 business leaders are chosen for their good character. But it is a hard philosophy to teach—just how much loyalty should you show to a manufacturer that keeps losing money? Show too little and you're a "greed is good" corporate raider; too much and you're wasting
40 money on unproductive capital. Aristotle thought there was a golden mean between the two extremes, and finding it was a matter of fine judgment. But if ethics is about character, it's not clear what those characteristics should be.

45 There is yet another approach: instead of rooting ethics in character or the consequences of actions, we can focus on our actions themselves. From this perspective some things are right, some wrong—we should buy fair trade goods, we shouldn't tell lies in
50 advertisements. Ethics becomes a list of commandments, a catalog of "dos" and "don'ts." When a finance official refuses to devalue a currency because they have promised not to, they are defining ethics this way. According to this approach
55 devaluation can still be bad, even if it would make everybody better off.

Many moral dilemmas arise when these three versions pull in different directions but clashes are not inevitable. Take fair trade coffee (coffee that is
60 sold with a certification that indicates the farmers and workers who produced it were paid a fair wage), for example: buying it might have good consequences, be virtuous, and also be the right way to act in a flawed market. Common ground like this
65 suggests that, even without agreement on where ethics applies, ethical economics is still possible.

Whenever we feel queasy about "perfect" competitive markets, the problem is often rooted in a phony conception of people. The model of man on
70 which classical economics is based—an entirely rational and selfish being—is a parody, as John Stuart Mill, the philosopher who pioneered the model, accepted. Most people—even economists— now accept that this "economic man" is a fiction.
75 We behave like a herd; we fear losses more than we hope for gains; rarely can our brains process all the relevant facts.

These human quirks mean we can never make purely "rational" decisions. A new wave of behavioral
80 economists, aided by neuroscientists, is trying to understand our psychology, both alone and in groups, so they can anticipate our decisions in the marketplace more accurately. But psychology can also help us understand why we react in disgust at
85 economic injustice, or accept a moral law as universal. Which means that the relatively new science of human behavior might also define ethics for us. Ethical economics would then emerge from one of the least likely places: economists themselves.

CONTINUE ➤

Regular Coffee Profits
Compared to Fair Trade Coffee
Profits in Tanzania

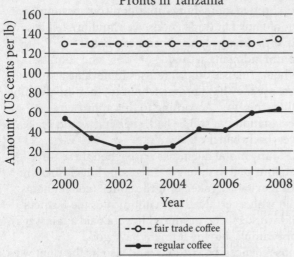

Adapted from the Fair Trade Vancouver website.

11

The main purpose of the passage is to

A) consider an ethical dilemma posed by cost-benefit analysis.

B) describe a psychology study of ethical economic behavior.

C) argue that the free market prohibits ethical economics.

D) examine ways of evaluating the ethics of economics.

12

In the passage, the author anticipates which of the following objections to criticizing the ethics of free markets?

A) Smith's association of free markets with ethical behavior still applies today.

B) Free markets are the best way to generate high profits, so ethics are a secondary consideration.

C) Free markets are ethical because they are made possible by devalued currency.

D) Free markets are ethical because they enable individuals to make choices.

13

Which choice provides the best evidence for the answer to the previous question?

A) Lines 4-5 ("Some . . . ethical")

B) Lines 7-10 ("But . . . about")

C) Lines 21-22 ("Smith . . . outcome")

D) Lines 52-54 ("When . . . way")

CONTINUE

14

As used in line 6, "embraced" most nearly means

A) lovingly held.

B) readily adopted.

C) eagerly hugged.

D) reluctantly used.

15

The main purpose of the fifth paragraph (lines 45-56) is to

A) develop a counterargument to the claim that greed is good.

B) provide support for the idea that ethics is about character.

C) describe a third approach to defining ethical economics.

D) illustrate that one's actions are a result of one's character.

16

As used in line 58, "clashes" most nearly means

A) conflicts.

B) mismatches.

C) collisions.

D) brawls.

17

Which choice best supports the author's claim that there is common ground shared by the different approaches to ethics described in the passage?

A) Lines 11-12 ("There . . . decision")

B) Lines 47-50 ("From . . . advertisements")

C) Lines 59-64 ("Take . . . market")

D) Lines 75-77 ("We . . . facts")

18

The main idea of the final paragraph is that

A) human quirks make it difficult to predict people's ethical decisions accurately.

B) people universally react with disgust when faced with economic injustice.

C) understanding human psychology may help to define ethics in economics.

D) economists themselves will be responsible for reforming the free market.

19

Data in the graph about per-pound coffee profits in Tanzania most strongly support which of the following statements?

A) Fair trade coffee consistently earned greater profits than regular coffee earned.

B) The profits earned from regular coffee did not fluctuate.

C) Fair trade coffee profits increased between 2004 and 2006.

D) Fair trade and regular coffee were earning equal profits by 2008.

20

Data in the graph indicate that the greatest difference between per-pound profits from fair trade coffee and those from regular coffee occurred during which period?

A) 2000 to 2002

B) 2002 to 2004

C) 2004 to 2005

D) 2006 to 2008

CONTINUE

21

Data in the graph provide most direct support for which idea in the passage?

A) Acting on empathy can be counterproductive.

B) Ethical economics is defined by character.

C) Ethical economics is still possible.

D) People fear losses more than they hope for gains.

Questions 22-32 are based on the following passages.

Passage 1 is adapted from Nicholas Carr, "Author Nicholas Carr: The Web Shatters Focus, Rewires Brains." ©2010 by Condé Nast. Passage 2 is from Steven Pinker, "Mind over Mass Media." ©2010 by The New York Times Company.

Passage 1

The mental consequences of our online info-crunching are not universally bad. Certain cognitive skills are strengthened by our use
Line of computers and the Net. These tend to involve
5 more primitive mental functions, such as hand-eye coordination, reflex response, and the processing of visual cues. One much-cited study of video gaming revealed that after just 10 days of playing action games on computers, a group of young people had
10 significantly boosted the speed with which they could shift their visual focus between various images and tasks.

It's likely that Web browsing also strengthens brain functions related to fast-paced problem
15 solving, particularly when it requires spotting patterns in a welter of data. A British study of the way women search for medical information online indicated that an experienced Internet user can, at least in some cases, assess the trustworthiness and
20 probable value of a Web page in a matter of seconds. The more we practice surfing and scanning, the more adept our brain becomes at those tasks.

But it would be a serious mistake to look narrowly at such benefits and conclude that the Web is making
25 us smarter. In a *Science* article published in early 2009, prominent developmental psychologist Patricia Greenfield reviewed more than 40 studies of the effects of various types of media on intelligence and learning ability. She concluded that "every medium
30 develops some cognitive skills at the expense of others." Our growing use of the Net and other screen-based technologies, she wrote, has led to the "widespread and sophisticated development of visual-spatial skills." But those gains go hand in hand
35 with a weakening of our capacity for the kind of "deep processing" that underpins "mindful knowledge acquisition, inductive analysis, critical thinking, imagination, and reflection."

We know that the human brain is highly
40 plastic; neurons and synapses change as circumstances change. When we adapt to a new cultural phenomenon, including the use of a new

CONTINUE ▶

medium, we end up with a different brain, says
Michael Merzenich, a pioneer of the field of
45 neuroplasticity. That means our online habits
continue to reverberate in the workings of our brain
cells even when we're not at a computer. We're
exercising the neural circuits devoted to skimming
and multitasking while ignoring those used for
50 reading and thinking deeply.

Passage 2

    Critics of new media sometimes use science itself
to press their case, citing research that shows how
"experience can change the brain." But cognitive
neuroscientists roll their eyes at such talk. Yes, every
55 time we learn a fact or skill the wiring of the brain
changes; it's not as if the information is stored in the
pancreas. But the existence of neural plasticity does
not mean the brain is a blob of clay pounded into
shape by experience.

60   Experience does not revamp the basic
information-processing capacities of the brain.
Speed-reading programs have long claimed to do just
that, but the verdict was rendered by Woody Allen
after he read Leo Tolstoy's famously long novel
65 *War and Peace* in one sitting: "It was about Russia."
Genuine multitasking, too, has been exposed as a
myth, not just by laboratory studies but by the
familiar sight of an SUV undulating between lanes as
the driver cuts deals on his cell phone.

70   Moreover, the effects of experience are highly
specific to the experiences themselves. If you train
people to do one thing (recognize shapes, solve math
puzzles, find hidden words), they get better at doing
that thing, but almost nothing else. Music doesn't
75 make you better at math, conjugating Latin doesn't
make you more logical, brain-training games don't
make you smarter. Accomplished people don't bulk
up their brains with intellectual calisthenics; they
immerse themselves in their fields. Novelists read
80 lots of novels, scientists read lots of science.

    The effects of consuming electronic media are
likely to be far more limited than the panic implies.
Media critics write as if the brain takes on the
qualities of whatever it consumes, the informational
85 equivalent of "you are what you eat." As with ancient
peoples who believed that eating fierce animals made
them fierce, they assume that watching quick cuts in
rock videos turns your mental life into quick cuts or
that reading bullet points and online postings turns
90 your thoughts into bullet points and online postings.

22

The author of Passage 1 indicates which of the
following about the use of screen-based technologies?

A) It should be thoroughly studied.

B) It makes the brain increasingly rigid.

C) It has some positive effects.

D) It should be widely encouraged.

23

Which choice provides the best evidence for the
answer to the previous question?

A) Lines 3-4 ("Certain . . . Net")

B) Lines 23-25 ("But . . . smarter")

C) Lines 25-29 ("In a . . . ability")

D) Lines 29-31 ("She . . . others")

24

The author of Passage 1 indicates that becoming
adept at using the Internet can

A) make people complacent about their health.

B) undermine the ability to think deeply.

C) increase people's social contacts.

D) improve people's self-confidence.

25

As used in line 40, "plastic" most nearly means

A) creative.

B) artificial.

C) malleable.

D) sculptural.

CONTINUE ▶

26

The author of Passage 2 refers to the novel *War and Peace* primarily to suggest that Woody Allen

A) did not like Tolstoy's writing style.

B) could not comprehend the novel by speed-reading it.

C) had become quite skilled at multitasking.

D) regretted having read such a long novel.

27

According to the author of Passage 2, what do novelists and scientists have in common?

A) They take risks when they pursue knowledge.

B) They are eager to improve their minds.

C) They are curious about other subjects.

D) They become absorbed in their own fields.

28

The analogy in the final sentence of Passage 2 has primarily which effect?

A) It uses ornate language to illustrate a difficult concept.

B) It employs humor to soften a severe opinion of human behavior.

C) It alludes to the past to evoke a nostalgic response.

D) It criticizes the view of a particular group.

29

The main purpose of each passage is to

A) compare brain function in those who play games on the Internet and those who browse on it.

B) report on the problem-solving skills of individuals with varying levels of Internet experience.

C) take a position on increasing financial support for studies related to technology and intelligence.

D) make an argument about the effects of electronic media use on the brain.

30

Which choice best describes the relationship between the two passages?

A) Passage 2 relates first-hand experiences that contrast with the clinical approach in Passage 1.

B) Passage 2 critiques the conclusions drawn from the research discussed in Passage 1.

C) Passage 2 takes a high-level view of a result that Passage 1 examines in depth.

D) Passage 2 predicts the negative reactions that the findings discussed in Passage 1 might produce.

31

On which of the following points would the authors of both passages most likely agree?

A) Computer-savvy children tend to demonstrate better hand-eye coordination than do their parents.

B) Those who criticize consumers of electronic media tend to overreact in their criticism.

C) Improved visual-spatial skills do not generalize to improved skills in other areas.

D) Internet users are unlikely to prefer reading onscreen text to reading actual books.

32

Which choice provides the best evidence that the author of Passage 2 would agree to some extent with the claim attributed to Michael Merzenich in lines 41-43, Passage 1?

A) Lines 51-53 ("Critics . . . brain")

B) Lines 54-56 ("Yes . . . changes")

C) Lines 57-59 ("But . . . experience")

D) Lines 83-84 ("Media . . . consumes")

CONTINUE ▶

Questions 33-42 are based on the following passage.

This passage is adapted from Elizabeth Cady Stanton's address to the 1869 Woman Suffrage Convention in Washington, DC.

I urge a sixteenth amendment, because "manhood suffrage," or a man's government, is civil, religious, and social disorganization. The male element is a
Line destructive force, stern, selfish, aggrandizing, loving
5 war, violence, conquest, acquisition, breeding in the material and moral world alike discord, disorder, disease, and death. See what a record of blood and cruelty the pages of history reveal! Through what slavery, slaughter, and sacrifice, through what
10 inquisitions and imprisonments, pains and persecutions, black codes and gloomy creeds, the soul of humanity has struggled for the centuries, while mercy has veiled her face and all hearts have been dead alike to love and hope!
15 The male element has held high carnival thus far; it has fairly run riot from the beginning, overpowering the feminine element everywhere, crushing out all the diviner qualities in human nature, until we know but little of true manhood and
20 womanhood, of the latter comparatively nothing, for it has scarce been recognized as a power until within the last century. Society is but the reflection of man himself, untempered by woman's thought; the hard iron rule we feel alike in the church, the state, and the
25 home. No one need wonder at the disorganization, at the fragmentary condition of everything, when we remember that man, who represents but half a complete being, with but half an idea on every subject, has undertaken the absolute control of all
30 sublunary matters.

People object to the demands of those whom they choose to call the strong-minded, because they say "the right of suffrage will make the women masculine." That is just the difficulty in which we are
35 involved today. Though disfranchised, we have few women in the best sense; we have simply so many reflections, varieties, and dilutions of the masculine gender. The strong, natural characteristics of womanhood are repressed and ignored in

40 dependence, for so long as man feeds woman she will try to please the giver and adapt herself to his condition. To keep a foothold in society, woman must be as near like man as possible, reflect his ideas, opinions, virtues, motives, prejudices, and vices. She
45 must respect his statutes, though they strip her of every inalienable right, and conflict with that higher law written by the finger of God on her own soul. . . .

. . . [M]an has been molding woman to his ideas by direct and positive influences, while she, if not a
50 negation, has used indirect means to control him, and in most cases developed the very characteristics both in him and herself that needed repression. And now man himself stands appalled at the results of his own excesses, and mourns in bitterness that
55 falsehood, selfishness, and violence are the law of life. The need of this hour is not territory, gold mines, railroads, or specie payments but a new evangel of womanhood, to exalt purity, virtue, morality, true religion, to lift man up into the higher realms of
60 thought and action.

We ask woman's enfranchisement, as the first step toward the recognition of that essential element in government that can only secure the health, strength, and prosperity of the nation. Whatever is done to lift
65 woman to her true position will help to usher in a new day of peace and perfection for the race.

In speaking of the masculine element, I do not wish to be understood to say that all men are hard, selfish, and brutal, for many of the most beautiful
70 spirits the world has known have been clothed with manhood; but I refer to those characteristics, though often marked in woman, that distinguish what is called the stronger sex. For example, the love of acquisition and conquest, the very pioneers of
75 civilization, when expended on the earth, the sea, the elements, the riches and forces of nature, are powers of destruction when used to subjugate one man to another or to sacrifice nations to ambition.

Here that great conservator of woman's love, if
80 permitted to assert itself, as it naturally would in freedom against oppression, violence, and war, would hold all these destructive forces in check, for woman knows the cost of life better than man does, and not with her consent would one drop of blood
85 ever be shed, one life sacrificed in vain.

CONTINUE

33

The central problem that Stanton describes in the passage is that women have been

A) denied equal educational opportunities, which has kept them from reaching their potential.

B) prevented from exerting their positive influence on men, which has led to societal breakdown.

C) prevented from voting, which has resulted in poor candidates winning important elections.

D) blocked by men from serving as legislators, which has allowed the creation of unjust laws.

34

Stanton uses the phrase "high carnival" (line 15) mainly to emphasize what she sees as the

A) utter domination of women by men.

B) freewheeling spirit of the age.

C) scandalous decline in moral values.

D) growing power of women in society.

35

Stanton claims that which of the following was a relatively recent historical development?

A) The control of society by men

B) The spread of war and injustice

C) The domination of domestic life by men

D) The acknowledgment of women's true character

36

Which choice provides the best evidence for the answer to the previous question?

A) Lines 3-7 ("The male . . . death")

B) Lines 15-22 ("The male . . . century")

C) Lines 22-25 ("Society . . . home")

D) Lines 48-52 ("[M]an . . . repression")

37

As used in line 24, "rule" most nearly refers to

A) a general guideline.

B) a controlling force.

C) an established habit.

D) a procedural method.

38

It can reasonably be inferred that "the strong-minded" (line 32) was a term generally intended to

A) praise women who fight for their long-denied rights.

B) identify women who demonstrate intellectual skill.

C) criticize women who enter male-dominated professions.

D) condemn women who agitate for the vote for their sex.

39

As used in line 36, "best" most nearly means

A) superior.

B) excellent.

C) genuine.

D) rarest.

40

Stanton contends that the situation she describes in the passage has become so dire that even men have begun to

A) lament the problems they have created.

B) join the call for woman suffrage.

C) consider women their social equals.

D) ask women how to improve civic life.

CONTINUE

Which choice provides the best evidence for the answer to the previous question?

A) Lines 25-30 ("No one . . . matters")

B) Lines 53-55 ("And now . . . life")

C) Lines 56-60 ("The need . . . action")

D) Lines 61-64 ("We ask . . . nation")

The sixth paragraph (lines 67-78) is primarily concerned with establishing a contrast between

A) men and women.

B) the spiritual world and the material world.

C) bad men and good men.

D) men and masculine traits.

CONTINUE

Questions 43-52 are based on the following passage and supplementary material.

This passage is adapted from Geoffrey Giller, "Long a Mystery, How 500-Meter-High Undersea Waves Form Is Revealed." ©2014 by Scientific American.

Some of the largest ocean waves in the world are nearly impossible to see. Unlike other large waves, these rollers, called internal waves, do not ride the
Line ocean surface. Instead, they move underwater,
5 undetectable without the use of satellite imagery or sophisticated monitoring equipment. Despite their hidden nature, internal waves are fundamental parts of ocean water dynamics, transferring heat to the ocean depths and bringing up cold water from below.
10 And they can reach staggering heights—some as tall as skyscrapers.

Because these waves are involved in ocean mixing and thus the transfer of heat, understanding them is crucial to global climate modeling, says Tom
15 Peacock, a researcher at the Massachusetts Institute of Technology. Most models fail to take internal waves into account. "If we want to have more and more accurate climate models, we have to be able to capture processes such as this," Peacock says.
20 Peacock and his colleagues tried to do just that. Their study, published in November in *Geophysical Research Letters*, focused on internal waves generated in the Luzon Strait, which separates Taiwan and the Philippines. Internal waves in this region, thought to
25 be some of the largest in the world, can reach about 500 meters high. "That's the same height as the Freedom Tower that's just been built in New York," Peacock says.

Although scientists knew of this phenomenon in
30 the South China Sea and beyond, they didn't know exactly how internal waves formed. To find out, Peacock and a team of researchers from M.I.T. and Woods Hole Oceanographic Institution worked with France's National Center for Scientific Research
35 using a giant facility there called the Coriolis Platform. The rotating platform, about 15 meters (49.2 feet) in diameter, turns at variable speeds and can simulate Earth's rotation. It also has walls, which means scientists can fill it with water and create
40 accurate, large-scale simulations of various oceanographic scenarios.

Peacock and his team built a carbon-fiber resin scale model of the Luzon Strait, including the islands and surrounding ocean floor topography. Then they
45 filled the platform with water of varying salinity to replicate the different densities found at the strait, with denser, saltier water below and lighter, less briny water above. Small particles were added to the solution and illuminated with lights from below in
50 order to track how the liquid moved. Finally, they re-created tides using two large plungers to see how the internal waves themselves formed.

The Luzon Strait's underwater topography, with a distinct double-ridge shape, turns out to be
55 responsible for generating the underwater waves. As the tide rises and falls and water moves through the strait, colder, denser water is pushed up over the ridges into warmer, less dense layers above it. This action results in bumps of colder water trailed
60 by warmer water that generate an internal wave. As these waves move toward land, they become steeper—much the same way waves at the beach become taller before they hit the shore—until they break on a continental shelf.
65 The researchers were also able to devise a mathematical model that describes the movement and formation of these waves. Whereas the model is specific to the Luzon Strait, it can still help researchers understand how internal waves are
70 generated in other places around the world. Eventually, this information will be incorporated into global climate models, making them more accurate. "It's very clear, within the context of these [global climate] models, that internal waves play a role in
75 driving ocean circulations," Peacock says.

CONTINUE

CHANGES IN DEPTH OF ISOTHERMS*
IN AN INTERNAL WAVE OVER A 24-HOUR PERIOD

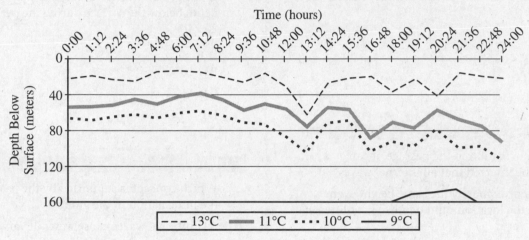

* Bands of water of constant temperatures

Adapted from Justin Small et al., "Internal Solitons in the Ocean: Prediction from SAR." ©1998 by Oceanography, Defence Evaluation and Research Agency.

43

The first paragraph serves mainly to

A) explain how a scientific device is used.

B) note a common misconception about an event.

C) describe a natural phenomenon and address its importance.

D) present a recent study and summarize its findings.

44

As used in line 19, "capture" is closest in meaning to

A) control.

B) record.

C) secure.

D) absorb.

45

According to Peacock, the ability to monitor internal waves is significant primarily because

A) it will allow scientists to verify the maximum height of such waves.

B) it will allow researchers to shift their focus to improving the quality of satellite images.

C) the study of wave patterns will enable regions to predict and prevent coastal damage.

D) the study of such waves will inform the development of key scientific models.

46

Which choice provides the best evidence for the answer to the previous question?

A) Lines 1-2 ("Some . . . see")

B) Lines 4-6 ("they . . . equipment")

C) Lines 17-19 ("If . . . this")

D) Lines 24-26 ("Internal . . . high")

CONTINUE ►

47

As used in line 65, "devise" most nearly means

A) create.

B) solve.

C) imagine.

D) begin.

48

Based on information in the passage, it can reasonably be inferred that all internal waves

A) reach approximately the same height even though the locations and depths of continental shelves vary.

B) may be caused by similar factors but are influenced by the distinct topographies of different regions.

C) can be traced to inconsistencies in the tidal patterns of deep ocean water located near islands.

D) are generated by the movement of dense water over a relatively flat section of the ocean floor.

49

Which choice provides the best evidence for the answer to the previous question?

A) Lines 29-31 ("Although . . . formed")

B) Lines 56-58 ("As the . . . it")

C) Lines 61-64 ("As these . . . shelf")

D) Lines 67-70 ("Whereas . . . world")

50

In the graph, which isotherm displays an increase in depth below the surface during the period 19:12 to 20:24?

A) 9°C

B) 10°C

C) 11°C

D) 13°C

51

Which concept is supported by the passage and by the information in the graph?

A) Internal waves cause water of varying salinity to mix.

B) Internal waves push denser water above layers of less dense water.

C) Internal waves push bands of cold water above bands of warmer water.

D) Internal waves do not rise to break the ocean's surface.

52

How does the graph support the author's point that internal waves affect ocean water dynamics?

A) It demonstrates that wave movement forces warmer water down to depths that typically are colder.

B) It reveals the degree to which an internal wave affects the density of deep layers of cold water.

C) It illustrates the change in surface temperature that takes place during an isolated series of deep waves.

D) It shows that multiple waves rising near the surface of the ocean disrupt the flow of normal tides.

STOP

If you finish before time is called, you may check your work on this section only.

Do not turn to any other section.

No Test Material On This Page

Writing and Language Test

35 MINUTES, 44 QUESTIONS

Turn to Section 2 of your answer sheet to answer the questions in this section.

DIRECTIONS

Each passage below is accompanied by a number of questions. For some questions, you will consider how the passage might be revised to improve the expression of ideas. For other questions, you will consider how the passage might be edited to correct errors in sentence structure, usage, or punctuation. A passage or a question may be accompanied by one or more graphics (such as a table or graph) that you will consider as you make revising and editing decisions.

Some questions will direct you to an underlined portion of a passage. Other questions will direct you to a location in a passage or ask you to think about the passage as a whole.

After reading each passage, choose the answer to each question that most effectively improves the quality of writing in the passage or that makes the passage conform to the conventions of standard written English. Many questions include a "NO CHANGE" option. Choose that option if you think the best choice is to leave the relevant portion of the passage as it is.

Questions 1-11 are based on the following passage.

Librarians Help Navigate in the Digital Age

In recent years, public libraries in the United States have experienced **1** reducing in their operating funds due to cuts imposed at the federal, state, and local government levels. **2** However, library staffing has been cut by almost four percent since 2008, and the demand for librarians continues to decrease, even though half of public libraries report that they have an insufficient number of staff to meet their patrons' needs. Employment in all job sectors in the United States is projected to grow by fourteen percent over the next

1
A) NO CHANGE
B) reductions
C) deducting
D) deducts

2
A) NO CHANGE
B) Consequently,
C) Nevertheless,
D) Previously,

Unauthorized copying or reuse of any part of this page is illegal.

468

CONTINUE ➡

decade, yet the expected growth rate for librarians is predicted to be only seven percent, or half of the overall rate. This trend, combined with the increasing accessibility of information via the Internet, **3** has led some to claim that librarianship is in decline as a profession. As public libraries adapt to rapid technological advances in information distribution, librarians' roles are actually expanding.

The share of library materials that is in nonprint formats **4** is increasing steadily; in 2010, at least 18.5 million e-books were available **5** for them to circulate. As a result, librarians must now be proficient curators of electronic information, compiling, **6** catalog, and updating these collections. But perhaps even more importantly, librarians function as first responders for their communities' computer needs. Since

3

A) NO CHANGE
B) have
C) which have
D) which has

4

At this point, the writer is considering adding the following information.

—e-books, audio and video materials, and online journals—

Should the writer make this addition here?

A) Yes, because it provides specific examples of the materials discussed in the sentence.
B) Yes, because it illustrates the reason for the increase mentioned later in the sentence.
C) No, because it interrupts the flow of the sentence by supplying irrelevant information.
D) No, because it weakens the focus of the passage by discussing a subject other than librarians.

5

A) NO CHANGE
B) to be circulated by them.
C) for their circulating.
D) for circulation.

6

A) NO CHANGE
B) librarians cataloging,
C) to catalog,
D) cataloging,

CONTINUE

one of the fastest growing library services is public access computer use, there is great demand for computer instruction. [7] In fact, librarians' training now includes courses on research and Internet search methods. Many of whom teach classes in Internet navigation, database and software use, and digital information literacy. While these classes are particularly helpful to young students developing basic research skills, [8] but adult patrons can also benefit from librarian assistance in that they can acquire job-relevant computer skills. [9] Free to all who utilize their services, public libraries and librarians are especially valuable, because they offer free resources that may be difficult to find elsewhere, such as help with online job

7

Which choice most effectively combines the underlined sentences?

A) In fact, librarians' training now includes courses on research and Internet search methods; many librarians teach classes in Internet navigation, database and software use, and digital information literacy is taught by them.

B) In fact, many librarians, whose training now includes courses on research and Internet search methods, teach classes in Internet navigation, database and software use, and digital information literacy.

C) Training now includes courses on research and Internet search methods; many librarians, in fact, are teaching classes in Internet navigation, database and software use, and digital information literacy.

D) Including courses on research and Internet search methods in their training is, in fact, why many librarians teach classes in Internet navigation, database and software use, and digital information literacy.

8

A) NO CHANGE
B) and
C) for
D) DELETE the underlined portion.

9

Which choice most effectively sets up the examples given at the end of the sentence?

A) NO CHANGE
B) During periods of economic recession,
C) Although their value cannot be measured,
D) When it comes to the free services libraries provide,

Unauthorized copying or reuse of any part of this page is illegal.

470

CONTINUE ▶

searches as well as résumé and job material development. An overwhelming number of public libraries also report that they provide help with electronic government resources related to income taxes, **10** law troubles, and retirement programs.

In sum, the Internet does not replace the need for librarians, and librarians are hardly obsolete. **11** Like books, librarians have been around for a long time, but the Internet is extremely useful for many types of research.

10

A) NO CHANGE

B) legal issues,

C) concerns related to law courts,

D) matters for the law courts,

11

Which choice most clearly ends the passage with a restatement of the writer's primary claim?

A) NO CHANGE

B) Although their roles have diminished significantly, librarians will continue to be employed by public libraries for the foreseeable future.

C) The growth of electronic information has led to a diversification of librarians' skills and services, positioning them as savvy resource specialists for patrons.

D) However, given their extensive training and skills, librarians who have been displaced by budget cuts have many other possible avenues of employment.

CONTINUE

Questions 12-22 are based on the following passage.

Tiny Exhibit, Big Impact

— 1 —

The first time I visited the Art Institute of Chicago, I expected to be impressed by its famous large paintings. **12** On one hand, I couldn't wait to view **13** painter, Georges Seurat's, 10-foot-wide *A Sunday Afternoon on the Island of La Grande Jatte* in its full size. It took me by surprise, then, when my favorite exhibit at the museum was one of **14** it's tiniest; the Thorne Miniature Rooms.

12

A) NO CHANGE
B) For instance,
C) However,
D) Similarly,

13

A) NO CHANGE
B) painter, Georges Seurat's
C) painter Georges Seurat's,
D) painter Georges Seurat's

14

A) NO CHANGE
B) its tiniest;
C) its tiniest:
D) it's tiniest,

Unauthorized copying or reuse of any part of this page is illegal.

472

CONTINUE

— 2 —

Viewing the exhibit, I was amazed by the intricate details of some of the more ornately decorated rooms. I marveled at a replica of a salon (a formal living room) dating back to the reign of French king Louis XV. **15** Built into the dark paneled walls are bookshelves stocked with leather-bound volumes. The couch and chairs, in keeping with the style of the time, are characterized by elegantly curved arms and **16** legs, they are covered in luxurious velvet. A dime-sized portrait of a French aristocratic woman hangs in a golden frame.

— 3 —

This exhibit showcases sixty-eight miniature rooms inserted into a wall at eye level. Each furnished room consists of three walls; the fourth wall is a glass pane through which museumgoers observe. The rooms and their furnishings were painstakingly created to scale at 1/12th their actual size, so that one inch in the exhibit correlates with one foot in real life. A couch, for example, is seven inches long, and **17** that is based on a seven-foot-long couch. Each room represents a distinctive style of European, American, or Asian interior design from the thirteenth to twentieth centuries.

15

At this point, the writer is considering adding the following sentence.

Some scholars argue that the excesses of King Louis XV's reign contributed significantly to the conditions that resulted in the French Revolution.

Should the writer make this addition here?

A) Yes, because it provides historical context for the Thorne Miniature Rooms exhibit.

B) Yes, because it explains why salons are often ornately decorated.

C) No, because it interrupts the paragraph's description of the miniature salon.

D) No, because it implies that the interior designer of the salon had political motivations.

16

A) NO CHANGE
B) legs, the couch and chairs
C) legs and
D) legs,

17

Which choice gives a second supporting example that is most similar to the example already in the sentence?

A) NO CHANGE
B) a tea cup is about a quarter of an inch.
C) there are even tiny cushions on some.
D) household items are also on this scale.

— 4 —

The plainer rooms are more sparsely **18** furnished. Their architectural features, furnishings, and decorations are just as true to the periods they represent. One of my favorite rooms in the whole exhibit, in fact, is an 1885 summer kitchen. The room is simple but spacious, with a small sink and counter along one wall, a cast-iron wood stove and some hanging pots and pans against another wall, and **19** a small table under a window of the third wall. Aside from a few simple wooden chairs placed near the edges of the room, the floor is open and obviously well worn.

18

Which choice most effectively combines the sentences at the underlined portion?

A) furnished by their

B) furnished, but their

C) furnished: their

D) furnished, whereas

19

Which choice most closely matches the stylistic pattern established earlier in the sentence?

A) NO CHANGE

B) a small table is under the third wall's window.

C) the third wall has a window and small table.

D) the third wall has a small table against it and a window.

CONTINUE ▶

— 5 —

As I walked through the exhibit, I overheard a [20] visitors' remark, "You know, that grandfather clock actually runs. Its glass door swings open, and the clock can be wound up." [21] Dotted with pin-sized knobs, another visitor noticed my fascination with a tiny writing desk and its drawers. "All of those little drawers pull out. And you see that hutch? Can you believe it has a secret compartment?" Given the exquisite craftsmanship and level of detail I'd already seen, I certainly could.

Question [22] asks about the previous passage as a whole.

20

A) NO CHANGE

B) visitors remarking,

C) visitor remarked,

D) visitor remark,

21

A) NO CHANGE

B) Another visitor, dotted with pin-sized knobs, noticed my fascination with a tiny writing desk and its drawers.

C) Another visitor dotted with pin-sized knobs noticed my fascination with a tiny writing desk and its drawers.

D) Another visitor noticed my fascination with a tiny writing desk and its drawers, dotted with pin-sized knobs.

Think about the previous passage as a whole as you answer question 22.

22

To make the passage most logical, paragraph 2 should be placed

A) where it is now.

B) after paragraph 3.

C) after paragraph 4.

D) after paragraph 5.

Unauthorized copying or reuse of any part of this page is illegal.

CONTINUE ▶

475

Questions 23-33 are based on the following passage and supplementary material.

Environmentalist Otters

It has long been known that the sea otters 23 living along the West Coast of North America help keep kelp forests in their habitat healthy and vital. They do this by feeding on sea urchins and other herbivorous invertebrates that graze voraciously on kelp. With sea otters to keep the population of sea urchins in check, kelp forests can flourish. In fact, 24 two years or less of sea otters can completely eliminate sea urchins in a coastal area (see chart).

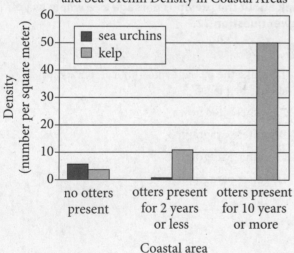

Effects of Sea Otter Presence on Kelp and Sea Urchin Density in Coastal Areas

Adapted from David O. Duggins, "Kelp Beds and Sea Otters: An Experimental Approach." ©1980 by the Ecological Society of America.

Without sea otters present, 25 nevertheless, kelp forests run the danger of becoming barren stretches of coastal wasteland known as urchin barrens.

23

A) NO CHANGE

B) living along the West Coast of North America, they help

C) that live along the West Coast of North America and help to

D) that live along the West Coast of North America, where they help

24

Which choice offers an accurate interpretation of the data in the chart?

A) NO CHANGE

B) even two years or less of sea otter presence can reduce the sea urchin threat

C) kelp density increases proportionally as sea urchin density increases

D) even after sea otters were present for ten years or more, kelp density was still lower than sea urchin density

25

A) NO CHANGE

B) however,

C) hence,

D) likewise,

CONTINUE

[1] What was less well-known, until recently at least, was how this relationship among sea otters, sea urchins, and kelp forests might help fight global warming. [2] The amount of carbon dioxide in the atmosphere has increased 40 percent **26** . [3] A recent study by two professors at the University of California, Santa Cruz, Chris Wilmers and James Estes, **27** suggests, that kelp forests protected by sea otters can absorb as much as twelve times the amount of carbon dioxide from the atmosphere as those where sea urchins are allowed to **28** devour the kelp. [4] Like **29** their terrestrial plant cousins, kelp removes carbon dioxide from the atmosphere, turning it into sugar fuel through photosynthesis, and releases oxygen back into the air.

26

At this point, the writer is considering adding the following information.

> since the start of the Industrial Revolution, resulting in a rise in global temperatures

Should the writer make this addition here?

A) Yes, because it establishes the relationship between the level of carbon dioxide in the atmosphere and global warming.

B) Yes, because it explains the key role sea otters, sea urchins, and kelp forests play in combating global warming.

C) No, because it contradicts the claim made in the previous paragraph that sea otters help keep kelp forests healthy.

D) No, because it mentions the Industrial Revolution, blurring the focus of the paragraph.

27

A) NO CHANGE

B) suggests—that

C) suggests, "that

D) suggests that

28

A) NO CHANGE

B) dispatch

C) overindulge on

D) dispose of

29

A) NO CHANGE

B) they're

C) its

D) it's

CONTINUE

[5] Scientists knew this but did not recognize [30] how large a role they played in helping kelp forests to significantly decrease the amount of carbon dioxide in the atmosphere. [6] Far from making no difference to the ecosystem, the presence of otters was found to increase the carbon storage of kelp forests by 4.4 to 8.7 megatons annually, offsetting the amount of carbon dioxide emitted by three million to six million passenger cars each year. [31]

Wilmers and Estes caution, however, that [32] having more otters will not automatically solve the problem of higher levels of carbon dioxide in the air. But they suggest that the presence of otters provides a good model of how carbon can be sequestered, [33] or removed; from the atmosphere through the management of animal populations. If ecologists can better understand what kinds of impacts animals might have on the environment, Wilmers contends, "there might be opportunities for win-win conservation scenarios, whereby animal species are protected or enhanced, and carbon gets sequestered."

[30]
A) NO CHANGE
B) how large a role that it played
C) how large a role sea otters played
D) that they played such a large role

[31]
Where is the most logical place in this paragraph to add the following sentence?

What Wilmers and Estes discovered in their study, therefore, surprised them.

A) After sentence 1
B) After sentence 3
C) After sentence 4
D) After sentence 5

[32]
A) NO CHANGE
B) increasing the otter population
C) the otters multiplying
D) having more otters than other locations

[33]
A) NO CHANGE
B) or removed from,
C) or, removed from,
D) or removed, from

CONTINUE

Questions 34-44 are based on the following passage.

A Quick Fix in a Throwaway Culture

    Planned obsolescence, a practice <u>34 at which</u> products are designed to have a limited period of 35 <u>usefulness,</u> has been a cornerstone of manufacturing strategy for the past 80 years. This approach increases sales, but it also stands in <u>36 austere</u> contrast to a time when goods were produced to be durable. Planned obsolescence wastes materials as well as energy in making and shipping new products. It also reinforces the belief that it is easier to replace goods than to mend them, as repair shops are rare and <u>37 repair methods are often specialized.</u> In 2009, an enterprising movement, the Repair Café, challenged this widely accepted belief.

34

A) NO CHANGE

B) from which

C) so that

D) whereby

35

A) NO CHANGE

B) usefulness—

C) usefulness;

D) usefulness

36

A) NO CHANGE

B) egregious

C) unmitigated

D) stark

37

Which choice provides information that best supports the claim made by this sentence?

A) NO CHANGE

B) obsolete goods can become collectible items.

C) no one knows whether something will fall into disrepair again.

D) new designs often have "bugs" that must be worked out.

CONTINUE

[1] More like a [38] fair then an actual café, the first Repair Café took place in Amsterdam, the Netherlands. [2] It was the brainchild of former journalist Martine Postma, [39] wanting to take a practical stand in a throwaway culture. [3] Her goals were [40] straightforward, however: reduce waste, maintain and perpetuate knowledge and skills, and strengthen community. [4] Participants bring all manner of damaged articles—clothing, appliances, furniture, and more—to be repaired by a staff of volunteer specialists including tailors, electricians, and carpenters. [5] Since the inaugural Repair Café, others have been hosted in theater foyers, community centers, hotels, and auditoriums. [6] While [41] they await for service, patrons can enjoy coffee and snacks and mingle with their neighbors in need. [42]

38

A) NO CHANGE
B) fair than
C) fare than
D) fair, then

39

A) NO CHANGE
B) whom wants
C) who wanted
D) she wanted

40

A) NO CHANGE
B) straightforward, therefore:
C) straightforward, nonetheless:
D) straightforward:

41

A) NO CHANGE
B) awaiting
C) they waited
D) waiting

42

To make this paragraph most logical, sentence 5 should be placed
A) where it is now.
B) before sentence 1.
C) after sentence 3.
D) after sentence 6.

CONTINUE

Though only about 3 percent of the Netherlands' municipal waste ends up in landfills, Repair Cafés still raise awareness about what may otherwise be mindless acts of waste by providing a venue for people to share and learn valuable skills that are in danger of being lost. **43** It is easy to classify old but fixable items as "junk" in an era that places great emphasis on the next big thing. In helping people consider how the goods they use on a daily basis work and are made, Repair Cafés restore a sense of relationship between human beings and material goods.

Though the concept remained a local trend at first, international Repair Cafés, all affiliated with the Dutch Repair Café via its website, have since arisen in France, Germany, South Africa, the United States, and other countries **44** on top of that. The original provides a central source for start-up tips and tools, as well as marketing advice to new Repair Cafés. As a result, the Repair Café has become a global network united by common ideals. Ironically, innovators are now looking back to old ways of doing things and applying them in today's cities in an effort to transform the way people relate to and think about the goods they consume.

43

At this point, the writer is considering adding the following sentence.

> As the number of corporate and service-based jobs has increased, the need for people who work with their hands has diminished.

Should the writer make this addition here?

A) Yes, because it provides an example of specific repair skills being lost.

B) Yes, because it elaborates on the statistic about the Netherlands' municipal waste.

C) No, because it blurs the paragraph's focus by introducing a topic that is not further explained.

D) No, because it contradicts the claims made in the rest of the paragraph.

44

A) NO CHANGE

B) in addition.

C) likewise.

D) DELETE the underlined portion, and end the sentence with a period.

STOP

If you finish before time is called, you may check your work on this section only.
Do not turn to any other section.

Math Test – No Calculator

25 MINUTES, 20 QUESTIONS

Turn to Section 3 of your answer sheet to answer the questions in this section.

DIRECTIONS

For questions 1-15, solve each problem, choose the best answer from the choices provided, and fill in the corresponding circle on your answer sheet. **For questions 16-20**, solve the problem and enter your answer in the grid on the answer sheet. Please refer to the directions before question 16 on how to enter your answers in the grid. You may use any available space in your test booklet for scratch work.

NOTES

1. The use of a calculator **is not permitted**.

2. All variables and expressions used represent real numbers unless otherwise indicated.

3. Figures provided in this test are drawn to scale unless otherwise indicated.

4. All figures lie in a plane unless otherwise indicated.

5. Unless otherwise indicated, the domain of a given function f is the set of all real numbers x for which $f(x)$ is a real number.

REFERENCE

    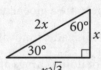

$A = \pi r^2$ $A = \ell w$ $A = \dfrac{1}{2} bh$ $c^2 = a^2 + b^2$ Special Right Triangles
$C = 2\pi r$

$V = \ell w h$ $V = \pi r^2 h$ $V = \dfrac{4}{3} \pi r^3$ $V = \dfrac{1}{3} \pi r^2 h$ $V = \dfrac{1}{3} \ell w h$

The number of degrees of arc in a circle is 360.
The number of radians of arc in a circle is 2π.
The sum of the measures in degrees of the angles of a triangle is 180.

CONTINUE

1

If $5x + 6 = 10$, what is the value of $10x + 3$?

A) 4

B) 9

C) 11

D) 20

2

$$x + y = 0$$
$$3x - 2y = 10$$

Which of the following ordered pairs (x, y) satisfies the system of equations above?

A) $(3, -2)$

B) $(2, -2)$

C) $(-2, 2)$

D) $(-2, -2)$

3

A landscaping company estimates the price of a job, in dollars, using the expression $60 + 12nh$, where n is the number of landscapers who will be working and h is the total number of hours the job will take using n landscapers. Which of the following is the best interpretation of the number 12 in the expression?

A) The company charges \$12 per hour for each landscaper.

B) A minimum of 12 landscapers will work on each job.

C) The price of every job increases by \$12 every hour.

D) Each landscaper works 12 hours a day.

4

$$9a^4 + 12a^2b^2 + 4b^4$$

Which of the following is equivalent to the expression shown above?

A) $(3a^2 + 2b^2)^2$

B) $(3a + 2b)^4$

C) $(9a^2 + 4b^2)^2$

D) $(9a + 4b)^4$

CONTINUE

5

$$\sqrt{2k^2 + 17} - x = 0$$

If $k > 0$ and $x = 7$ in the equation above, what is the value of k ?

A) 2

B) 3

C) 4

D) 5

6

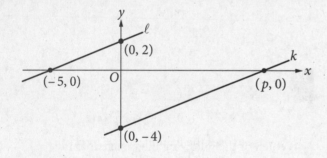

In the xy-plane above, line ℓ is parallel to line k. What is the value of p ?

A)   4

B)   5

C)   8

D) 10

7

If $\dfrac{x^{a^2}}{x^{b^2}} = x^{16}$, $x > 1$, and $a + b = 2$, what is the value

of $a - b$?

A)   8

B) 14

C) 16

D) 18

8

$$nA = 360$$

The measure A, in degrees, of an exterior angle of a regular polygon is related to the number of sides, n, of the polygon by the formula above. If the measure of an exterior angle of a regular polygon is greater than $50°$, what is the greatest number of sides it can have?

A) 5

B) 6

C) 7

D) 8

CONTINUE

9

The graph of a line in the xy-plane has slope 2 and contains the point $(1, 8)$. The graph of a second line passes through the points $(1, 2)$ and $(2, 1)$. If the two lines intersect at the point (a, b), what is the value of $a + b$?

A)   4

B)   3

C)   −1

D)   −4

10

Which of the following equations has a graph in the xy-plane for which y is always greater than or equal to -1 ?

A) $y = |x| - 2$

B) $y = x^2 - 2$

C) $y = (x - 2)^2$

D) $y = x^3 - 2$

11

Which of the following complex numbers is equivalent to $\dfrac{3 - 5i}{8 + 2i}$? (Note: $i = \sqrt{-1}$)

A) $\dfrac{3}{8} - \dfrac{5i}{2}$

B) $\dfrac{3}{8} + \dfrac{5i}{2}$

C) $\dfrac{7}{34} - \dfrac{23i}{34}$

D) $\dfrac{7}{34} + \dfrac{23i}{34}$

12

$$R = \frac{F}{N + F}$$

A website uses the formula above to calculate a seller's rating, R, based on the number of favorable reviews, F, and unfavorable reviews, N. Which of the following expresses the number of favorable reviews in terms of the other variables?

A) $F = \dfrac{RN}{R - 1}$

B) $F = \dfrac{RN}{1 - R}$

C) $F = \dfrac{N}{1 - R}$

D) $F = \dfrac{N}{R - 1}$

CONTINUE

13

What is the sum of all values of m that satisfy $2m^2 - 16m + 8 = 0$?

A) -8

B) $-4\sqrt{3}$

C) $4\sqrt{3}$

D) 8

14

A radioactive substance decays at an annual rate of 13 percent. If the initial amount of the substance is 325 grams, which of the following functions f models the remaining amount of the substance, in grams, t years later?

A) $f(t) = 325(0.87)^t$

B) $f(t) = 325(0.13)^t$

C) $f(t) = 0.87(325)^t$

D) $f(t) = 0.13(325)^t$

15

The expression $\dfrac{5x-2}{x+3}$ is equivalent to which of the following?

A) $\dfrac{5-2}{3}$

B) $5 - \dfrac{2}{3}$

C) $5 - \dfrac{2}{x+3}$

D) $5 - \dfrac{17}{x+3}$

CONTINUE

DIRECTIONS

For questions 16–20, solve the problem and enter your answer in the grid, as described below, on the answer sheet.

1. Although not required, it is suggested that you write your answer in the boxes at the top of the columns to help you fill in the circles accurately. You will receive credit only if the circles are filled in correctly.

2. Mark no more than one circle in any column.

3. No question has a negative answer.

4. Some problems may have more than one correct answer. In such cases, grid only one answer.

5. **Mixed numbers** such as $3\frac{1}{2}$ must be gridded as 3.5 or 7/2. (If | 3 | 1 | / | 2 | is entered into the grid, it will be interpreted as $\frac{31}{2}$, not $3\frac{1}{2}$.)

6. **Decimal answers:** If you obtain a decimal answer with more digits than the grid can accommodate, it may be either rounded or truncated, but it must fill the entire grid.

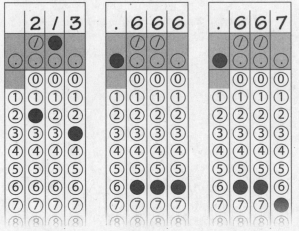

Acceptable ways to grid $\frac{2}{3}$ are:

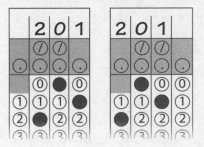

Answer: 201 – either position is correct

NOTE: You may start your answers in any column, space permitting. Columns you don't need to use should be left blank.

CONTINUE ▶

16

The sales manager of a company awarded a total of $3000 in bonuses to the most productive salespeople. The bonuses were awarded in amounts of $250 or $750. If at least one $250 bonus and at least one $750 bonus were awarded, what is one possible number of $250 bonuses awarded?

17

$$2x(3x + 5) + 3(3x + 5) = ax^2 + bx + c$$

In the equation above, a, b, and c are constants. If the equation is true for all values of x, what is the value of b ?

18

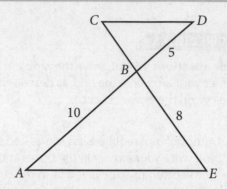

In the figure above, $\overline{AE} \parallel \overline{CD}$ and segment AD intersects segment CE at B. What is the length of segment CE ?

CONTINUE

19

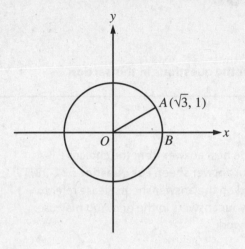

In the xy-plane above, O is the center of the circle, and the measure of $\angle AOB$ is $\dfrac{\pi}{a}$ radians. What is the value of a ?

20

$$ax + by = 12$$
$$2x + 8y = 60$$

In the system of equations above, a and b are constants. If the system has infinitely many solutions, what is the value of $\dfrac{a}{b}$?

STOP

If you finish before time is called, you may check your work on this section only.
Do not turn to any other section.

Math Test – Calculator

55 MINUTES, 38 QUESTIONS

Turn to Section 4 of your answer sheet to answer the questions in this section.

DIRECTIONS

For questions 1-30, solve each problem, choose the best answer from the choices provided, and fill in the corresponding circle on your answer sheet. **For questions 31-38,** solve the problem and enter your answer in the grid on the answer sheet. Please refer to the directions before question 31 on how to enter your answers in the grid. You may use any available space in your test booklet for scratch work.

NOTES

1. The use of a calculator **is permitted**.

2. All variables and expressions used represent real numbers unless otherwise indicated.

3. Figures provided in this test are drawn to scale unless otherwise indicated.

4. All figures lie in a plane unless otherwise indicated.

5. Unless otherwise indicated, the domain of a given function f is the set of all real numbers x for which $f(x)$ is a real number.

REFERENCE

$A = \pi r^2$
$C = 2\pi r$

$A = \ell w$

$A = \dfrac{1}{2}bh$

$c^2 = a^2 + b^2$

Special Right Triangles

$V = \ell w h$

$V = \pi r^2 h$

$V = \dfrac{4}{3}\pi r^3$

$V = \dfrac{1}{3}\pi r^2 h$

$V = \dfrac{1}{3}\ell w h$

The number of degrees of arc in a circle is 360.
The number of radians of arc in a circle is 2π.
The sum of the measures in degrees of the angles of a triangle is 180.

CONTINUE

1

A musician has a new song available for downloading or streaming. The musician earns $0.09 each time the song is downloaded and $0.002 each time the song is streamed. Which of the following expressions represents the amount, in dollars, that the musician earns if the song is downloaded d times and streamed s times?

A) $0.002d + 0.09s$

B) $0.002d - 0.09s$

C) $0.09d + 0.002s$

D) $0.09d - 0.002s$

2

A quality control manager at a factory selects 7 lightbulbs at random for inspection out of every 400 lightbulbs produced. At this rate, how many lightbulbs will be inspected if the factory produces 20,000 lightbulbs?

A) 300

B) 350

C) 400

D) 450

3

$$\ell = 24 + 3.5m$$

One end of a spring is attached to a ceiling. When an object of mass m kilograms is attached to the other end of the spring, the spring stretches to a length of ℓ centimeters as shown in the equation above. What is m when ℓ is 73 ?

A) 14

B) 27.7

C) 73

D) 279.5

CONTINUE

Questions 4 and 5 refer to the following information.

The amount of money a performer earns is directly proportional to the number of people attending the performance. The performer earns $120 at a performance where 8 people attend.

4

How much money will the performer earn when 20 people attend a performance?

A) $960

B) $480

C) $300

D) $240

5

The performer uses 43% of the money earned to pay the costs involved in putting on each performance. The rest of the money earned is the performer's profit. What is the profit the performer makes at a performance where 8 people attend?

A) $51.60

B) $57.00

C) $68.40

D) $77.00

6

When 4 times the number x is added to 12, the result is 8. What number results when 2 times x is added to 7 ?

A) -1

B) 5

C) 8

D) 9

7

$$y = x^2 - 6x + 8$$

The equation above represents a parabola in the xy-plane. Which of the following equivalent forms of the equation displays the x-intercepts of the parabola as constants or coefficients?

A) $y - 8 = x^2 - 6x$

B) $y + 1 = (x - 3)^2$

C) $y = x(x - 6) + 8$

D) $y = (x - 2)(x - 4)$

CONTINUE

8

In a video game, each player starts the game with k points and loses 2 points each time a task is not completed. If a player who gains no additional points and fails to complete 100 tasks has a score of 200 points, what is the value of k ?

A)   0

B)   150

C)   250

D)   400

9

A worker uses a forklift to move boxes that weigh either 40 pounds or 65 pounds each. Let x be the number of 40-pound boxes and y be the number of 65-pound boxes. The forklift can carry up to either 45 boxes or a weight of 2,400 pounds. Which of the following systems of inequalities represents this relationship?

A) $\begin{cases} 40x + 65y \leq 2,400 \\ x + y \leq 45 \end{cases}$

B) $\begin{cases} \dfrac{x}{40} + \dfrac{y}{65} \leq 2,400 \\ x + y \leq 45 \end{cases}$

C) $\begin{cases} 40x + 65y \leq 45 \\ x + y \leq 2,400 \end{cases}$

D) $\begin{cases} x + y \leq 2,400 \\ 40x + 65y \leq 2,400 \end{cases}$

10

A function f satisfies $f(2) = 3$ and $f(3) = 5$. A function g satisfies $g(3) = 2$ and $g(5) = 6$. What is the value of $f(g(3))$?

A) 2

B) 3

C) 5

D) 6

11

Number of hours Tony plans to read the novel per day	3
Number of parts in the novel	8
Number of chapters in the novel	239
Number of words Tony reads per minute	250
Number of pages in the novel	1,078
Number of words in the novel	349,168

Tony is planning to read a novel. The table above shows information about the novel, Tony's reading speed, and the amount of time he plans to spend reading the novel each day. If Tony reads at the rates given in the table, which of the following is closest to the number of days it would take Tony to read the entire novel?

A)   6

B)   8

C)   23

D) 324

CONTINUE

12

On January 1, 2000, there were 175,000 tons of trash in a landfill that had a capacity of 325,000 tons. Each year since then, the amount of trash in the landfill increased by 7,500 tons. If y represents the time, in years, after January 1, 2000, which of the following inequalities describes the set of years where the landfill is at or above capacity?

A) $325,000 - 7,500 \leq y$

B) $325,000 \leq 7,500y$

C) $150,000 \geq 7,500y$

D) $175,000 + 7,500y \geq 325,000$

13

A researcher conducted a survey to determine whether people in a certain large town prefer watching sports on television to attending the sporting event. The researcher asked 117 people who visited a local restaurant on a Saturday, and 7 people refused to respond. Which of the following factors makes it least likely that a reliable conclusion can be drawn about the sports-watching preferences of all people in the town?

A) Sample size

B) Population size

C) The number of people who refused to respond

D) Where the survey was given

14

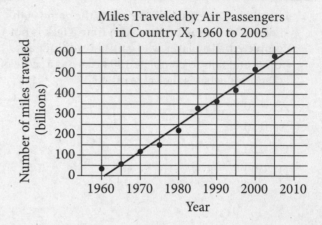

Miles Traveled by Air Passengers in Country X, 1960 to 2005

According to the line of best fit in the scatterplot above, which of the following best approximates the year in which the number of miles traveled by air passengers in Country X was estimated to be 550 billion?

A) 1997

B) 2000

C) 2003

D) 2008

CONTINUE

15

The distance traveled by Earth in one orbit around the Sun is about 580,000,000 miles. Earth makes one complete orbit around the Sun in one year. Of the following, which is closest to the average speed of Earth, in miles per hour, as it orbits the Sun?

A) 66,000

B) 93,000

C) 210,000

D) 420,000

16

Results on the Bar Exam of Law School Graduates

	Passed bar exam	Did not pass bar exam
Took review course	18	82
Did not take review course	7	93

The table above summarizes the results of 200 law school graduates who took the bar exam. If one of the surveyed graduates who passed the bar exam is chosen at random for an interview, what is the probability that the person chosen did <u>not</u> take the review course?

A) $\dfrac{18}{25}$

B) $\dfrac{7}{25}$

C) $\dfrac{25}{200}$

D) $\dfrac{7}{200}$

17

The atomic weight of an unknown element, in atomic mass units (amu), is approximately 20% less than that of calcium. The atomic weight of calcium is 40 amu. Which of the following best approximates the atomic weight, in amu, of the unknown element?

A) 8

B) 20

C) 32

D) 48

18

A survey was taken of the value of homes in a county, and it was found that the mean home value was $165,000 and the median home value was $125,000. Which of the following situations could explain the difference between the mean and median home values in the county?

A) The homes have values that are close to each other.

B) There are a few homes that are valued much less than the rest.

C) There are a few homes that are valued much more than the rest.

D) Many of the homes have values between $125,000 and $165,000.

CONTINUE

Questions 19 and 20 refer to the following information.

A sociologist chose 300 students at random from each of two schools and asked each student how many siblings he or she has. The results are shown in the table below.

Students' Sibling Survey

Number of siblings	Lincoln School	Washington School
0	120	140
1	80	110
2	60	30
3	30	10
4	10	10

There are a total of 2,400 students at Lincoln School and 3,300 students at Washington School.

19

What is the median number of siblings for all the students surveyed?

A) 0

B) 1

C) 2

D) 3

20

Based on the survey data, which of the following most accurately compares the expected total number of students with 4 siblings at the two schools?

A) The total number of students with 4 siblings is expected to be equal at the two schools.

B) The total number of students with 4 siblings at Lincoln School is expected to be 30 more than at Washington School.

C) The total number of students with 4 siblings at Washington School is expected to be 30 more than at Lincoln School.

D) The total number of students with 4 siblings at Washington School is expected to be 900 more than at Lincoln School.

21

A project manager estimates that a project will take x hours to complete, where $x > 100$. The goal is for the estimate to be within 10 hours of the time it will actually take to complete the project. If the manager meets the goal and it takes y hours to complete the project, which of the following inequalities represents the relationship between the estimated time and the actual completion time?

A) $x + y < 10$

B) $y > x + 10$

C) $y < x - 10$

D) $-10 < y - x < 10$

Unauthorized copying or reuse of any part of this page is illegal.

496

CONTINUE

Questions 22 and 23 refer to the following information.

$$I = \frac{P}{4\pi r^2}$$

At a large distance r from a radio antenna, the intensity of the radio signal I is related to the power of the signal P by the formula above.

22

Which of the following expresses the square of the distance from the radio antenna in terms of the intensity of the radio signal and the power of the signal?

A) $r^2 = \dfrac{IP}{4\pi}$

B) $r^2 = \dfrac{P}{4\pi I}$

C) $r^2 = \dfrac{4\pi I}{P}$

D) $r^2 = \dfrac{I}{4\pi P}$

23

For the same signal emitted by a radio antenna, Observer A measures its intensity to be 16 times the intensity measured by Observer B. The distance of Observer A from the radio antenna is what fraction of the distance of Observer B from the radio antenna?

A) $\dfrac{1}{4}$

B) $\dfrac{1}{16}$

C) $\dfrac{1}{64}$

D) $\dfrac{1}{256}$

24

$$x^2 + y^2 + 4x - 2y = -1$$

The equation of a circle in the xy-plane is shown above. What is the radius of the circle?

A) 2

B) 3

C) 4

D) 9

CONTINUE

25

The graph of the linear function f has intercepts at $(a, 0)$ and $(0, b)$ in the xy-plane. If $a + b = 0$ and $a \neq b$, which of the following is true about the slope of the graph of f ?

A) It is positive.

B) It is negative.

C) It equals zero.

D) It is undefined.

26

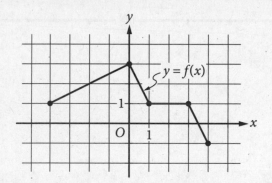

The complete graph of the function f is shown in the xy-plane above. Which of the following are equal to 1 ?

    I. $f(-4)$

    II. $f\left(\dfrac{3}{2}\right)$

    III. $f(3)$

A) III only

B) I and III only

C) II and III only

D) I, II, and III

27

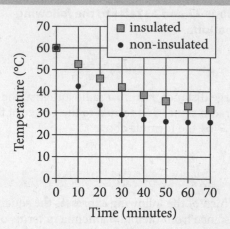

Two samples of water of equal mass are heated to 60 degrees Celsius (°C). One sample is poured into an insulated container, and the other sample is poured into a non-insulated container. The samples are then left for 70 minutes to cool in a room having a temperature of 25°C. The graph above shows the temperature of each sample at 10-minute intervals. Which of the following statements correctly compares the average rates at which the temperatures of the two samples change?

A) In every 10-minute interval, the magnitude of the rate of change of temperature of the insulated sample is greater than that of the non-insulated sample.

B) In every 10-minute interval, the magnitude of the rate of change of temperature of the non-insulated sample is greater than that of the insulated sample.

C) In the intervals from 0 to 10 minutes and from 10 to 20 minutes, the rates of change of temperature of the insulated sample are of greater magnitude, whereas in the intervals from 40 to 50 minutes and from 50 to 60 minutes, the rates of change of temperature of the non-insulated sample are of greater magnitude.

D) In the intervals from 0 to 10 minutes and from 10 to 20 minutes, the rates of change of temperature of the non-insulated sample are of greater magnitude, whereas in the intervals from 40 to 50 minutes and from 50 to 60 minutes, the rates of change of temperature of the insulated sample are of greater magnitude.

CONTINUE

28

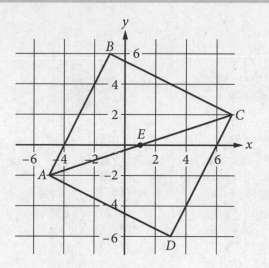

In the *xy*-plane above, *ABCD* is a square and point *E* is the center of the square. The coordinates of points *C* and *E* are $(7, 2)$ and $(1, 0)$, respectively. Which of the following is an equation of the line that passes through points *B* and *D* ?

A) $y = -3x - 1$

B) $y = -3(x - 1)$

C) $y = -\frac{1}{3}x + 4$

D) $y = -\frac{1}{3}x - 1$

29

$$y = 3$$
$$y = ax^2 + b$$

In the system of equations above, *a* and *b* are constants. For which of the following values of *a* and *b* does the system of equations have exactly two real solutions?

A) $a = -2, b = 2$

B) $a = -2, b = 4$

C) $a = 2, b = 4$

D) $a = 4, b = 3$

30

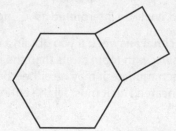

The figure above shows a regular hexagon with sides of length *a* and a square with sides of length *a*. If the area of the hexagon is $384\sqrt{3}$ square inches, what is the area, in square inches, of the square?

A) 256

B) 192

C) $64\sqrt{3}$

D) $16\sqrt{3}$

CONTINUE

DIRECTIONS

For questions 31-38, solve the problem and enter your answer in the grid, as described below, on the answer sheet.

1. Although not required, it is suggested that you write your answer in the boxes at the top of the columns to help you fill in the circles accurately. You will receive credit only if the circles are filled in correctly.

2. Mark no more than one circle in any column.

3. No question has a negative answer.

4. Some problems may have more than one correct answer. In such cases, grid only one answer.

5. **Mixed numbers** such as $3\frac{1}{2}$ must be gridded as 3.5 or 7/2. (If ⌊3|1|/|2⌋ is entered into the grid, it will be interpreted as $\frac{31}{2}$, not $3\frac{1}{2}$.)

6. **Decimal answers:** If you obtain a decimal answer with more digits than the grid can accommodate, it may be either rounded or truncated, but it must fill the entire grid.

Answer: $\frac{7}{12}$ — Write answer in boxes. ← Fraction line — Grid in result.

Answer: 2.5 ← Decimal point

Acceptable ways to grid $\frac{2}{3}$ are:

Answer: 201 – either position is correct

NOTE: You may start your answers in any column, space permitting. Columns you don't need to use should be left blank.

CONTINUE ➤

31

A coastal geologist estimates that a certain country's beaches are eroding at a rate of 1.5 feet per year. According to the geologist's estimate, how long will it take, in years, for the country's beaches to erode by 21 feet?

32

If h hours and 30 minutes is equal to 450 minutes, what is the value of h ?

33

In the xy-plane, the point $(3, 6)$ lies on the graph of the function $f(x) = 3x^2 - bx + 12$. What is the value of b ?

34

In one semester, Doug and Laura spent a combined 250 hours in the tutoring lab. If Doug spent 40 more hours in the lab than Laura did, how many hours did Laura spend in the lab?

CONTINUE

35

$$a = 18t + 15$$

Jane made an initial deposit to a savings account. Each week thereafter she deposited a fixed amount to the account. The equation above models the amount a, in dollars, that Jane has deposited after t weekly deposits. According to the model, how many dollars was Jane's initial deposit? (Disregard the $ sign when gridding your answer.)

36

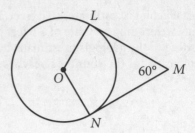

In the figure above, point O is the center of the circle, line segments LM and MN are tangent to the circle at points L and N, respectively, and the segments intersect at point M as shown. If the circumference of the circle is 96, what is the length of minor arc $\overset{\frown}{LN}$?

CONTINUE

Questions 37 and 38 refer to the following information.

A botanist is cultivating a rare species of plant in a controlled environment and currently has 3000 of these plants. The population of this species that the botanist expects to grow next year, $N_{\text{next year}}$, can be estimated from the number of plants this year, $N_{\text{this year}}$, by the equation below.

$$N_{\text{next year}} = N_{\text{this year}} + 0.2\left(N_{\text{this year}}\right)\left(1 - \frac{N_{\text{this year}}}{K}\right)$$

The constant K in this formula is the number of plants the environment is able to support.

37

According to the formula, what will be the number of plants two years from now if $K = 4000$? (Round your answer to the nearest whole number.)

38

The botanist would like to increase the number of plants that the environment can support so that the population of the species will increase more rapidly. If the botanist's goal is that the number of plants will increase from 3000 this year to 3360 next year, how many plants must the modified environment support?

STOP

If you finish before time is called, you may check your work on this section only.

Do not turn to any other section.

YOUR NAME (PRINT) ....

LAST · FIRST MI

TEST CENTER ....

NUMBER NAME OF TEST CENTER ROOM NUMBER

The SAT

GENERAL DIRECTIONS

- You may work on only one section at a time.
- If you finish a section before time is called, check your work on that section. You may NOT turn to any other section.

MARKING ANSWERS

- Be sure to mark your answer sheet properly.

COMPLETE MARK ● EXAMPLES OF INCOMPLETE MARKS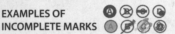

- You must use a No. 2 pencil.
- Carefully mark only one answer for each question.
- Make sure you fill the entire circle darkly and completely.
- Do not make any stray marks on your answer sheet.
- If you erase, do so completely. Incomplete erasures may be scored as intended answers.
- Use only the answer spaces that correspond to the question numbers.

USING YOUR TEST BOOK

- You may use the test book for scratch work, but you will not receive credit for anything that you write in your test book.
- After time has been called, you may not transfer answers from your test book to your answer sheet or fill in circles.
- You may not fold or remove pages or portions of a page from this book, or take the book or answer sheet from the testing room.

SCORING

- For each correct answer, you receive one point.
- You do not lose points for wrong answers; therefore, you should try to answer every question even if you are not sure of the correct answer.

IMPORTANT

The codes below are unique to your test book.
Copy them on your answer sheet in boxes 8 and 9 and fill in the corresponding circles exactly as shown.

9	TEST ID
	(Copy from back of test book.)

8 FORM CODE
(Copy and grid as on back of test book.)

Follow this link for more information on scoring your practice test:
www.sat.org/scoring

5LSA07

DO NOT OPEN THIS BOOK UNTIL THE SUPERVISOR TELLS YOU TO DO SO.

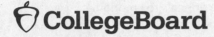
CollegeBoard

SAT® Practice Essay #2

ESSAY BOOK

DIRECTIONS

The essay gives you an opportunity to show how effectively you can read and comprehend a passage and write an essay analyzing the passage. In your essay, you should demonstrate that you have read the passage carefully, present a clear and logical analysis, and use language precisely.

Your essay must be written on the lines provided in your answer booklet; except for the Planning Page of the answer booklet, you will receive no other paper on which to write. You will have enough space if you write on every line, avoid wide margins, and keep your handwriting to a reasonable size. Remember that people who are not familiar with your handwriting will read what you write. Try to write or print so that what you are writing is legible to those readers.

You have <u>50 minutes</u> to read the passage and write an essay in response to the prompt provided inside this booklet.

REMINDERS

— Do not write your essay in this booklet. Only what you write on the lined pages of your answer booklet will be evaluated.

— An off-topic essay will not be evaluated.

Follow this link for more information on scoring your practice test: **www.sat.org/scoring**

This cover is representative of what you'll see on test day.

As you read the passage below, consider how Martin Luther King Jr. uses

- evidence, such as facts or examples, to support claims.
- reasoning to develop ideas and to connect claims and evidence.
- stylistic or persuasive elements, such as word choice or appeals to emotion, to add power to the ideas expressed.

Adapted from Martin Luther King Jr., "Beyond Vietnam—A Time to Break Silence." The speech was delivered at Riverside Church in New York City on April 4, 1967.

1   Since I am a preacher by calling, I suppose it is not surprising that I have . . . major reasons for bringing Vietnam into the field of my moral vision. There is at the outset a very obvious and almost facile connection between the war in Vietnam and the struggle I, and others, have been waging in America. A few years ago there was a shining moment in that struggle. It seemed as if there was a real promise of hope for the poor—both black and white—through the poverty program. There were experiments, hopes, new beginnings. Then came the buildup in Vietnam, and I watched this program broken and eviscerated, as if it were some idle political plaything of a society gone mad on war, and I knew that America would never invest the necessary funds or energies in rehabilitation of its poor so long as adventures like Vietnam continued to draw men and skills and money like some demonic destructive suction tube. So, I was increasingly compelled to see the war as an enemy of the poor and to attack it as such.

2   Perhaps a more tragic recognition of reality took place when it became clear to me that the war was doing far more than devastating the hopes of the poor at home. It was sending their sons and their brothers and their husbands to fight and to die in extraordinarily high proportions relative to the rest of the population. We were taking the black young men who had been crippled by our society and sending them eight thousand miles away to guarantee liberties in Southeast Asia which they had not found in southwest Georgia and East Harlem. And so we have been repeatedly faced with the cruel irony of watching Negro and white boys on TV screens as they kill and die together for a nation that has been unable to seat them together in the same schools. And so we watch them in brutal solidarity burning the huts of a poor village, but we realize that they would hardly live on the same block in Chicago. I could not be silent in the face of such cruel manipulation of the poor.

3   My [next] reason moves to an even deeper level of awareness, for it grows out of my experience in the ghettoes of the North over the last three years—especially the last three summers. As I have walked among the desperate, rejected, and angry young men, I have told them that Molotov cocktails[1] and rifles would not solve their problems. I have tried to offer them my deepest compassion while maintaining my conviction that social change comes most meaningfully through nonviolent action. But they ask—and rightly so—what about Vietnam? They ask if our own nation wasn't using massive doses of violence to solve its problems, to bring about the changes it wanted. Their questions hit home, and I knew that I could never again raise my voice against the violence of the oppressed in the ghettos without having first spoken clearly to the greatest purveyor of violence in the world today—my own government. For the sake of those boys, for the sake of this government, for the sake of the hundreds of thousands trembling under our violence, I cannot be silent.

4   For those who ask the question, "Aren't you a civil rights leader?" and thereby mean to exclude me from the movement for peace, I have this further answer. In 1957 when a group of us formed the Southern Christian Leadership Conference, we chose as our motto: "To save the soul of America." We were convinced that we could not limit our vision to certain rights for black people, but instead affirmed the conviction that America would never be free or saved from itself until the descendants of its slaves were loosed completely from the shackles they still wear. . . . Now, it should be incandescently clear that no one who has any concern for the integrity and life of America today can ignore the present war. If America's soul becomes totally poisoned, part of the autopsy must read: Vietnam. It can never be saved so long as it destroys the deepest hopes of men the world over. So it is that those of us who are yet determined that America will be—are—are led down the path of protest and dissent, working for the health of our land.

Write an essay in which you explain how Martin Luther King Jr. builds an argument to persuade his audience that American involvement in the Vietnam War is unjust. In your essay, analyze how King uses one or more of the features listed in the box above (or features of your own choice) to strengthen the logic and persuasiveness of his argument. Be sure that your analysis focuses on the most relevant features of the passage.

Your essay should not explain whether you agree with King's claims, but rather explain how King builds an argument to persuade his audience.

---

[1] A crude bomb made from glass bottles filled with flammable liquids and topped with wicks

YOUR NAME (PRINT) ....

LAST FIRST MI

TEST CENTER ....

NUMBER NAME OF TEST CENTER ROOM NUMBER

This page represents the back cover of the Practice Essay.

5LS07E

Ideas contained in the passage for this test, which is excerpted or adapted from published material, do not necessarily represent the opinions of the College Board.

DO NOT OPEN THIS BOOK UNTIL THE SUPERVISOR TELLS YOU TO DO SO.

CollegeBoard

■ **TEST NUMBER**   ■ **SECTION 1**

ENTER TEST NUMBER

For instance, for Practice Test #1, fill in the circle for 0 in the **first column** and for 1 in the **second column.**

0 ○ ○
1 ○ ○
2 ○ ○
3 ○ ○
4 ○ ○
5 ○ ○
6 ○ ○
7 ○ ○
8 ○ ○
9 ○ ○

	A	B	C	D		A	B	C	D		A	B	C	D		A	B	C	D
1	○	○	○	○	14	○	○	○	○	27	○	○	○	○	40	○	○	○	○
2	○	○	○	○	15	○	○	○	○	28	○	○	○	○	41	○	○	○	○
3	○	○	○	○	16	○	○	○	○	29	○	○	○	○	42	○	○	○	○
4	○	○	○	○	17	○	○	○	○	30	○	○	○	○	43	○	○	○	○
5	○	○	○	○	18	○	○	○	○	31	○	○	○	○	44	○	○	○	○
6	○	○	○	○	19	○	○	○	○	32	○	○	○	○	45	○	○	○	○
7	○	○	○	○	20	○	○	○	○	33	○	○	○	○	46	○	○	○	○
8	○	○	○	○	21	○	○	○	○	34	○	○	○	○	47	○	○	○	○
9	○	○	○	○	22	○	○	○	○	35	○	○	○	○	48	○	○	○	○
10	○	○	○	○	23	○	○	○	○	36	○	○	○	○	49	○	○	○	○
11	○	○	○	○	24	○	○	○	○	37	○	○	○	○	50	○	○	○	○
12	○	○	○	○	25	○	○	○	○	38	○	○	○	○	51	○	○	○	○
13	○	○	○	○	26	○	○	○	○	39	○	○	○	○	52	○	○	○	○

Download the College Board SAT Practice app to instantly score this test.
Learn more at sat.org/scoring.

● ● ● ● ●   ●   ●

CollegeBoard

■ SECTION 2

	A B C D		A B C D		A B C D		A B C D		A B C D
1	○○○○	10	○○○○	19	○○○○	28	○○○○	37	○○○○
2	○○○○	11	○○○○	20	○○○○	29	○○○○	38	○○○○
3	○○○○	12	○○○○	21	○○○○	30	○○○○	39	○○○○
4	○○○○	13	○○○○	22	○○○○	31	○○○○	40	○○○○
5	○○○○	14	○○○○	23	○○○○	32	○○○○	41	○○○○
6	○○○○	15	○○○○	24	○○○○	33	○○○○	42	○○○○
7	○○○○	16	○○○○	25	○○○○	34	○○○○	43	○○○○
8	○○○○	17	○○○○	26	○○○○	35	○○○○	44	○○○○
9	○○○○	18	○○○○	27	○○○○	36	○○○○		

If you're scoring with our mobile app we recommend that you cut these pages out of the back of this book. The scoring does best with a flat page.

● ● ● ● ●   ●   ●

CollegeBoard

SAT PRACTICE ANSWER SHEET

| COMPLETE MARK ● | EXAMPLES OF INCOMPLETE MARKS | It is recommended that you use a No. 2 pencil. It is very important that you fill in the entire circle darkly and completely. If you change your response, erase as completely as possible. Incomplete marks or erasures may affect your score. |

■ SECTION 3

1 A B C D ○○○○
2 A B C D ○○○○
3 A B C D ○○○○

4 A B C D ○○○○
5 A B C D ○○○○
6 A B C D ○○○○

7 A B C D ○○○○
8 A B C D ○○○○
9 A B C D ○○○○

10 A B C D ○○○○
11 A B C D ○○○○
12 A B C D ○○○○

13 A B C D ○○○○
14 A B C D ○○○○
15 A B C D ○○○○

Only answers that are gridded will be scored. You will not receive credit for anything written in the boxes.

16

/ ○○
. ○○○○
0 ○○○○
1 ○○○○
2 ○○○○
3 ○○○○
4 ○○○○
5 ○○○○
6 ○○○○
7 ○○○○
8 ○○○○
9 ○○○○

17

/ ○○
. ○○○○
0 ○○○○
1 ○○○○
2 ○○○○
3 ○○○○
4 ○○○○
5 ○○○○
6 ○○○○
7 ○○○○
8 ○○○○
9 ○○○○

18

/ ○○
. ○○○○
0 ○○○○
1 ○○○○
2 ○○○○
3 ○○○○
4 ○○○○
5 ○○○○
6 ○○○○
7 ○○○○
8 ○○○○
9 ○○○○

19

/ ○○
. ○○○○
0 ○○○○
1 ○○○○
2 ○○○○
3 ○○○○
4 ○○○○
5 ○○○○
6 ○○○○
7 ○○○○
8 ○○○○
9 ○○○○

20

/ ○○
. ○○○○
0 ○○○○
1 ○○○○
2 ○○○○
3 ○○○○
4 ○○○○
5 ○○○○
6 ○○○○
7 ○○○○
8 ○○○○
9 ○○○○

NO CALCULATOR ALLOWED

! Did you know that you can print out these test sheets from the web? Learn more at sat.org/scoring.

● ● ● ● ●   ●   ●

CollegeBoard

COMPLETE MARK ● EXAMPLES OF INCOMPLETE MARKS

It is recommended that you use a No. 2 pencil. It is very important that you fill in the entire circle darkly and completely. If you change your response, erase as completely as possible. Incomplete marks or erasures may affect your score.

■ SECTION 4

	A B C D		A B C D		A B C D		A B C D		A B C D
1	○○○○	7	○○○○	13	○○○○	19	○○○○	25	○○○○
2	○○○○	8	○○○○	14	○○○○	20	○○○○	26	○○○○
3	○○○○	9	○○○○	15	○○○○	21	○○○○	27	○○○○
4	○○○○	10	○○○○	16	○○○○	22	○○○○	28	○○○○
5	○○○○	11	○○○○	17	○○○○	23	○○○○	29	○○○○
6	○○○○	12	○○○○	18	○○○○	24	○○○○	30	○○○○

CALCULATOR ALLOWED

If you're using our mobile app keep in mind that bad lighting and even shadows cast over the answer sheet can affect your score. Be sure to scan this in a well-lit area for best results.

● ● ● ● ●   ●   ●

CollegeBoard

SECTION 4 (Continued)

Only answers that are gridded will be scored. You will not receive credit for anything written in the boxes.

31 **32** **33** **34** **35**

36 **37** **38**

Only answers that are gridded will be scored. You will not receive credit for anything written in the boxes.

CALCULATOR ALLOWED

513

PLANNING PAGE You may plan your essay in the unlined planning space below, but use only the lined pages following this one to write your essay. Any work on this planning page will not be scored.

Use pages 7 through 10 for your ESSAY ⟶

FOR PLANNING ONLY

Use pages 7 through 10 for your ESSAY ⟶

Page 6

SERIAL #

514

515

You may continue on the next page.

You may continue on the next page.

SERIAL #

STOP.

Answer Explanations

SAT Practice Test #2

Section 1: Reading Test

QUESTION 1.

Choice A is the best answer. The narrator admits that his job is "irksome" (line 7) and reflects on the reasons for his dislike. The narrator admits that his work is a "dry and tedious task" (line 9) and that he has a poor relationship with his superior: "the antipathy which had sprung up between myself and my employer striking deeper root and spreading denser shade daily, excluded me from every glimpse of the sunshine of life" (lines 28-31).

Choices B, C, and D are incorrect because the narrator does not become increasingly competitive with his employer, publicly defend his choice of occupation, or exhibit optimism about his job.

QUESTION 2.

Choice B is the best answer. The first sentence of the passage explains that people do not like to admit when they've chosen the wrong profession and that they will continue in their profession for a while before admitting their unhappiness. This statement mirrors the narrator's own situation, as the narrator admits he finds his own occupation "irksome" (line 7) but that he might "long have borne with the nuisance" (line 10) if not for his poor relationship with his employer.

Choices A, C, and D are incorrect because the first sentence does not discuss a controversy, focus on the narrator's employer, Edward Crimsworth, or provide any evidence of malicious conduct.

QUESTION 3.

Choice C is the best answer. The first paragraph shifts from a general discussion of how people deal with choosing an occupation they later regret (lines 1-6) to the narrator's description of his own dissatisfaction with his occupation (lines 6-33).

Choices A, B, and D are incorrect because the first paragraph does not focus on the narrator's self-doubt, his expectations of life as a tradesman, or his identification of alternatives to his current occupation.

QUESTION 4.

Choice A is the best answer. In lines 27-33, the narrator is describing the hostile relationship between him and his superior, Edward Crimsworth. This relationship causes the narrator to feel like he lives in the "shade" and in "humid darkness." These words evoke the narrator's feelings of dismay toward his current occupation and his poor relationship with his superior—factors that cause him to live without "the sunshine of life."

Choices B, C, and D are incorrect because the words "shade" and "darkness" do not reflect the narrator's sinister thoughts, his fear of confinement, or his longing for rest.

QUESTION 5.

Choice D is the best answer. The narrator states that Crimsworth dislikes him because the narrator may "one day make a successful tradesman" (line 43). Crimsworth recognizes that the narrator is not "inferior to him" but rather more intelligent, someone who keeps "the padlock of silence on mental wealth which [Crimsworth] was no sharer" (lines 44-48). Crimsworth feels inferior to the narrator and is jealous of the narrator's intellectual and professional abilities.

Choices A and C are incorrect because the narrator is not described as exhibiting "high spirits" or "rash actions," but "Caution, Tact, [and] Observation" (line 51). Choice B is incorrect because the narrator's "humble background" is not discussed.

QUESTION 6.

Choice B is the best answer. Lines 61-62 state that the narrator "had long ceased to regard Mr. Crimsworth as my brother." In these lines, the term "brother" means friend or ally, which suggests that the narrator and Crimsworth were once friendly toward one another.

Choices A, C, and D are incorrect because the narrator originally viewed Crimsworth as a friend, or ally, and later as a hostile superior; he never viewed Crimsworth as a harmless rival, perceptive judge, or demanding mentor.

QUESTION 7.

Choice D is the best answer. In lines 61-62, the narrator states that he once regarded Mr. Crimsworth as his "brother." This statement provides evidence that the narrator originally viewed Crimsworth as a sympathetic ally.

Choices A, B, and C do not provide the best evidence for the claim that Crimsworth was a sympathetic ally. Rather, choices A, B, and C provide evidence of the hostile relationship that currently exists between the narrator and Crimsworth.

QUESTION 8.

Choice D is the best answer. In lines 48-53, the narrator states that he exhibited "Caution, Tact, [and] Observation" at work and watched Mr. Crimsworth with "lynx-eyes." The narrator acknowledges that Crimsworth was "prepared to steal snake-like" if he caught the narrator acting without tact or being disrespectful toward his superiors (lines 53-56). Thus, Crimsworth was trying to find a reason to place the narrator "in a ridiculous or mortifying position" (lines 49-50) by accusing the narrator of acting unprofessionally. The use of the lynx and snake serve to emphasize the narrator and Crimsworth's adversarial, or hostile, relationship.

Choices A and B are incorrect because the description of the lynx and snake does not contrast two hypothetical courses of action or convey a resolution. Choice C is incorrect because while lines 48-56 suggest that Crimsworth is trying to find a reason to fault the narrator's work, they do not imply that an altercation, or heated dispute, between the narrator and Crimsworth is likely to occur.

QUESTION 9.

Choice B is the best answer. Lines 73-74 state that the narrator noticed there was no "cheering red gleam" of fire in his sitting-room fireplace. The lack of a "cheering," or comforting, fire suggests that the narrator sometimes found his lodgings to be dreary or bleak.

Choices A and D are incorrect because the narrator does not find his living quarters to be treacherous or intolerable. Choice C is incorrect because while the narrator is walking home he speculates about the presence of a fire in his sitting-room's fireplace (lines 69-74), which suggests that he could not predict the state of his living quarters.

QUESTION 10.

Choice D is the best answer. In lines 68-74, the narrator states that he did not see the "cheering" glow of a fire in his sitting-room fireplace. This statement provides evidence that the narrator views his lodgings as dreary or bleak.

Choices A, B, and C do not provide the best evidence that the narrator views his lodgings as dreary. Choices A and C are incorrect because they do not provide the narrator's opinion of his lodgings, and choice B is incorrect because lines 21-23 describe the narrator's lodgings only as "small."

QUESTION 11.

Choice D is the best answer. In lines 11-12, the author introduces the main purpose of the passage, which is to examine the "different views on where ethics should apply when someone makes an economic decision." The passage examines what historical figures Adam Smith, Aristotle, and John Stuart Mill believed about the relationship between ethics and economics.

Choices A, B, and C are incorrect because they identify certain points addressed in the passage (cost-benefit analysis, ethical economic behavior, and the role of the free market), but do not describe the passage's main purpose.

QUESTION 12.

Choice D is the best answer. In lines 4-5, the author suggests that people object to criticizing ethics in free markets because they believe free markets are inherently ethical, and therefore, the role of ethics in free markets is unnecessary to study. In the opinion of the critics, free markets are ethical because they allow individuals to make their own choices about which goods to purchase and which goods to sell.

Choices A and B are incorrect because they are not objections that criticize the ethics of free markets. Choice C is incorrect because the author does not present the opinion that free markets depend on devalued currency.

QUESTION 13.

Choice A is the best answer. In lines 4-5, the author states that some people believe that free markets are "already ethical" because they "allow for personal choice." This statement provides evidence that some people believe criticizing the ethics of free markets is unnecessary because free markets permit individuals to make their own choices.

Choices B, C, and D are incorrect because they do not provide the best evidence of an objection to a critique of the ethics of free markets.

QUESTION 14.

Choice B is the best answer. In lines 6-7, the author states that people "have accepted the ethical critique and embraced corporate social responsibility." In this context, people "embrace," or readily adopt, corporate social responsibility by acting in a certain way.

Choices A, C, and D are incorrect because in this context "embraced" does not mean lovingly held, eagerly hugged, or reluctantly used.

QUESTION 15.

Choice C is the best answer. The third and fourth paragraphs of the passage present Adam Smith's and Aristotle's different approaches to defining ethics in economics. The fifth paragraph offers a third approach to defining ethical economics, how "instead of rooting ethics in character or the consequences of actions, we can focus on our actions themselves. From this perspective some things are right, some wrong" (lines 45-48).

Choice A is incorrect because the fifth paragraph does not develop a counterargument. Choices B and D are incorrect because although "character" is briefly mentioned in the fifth paragraph, its relationship to ethics is examined in the fourth paragraph.

QUESTION 16.

Choice A is the best answer. In lines 57-59, the author states that "Many moral dilemmas arise when these three versions pull in different directions but clashes are not inevitable." In this context, the three different perspectives on ethical economics may "clash," or conflict, with one another.

Choices B, C, and D are incorrect because in this context "clashes" does not mean mismatches, collisions, or brawls.

QUESTION 17.

Choice C is the best answer. In lines 59-64, the author states, "Take fair trade coffee . . . for example: buying it might have good consequences, be virtuous, and also be the right way to act in a flawed market." The author is suggesting that in the example of fair trade coffee, all three perspectives about ethical economics—Adam Smith's belief in consequences dictating action, Aristotle's emphasis on character, and the third approach emphasizing the virtue of good actions—can be applied. These three approaches share "common ground" (line 64), as they all can be applied to the example of fair trade coffee without contradicting one another.

Choices A, B, and D are incorrect because they do not show how the three different approaches to ethical economics share common ground. Choice A simply states that there are "different views on ethics" in economics, choice B explains the third ethical economics approach, and choice D suggests that people "behave like a herd" when considering economics.

QUESTION 18.

Choice C is the best answer. In lines 83-88, the author states that psychology can help "define ethics for us," which can help explain why people "react in disgust at economic injustice, or accept a moral law as universal."

Choices A and B are incorrect because they identify topics discussed in the final paragraph (human quirks and people's reaction to economic injustice) but not its main idea. Choice D is incorrect because the final paragraph does not suggest that economists may be responsible for reforming the free market.

QUESTION 19.

Choice A is the best answer. The data in the graph show that in Tanzania between the years 2000 and 2008, fair trade coffee profits were around $1.30 per pound, while profits of regular coffee were in the approximate range of 20–60 cents per pound.

Choices B, C, and D are incorrect because they are not supported by information in the graph.

QUESTION 20.

Choice B is the best answer. The data in the graph indicate that between 2002 and 2004 the difference in per-pound profits between fair trade and regular coffee was about $1. In this time period, fair trade coffee was valued at around $1.30 per pound and regular coffee was valued at around 20 cents per pound. The graph also shows that regular coffee recorded the lowest profits between the years 2002 and 2004, while fair trade coffee remained relatively stable throughout the entire eight-year span (2000 to 2008).

Choices A, C, and D are incorrect because they do not indicate the greatest difference between per-pound profits for fair trade and regular coffee.

QUESTION 21.

Choice C is the best answer. In lines 59-61, the author defines fair trade coffee as "coffee that is sold with a certification that indicates the farmers and workers who produced it were paid a fair wage." This definition suggests that purchasing fair trade coffee is an ethically responsible choice, and the fact that fair trade coffee is being produced and is profitable suggests that ethical economics is still a consideration. The graph's data support this claim by showing how fair trade coffee was more than twice as profitable as regular coffee.

Choice A is incorrect because the graph suggests that people acting on empathy (by buying fair trade coffee) is productive for fair trade coffee farmers and workers. Choices B and D are incorrect because the graph does not provide support for the idea that character or people's fears factor into economic choices.

QUESTION 22.

Choice C is the best answer. The author of Passage 1 indicates that people can benefit from using screen-based technologies as these technologies strengthen "certain cognitive skills" (line 3) and the "brain functions related to fast-paced problem solving" (lines 14-15).

Choice A is incorrect because the author of Passage 1 cites numerous studies of screen-based technologies. Choice B is incorrect because it is not supported by Passage 1, and choice D is incorrect because while the author mentions some benefits to screen-based technologies, he does not encourage their use.

QUESTION 23.

Choice A is the best answer. In lines 3-4, the author of Passage 1 provides evidence that the use of screen-based technologies has some positive effects: "Certain cognitive skills are strengthened by our use of computers and the Net."

Choices B, C, and D are incorrect because they do not provide the best evidence that the use of screen-based technologies has some positive effects. Choices B, C, and D introduce and describe the author's reservations about screen-based technologies.

QUESTION 24.

Choice B is the best answer. The author of Passage 1 cites Patricia Greenfield's study, which found that people's use of screen-based technologies weakened their ability to acquire knowledge, perform "inductive analysis" and "critical thinking," and be imaginative and reflective (lines 34-38). The author of Passage 1 concludes that the use of screen-based technologies interferes with people's ability to think "deeply" (lines 47-50).

Choices A, C, and D are incorrect because the author of Passage 1 does not address how using the Internet affects people's health, social contacts, or self-confidence.

QUESTION 25.

Choice C is the best answer. In lines 39-41, the author states, "We know that the human brain is highly plastic; neurons and synapses change as circumstances change." In this context, the brain is "plastic" because it is malleable, or able to change.

Choices A, B, and D are incorrect because in this context "plastic" does not mean creative, artificial, or sculptural.

QUESTION 26.

Choice B is the best answer. In lines 60-65, the author of Passage 2 explains how speed-reading does not "revamp," or alter, how the brain processes information. He supports this statement by explaining how Woody Allen's reading of *War and Peace* in one sitting caused him to describe the novel as "about Russia." Woody Allen was not able to comprehend the "famously long" novel by speed-reading it.

Choices A and D are incorrect because Woody Allen's description of *War and Peace* does not suggest he disliked Tolstoy's writing style or that he regretted reading the book. Choice C is incorrect because the anecdote about Woody Allen is unrelated to multitasking.

QUESTION 27.

Choice D is the best answer. The author of Passage 2 states that people like novelists and scientists improve in their profession by "immers[ing] themselves in their fields" (line 79). Both novelists and scientists, in other words, become absorbed in their areas of expertise.

Choices A and C are incorrect because the author of Passage 2 does not suggest that novelists and scientists both take risks when they pursue knowledge or are curious about other subjects. Choice B is incorrect because the author of Passage 2 states that "accomplished people" don't perform "intellectual calisthenics," or exercises that improve their minds (lines 77-78).

QUESTION 28.

Choice D is the best answer. In lines 83-90, the author of Passage 2 criticizes media critics for their alarmist writing: "Media critics write as if the brain takes on the qualities of whatever it consumes, the informational equivalent of 'you are what you eat.'" The author then compares media critics' "you are what you eat" mentality to ancient people's belief that "eating fierce animals made them fierce." The author uses this analogy to discredit media critics' belief that consumption of electronic media alters the brain.

Choices A, B, and C are incorrect because the final sentence of Passage 2 does not use ornate language, employ humor, or evoke nostalgia for the past.

QUESTION 29.

Choice D is the best answer. The author of Passage 1 argues that online and other screen-based technologies affect people's abilities to think deeply (lines 47-50). The author of Passage 2 argues that the effects of consuming electronic media are less drastic than media critics suggest (lines 81-82).

Choices A and B are incorrect because they discuss points made in the passages but not the main purpose of the passages. Choice C is incorrect because neither passage argues in favor of increasing financial support for certain studies.

QUESTION 30.

Choice B is the best answer. The author of Passage 1 cites scientific research that suggests online and screen-based technologies have a negative effect on the brain (lines 25-38). The author of Passage 2 is critical of the research highlighted in Passage 1: "Critics of new media sometimes use science itself to press their case, citing research that shows how 'experience can change the brain.' But cognitive neuroscientists roll their eyes at such talk" (lines 51-54).

Choices A, C, and D are incorrect because they do not accurately describe the relationship between the two passages. Passage 1 does not take a clinical approach to the topic. Passage 2 does not take a high-level view of a finding examined in depth in Passage 1, nor does it predict negative reactions to the findings discussed in paragraph 1.

QUESTION 31.

Choice C is the best answer. In Passage 1, the author cites psychologist Patricia Greenfield's finding that "'every medium develops some cognitive skills at the expense of others'" (lines 29-31). In Passage 2, the author states "If you train people to do one thing (recognize shapes, solve math puzzles, find hidden words), they get better at doing that thing, but almost nothing else" (lines 71-74). Both authors would agree than an improvement in one cognitive area, such as visual-spatial skills, would not result in improved skills in other areas.

Choice A is incorrect because hand-eye coordination is not discussed in Passage 2. Choice B is incorrect because Passage 1 does not suggest that critics of electronic media tend to overreact. Choice D is incorrect because neither passage discusses whether Internet users prefer reading printed texts or digital texts.

QUESTION 32.

Choice B is the best answer. In Passage 1, the author cites Michael Merzenich's claim that when people adapt to a new cultural phenomenon, including the use of a new medium, we end up with a "different brain" (lines 41-43). The author of Passage 2 somewhat agrees with Merzenich's claim by stating, "Yes, every time we learn a fact or skill the wiring of the brain changes" (lines 54-56).

Choices A, C, and D do not provide the best evidence that the author of Passage 2 would agree to some extent with Merzenich's claim. Choices A and D are incorrect because the claims are attributed to critics of new media. Choice C is incorrect because it shows that the author of Passage 2 does not completely agree with Merzenich's claim about brain plasticity.

QUESTION 33.

Choice B is the best answer. In lines 16-31, Stanton argues that men make all the decisions in "the church, the state, and the home." This absolute power has led to a disorganized society, a "fragmentary condition of everything." Stanton confirms this claim when she states that society needs women to "lift man up into the higher realms of thought and action" (lines 60-61).

Choices A and D are incorrect because Stanton does not focus on women's lack of equal educational opportunities or inability to hold political positions. Choice C is incorrect because although Stanton implies women are not allowed to vote, she never mentions that "poor candidates" are winning elections.

QUESTION 34.

Choice A is the best answer. Stanton argues that women are repressed in society because men hold "high carnival," or have all the power, and make the rules in "the church, the state, and the home" (lines 16-31). Stanton claims that men have total control over women, "overpowering the feminine element everywhere" (line 18).

Choices B, C, and D are incorrect because Stanton does not use the term "high carnival" to emphasize that the time period is freewheeling, or unrestricted; that there has been a scandalous decline in moral values; or that the power of women is growing.

QUESTION 35.

Choice D is the best answer. In lines 16-23, Stanton states that men's absolute rule in society is "crushing out all the diviner qualities in human nature," such that society knows very "little of true manhood and womanhood." Stanton argues that society knows less about womanhood than manhood, because womanhood has "scarce been recognized as a power until within the last century." This statement indicates that society's acknowledgement of "womanhood," or women's true character, is a fairly recent historical development.

Choices A, B, and C are incorrect because Stanton describes men's control of society, their domination of the domestic sphere, and the prevalence of war and injustice as long-established realities.

QUESTION 36.

Choice B is the best answer. In lines 16-23, Stanton provides evidence for the claim that society's acknowledgement of "womanhood," or women's true character, is a fairly recent historical development: "[womanhood] has scarce been recognized as a power until within the last century."

Choices A, C, and D are incorrect because they do not provide the best evidence that society's acknowledgement of "womanhood," or women's true character, is a fairly recent historical development. Rather, choices A, C, and D discuss men's character, power, and influence.

QUESTION 37.

Choice B is the best answer. In lines 23-26, Stanton states, "Society is but the reflection of man himself, untempered by woman's thought; the hard iron rule we feel alike in the church, the state, and the home." In this context, man's "rule" in "the church, the state, and the home" means that men have a controlling force in all areas of society.

Choices A, C, and D are incorrect because in this context "rule" does not mean a general guideline, an established habit, or a procedural method.

QUESTION 38.

Choice D is the best answer. In lines 32-35, Stanton argues that people use the term "the strong-minded" to refer to women who advocate for "the right to suffrage," or the right to vote in elections. In this context, people use the term "the strong-minded" to criticize female suffragists, as they believe voting will make women too "masculine."

Choices A and B are incorrect because Stanton does not suggest that people use the term "the strong-minded" as a compliment. Choice C is incorrect because Stanton suggests that "the strong-minded" is a term used to criticize women who want to vote, not those who enter male-dominated professions.

QUESTION 39.

Choice C is the best answer. In lines 36-39, Stanton states that society contains hardly any women in the "best sense," and clarifies that too many women are "reflections, varieties, and dilutions of the masculine gender." Stanton is suggesting that there are few "best," or genuine, women who are not completely influenced or controlled by men.

Choices A, B, and D are incorrect because in this context "best" does not mean superior, excellent, or rarest.

QUESTION 40.

Choice A is the best answer. In lines 54-56, Stanton argues that man "mourns," or regrets, how his power has caused "falsehood, selfishness, and violence" to become the "law" of society. Stanton is arguing that men are lamenting, or expressing regret about, how their governance has created problems.

Choices B, C, and D are incorrect because Stanton does not suggest that men are advocating for women's right to vote or for female equality, nor are they requesting women's opinions about improving civic life.

QUESTION 41.

Choice B is the best answer. In lines 54-56, Stanton provides evidence that men are lamenting the problems they have created, as they recognize that their actions have caused "falsehood, selfishness, and violence [to become] the law of life."

Choices A, C, and D are incorrect because they do not provide the best evidence that men are lamenting the problems they have created. Choice A explains society's current fragmentation. Choices C and D present Stanton's main argument for women's enfranchisement.

QUESTION 42.

Choice D is the best answer. In the sixth paragraph, Stanton differentiates between men and masculine traits. Stanton argues that masculine traits or "characteristics," such as a "love of acquisition and conquest," serve to "subjugate one man to another" (lines 69-80). Stanton is suggesting that some masculine traits position men within certain power structures.

Choices A and B are incorrect because the sixth paragraph does not primarily establish a contrast between men and women or between the spiritual and material worlds. Choice C is incorrect because although Stanton argues that not "all men are hard, selfish, and brutal," she does not discuss what constitutes a "good" man.

QUESTION 43.

Choice C is the best answer. In the first paragraph, the author identifies the natural phenomenon "internal waves" (line 3), and explains why they are important: "internal waves are fundamental parts of ocean water dynamics, transferring heat to the ocean depths and bringing up cold water from below" (lines 7-9).

Choices A, B, and D are incorrect because they do not identify the main purpose of the first paragraph, as that paragraph does not focus on a scientific device, a common misconception, or a recent study.

QUESTION 44.

Choice B is the best answer. In lines 17-19, researcher Tom Peacock argues that in order to create precise global climate models, scientists must be able to "capture processes" such as how internal waves are formed. In this context, to "capture" a process means to record it for scientific study.

Choices A, C, and D are incorrect because in this context "capture" does not mean to control, secure, or absorb.

QUESTION 45.

Choice D is the best answer. In lines 17-19, researcher Tom Peacock argues that scientists need to "capture processes" of internal waves to develop "more and more accurate climate models." Peacock is suggesting that studying internal waves will inform the development of scientific models.

Choices A, B, and C are incorrect because Peacock does not state that monitoring internal waves will allow people to verify wave heights, improve satellite image quality, or prevent coastal damage.

QUESTION 46.

Choice C is the best answer. In lines 17-19, researcher Tom Peacock provides evidence that studying internal waves will inform the development of key scientific models, such as "more accurate climate models."

Choices A, B, and D are incorrect because they do not provide the best evidence that studying internal waves will inform the development of key scientific models; rather, they provide general information about internal waves.

QUESTION 47.

Choice A is the best answer. In lines 65-67, the author notes that Tom Peacock and his team "were able to devise a mathematical model that describes the movement and formation of these waves." In this context, the researchers devised, or created, a mathematical model.

Choices B, C, and D are incorrect because in this context "devise" does not mean to solve, imagine, or begin.

QUESTION 48.

Choice B is the best answer. Tom Peacock and his team created a model of the "Luzon's Strait's underwater topography" and determined that its "distinct double-ridge shape . . . [is] responsible for generating the underwater [internal] waves" (lines 53-55). The author notes that this model describes only internal waves in the Luzon Strait but that the team's findings may "help researchers understand how internal waves are generated in other places around the world" (lines 67-70). The author's claim suggests that while internal waves in the Luzon Strait are "some of the largest in the world" (line 25) due to the region's topography, internal waves occurring in other regions may be caused by some similar factors.

Choice A is incorrect because the author notes that the internal waves in the Luzon Strait are "some of the largest in the world" (line 25), which suggests that internal waves reach varying heights. Choices C and D are incorrect because they are not supported by the researchers' findings.

QUESTION 49.

Choice D is the best answer. In lines 67-70, the author provides evidence that, while the researchers' findings suggest the internal waves in the Luzon Strait are influenced by the region's topography, the findings may "help researchers understand how internal waves are generated in other places around the world." This statement suggests that all internal waves may be caused by some similar factors.

Choices A, B, and C are incorrect because they do not provide the best evidence that internal waves are caused by similar factors but influenced by the distinct topographies of different regions. Rather, choices A, B, and C reference general information about internal waves or focus solely on those that occur in the Luzon Strait.

QUESTION 50.

Choice D is the best answer. During the period 19:12 to 20:24, the graph shows the 13°C isotherm increasing in depth from about 20 to 40 meters.

Choices A, B, and C are incorrect because during the time period 19:12 to 20:24 the 9°C, 10°C, and 11°C isotherms all decreased in depth.

QUESTION 51.

Choice D is the best answer. In lines 3-6, the author notes that internal waves "do not ride the ocean surface" but "move underwater, undetectable without the use of satellite imagery or sophisticated monitoring equipment." The graph shows that the isotherms in an internal wave never reach the ocean's surface, as the isotherms do not record a depth of 0.

Choice A is incorrect because the graph provides no information about salinity. Choice B is incorrect because the graph shows layers of less dense water (which, based on the passage, are warmer) riding above layers of denser water (which, based on the passage, are cooler). Choice C is incorrect because the graph shows that internal waves push isotherms of warmer water above bands of colder water.

QUESTION 52.

Choice A is the best answer. In lines 7-9, the author notes that internal waves are "fundamental parts of ocean water dynamics" because they transfer "heat to the ocean depths and brin[g] up cold water from below." The graph shows an internal wave forcing the warm isotherms to depths that typically are colder. For example, at 13:12, the internal wave transfers "heat to the ocean depths" by forcing the 10°C, 11°C, and 13°C isotherms to depths that typically are colder.

Choices B, C, and D are incorrect because the graph does not show how internal waves affect the ocean's density, surface temperature, or tide flow.

Section 2: Writing and Language Test

QUESTION 1.

Choice B is the best answer because it provides a noun, "reductions," yielding a grammatically complete and coherent sentence.

Choices A, C, and D are incorrect because each provides a verb or gerund, while the underlined portion calls for a noun.

QUESTION 2.

Choice B is the best answer because it offers a transitional adverb, "Consequently," that communicates a cause-effect relationship between the funding reduction identified in the previous sentence and the staffing decrease described in this sentence.

Choices A, C, and D are incorrect because each misidentifies the relationship between the preceding sentence and the sentence of which it is a part.

QUESTION 3.

Choice A is the best answer because the singular verb "has" agrees with the singular noun "trend" that appears earlier in the sentence.

Choices B, C, and D are incorrect because the plural verb "have" does not agree with the singular subject "trend," and the relative pronoun "which" unnecessarily interrupts the direct relationship between "trend" and the verb.

QUESTION 4.

Choice A is the best answer because it states accurately why the proposed clause should be added to the sentence. Without these specific examples, readers have only a vague sense of what "nonprint" formats might be.

Choices B, C, and D are incorrect because each represents a misinterpretation of the relationship between the proposed clause to be added and the surrounding text in the passage.

QUESTION 5.

Choice D is the best answer because it includes only the preposition and noun that the sentence requires.

Choices A, B, and C are incorrect because each includes an unnecessary pronoun, either "them" or "their." The sentence contains no referents that would circulate e-books.

QUESTION 6.

Choice D is the best answer because the verb form "cataloging" parallels the other verbs in the series.

Choices A, B, and C are incorrect because each interrupts the parallel structure in the verb series, either through an incorrect verb form or with an unnecessary subject.

QUESTION 7.

Choice B is the best answer because it consolidates references to the subject, "librarians," by placing the relative pronoun "whose" immediately following "librarians." This results in a logical flow of information within the sentence.

Choices A, C, and D are incorrect because each fails to place "librarians" as the main subject of the sentence without redundancy, resulting in a convoluted sentence whose relevance to the preceding and subsequent sentences is unclear.

QUESTION 8.

Choice D is the best answer because no conjunction is necessary to communicate the relationship between the clauses in the sentence. The conjunction "While" at the beginning of the sentence already creates a comparison.

Choices A, B, and C are incorrect because each provides an unnecessary coordinating conjunction.

QUESTION 9.

Choice B is the best answer because it mentions time periods when the free services described later in the sentence are particularly useful to library patrons.

Choices A, C, and D are incorrect because each creates redundancy or awkwardness in the remainder of the sentence.

QUESTION 10.

Choice B is the best answer because it is concise; it is also consistent with the formal language in the rest of the sentence and the passage overall.

Choices A, C, and D are incorrect because each is either unnecessarily wordy or uses colloquial language that does not correspond with the tone of the passage.

QUESTION 11.

Choice C is the best answer because it restates the writer's primary argument, which may be found at the end of the first paragraph: "As public libraries adapt to rapid technological advances in information distribution, librarians' roles are actually expanding."

Choices A, B, and D are incorrect because they do not paraphrase the writer's primary claim.

QUESTION 12.

Choice B is the best answer because it clarifies that the sentence, which mentions a specific large-scale painting at the Art Institute of Chicago, is an example supporting the preceding claim about large-scale paintings.

Choices A, C, and D are incorrect because they propose transitional words or phrases that do not accurately represent the relationship between the preceding sentence and the sentence containing the underlined portion.

QUESTION 13.

Choice D is the best answer because no punctuation is necessary in the underlined phrase.

Choices A, B, and C are incorrect because each separates parts of the noun phrase "painter Georges Seurat's 10-foot-wide *A Sunday Afternoon on the Island of La Grande Jatte*" from one another with one or more unnecessary commas.

QUESTION 14.

Choice C is the best answer because it provides the appropriate possessive form, "its," and a colon to introduce the identifying phrase that follows.

Choices A, B, and D are incorrect because none contains both the appropriate possessive form of "it" and the punctuation that creates a grammatically standard sentence.

QUESTION 15.

Choice C is the best answer because an analysis of the consequences of King Louis XV's reign is irrelevant to the paragraph.

Choices A, B, and D are incorrect because each represents a misinterpretation of the relationship between the proposed sentence to be added and the main point of the paragraph.

QUESTION 16.

Choice C is the best answer because it provides a coordinating conjunction, "and," to connect the two verb phrases "are characterized" and "are covered."

Choices A, B, and D are incorrect because each lacks the conjunction needed to connect the two verb phrases "are characterized" and "are covered."

QUESTION 17.

Choice B is the best answer because it offers an example of an additional household item, a "tea cup," with a specific measurement that is one-twelfth of its actual size.

Choices A, C, D are incorrect because, compared to the example preceding the underlined portion, each is vague and fails to offer a specific measurement of an additional household item.

QUESTION 18.

Choice B is the best answer because it provides correct punctuation and the coordinating conjunction "but," which acknowledges the possible contrast between being "sparsely furnished" and displaying "just as true" period details.

Choices A, C, and D are incorrect because each communicates an illogical relationship between the phrases that precede and follow the underlined portion.

QUESTION 19.

Choice A is the best answer because it provides a clause that is the most similar to the two preceding clauses, which both end with a reference to a specific wall.

Choices B, C, and D are incorrect because each deviates from the stylistic pattern of the preceding two clauses.

QUESTION 20.

Choice D is the best answer because the article "a" requires the singular noun "visitor," and the simple present verb "remark" is the appropriate verb tense in this context.

Choices A, B, and C are incorrect because each contains either a noun or verb that does not fit the context.

QUESTION 21.

Choice D is the best answer because it identifies the drawers, rather than the visitor, as being "dotted with pin-sized knobs."

Choices A, B, and C are incorrect because all three contain dangling modifiers that obscure the relationship between the visitor, the drawers, and the pin-sized knobs.

QUESTION 22.

Choice B is the best answer because paragraph 3 offers an overview of the exhibit and so serves to introduce the specific aspects of particular miniature rooms described in paragraphs 2 and 4.

Choices A, C, and D are incorrect because each proposes a placement of paragraph 2 that prevents the passage from developing in a logical sequence.

QUESTION 23.

Choice A is the best answer because it correctly completes the noun phrase that begins with "sea otters," and directly follows the noun phrase with the verb "help."

Choices B, C, and D are incorrect because each separates the noun "otters" from the verb "help" in a way that results in a grammatically incomplete sentence.

QUESTION 24.

Choice B is the best answer because the data in the chart show lower sea urchin density in areas where sea otters have lived for two years or less than in areas where no otters are present.

Choices A, C, and D are incorrect because none accurately describes the data in the chart.

QUESTION 25.

Choice B is the best answer because the conjunctive adverb "however" accurately communicates the contrast between an environment shaped by the presence of sea otters, described in the preceding sentence, and an environment shaped by the absence of sea otters, described in this sentence.

Choices A, C, and D are incorrect because each presents a conjunctive adverb that does not accurately depict the relationship between the preceding sentence and the sentence with the underlined word.

QUESTION 26.

Choice A is the best answer because the additional information usefully connects the carbon dioxide levels mentioned in this sentence with the global warming mentioned in the previous sentence.

Choices B, C, and D are incorrect because each misinterprets the relationship between the proposed information and the main points of the paragraph and the passage.

QUESTION 27.

Choice D is the best answer because it offers the verb "suggests" followed directly by its object, a that-clause, without interruption.

Choices A, B, and C are incorrect because each contains punctuation that unnecessarily separates the study from its findings—that is, separates the verb from its object.

QUESTION 28.

Choice A is the best answer because it accurately reflects the fact that sea urchins "graze voraciously on kelp," as stated in the first paragraph, and it also maintains the tone of the passage.

Choices B, C, and D are incorrect because each offers a term that does not accurately describe the behavior of sea otters.

QUESTION 29.

Choice C is the best answer because the possessive singular pronoun "its" corresponds with the referent "kelp," which appears later in the sentence, and with the possessive relationship between the pronoun and the "terrestrial plant cousins."

Choices A, B, and D are incorrect because none provides a pronoun that is both singular and possessive.

QUESTION 30.

Choice C is the best answer because it provides the noun "sea otters" to identify who or what "played a role."

Choices A, B, and D are incorrect because each provides a pronoun that makes no sense in the context of the paragraph and the passage, which is about the role sea otters play—not the role scientists play or the role kelp plays.

QUESTION 31.

Choice D is the best answer because sentence 5 indicates that sea otters' importance in decreasing atmospheric carbon dioxide was not known, and the sentence to be added indicates that a surprise will follow. Sentence 6 provides that surprise: sea otters have a large impact on the amount of carbon dioxide kelp can remove from the atmosphere.

Choices A, B, and C are incorrect because each interrupts the logical flow of ideas in the paragraph.

QUESTION 32.

Choice B is the best answer because its clear wording and formal tone correspond with the passage's established style.

Choices A, C, and D are incorrect because each contains vague language that is inconsistent with the passage's clear wording and formal tone.

QUESTION 33.

Choice D is the best answer because it provides punctuation that appropriately identifies "removed" as the definition of "sequestered."

Choices A, B, and C are incorrect because each contains punctuation that obscures the relationship between "sequestered," "removed," and the text that follows.

QUESTION 34.

Choice D is the best answer because it provides a conjunction that correctly identifies the relationship between "a practice" and the actions involved in the practice.

Choices A, B, and C are incorrect because each contains a conjunction that miscommunicates the relationship between the text that precedes and follows the underlined portion.

QUESTION 35.

Choice A is the best answer because it provides a comma to close the appositive clause "a practice whereby products are designed to have a limited period of usefulness," which also begins with a comma.

Choices B, C, and D are incorrect because each provides closing punctuation inconsistent with the punctuation at the beginning of the clause.

QUESTION 36.

Choice D is the best answer because it provides an adjective that accurately describes the clear "contrast" between products "designed to have a limited period of usefulness" and those "produced to be durable."

Choices A, B, and C are incorrect because none provides an adjective that appropriately modifies "contrast" in the context of the paragraph.

QUESTION 37.

Choice A is the best answer because by mentioning the "specialized" methods used in repair shops, it suggests that repairing goods is seen as a specialty rather than as a common activity. This connects logically with the "rare" repair shops introduced just before the underlined portion.

Choices B, C, and D are incorrect because none provides information that supports the claim made in the sentence.

QUESTION 38.

Choice B is the best answer because it provides the correct spelling of the noun "fair," meaning exhibition, and uses the correct word "than" to create the comparison between a "fair" and a "café."

Choices A, C, and D are incorrect because each contains a misspelling of either "fair" or "than."

QUESTION 39.

Choice C is the best answer because it offers a relative pronoun that properly links the noun "Martine Postma" with the appropriate verb "wanted."

Choices A, B, and D are incorrect because none contains a pronoun that is appropriate for the referent and placement of the clause.

QUESTION 40.

Choice D is the best answer because it provides the most concise phrasing and links the sentence appropriately to the previous sentence.

Choices A, B, and C are incorrect because each provides an unnecessary adverb that obscures the relationship between this sentence and the previous one.

QUESTION 41.

Choice D is the best answer because the gerund "waiting" corresponds with the preposition "for" and the present tense used in the rest of the sentence.

Choices A, B, and C are incorrect because each contains a verb form not used with the preposition "for."

QUESTION 42.

Choice C is the best answer because it appropriately places sentence 5, which describes the places Repair Cafés can be found today, between a sentence that gives the first Repair Café's location and purpose and a statement about current customers and how they use Repair Cafés.

Choices A, B, and D are incorrect because each creates a paragraph with an inappropriate shift in verb tense and, therefore, an illogical sequence of information.

QUESTION 43.

Choice C is the best answer because it accurately states that the issue of "corporate and service-based jobs" is not particularly relevant at this point in the paragraph. The focus here is on repairing objects in a "throwaway culture," not jobs.

Choices A, B, and D are incorrect because each misinterprets the relationship between the proposed text and the information in the paragraph.

QUESTION 44.

Choice D is the best answer because the phrase "and other countries" communicates the fact that there are additional items not being named that could be added to the list; no other wording is required to clarify that point.

Choices A, B, and C are incorrect because each presents a word or phrase that results in a redundancy with "and other countries."

Section 3: Math Test — No Calculator

QUESTION 1.

Choice C is correct. Subtracting 6 from each side of $5x + 6 = 10$ yields $5x = 4$. Dividing both sides of $5x = 4$ by 5 yields $x = \frac{4}{5}$. The value of x can now be substituted into the expression $10x + 3$, giving $10\left(\frac{4}{5}\right) + 3 = 11$.

Alternatively, the expression $10x + 3$ can be rewritten as $2(5x + 6) - 9$, and 10 can be substituted for $5x + 6$, giving $2(10) - 9 = 11$.

Choices A, B, and D are incorrect. Each of these choices leads to $5x + 6 \neq 10$, contradicting the given equation, $5x + 6 = 10$. For example, choice A is incorrect because if the value of $10x + 3$ were 4, then it would follow that $x = 0.1$, and the value of $5x + 6$ would be 6.5, not 10.

QUESTION 2.

Choice B is correct. Multiplying each side of $x + y = 0$ by 2 gives $2x + 2y = 0$. Then, adding the corresponding sides of $2x + 2y = 0$ and $3x - 2y = 10$ gives $5x = 10$. Dividing each side of $5x = 10$ by 5 gives $x = 2$. Finally, substituting 2 for x in $x + y = 0$ gives $2 + y = 0$, or $y = -2$. Therefore, the solution to the given system of equations is $(2, -2)$.

Alternatively, the equation $x + y = 0$ can be rewritten as $x = -y$, and substituting x for $-y$ in $3x - 2y = 10$ gives $5x = 10$, or $x = 2$. The value of y can then be found in the same way as before.

Choices A, C, and D are incorrect because when the given values of x and y are substituted into $x + y = 0$ and $3x - 2y = 10$, either one or both of the equations are not true. These answers may result from sign errors or other computational errors.

QUESTION 3.

Choice A is correct. The price of the job, in dollars, is calculated using the expression $60 + 12nh$, where 60 is a fixed price and $12nh$ depends on the number of landscapers, n, working the job and the number of hours, h, the job takes those n landscapers. Since nh is the total number of hours of work done when n landscapers work h hours, the cost of the job increases by \$12 for each hour a landscaper works. Therefore, of the choices given, the best interpretation of the number 12 is that the company charges \$12 per hour for each landscaper.

Choice B is incorrect because the number of landscapers that will work each job is represented by n in the equation, not by the number 12. Choice C is incorrect because the price of the job increases by $12n$ dollars each hour, which will not be equal to 12 dollars unless $n = 1$. Choice D is incorrect because the total number of hours each landscaper works is equal to h. The number of hours each landscaper works in a day is not provided.

QUESTION 4.

Choice A is correct. If a polynomial expression is in the form $(x)^2 + 2(x)(y) + (y)^2$, then it is equivalent to $(x + y)^2$. Because $9a^4 + 12a^2b^2 + 4b^4 = (3a^2)^2 + 2(3a^2)(2b^2) + (2b^2)^2$, it can be rewritten as $(3a^2 + 2b^2)^2$.

Choice B is incorrect. The expression $(3a + 2b)^4$ is equivalent to the product $(3a + 2b)(3a + 2b)(3a + 2b)(3a + 2b)$. This product will contain the term $4(3a)^3(2b) = 216a^3b$. However, the given polynomial, $9a^4 + 12a^2b^2 + 4b^4$, does not contain the term $216a^3b$. Therefore, $9a^4 + 12a^2b^2 + 4b^4 \neq (3a + 2b)^4$. Choice C is incorrect. The expression $(9a^2 + 4b^2)^2$ is equivalent to the product $(9a^2 + 4b^2)(9a^2 + 4b^2)$. This product will contain the term $(9a^2)(9a^2) = 81a^4$. However, the given polynomial, $9a^4 + 12a^2b^2 + 4b^4$, does not contain the term $81a^4$. Therefore, $9a^4 + 12a^2b^2 + 4b^4 \neq (9a^2 + 4b^2)^2$. Choice D is incorrect. The expression $(9a + 4b)^4$ is equivalent to the product $(9a + 4b)(9a + 4b)(9a + 4b)(9a + 4b)$. This product will contain the term $(9a)(9a)(9a)(9a) = 6,561a^4$. However, the given polynomial, $9a^4 + 12a^2b^2 + 4b^4$, does not contain the term $6,561a^4$. Therefore, $9a^4 + 12a^2b^2 + 4b^4 \neq (9a + 4b)^4$.

QUESTION 5.

Choice C is correct. Since $\sqrt{2k^2 + 17} - x = 0$, and $x = 7$, one can substitute 7 for x, which gives $\sqrt{2k^2 + 17} - 7 = 0$. Adding 7 to each side of $\sqrt{2k^2 + 17} - 7 = 0$ gives $\sqrt{2k^2 + 17} = 7$. Squaring each side of $\sqrt{2k^2 + 17} = 7$ will remove the square root symbol: $\left(\sqrt{2k^2 + 17}\right)^2 = (7)^2$, or $2k^2 + 17 = 49$. Then subtracting 17 from each side of $2k^2 + 17 = 49$ gives $2k^2 = 49 - 17 = 32$, and dividing each side of $2k^2 = 32$ by 2 gives $k^2 = 16$. Finally, taking the square root of each side of $k^2 = 16$ gives $k = \pm 4$, and since the problem states that $k > 0$, it follows that $k = 4$.

Since the sides of an equation were squared while solving $\sqrt{2k^2 + 17} - 7 = 0$, it is possible that an extraneous root was produced. However, substituting 4 for k in $\sqrt{2k^2 + 17} - 7 = 0$ confirms that 4 is a solution for k: $\sqrt{2(4)^2 + 17} - 7 = \sqrt{32 + 17} - 7 = \sqrt{49} - 7 = 7 - 7 = 0$.

Choices A, B, and D are incorrect because substituting any of these values for k in $\sqrt{2k^2 + 17} - 7 = 0$ does not yield a true statement.

QUESTION 6.

Choice D is correct. Since lines ℓ and k are parallel, the lines have the same slope. Line ℓ passes through the points $(-5, 0)$ and $(0, 2)$, so its slope is $\frac{0 - 2}{-5 - 0}$, which is $\frac{2}{5}$. The slope of line k must also be $\frac{2}{5}$. Since line k has slope $\frac{2}{5}$ and passes through the points $(0, -4)$ and $(p, 0)$, it follows that $\frac{-4 - 0}{0 - p} = \frac{2}{5}$, or $\frac{4}{p} = \frac{2}{5}$. Multiplying each side of $\frac{4}{p} = \frac{2}{5}$ by $5p$ gives $20 = 2p$, and therefore, $p = 10$.

Choices A, B, and C are incorrect and may result from conceptual or calculation errors.

QUESTION 7.

Choice A is correct. Since the numerator and denominator of $\frac{x^{a^2}}{x^{b^2}}$ have a common base, it follows by the laws of exponents that this expression can be rewritten as $x^{a^2 - b^2}$. Thus, the equation $\frac{x^{a^2}}{x^{b^2}} = 16$ can be rewritten as $x^{a^2 - b^2} = x^{16}$. Because the equivalent expressions have the common base x, and $x > 1$, it follows that the exponents of the two expressions must also be equivalent. Hence, the equation $a^2 - b^2 = 16$ must be true. The left-hand side of this new equation is a difference of squares, and so it can be factored: $(a + b)(a - b) = 16$. It is given that $(a + b) = 2$; substituting 2 for the factor $(a + b)$ gives $2(a - b) = 16$. Finally, dividing both sides of $2(a - b) = 16$ by 2 gives $a - b = 8$.

Choices B, C, and D are incorrect and may result from errors in applying the laws of exponents or errors in solving the equation $a^2 - b^2 = 16$.

QUESTION 8.

Choice C is correct. The relationship between n and A is given by the equation $nA = 360$. Since n is the number of sides of a polygon, n must be a positive integer, and so $nA = 360$ can be rewritten as $A = \frac{360}{n}$. If the value of A is greater than 50, it follows that $\frac{360}{n} > 50$ is a true statement. Thus, $50n < 360$, or $n < \frac{360}{50} = 7.2$. Since n must be an integer, the greatest possible value of n is 7.

Choices A and B are incorrect. These are possible values for n, the number of sides of a regular polygon, if $A > 50$, but neither is the greatest possible value of n. Choice D is incorrect. If $A < 50$, then $n = 8$ is the least possible value of n, the number of sides of a regular polygon. However, the question asks for the <u>greatest</u> possible value of n if $A > 50$, which is $n = 7$.

QUESTION 9.

Choice B is correct. Since the slope of the first line is 2, an equation of this line can be written in the form $y = 2x + c$, where c is the y-intercept of the line. Since the line contains the point $(1, 8)$, one can substitute 1 for x and 8 for y in $y = 2x + c$, which gives $8 = 2(1) + c$, or $c = 6$. Thus, an equation of the first line is $y = 2x + 6$. The slope of the second line is equal to $\frac{1 - 2}{2 - 1}$ or -1. Thus, an equation of the second line can be written in the form $y = -x + d$, where d is the y-intercept of the line. Substituting 2 for x and 1 for y gives $1 = -2 + d$, or $d = 3$. Thus, an equation of the second line is $y = -x + 3$.

Since a is the x-coordinate and b is the y-coordinate of the intersection point of the two lines, one can substitute a for x and b for y in the two equations, giving the system $b = 2a + 6$ and $b = -a + 3$. Thus, a can be found by solving the equation $2a + 6 = -a + 3$, which gives $a = -1$. Finally, substituting -1 for a into the equation $b = -a + 3$ gives $b = -(-1) + 3$, or $b = 4$. Therefore, the value of $a + b$ is 3.

Alternatively, since the second line passes through the points $(1, 2)$ and $(2, 1)$, an equation for the second line is $x + y = 3$. Thus, the intersection point of the first line and the second line, (a, b) lies on the line with equation $x + y = 3$. It follows that $a + b = 3$.

Choices A and C are incorrect and may result from finding the value of only a or b, but not calculating the value of $a + b$. Choice D is incorrect and may result from a computation error in finding equations of the two lines or in solving the resulting system of equations.

QUESTION 10.

Choice C is correct. Since the square of any real number is nonnegative, every point on the graph of the quadratic equation $y = (x - 2)^2$ in the xy-plane has a nonnegative y-coordinate. Thus, $y \geq 0$ for every point on the graph. Therefore, the equation $y = (x - 2)^2$ has a graph for which y is always greater than or equal to -1.

Choices A, B, and D are incorrect because the graph of each of these equations in the xy-plane has a y-intercept at $(0, -2)$. Therefore, each of these equations contains at least one point where y is less than -1.

QUESTION 11.

Choice C is correct. To perform the division $\dfrac{3 - 5i}{8 + 2i}$, multiply the numerator and denominator of $\dfrac{3 - 5i}{8 + 2i}$ by the conjugate of the denominator, $8 - 2i$. This gives $\dfrac{(3 - 5i)(8 - 2i)}{(8 + 2i)(8 - 2i)} = \dfrac{24 - 6i - 40i + (-5i)(-2i)}{8^2 - (2i)^2}$. Since $i^2 = -1$, this can be simplified to $\dfrac{24 - 6i - 40i - 10}{64 + 4} = \dfrac{14 - 46i}{68}$, which then simplifies to $\dfrac{7}{34} - \dfrac{23i}{34}$.

Choices A and B are incorrect and may result from misconceptions about fractions. For example, $\dfrac{a + b}{c + d}$ is equal to $\dfrac{a}{c + d} + \dfrac{b}{c + d}$, not $\dfrac{a}{c} + \dfrac{b}{d}$. Choice D is incorrect and may result from a calculation error.

QUESTION 12.

Choice B is correct. Multiplying each side of $R = \dfrac{F}{N + F}$ by $N + F$ gives $R(N + F) = F$, which can be rewritten as $RN + RF = F$. Subtracting RF from each side of $RN + RF = F$ gives $RN = F - RF$, which can be factored as $RN = F(1 - R)$. Finally, dividing each side of $RN = F(1 - R)$ by $1 - R$, expresses F in terms of the other variables: $F = \dfrac{RN}{1 - R}$.

Choices A, C, and D are incorrect and may result from calculation errors when rewriting the given equation.

QUESTION 13.

Choice D is correct. The problem asks for the sum of the roots of the quadratic equation $2m^2 - 16m + 8 = 0$. Dividing each side of the equation by 2 gives $m^2 - 8m + 4 = 0$. If the roots of $m^2 - 8m + 4 = 0$ are s_1 and s_2, then the equation can be factored as $m^2 - 8m + 4 = (m - s_1)(m - s_2) = 0$. Looking at the coefficient of x on each side of $m^2 - 8m + 4 = (m - s_1)(m - s_2)$ gives $-8 = -s_1 - s_2$, or $s_1 + s_2 = 8$.

Alternatively, one can apply the quadratic formula to either $2m^2 - 16m + 8 = 0$ or $m^2 - 8m + 4 = 0$. The quadratic formula gives two solutions, $4 - 2\sqrt{3}$ and $4 + 2\sqrt{3}$ whose sum is 8.

Choices A, B, and C are incorrect and may result from calculation errors when applying the quadratic formula or a sign error when determining the sum of the roots of a quadratic equation from its coefficients.

QUESTION 14.

Choice A is correct. Each year, the amount of the radioactive substance is reduced by 13 percent from the prior year's amount; that is, each year, 87 percent of the previous year's amount remains. Since the initial amount of the radioactive substance was 325 grams, after 1 year, $325(0.87)$ grams remains; after 2 years $325(0.87)(0.87) = 325(0.87)^2$ grams remains; and after t years, $325(0.87)^t$ grams remains. Therefore, the function $f(t) = 325(0.87)^t$ models the remaining amount of the substance, in grams, after t years.

Choice B is incorrect and may result from confusing the amount of the substance remaining with the decay rate. Choices C and D are incorrect and may result from confusing the original amount of the substance and the decay rate.

QUESTION 15.

Choice D is correct. Dividing $5x - 2$ by $x + 3$ gives:

$$x + 3 \overline{)\begin{array}{r} 5 \\ 5x - 2 \end{array}}$$
$$\underline{5x + 15}$$
$$-17$$

Therefore, the expression $\dfrac{5x - 2}{x + 3}$ can be rewritten as $5 - \dfrac{17}{x + 3}$.

Alternatively, $\dfrac{5x - 2}{x + 3}$ can be rewritten as

$$\dfrac{5x - 2}{x + 3} = \dfrac{(5x + 15) - 15 - 2}{x + 3} = \dfrac{5(x + 3) - 17}{x + 3} = 5 - \dfrac{17}{x + 3}.$$

Choices A and B are incorrect and may result from incorrectly canceling out the x in the expression $\dfrac{5x-2}{x+3}$. Choice C is incorrect and may result from finding an incorrect remainder when performing long division.

QUESTION 16.

The correct answer is 3, 6, or 9. Let x be the number of \$250 bonuses awarded, and let y be the number of \$750 bonuses awarded. Since \$3000 in bonuses were awarded, and this included at least one \$250 bonus and one \$750 bonus, it follows that $250x + 750y = 3000$, where x and y are positive integers. Dividing each side of $250x + 750y = 3000$ by 250 gives $x + 3y = 12$, where x and y are positive integers. Since $3y$ and 12 are each divisible by 3, it follows that $x = 12 - 3y$ must also be divisible by 3. If $x = 3$, then $y = 3$; if $x = 6$, then $y = 2$; and if $x = 9$, then $y = 1$. If $x = 12$, then $y = 0$, but this is not possible since there was at least one \$750 bonus awarded. Therefore, the possible numbers of \$250 bonuses awarded are 3, 6, and 9. Any of the numbers 3, 6, or 9 may be gridded as the correct answer.

QUESTION 17.

The correct answer is 19. Since $2x(3x+5) + 3(3x+5) = ax^2 + bx + c$ for all values of x, the two sides of the equation are equal, and the value of b can be determined by simplifying the left-hand side of the equation and writing it in the same form as the right-hand side. Using the distributive property, the equation becomes $(6x^2 + 10x) + (9x + 15) = ax^2 + bx + c$. Combining like terms gives $6x^2 + 19x + 15 = ax^2 + bx + c$. The value of b is the coefficient of x, which is 19.

QUESTION 18.

The correct answer is 12. Angles ABE and DBC are vertical angles and thus have the same measure. Since segment AE is parallel to segment CD, angles A and D are of the same measure by the alternate interior angle theorem. Thus, by the angle-angle theorem, triangle ABE is similar to triangle DBC, with vertices A, B, and E corresponding to vertices D, B, and C, respectively. Thus, $\dfrac{AB}{DB} = \dfrac{EB}{CB}$ or $\dfrac{10}{5} = \dfrac{8}{CB}$. It follows that $CB = 4$, and so $CE = CB + BE = 4 + 8 = 12$.

QUESTION 19.

The correct answer is 6. By the distance formula, the length of radius OA is $\sqrt{(\sqrt{3})^2 + 1^2} = \sqrt{3+1} = 2$. Thus, $\sin(\angle AOB) = \dfrac{1}{2}$. Therefore, the measure of $\angle AOB$ is 30°, which is equal to $30\left(\dfrac{\pi}{180}\right) = \dfrac{\pi}{6}$ radians. Hence, the value of a is 6.

QUESTION 20.

The correct answer is $\dfrac{1}{4}$ or .25. In order for a system of two linear equations to have infinitely many solutions, the two equations must be equivalent.

Thus, the equation $ax + by = 12$ must be equivalent to the equation $2x + 8y = 60$. Multiplying each side of $ax + by = 12$ by 5 gives $5ax + 5by = 60$, which must be equivalent to $2x + 8y = 60$. Since the right-hand sides of $5ax + 5by = 60$ and $2x + 8y = 60$ are the same, equating coefficients gives $5a = 2$, or $a = \frac{2}{5}$, and $5b = 8$, or $b = \frac{8}{5}$. Therefore, the value of $\frac{a}{b} = \left(\frac{2}{5}\right) \div \left(\frac{8}{5}\right)$, which is equal to $\frac{1}{4}$. Either the fraction $\frac{1}{4}$ or its equivalent decimal, .25, may be gridded as the correct answer.

Alternatively, since $ax + by = 12$ is equivalent to $2x + 8y = 60$, the equation $ax + by = 12$ is equal to $2x + 8y = 60$ multiplied on each side by the same constant. Since multiplying $2x + 8y = 60$ by a constant does not change the ratio of the coefficient of x to the coefficient of y, it follows that $\frac{a}{b} = \frac{2}{8} = \frac{1}{4}$.

Section 4: Math Test — Calculator

QUESTION 1.

Choice C is correct. Since the musician earns $0.09 for each download, the musician earns $0.09d$ dollars when the song is downloaded d times. Similarly, since the musician earns $0.002 each time the song is streamed, the musician earns $0.002s$ dollars when the song is streamed s times. Therefore, the musician earns a total of $0.09d + 0.002s$ dollars when the song is downloaded d times and streamed s times.

Choice A is incorrect because the earnings for each download and the earnings for time streamed are interchanged in the expression. Choices B and D are incorrect because in both answer choices, the musician will lose money when a song is either downloaded or streamed. However, the musician only earns money, not loses money, when the song is downloaded or streamed.

QUESTION 2.

Choice B is correct. The quality control manager selects 7 lightbulbs at random for inspection out of every 400 lightbulbs produced. A quantity of 20,000 lightbulbs is equal to $\frac{20,000}{400} = 50$ batches of 400 lightbulbs. Therefore, at the rate of 7 lightbulbs per 400 lightbulbs produced, the quality control manager will inspect a total of $50 \times 7 = 350$ lightbulbs.

Choices A, C, and D are incorrect and may result from calculation errors or misunderstanding of the proportional relationship.

QUESTION 3.

Choice A is correct. The value of m when ℓ is 73 can be found by substituting the 73 for ℓ in $\ell = 24 + 3.5m$ and then solving for m. The resulting equation is $73 = 24 + 3.5m$; subtracting 24 from each side gives $49 = 3.5m$. Then, dividing each side of $49 = 3.5m$ by 3.5 gives $14 = m$. Therefore, when ℓ is 73, m is 14.

Choice B is incorrect and may result from adding 24 to 73, instead of subtracting 24 from 73, when solving $73 = 24 + 3.5m$. Choice C is incorrect because 73 is the given value for ℓ, not for m. Choice D is incorrect and may result from substituting 73 for m, instead of for ℓ, in the equation $\ell = 24 + 3.5m$.

QUESTION 4.

Choice C is correct. The amount of money the performer earns is directly proportional to the number of people who attend the performance. Thus, by the definition of direct proportionality, $M = kP$, where M is the amount of money the performer earns, in dollars, P is the number of people who attend the performance, and k is a constant. Since the performer earns $120 when 8 people attend the performance, one can substitute 120 for M and 8 for P, giving $120 = 8k$. Hence, $k = 15$, and the relationship between the number of people who attend the performance and the amount of money, in dollars, the performer earns is $M = 15P$. Therefore, when 20 people attend the performance, the performer earns $15(20) = 300$ dollars.

Choices A, B, and D are incorrect and may result from either misconceptions about proportional relationships or computational errors.

QUESTION 5.

Choice C is correct. If 43% of the money earned is used to pay for costs, then the rest, 57%, is profit. A performance where 8 people attend earns the performer $120, and 57% of $120 is $120 \times 0.57 = \$68.40$.

Choice A is incorrect. The amount $51.60 is 43% of the money earned from a performance where 8 people attend, which is the cost of putting on the performance, not the profit from the performance. Choice B is incorrect. It is given that 57% of the money earned is profit, but 57% of $120 is not equal to $57.00. Choice D is incorrect. The profit can be found by subtracting 43% of $120 from $120, but 43% of $120 is $51.60, not $43.00. Thus, the profit is $120 − \$51.60 = \$68.40$, not $120 − \$43.00 = \$77.00$.

QUESTION 6.

Choice B is correct. When 4 times the number x is added to 12, the result is $12 + 4x$. Since this result is equal to 8, the equation $12 + 4x = 8$ must be true. Subtracting 12 from each side of $12 + 4x = 8$ gives $4x = -4$, and then dividing both sides of $4x = -4$ by 4 gives $x = -1$. Therefore, 2 times x added to 7, or $7 + 2x$, is equal to $7 + 2(-1) = 5$.

Choice A is incorrect because -1 is the value of x, not the value of $7 + 2x$. Choices C and D are incorrect and may result from calculation errors.

QUESTION 7.

Choice D is correct. The x-intercepts of the parabola represented by $y = x^2 - 6x + 8$ in the xy-plane are the values of x for which y is equal to 0. The factored form of the equation, $y = (x - 2)(x - 4)$, shows that y equals 0 if and only if $x = 2$ or $x = 4$. Thus, the factored form, $y = (x - 2)(x - 4)$, displays the x-intercepts of the parabola as the constants 2 and 4.

Choices A, B, and C are incorrect because none of these forms shows the x-intercepts 2 and 4 as constants or coefficients.

QUESTION 8.

Choice D is correct. Since a player starts with k points and loses 2 points each time a task is not completed, the player's score will be $k - 2n$ after n tasks are not completed (and no additional points are gained). Since a player who fails to complete 100 tasks has a score of 200 points, the equation $200 = k - 100(2)$ must be true. This equation can be solved by adding 200 to each side, giving $k = 400$.

Choices A, B, and C are incorrect and may result from errors in setting up or solving the equation relating the player's score to the number of tasks the player fails to complete. For example, choice A may result from subtracting 200 from the left-hand side of $200 = k - 100(2)$ and adding 200 to the right-hand side.

QUESTION 9.

Choice A is correct. Since x is the number of 40-pound boxes, $40x$ is the total weight, in pounds, of the 40-pound boxes; and since y is the number of 65-pound boxes, $65y$ is the total weight, in pounds, of the 65-pound boxes. The combined weight of the boxes is therefore $40x + 65y$, and the total number of boxes is $x + y$. Since the forklift can carry up to 45 boxes or up to 2,400 pounds, the inequalities that represent these relationships are $40x + 65y \leq 2,400$ and $x + y \leq 45$.

Choice B is incorrect. The second inequality correctly represents the maximum number of boxes on the forklift, but the first inequality divides, rather than multiplies, the number of boxes by their respective weights. Choice C is incorrect. The combined weight of the boxes, $40x + 65y$, must be less than or equal to 2,400 pounds, not 45; the total number of boxes, $x + y$, must be less than or equal to 45, not 2,400. Choice D is incorrect. The second inequality correctly represents the maximum weight, in pounds, of the boxes on the forklift, but the total number of boxes, $x + y$, must be less than or equal to 45, not 2,400.

QUESTION 10.

Choice B is correct. It is given that $g(3) = 2$. Therefore, to find the value of $f(g(3))$, substitute 2 for $g(3)$: $f(g(3)) = f(2) = 3$.

Choices A, C, and D are incorrect and may result from misunderstandings about function notation.

QUESTION 11.

Choice B is correct. Tony reads 250 words per minute, and he plans to read for 3 hours, which is 180 minutes, each day. Thus, Tony is planning to read $250 \times 180 = 45,000$ words of the novel per day. Since the novel has 349,168 words, it will take Tony $\frac{349,168}{45,000} \approx 7.76$ days of reading to finish the novel. That is, it will take Tony 7 full days of reading and most of an 8th day of reading to finish the novel. Therefore, it will take Tony 8 days to finish the novel.

Choice A is incorrect and may result from an incorrect calculation or incorrectly using the numbers provided in the table. Choice C is incorrect and may result from taking the total number of words in the novel divided by the rate Tony reads per hour. Choice D is incorrect and may result from taking the total number of words in the novel divided by the number of pages in the novel.

QUESTION 12.

Choice D is correct. Since there were 175,000 tons of trash in the landfill on January 1, 2000, and the amount of trash in the landfill increased by 7,500 tons each year after that date, the amount of trash, in tons, in the landfill y years after January 1, 2000 can be expressed as $175,000 + 7,500y$. The landfill has a capacity of 325,000 tons. Therefore, the set of years where the amount of trash in the landfill is at (equal to) or above (greater than) capacity is described by the inequality $175,000 + 7,500y \geq 325,000$.

Choice A is incorrect. This inequality does not account for the 175,000 tons of trash in the landfill on January 1, 2000, nor does it accurately account for the 7,500 tons of trash that are added to the landfill each <u>year</u> after January 1, 2000. Choice B is incorrect. This inequality does not account for the 175,000 tons of trash in the landfill on January 1, 2000. Choice C is incorrect. This inequality represents the set of years where the amount of trash in the landfill is at or <u>below</u> capacity.

QUESTION 13.

Choice D is correct. Survey research is an efficient way to estimate the preferences of a large population. In order to reliably generalize the results of survey research to a larger population, the participants should be randomly selected from all people in that population. Since this survey was conducted with a population that was not randomly selected, the results are not reliably representative of all people in the town. Therefore, of the given factors, where the survey was given makes it least likely that a reliable conclusion can be drawn about the sports-watching preferences of all people in the town.

Choice A is incorrect. In general, larger sample sizes are preferred over smaller sample sizes. However, a sample size of 117 people would have allowed a reliable conclusion about the population if the participants had been selected at random. Choice B is incorrect. Whether the population is large or small, a large enough sample taken from the population is reliably generalizable if the participants are selected at random from that population. Thus, a reliable conclusion could have been drawn about the population if the 117 survey participants had been selected at random. Choice C is incorrect. When giving a survey, participants are not forced to respond. Even though some people refused to respond, a reliable conclusion could have been drawn about the population if the participants had been selected at random.

QUESTION 14.

Choice C is correct. According to the graph, the horizontal line that represents 550 billion miles traveled intersects the line of best fit at a point whose horizontal coordinate is between 2000 and 2005, and slightly closer to 2005 than to 2000. Therefore, of the choices given, 2003 best approximates the year in which the number of miles traveled by air passengers in Country X was estimated to be 550 billion.

Choice A is incorrect. According to the line of best fit, in 1997 the estimated number of miles traveled by air passengers in Country X was about 450 billion, not 550 billion. Choice B is incorrect. According to the line of best fit, in 2000 the estimated number of miles traveled by air passengers in Country X was about 500 billion, not 550 billion. Choice D is incorrect. According to the line of best fit, in 2008 the estimated number of miles traveled by air passengers in Country X was about 600 billion, not 550 billion.

QUESTION 15.

Choice A is correct. The number of miles Earth travels in its one-year orbit of the Sun is 580,000,000. Because there are about 365 days per year, the number of miles Earth travels per day is $\frac{580,000,000}{365} \approx 1,589,041$. There are 24 hours in one day, so Earth travels at $\frac{1,589,041}{24} \approx 66,210$ miles per hour. Therefore, of the choices given, 66,000 miles per hour is closest to the average speed of Earth as it orbits the Sun.

Choices B, C, and D are incorrect and may result from calculation errors.

QUESTION 16.

Choice B is correct. According to the table, there are $18 + 7 = 25$ graduates who passed the bar exam, and 7 of them did not take the review course. Therefore, if one of the surveyed graduates who passed the bar exam is chosen at random, the probability that the person chosen did not take the review course is $\frac{7}{25}$.

Choices A, C, and D are incorrect. Each of these choices represents a different probability from the conditional probability that the question asks for. Choice A represents the following probability. If one of the surveyed graduates who passed the bar exam is chosen at random, the probability that the person chosen <u>did</u> take the review course is $\frac{18}{25}$. Choice C represents the following probability. If one of the surveyed graduates is chosen at random, the probability that the person chosen passed the bar exam is $\frac{25}{200}$. Choice D represents the following probability. If one of the surveyed graduates is chosen at random, the probability that the person chosen passed the exam and took the review course is $\frac{7}{200}$.

QUESTION 17.

Choice C is correct. To find the atomic weight of an unknown element that is 20% less than the atomic weight of calcium, multiply the atomic weight, in amu, of calcium by $(1 - 0.20)$: $(40)(1 - 0.20) = (40)(0.8) = 32$.

Choice A is incorrect. This value is 20% of the atomic weight of calcium, not an atomic weight 20% less than that atomic weight of calcium. Choice B is incorrect. This value is 20 amu less, not 20% less, than the atomic weight of calcium. Choice D is incorrect. This value is 20% more, not 20% less, than the atomic weight of calcium.

QUESTION 18.

Choice C is correct. The mean and median values of a data set are equal when there is a symmetrical distribution. For example, a normal distribution is symmetrical. If the mean and the median values are not equal, then the distribution is not symmetrical. Outliers are a small group of values that are significantly smaller or larger than the other values in the data. When there are outliers in the data, the mean will be pulled in their direction (either smaller or larger) while the median remains the same. The example in the question has a mean that is larger than the median, and so an appropriate conjecture is that large outliers are present in the data; that is, that there are a few homes that are valued much more than the rest.

Choice A is incorrect because a set of home values that are close to each other will have median and mean values that are also close to each other.

Choice B is incorrect because outliers with small values will tend to make the mean lower than the median. Choice D is incorrect because a set of data where many homes are valued between $125,000 and $165,000 will likely have both a mean and a median between $125,000 and $165,000.

QUESTION 19.

Choice B is correct. The median of a data set is the middle value when the data points are sorted in either ascending or descending order. There are a total of 600 data points provided, so the median will be the average of the 300th and 301st data points. When the data points are sorted in order:

▶ Values 1 through 260 will be 0.

▶ Values 261 through 450 will be 1.

▶ Values 451 through 540 will be 2.

▶ Values 541 through 580 will be 3.

▶ Values 581 through 600 will be 4.

Therefore, both the 300th and 301st values are 1, and hence the median is 1.

Choices A, C, and D are incorrect and may result from either a calculation error or a conceptual error.

QUESTION 20.

Choice C is correct. When survey participants are selected at random from a larger population, the sample statistics calculated from the survey can be generalized to the larger population. Since 10 of 300 students surveyed at Lincoln School have 4 siblings, one can estimate that this same ratio holds for all 2,400 students at Lincoln School. Also, since 10 of 300 students surveyed at Washington School have 4 siblings, one can estimate that this same ratio holds for all 3,300 students at Washington School. Therefore, approximately $\frac{10}{300} \times 2,400 = 80$ students at Lincoln School and $\frac{10}{300} \times 3,300 = 110$ students at Washington School are expected to have 4 siblings. Thus, the total number of students with 4 siblings at Washington School is expected to be $110 - 80 = 30$ more than the total number of students with 4 siblings at Lincoln School.

Choices A, B, and D are incorrect and may result from either conceptual or calculation errors. For example, choice A is incorrect; even though there is the same <u>ratio</u> of survey participants from Lincoln School and Washington School with 4 siblings, the two schools have a different <u>total</u> number of students, and thus, a different expected total number of students with 4 siblings.

QUESTION 21.

Choice D is correct. The difference between the number of hours the project takes, y, and the number of hours the project was estimated to take, x, is $|y - x|$. If the goal is met, the difference is less than 10, which can be represented as $|y - x| < 10$ or $-10 < y - x < 10$.

Choice A is incorrect. This inequality states that the estimated number of hours plus the actual number of hours is less than 10, which cannot be true because the estimate is greater than 100. Choice B is incorrect. This inequality states that the actual number of hours is greater than the estimated number of hours plus 10, which could be true only if the goal of being within 10 hours of the estimate were not met. Choice C is incorrect. This inequality states that the actual number of hours is less than the estimated number of hours minus 10, which could be true only if the goal of being within 10 hours of the estimate were not met.

QUESTION 22.

Choice B is correct. To rearrange the formula $I = \dfrac{P}{4\pi r^2}$ in terms of r^2, first multiply each side of the equation by r^2. This yields $r^2 I = \dfrac{P}{4\pi}$. Then dividing each side of $r^2 I = \dfrac{P}{4\pi}$ by I gives $r^2 = \dfrac{P}{4\pi I}$.

Choices A, C, and D are incorrect and may result from algebraic errors during the rearrangement of the formula.

QUESTION 23.

Choice A is correct. If I_A is the intensity measured by Observer A from a distance of r_A and I_B is the intensity measured by Observer B from a distance of r_B, then $I_A = 16 I_B$. Using the formula $I = \dfrac{P}{4\pi^2}$, the intensity measured by Observer A is $I_A = \dfrac{P}{4\pi r_A^2}$, which can also be written in terms of I_B as $I_A = 16 I_B = 16\left(\dfrac{P}{4\pi r_B^2}\right)$. Setting the right-hand sides of these two equations equal to each other gives $\dfrac{P}{4\pi r_A^2} = 16\left(\dfrac{P}{4\pi r_B^2}\right)$, which relates the distance of Observer A from the radio antenna to the distance of Observer B from the radio antenna. Canceling the common factor $\dfrac{P}{4\pi}$ and rearranging the equation gives $r_B^2 = 16 r_A^2$. Taking the square root of each side of $r_B^2 = 16 r_A^2$ gives $r_B = 4 r_A$, and then dividing each side by 4 yields $r_A = \dfrac{1}{4} r_B$. Therefore, the distance of Observer A from the radio antenna is $\dfrac{1}{4}$ the distance of Observer B from the radio antenna.

Choices B, C, and D are incorrect and may result from errors in deriving or using the formula $\dfrac{P}{4\pi r_A^2} = (16)\left(\dfrac{P}{4\pi r_B^2}\right)$.

QUESTION 24.

Choice A is correct. The equation of a circle with center (h, k) and radius r is $(x - h)^2 + (y - k)^2 = r^2$. To put the equation $x^2 + y^2 + 4x - 2y = -1$ in this form, complete the square as follows:

$$x^2 + y^2 + 4x - 2y = -1$$
$$(x^2 + 4x) + (y^2 - 2y) = -1$$
$$(x^2 + 4x + 4) - 4 + (y^2 - 2y + 1) - 1 = -1$$
$$(x + 2)^2 + (y - 1)^2 - 4 - 1 = -1$$
$$(x + 2)^2 + (y - 1)^2 = 4 = 2^2$$

Therefore, the radius of the circle is 2.

Choice C is incorrect because it is the square of the radius, not the radius. Choices B and D are incorrect and may result from errors in rewriting the given equation in standard form.

QUESTION 25.

Choice A is correct. In the xy-plane, the slope m of the line that passes through the points (x_1, y_1) and (x_2, y_2) is given by the formula $m = \dfrac{y_2 - y_1}{x_2 - x_1}$. Thus, if the graph of the linear function f has intercepts at $(a, 0)$ and $(0, b)$, then the slope of the line that is the graph of $y = f(x)$ is $m = \dfrac{0 - b}{a - 0} = -\dfrac{b}{a}$. It is given that $a + b = 0$, and so $a = -b$. Finally, substituting $-b$ for a in $m = -\dfrac{b}{a}$ gives $m = -\dfrac{b}{-b} = 1$, which is positive.

Choices B, C, and D are incorrect and may result from a conceptual misunderstanding or a calculation error.

QUESTION 26.

Choice D is correct. The definition of the graph of a function f in the xy-plane is the set of all points $(x, f(x))$. Thus, for $-4 \le a \le 4$, the value of $f(a)$ is 1 if and only if the unique point on the graph of f with x-coordinate a has y-coordinate equal to 1. The points on the graph of f with x-coordinates $-4, \dfrac{3}{2}$, and 3 are, respectively, $(-4, 1), \left(\dfrac{3}{2}, 1\right)$, and $(3, 1)$. Therefore, all of the values of f given in I, II, and III are equal to 1.

Choices A, B, and C are incorrect because they each omit at least one value of x for which $f(x) = 1$.

QUESTION 27.

Choice D is correct. According to the graph, in the interval from 0 to 10 minutes, the non-insulated sample decreased in temperature by about 18°C, while the insulated sample decreased by about 8°C; in the interval from 10 to 20 minutes, the non-insulated sample decreased in temperature by about 9°C, while the insulated sample decreased by about 5°C; in the interval from 40 to 50 minutes, the non-insulated sample decreased in temperature by about 1°C, while the insulated sample decreased by about 3°C; and in the interval from 50 to 60 minutes, the non-insulated sample decreased in temperature by about 1°C, while the insulated sample decreased by about 2°C. The description in choice D accurately summarizes these rates of temperature change over the given intervals. (Note that since the two samples of water have equal mass and so must lose the same amount of heat to cool from 60°C to 25°C, the faster cooling of the non-insulated sample at the start of the cooling process must be balanced out by faster cooling of the insulated sample at the end of the cooling process.)

Choices A, B, and C are incorrect. None of these descriptions accurately compares the rates of temperature change shown in the graph for the 10-minute intervals.

QUESTION 28.

Choice B is correct. In the xy-plane, the slope m of the line that passes through the points (x_1, y_1) and (x_2, y_2) is $m = \dfrac{y_2 - y_1}{x_2 - x_1}$. Thus, the slope of the line through the points $C(7, 2)$ and $E(1, 0)$ is $\dfrac{2 - 0}{7 - 1}$, which simplifies to $\dfrac{2}{6} = \dfrac{1}{3}$. Therefore, diagonal AC has a slope of $\dfrac{1}{3}$. The other diagonal of the square is a segment of the line that passes through points B and D. The diagonals of a square are perpendicular, and so the product of the slopes of the diagonals is equal to -1. Thus, the slope of the line that passes through B and D is -3 because $\dfrac{1}{3}(-3) = -1$. Hence, an equation of the line that passes through B and D can be written as $y = -3x + b$, where b is the y-intercept of the line. Since diagonal BD will pass through the center of the square, $E(1, 0)$, the equation $0 = -3(1) + b$ holds. Solving this equation for b gives $b = 3$. Therefore, an equation of the line that passes through points B and D is $y = -3x + 3$, which can be rewritten as $y = -3(x - 1)$.

Choices A, C, and D are incorrect and may result from a conceptual error or a calculation error.

QUESTION 29.

Choice B is correct. Substituting 3 for y in $y = ax^2 + b$ gives $3 = ax^2 + b$, which can be rewritten as $3 - b = ax^2$. Since $y = 3$ is one of the equations in the given system, any solution x of $3 - b = ax^2$ corresponds to the solution $(x, 3)$ of the given system. Since the square of a real number is always nonnegative, and a positive number has two square roots, the equation $3 - b = ax^2$ will have two solutions for x if and only if (1) $a > 0$ and $b < 3$ or (2) $a < 0$ and $b > 3$. Of the values for a and b given in the choices, only $a = -2$, $b = 4$ satisfy one of these pairs of conditions.

Alternatively, if $a = -2$ and b $= 4$, then the second equation would be $y = -2x^2 + 4$. The graph of this quadratic equation in the xy-plane is a parabola with y-intercept $(0, 4)$ that opens downward. The graph of the first equation, $y = 3$, is the horizontal line that contains the point $(0, 3)$. As shown below, these two graphs have two points of intersection, and therefore, this system of equations has exactly two real solutions. (Graphing shows that none of the other three choices produces a system with exactly two real solutions.)

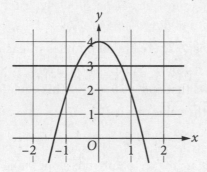

Choices A, C, and D are incorrect and may result from calculation or conceptual errors.

QUESTION 30.

Choice A is correct. The regular hexagon can be divided into 6 equilateral triangles of side length a by drawing the six segments from the center of the regular hexagon to each of its 6 vertices. Since the area of the hexagon is $384\sqrt{3}$ square inches, the area of each equilateral triangle will be $\dfrac{384\sqrt{3}}{6} = 64\sqrt{3}$ square inches.

Drawing any altitude of an equilateral triangle divides it into two 30°-60°-90° triangles. If the side length of the equilateral triangle is a, then the hypotenuse of each 30°-60°-90° triangle is a, and the altitude of the equilateral triangle will be the side opposite the 60° angle in each of the 30°-60°-90° triangles. Thus, the altitude of the equilateral triangle is $\dfrac{\sqrt{3}}{2}a$, and the area of the equilateral triangle is $\dfrac{1}{2}(a)\left(\dfrac{\sqrt{3}}{2}a\right) = \dfrac{\sqrt{3}}{4}a^2$. Since the area of each equilateral triangle is $64\sqrt{3}$ square inches, it follows that $a^2 = \dfrac{4}{\sqrt{3}}(64\sqrt{3})$ $= 256$ square inches. And since the area of the square with side length a is a^2, it follows that the square has area 256 square inches.

Choices B, C, and D are incorrect and may result from calculation or conceptual errors.

QUESTION 31.

The correct answer is 14. Since the coastal geologist estimates that the country's beaches are eroding at a rate of 1.5 feet every year, they will erode by $1.5x$ feet in x years. Thus, if the beaches erode by 21 feet in x years, the equation $1.5x = 21$ must hold. The value of x is then $\frac{21}{1.5} = 14$. Therefore, according to the geologist's estimate, it will take 14 years for the country's beaches to erode by 21 feet.

QUESTION 32.

The correct answer is 7. There are 60 minutes in each hour, and so there are $60h$ minutes in h hours. Since h hours and 30 minutes is equal to 450 minutes, it follows that $60h + 30 = 450$. This equation can be simplified to $60h = 420$, and so the value of h is $\frac{420}{60} = 7$.

QUESTION 33.

The correct answer is 11. It is given that the function $f(x)$ passes through the point $(3, 6)$. Thus, if $x = 3$, the value of $f(x)$ is 6 (since the graph of f in the xy-plane is the set of all points $(x, f(x))$. Substituting 3 for x and 6 for $f(x)$ in $f(x) = 3x^2 - bx + 12$ gives $6 = 3(3)^2 - b(3) + 12$. Performing the operations on the right-hand side of this equation gives $6 = 3(9) - 3b + 12 = 27 - 3b + 12 = 39 - 3b$. Subtracting 39 from each side of $6 = 39 - 3b$ gives $-33 = -3b$, and then dividing each side of $-3b = -33$ by -3 gives the value of b as 11.

QUESTION 34.

The correct answer is 105. Let D be the number of hours Doug spent in the tutoring lab, and let L be the number of hours Laura spent in the tutoring lab. Since Doug and Laura spent a combined total of 250 hours in the tutoring lab, the equation $D + L = 250$ holds. The number of hours Doug spent in the lab is 40 more than the number of hours Laura spent in the lab, and so the equation $D = L + 40$ holds. Substituting $L + 40$ for D in $D + L = 250$ gives $(L + 40) + L = 250$, or $40 + 2L = 250$. Solving this equation gives $L = 105$. Therefore, Laura spent 105 hours in the tutoring lab.

QUESTION 35.

The correct answer is 15. The amount, a, that Jane has deposited after t fixed weekly deposits is equal to the initial deposit plus the total amount of money Jane has deposited in the t fixed weekly deposits. This amount a is given to be $a = 18t + 15$. The amount she deposited in the t fixed weekly deposits is the amount of the weekly deposit times t; hence, this amount must be given by the term $18t$ in $a = 18t + 15$ (and so Jane must have deposited 18 dollars each week after the initial deposit). Therefore, the amount of Jane's original deposit, in dollars, is $a - 18t = 15$.

QUESTION 36.

The correct answer is 32. Since segments LM and MN are tangent to the circle at points L and N, respectively, angles OLM and ONM are right angles. Thus, in quadrilateral $OLMN$, the measure of angle O is $360° - (90° + 60° + 90°) = 120°$. Thus, in the circle, central angle O cuts off $\frac{120}{360} = \frac{1}{3}$ of the circumference; that is, minor arc $\overarc{LN}$ is $\frac{1}{3}$ of the circumference. Since the circumference is 96, the length of minor arc $\overarc{LN}$ is $\frac{1}{3} \times 96 = 32$.

QUESTION 37.

The correct answer is 3284. According to the formula, the number of plants one year from now will be $3000 + 0.2(3000)\left(1 - \frac{3000}{4000}\right)$, which is equal to 3150. Then, using the formula again, the number of plants two years from now will be $3150 + 0.2(3150)\left(1 - \frac{3150}{4000}\right)$, which is 3283.875. Rounding this value to the nearest whole number gives 3284.

QUESTION 38.

The correct answer is 7500. If the number of plants is to be increased from 3000 this year to 3360 next year, then the number of plants that the environment can support, K, must satisfy the equation $3360 = 3000 + 0.2(3000)\left(1 - \frac{3000}{K}\right)$. Dividing both sides of this equation by 3000 gives $1.12 = 1 + 0.2\left(1 - \frac{3000}{K}\right)$, and therefore, it must be true that $0.2\left(1 - \frac{3000}{K}\right) = 0.12$, or equivalently, $1 - \frac{3000}{K} = 0.6$. It follows that $\frac{3000}{K} = 0.4$, and so $K = \frac{3000}{0.4} = 7500$.

CollegeBoard

SAT® Practice Test #3

IMPORTANT REMINDERS

A No. 2 pencil is required for the test.
Do not use a mechanical pencil or pen.

Sharing any questions with anyone
is a violation of Test Security
and Fairness policies and may result
in your scores being canceled.

This cover is representative of what you'll see on test day.

Test begins on the next page.

Reading Test

65 MINUTES, 52 QUESTIONS

Turn to Section 1 of your answer sheet to answer the questions in this section.

DIRECTIONS

Each passage or pair of passages below is followed by a number of questions. After reading each passage or pair, choose the best answer to each question based on what is stated or implied in the passage or passages and in any accompanying graphics (such as a table or graph).

Questions 1-10 are based on the following passage.

This passage is adapted from Saki, "The Schartz-Metterklume Method." Originally published in 1911.

Lady Carlotta stepped out on to the platform of the small wayside station and took a turn or two up and down its uninteresting length, to kill time till the
Line train should be pleased to proceed on its way. Then,
5 in the roadway beyond, she saw a horse struggling with a more than ample load, and a carter of the sort that seems to bear a sullen hatred against the animal that helps him to earn a living. Lady Carlotta promptly betook her to the roadway, and put rather a
10 different complexion on the struggle. Certain of her acquaintances were wont to give her plentiful admonition as to the undesirability of interfering on behalf of a distressed animal, such interference being "none of her business." Only once had she put the
15 doctrine of non-interference into practice, when one of its most eloquent exponents had been besieged for nearly three hours in a small and extremely uncomfortable may-tree by an angry boar-pig, while Lady Carlotta, on the other side of the fence, had
20 proceeded with the water-colour sketch she was engaged on, and refused to interfere between the boar and his prisoner. It is to be feared that she lost the friendship of the ultimately rescued lady. On this occasion she merely lost the train, which gave way to
25 the first sign of impatience it had shown throughout the journey, and steamed off without her. She bore the desertion with philosophical indifference; her

friends and relations were thoroughly well used to the fact of her luggage arriving without her.
30 She wired a vague non-committal message to her destination to say that she was coming on "by another train." Before she had time to think what her next move might be she was confronted by an imposingly attired lady, who seemed to be taking a
35 prolonged mental inventory of her clothes and looks.
"You must be Miss Hope, the governess I've come to meet," said the apparition, in a tone that admitted of very little argument.
"Very well, if I must I must," said Lady Carlotta to
40 herself with dangerous meekness.
"I am Mrs. Quabarl," continued the lady; "and where, pray, is your luggage?"
"It's gone astray," said the alleged governess, falling in with the excellent rule of life that the absent
45 are always to blame; the luggage had, in point of fact, behaved with perfect correctitude. "I've just telegraphed about it," she added, with a nearer approach to truth.
"How provoking," said Mrs. Quabarl; "these
50 railway companies are so careless. However, my maid can lend you things for the night," and she led the way to her car.
During the drive to the Quabarl mansion Lady Carlotta was impressively introduced to the
55 nature of the charge that had been thrust upon her; she learned that Claude and Wilfrid were delicate, sensitive young people, that Irene had the artistic temperament highly developed, and that Viola was

CONTINUE

something or other else of a mould equally
60 commonplace among children of that class and type
in the twentieth century.

"I wish them not only to be TAUGHT," said Mrs.
Quabarl, "but INTERESTED in what they learn. In
their history lessons, for instance, you must try to
65 make them feel that they are being introduced to the
life-stories of men and women who really lived, not
merely committing a mass of names and dates to
memory. French, of course, I shall expect you to talk
at meal-times several days in the week."
70 "I shall talk French four days of the week and
Russian in the remaining three."

"Russian? My dear Miss Hope, no one in the
house speaks or understands Russian."

"That will not embarrass me in the least," said
75 Lady Carlotta coldly.

Mrs. Quabarl, to use a colloquial expression, was
knocked off her perch. She was one of those
imperfectly self-assured individuals who are
magnificent and autocratic as long as they are not
80 seriously opposed. The least show of unexpected
resistance goes a long way towards rendering them
cowed and apologetic. When the new governess
failed to express wondering admiration of the large
newly-purchased and expensive car, and lightly
85 alluded to the superior advantages of one or two
makes which had just been put on the market, the
discomfiture of her patroness became almost abject.
Her feelings were those which might have animated a
general of ancient warfaring days, on beholding his
90 heaviest battle-elephant ignominiously driven off the
field by slingers and javelin throwers.

1

Which choice best summarizes the passage?

A) A woman weighs the positive and negative
aspects of accepting a new job.

B) A woman does not correct a stranger who
mistakes her for someone else.

C) A woman impersonates someone else to seek
revenge on an acquaintance.

D) A woman takes an immediate dislike to her new
employer.

2

In line 2, "turn" most nearly means

A) slight movement.

B) change in rotation.

C) short walk.

D) course correction.

3

The passage most clearly implies that other people
regarded Lady Carlotta as

A) outspoken.

B) tactful.

C) ambitious.

D) unfriendly.

4

Which choice provides the best evidence for the
answer to the previous question?

A) Lines 10-14 ("Certain . . . business")

B) Lines 22-23 ("It is . . . lady")

C) Lines 23-26 ("On this . . . her")

D) Lines 30-32 ("She . . . train")

CONTINUE

5

The description of how Lady Carlotta "put the doctrine of non-interference into practice" (lines 14-15) mainly serves to

A) foreshadow her capacity for deception.

B) illustrate the subtle cruelty in her nature.

C) provide a humorous insight into her character.

D) explain a surprising change in her behavior.

6

In line 55, "charge" most nearly means

A) responsibility.

B) attack.

C) fee.

D) expense.

7

The narrator indicates that Claude, Wilfrid, Irene, and Viola are

A) similar to many of their peers.

B) unusually creative and intelligent.

C) hostile to the idea of a governess.

D) more educated than others of their age.

8

The narrator implies that Mrs. Quabarl favors a form of education that emphasizes

A) traditional values.

B) active engagement.

C) artistic experimentation.

D) factual retention.

9

As presented in the passage, Mrs. Quabarl is best described as

A) superficially kind but actually selfish.

B) outwardly imposing but easily defied.

C) socially successful but irrationally bitter.

D) naturally generous but frequently imprudent.

10

Which choice provides the best evidence for the answer to the previous question?

A) Lines 49-50 ("How . . . careless")

B) Lines 62-68 ("I wish . . . memory")

C) Lines 70-73 ("I shall . . . Russian")

D) Lines 77-82 ("She was . . . apologetic")

CONTINUE

Questions 11-20 are based on the following passage and supplementary material.

This passage is adapted from Taras Grescoe, *Straphanger: Saving Our Cities and Ourselves from the Automobile.* ©2012 by Taras Grescoe.

Though there are 600 million cars on the planet, and counting, there are also seven billion people, which means that for the vast majority of us getting
Line around involves taking buses, ferryboats, commuter
5 trains, streetcars, and subways. In other words, traveling to work, school, or the market means being a straphanger: somebody who, by choice or necessity, relies on public transport, rather than a privately owned automobile.
10 Half the population of New York, Toronto, and London do not own cars. Public transport is how most of the people of Asia and Africa, the world's most populous continents, travel. Every day, subway systems carry 155 million passengers, thirty-four
15 times the number carried by all the world's airplanes, and the global public transport market is now valued at $428 billion annually. A century and a half after the invention of the internal combustion engine, private car ownership is still an anomaly.
20 And yet public transportation, in many minds, is the opposite of glamour—a squalid last resort for those with one too many impaired driving charges, too poor to afford insurance, or too decrepit to get behind the wheel of a car. In much of North
25 America, they are right: taking transit is a depressing experience. Anybody who has waited far too long on a street corner for the privilege of boarding a lurching, overcrowded bus, or wrestled luggage onto subways and shuttles to get to a big city airport,
30 knows that transit on this continent tends to be underfunded, ill-maintained, and ill-planned. Given the opportunity, who wouldn't drive? Hopping in a car almost always gets you to your destination more quickly.
35 It doesn't have to be like this. Done right, public transport can be faster, more comfortable, and cheaper than the private automobile. In Shanghai, German-made magnetic levitation trains skim over elevated tracks at 266 miles an hour, whisking people
40 to the airport at a third of the speed of sound. In provincial French towns, electric-powered streetcars run silently on rubber tires, sliding through narrow streets along a single guide rail set into cobblestones. From Spain to Sweden, Wi-Fi equipped high-speed
45 trains seamlessly connect with highly ramified metro networks, allowing commuters to work on laptops as they prepare for same-day meetings in once distant capital cities. In Latin America, China, and India, working people board fast-loading buses that move
50 like subway trains along dedicated busways, leaving the sedans and SUVs of the rich mired in dawn-to-dusk traffic jams. And some cities have transformed their streets into cycle-path freeways, making giant strides in public health and safety and
55 the sheer livability of their neighborhoods—in the process turning the workaday bicycle into a viable form of mass transit.
    If you credit the demographers, this transit trend has legs. The "Millenials," who reached adulthood
60 around the turn of the century and now outnumber baby boomers, tend to favor cities over suburbs, and are far more willing than their parents to ride buses and subways. Part of the reason is their ease with iPads, MP3 players, Kindles, and smartphones: you
65 can get some serious texting done when you're not driving, and earbuds offer effective insulation from all but the most extreme commuting annoyances. Even though there are more teenagers in the country than ever, only ten million have a driver's license
70 (versus twelve million a generation ago). Baby boomers may have been raised in Leave It to Beaver suburbs, but as they retire, a significant contingent is favoring older cities and compact towns where they have the option of walking and riding bikes. Seniors,
75 too, are more likely to use transit, and by 2025, there will be 64 million Americans over the age of sixty-five. Already, dwellings in older neighborhoods in Washington, D.C., Atlanta, and Denver, especially those near light-rail or subway stations, are
80 commanding enormous price premiums over suburban homes. The experience of European and Asian cities shows that if you make buses, subways, and trains convenient, comfortable, fast, and safe, a surprisingly large percentage of citizens will opt to
85 ride rather than drive.

CONTINUE

Figure 1

Primary Occupation of Public
Transportation Passengers
in US Cities

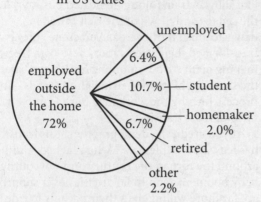

Figure 2

Purpose of Public Transportation
Trips in US Cities

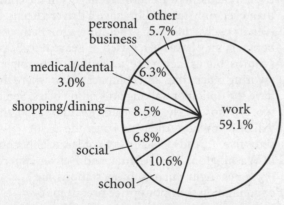

Figure 1 and figure 2 are adapted from the American Public
Transportation Association, "A Profile of Public Transportation
Passenger Demographics and Travel Characteristics Reported in
On-Board Surveys." ©2007 by American Public Transportation
Association.

11

What function does the third paragraph (lines 20-34)
serve in the passage as a whole?

A) It acknowledges that a practice favored by the
author of the passage has some limitations.

B) It illustrates with detail the arguments made in
the first two paragraphs of the passage.

C) It gives an overview of a problem that has not
been sufficiently addressed by the experts
mentioned in the passage.

D) It advocates for abandoning a practice for which
the passage as a whole provides mostly
favorable data.

12

Which choice does the author explicitly cite as
an advantage of automobile travel in North America?

A) Environmental impact

B) Convenience

C) Speed

D) Cost

13

Which choice provides the best evidence for the
answer to the previous question?

A) Lines 5-9 ("In . . . automobile")

B) Lines 20-24 ("And . . . car")

C) Lines 24-26 ("In . . . experience")

D) Lines 32-34 ("Hopping . . . quickly")

CONTINUE

14

The central idea of the fourth paragraph (lines 35-57) is that

A) European countries excel at public transportation.

B) some public transportation systems are superior to travel by private automobile.

C) Americans should mimic foreign public transportation systems when possible.

D) much international public transportation is engineered for passengers to work while on board.

15

Which choice provides the best evidence for the answer to the previous question?

A) Line 35 ("It . . . this")

B) Lines 35-37 ("Done . . . automobile")

C) Lines 37-40 ("In . . . sound")

D) Lines 44-48 ("From . . . cities")

16

As used in line 58, "credit" most nearly means

A) endow.

B) attribute.

C) believe.

D) honor.

17

As used in line 61, "favor" most nearly means

A) indulge.

B) prefer.

C) resemble.

D) serve.

18

Which choice best supports the conclusion that public transportation is compatible with the use of personal electronic devices?

A) Lines 59-63 ("The . . . subways")

B) Lines 63-67 ("Part . . . annoyances")

C) Lines 68-70 ("Even . . . ago")

D) Lines 77-81 ("Already . . . homes")

19

Which choice is supported by the data in the first figure?

A) The number of students using public transportation is greater than the number of retirees using public transportation.

B) The number of employed people using public transportation and the number of unemployed people using public transportation is roughly the same.

C) People employed outside the home are less likely to use public transportation than are homemakers.

D) Unemployed people use public transportation less often than do people employed outside the home.

20

Taken together, the two figures suggest that most people who use public transportation

A) are employed outside the home and take public transportation to work.

B) are employed outside the home but take public transportation primarily in order to run errands.

C) use public transportation during the week but use their private cars on weekends.

D) use public transportation only until they are able to afford to buy a car.

CONTINUE ▶

Questions 21-30 are based on the following passage.

This passage is adapted from Thor Hanson, *Feathers*. ©2011 by Thor Hanson. Scientists have long debated how the ancestors of birds evolved the ability to fly. The ground-up theory assumes they were fleet-footed ground dwellers that captured prey by leaping and flapping their upper limbs. The tree-down theory assumes they were tree climbers that leapt and glided among branches.

At field sites around the world, Ken Dial saw a
pattern in how young pheasants, quail, tinamous,
and other ground birds ran along behind their
Line parents. "They jumped up like popcorn," he said,
5 describing how they would flap their half-formed
wings and take short hops into the air. So when a
group of graduate students challenged him
to come up with new data on the age-old
ground-up-tree-down debate, he designed a project
10 to see what clues might lie in how baby game birds
learned to fly.
   Ken settled on the Chukar Partridge as a
model species, but he might not have made his
discovery without a key piece of advice from the local
15 rancher in Montana who was supplying him with
birds. When the cowboy stopped by to see how
things were going, Ken showed him his nice, tidy
laboratory setup and explained how the birds' first
hops and flights would be measured. The rancher
20 was incredulous. "He took one look and said, in
pretty colorful language, 'What are those birds doing
on the ground? They hate to be on the ground! Give
them something to climb on!' " At first it seemed
unnatural—ground birds don't like the ground? But
25 as he thought about it Ken realized that all the
species he'd watched in the wild preferred to rest on
ledges, low branches, or other elevated perches where
they were safe from predators. They really only used
the ground for feeding and traveling. So he brought
30 in some hay bales for the Chukars to perch on and
then left his son in charge of feeding and data
collection while he went away on a short work trip.
   Barely a teenager at the time, young Terry Dial
was visibly upset when his father got back. "I asked
35 him how it went," Ken recalled, "and he said,

'Terrible! The birds are cheating!' " Instead of flying
up to their perches, the baby Chukars were using
their legs. Time and again Terry had watched them
run right up the side of a hay bale, flapping all the
40 while. Ken dashed out to see for himself, and that
was the "aha" moment. "The birds were using their
wings and legs cooperatively," he told me, and that
single observation opened up a world of possibilities.
   Working together with Terry (who has since gone
45 on to study animal locomotion), Ken came up with a
series of ingenious experiments, filming the birds as
they raced up textured ramps tilted at increasing
angles. As the incline increased, the partridges began
to flap, but they angled their wings differently from
50 birds in flight. They aimed their flapping down and
backward, using the force not for lift but to keep
their feet firmly pressed against the ramp. "It's like
the spoiler on the back of a race car," he explained,
which is a very apt analogy. In Formula One racing,
55 spoilers are the big aerodynamic fins that push the
cars downward as they speed along, increasing
traction and handling. The birds were doing the very
same thing with their wings to help them scramble
up otherwise impossible slopes.
60   Ken called the technique WAIR, for wing-assisted
incline running, and went on to document it in a
wide range of species. It not only allowed young
birds to climb vertical surfaces within the first few
weeks of life but also gave adults an energy-efficient
65 alternative to flying. In the Chukar experiments,
adults regularly used WAIR to ascend ramps steeper
than 90 degrees, essentially running up the wall and
onto the ceiling.
   In an evolutionary context, WAIR takes on
70 surprising explanatory powers. With one fell swoop,
the Dials came up with a viable origin for the
flapping flight stroke of birds (something gliding
animals don't do and thus a shortcoming of the
tree-down theory) and an aerodynamic function for
75 half-formed wings (one of the main drawbacks to the
ground-up hypothesis).

CONTINUE

21

Which choice best reflects the overall sequence of events in the passage?

A) An experiment is proposed but proves unworkable; a less ambitious experiment is attempted, and it yields data that give rise to a new set of questions.

B) A new discovery leads to reconsideration of a theory; a classic study is adapted, and the results are summarized.

C) An anomaly is observed and simulated experimentally; the results are compared with previous findings, and a novel hypothesis is proposed.

D) An unexpected finding arises during the early phase of a study; the study is modified in response to this finding, and the results are interpreted and evaluated.

22

As used in line 7, "challenged" most nearly means

A) dared.

B) required.

C) disputed with.

D) competed with.

23

Which statement best captures Ken Dial's central assumption in setting up his research?

A) The acquisition of flight in young birds sheds light on the acquisition of flight in their evolutionary ancestors.

B) The tendency of certain young birds to jump erratically is a somewhat recent evolved behavior.

C) Young birds in a controlled research setting are less likely than birds in the wild to require perches when at rest.

D) Ground-dwelling and tree-climbing predecessors to birds evolved in parallel.

24

Which choice provides the best evidence for the answer to the previous question?

A) Lines 1-4 ("At field . . . parents")

B) Lines 6-11 ("So when . . . fly")

C) Lines 16-19 ("When . . . measured")

D) Lines 23-24 ("At first . . . the ground")

25

In the second paragraph (lines 12-32), the incident involving the local rancher mainly serves to

A) reveal Ken Dial's motivation for undertaking his project.

B) underscore certain differences between laboratory and field research.

C) show how an unanticipated piece of information influenced Ken Dial's research.

D) introduce a key contributor to the tree-down theory.

26

After Ken Dial had his "'aha' moment" (line 41), he

A) tried to train the birds to fly to their perches.

B) studied videos to determine why the birds no longer hopped.

C) observed how the birds dealt with gradually steeper inclines.

D) consulted with other researchers who had studied Chukar Partridges.

27

The passage identifies which of the following as a factor that facilitated the baby Chukars' traction on steep ramps?

A) The speed with which they climbed

B) The position of their flapping wings

C) The alternation of wing and foot movement

D) Their continual hopping motions

CONTINUE ▶

28

As used in line 61, "document" most nearly means

A) portray.

B) record.

C) publish.

D) process.

29

What can reasonably be inferred about gliding animals from the passage?

A) Their young tend to hop along beside their parents instead of flying beside them.

B) Their method of locomotion is similar to that of ground birds.

C) They use the ground for feeding more often than for perching.

D) They do not use a flapping stroke to aid in climbing slopes.

30

Which choice provides the best evidence for the answer to the previous question?

A) Lines 4-6 ("They jumped . . . air")

B) Lines 28-29 ("They really . . . traveling")

C) Lines 57-59 ("The birds . . . slopes")

D) Lines 72-74 ("something . . . theory")

Questions 31-41 are based on the following passages.

Passage 1 is adapted from Talleyrand et al., *Report on Public Instruction*. Originally published in 1791. Passage 2 is adapted from Mary Wollstonecraft, *A Vindication of the Rights of Woman*. Originally published in 1792. Talleyrand was a French diplomat; the *Report* was a plan for national education. Wollstonecraft, a British novelist and political writer, wrote *Vindication* in response to Talleyrand.

Passage 1

That half the human race is excluded by the other half from any participation in government; that they are native by birth but foreign by law in the very land
Line where they were born; and that they are
5 property-owners yet have no direct influence or representation: are all political phenomena apparently impossible to explain on abstract principle. But on another level of ideas, the question changes and may be easily resolved. The purpose of
10 all these institutions must be the happiness of the greatest number. Everything that leads us farther from this purpose is in error; everything that brings us closer is truth. If the exclusion from public employments decreed against women leads to a
15 greater sum of mutual happiness for the two sexes, then this becomes a law that all Societies have been compelled to acknowledge and sanction.

Any other ambition would be a reversal of our primary destinies; and it will never be in women's
20 interest to change the assignment they have received.

It seems to us incontestable that our common happiness, above all that of women, requires that they never aspire to the exercise of political rights and functions. Here we must seek their interests in
25 the wishes of nature. Is it not apparent, that their delicate constitutions, their peaceful inclinations, and the many duties of motherhood, set them apart from strenuous habits and onerous duties, and summon them to gentle occupations and the cares of the
30 home? And is it not evident that the great conserving principle of Societies, which makes the division of powers a source of harmony, has been expressed and revealed by nature itself, when it divided the functions of the two sexes in so obviously distinct a
35 manner? This is sufficient; we need not invoke principles that are inapplicable to the question. Let us not make rivals of life's companions. You must, you truly must allow the persistence of a union that no interest, no rivalry, can possibly undo. Understand
40 that the good of all demands this of you.

Unauthorized copying or reuse of any part of this page is illegal.

572

CONTINUE ▶

Passage 2

Contending for the rights of woman, my main argument is built on this simple principle, that if she be not prepared by education to become the companion of man, she will stop the progress of
45 knowledge and virtue; for truth must be common to all, or it will be inefficacious with respect to its influence on general practice. And how can woman be expected to co-operate unless she know why she ought to be virtuous? unless freedom strengthen her
50 reason till she comprehend her duty, and see in what manner it is connected with her real good? If children are to be educated to understand the true principle of patriotism, their mother must be a patriot; and the love of mankind, from which an
55 orderly train of virtues spring, can only be produced by considering the moral and civil interest of mankind; but the education and situation of woman, at present, shuts her out from such investigations. . . .

Consider, sir, dispassionately, these
60 observations—for a glimpse of this truth seemed to open before you when you observed, "that to see one half of the human race excluded by the other from all participation of government, was a political phenomenon that, according to abstract principles, it
65 was impossible to explain." If so, on what does your constitution rest? If the abstract rights of man will bear discussion and explanation, those of woman, by a parity of reasoning, will not shrink from the same test: though a different opinion prevails in this
70 country, built on the very arguments which you use to justify the oppression of woman—prescription.

Consider—I address you as a legislator— whether, when men contend for their freedom, and to be allowed to judge for themselves respecting their
75 own happiness, it be not inconsistent and unjust to subjugate women, even though you firmly believe that you are acting in the manner best calculated to promote their happiness? Who made man the exclusive judge, if woman partake with him the gift
80 of reason?

In this style, argue tyrants of every denomination, from the weak king to the weak father of a family; they are all eager to crush reason; yet always assert that they usurp its throne only to be
85 useful. Do you not act a similar part, when you force all women, by denying them civil and political rights, to remain immured in their families groping in the dark?

31

As used in line 21, "common" most nearly means

A) average.

B) shared.

C) coarse.

D) similar.

32

It can be inferred that the authors of Passage 1 believe that running a household and raising children

A) are rewarding for men as well as for women.

B) yield less value for society than do the roles performed by men.

C) entail very few activities that are difficult or unpleasant.

D) require skills similar to those needed to run a country or a business.

33

Which choice provides the best evidence for the answer to the previous question?

A) Lines 4-6 ("they are . . . representation")

B) Lines 13-17 ("If the . . . sanction")

C) Lines 25-30 ("Is it . . . home")

D) Lines 30-35 ("And . . . manner")

34

According to the author of Passage 2, in order for society to progress, women must

A) enjoy personal happiness and financial security.

B) follow all currently prescribed social rules.

C) replace men as figures of power and authority.

D) receive an education comparable to that of men.

CONTINUE

35

As used in line 50, "reason" most nearly means

A) motive.

B) sanity.

C) intellect.

D) explanation.

36

In Passage 2, the author claims that freedoms granted by society's leaders have

A) privileged one gender over the other.

B) resulted in a general reduction in individual virtue.

C) caused arguments about the nature of happiness.

D) ensured equality for all people.

37

Which choice provides the best evidence for the answer to the previous question?

A) Lines 41-45 ("Contending . . . virtue")

B) Lines 45-47 ("truth . . . practice")

C) Lines 65-66 ("If so . . . rest")

D) Lines 72-75 ("Consider . . . happiness")

38

In lines 61-65, the author of Passage 2 refers to a statement made in Passage 1 in order to

A) call into question the qualifications of the authors of Passage 1 regarding gender issues.

B) dispute the assertion made about women in the first sentence of Passage 1.

C) develop her argument by highlighting what she sees as flawed reasoning in Passage 1.

D) validate the concluding declarations made by the authors of Passage 1 about gender roles.

39

Which best describes the overall relationship between Passage 1 and Passage 2?

A) Passage 2 strongly challenges the point of view in Passage 1.

B) Passage 2 draws alternative conclusions from the evidence presented in Passage 1.

C) Passage 2 elaborates on the proposal presented in Passage 1.

D) Passage 2 restates in different terms the argument presented in Passage 1.

40

The authors of both passages would most likely agree with which of the following statements about women in the eighteenth century?

A) Their natural preferences were the same as those of men.

B) They needed a good education to be successful in society.

C) They were just as happy in life as men were.

D) They generally enjoyed fewer rights than men did.

41

How would the authors of Passage 1 most likely respond to the points made in the final paragraph of Passage 2?

A) Women are not naturally suited for the exercise of civil and political rights.

B) Men and women possess similar degrees of reasoning ability.

C) Women do not need to remain confined to their traditional family duties.

D) The principles of natural law should not be invoked when considering gender roles.

CONTINUE

Questions 42-52 are based on the following passage and supplementary material.

This passage is adapted from Richard J. Sharpe and Lisa Heyden, "Honey Bee Colony Collapse Disorder is Possibly Caused by a Dietary Pyrethrum Deficiency." ©2009 by Elsevier Ltd. Colony collapse disorder is characterized by the disappearance of adult worker bees from hives.

Honey bees are hosts to the pathogenic large ectoparasitic mite *Varroa destructor* (Varroa mites). These mites feed on bee hemolymph (blood) and can
Line kill bees directly or by increasing their susceptibility
5 to secondary infection with fungi, bacteria or viruses. Little is known about the natural defenses that keep the mite infections under control.

Pyrethrums are a group of flowering plants which include *Chrysanthemum coccineum*, *Chrysanthemum*
10 *cinerariifolium*, *Chrysanthemum marschalli*, and related species. These plants produce potent insecticides with anti-mite activity. The naturally occurring insecticides are known as pyrethrums. A synonym for the naturally occurring pyrethrums is
15 pyrethrin and synthetic analogues of pyrethrums are known as pyrethroids. In fact, the human mite infestation known as scabies (*Sarcoptes scabiei*) is treated with a topical pyrethrum cream.

We suspect that the bees of commercial bee
20 colonies which are fed mono-crops are nutritionally deficient. In particular, we postulate that the problem is a diet deficient in anti-mite toxins: pyrethrums, and possibly other nutrients which are inherent in such plants. Without, at least, intermittent feeding on
25 the pyrethrum producing plants, bee colonies are susceptible to mite infestations which can become fatal either directly or due to a secondary infection of immunocompromised or nutritionally deficient bees. This secondary infection can be viral, bacterial or
30 fungal and may be due to one or more pathogens. In addition, immunocompromised or nutritionally deficient bees may be further weakened when commercially produced insecticides are introduced into their hives by bee keepers in an effort to fight
35 mite infestation. We further postulate that the proper dosage necessary to prevent mite infestation may be better left to the bees, who may seek out or avoid pyrethrum containing plants depending on the amount necessary to defend against mites and the
40 amount already consumed by the bees, which in higher doses could be potentially toxic to them.

This hypothesis can best be tested by a trial wherein a small number of commercial honey bee colonies are offered a number of pyrethrum
45 producing plants, as well as a typical bee food source such as clover, while controls are offered only the clover. Mites could then be introduced to each hive with note made as to the choice of the bees, and the effects of the mite parasites on the experimental
50 colonies versus control colonies.

It might be beneficial to test wild-type honey bee colonies in this manner as well, in case there could be some genetic difference between them that affects the bees' preferences for pyrethrum producing flowers.

Pathogen Occurence in Honey Bee Colonies With and Without Colony Collapse Disorder

Pathogen	Percent of colonies affected by pathogen	
	Colonies with colony collapse disorder (%)	Colonies without colony collapse disorder (%)
Viruses		
IAPV	83	5
KBV	100	76
Fungi		
Nosema apis	90	48
Nosema ceranae	100	81
All four pathogens	77	0

Adapted from Diana L. Cox-Foster et al., "A Metagenomic Survey of Microbes in Honey Bee Colony Collapse Disorder." ©2007 by American Association for the Advancement of Science.

The table above shows, for colonies with colony collapse disorder and for colonies without colony collapse disorder, the percent of colonies having honey bees infected by each of four pathogens and by all four pathogens together.

CONTINUE

42

How do the words "can," "may," and "could" in the third paragraph (lines 19-41) help establish the tone of the paragraph?

A) They create an optimistic tone that makes clear the authors are hopeful about the effects of their research on colony collapse disorder.

B) They create a dubious tone that makes clear the authors do not have confidence in the usefulness of the research described.

C) They create a tentative tone that makes clear the authors suspect but do not know that their hypothesis is correct.

D) They create a critical tone that makes clear the authors are skeptical of claims that pyrethrums are inherent in mono-crops.

43

In line 42, the authors state that a certain hypothesis "can best be tested by a trial." Based on the passage, which of the following is a hypothesis the authors suggest be tested in a trial?

A) Honeybees that are exposed to both pyrethrums and mites are likely to develop a secondary infection by a virus, a bacterium, or a fungus.

B) Beekeepers who feed their honeybee colonies a diet of a single crop need to increase the use of insecticides to prevent mite infestations.

C) A honeybee diet that includes pyrethrums results in honeybee colonies that are more resistant to mite infestations.

D) Humans are more susceptible to varroa mites as a result of consuming nutritionally deficient food crops.

44

Which choice provides the best evidence for the answer to the previous question?

A) Lines 3-5 ("These mites . . . viruses")

B) Lines 16-18 ("In fact . . . cream")

C) Lines 19-21 ("We suspect . . . deficient")

D) Lines 24-28 ("Without . . . bees")

45

The passage most strongly suggests that beekeepers' attempts to fight mite infestations with commercially produced insecticides have what unintentional effect?

A) They increase certain mite populations.

B) They kill some beneficial forms of bacteria.

C) They destroy bees' primary food source.

D) They further harm the health of some bees.

46

Which choice provides the best evidence for the answer to the previous question?

A) Lines 1-2 ("Honey bees . . . mites")

B) Lines 6-7 ("Little . . . control")

C) Lines 31-35 ("In addition . . . infestation")

D) Lines 47-50 ("Mites . . . control colonies")

47

As used in line 35, "postulate" most nearly means to

A) make an unfounded assumption.

B) put forth an idea or claim.

C) question a belief or theory.

D) conclude based on firm evidence.

48

The main purpose of the fourth paragraph (lines 42-50) is to

A) summarize the results of an experiment that confirmed the authors' hypothesis about the role of clover in the diets of wild-type honeybees.

B) propose an experiment to investigate how different diets affect commercial honeybee colonies' susceptibility to mite infestations.

C) provide a comparative nutritional analysis of the honey produced by the experimental colonies and by the control colonies.

D) predict the most likely outcome of an unfinished experiment summarized in the third paragraph (lines 19-41).

CONTINUE

49

An unstated assumption made by the authors about clover is that the plants

A) do not produce pyrethrums.

B) are members of the *Chrysanthemum* genus.

C) are usually located near wild-type honeybee colonies.

D) will not be a good food source for honeybees in the control colonies.

50

Based on data in the table, in what percent of colonies with colony collapse disorder were the honeybees infected by all four pathogens?

A)   0 percent

B)   77 percent

C)   83 percent

D) 100 percent

51

Based on data in the table, which of the four pathogens infected the highest percentage of honeybee colonies without colony collapse disorder?

A) IAPV

B) KBV

C) *Nosema apis*

D) *Nosema ceranae*

52

Do the data in the table provide support for the authors' claim that infection with varroa mites increases a honeybee's susceptibility to secondary infections?

A) Yes, because the data provide evidence that infection with a pathogen caused the colonies to undergo colony collapse disorder.

B) Yes, because for each pathogen, the percent of colonies infected is greater for colonies with colony collapse disorder than for colonies without colony collapse disorder.

C) No, because the data do not provide evidence about bacteria as a cause of colony collapse disorder.

D) No, because the data do not indicate whether the honeybees had been infected with mites.

STOP

If you finish before time is called, you may check your work on this section only.

Do not turn to any other section.

Writing and Language Test

35 MINUTES, 44 QUESTIONS

Turn to Section 2 of your answer sheet to answer the questions in this section.

Each passage below is accompanied by a number of questions. For some questions, you will consider how the passage might be revised to improve the expression of ideas. For other questions, you will consider how the passage might be edited to correct errors in sentence structure, usage, or punctuation. A passage or a question may be accompanied by one or more graphics (such as a table or graph) that you will consider as you make revising and editing decisions.

Some questions will direct you to an underlined portion of a passage. Other questions will direct you to a location in a passage or ask you to think about the passage as a whole.

After reading each passage, choose the answer to each question that most effectively improves the quality of writing in the passage or that makes the passage conform to the conventions of standard written English. Many questions include a "NO CHANGE" option. Choose that option if you think the best choice is to leave the relevant portion of the passage as it is.

Questions 1-11 are based on the following passage.

Shed Some Light on the Workplace

　　Studies have shown that employees are happier, **[1]** healthier, and more productive when they work in an environment **[2]** in which temperatures are carefully controlled. New buildings may be designed with these studies in mind, but many older buildings were not, resulting in spaces that often depend primarily on artificial lighting. While employers may balk at the expense of reconfiguring such buildings to increase the amount of natural light, the investment has been shown to be well worth it in the long run—for both employees and employers.

1

A) NO CHANGE
B) healthy, and more
C) healthier, and they are
D) healthier, being more

2

Which choice provides the most appropriate introduction to the passage?

A) NO CHANGE
B) that affords them adequate amounts of natural light.
C) that is thoroughly sealed to prevent energy loss.
D) in which they feel comfortable asking managers for special accommodations.

Unauthorized copying or reuse of any part of this page is illegal.

CONTINUE ▶

578

For one thing, lack of exposure to natural light has a significant impact on employees' health. A study conducted in 2013 by Northwestern University in Chicago showed that inadequate natural light could result in eye strain, headaches, and fatigue, as well as interference with the body's circadian rhythms. **3** Circadian rhythms, which are controlled by the **4** bodies biological clocks, influence body temperature, hormone release, cycles of sleep and wakefulness, and other bodily functions. Disruptions of circadian rhythms have been linked to sleep disorders, diabetes, depression, and bipolar disorder. Like any other health problems, these ailments can increase employee absenteeism, which, in turn, **5** is costly for employers. Employees who feel less than 100 percent and are sleep deprived are also less prone to work at their maximal productivity. One company in California **6** gained a huge boost in its employees' morale when it moved from an artificially lit distribution facility to one with natural illumination.

3

At this point, the writer is considering adding the following sentence.

> Workers in offices with windows sleep an average of 46 minutes more per night than workers in offices without windows.

Should the writer make this addition here?

A) Yes, because it supplies quantitative data that will be examined in the rest of the paragraph.

B) Yes, because it explains the nature of the bodily functions referred to in the next sentence.

C) No, because it interrupts the discussion of circadian rhythms.

D) No, because it does not take into account whether workers were exposed to sunlight outside the office.

4

A) NO CHANGE

B) bodies' biological clocks',

C) body's biological clocks,

D) body's biological clock's,

5

A) NO CHANGE

B) are

C) is being

D) have been

6

Which choice best supports the statement made in the previous sentence?

A) NO CHANGE

B) saw a 5 percent increase in productivity

C) saved a great deal on its operational costs

D) invested large amounts of time and capital

CONTINUE

[7] Artificial light sources are also costly aside from lowering worker productivity. They typically constitute anywhere from 25 to 50 percent of a building's energy use. When a plant in Seattle, Washington, was redesigned for more natural light, the company was able to enjoy annual electricity cost reductions of $500,000 **[8]** each year.

7

In context, which choice best combines the underlined sentences?

A) Aside from lowering worker productivity, artificial light sources are also costly, typically constituting anywhere from 25 to 50 percent of a building's energy use.

B) The cost of artificial light sources, aside from lowering worker productivity, typically constitutes anywhere from 25 to 50 percent of a building's energy use.

C) Typically constituting 25 to 50 percent of a building's energy use, artificial light sources lower worker productivity and are costly.

D) Artificial lights, which lower worker productivity and are costly, typically constitute anywhere from 25 to 50 percent of a building's energy use.

8

A) NO CHANGE

B) every year.

C) per year.

D) DELETE the underlined portion and end the sentence with a period.

CONTINUE

Among the possibilities to reconfigure a building's lighting is the installation of full-pane windows to allow the greatest degree of sunlight to reach office interiors. **9** Thus, businesses can install light tubes, **10** these are pipes placed in workplace roofs to capture and funnel sunlight down into a building's interior. Glass walls and dividers can also be used to replace solid walls as a means **11** through distributing natural light more freely. Considering the enormous costs of artificial lighting, both in terms of money and productivity, investment in such improvements should be a natural choice for businesses.

9

A) NO CHANGE
B) Nevertheless,
C) Alternatively,
D) Finally,

10

A) NO CHANGE
B) they are
C) which are
D) those being

11

A) NO CHANGE
B) of
C) from
D) DELETE the underlined portion.

CONTINUE ▶

Questions 12-22 are based on the following passage.

Transforming the American West Through Food and Hospitality

Just as travelers taking road trips today may need to take a break for food at a rest area along the highway, settlers traversing the American West by train in the mid-1800s often found **12** themselves in need of refreshment. However, food available on rail lines was generally of terrible quality. **13** Despite having worked for railroad companies, Fred Harvey, an English-born **14** entrepreneur. He decided to open his own restaurant business to serve rail customers. Beginning in the 1870s, he opened dozens of restaurants in rail stations and dining cars. These Harvey Houses, which constituted the first restaurant chain in the United States, **15** was unique for its high standards of service and quality. The menu was modeled after those of fine restaurants, so the food was leagues beyond the **16** sinister fare travelers were accustomed to receiving in transit.

12

A) NO CHANGE
B) himself or herself
C) their selves
D) oneself

13

Which choice provides the most logical introduction to the sentence?
A) NO CHANGE
B) He had lived in New York and New Orleans, so
C) To capitalize on the demand for good food,
D) DELETE the underlined portion.

14

A) NO CHANGE
B) entrepreneur:
C) entrepreneur; he
D) entrepreneur,

15

A) NO CHANGE
B) were unique for their
C) was unique for their
D) were unique for its

16

Which choice best maintains the tone established in the passage?
A) NO CHANGE
B) surly
C) abysmal
D) icky

CONTINUE

His restaurants were immediately successful, but Harvey was not content to follow conventional business practices. [17] Although women did not traditionally work in restaurants in the nineteenth century, Harvey decided to try employing women as waitstaff. In 1883, he placed an advertisement seeking educated, well-mannered, articulate young women between the ages of 18 and 30. [18] Response to the advertisement was overwhelming, even tremendous, and Harvey soon replaced the male servers at his restaurants with women. Those who were hired as "Harvey Girls" joined an elite group of workers, who were expected to complete a 30-day training program and follow a strict code of rules for conduct and curfews. In the workplace, the women donned identical black-and-white uniforms and carried out their duties with precision. Not only were such regulations meant to ensure the efficiency of the business and the safety of the workers, [19] but also helped to raise people's generally low opinion of the restaurant industry.

17

The writer is considering deleting the previous sentence. Should the writer make this change?

A) Yes, because it introduces information that is irrelevant at this point in the passage.

B) Yes, because it does not logically follow from the previous paragraph.

C) No, because it provides a logical introduction to the paragraph.

D) No, because it provides a specific example in support of arguments made elsewhere in the passage.

18

A) NO CHANGE

B) Response to the advertisement was overwhelming,

C) Overwhelming, even tremendous, was the response to the advertisement,

D) There was an overwhelming, even tremendous, response to the advertisement,

19

A) NO CHANGE

B) but also helping

C) also helping

D) but they also helped

CONTINUE ▶

In return for the servers' work, the position paid quite well for the time: $17.50 a month, plus tips, meals, room and board, laundry service, and travel expenses. **20**

For as long as Harvey Houses served rail travelers through the mid-twentieth century, working there was a steady and lucrative position for women. Living independently and demonstrating an intense work **21** ethic; the Harvey Girls became known as a transformative force in the American **22** West. Advancing the roles of women in the restaurant industry and the American workforce as a whole, the Harvey Girls raised the standards for restaurants and blazed a trail in the fast-changing landscape of the western territories.

20

Which choice most logically follows the previous sentence?

A) The growth of Harvey's business coincided with the expansion of the Santa Fe Railway, which served large sections of the American West.

B) Harvey would end up opening dozens of restaurants and dining cars, plus 15 hotels, over his lucrative career.

C) These benefits enabled the Harvey Girls to save money and build new and exciting lives for themselves in the so-called Wild West.

D) The compensation was considered excellent at the time, though it may not seem like much money by today's standards.

21

A) NO CHANGE
B) ethic:
C) ethic, and
D) ethic,

22

The writer is considering revising the underlined portion of the sentence to read:

West, inspiring books, documentaries, and even a musical.

Should the writer add this information here?

A) Yes, because it provides examples of the Harvey Girls' influence.

B) Yes, because it serves as a transitional point in the paragraph.

C) No, because it should be placed earlier in the passage.

D) No, because it contradicts the main claim of the passage.

Unauthorized copying or reuse of any part of this page is illegal.

CONTINUE

584

Questions 23-33 are based on the following passage and supplementary material.

How Do You Like Those Apples?

Marketed as SmartFresh, the chemical 1-MCP (1-methylcyclopropene) has been used by fruit growers since 2002 in the United States and elsewhere to preserve the crispness and lengthen the storage life of apples and other fruit, which often must travel long distances before being eaten by consumers. **23** 1-MCP lengthens storage life by three to four times when applied to apples. This extended life allows producers to sell their apples in the off-season, months after the apples have been harvested. And at a cost of about one cent per pound of apples, 1-MCP is a highly cost-effective treatment. However, 1-MCP is not a panacea for fruit producers or sellers: there are problems and limitations associated with its use.

23

Which choice most effectively combines the underlined sentences?

A) When applied to apples, 1-MCP lengthens storage life by three to four times, allowing producers to sell their apples in the off-season, months after the apples have been harvested.

B) Producers are allowed to sell their apples months after they have been harvested—in the off-season—because 1-MCP, when applied to apples, lengthens their storage life by three to four times.

C) 1-MCP lengthens storage life, when applied to apples, by three to four times, allowing producers to sell their apples months after the apples have been harvested in the off-season.

D) Months after apples have been harvested, producers are allowed to sell their apples, in the off-season, because 1-MCP lengthens storage life when applied to apples by three to four times.

CONTINUE

[1] 1-MCP works by limiting a fruit's production of ethylene, 24 it is a chemical that causes fruit to ripen and eventually rot. [2] While 1-MCP keeps apples 25 tight and crisp for months, it also limits 26 their scent production. [3] This may not be much of a problem with certain kinds of apples that are not naturally very fragrant, such as Granny Smith, but for apples that are prized for their fruity fragrance, such as McIntosh, this can be a problem with consumers, 27 that will reject apples lacking the expected aroma. [4] But some fruits do not respond as well to 1-MCP as others 28 did, and some even respond adversely. [5] Furthermore, some fruits, particularly those that naturally produce a large

24
A) NO CHANGE
B) being
C) that is
D) DELETE the underlined portion.

25
A) NO CHANGE
B) firm
C) stiff
D) taut

26
A) NO CHANGE
B) there
C) its
D) it's

27
A) NO CHANGE
B) they
C) which
D) who

28
A) NO CHANGE
B) do,
C) have,
D) will,

CONTINUE

amount of ethylene, do not respond as well to 1-MCP treatment. [6] Take Bartlett 29 pears, for instance, unless they are treated with exactly the right amount of 1-MCP at exactly the right time, they will remain hard and green until they rot, and consumers who experience this will be unlikely to purchase them again. 30

29

A) NO CHANGE
B) pears, for instance:
C) pears for instance,
D) pears. For instance,

30

To make this paragraph most logical, sentence 4 should be placed

A) where it is now.
B) after sentence 1.
C) after sentence 2.
D) after sentence 5.

CONTINUE

Finally, researchers have found that 1-MCP actually increases susceptibility to some pathologies in certain apple varieties. For example, Empire apples are prone to a condition that causes the flesh of the apple to turn brown. Traditionally, apple producers have dealt with this problem by leaving the apples in the open air for three weeks before storing them in a controlled atmosphere with tightly regulated temperature, humidity, and carbon dioxide levels. As the graph shows, the flesh of untreated Empire apples that are first stored in the open air undergoes **31** roughly five percent less browning than the flesh of untreated Empire apples that are immediately put into storage in a controlled environment. However, when Empire apples are treated with 1-MCP, **32** their flesh turns brown when the apples are first stored in the open air, though not under other conditions. Although

31

Which choice offers an accurate interpretation of the data in the graph?

A) NO CHANGE

B) slightly more browning than

C) twice as much browning as

D) substantially less browning than

32

Which choice offers an accurate interpretation of the data in the graph?

A) NO CHANGE

B) roughly half of their flesh turns brown, regardless of whether the apples are first stored in the open air.

C) their flesh browns when they are put directly into a controlled atmosphere but not when they are first stored in the open air.

D) their flesh turns brown when they are first stored in the open air, though not as quickly as the apple flesh in an untreated group does.

CONTINUE

researchers continue to search for the right combination of factors that will keep fruits fresh and attractive, **33** the problem may be that consumers are overly concerned with superficial qualities rather than the actual freshness of the fruit.

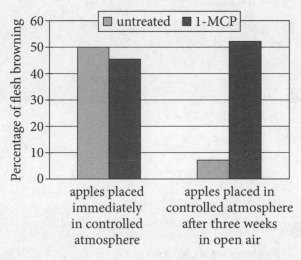

Results of Treatment to Control Browning of Empire Apples

Adapted from Hannah J. James, Jacqueline F. Nock, and Chris B. Watkins, "The Failure of Postharvest Treatments to Control Firm Flesh Browning in Empire Apples." ©2010 by The New York State Horticultural Society.

33

The writer wants a conclusion that conveys how the shortcomings of 1-MCP presented in the passage affect the actions of people in the fruit industry. Which choice best accomplishes this goal?

A) NO CHANGE

B) many of the improvements to fruit quality they have discovered so far have required trade-offs in other properties of the fruit.

C) for now many fruit sellers must weigh the relative values of aroma, color, and freshness when deciding whether to use 1-MCP.

D) it must be acknowledged that 1-MCP, despite some inadequacies, has enabled the fruit industry to ship and store fruit in ways that were impossible before.

CONTINUE

Questions 34-44 are based on the following passage.

More than One Way to Dress a Cat

From Michelangelo's *David* to Vincent van Gogh's series of self-portraits to Grant Wood's iconic image of a farming couple in *American* **34** *Gothic. These works* by human artists have favored representations of members of their own species to those of other species. Indeed, when we think about animals depicted in well-known works of art, the image of dogs playing poker—popularized in a series of paintings by American artist C. M. **35** Coolidge, may be the first and only one that comes to mind. Yet some of the earliest known works of art, including paintings and drawings tens of thousands of years old found on cave walls in Spain and France, **36** portrays animals. Nor has artistic homage to our fellow creatures entirely died out in the millennia since, **37** despite the many years that have passed between then and now.

34

A) NO CHANGE
B) *Gothic*. Works
C) *Gothic*; these works
D) *Gothic*, works

35

A) NO CHANGE
B) Coolidge—
C) Coolidge;
D) Coolidge

36

A) NO CHANGE
B) portraying
C) portray
D) has portrayed

37

The writer wants to link the first paragraph with the ideas that follow. Which choice best accomplishes this goal?

A) NO CHANGE
B) with special attention being paid to domestic animals such as cats.
C) even though most paintings in museums are of people, not animals.
D) as the example of one museum in Russia shows.

Unauthorized copying or reuse of any part of this page is illegal.

590

CONTINUE

[1] The State Hermitage Museum in St. Petersburg, one of Russia's greatest art museums, has long had a productive partnership with a much loved animal: the cat. [2] For centuries, cats have guarded this famous museum, ridding it of mice, rats, and other rodents that could damage the art, not to mention **38** scared off visitors. [3] Peter the Great introduced the first cat to the Hermitage in the early eighteenth century. [4] Later Catherine the Great declared the cats to be official guardians of the galleries. [5] Continuing the tradition, Peter's daughter Elizaveta introduced the best and strongest cats in Russia to the Hermitage. [6] Today, the museum holds a yearly festival honoring these faithful workers. **39**

38

A) NO CHANGE
B) scaring
C) scare
D) have scared

39

To make this paragraph most logical, sentence 5 should be placed

A) where it is now.
B) after sentence 1.
C) after sentence 3.
D) after sentence 6.

Unauthorized copying or reuse of any part of this page is illegal.

CONTINUE

591

These cats are so cherished by the museum that officials recently **40** decreed original paintings to be made of six of them. In each, a cat is depicted upright in a humanlike pose and clothed in imperial-era Russian attire. The person chosen for this **41** task, digital artist, Eldar Zakirov painted the cats in the style traditionally used by portrait artists, in so doing **42** presenting the cats as noble individuals worthy of respect. One portrait, *The Hermitage Court Chamber Herald Cat*, includes an

40

A) NO CHANGE
B) commissioned
C) forced
D) licensed

41

A) NO CHANGE
B) task, digital artist, Eldar Zakirov,
C) task digital artist Eldar Zakirov,
D) task, digital artist Eldar Zakirov,

42

Which choice most effectively sets up the examples that follow?

A) NO CHANGE
B) managing to capture unique characteristics of each cat.
C) commenting on the absurdity of dressing up cats in royal robes.
D) indicating that the cats were very talented mouse catchers.

CONTINUE

aristocratic tilt of feline ears as well as a stately sweep of tail emerging from the stiff scarlet and gold of royal court dress. The wise, thoughtful green eyes of the subject of *The Hermitage Court Outrunner Cat* mimic those of a trusted royal advisor. **43** Some may find it peculiar to observe cats portrayed in formal court poses, but these felines, by **44** mastering the art of killing mice and rats, are benefactors of the museum as important as any human.

43

At this point, the writer is considering adding the following sentence.

> The museum occupies six historic buildings, including the Winter Palace, a former residence of Russian emperors.

Should the writer make this addition here?

A) Yes, because it shows the link between Peter the Great and the cat paintings.

B) Yes, because it helps explain why Russian art celebrates animals.

C) No, because it fails to indicate why the Winter Palace became an art museum.

D) No, because it provides background information that is irrelevant to the paragraph.

44

A) NO CHANGE

B) acting as the lead predator in the museum's ecosystem,

C) hunting down and killing all the mice and rats one by one,

D) protecting the museum's priceless artworks from destructive rodents,

STOP

If you finish before time is called, you may check your work on this section only.
Do not turn to any other section.

Math Test – No Calculator

25 MINUTES, 20 QUESTIONS

Turn to Section 3 of your answer sheet to answer the questions in this section.

DIRECTIONS

For questions 1-15, solve each problem, choose the best answer from the choices provided, and fill in the corresponding circle on your answer sheet. **For questions 16-20**, solve the problem and enter your answer in the grid on the answer sheet. Please refer to the directions before question 16 on how to enter your answers in the grid. You may use any available space in your test booklet for scratch work.

NOTES

1. The use of a calculator **is not permitted**.

2. All variables and expressions used represent real numbers unless otherwise indicated.

3. Figures provided in this test are drawn to scale unless otherwise indicated.

4. All figures lie in a plane unless otherwise indicated.

5. Unless otherwise indicated, the domain of a given function f is the set of all real numbers x for which $f(x)$ is a real number.

REFERENCE

$A = \pi r^2$
$C = 2\pi r$

$A = \ell w$

$A = \frac{1}{2} bh$

$c^2 = a^2 + b^2$

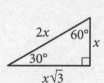
Special Right Triangles

$V = \ell wh$

$V = \pi r^2 h$

$V = \frac{4}{3} \pi r^3$

$V = \frac{1}{3} \pi r^2 h$

$V = \frac{1}{3} \ell wh$

The number of degrees of arc in a circle is 360.
The number of radians of arc in a circle is 2π.
The sum of the measures in degrees of the angles of a triangle is 180.

Unauthorized copying or reuse of any part of this page is illegal.

CONTINUE ➤

1

A painter will paint n walls with the same size and shape in a building using a specific brand of paint. The painter's fee can be calculated by the expression $nK\ell h$, where n is the number of walls, K is a constant with units of dollars per square foot, ℓ is the length of each wall in feet, and h is the height of each wall in feet. If the customer asks the painter to use a more expensive brand of paint, which of the factors in the expression would change?

A) h

B) ℓ

C) K

D) n

2

If $3r = 18$, what is the value of $6r + 3$?

A) 6

B) 27

C) 36

D) 39

3

Which of the following is equal to $a^{\frac{2}{3}}$, for all values of a ?

A) $\sqrt{a^{\frac{1}{3}}}$

B) $\sqrt{a^3}$

C) $\sqrt[3]{a^{\frac{1}{2}}}$

D) $\sqrt[3]{a^2}$

4

The number of states that joined the United States between 1776 and 1849 is twice the number of states that joined between 1850 and 1900. If 30 states joined the United States between 1776 and 1849 and x states joined between 1850 and 1900, which of the following equations is true?

A) $30x = 2$

B) $2x = 30$

C) $\dfrac{x}{2} = 30$

D) $x + 30 = 2$

CONTINUE

5

If $\dfrac{5}{x} = \dfrac{15}{x+20}$, what is the value of $\dfrac{x}{5}$?

A) 10

B) 5

C) 2

D) $\dfrac{1}{2}$

6

$$2x - 3y = -14$$
$$3x - 2y = -6$$

If (x, y) is a solution to the system of equations above, what is the value of $x - y$?

A) -20

B) -8

C) -4

D) 8

7

x	$f(x)$
0	3
2	1
4	0
5	-2

The function f is defined by a polynomial. Some values of x and $f(x)$ are shown in the table above. Which of the following must be a factor of $f(x)$?

A) $x - 2$

B) $x - 3$

C) $x - 4$

D) $x - 5$

8

The line $y = kx + 4$, where k is a constant, is graphed in the xy-plane. If the line contains the point (c, d), where $c \neq 0$ and $d \neq 0$, what is the slope of the line in terms of c and d ?

A) $\dfrac{d-4}{c}$

B) $\dfrac{c-4}{d}$

C) $\dfrac{4-d}{c}$

D) $\dfrac{4-c}{d}$

CONTINUE

9

$$kx - 3y = 4$$

$$4x - 5y = 7$$

In the system of equations above, k is a constant and x and y are variables. For what value of k will the system of equations have no solution?

A) $\dfrac{12}{5}$

B) $\dfrac{16}{7}$

C) $-\dfrac{16}{7}$

D) $-\dfrac{12}{5}$

10

In the xy-plane, the parabola with equation $y = (x - 11)^2$ intersects the line with equation $y = 25$ at two points, A and B. What is the length of $\overline{AB}$?

A) 10

B) 12

C) 14

D) 16

11

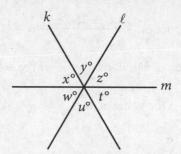

Note: Figure not drawn to scale.

In the figure above, lines k, ℓ, and m intersect at a point. If $x + y = u + w$, which of the following must be true?

    I. $x = z$

    II. $y = w$

    III. $z = t$

A) I and II only

B) I and III only

C) II and III only

D) I, II, and III

12

$$y = a(x - 2)(x + 4)$$

In the quadratic equation above, a is a nonzero constant. The graph of the equation in the xy-plane is a parabola with vertex (c, d). Which of the following is equal to d ?

A) $-9a$

B) $-8a$

C) $-5a$

D) $-2a$

CONTINUE

13

The equation $\dfrac{24x^2 + 25x - 47}{ax - 2} = -8x - 3 - \dfrac{53}{ax - 2}$ is

true for all values of $x \neq \dfrac{2}{a}$, where a is a constant.

What is the value of a ?

A) -16

B) -3

C) 3

D) 16

14

What are the solutions to $3x^2 + 12x + 6 = 0$?

A) $x = -2 \pm \sqrt{2}$

B) $x = -2 \pm \dfrac{\sqrt{30}}{3}$

C) $x = -6 \pm \sqrt{2}$

D) $x = -6 \pm 6\sqrt{2}$

15

$$C = \frac{5}{9}(F - 32)$$

The equation above shows how a temperature F, measured in degrees Fahrenheit, relates to a temperature C, measured in degrees Celsius. Based on the equation, which of the following must be true?

I.   A temperature increase of 1 degree Fahrenheit is equivalent to a temperature increase of $\dfrac{5}{9}$ degree Celsius.

II. A temperature increase of 1 degree Celsius is equivalent to a temperature increase of 1.8 degrees Fahrenheit.

III. A temperature increase of $\dfrac{5}{9}$ degree Fahrenheit is equivalent to a temperature increase of 1 degree Celsius.

A) I only

B) II only

C) III only

D) I and II only

CONTINUE

DIRECTIONS

For questions 16–20, solve the problem and enter your answer in the grid, as described below, on the answer sheet.

1. Although not required, it is suggested that you write your answer in the boxes at the top of the columns to help you fill in the circles accurately. You will receive credit only if the circles are filled in correctly.
2. Mark no more than one circle in any column.
3. No question has a negative answer.
4. Some problems may have more than one correct answer. In such cases, grid only one answer.
5. **Mixed numbers** such as $3\frac{1}{2}$ must be gridded as 3.5 or 7/2. (If $\boxed{3\,1\,/\,2}$ is entered into the grid, it will be interpreted as $\frac{31}{2}$, not $3\frac{1}{2}$.)
6. **Decimal answers:** If you obtain a decimal answer with more digits than the grid can accommodate, it may be either rounded or truncated, but it must fill the entire grid.

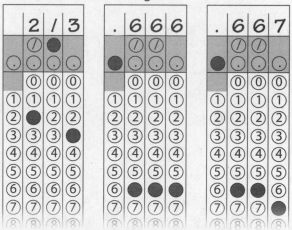

Answer: $\frac{7}{12}$ Answer: 2.5

Write answer in boxes. ← Fraction line

Grid in result. ← Decimal point

Acceptable ways to grid $\frac{2}{3}$ are:

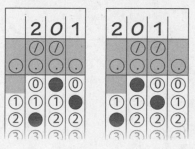

Answer: 201 – either position is correct

NOTE: You may start your answers in any column, space permitting. Columns you don't need to use should be left blank.

CONTINUE ➡

16

$$x^3(x^2 - 5) = -4x$$

If $x > 0$, what is one possible solution to the equation above?

17

If $\dfrac{7}{9}x - \dfrac{4}{9}x = \dfrac{1}{4} + \dfrac{5}{12}$, what is the value of x ?

18

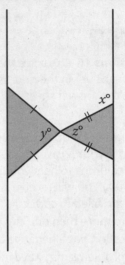

Note: Figure not drawn to scale.

Two isosceles triangles are shown above. If $180 - z = 2y$ and $y = 75$, what is the value of x ?

CONTINUE

19

At a lunch stand, each hamburger has 50 more calories than each order of fries. If 2 hamburgers and 3 orders of fries have a total of 1700 calories, how many calories does a hamburger have?

20

In triangle ABC, the measure of $\angle B$ is 90°, $BC = 16$, and $AC = 20$. Triangle DEF is similar to triangle ABC, where vertices D, E, and F correspond to vertices A, B, and C, respectively, and each side of triangle DEF is $\frac{1}{3}$ the length of the corresponding side of triangle ABC. What is the value of $\sin F$?

STOP

If you finish before time is called, you may check your work on this section only.
Do not turn to any other section.

Math Test – Calculator

55 MINUTES, 38 QUESTIONS

Turn to Section 4 of your answer sheet to answer the questions in this section.

DIRECTIONS

For questions 1-30, solve each problem, choose the best answer from the choices provided, and fill in the corresponding circle on your answer sheet. **For questions 31-38,** solve the problem and enter your answer in the grid on the answer sheet. Please refer to the directions before question 31 on how to enter your answers in the grid. You may use any available space in your test booklet for scratch work.

NOTES

1. The use of a calculator **is permitted**.

2. All variables and expressions used represent real numbers unless otherwise indicated.

3. Figures provided in this test are drawn to scale unless otherwise indicated.

4. All figures lie in a plane unless otherwise indicated.

5. Unless otherwise indicated, the domain of a given function f is the set of all real numbers x for which $f(x)$ is a real number.

REFERENCE

$A = \pi r^2$
$C = 2\pi r$

$A = \ell w$

$A = \frac{1}{2}bh$

$c^2 = a^2 + b^2$

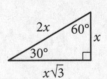

Special Right Triangles

$V = \ell w h$

$V = \pi r^2 h$

$V = \frac{4}{3}\pi r^3$

$V = \frac{1}{3}\pi r^2 h$

$V = \frac{1}{3}\ell w h$

The number of degrees of arc in a circle is 360.
The number of radians of arc in a circle is 2π.
The sum of the measures in degrees of the angles of a triangle is 180.

CONTINUE

1

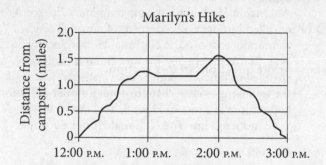

Marilyn's Hike

The graph above shows Marilyn's distance from her campsite during a 3-hour hike. She stopped for 30 minutes during her hike to have lunch. Based on the graph, which of the following is closest to the time she finished lunch and continued her hike?

A) 12:40 P.M.

B) 1:10 P.M.

C) 1:40 P.M.

D) 2:00 P.M.

2

| | Age | | Total |
Gender	Under 40	40 or older	
Male	12	2	14
Female	8	3	11
Total	20	5	25

The table above shows the distribution of age and gender for 25 people who entered a contest. If the contest winner will be selected at random, what is the probability that the winner will be either a female under age 40 or a male age 40 or older?

A) $\dfrac{4}{25}$

B) $\dfrac{10}{25}$

C) $\dfrac{11}{25}$

D) $\dfrac{16}{25}$

CONTINUE

3

The graph below shows the total number of music album sales, in millions, each year from 1997 through 2009.

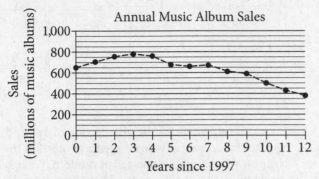

Annual Music Album Sales

Based on the graph, which of the following best describes the general trend in music album sales from 1997 through 2009 ?

A) Sales generally increased each year since 1997.

B) Sales generally decreased each year since 1997.

C) Sales increased until 2000 and then generally decreased.

D) Sales generally remained steady from 1997 through 2009.

4

n	1	2	3	4
$f(n)$	–2	1	4	7

The table above shows some values of the linear function f. Which of the following defines f ?

A) $f(n) = n - 3$

B) $f(n) = 2n - 4$

C) $f(n) = 3n - 5$

D) $f(n) = 4n - 6$

5

At Lincoln High School, approximately 7 percent of enrolled juniors and 5 percent of enrolled seniors were inducted into the National Honor Society last year. If there were 562 juniors and 602 seniors enrolled at Lincoln High School last year, which of the following is closest to the total number of juniors and seniors at Lincoln High School last year who were inducted into the National Honor Society?

A) 140

B) 69

C) 39

D) 30

6

$$3x^2 - 5x + 2$$
$$5x^2 - 2x - 6$$

Which of the following is the sum of the two polynomials shown above?

A) $8x^2 - 7x - 4$

B) $8x^2 + 7x - 4$

C) $8x^4 - 7x^2 - 4$

D) $8x^4 + 7x^2 - 4$

CONTINUE

7

If $\dfrac{3}{5}w = \dfrac{4}{3}$, what is the value of w ?

A) $\dfrac{9}{20}$

B) $\dfrac{4}{5}$

C) $\dfrac{5}{4}$

D) $\dfrac{20}{9}$

8

The average number of students per classroom at Central High School from 2000 to 2010 can be modeled by the equation $y = 0.56x + 27.2$, where x represents the number of years since 2000, and y represents the average number of students per classroom. Which of the following best describes the meaning of the number 0.56 in the equation?

A) The total number of students at the school in 2000

B) The average number of students per classroom in 2000

C) The estimated increase in the average number of students per classroom each year

D) The estimated difference between the average number of students per classroom in 2010 and in 2000

9

Nate walks 25 meters in 13.7 seconds. If he walks at this same rate, which of the following is closest to the distance he will walk in 4 minutes?

A)   150 meters

B)   450 meters

C)   700 meters

D) 1,400 meters

CONTINUE

Questions 10 and 11 refer to the following information.

Planet	Acceleration due to gravity $\left(\dfrac{\text{m}}{\text{sec}^2}\right)$
Mercury	3.6
Venus	8.9
Earth	9.8
Mars	3.8
Jupiter	26.0
Saturn	11.1
Uranus	10.7
Neptune	14.1

The chart above shows approximations of the acceleration due to gravity in meters per second squared $\left(\dfrac{\text{m}}{\text{sec}^2}\right)$ for the eight planets in our solar system. The weight of an object on a given planet can be found by using the formula $W = mg$, where W is the weight of the object measured in newtons, m is the mass of the object measured in kilograms, and g is the acceleration due to gravity on the planet measured in $\dfrac{\text{m}}{\text{sec}^2}$.

10

What is the weight, in newtons, of an object on Mercury with a mass of 90 kilograms?

A) 25

B) 86

C) 101

D) 324

11

An object on Earth has a weight of 150 newtons. On which planet would the same object have an approximate weight of 170 newtons?

A) Venus

B) Saturn

C) Uranus

D) Neptune

CONTINUE

12

If the function f has five distinct zeros, which of the following could represent the complete graph of f in the xy-plane?

A)

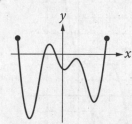

B)

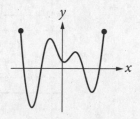

C)

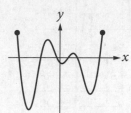

D)

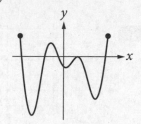

13

$$h = -16t^2 + vt + k$$

The equation above gives the height h, in feet, of a ball t seconds after it is thrown straight up with an initial speed of v feet per second from a height of k feet. Which of the following gives v in terms of h, t, and k ?

A) $v = h + k - 16t$

B) $v = \dfrac{h - k + 16}{t}$

C) $v = \dfrac{h + k}{t} - 16t$

D) $v = \dfrac{h - k}{t} + 16t$

14

The cost of using a telephone in a hotel meeting room is \$0.20 per minute. Which of the following equations represents the total cost c, in dollars, for h <u>hours</u> of phone use?

A) $c = 0.20(60h)$

B) $c = 0.20h + 60$

C) $c = \dfrac{60h}{0.20}$

D) $c = \dfrac{0.20h}{60}$

CONTINUE

15

In order to determine if treatment X is successful in improving eyesight, a research study was conducted. From a large population of people with poor eyesight, 300 participants were selected at random. Half of the participants were randomly assigned to receive treatment X, and the other half did not receive treatment X. The resulting data showed that participants who received treatment X had significantly improved eyesight as compared to those who did not receive treatment X. Based on the design and results of the study, which of the following is an appropriate conclusion?

A) Treatment X is likely to improve the eyesight of people who have poor eyesight.

B) Treatment X improves eyesight better than all other available treatments.

C) Treatment X will improve the eyesight of anyone who takes it.

D) Treatment X will cause a substantial improvement in eyesight.

16

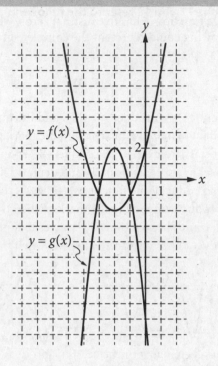

Graphs of the functions f and g are shown in the xy-plane above. For which of the following values of x does $f(x) + g(x) = 0$?

A) -3

B) -2

C) -1

D) $\;\;0$

CONTINUE

Questions 17 and 18 refer to the following information.

$$S(P) = \frac{1}{2}P + 40$$
$$D(P) = 220 - P$$

The quantity of a product supplied and the quantity of the product demanded in an economic market are functions of the price of the product. The functions above are the estimated supply and demand functions for a certain product. The function $S(P)$ gives the quantity of the product supplied to the market when the price is P dollars, and the function $D(P)$ gives the quantity of the product demanded by the market when the price is P dollars.

17

How will the quantity of the product supplied to the market change if the price of the product is increased by $10 ?

A) The quantity supplied will decrease by 5 units.

B) The quantity supplied will increase by 5 units.

C) The quantity supplied will increase by 10 units.

D) The quantity supplied will increase by 50 units.

18

At what price will the quantity of the product supplied to the market equal the quantity of the product demanded by the market?

A) $90

B) $120

C) $133

D) $155

19

Graphene, which is used in the manufacture of integrated circuits, is so thin that a sheet weighing one ounce can cover up to 7 football fields. If a football field has an area of approximately $1\frac{1}{3}$ acres, about how many acres could 48 ounces of graphene cover?

A)   250

B)   350

C)   450

D)   1,350

CONTINUE

20

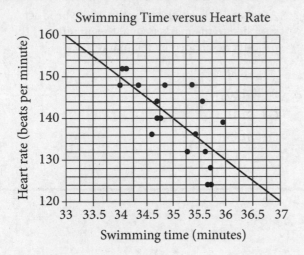

Swimming Time versus Heart Rate

Michael swam 2,000 yards on each of eighteen days. The scatterplot above shows his swim time for and corresponding heart rate after each swim. The line of best fit for the data is also shown. For the swim that took 34 minutes, Michael's actual heart rate was about how many beats per minutes less than the rate predicted by the line of best fit?

A) 1

B) 2

C) 3

D) 4

21

Of the following four types of savings account plans, which option would yield exponential growth of the money in the account?

A) Each successive year, 2% of the initial savings is added to the value of the account.

B) Each successive year, 1.5% of the initial savings and $100 is added to the value of the account.

C) Each successive year, 1% of the current value is added to the value of the account.

D) Each successive year, $100 is added to the value of the account.

22

The sum of three numbers is 855. One of the numbers, x, is 50% more than the sum of the other two numbers. What is the value of x ?

A) 570

B) 513

C) 214

D) 155

CONTINUE

23

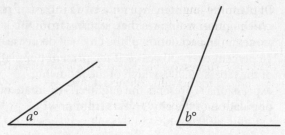

Note: Figures not drawn to scale.

The angles shown above are acute and
$\sin(a°) = \cos(b°)$. If $a = 4k - 22$ and $b = 6k - 13$,
what is the value of k ?

A)   4.5

B)   5.5

C)   12.5

D)   21.5

24

Mr. Kohl has a beaker containing n milliliters of
solution to distribute to the students in his chemistry
class. If he gives each student 3 milliliters of solution,
he will have 5 milliliters left over. In order to give
each student 4 milliliters of solution, he will need an
additional 21 milliliters. How many students are in
the class?

A) 16

B) 21

C) 23

D) 26

25

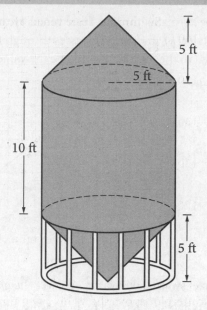

A grain silo is built from two right circular cones and
a right circular cylinder with internal measurements
represented by the figure above. Of the following,
which is closest to the volume of the grain silo, in
cubic feet?

A)   261.8

B)   785.4

C)   916.3

D) 1,047.2

CONTINUE

26

In the xy-plane, the line determined by the points $(2, k)$ and $(k, 32)$ passes through the origin. Which of the following could be the value of k ?

A) 0

B) 4

C) 8

D) 16

27

A rectangle was altered by increasing its length by 10 percent and decreasing its width by p percent. If these alterations decreased the area of the rectangle by 12 percent, what is the value of p ?

A) 12

B) 15

C) 20

D) 22

28

In planning maintenance for a city's infrastructure, a civil engineer estimates that, starting from the present, the population of the city will decrease by 10 percent every 20 years. If the present population of the city is 50,000, which of the following expressions represents the engineer's estimate of the population of the city t years from now?

A) $50,000(0.1)^{20t}$

B) $50,000(0.1)^{\frac{t}{20}}$

C) $50,000(0.9)^{20t}$

D) $50,000(0.9)^{\frac{t}{20}}$

CONTINUE

29

	Handedness	
Gender	Left	Right
Female		
Male		
Total	18	122

The incomplete table above summarizes the number of left-handed students and right-handed students by gender for the eighth-grade students at Keisel Middle School. There are 5 times as many right-handed female students as there are left-handed female students, and there are 9 times as many right-handed male students as there are left-handed male students. If there is a total of 18 left-handed students and 122 right-handed students in the school, which of the following is closest to the probability that a right-handed student selected at random is female? (Note: Assume that none of the eighth-grade students are both right-handed and left-handed.)

A) 0.410

B) 0.357

C) 0.333

D) 0.250

30

$$3x + b = 5x - 7$$
$$3y + c = 5y - 7$$

In the equations above, b and c are constants.

If b is c minus $\frac{1}{2}$, which of the following is true?

A) x is y minus $\frac{1}{4}$.

B) x is y minus $\frac{1}{2}$.

C) x is y minus 1.

D) x is y plus $\frac{1}{2}$.

CONTINUE

DIRECTIONS

For questions 31-38, solve the problem and enter your answer in the grid, as described below, on the answer sheet.

1. Although not required, it is suggested that you write your answer in the boxes at the top of the columns to help you fill in the circles accurately. You will receive credit only if the circles are filled in correctly.
2. Mark no more than one circle in any column.
3. No question has a negative answer.
4. Some problems may have more than one correct answer. In such cases, grid only one answer.
5. **Mixed numbers** such as $3\frac{1}{2}$ must be gridded as 3.5 or 7/2. (If [3|1|/|2] is entered into the grid, it will be interpreted as $\frac{31}{2}$, not $3\frac{1}{2}$.)
6. **Decimal answers:** If you obtain a decimal answer with more digits than the grid can accommodate, it may be either rounded or truncated, but it must fill the entire grid.

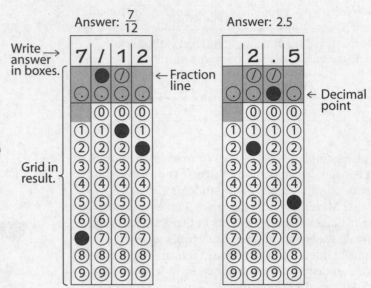

Answer: $\frac{7}{12}$ — Write answer in boxes. ← Fraction line. Grid in result. — Answer: 2.5 ← Decimal point

Acceptable ways to grid $\frac{2}{3}$ are:

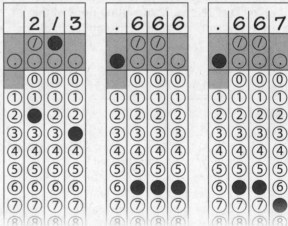

Answer: 201 – either position is correct

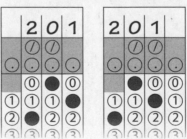

NOTE: You may start your answers in any column, space permitting. Columns you don't need to use should be left blank.

CONTINUE ➡

31

Tickets for a school talent show cost $2 for students and $3 for adults. If Chris spends at least $11 but no more than $14 on x student tickets and 1 adult ticket, what is one possible value of x ?

32

Ages of the First 12 United States Presidents at the Beginning of Their Terms in Office

President	Age (years)	President	Age (years)
Washington	57	Jackson	62
Adams	62	Van Buren	55
Jefferson	58	Harrison	68
Madison	58	Tyler	51
Monroe	59	Polk	50
Adams	58	Taylor	65

The table above lists the ages of the first 12 United States presidents when they began their terms in office. According to the table, what was the mean age, in years, of these presidents at the beginning of their terms? (Round your answer to the nearest tenth.)

33

$$(-3x^2 + 5x - 2) - 2(x^2 - 2x - 1)$$

If the expression above is rewritten in the form $ax^2 + bx + c$, where a, b, and c are constants, what is the value of b ?

34

In a circle with center O, central angle AOB has a measure of $\dfrac{5\pi}{4}$ radians. The area of the sector formed by central angle AOB is what fraction of the area of the circle?

Unauthorized copying or reuse of any part of this page is illegal.

CONTINUE ➤

615

35

An online store receives customer satisfaction ratings between 0 and 100, inclusive. In the first 10 ratings the store received, the average (arithmetic mean) of the ratings was 75. What is the least value the store can receive for the 11th rating and still be able to have an average of at least 85 for the first 20 ratings?

36

$$y \leq -15x + 3000$$
$$y \leq 5x$$

In the xy-plane, if a point with coordinates (a, b) lies in the solution set of the system of inequalities above, what is the maximum possible value of b ?

Unauthorized copying or reuse of any part of this page is illegal.

616

CONTINUE

Questions 37 and 38 refer to the following information.

If shoppers enter a store at an average rate of r shoppers per minute and each stays in the store for an average time of T minutes, the average number of shoppers in the store, N, at any one time is given by the formula $N = rT$. This relationship is known as Little's law.

The owner of the Good Deals Store estimates that during business hours, an average of 3 shoppers per minute enter the store and that each of them stays an average of 15 minutes. The store owner uses Little's law to estimate that there are 45 shoppers in the store at any time.

37

Little's law can be applied to any part of the store, such as a particular department or the checkout lines. The store owner determines that, during business hours, approximately 84 shoppers per hour make a purchase and each of these shoppers spend an average of 5 minutes in the checkout line. At any time during business hours, about how many shoppers, on average, are waiting in the checkout line to make a purchase at the Good Deals Store?

38

The owner of the Good Deals Store opens a new store across town. For the new store, the owner estimates that, during business hours, an average of 90 shoppers per <u>hour</u> enter the store and each of them stays an average of 12 minutes. The average number of shoppers in the new store at any time is what percent less than the average number of shoppers in the original store at any time? (Note: Ignore the percent symbol when entering your answer. For example, if the answer is 42.1%, enter 42.1)

STOP

If you finish before time is called, you may check your work on this section only.
Do not turn to any other section.

The SAT

GENERAL DIRECTIONS

– You may work on only one section at a time.
– If you finish a section before time is called, check your work on that section. You may NOT turn to any other section.

MARKING ANSWERS

– Be sure to mark your answer sheet properly.

COMPLETE MARK ●   EXAMPLES OF INCOMPLETE MARKS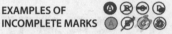

– You must use a No. 2 pencil.
– Carefully mark only one answer for each question.
– Make sure you fill the entire circle darkly and completely.
– Do not make any stray marks on your answer sheet.
– If you erase, do so completely. Incomplete erasures may be scored as intended answers.
– Use only the answer spaces that correspond to the question numbers.

USING YOUR TEST BOOK

– You may use the test book for scratch work, but you will not receive credit for anything that you write in your test book.
– After time has been called, you may not transfer answers from your test book to your answer sheet or fill in circles.
– You may not fold or remove pages or portions of a page from this book, or take the book or answer sheet from the testing room.

SCORING

– For each correct answer, you receive one point.
– You do not lose points for wrong answers; therefore, you should try to answer every question even if you are not sure of the correct answer.

IMPORTANT

The codes below are unique to your test book.
Copy them on your answer sheet in boxes 8 and 9 and fill in the corresponding circles exactly as shown.

9	TEST ID
	(Copy from back of test book.)

8	FORM CODE
	(Copy and grid as on back of test book.)

Follow this link for more information on scoring your practice test:
www.sat.org/scoring

Ideas contained in passages for this test, some of which are excerpted or adapted from published material, do not necessarily represent the opinions of the College Board.

5LSA08

DO NOT OPEN THIS BOOK UNTIL THE SUPERVISOR TELLS YOU TO DO SO.

SAT® Practice Essay #3

 ESSAY BOOK

DIRECTIONS

The essay gives you an opportunity to show how effectively you can read and comprehend a passage and write an essay analyzing the passage. In your essay, you should demonstrate that you have read the passage carefully, present a clear and logical analysis, and use language precisely.

Your essay must be written on the lines provided in your answer booklet; except for the Planning Page of the answer booklet, you will receive no other paper on which to write. You will have enough space if you write on every line, avoid wide margins, and keep your handwriting to a reasonable size. Remember that people who are not familiar with your handwriting will read what you write. Try to write or print so that what you are writing is legible to those readers.

You have 50 minutes to read the passage and write an essay in response to the prompt provided inside this booklet.

REMINDERS

— Do not write your essay in this booklet. Only what you write on the lined pages of your answer booklet will be evaluated.

— An off-topic essay will not be evaluated.

Follow this link for more information on scoring your practice test: **www.sat.org/scoring**

This cover is representative of what you'll see on test day.

As you read the passage below, consider how Eliana Dockterman uses

- evidence, such as facts or examples, to support claims.
- reasoning to develop ideas and to connect claims and evidence.
- stylistic or persuasive elements, such as word choice or appeals to emotion, to add power to the ideas expressed.

Adapted from Eliana Dockterman, "The Digital Parent Trap." ©2013 by Time Inc. Originally published August 19, 2013.

1   By all measures, this generation of American kids (ages 3 to 18) is the tech-savviest in history: 27% of them use tablets, 43% use smartphones, and 52% use laptops. And in just a few weeks they will start the most tech-saturated school year ever: Los Angeles County alone will spend $30 million on classroom iPads this year, outfitting 640,000 kids by late 2014.

2   Yet, according to the latest findings from the research firm Grunwald Associates, barely half of U.S. parents agree that mobile technology should play a more prominent role in schools. Some are even paying as much as $24,000 to send their kids to monthlong "digital detox" programs like the one at Capio Nightingale Hospital in the U.K. . . .

3   So who's right—the mom trying to protect her kids from the perils of new technology or the dad who's coaching his kids to embrace it? It's an urgent question at a time when more than 80% of U.S. school districts say they are on the cusp of incorporating Web-enabled tablets into everyday curriculums.

4   For years, the Parental Adage was simple: The less time spent with screens, the better. That thinking stems from, among other things, reports about the rise of cyberbullying . . . as well as the fact that social media—specifically the sight of others looking happy in photos—can make kids feel depressed and insecure.

5   There's also a fundamental aversion to sitting kids in front of screens, thanks to decades of studies proving that watching too much TV can lead to obesity, violence and attention-deficit/hyperactivity disorder.

6   In that vein, the Waldorf Schools—a consortium of private K-12 schools in North America designed to "connect children to nature" and "ignite passion for lifelong learning"—limit tech in the classroom and bar the use of smartphones, laptops, televisions and even radios at home. "You could say some computer games develop creativity," says Lucy Wurtz, an administrator at the Waldorf School in Los Altos, Calif., minutes from Silicon Valley. "But I don't see any benefit. Waldorf kids knit and build things and paint—a lot of really practical and creative endeavors."

7   But it's not that simple. While there are dangers inherent in access to Facebook, new research suggests that social-networking sites also offer unprecedented learning opportunities. "Online, kids can engage with specialized communities of interest,"

says Mimi Ito, an anthropologist at the University of California at Irvine who's studying how technology affects young adults. "They're no longer limited by what's offered in school."

8   Early tech use has cognitive benefits as well. Although parenting experts have questioned the value of educational games—as Jim Taylor, author of *Raising Generation Tech*, puts it, "they're a load of crap . . . meant to make money"—new studies have shown they can add real value. In a recent study by SRI, a nonprofit research firm, kids who played games like Samorost (solving puzzles) did 12% better on logic tests than those who did not. And at MIT's Education Arcade, playing the empire-building game Civilization piqued students' interest in history and was directly linked to an improvement in the quality of their history-class reports.

9   The reason: engagement. On average, according to research cited by MIT, students can remember only 10% of what they read, 20% of what they hear and 50% of what they see demonstrated. But when they're actually doing something themselves—in the virtual worlds on iPads or laptops—that retention rate skyrockets to 90%.

10 This is a main reason researchers like Ito say the American Academy of Pediatrics' recommendation of a two-hour screen-time limit is an outdated concept: actively browsing pages on a computer or tablet is way more brain-stimulating than vegging out in front of the TV.

11 The most convincing argument for early-age tech fluency, however, is more basic: staying competitive. "If you look at applying for college or a job, that's on the computer," says Shawn Jackson, principal of Spencer Tech, a public school in one of Chicago's lower-income neighborhoods. Ditto the essential skills for jobs in fast-growing sectors such as programming, engineering and biotechnology. "If we're not exposing our students to this stuff early," Jackson continues, "they're going to be left behind." . . .

12 None of this means kids deserve unfettered access to the gadget of their choice—especially if, as McGrath notes, they've already been caught abusing it. As with any childhood privilege, monitoring is key. But parents should keep an open mind about the benefits of tech fluency.

Write an essay in which you explain how Eliana Dockterman builds an argument to persuade her audience that there are benefits to early exposure to technology. In your essay, analyze how Dockterman uses one or more of the features listed in the box above (or features of your own choice) to strengthen the logic and persuasiveness of her argument. Be sure that your analysis focuses on the most relevant features of the passage.

Your essay should not explain whether you agree with Dockterman's claims, but rather explain how Dockterman builds an argument to persuade her audience.

YOUR NAME (PRINT) ....

LAST FIRST MI

TEST CENTER ....

NUMBER NAME OF TEST CENTER ROOM NUMBER

This page represents the back cover of the Practice Essay.

5LS06E

Ideas contained in the passage for this test, which is excerpted or adapted from published material, do not necessarily represent the opinions of the College Board.

DO NOT OPEN THIS BOOK UNTIL THE SUPERVISOR TELLS YOU TO DO SO.

CollegeBoard

SAT PRACTICE ANSWER SHEET

COMPLETE MARK ● **EXAMPLES OF INCOMPLETE MARKS** ⊗ ⊖ ◖ ◑ ✏ ⬗ ⓐ

It is recommended that you use a No. 2 pencil. It is very important that you fill in the entire circle darkly and completely. If you change your response, erase as completely as possible. Incomplete marks or erasures may affect your score.

◼ **TEST NUMBER**   ◼ **SECTION 1**

ENTER TEST NUMBER
For instance, for Practice Test #1, fill in the circle for 0 in the **first column** and for 1 in the **second column.**

0 ○ ○
1 ○ ○
2 ○ ○
3 ○ ○
4 ○ ○
5 ○ ○
6 ○ ○
7 ○ ○
8 ○ ○
9 ○ ○

1   A B C D ○ ○ ○ ○
2   A B C D ○ ○ ○ ○
3   A B C D ○ ○ ○ ○
4   A B C D ○ ○ ○ ○
5   A B C D ○ ○ ○ ○
6   A B C D ○ ○ ○ ○
7   A B C D ○ ○ ○ ○
8   A B C D ○ ○ ○ ○
9   A B C D ○ ○ ○ ○
10 A B C D ○ ○ ○ ○
11 A B C D ○ ○ ○ ○
12 A B C D ○ ○ ○ ○
13 A B C D ○ ○ ○ ○

14 A B C D ○ ○ ○ ○
15 A B C D ○ ○ ○ ○
16 A B C D ○ ○ ○ ○
17 A B C D ○ ○ ○ ○
18 A B C D ○ ○ ○ ○
19 A B C D ○ ○ ○ ○
20 A B C D ○ ○ ○ ○
21 A B C D ○ ○ ○ ○
22 A B C D ○ ○ ○ ○
23 A B C D ○ ○ ○ ○
24 A B C D ○ ○ ○ ○
25 A B C D ○ ○ ○ ○
26 A B C D ○ ○ ○ ○

27 A B C D ○ ○ ○ ○
28 A B C D ○ ○ ○ ○
29 A B C D ○ ○ ○ ○
30 A B C D ○ ○ ○ ○
31 A B C D ○ ○ ○ ○
32 A B C D ○ ○ ○ ○
33 A B C D ○ ○ ○ ○
34 A B C D ○ ○ ○ ○
35 A B C D ○ ○ ○ ○
36 A B C D ○ ○ ○ ○
37 A B C D ○ ○ ○ ○
38 A B C D ○ ○ ○ ○
39 A B C D ○ ○ ○ ○

40 A B C D ○ ○ ○ ○
41 A B C D ○ ○ ○ ○
42 A B C D ○ ○ ○ ○
43 A B C D ○ ○ ○ ○
44 A B C D ○ ○ ○ ○
45 A B C D ○ ○ ○ ○
46 A B C D ○ ○ ○ ○
47 A B C D ○ ○ ○ ○
48 A B C D ○ ○ ○ ○
49 A B C D ○ ○ ○ ○
50 A B C D ○ ○ ○ ○
51 A B C D ○ ○ ○ ○
52 A B C D ○ ○ ○ ○

Download the College Board SAT Practice app to instantly score this test.
Learn more at sat.org/scoring.

● ● ● ● ●   ●   ●

623

CollegeBoard

COMPLETE MARK ●	EXAMPLES OF INCOMPLETE MARKS	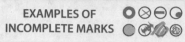	It is recommended that you use a No. 2 pencil. It is very important that you fill in the entire circle darkly and completely. If you change your response, erase as completely as possible. Incomplete marks or erasures may affect your score.

■ SECTION 2

	A B C D		A B C D		A B C D		A B C D		A B C D
1	○○○○	10	○○○○	19	○○○○	28	○○○○	37	○○○○
2	○○○○	11	○○○○	20	○○○○	29	○○○○	38	○○○○
3	○○○○	12	○○○○	21	○○○○	30	○○○○	39	○○○○
4	○○○○	13	○○○○	22	○○○○	31	○○○○	40	○○○○
5	○○○○	14	○○○○	23	○○○○	32	○○○○	41	○○○○
6	○○○○	15	○○○○	24	○○○○	33	○○○○	42	○○○○
7	○○○○	16	○○○○	25	○○○○	34	○○○○	43	○○○○
8	○○○○	17	○○○○	26	○○○○	35	○○○○	44	○○○○
9	○○○○	18	○○○○	27	○○○○	36	○○○○		

If you're scoring with our mobile app we recommend that you cut these pages out of the back of this book. The scoring does best with a flat page.

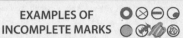

SAT PRACTICE ANSWER SHEET

COMPLETE MARK ●

EXAMPLES OF INCOMPLETE MARKS ⊘ ⊗ ⊖ ◐ ◑ ⌦ ⬮ ⬯

It is recommended that you use a No. 2 pencil. It is very important that you fill in the entire circle darkly and completely. If you change your response, erase as completely as possible. Incomplete marks or erasures may affect your score.

■ SECTION 3

1 Ⓐ Ⓑ Ⓒ Ⓓ
2 Ⓐ Ⓑ Ⓒ Ⓓ
3 Ⓐ Ⓑ Ⓒ Ⓓ

4 Ⓐ Ⓑ Ⓒ Ⓓ
5 Ⓐ Ⓑ Ⓒ Ⓓ
6 Ⓐ Ⓑ Ⓒ Ⓓ

7 Ⓐ Ⓑ Ⓒ Ⓓ
8 Ⓐ Ⓑ Ⓒ Ⓓ
9 Ⓐ Ⓑ Ⓒ Ⓓ

10 Ⓐ Ⓑ Ⓒ Ⓓ
11 Ⓐ Ⓑ Ⓒ Ⓓ
12 Ⓐ Ⓑ Ⓒ Ⓓ

13 Ⓐ Ⓑ Ⓒ Ⓓ
14 Ⓐ Ⓑ Ⓒ Ⓓ
15 Ⓐ Ⓑ Ⓒ Ⓓ

Only answers that are gridded will be scored. You will not receive credit for anything written in the boxes.

16   17   18   19   20

/ ○ ○
. ○ ○ ○ ○
0 ○ ○ ○ ○
1 ○ ○ ○ ○
2 ○ ○ ○ ○
3 ○ ○ ○ ○
4 ○ ○ ○ ○
5 ○ ○ ○ ○
6 ○ ○ ○ ○
7 ○ ○ ○ ○
8 ○ ○ ○ ○
9 ○ ○ ○ ○

Did you know that you can print out these test sheets from the web? Learn more at sat.org/scoring.

NO CALCULATOR ALLOWED

● ● ● ● ●   ●   ●

625

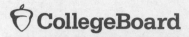 **CollegeBoard**

■ SECTION 4

	A B C D		A B C D		A B C D		A B C D		A B C D
1	○○○○	7	○○○○	13	○○○○	19	○○○○	25	○○○○
2	○○○○	8	○○○○	14	○○○○	20	○○○○	26	○○○○
3	○○○○	9	○○○○	15	○○○○	21	○○○○	27	○○○○
4	○○○○	10	○○○○	16	○○○○	22	○○○○	28	○○○○
5	○○○○	11	○○○○	17	○○○○	23	○○○○	29	○○○○
6	○○○○	12	○○○○	18	○○○○	24	○○○○	30	○○○○

 If you're using our mobile app keep in mind that bad lighting and even shadows cast over the answer sheet can affect your score. Be sure to scan this in a well-lit area for best results.

CALCULATOR ALLOWED

●●●●●   ●   ●

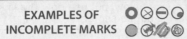

SAT PRACTICE ANSWER SHEET

COMPLETE MARK ●

EXAMPLES OF
INCOMPLETE MARKS ⊘ ⊗ ⊖ ◓ ◐ ⊙ ◑ Ⓐ

It is recommended that you use a No. 2 pencil. It is very important that you fill in the entire circle darkly and completely. If you change your response, erase as completely as possible. Incomplete marks or erasures may affect your score.

■ SECTION 4 (Continued)

Only answers that are gridded will be scored. You will not receive credit for anything written in the boxes.

31   **32**   **33**   **34**   **35**

Only answers that are gridded will be scored. You will not receive credit for anything written in the boxes.

36   **37**   **38**

CALCULATOR
ALLOWED

● ● ● ● ●   ●   ●

627

SECTION 5

IMPORTANT: **USE A NO. 2 PENCIL. DO NOT WRITE OUTSIDE THE BORDER!**
Words written outside the essay box or written in ink **WILL NOT APPEAR** in the copy sent to be scored, and your score will be affected.

PLANNING PAGE You may plan your essay in the unlined planning space below, but use only the lined pages following this one to write your essay. Any work on this planning page will not be scored.

Use pages 7 through 10 for your ESSAY ⟶

FOR PLANNING ONLY

Use pages 7 through 10 for your ESSAY ⟶

Page 6

SERIAL #

628

You may continue on the next page.

You may continue on the next page.

SERIAL #

Answer Explanations

SAT Practice Test #3

Section 1: Reading Test

QUESTION 1.

Choice B is the best answer. In the passage, Lady Carlotta is approached by the "imposingly attired lady" Mrs. Quabarl while standing at a train station (lines 32-35). Mrs. Quabarl assumes Lady Carlotta is her new nanny, Miss Hope: "You must be Miss Hope, the governess I've come to meet" (lines 36-37). Lady Carlotta does not correct Mrs. Quabarl's mistake and replies, "Very well, if I must I must" (line 39).

Choices A, C, and D are incorrect because the passage is not about a woman weighing a job choice, seeking revenge on an acquaintance, or disliking her new employer.

QUESTION 2.

Choice C is the best answer. In lines 1-3, the narrator states that Lady Carlotta "stepped out on to the platform of the small wayside station and took a turn or two up and down its uninteresting length" in order to "kill time." In this context, Lady Carlotta was taking a "turn," or a short walk, along the platform while waiting for the train to leave the station.

Choices A, B, and D are incorrect because in this context "turn" does not mean slight movement, change in rotation, or course correction. While Lady Carlotta may have had to rotate her body while moving across the station, "took a turn" implies that Lady Carlotta took a short walk along the platform's length.

QUESTION 3.

Choice A is the best answer. In lines 10-14, the narrator states that some of Lady Carlotta's acquaintances would often admonish, or criticize, Lady Carlotta for meddling in or openly expressing her opinion on other people's affairs.

Choices B, C, and D are incorrect because the narrator does not suggest that other people viewed Lady Carlotta as tactful, ambitious, or unfriendly.

QUESTION 4.

Choice A is the best answer. In lines 10-14, the narrator states that people often criticized Lady Carlotta and suggested that she not interfere in other people's affairs, which were "none of her business." The fact that people often were critical of Lady Carlotta's behavior provides evidence that Lady Carlotta was outspoken.

Choices B, C, and D do not provide the best evidence that Lady Carlotta was outspoken. Choices B, C, and D mention Lady Carlotta, but do not specify how others view her.

QUESTION 5.

Choice C is the best answer. The narrator notes that Lady Carlotta decided not to interfere when one of her "most eloquent exponents" was stuck in a tree because an angry boar was nearby (lines 14-22). This "eloquent exponent" was a woman who often criticized Lady Carlotta for interfering in other people's affairs. Lady Carlotta's decision to "put the doctrine of non-interference into practice" (to not help her female acquaintance who was "besieged" in a tree) suggests that Lady Carlotta has a sense of humor.

Choices A, B, and D are incorrect because the description of how she "put the doctrine of non-interference into practice" does not suggest that Lady Carlotta is deceptive or cruel, or explain a surprising change in her behavior.

QUESTION 6.

Choice A is the best answer. The narrator explains that Mrs. Quabarl told Lady Carlotta about the "nature of the charge" when she gave Lady Carlotta details about the Quabarl children (line 53-61). Since Lady Carlotta is pretending to be a governess, the term "charge" refers to her responsibilities, or job duties, when caring for the Quabarl children.

Choices B, C, and D are incorrect because in this context "charge" does not mean attack, fee, or expense.

QUESTION 7.

Choice A is the best answer. Lady Carlotta learns about Mrs. Quabarl's children Claude, Wilfrid, and Irene (lines 53-58). The narrator then describes Mrs. Quabarl's child Viola as "something or other else of a mould equally commonplace among children of that class and type in the twentieth century" (lines 58-61). This statement about Viola implies that all of the Quabarl children have skills typical, or "of a mould equally commonplace," to other peers in their social class.

Choices B, C, and D are incorrect because the narrator does not indicate that all of the Quabarl children are unusually creative and intelligent, hostile to the idea of having a governess, or more educated than their peers.

QUESTION 8.

Choice B is the best answer. In lines 62-69, Mrs. Quabarl explains to Lady Carlotta that she wants her children to actively participate in their education, and that Lady Carlotta should not create lessons that require her children to simply memorize historical figures and dates. Mrs. Quabarl emphasizes an education centered on active engagement when she states that her children should "not only be TAUGHT . . . but INTERESTED in what they learn."

Choices A, C, and D are incorrect because the narrator does not suggest that Mrs. Quabarl favors an education that emphasizes traditional values, artistic experimentation, or factual retention.

QUESTION 9.

Choice B is the best answer. In lines 77-82, the narrator describes Mrs. Quabarl as appearing "magnificent and autocratic," or outwardly domineering, but easily "cowed and apologetic" when someone challenges, or defies, her authority.

Choices A, C, and D are incorrect because the narrator does not describe Mrs. Quabarl as selfish, bitter, or frequently imprudent.

QUESTION 10.

Choice D is the best answer. In lines 77-82, the narrator provides evidence that Mrs. Quabarl appears imposing, or autocratic, but is easily defied, or opposed: "She was one of those imperfectly self-assured individuals who are magnificent and autocratic as long as they are not seriously opposed. The least show of unexpected resistance goes a long way towards rendering them cowed and apologetic."

Choices A, B, and C do not provide the best evidence that Mrs. Quabarl appears imposing but is easily defied. Choices A and B are incorrect because they present Mrs. Quabarl's opinions on railway companies and education, and choice C is incorrect because it focuses on Lady Carlotta, not Mrs. Quabarl.

QUESTION 11.

Choice A is the best answer. While the author predominantly supports the use of public transportation, in the third paragraph he recognizes some limitations to the public transportation system: it is a "depressing experience" (lines 25-26) and "underfunded, ill-maintained, and ill-planned" (line 31).

Choices B, C, and D are incorrect because the third paragraph does not expand upon an argument made in the first two paragraphs, provide an overview of a problem, or advocate ending the use of public transportation.

QUESTION 12.

Choice C is the best answer. The author notes that in North America "hopping in a car almost always gets you to your destination more quickly" (lines 32-34). This statement suggests that speed is one advantage to driving in North America.

Choices A, B, and D are incorrect because the author does not cite environmental impact, convenience, or cost as advantages of driving in North America.

QUESTION 13.

Choice D is the best answer. In lines 32-34, the author provides evidence that speed is one advantage to driving in North America, because driving "almost always gets you to your destination more quickly."

Choices A, B, and C do not provide the best evidence that speed is one advantage to driving in North America. Choices A and B are incorrect because they offer general information about using public transportation. Choice C is incorrect because although these lines mention North America, they focus on the disadvantages of public transportation.

QUESTION 14.

Choice B is the best answer. The author argues in the fourth paragraph that public transportation "can be faster, more comfortable, and cheaper than the private automobile" (lines 36-37) and provides examples of fast and convenient public transportation systems.

Choices A, C, and D are incorrect because they focus on points made in the fourth paragraph rather than the paragraph's central idea.

QUESTION 15.

Choice B is the best answer. In lines 35-37, the author provides evidence that some public transportation systems are superior to driving, because public transportation "can be faster, more comfortable, and cheaper than the private automobile."

Choices A, C, and D do not provide the best evidence that some public transportation systems are superior to driving, as they highlight points made in the fourth paragraph rather than the paragraph's central idea.

QUESTION 16.

Choice C is the best answer. In the last paragraph, the author explains the trend that people who became adults around the end of the twentieth century are more willing to use public transportation than people from older generations. The author notes, "If you credit the demographers, this transit trend has legs" (lines 58-59). In this context, "credit" means to believe the demographers' claims about the trend.

Choices A, B, and D are incorrect because in this context, "credit" does not mean endow, attribute, or honor.

QUESTION 17.

Choice B is the best answer. In lines 59-63, the author explains the trend of people who became adults around the end of the twentieth century "tend[ing] to favor cities over suburbs." In this context, these adults "favor," or prefer, cities over suburbs.

Choices A, C, and D are incorrect because in this context "favor" does not mean indulge, resemble, or serve.

QUESTION 18.

Choice B is the best answer. In lines 63-67, the author explains that while riding on public transportation, people can use personal electronic devices, such as "iPads, MP3 players, Kindles, and smartphones."

Choices A, C, and D are incorrect because they do not show that public transportation is compatible with the use of personal electronic devices.

QUESTION 19.

Choice A is the best answer. Figure 1 shows that 10.7% of public transportation passengers are students and 6.7% of public transportation passengers are retirees. Thus, more students than retirees use public transportation.

Choices B and C are incorrect because figure 1 shows that more employed than unemployed people use public transportation and that more employed people than homemakers use public transportation. Choice D is incorrect because figure 1 does not explain how frequently passengers use public transportation; it only identifies public transportation passengers by their primary occupation.

QUESTION 20.

Choice A is the best answer. Figure 1 shows that 72% of public transportation passengers are "employed outside the home," and figure 2 indicates that 59.1% of public transportation trips are for "work." It can be inferred from these figures that many public transportation passengers take public transportation to their place of employment.

Choices B, C, and D are incorrect because figure 1 and figure 2 do not indicate that public transportation passengers primarily use the system to run errands, use their own car on weekends, or are planning to purchase a car.

QUESTION 21.

Choice D is the best answer. The author explains that Ken Dial created an experiment to study the evolution of flight by observing how baby Chukars learn to fly. During the experiment, Dial noticed the unusual way Chukars use their "'wings and legs cooperatively'" to scale hay bales (lines 38-43), and he created "a series of ingenious experiments" (line 46) to study this observation. After his additional experiments, Dial determined that these baby birds angle "their wings differently from birds in flight" (lines 49-50).

Choices A, B, and C are incorrect because they do not accurately reflect the sequence of events in the passage.

QUESTION 22.

Choice A is the best answer. In lines 6-9, the author explains that Dial was "challenged," or dared, by graduate students to develop "new data" on a long-standing scientific debate (the "ground-up-tree-down" theory).

Choices B, C, and D are incorrect because in this context "challenged" does not mean required, disputed with, or competed with.

QUESTION 23.

Choice A is the best answer. The author explains that Dial created his initial experiment to try and create "new data on the age-old ground-up-tree-down debate," and that he looked for "clues" in "how baby game birds learned to fly" (lines 8-11). The note at the beginning of the passage explains the "age-old ground-up-tree down debate" and offers two different theories on how birds evolved to fly. Finally, the last paragraph of the passage discusses WAIR in an evolutionary context.

Choices B, C, and D are incorrect because they do not identify Dial's central assumption in setting up his research.

QUESTION 24.

Choice B is the best answer. In lines 6-11, the author provides evidence that Dial's central assumption in setting up his research is that the acquisition of flight in young birds is linked to the acquisition of flight in their ancestors. The author notes that Dial created a project to "come up with new data on the age-old ground-up-tree-down debate."

Choices A, C, and D do not provide the best evidence that Dial's central assumption in setting up his research is that the acquisition of flight in young birds is linked to the acquisition of flight in their ancestors. Choices A, C, and D are incorrect because they focus on Dial's experiment and his observations on ground birds.

QUESTION 25.

Choice C is the best answer. When a rancher observed Dial's laboratory setup, he was "incredulous" that the Chukars were living on the ground, and he advised Dial to give the birds "something to climb on" (lines 16-23). This "key piece of advice" (line 14) led Dial to add hay bales to his laboratory. Dial later noticed that the Chukars were using their legs and wings to scale the hay bales, and this observation became the focal point of his research.

Choices A, B, and D are incorrect because the incident with the local rancher did not serve to reveal Dial's motivation for creating the project, emphasize differences in laboratory and field research, or introduce a contributor to a scientific theory.

QUESTION 26.

Choice C is the best answer. The author explains that Dial's "aha moment" came when he determined the Chukars used "their legs and wings cooperatively" to scale the hay bales (lines 40-42). Dial then created additional experiments to study how the birds dealt with gradually steeper inclines: "[he filmed] the birds as they raced up textured ramps tilted at increasing angles" (lines 46-48).

Choices A, B, and D are incorrect because Dial's "aha moment" was not followed by Dial teaching the birds to fly, studying videos to find out why the birds no longer hopped, or consulting with other researchers.

QUESTION 27.

Choice B is the best answer. Dial observed that as the Chukars raced up steep ramps, they "began to flap" and "aimed their flapping down and backward, using the force . . . to keep their feet firmly pressed against the ramp" (lines 49-53). Dial determined that the position of their flapping wings facilitated the baby Chukars' traction on the steep ramps.

Choices A, C, and D are incorrect because the passage does not indicate that the Chukars' speed, alternation of wing and foot movement, or continual hopping motions facilitated their traction on steep ramps.

QUESTION 28.

Choice B is the best answer. In lines 61-63, the author explains that Dial named his scientific finding "WAIR, for wing-assisted incline running, and went on to document it in a wide range of species." In this context, Dial "documented," or recorded, the existence of WAIR in numerous bird species.

Choices A, C, and D are incorrect because in this context, "document" does not mean to portray, publish, or process.

QUESTION 29.

Choice D is the best answer. In lines 70-74, the author explains that gliding animals do not use a "flapping flight stroke," or WAIR, wing-assisted incline running. Since Chukars, a ground bird, use WAIR to help scale steep inclines, it can be reasonably inferred that gliding animals do not use WAIR to aid in climbing slopes.

Choices A, B, and C are incorrect because the passage does not include information on gliding animals' offspring, their method of locomotion, or their feeding habits.

QUESTION 30.

Choice D is the best answer. In lines 73-75, the author provides evidence that "the flapping flight stroke" is "something gliding animals don't do."

Choices A, B, and C do not provide the best evidence that gliding animals do not use a flapping stroke to aid in climbing slopes. These choices do not contain information about gliding animals.

QUESTION 31.

Choice B is the best answer. In lines 21-24, the authors of Passage 1 state society's "common happiness" is dependent on women never becoming involved in politics. In this context, the authors of Passage 1 are suggesting that all members of society can have a "common," or shared, happiness.

Choices A, C, and D are incorrect because in this context, "common" does not mean average, coarse, or similar.

QUESTION 32.

Choice C is the best answer. In lines 25-30, the authors of Passage 1 state that women should seek "gentle occupations and the cares of the home" so they can avoid performing difficult, or "strenuous," and unpleasant, or "onerous," tasks.

Choices A, B, and D are incorrect because the authors of Passage 1 do not suggest that running a household and raising children are rewarding for both sexes, yield less value for society, or require professional or political skills.

QUESTION 33.

Choice C is the best answer. In lines 25-30, the authors of Passage 1 provide evidence that women should run households and raise children because these roles do not require "strenuous habits and onerous duties."

Choices A, B, and D do not provide the best evidence that running a household and raising children entail very few activities that are difficult or unpleasant; rather, these lines offer general information about the differences between the sexes.

QUESTION 34.

Choice D is the best answer. In lines 41-46, Wollstonecraft argues that if women do not receive an education "to become the companion of man," or one that is comparable to men's education, then society will not progress in "knowledge and virtue."

Choices A, B, and C are incorrect because Wollstonecraft does not suggest that society can progress only if women have happiness and financial security, follow societal rules, or replace men as figures of power.

QUESTION 35.

Choice C is the best answer. Wollstonecraft argues that women should be granted an education comparable to men's so that truth is "common to all" (lines 41-46). Wollstonecraft states that education will "strengthen [women's] reason till she comprehend her duty" (lines 49-50). In this context, Wollstonecraft is arguing that education will improve women's "reason," or intellect, and allow women to consider their role in society.

Choices A, B, and D are incorrect because in this context "reason" does not mean motive, sanity, or explanation.

QUESTION 36.

Choice A is the best answer. In lines 72-78, Wollstonecraft argues that the laws passed by society's leaders allow men to "contend for their freedom" but serve to "subjugate women." In this context, "subjugate" means to control. Wollstonecraft is arguing that society's leaders grant men freedoms that are denied to women.

Choices B, C, and D are incorrect because Wollstonecraft does not claim that society's leaders have granted freedoms that created a general reduction in individual virtue, caused arguments about happiness, or ensured equality for all people.

QUESTION 37.

Choice D is the best answer. In lines 72-75, Wollstonecraft provides evidence that society's leaders grant freedoms that privilege men. She argues that while society's leaders believe they "are acting in the manner best calculated to promote [women's] happiness," their decisions don't allow women to "contend for their freedom."

Choices A, B, and C do not provide the best evidence that society's leaders grant freedoms that privilege men over women.

QUESTION 38.

Choice C is the best answer. Wollstonecraft cites the statement made by the authors of Passage 1 that excluding women from political participation is "according to abstract principles . . . impossible to explain" (lines 61-65). Wollstonecraft then states that if the authors of Passage 1 can discuss "the abstract rights of man" they should be able to discuss the abstract rights of women (lines 66-69). In these lines, Wollstonecraft is developing her argument by highlighting a flaw in the reasoning presented by the authors of Passage 1.

Choices A, B, and D are incorrect because Wollstonecraft does not refer to the statement made in Passage 1 to call into question the authors' qualifications, dispute the assertion that women are excluded by their own government (sentence one of Passage 1), or validate the authors' conclusions on gender roles.

QUESTION 39.

Choice A is the best answer. The authors of Passage 1 argue that while restricting women's freedoms may be "impossible to explain" (line 7), this restriction is necessary for society's overall happiness (lines 13-17). Wollstonecraft, however, strongly challenges this argument, asking the authors of Passage 1, "Who made man the exclusive judge" of which freedoms are granted to women, and likening society's male leaders to tyrants as they deny women their "civil and political rights" and leave them "groping in the dark" (lines 78-88).

Choices B, C, and D are incorrect because they do not characterize the overall relationship between Passage 1 and Passage 2.

QUESTION 40.

Choice D is the best answer. The authors of Passage 1 admit that women are "excluded by the other half [men] from any participation in government" (lines 1-2), and Wollstonecraft states that society's male leaders create laws that deny women "civil and political rights" (line 86).

Choices A, B, and C are incorrect because the authors of both passages would not agree that women had the same preferences as men, required a good education, or were as happy as men.

QUESTION 41.

Choice A is the best answer. Wollstonecraft argues in the final paragraph of Passage 2 that society's male leaders are like "tyrants" that deny women "civil and political rights" (lines 81-88). The authors of Passage 1 would most likely argue that allowing women these rights would be "a reversal of [society's] primary destines" as society's leaders should only seek women's interests as they pertain to the "wishes of nature," such as women's role as mothers (lines 18-30). The authors of Passage 1 clarify that "nature" created two sexes for a particular reason, so while men can exercise civil and political rights, women are not naturally suited to these activities (lines 30-36).

Choices B and C are incorrect because they are not supported by information in Passage 1. Choice D is incorrect because the authors of Passage 1 do not mention "natural law," only the "wishes of nature."

QUESTION 42.

Choice C is the best answer. When discussing problems with bee colonies, the authors use phrases like "we suspect" (line 19) and "we postulate" (line 21) to show they are hypothesizing reasons for bee colonies' susceptibility to mite infestations. The use of "can," "may," and "could" creates a tentative tone and provides further evidence that the authors believe, but are not certain, that their hypothesis is correct.

Choices A, B, and D are incorrect because the authors' use of "can," "may," and "could" does not create an optimistic, dubious, or critical tone.

QUESTION 43.

Choice C is the best answer. In lines 24-28, the authors hypothesize that bee colonies will be susceptible to mite infestations if they do not occasionally feed on pyrethrum producing plants. In lines 42-46, they suggest creating a trial where a "small number of commercial honey bee colonies are offered a number of pyrethrum producing plants" to test their hypothesis.

Choices A, B, and D are incorrect because the authors do not hypothesize that honeybees' exposure to both pyrethrums and mites will cause the honeybees to develop secondary infections, that beekeepers should increase their use of insecticides, or that humans are more susceptible to varroa mites.

QUESTION 44.

Choice D is the best answer. In lines 24-28, the authors provide evidence that a bee colony may be more resistant to mite infections if the bees eat pyrethrums because this diet may help prevent bees from becoming "immunocompromised or nutritionally deficient." In lines 42-50, the authors suggest testing this hypothesis in a trial on honeybees.

Choices A, B, and C do not describe any of the authors' hypotheses.

QUESTION 45.

Choice D is the best answer. The authors explain that when beekeepers use commercially produced insecticides to fight mite infections, they may "further weaken" bees that are "immunocompromised or nutritionally deficient" (lines 31-35).

Choices A, B, and C are incorrect because the authors do not suggest that beekeepers' use of commercially produced insecticides increases mite populations, kills bacteria, or destroys bees' primary food source.

QUESTION 46.

Choice C is the best answer. In lines 31-35, the authors provide evidence that beekeepers' use of commercially produced insecticides may cause further harm to "immunocompromised or nutritionally deficient bees."

Choices A, B, and D are incorrect because they do not provide the best evidence that beekeepers' use of commercially produced insecticides may be harmful to bees; choices A, B, and D focus on mite infestations' impact on honeybees.

QUESTION 47.

Choice B is the best answer. In lines 31-35, the authors argue that beekeepers' use of insecticides to control mite infestations may be harmful to some bees. The authors then state, "We further postulate that the proper dosage necessary to prevent mite infestation may be better left to the bees" (lines 35-37). In this context, the authors "postulate," or put forth the idea that the bees may naturally control mite infestations better than insecticides.

Choices A, C, and D are incorrect because in this context, "postulate" does not mean to make an unfounded assumption, question a belief or theory, or conclude based on firm evidence.

QUESTION 48.

Choice B is the best answer. In the fourth paragraph the authors propose a trial to study if honeybees' consumption of pyrethrum producing plants helps the honeybees defend against mite infestations. In the experiment, the authors plan to offer honey bee colonies both pyrethrum producing plants and "a typical bee food source such as clover" to determine if these different diets affect the bees' susceptibility to mite infestations.

Choices A, C, and D are incorrect because the main purpose of the fourth paragraph is not to summarize the results of an experiment, provide a comparative nutritional analysis, or predict an outcome of an unfinished experiment.

QUESTION 49.

Choice A is the best answer. In lines 43-45, the authors propose a scientific trial in which honeybees are "offered a number of pyrethrum producing plants, as well as a typical bee food source such as clover." Since the authors contrast the "pyrethrum producing plants" with clover, a "typical bee food source," it can be assumed that clover does not produce pyrethrums.

Choice B is incorrect because it is stated in the passage. Choices C and D are incorrect because they are not assumptions made by the authors.

QUESTION 50.

Choice B is the best answer. The table shows that 77 percent of the honeybee colonies with colony collapse disorder were infected by all four pathogens.

Choices A, C, and D are incorrect because they do not identify the percent of honeybee colonies with colony collapse disorder that were infected by all four pathogens as based on data in the table.

QUESTION 51.

Choice D is the best answer. The table shows that 81 percent of colonies without colony collapse disorder were affected by the pathogen *Nosema ceranae*.

Choices A, B, and C are incorrect because they do not identify the pathogen that infected the highest percentage of honeybee colonies without colony collapse disorder as based on data in the table.

QUESTION 52.

Choice D is the best answer. The table discusses pathogen occurrence in honeybee colonies, but it includes no information as to whether these honeybees were infected with mites. Because the table does not suggest mites infested the honeybee colonies, no conclusions can be made as to whether mites increased the honeybees' "susceptibility to secondary infection with fungi, bacteria or viruses" (lines 4-5).

Choices A, B, and C are incorrect because the table provides no information about whether these honeybees were infected with mites.

Section 2: Writing and Language Test

QUESTION 1.

Choice A is the best answer because by providing the comparative adjective "healthier" and the word "more" to make "productive" comparative, it creates a parallel structure within the list that begins with "happier."

Choices B, C, and D are incorrect because none creates a parallel structure within the list of qualities.

QUESTION 2.

Choice B is the best answer. The ways in which exposure to natural light affects employees is the main subject of the passage.

Choices A, C, and D are incorrect because none introduces the topic discussed in the remainder of the passage.

QUESTION 3.

Choice C is the best answer. It accurately notes that the proposed sentence would be placed directly between the first mention of circadian rhythms and the explanation of the term.

Choices A, B, and D are incorrect because each misinterprets the relationship between the proposed additional text and the ideas in the paragraph.

QUESTION 4.

Choice C is the best answer. It provides the correct possessive construction for "body," which must be a singular noun when discussed in general terms as in this sentence. Choice C also provides the correct plural construction for "clocks."

Choices A, B, and D are incorrect because each applies either a possessive or a plural construction in a place where it doesn't belong.

QUESTION 5.

Choice A is the best answer. The singular verb "is" agrees with the singular noun "absenteeism."

Choices B, C, and D are incorrect because each provides a verb that either fails to agree with the singular subject "absenteeism" or introduces redundancy.

QUESTION 6.

Choice B is the best answer. It contains a direct reference to productivity, the topic introduced in the previous sentence.

Choices A, C, and D are incorrect because none directly addresses employee productivity, the primary subject of the previous sentence.

QUESTION 7.

Choice A is the best answer. It opens with a reference to lowered worker productivity, creating a transition from the previous paragraph, and clearly positions the high energy costs of artificial light sources as an additional disadvantage.

Choices B, C, and D are incorrect because none of the choices offer an adequate transition from the previous paragraph: Each awkwardly inserts the issue of lower worker productivity into a statement about the high energy costs of artificial light sources.

QUESTION 8.

Choice D is the best answer. The word "annual" is adequate to communicate that the savings occurred every year.

Choices A, B, and C are incorrect because each proposes an option that would result in a redundancy with "annual."

QUESTION 9.

Choice C is the best answer. It provides a transitional adverb that accurately communicates that this sentence describes an option that companies could choose ("light tubes") instead of the option described in the previous sentence ("full-pane windows").

Choices A, B, and D are incorrect because each proposes a transitional adverb that does not accurately reflect the relationship between this sentence and the one preceding it.

QUESTION 10.

Choice C is the best answer. It provides the correct relative pronoun to correspond with the plural referent "light tubes" and the correct verb to introduce the definition that follows.

Choices A, B, and D are incorrect because each offers a pronoun inappropriate for opening a dependent clause defining "light tubes."

QUESTION 11.

Choice B is the best answer. The preposition "of" idiomatically follows the noun "means," particularly as a way to connect it to another noun or verb.

Choices A, C, and D are incorrect because each results in nonstandard phrasing with "means."

QUESTION 12.

Choice A is the best answer. The plural reflexive pronoun "themselves" corresponds with the plural noun "settlers."

Choices B, C, and D are incorrect because each provides either a nonstandard phrase or a singular pronoun that does not correspond with "settlers."

QUESTION 13.

Choice C is the best answer. It creates a transition from the poor food quality mentioned in the previous sentence to the information about Harvey in the remainder of the sentence.

Choices A, B, and D are incorrect because none offers a transition from the previous sentence or a detail that corresponds precisely with the information in the remainder of the sentence.

QUESTION 14.

Choice D is the best answer. It correctly provides a comma to close the modifying clause "an English-born entrepreneur," which opens with a comma.

Choices A, B, and C are incorrect because each proposes punctuation that creates an inappropriately strong separation between the subject "Fred Harvey" and the verb "decided."

QUESTION 15.

Choice B is the best answer. It provides the plural verb and plural possessive pronoun that grammatically correspond to the plural referent "Harvey Houses."

Choices A, C, and D are incorrect because each either fails to provide a verb that corresponds with the plural referent "Harvey Houses" or fails to provide the appropriate possessive pronoun.

QUESTION 16.

Choice C is the best answer. It accurately echoes an earlier characterization of the food as being of "terrible quality," while maintaining the established tone of the passage.

Choices A, B, and D are incorrect either because the word is less formal than the established tone of the passage ("icky") or because it illogically attributes agency to food ("sinister," "surly").

QUESTION 17.

Choice C is the best answer. It accurately interprets "not content to follow conventional business practices" as logically introducing the new practice of "employing women" described in the following sentences.

Choices A, B, and D are incorrect because none recognizes why the sentence is relevant to this particular location in the passage.

QUESTION 18.

Choice B is the best answer. It is concise and free of redundancies.

Choices A, C, and D are incorrect because each pairs "overwhelming" and "tremendous," adjectives so close in meaning that together they present a redundancy.

QUESTION 19.

Choice D is the best answer. It contains the pronoun "they," a necessary reference to "such regulations" in the previous clause.

Choices A, B, and C are incorrect because each lacks a necessary subject, such as a pronoun or noun.

QUESTION 20.

Choice C is the best answer. It refers directly to benefits for the restaurants' female employees, the subject of the previous sentence.

Choices A, B, and D are incorrect because none logically builds upon the sentence that precedes it.

QUESTION 21.

Choice D is the best answer. It provides punctuation that indicates that the opening dependent clause modifies the subject "Harvey Girls."

Choices A, B, and C are incorrect because each uses the punctuation for a dependent clause ("Living independently and demonstrating an intense work ethic") as if it were an independent clause.

QUESTION 22.

Choice A is the best answer. It recognizes that the new information supports the previous sentence's claim that "the Harvey Girls became known as a transformative force."

Choices B, C, and D are incorrect because each misinterprets the relationship between the proposed text and the passage.

QUESTION 23.

Choice A is the best answer. It opens with a clause that identifies how 1-MCP affects apples, which focuses the sentence on 1-MCP as the subject and allows the ideas in the sentence to progress logically.

Choices B, C, and D are incorrect because each displays awkward or flawed modification and progression of ideas, or creates redundancy.

QUESTION 24.

Choice D is the best answer. Only the comma is necessary to separate "ethylene" from the appositive noun phrase that defines it.

Choices A, B, and C are incorrect because each creates a comma splice and/ or adds unnecessary words.

QUESTION 25.

Choice B is the best answer. It offers an adjective that accurately describes fresh apples.

Choices A, C, and D are incorrect because each proposes an adjective that does not describe a plausible fruit texture.

QUESTION 26.

Choice A is the best answer. The plural possessive pronoun "their" corresponds with the plural referent "apples."

Choices B, C, and D are incorrect because none provides a pronoun that is both possessive and plural.

QUESTION 27.

Choice D is the best answer. It provides the pronoun "who," which accurately identifies the referent "consumers" as people and appropriately begins the relative clause.

Choices A, B, and C are incorrect because each contains a pronoun that either does not correspond with the human referent "consumers" or does not correctly begin the relative clause.

QUESTION 28.

Choice B is the best answer. It provides the present tense verb "do," which corresponds to the present tense established earlier in the sentence.

Choices A, C, and D are incorrect because each contains a verb that deviates from the simple present tense established in the sentence.

QUESTION 29.

Choice B is the best answer. It provides a colon to appropriately introduce the clause that follows, an elaboration on the preceding claim that Bartlett pears are an example of fruit that "do not respond as well to 1-MCP treatment."

Choices A, C, and D are incorrect because each either creates a comma splice or uses a transitional phrase ("For instance") illogically.

QUESTION 30.

Choice B is the best answer. Sentence 4 begins with "But," indicating a contrast with a previous idea, and goes on to mention that 1-MCP can have negative effects. Sentence 1 continues the discussion of benefits of 1-MCP, and sentence 2 names the adverse effect of limiting scent production, so the most logical spot for sentence 4 is between these sentences.

Choices A, C, and D are incorrect because each proposes placing the sentence at a point where it would compromise the logical development of ideas in the paragraph.

QUESTION 31.

Choice D is the best answer. It most accurately reflects the data in the graph, which shows a steep decrease in percentage of flesh browning when untreated apples are left in the open air for three weeks rather than placed immediately into a controlled atmosphere.

Choices A, B, and C are incorrect because each presents an inaccurate interpretation of the data in the graph.

QUESTION 32.

Choice B is the best answer. It accurately interprets the data as indicating that "roughly half of their flesh turns brown" when apples are treated with 1-MCP: both bars representing 1-MCP treatment are near the 50% line.

Choices A, C, and D are incorrect because each proposes an inaccurate interpretation of the data.

QUESTION 33.

Choice C is the best answer. It describes an action, weighing the relative values, that fruit sellers must take as a result of 1-MCP's limitations.

Choices A, B, and D are incorrect because none specifically connects the shortcomings of 1-MCP with any action on the part of fruit sellers.

QUESTION 34.

Choice D is the best answer. It clearly communicates that the preceding dependent clause modifies "works by human artists."

Choices A, B, and C are incorrect because each fails to link the preceding dependent clause to an independent clause, resulting in an incomplete sentence.

QUESTION 35.

Choice B is the best answer. It provides the necessary em dash to close the aside about artist C.M. Coolidge, which opens with an em dash.

Choices A, C, and D are incorrect because each provides closing punctuation for the aside that does not correspond with the opening punctuation.

QUESTION 36.

Choice C is the best answer. The plural verb "portray" corresponds with the plural noun "works of art."

Choices A, B, and D are incorrect because none provides the plural verb in the present tense that the sentence requires.

QUESTION 37.

Choice D is the best answer. It names a "museum in Russia," which is the subject of the next paragraph.

Choices A, B, and C are incorrect because each provides an overly general phrase that does not specifically link to the paragraph that follows.

QUESTION 38.

Choice C is the best answer. It creates parallelism with the verb "could damage" that appears earlier in the clause ("rodents that could damage . . . [and could] scare off visitors").

Choices A, B, and D are incorrect because each presents a verb tense that is inconsistent with the sentence's other present-tense verb ("could damage") that shares "mice, rats, and other rodents" as its subject.

QUESTION 39.

Choice C is the best answer. Sentence 5, which discusses Peter the Great's daughter continuing his tradition, most logically follows the sentence about Peter the Great.

Choices A, B, and D are incorrect because each presents a placement that would compromise the logical development of the paragraph.

QUESTION 40.

Choice B is the best answer. "Commissioned" describes the act of hiring an artist to create a specific work.

Choices A, C, and D are incorrect because each provides a word that does not correspond logically with the context.

QUESTION 41.

Choice D is the best answer. It provides punctuation that clearly places the noun phrase "digital artist Eldar Zakirov" as an appositive identifying the person mentioned in the previous phrase, "The person chosen for this task."

Choices A, B, and C are incorrect because each fails to open and close the uninterrupted appositive noun phrase "digital artist Eldar Zakirov" with commas.

QUESTION 42.

Choice A is the best answer. The phrase "noble individuals" corresponds with the subsequent examples of portraits where the cats are depicted as "aristocratic," "stately," and like a "trusted royal advisor."

Choices B, C, and D are incorrect because each provides a statement that does not logically connect to the examples that follow.

QUESTION 43.

Choice D is the best answer. It accurately states that the information in the proposed additional sentence is not related to formal portraits of cats, the main topic of the paragraph.

Choices A, B, and C are incorrect because each fails to recognize that the proposed sentence interrupts the logical development of the paragraph.

QUESTION 44.

Choice D is the best answer. The tone corresponds with that established in the passage, and the phrasing appropriately focuses on the cats' contribution to protecting artwork rather than on simply killing rodents.

Choices A, B, and C are incorrect because none makes explicit the link between the cats' hunting activities and the service to the museum.

Section 3: Math Test — No Calculator

QUESTION 1.

Choice C is correct. The painter's fee is given by $nK\ell h$, where n is the number of walls, K is a constant with units of dollars per square foot, ℓ is the length of each wall in feet, and h is the height of each wall in feet. Examining this equation shows that ℓ and h will be used to determine the area of each wall. The variable n is the number of walls, so n times the area of the walls will give the amount of area that will need to be painted. The only remaining variable is K, which represents the cost per square foot and is determined by the painter's time and the price of paint. Therefore, K is the only factor that will change if the customer asks for a more expensive brand of paint.

Choice A is incorrect because a more expensive brand of paint would not cause the height of each wall to change. Choice B is incorrect because a more expensive brand of paint would not cause the length of each wall to change. Choice D is incorrect because a more expensive brand of paint would not cause the number of walls to change.

QUESTION 2.

Choice D is correct. Dividing each side of the equation $3r = 18$ by 3 gives $r = 6$. Substituting 6 for r in the expression $6r + 3$ gives $6(6) + 3 = 39$.

Alternatively, the expression $6r + 3$ can be rewritten as $2(3r) + 3$. Substituting 18 for $3r$ in the expression $2(3r) + 3$ yields $2(18) + 3 = 36 + 3 = 39$.

Choice A is incorrect because 6 is the value of r; however, the question asks for the value of the expression $6r + 3$. Choices B and C are incorrect because if $6r + 3$ were equal to either of these values, then it would not be possible for $3r$ to be equal to 18, as stated in the question.

QUESTION 3.

Choice D is correct. By definition, $a^{\frac{m}{n}} = \sqrt[n]{a^m}$ for any positive integers m and n. It follows, therefore, that $a^{\frac{2}{3}} = \sqrt[3]{a^2}$.

Choice A is incorrect. By definition, $a^{\frac{1}{n}} = \sqrt[n]{a}$ for any positive integer n. Applying this definition as well as the power property of exponents to the expression $\sqrt{a^{\frac{1}{3}}}$ yields $\sqrt{a^{\frac{1}{3}}} = \left(a^{\frac{1}{3}}\right)^{\frac{1}{2}} = a^{\frac{1}{6}}$. Because $a^{\frac{1}{6}} \neq a^{\frac{2}{3}}$, $\sqrt{a^{\frac{1}{3}}}$ is not the correct answer. Choice B is incorrect. By definition, $a^{\frac{1}{n}} = \sqrt[n]{a}$ for any positive integer n. Applying this definition as well as the power property of exponents to the expression $\sqrt{a^3}$ yields $\sqrt{a^3} = (a^3)^{\frac{1}{2}} = a^{\frac{3}{2}}$. Because $a^{\frac{3}{2}} \neq a^{\frac{2}{3}}$, $\sqrt{a^3}$ is not the correct answer. Choice C is incorrect. By definition, $a^{\frac{1}{n}} = \sqrt[n]{a}$ for any positive integer n. Applying this definition as well as the power property of exponents to the expression $\sqrt[3]{a^{\frac{1}{2}}}$ yields $\sqrt[3]{a^{\frac{1}{2}}} = \left(a^{\frac{1}{2}}\right)^{\frac{1}{3}} = a^{\frac{1}{6}}$. Because $a^{\frac{1}{6}} \neq a^{\frac{2}{3}}$, $\sqrt[3]{a^{\frac{1}{2}}}$ is not the correct answer.

QUESTION 4.

Choice B is correct. To fit the scenario described, 30 must be twice as large as x. This can be written as $2x = 30$.

Choices A, C, and D are incorrect. These equations do not correctly relate the numbers and variables described in the stem. For example, the expression in choice C states that 30 is half as large as x, not twice as large as x.

QUESTION 5.

Choice C is correct. Multiplying each side of $\dfrac{5}{x} = \dfrac{15}{x + 20}$ by $x(x + 20)$ gives $15x = 5(x + 20)$. Distributing the 5 over the values within the parentheses yields $15x = 5x + 100$, and then subtracting $5x$ from each side gives $10x = 100$. Finally, dividing both sides by 10 gives $x = 10$. Therefore, the value of $\dfrac{x}{5}$ is $\dfrac{10}{5} = 2$.

Choice A is incorrect because it is the value of x, not $\dfrac{x}{5}$. Choices B and D are incorrect and may be the result of errors in arithmetic operations on the given equation.

QUESTION 6.

Choice C is correct. Multiplying each side of the equation $2x - 3y = -14$ by 3 gives $6x - 9y = -42$. Multiplying each side of the equation $3x - 2y = -6$ by 2 gives $6x - 4y = -12$. Then, subtracting the sides of $6x - 4y = -12$ from the corresponding sides of $6x - 9y = -42$ gives $-5y = -30$. Dividing each side of the equation $-5y = -30$ by -5 gives $y = 6$. Finally, substituting 6 for y in $2x - 3y = -14$ gives $2x - 3(6) = -14$, or $x = 2$. Therefore, the value of $x - y$ is $2 - 6 = -4$.

Alternatively, adding the corresponding sides of $2x - 3y = -14$ and $3x - 2y = -6$ gives $5x - 5y = -20$, from which it follows that $x - y = -4$.

Choices A, B, and D are incorrect and may be the result of an arithmetic error when solving the system of equations.

QUESTION 7.

Choice C is correct. If $x - b$ is a factor of $f(x)$, then $f(b)$ must equal 0. Based on the table, $f(4) = 0$. Therefore, $x - 4$ must be a factor of $f(x)$.

Choice A is incorrect because $f(2) \neq 0$; choice B is incorrect because no information is given about the value of $f(3)$, so $x - 3$ may or may not be a factor of $f(x)$; and choice D is incorrect because $f(5) \neq 0$.

QUESTION 8.

Choice A is correct. The linear equation $y = kx + 4$ is in slope-intercept form, and so the slope of the line is k. Since the line contains the point (c, d), the coordinates of this point satisfy the equation $y = kx + 4$: $d = kc + 4$. Solving this equation for the slope, k, gives $k = \dfrac{d - 4}{c}$.

Choices B, C, and D are incorrect and may be the result of errors in substituting the coordinates of (c, d) in $y = kx + 4$ or of errors in solving for k in the resulting equation.

QUESTION 9.

Choice A is correct. If a system of two linear equations has no solution, then the lines represented by the equations in the coordinate plane are parallel. The equation $kx - 3y = 4$ can be rewritten as $y = \dfrac{k}{3}x - \dfrac{4}{3}$, where $\dfrac{k}{3}$ is the slope of the line, and the equation $4x - 5y = 7$ can be rewritten as $y = \dfrac{4}{5}x - \dfrac{7}{5}$, where $\dfrac{4}{5}$ is the slope of the line. If two lines are parallel, then the slopes of the line are equal. Therefore, $\dfrac{4}{5} = \dfrac{k}{3}$, or $k = \dfrac{12}{5}$. (Since the y-intercepts of the lines represented by the equations are $-\dfrac{4}{3}$ and $-\dfrac{7}{5}$, the lines are parallel, not identical.)

Choices B, C, and D are incorrect and may be the result of a computational error when rewriting the equations or solving the equation representing the equality of the slopes for k.

QUESTION 10.

Choice A is correct. Substituting 25 for y in the equation $y = (x - 11)^2$ gives $25 = (x - 11)^2$. It follows that $x - 11 = 5$ or $x - 11 = -5$, so the x-coordinates of the two points of intersection are $x = 16$ and $x = 6$, respectively. Since both points of intersection have a y-coordinate of 25, it follows that the two points are $(16, 25)$ and $(6, 25)$. Since these points lie on the horizontal line $y = 25$, the distance between these points is the positive difference of the x-coordinates: $16 - 6 = 10$.

Choices B, C, and D are incorrect and may be the result of an error in solving the quadratic equation that results when substituting 25 for y in the given quadratic equation.

QUESTION 11.

Choice B is correct. Since the angles marked $y°$ and $u°$ are vertical angles, $y = u$. Subtracting the sides of $y = u$ from the corresponding sides of $x + y = u + w$ gives $x = w$. Since the angles marked $w°$ and $z°$ are vertical angles, $w = z$. Therefore, $x = z$, and so I must be true.

The equation in II need not be true. For example, if $x = w = z = t = 70$ and $y = u = 40$, then all three pairs of vertical angles in the figure have equal measure and the given condition $x + y = u + w$ holds. But it is not true in this case that y is equal to w. Therefore, II need not be true.

Since the top three angles in the figure form a straight angle, it follows that $x + y + z = 180$. Similarly, $w + u + t = 180$, and so $x + y + z = w + u + t$. Subtracting the sides of the given equation $x + y = u + w$ from the corresponding sides of $x + y + z = w + u + t$ gives $z = t$. Therefore, III must be true. Since only I and III must be true, the correct answer is choice B.

Choices A, C, and D are incorrect because each of these choices includes II, which need not be true.

QUESTION 12.

Choice A is correct. The parabola with equation $y = a(x - 2)(x + 4)$ crosses the x-axis at the points $(-4, 0)$ and $(2, 0)$. The x-coordinate of the vertex of the parabola is halfway between the x-coordinates of $(-4, 0)$ and $(2, 0)$. Thus, the x-coordinate of the vertex is $\frac{-4 + 2}{2} = -1$. This is the value of c. To find the y-coordinate of the vertex, substitute -1 for x in $y = a(x - 2)(x + 4)$: $y = a(x - 2)(x + 4) = a(-1 - 2)(-1 + 4) = a(-3)(3) = -9a$.

Therefore, the value of d is $-9a$.

Choice B is incorrect because the value of the constant term in the equation is not the y-coordinate of the vertex, unless there were no linear terms in the quadratic. Choice C is incorrect and may be the result of a sign error in finding the x-coordinate of the vertex. Choice D is incorrect because the negative of the coefficient of the linear term in the quadratic is not the y-coordinate of the vertex.

QUESTION 13.

Choice B is correct. Since $24x^2 + 25x - 47$ divided by $ax - 2$ is equal to $-8x - 3$ with remainder -53, it is true that $(-8x - 3)(ax - 2) - 53 = 24x^2 + 25x - 47$. (This can be seen by multiplying each side of the given equation by $ax - 2$). This can be rewritten as $-8ax^2 + 16x - 3ax = 24x^2 + 25x - 47$. Since the coefficients of the x^2-term have to be equal on both sides of the equation, $-8a = 24$, or $a = -3$.

Choices A, C, and D are incorrect and may be the result of either a conceptual misunderstanding or a computational error when trying to solve for the value of a.

QUESTION 14.

Choice A is correct. Dividing each side of the given equation by 3 gives the equivalent equation $x^2 + 4x + 2 = 0$. Then using the quadratic formula, $\dfrac{-b \pm \sqrt{b^2 - 4ac}}{2a}$, with $a = 1$, $b = 4$, and $c = 2$, gives the solutions $x = -2 \pm \sqrt{2}$.

Choices B, C, and D are incorrect and may be the result of errors when applying the quadratic formula.

QUESTION 15.

Choice D is correct. If C is graphed against F, the slope of the graph is equal to $\dfrac{5}{9}$ degrees Celsius/degrees Fahrenheit, which means that for an increase of 1 degree Fahrenheit, the increase is $\dfrac{5}{9}$ of 1 degree Celsius. Thus, statement I is true. This is the equivalent to saying that an increase of 1 degree Celsius is equal to an increase of $\dfrac{9}{5}$ degrees Fahrenheit. Since $\dfrac{9}{5} = 1.8$, statement II is true. On the other hand, statement III is not true, since a temperature increase of $\dfrac{9}{5}$ degrees Fahrenheit, not $\dfrac{5}{9}$ degree Fahrenheit, is equal to a temperature increase of 1 degree Celsius.

Choices A, B, and C are incorrect because each of these choices omits a true statement or includes a false statement.

QUESTION 16.

The correct answer is either 1 or 2. The given equation can be rewritten as $x^5 - 5x^3 + 4x = 0$. Since the polynomial expression on the left has no constant term, it has x as a factor: $x(x^4 - 5x^2 + 4) = 0$. The expression in parentheses is a quadratic equation in x^2 that can be factored, giving $x(x^2 - 1)(x^2 - 4) = 0$. This further factors as $x(x - 1)(x + 1)(x - 2)(x + 2) = 0$. The solutions for x are $x = 0$, $x = 1$, $x = -1$, $x = 2$, and $x = -2$. Since it is given that $x > 0$, the possible values of x are $x = 1$ and $x = 2$. Either 1 or 2 may be gridded as the correct answer.

QUESTION 17.

The correct answer is 2. First, clear the fractions from the given equation by multiplying each side of the equation by 36 (the least common multiple of 4, 9, and 12). The equation becomes $28x - 16x = 9 + 15$. Combining like terms on each side of the equation yields $12x = 24$. Finally, dividing both sides of the equation by 12 yields $x = 2$.

Alternatively, since $\frac{7}{9}x - \frac{4}{9}x = \frac{3}{9}x = \frac{1}{3}x$ and $\frac{1}{4} + \frac{5}{12} = \frac{3}{12} + \frac{5}{12} = \frac{8}{12} = \frac{2}{3}$, the given equation simplifies to $\frac{1}{3}x = \frac{2}{3}$. Multiplying each side of $\frac{1}{3}x = \frac{2}{3}$ by 3 yields $x = 2$.

QUESTION 18.

The correct answer is 105. Since $180 - z = 2y$ and $y = 75$, it follows that $180 - z = 150$, and so $z = 30$. Thus, each of the base angles of the isosceles triangle on the right has measure $\frac{180° - 30°}{2} = 75°$. Therefore, the measure of the angle marked $x°$ is $180° - 75° = 105°$, and so the value of x is 105.

QUESTION 19.

The correct answer is 370. A system of equations can be used where h represents the number of calories in a hamburger and f represents the number of calories in an order of fries. The equation $2h + 3f = 1700$ represents the fact that 2 hamburgers and 3 orders of fries contain a total of 1700 calories, and the equation $h = f + 50$ represents the fact that one hamburger contains 50 more calories than an order of fries. Substituting $f + 50$ for h in $2h + 3f = 1700$ gives $2(f + 50) + 3f = 1700$. This equation can be solved as follows:

$$2f + 100 + 3f = 1700$$
$$5f + 100 = 1700$$
$$5f = 1600$$
$$f = 320$$

The number of calories in an order of fries is 320, so the number of calories in a hamburger is 50 more than 320, or 370.

QUESTION 20.

The correct answer is $\frac{3}{5}$ **or .6.** Triangle ABC is a right triangle with its right angle at B. Thus, $\overline{AC}$ is the hypotenuse of right triangle ABC, and $\overline{AB}$ and $\overline{BC}$ are the legs of right triangle ABC. By the Pythagorean theorem, $AB = \sqrt{20^2 - 16^2} = \sqrt{400 - 256} = \sqrt{144} = 12$. Since triangle DEF is similar to triangle ABC, with vertex F corresponding to vertex C, the measure of angle F equals the measure of angle C. Thus, $\sin F = \sin C$. From the side lengths of triangle ABC, $\sin C = \dfrac{\text{opposite side}}{\text{hypotenuse}} = \dfrac{AB}{AC} = \dfrac{12}{20} = \dfrac{3}{5}$. Therefore, $\sin F = \dfrac{3}{5}$. Either $\frac{3}{5}$ or its decimal equivalent, .6, may be gridded as the correct answer.

Section 4: Math Test – Calculator

QUESTION 1.

Choice C is correct. Marilyn's distance from her campsite remained the same during the time she ate lunch. This is represented by a horizontal segment in the graph. The only horizontal segment in the graph starts at a time of about 1:10 P.M. and ends at about 1:40 P.M. Therefore, Marilyn finished her lunch and continued her hike at about 1:40 P.M.

Choices A, B, and D are incorrect and may be the result of a misinterpretation of the graph. For example, choice B is the time Marilyn started her lunch, and choice D is the time Marilyn was at the maximum distance from her campsite.

QUESTION 2.

Choice B is correct. Of the 25 people who entered the contest, there are 8 females under age 40 and 2 males age 40 or older. Therefore, the probability that the contest winner will be either a female under age 40 or a male age 40 or older is $\dfrac{8}{25} + \dfrac{2}{25} = \dfrac{10}{25}$.

Choice A is incorrect and may be the result of dividing 8 by 2, instead of adding 8 to 2, to find the probability. Choice C is incorrect; it is the probability that the contest winner will be either a female under age 40 or a female age 40 or older. Choice D is incorrect and may be the result of multiplying 8 and 2, instead of adding 8 and 2, to find the probability.

QUESTION 3.

Choice C is correct. Based on the graph, sales increased in the first 3 years since 1997, which is until year 2000, and then generally decreased thereafter.

Choices A, B, and D are incorrect; each of these choices contains inaccuracies in describing the general trend of music album sales from 1997 to 2000.

QUESTION 4.

Choice C is correct. The graph of $y = f(n)$ in the coordinate plane is a line that passes through each of the points given in the table. From the table, one can see that an increase of 1 unit in n results in an increase of 3 units in $f(n)$; for example, $f(2) - f(1) = 1 - (-2) = 3$. Therefore, the graph of $y = f(n)$ in the coordinate plane is a line with slope 3. Only choice C is a line with slope 3. The y-intercept of the line is the value of $f(0)$. Since an increase of 1 unit in n results in an increase of 3 units in $f(n)$, it follows that $f(1) - f(0) = 3$. Since $f(1) = -2$, it follows that $f(0) = f(1) - 3 = -5$. Therefore, the y-intercept of the graph of $f(n)$ is -5, and the slope-intercept equation for $f(n)$ is $f(n) = 3n - 5$.

Choices A, B, and D are incorrect because each equation has the incorrect slope of the line (the y-intercept in each equation is also incorrect).

QUESTION 5.

Choice B is correct. Since 7 percent of the 562 juniors is 0.07(562) and 5 percent of the 602 seniors is 0.05(602), the expression 0.07(562) + 0.05(602) can be evaluated to determine the total number of juniors and seniors inducted into the honor society. Of the given choices, 69 is closest to the value of the expression.

Choice A is incorrect and may be the result of adding the number of juniors and seniors and the percentages given and then using the expression (0.07 + 0.05)(562 + 602). Choices C and D are incorrect and may be the result of finding either only the number of juniors inducted or only the number of seniors inducted.

QUESTION 6.

Choice A is correct. The sum of the two polynomials is $(3x^2 - 5x + 2) + (5x^2 - 2x - 6)$. This can be rewritten by combining like terms:

$$(3x^2 - 5x + 2) + (5x^2 - 2x - 6) = (3x^2 + 5x^2) + (-5x - 2x) + (2 - 6) = 8x^2 - 7x - 4.$$

Choice B is incorrect and may be the result of a sign error when combining the coefficients of the x-term. Choice C is incorrect and may be the result of adding the exponents, as well as the coefficients, of like terms. Choice D is incorrect and may be the result of a combination of the errors described in B and C.

QUESTION 7.

Choice D is correct. To solve the equation for w, multiply both sides of the equation by the reciprocal of $\frac{3}{5}$, which is $\frac{5}{3}$. This gives $\left(\frac{5}{3}\right) \cdot \frac{3}{5}w = \frac{4}{5} \cdot \left(\frac{5}{3}\right)$, which simplifies to $w = \frac{20}{9}$.

Choices A, B, and C are incorrect and may be the result of errors in arithmetic when simplifying the given equation.

QUESTION 8.

Choice C is correct. In the equation $y = 0.56x + 27.2$, the value of x increases by 1 for each year that passes. Each time x increases by 1, y increases by 0.56 since 0.56 is the slope of the graph of this equation. Since y represents the average number of students per classroom in the year represented by x, it follows that, according to the model, the estimated increase each year in the average number of students per classroom at Central High School is 0.56.

Choice A is incorrect because the total number of students in the school in 2000 is the product of the average number of students per classroom and the total number of classrooms, which would appropriately be approximated by the y-intercept (27.2) times the total number of classrooms, which is not given. Choice B is incorrect because the average number of students per classroom in 2000 is given by the y-intercept of the graph of the equation, but the question is asking for the meaning of the number 0.56, which is the slope. Choice D is incorrect because 0.56 represents the estimated <u>yearly</u> change in the average number of students per classroom. The estimated difference between the average number of students per classroom in 2010 and 2000 is 0.56 times the number of years that have passed between 2000 and 2010, that is, $0.56 \times 10 = 5.6$.

QUESTION 9.

Choice B is correct. Because Nate walks 25 meters in 13.7 seconds, and 4 minutes is equal to 240 seconds, the proportion $\dfrac{25 \text{ meters}}{13.7 \text{ sec}} = \dfrac{x \text{ meters}}{240 \text{ sec}}$ can be used to find out how many meters, x, Nate walks in 4 minutes. The proportion can be simplified to $\dfrac{25}{13.7} = \dfrac{x}{240}$, because the units of meters per second cancel, and then each side of the equation can be multiplied by 240, giving $\dfrac{(240)(25)}{13.7} = x \approx 438$. Therefore, of the given options, 450 meters is closest to the distance Nate will walk in 4 minutes.

Choice A is incorrect and may be the result of setting up the proportion as $\dfrac{13.7 \text{ sec}}{25 \text{ meters}} = \dfrac{x \text{ meters}}{240 \text{ sec}}$ and finding that $x \approx 132$, which is close to 150. Choices C and D are incorrect and may be the result of errors in calculation.

QUESTION 10.

Choice D is correct. On Mercury, the acceleration due to gravity is 3.6 m/sec^2. Substituting 3.6 for g and 90 for m in the formula $W = mg$ gives $W = 90(3.6) = 324$ newtons.

Choice A is incorrect and may be the result of dividing 90 by 3.6. Choice B is incorrect and may be the result of subtracting 3.6 from 90 and rounding to the nearest whole number. Choice C is incorrect because an object with a weight of 101 newtons on Mercury would have a mass of about 28 kilograms, not 90 kilograms.

QUESTION 11.

Choice B is correct. On Earth, the acceleration due to gravity is 9.8 m/sec^2. Thus, for an object with a weight of 150 newtons, the formula $W = mg$ becomes $150 = m(9.8)$, which shows that the mass of an object with a weight of 150 newtons on Earth is about 15.3 kilograms. Substituting this mass into the formula $W = mg$ and now using the weight of 170 newtons gives $170 = 15.3g$, which shows that the second planet's acceleration due to gravity is about 11.1 m/sec^2. According to the table, this value for the acceleration due to gravity holds on Saturn.

Choices A, C, and D are incorrect. Using the formula $W = mg$ and the values for g in the table shows that an object with a weight of 170 newtons on these planets would not have the same mass as an object with a weight of 150 newtons on Earth.

QUESTION 12.

Choice D is correct. A zero of a function corresponds to an x-intercept of the graph of the function in the xy-plane. Therefore, the complete graph of the function f, which has five distinct zeros, must have five x-intercepts. Only the graph in choice D has five x-intercepts, and therefore, this is the only one of the given graphs that could be the complete graph of f in the xy-plane.

Choices A, B, and C are incorrect. The number of x-intercepts of each of these graphs is not equal to five; therefore, none of these graphs could be the complete graph of f, which has five distinct zeros.

QUESTION 13.

Choice D is correct. Starting with the original equation, $h = -16t^2 + vt + k$, in order to get v in terms of the other variables, $-16t^2$ and k need to be subtracted from each side. This yields $vt = h + 16t^2 - k$, which when divided by t will give v in terms of the other variables. However, the equation $v = \dfrac{h + 16t^2 - k}{t}$ is not one of the options, so the right side needs to be further simplified. Another way to write the previous equation is $v = \dfrac{h - k}{t} + \dfrac{16t^2}{t}$, which can be simplified to $v = \dfrac{h - k}{t} + 16t$.

Choices A, B, and C are incorrect and may be the result of arithmetic errors when rewriting the original equation to express v in terms of h, t, and k.

QUESTION 14.

Choice A is correct. The hotel charges $0.20 per minute to use the meeting-room phone. This per-minute rate can be converted to the hourly rate using the conversion 1 hour = 60 minutes, as shown below.

$$\frac{\$0.20}{\text{minute}} \times \frac{60 \text{ minutes}}{1 \text{ hour}} = \frac{\$(0.20 \times 60)}{\text{hour}}$$

Thus, the hotel charges $(0.20 × 60) per hour to use the meeting-room phone. Therefore, the cost c, in dollars, for h hours of use is $c = (0.20 \times 60)h$, which is equivalent to $c = 0.20(60h)$.

Choice B is incorrect because in this expression the per-minute rate is multiplied by h, the number of <u>hours</u> of phone use. Furthermore, the equation indicates that there is a flat fee of $60 in addition to the per-minute or per-hour rate. This is not the case. Choice C is incorrect because the expression indicates that the hotel charges $\left(\dfrac{60}{0.20}\right)$ per hour for use of the meeting-room phone, not $0.20(60) per hour. Choice D is incorrect because the expression indicates that the hourly rate is $\dfrac{1}{60}$ times the per-minute rate, not 60 times the per-minute rate.

QUESTION 15.

Choice A is the correct answer. Experimental research is a method used to study a small group of people and generalize the results to a larger population. However, in order to make a generalization involving cause and effect:

▶ The population must be well defined.

▶ The participants must be selected at random.

▶ The participants must be randomly assigned to treatment groups.

When these conditions are met, the results of the study can be generalized to the population with a conclusion about cause and effect. In this study, all conditions are met and the population from which the participants were selected are people with poor eyesight. Therefore, a general conclusion can be drawn about the effect of Treatment X on the population of people with poor eyesight.

Choice B is incorrect. The study did not include all available treatments, so no conclusion can be made about the relative effectiveness of all available treatments. Choice C is incorrect. The participants were selected at random from a large population of people with poor eyesight. Therefore, the results can be generalized only to that population and not to anyone in general. Also, the conclusion is too strong: an experimental study might show that people are likely to be helped by a treatment, but it cannot show that <u>anyone</u> who takes the treatment will be helped. Choice D is incorrect.

This conclusion is too strong. The study shows that Treatment X is <u>likely</u> to improve the eyesight of people with poor eyesight, but it cannot show that the treatment definitely <u>will</u> cause improvement in eyesight for every person. Furthermore, since the people undergoing the treatment in the study were selected from people with poor eyesight, the results can be generalized only to this population, not to all people.

QUESTION 16.

Choice B is correct. For any value of x, say $x = x_0$, the point $(x_0, f(x_0))$ lies on the graph of f and the point $(x_0, g(x_0))$ lies on the graph of g. Thus, for any value of x, say $x = x_0$, the value of $f(x_0) + g(x_0)$ is equal to the sum of the y-coordinates of the points on the graphs of f and g with x-coordinate equal to x_0. Therefore, the value of x for which $f(x) + g(x)$ is equal to 0 will occur when the y-coordinates of the points representing $f(x)$ and $g(x)$ at the same value of x are equidistant from the x-axis and are on opposite sides of the x-axis. Looking at the graphs, one can see that this occurs at $x = -2$: the point $(-2, -2)$ lies on the graph of f, and the point $(-2, 2)$ lies on the graph of g. Thus, at $x = -2$, the value of $f(x) + g(x)$ is $-2 + 2 = 0$.

Choices A, C, and D are incorrect because none of these x-values satisfy the given equation, $f(x) + g(x) = 0$.

QUESTION 17.

Choice B is correct. The quantity of the product supplied to the market is given by the function $S(P) = \frac{1}{2}P + 40$. If the price P of the product increases by \$10, the effect on the quantity of the product supplied can be determined by substituting $P + 10$ for P as the argument in the function. This gives $S(P + 10) = \frac{1}{2}(P + 10) + 40 = \frac{1}{2}P + 45$, which shows that $S(P + 10) = S(P) + 5$. Therefore, the quantity supplied to the market will increase by 5 units when the price of the product is increased by \$10.

Alternatively, look at the coefficient of P in the linear function S. This is the slope of the graph of the function, where P is on the horizontal axis and $S(P)$ is on the vertical axis. Since the slope is $\frac{1}{2}$, for every increase of 1 in P, there will be an increase of $\frac{1}{2}$ in $S(P)$, and therefore, an increase of 10 in P will yield an increase of 5 in $S(P)$.

Choice A is incorrect. If the quantity supplied decreases as the price of the product increases, the function $S(P)$ would be decreasing, but $S(P) = \frac{1}{2}P + 40$ is an increasing function. Choice C is incorrect and may be the result of assuming the slope of the graph of $S(P)$ is equal to 1. Choice D is incorrect and may be the result of confusing the y-intercept of the graph of $S(P)$ with the slope, and then adding 10 to the y-intercept.

QUESTION 18.

Choice B is correct. The quantity of the product supplied to the market will equal the quantity of the product demanded by the market if $S(P)$ is equal to $D(P)$, that is, if $\frac{1}{2}P + 40 = 220 - P$. Solving this equation gives $P = 120$, and so \$120 is the price at which the quantity of the product supplied will equal the quantity of the product demanded.

Choices A, C, and D are incorrect. At these dollar amounts, the quantities given by $S(P)$ and $D(P)$ are not equal.

QUESTION 19.

Choice C is correct. It is given that 1 ounce of graphene covers 7 football fields. Therefore, 48 ounces can cover $7 \times 48 = 336$ football fields. If each football field has an area of $1\frac{1}{3}$ acres, than 336 football fields have a total area of $336 \times 1\frac{1}{3} = 448$ acres. Therefore, of the choices given, 450 acres is closest to the number of acres 48 ounces of graphene could cover.

Choice A is incorrect and may be the result of dividing, instead of multiplying, the number of football fields by $1\frac{1}{3}$. Choice B is incorrect and may be the result of finding the number of football fields, not the number of acres, that can be covered by 48 ounces of graphene. Choice D is incorrect and may be the result of setting up the expression $\frac{7 \times 48 \times 4}{3}$ and then finding only the numerator of the fraction.

QUESTION 20.

Choice B is correct. To answer this question, find the point in the graph that represents Michael's 34-minute swim and then compare the actual heart rate for that swim with the expected heart rate as defined by the line of best fit. To find the point that represents Michael's swim that took 34 minutes, look along the vertical line of the graph that is marked "34" on the horizontal axis. That vertical line intersects only one point in the scatterplot, at 148 beats per minute. On the other hand, the line of best fit intersects the vertical line representing 34 minutes at 150 beats per minute. Therefore, for the swim that took 34 minutes, Michael's actual heart rate was $150 - 148 = 2$ beats per minute less than predicted by the line of best fit.

Choices A, C, and D are incorrect and may be the result of misreading the scale of the graph.

QUESTION 21.

Choice C is correct. Let I be the initial savings. If each successive year, 1% of the current value is added to the value of the account, then after 1 year, the amount in the account will be $I + 0.01I = I(1 + 0.01)$; after 2 years, the amount in the account will be $I(1 + 0.01) + 0.01I(1 + 0.01) = (1 + 0.01)I(1 + 0.01) = I(1 + 0.01)^2$; and after t years, the amount in the account will be $I(1 + 0.01)^t$. This is exponential growth of the money in the account.

Choice A is incorrect. If each successive year, 2% of the initial savings, I, is added to the value of the account, then after t years, the amount in the account will be $I + 0.02It$, which is linear growth. Choice B is incorrect. If each successive year, 1.5% of the initial savings, I, and \$100 is added to the value of the the account, then after t years the amount in the account will be $I + (0.015I + 100)t$, which is linear growth. Choice D is incorrect. If each successive year, \$100 is added to the value of the account, then after t years the amount in the account will be $I + 100t$, which is linear growth.

QUESTION 22.

Choice B is correct. One of the three numbers is x; let the other two numbers be y and z. Since the sum of three numbers is 855, the equation $x + y + z = 855$ is true. The statement that x is 50% more than the sum of the other two numbers can be represented as $x = 1.5(y + z)$, or $\frac{x}{1.5} = y + z$. Substituting $\frac{x}{1.5}$ for $y + z$ in $x + y + z = 855$ gives $x + \frac{x}{1.5} = 855$. This last equation can be rewritten as $x + \frac{2x}{3} = 855$, or $\frac{5x}{3} = 855$. Therefore, x equals $\frac{3}{5} \times 855 = 513$.

Choices A, C, and D are incorrect and may be the result of calculation errors.

QUESTION 23.

Choice C is correct. Since the angles are acute and $\sin(a°) = \cos(b°)$, it follows from the complementary angle property of sines and cosines that $a + b = 90$. Substituting $4k - 22$ for a and $6k - 13$ for b gives $(4k - 22) + (6k - 13) = 90$, which simplifies to $10k - 35 = 90$. Therefore, $10k = 125$, and $k = 12.5$.

Choice A is incorrect and may be the result of mistakenly assuming that $a + b$ and making a sign error. Choices B and D are incorrect because they result in values for a and b such that $\sin(a°) \neq \cos(b°)$.

QUESTION 24.

Choice D is correct. Let c be the number of students in Mr. Kohl's class. The conditions described in the question can be represented by the equations $n = 3c + 5$ and $n + 21 = 4c$. Substituting $3c + 5$ for n in the second equation gives $3c + 5 + 21 = 4c$, which can be solved to find $c = 26$.

Choices A, B, and C are incorrect because the values given for the number of students in the class cannot fulfill both conditions given in the question. For example, if there were 16 students in the class, then the first condition would imply that there are 3(16) + 5 = 53 milliliters of solution in the beaker, but the second condition would imply that there are 4(16) − 21 = 43 milliliters of solution in the beaker. This contradiction shows that there cannot be 16 students in the class.

QUESTION 25.

Choice D is correct. The volume of the grain silo can be found by adding the volumes of all the solids of which it is composed. The silo is made up of a cylinder with height 10 feet (ft) and base radius 5 feet and two cones, each having height 5 ft and base radius 5 ft. The formulas $V_{cylinder} = \pi r^2 h$ and $V_{cone} = \frac{1}{3}\pi r^2 h$ can be used to determine the total volume of the silo. Since the two cones have identical dimensions, the total volume, in cubic feet, of the silo is given by $V_{silo} = \pi(5)^2(10) + (2)\left(\frac{1}{3}\right)\pi(5)^2(5) = \left(\frac{4}{3}\right)(250)\pi$, which is approximately equal to 1,047.2 cubic feet.

Choice A is incorrect because this is the volume of only the two cones. Choice B is incorrect because this is the volume of only the cylinder. Choice C is incorrect because this is the volume of only one of the cones plus the cylinder.

QUESTION 26.

Choice C is correct. The line passes through the origin, (2, k), and (k, 32). Any two of these points can be used to find the slope of the line. Since the line passes through (0, 0) and (2, k), the slope of the line is equal to $\frac{k-0}{2-0} = \frac{k}{2}$. Similarly, since the line passes through (0, 0) and (k, 32), the slope of the line is equal to $\frac{32-0}{k-0} = \frac{32}{k}$. Since each expression gives the slope of the same line, it must be true that $\frac{k}{2} = \frac{32}{k}$. Multiplying each side of $\frac{k}{2} = \frac{32}{k}$ by 2k gives $k^2 = 64$, from which it follows that $k = 8$ or $k = -8$. Therefore, of the given choices, only 8 could be the value of k.

Choices A, B, and D are incorrect and may be the result of calculation errors.

QUESTION 27.

Choice C is correct. Let ℓ and w be the length and width, respectively, of the original rectangle. The area of the original rectangle is $A = \ell w$. The rectangle is altered by increasing its length by 10 percent and decreasing its width by p percent; thus, the length of the altered rectangle is 1.1ℓ, and the width of the altered rectangle is $\left(1 - \frac{p}{100}\right)w$. The alterations decrease the area by 12 percent, so the area of the altered rectangle is $(1 - 0.12)A = 0.88A$.

The altered rectangle is the product of its length and width, so $0.88A = (1.1\ell)\left(1 - \dfrac{P}{100}\right)w$. Since $A = \ell w$, this last equation can be rewritten as $0.88A = (1.1)\left(1 - \dfrac{P}{100}\right)\ell w = (1.1)\left(1 - \dfrac{P}{100}\right)A$, from which it follows that $0.88 = (1.1)\left(1 - \dfrac{P}{100}\right)$, or $0.8 = \left(1 - \dfrac{P}{100}\right)$. Therefore, $\dfrac{P}{100} = 0.2$, and so the value of p is 20.

Choice A is incorrect and may be the result of confusing the 12 percent decrease in area with the percent decrease in width. Choice B is incorrect because decreasing the width by 15 percent results in a 6.5 percent decrease in area, not a 12 percent decrease. Choice D is incorrect and may be the result of adding the percents given in the question $(10 + 12)$.

QUESTION 28.

Choice D is correct. For the present population to decrease by 10 percent, it must be multiplied by the factor 0.9. Since the engineer estimates that the population will decrease by 10 percent every 20 years, the present population, 50,000, must be multiplied by $(0.9)^n$, where n is the number of 20-year periods that will have elapsed t years from now. After t years, the number of 20-year periods that have elapsed is $\dfrac{t}{20}$. Therefore, $50{,}000(0.9)^{\frac{t}{20}}$ represents the engineer's estimate of the population of the city t years from now.

Choices A, B, and C are incorrect because each of these choices either confuses the percent decrease with the multiplicative factor that represents the percent decrease or mistakenly multiplies t by 20 to find the number of 20-year periods that will have elapsed in t years.

QUESTION 29.

Choice A is correct. Let x be the number of left-handed female students and let y be the number of left-handed male students. Then the number of right-handed female students will be $5x$ and the number of right-handed male students will be $9y$. Since the total number of left-handed students is 18 and the total number of right-handed students is 122, the system of equations below must be satisfied.

$$\begin{cases} x + y = 18 \\ 5x + 9y = 122 \end{cases}$$

Solving this system gives $x = 10$ and $y = 8$. Thus, 50 of the 122 right-handed students are female. Therefore, the probability that a right-handed student selected at random is female is $\dfrac{50}{122}$, which to the nearest thousandth is 0.410.

Choices B, C, and D are incorrect and may be the result of incorrect calculation of the missing values in the table.

QUESTION 30.

Choice A is correct. Subtracting the sides of $3y + c = 5y - 7$ from the corresponding sides of $3x + b = 5x - 7$ gives $(3x - 3y) + (b - c) = (5x - 5y)$. Since $b = c - \frac{1}{2}$, or $b - c = -\frac{1}{2}$, it follows that $(3x - 3y) + \left(-\frac{1}{2}\right) = (5x - 5y)$. Solving this equation for x in terms of y gives $x = y - \frac{1}{4}$. Therefore, x is y minus $\frac{1}{4}$.

Choices B, C, and D are incorrect and may be the result of making a computational error when solving the equations for x in terms of y.

QUESTION 31.

The correct answer is either 4 or 5. Because each student ticket costs \$2 and each adult ticket costs \$3, the total amount, in dollars, that Chris spends on x student tickets and 1 adult ticket is $2(x) + 3(1)$. Because Chris spends at least \$11 but no more than \$14 on the tickets, one can write the compound inequality $2x + 3 \geq 11$ and $2x + 3 \leq 14$. Subtracting 3 from each side of both inequalities and then dividing each side of both inequalities by 2 yields $x \geq 4$ and $x \leq 5.5$. Thus, the value of x must be an integer that is both greater than or equal to 4 and less than or equal to 5.5. Therefore, $x = 4$ or $x = 5$. Either 4 or 5 may be gridded as the correct answer.

QUESTION 32.

The correct answer is 58.6. The mean of a data set is determined by calculating the sum of the values and dividing by the number of values in the data set. The sum of the ages, in years, in the data set is 703, and the number of values in the data set is 12. Thus, the mean of the ages, in years, of the first 12 United States presidents at the beginning of their terms is $\frac{703}{12}$. The fraction $\frac{703}{12}$ cannot be entered into the grid, so the decimal equivalent, rounded to the nearest tenth, is the correct answer. This rounded decimal equivalent is 58.6.

QUESTION 33.

The correct answer is 9. To rewrite the difference $(-3x^2 + 5x - 2) - 2(x^2 - 2x - 1)$ in the form $ax^2 + bx + c$, the expression can be simplified by using the distributive property and combining like terms as follows:

$(-3x^2 + 5x - 2) - (2x^2 - 4x - 2)$

$(-3x^2 - 2x^2) + (5x - (-4x)) + (-2 - (-2))$

$-5x^2 + 9x + 0$

The coefficient of x is the value of b, which is 9.

Alternatively, since b is the coefficient of x in the difference $(-3x^2 + 5x - 2) - 2(x^2 - 2x - 1)$, one need only compute the x-term in the difference. The x-term is $5x - 2(-2x) = 5x + 4x = 9x$, so the value of b is 9.

QUESTION 34.

The correct answer is $\frac{5}{8}$ **or .625.** A complete rotation around a point is 360° or 2π radians. Since the central angle AOB has measure $\frac{5\pi}{4}$ radians, it rep-

resents $\dfrac{\frac{5\pi}{4}}{2\pi} = \dfrac{5}{8}$ of a complete rotation around point O. Therefore, the sector

formed by central angle AOB has area equal to $\frac{5}{8}$ the area of the entire circle. Either the fraction $\frac{5}{8}$ or its decimal equivalent, .625, may be gridded as the correct answer.

QUESTION 35.

The correct answer is 50. The mean of a data set is the sum of the values in the data set divided by the number of values in the data set. The mean of 75 is obtained by finding the sum of the first 10 ratings and dividing by 10. Thus, the sum of the first 10 ratings was 750. In order for the mean of the first 20 ratings to be at least 85, the sum of the first 20 ratings must be at least $(85)(20) = 1700$. Therefore, the sum of the next 10 ratings must be at least $1700 - 750 = 950$. The maximum rating is 100, so the maximum possible value of the sum of the 12th through 20th ratings is $9 \times 100 = 900$. Therefore, for the store to be able to have an average of at least 85 for the first 20 ratings, the least possible value for the 11th rating is $950 - 900 = 50$.

QUESTION 36.

The correct answer is 750. The inequalities $y \leq -15x + 3000$ and $y \leq 5x$ can be graphed in the xy-plane. They are represented by the half-planes below and include the boundary lines $y = -15x + 3000$ and $y = 5x$, respectively. The solution set of the system of inequalities will be the intersection of these half-planes, including the boundary lines, and the solution (a, b) with the greatest possible value of b will be the point of intersection of the boundary lines. The intersection of boundary lines of these inequalities can be found by setting them equal to each other: $5x = -15x + 3000$, which has solution $x = 150$. Thus, the x-coordinate of the point of intersection is 150. Therefore, the y-coordinate of the point of intersection of the boundary lines is $5(150) = -15(150) + 3000 = 750$. This is the maximum possible value of b for a point (a, b) that is in the solution set of the system of inequalities.

QUESTION 37.

The correct answer is 7. The average number of shoppers, N, in the checkout line at any time is $N = rt$, where r is the number of shoppers entering the checkout line per minute and T is the average number of minutes each shopper spends in the checkout line. Since 84 shoppers per hour make a purchase, 84 shoppers per hour enter the checkout line. This needs to be converted to the number of shoppers per minute. Since there are 60 minutes in one hour, the rate is $\frac{84 \text{ shoppers}}{60 \text{ minutes}} = 1.4$ shoppers per minute. Using the given formula with $r = 1.4$ and $t = 5$ yields $N = rt = (1.4)(5) = 7$. Therefore, the average number of shoppers, N, in the checkout line at any time during business hours is 7.

QUESTION 38.

The correct answer is 60. The estimated average number of shoppers in the original store at any time is 45. In the new store, the manager estimates that an average of 90 shoppers per <u>hour</u> enter the store, which is equivalent to 1.5 shoppers per minute. The manager also estimates that each shopper stays in the store for an average of 12 minutes. Thus, by Little's law, there are, on average, $N = rt = (1.5)(12) = 18$ shoppers in the new store at any time. This is $\frac{45 - 18}{45} \times 100 = 60$ percent less than the average number of shoppers in the original store at any time.

SAT® Practice Test #4

IMPORTANT REMINDERS

A No. 2 pencil is required for the test.
Do not use a mechanical pencil or pen.

Sharing any questions with anyone
is a violation of Test Security
and Fairness policies and may result
in your scores being canceled.

This cover is representative of what you'll see on test day.

Test begins on the next page.

Reading Test

65 MINUTES, 52 QUESTIONS

Turn to Section 1 of your answer sheet to answer the questions in this section.

DIRECTIONS

Each passage or pair of passages below is followed by a number of questions. After reading each passage or pair, choose the best answer to each question based on what is stated or implied in the passage or passages and in any accompanying graphics (such as a table or graph).

Questions 1-10 are based on the following passage.

This passage is adapted from MacDonald Harris, *The Balloonist*. ©2011 by The Estate of Donald Heiney. During the summer of 1897, the narrator of this story, a fictional Swedish scientist, has set out for the North Pole in a hydrogen-powered balloon.

My emotions are complicated and not readily verifiable. I feel a vast yearning that is simultaneously a pleasure and a pain. I am certain
Line of the consummation of this yearning, but I don't
5 know yet what form it will take, since I do not understand quite what it is that the yearning desires. For the first time there is borne in upon me the full truth of what I myself said to the doctor only an hour ago: that my motives in this undertaking are not
10 entirely clear. For years, for a lifetime, the machinery of my destiny has worked in secret to prepare for this moment; its clockwork has moved exactly toward this time and place and no other. Rising slowly from the earth that bore me and gave me sustenance, I am
15 carried helplessly toward an uninhabited and hostile, or at best indifferent, part of the earth, littered with the bones of explorers and the wrecks of ships, frozen supply caches, messages scrawled with chilled fingers and hidden in cairns that no eye will ever see.
20 Nobody has succeeded in this thing, and many have died. Yet in freely willing this enterprise, in choosing this moment and no other when the south wind will carry me exactly northward at a velocity of eight knots, I have converted the machinery of my

25 fate into the servant of my will. All this I understand, as I understand each detail of the technique by which this is carried out. What I don't understand is why I am so intent on going to this particular place. Who wants the North Pole! What good is it! Can you eat
30 it? Will it carry you from Gothenburg to Malmö like a railway? The Danish ministers have declared from their pulpits that participation in polar expeditions is beneficial to the soul's eternal well-being, or so I read in a newspaper. It isn't clear how this doctrine is to
35 be interpreted, except that the Pole is something difficult or impossible to attain which must nevertheless be sought for, because man is condemned to seek out and know everything whether or not the knowledge gives him pleasure. In
40 short, it is the same unthinking lust for knowledge that drove our First Parents out of the garden.

And suppose you were to find it in spite of all, this wonderful place that everybody is so anxious to stand on! *What* would you find? Exactly nothing.
45 A point precisely identical to all the others in a completely featureless wasteland stretching around it for hundreds of miles. It is an abstraction, a mathematical fiction. No one but a Swedish madman could take the slightest interest in it. Here I am. The
50 wind is still from the south, bearing us steadily northward at the speed of a trotting dog. Behind us, perhaps forever, lie the Cities of Men with their

CONTINUE ➡

teacups and their brass bedsteads. I am going forth of
my own volition to join the ghosts of Bering and
55 poor Franklin, of frozen De Long and his men.
What I am on the brink of knowing, I now see, is not
an ephemeral mathematical spot but myself. The
doctor was right, even though I dislike him.
Fundamentally I am a dangerous madman, and what
60 I do is both a challenge to my egotism and a
surrender to it.

1

Over the course of the passage, the narrator's attitude
shifts from

A) fear about the expedition to excitement about it.

B) doubt about his abilities to confidence in them.

C) uncertainty of his motives to recognition of
them.

D) disdain for the North Pole to appreciation of it.

2

Which choice provides the best evidence for the
answer to the previous question?

A) Lines 10-12 ("For . . . moment")

B) Lines 21-25 ("Yet . . . will")

C) Lines 42-44 ("And . . . stand on")

D) Lines 56-57 ("What . . . myself")

3

As used in lines 1-2, "not readily verifiable" most
nearly means

A) unable to be authenticated.

B) likely to be contradicted.

C) without empirical support.

D) not completely understood.

4

The sentence in lines 10-13 ("For years . . . other")
mainly serves to

A) expose a side of the narrator that he prefers to
keep hidden.

B) demonstrate that the narrator thinks in a
methodical and scientific manner.

C) show that the narrator feels himself to be
influenced by powerful and independent forces.

D) emphasize the length of time during which the
narrator has prepared for his expedition.

5

The narrator indicates that many previous explorers
seeking the North Pole have

A) perished in the attempt.

B) made surprising discoveries.

C) failed to determine its exact location.

D) had different motivations than his own.

6

Which choice provides the best evidence for the
answer to the previous question?

A) Lines 20-21 ("Nobody . . . died")

B) Lines 25-27 ("All . . . out")

C) Lines 31-34 ("The . . . newspaper")

D) Lines 51-53 ("Behind . . . bedsteads")

7

Which choice best describes the narrator's view of
his expedition to the North Pole?

A) Immoral but inevitable

B) Absurd but necessary

C) Socially beneficial but misunderstood

D) Scientifically important but hazardous

CONTINUE

8

The question the narrator asks in lines 30-31 ("Will it . . . railway") most nearly implies that

A) balloons will never replace other modes of transportation.

B) the North Pole is farther away than the cities usually reached by train.

C) people often travel from one city to another without considering the implications.

D) reaching the North Pole has no foreseeable benefit to humanity.

9

As used in line 49, "take the slightest interest in" most nearly means

A) accept responsibility for.

B) possess little regard for.

C) pay no attention to.

D) have curiosity about.

10

As used in line 50, "bearing" most nearly means

A) carrying.

B) affecting.

C) yielding.

D) enduring.

Questions 11-21 are based on the following passage and supplementary material.

This passage is adapted from Alan Ehrenhalt, *The Great Inversion and the Future of the American City*. ©2013 by Vintage. Ehrenhalt is an urbanologist—a scholar of cities and their development. Demographic inversion is a phenomenon that describes the rearrangement of living patterns throughout a metropolitan area.

We are not witnessing the abandonment of the suburbs, or a movement of millions of people back to the city all at once. The 2010 census certainly did not
Line turn up evidence of a middle-class stampede to the
5 nation's cities. The news was mixed: Some of the larger cities on the East Coast tended to gain population, albeit in small increments. Those in the Midwest, including Chicago, tended to lose substantial numbers. The cities that showed gains in
10 overall population during the entire decade tended to be in the South and Southwest. But when it comes to measuring demographic inversion, raw census numbers are an ineffective blunt instrument. A closer look at the results shows that the most powerful
15 demographic events of the past decade were the movement of African Americans out of central cities (180,000 of them in Chicago alone) and the settlement of immigrant groups in suburbs, often ones many miles distant from downtown.
20 Central-city areas that gained affluent residents in the first part of the decade maintained that population in the recession years from 2007 to 2009. They also, according to a 2011 study by Brookings, suffered considerably less from increased
25 unemployment than the suburbs did. Not many young professionals moved to new downtown condos in the recession years because few such residences were being built. But there is no reason to believe that the demographic trends prevailing prior
30 to the construction bust will not resume once that bust is over. It is important to remember that demographic inversion is not a proxy for population growth; it can occur in cities that are growing, those whose numbers are flat, and even in those
35 undergoing a modest decline in size.

America's major cities face enormous fiscal problems, many of them the result of public pension obligations they incurred in the more prosperous years of the past two decades. Some, Chicago

CONTINUE

prominent among them, simply are not producing
enough revenue to support the level of public
services to which most of the citizens have grown to
feel entitled. How the cities are going to solve this
problem, I do not know. What I do know is that if
fiscal crisis were going to drive affluent professionals
out of central cities, it would have done so by now.
There is no evidence that it has.

The truth is that we are living at a moment in
which the massive outward migration of the affluent
that characterized the second half of the
twentieth century is coming to an end. And we need
to adjust our perceptions of cities, suburbs, and
urban mobility as a result.

Much of our perspective on the process of
metropolitan settlement dates, whether we realize it
or not, from a paper written in 1925 by the
University of Chicago sociologist Ernest W. Burgess.
It was Burgess who defined four urban/suburban
zones of settlement: a central business district; an
area of manufacturing just beyond it; then a
residential area inhabited by the industrial and
immigrant working class; and finally an outer
enclave of single-family dwellings.

Burgess was right about the urban America of
1925; he was right about the urban America of 1974.
Virtually every city in the country had a downtown,
where the commercial life of the metropolis was
conducted; it had a factory district just beyond; it had
districts of working-class residences just beyond that;
and it had residential suburbs for the wealthy and the
upper middle class at the far end of the continuum.
As a family moved up the economic ladder, it also
moved outward from crowded working-class
districts to more spacious apartments and,
eventually, to a suburban home. The suburbs of
Burgess's time bore little resemblance to those at the
end of the twentieth century, but the theory still
essentially worked. People moved ahead in life by
moving farther out.

But in the past decade, in quite a few places, this
model has ceased to describe reality. There are still
downtown commercial districts, but there are no
factory districts lying next to them. There are
scarcely any factories at all. These close-in parts of
the city, whose few residents Burgess described as
dwelling in "submerged regions of poverty,
degradation and disease," are increasingly the
preserve of the affluent who work in the commercial
core. And just as crucially newcomers to America are
not settling on the inside and accumulating the
resources to move out; they are living in the suburbs
from day one.

United States Population by Metropolitan Size/Status, 1980–2010

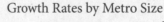

Chart 1	Chart 2

2010 Population Shares by Metro Size (%)

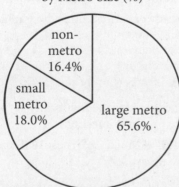

non-metro 16.4%

small metro 18.0%

large metro 65.6%

Growth Rates by Metro Size

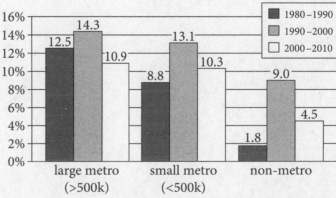

Adapted from William H. Frey, "Population Growth in Metro America since 1980: Putting the Volatile 2000s in Perspective." Published 2012 by Metropolitan Policy Program, Brookings Institution.

CONTINUE

11

Which choice best summarizes the first paragraph of the passage (lines 1-35)?

A) The 2010 census demonstrated a sizeable growth in the number of middle-class families moving into inner cities.

B) The 2010 census is not a reliable instrument for measuring population trends in American cities.

C) Population growth and demographic inversion are distinct phenomena, and demographic inversion is evident in many American cities.

D) Population growth in American cities has been increasing since roughly 2000, while suburban populations have decreased.

12

According to the passage, members of which group moved away from central-city areas in large numbers in the early 2000s?

A) The unemployed

B) Immigrants

C) Young professionals

D) African Americans

13

In line 34, "flat" is closest in meaning to

A) static.

B) deflated.

C) featureless.

D) obscure.

14

According to the passage, which choice best describes the current financial situation in many major American cities?

A) Expected tax increases due to demand for public works

B) Economic hardship due to promises made in past years

C) Greater overall prosperity due to an increased inner-city tax base

D) Insufficient revenues due to a decrease in manufacturing

15

Which choice provides the best evidence for the answer to the previous question?

A) Lines 36-39 ("America's . . . decades")

B) Lines 43-44 ("How . . . not know")

C) Lines 44-46 ("What . . . now")

D) Lines 48-51 ("The truth . . . end")

16

The passage implies that American cities in 1974

A) were witnessing the flight of minority populations to the suburbs.

B) had begun to lose their manufacturing sectors.

C) had a traditional four-zone structure.

D) were already experiencing demographic inversion.

17

Which choice provides the best evidence for the answer to the previous question?

A) Lines 54-57 ("Much . . . Ernest W. Burgess")

B) Lines 58-59 ("It was . . . settlement")

C) Lines 66-71 ("Virtually . . . continuum")

D) Lines 72-75 ("As . . . home")

CONTINUE

18

As used in line 68, "conducted" is closest in meaning to

A) carried out.

B) supervised.

C) regulated.

D) inhibited.

19

The author of the passage would most likely consider the information in chart 1 to be

A) excellent evidence for the arguments made in the passage.

B) possibly accurate but too crude to be truly informative.

C) compelling but lacking in historical information.

D) representative of a perspective with which the author disagrees.

20

According to chart 2, the years 2000–2010 were characterized by

A) less growth in metropolitan areas of all sizes than had taken place in the 1990s.

B) more growth in small metropolitan areas than in large metropolitan areas.

C) a significant decline in the population of small metropolitan areas compared to the 1980s.

D) roughly equal growth in large metropolitan areas and nonmetropolitan areas.

21

Chart 2 suggests which of the following about population change in the 1990s?

A) Large numbers of people moved from suburban areas to urban areas in the 1990s.

B) Growth rates fell in smaller metropolitan areas in the 1990s.

C) Large numbers of people moved from metropolitan areas to nonmetropolitan areas in the 1990s.

D) The US population as a whole grew more in the 1990s than in the 1980s.

CONTINUE

Questions 22-31 are based on the following passage.

This passage is adapted from Emily Anthes, *Frankenstein's Cat.* ©2013 by Emily Anthes.

When scientists first learned how to edit the genomes of animals, they began to imagine all the ways they could use this new power. Creating
Line brightly colored novelty pets was not a high priority.
5 Instead, most researchers envisioned far more consequential applications, hoping to create genetically engineered animals that saved human lives. One enterprise is now delivering on this dream. Welcome to the world of "pharming," in which
10 simple genetic tweaks turn animals into living pharmaceutical factories.

Many of the proteins that our cells crank out naturally make for good medicine. Our bodies' own enzymes, hormones, clotting factors, and antibodies
15 are commonly used to treat cancer, diabetes, autoimmune diseases, and more. The trouble is that it's difficult and expensive to make these compounds on an industrial scale, and as a result, patients can face shortages of the medicines they need. Dairy
20 animals, on the other hand, are expert protein producers, their udders swollen with milk. So the creation of the first transgenic animals—first mice, then other species—in the 1980s gave scientists an idea: What if they put the gene for a human antibody
25 or enzyme into a cow, goat, or sheep? If they put the gene in just the right place, under the control of the right molecular switch, maybe they could engineer animals that produced healing human proteins in their milk. Then doctors could collect medicine by
30 the bucketful.

Throughout the 1980s and '90s, studies provided proof of principle, as scientists created transgenic mice, sheep, goats, pigs, cattle, and rabbits that did in fact make therapeutic compounds in their milk.
35 At first, this work was merely gee-whiz, scientific geekery, lab-bound thought experiments come true. That all changed with ATryn, a drug produced by the Massachusetts firm GTC Biotherapeutics. ATryn is antithrombin, an anticoagulant that can be used to
40 prevent life-threatening blood clots. The compound, made by our liver cells, plays a key role in keeping our bodies clot-free. It acts as a molecular bouncer, sidling up to clot-forming compounds and escorting them out of the bloodstream. But as many as 1 in

45 2,000 Americans are born with a genetic mutation that prevents them from making antithrombin. These patients are prone to clots, especially in their legs and lungs, and they are at elevated risk of suffering from fatal complications during surgery
50 and childbirth. Supplemental antithrombin can reduce this risk, and GTC decided to try to manufacture the compound using genetically engineered goats.

To create its special herd of goats, GTC used
55 microinjection, the same technique that produced GloFish and AquAdvantage salmon. The company's scientists took the gene for human antithrombin and injected it directly into fertilized goat eggs. Then they implanted the eggs in the wombs of female goats.
60 When the kids were born, some of them proved to be transgenic, the human gene nestled safely in their cells. The researchers paired the antithrombin gene with a promoter (which is a sequence of DNA that controls gene activity) that is normally active in the
65 goat's mammary glands during milk production. When the transgenic females lactated, the promoter turned the transgene on and the goats' udders filled with milk containing antithrombin. All that was left to do was to collect the milk, and extract and purify
70 the protein. *Et voilà*—human medicine! And, for GTC, liquid gold. ATryn hit the market in 2006, becoming the world's first transgenic animal drug. Over the course of a year, the "milking parlors" on GTC's 300-acre farm in Massachusetts can collect
75 more than a kilogram of medicine from a single animal.

22

The primary purpose of the passage is to

A) present the background of a medical breakthrough.

B) evaluate the research that led to a scientific discovery.

C) summarize the findings of a long-term research project.

D) explain the development of a branch of scientific study.

CONTINUE

23

The author's attitude toward pharming is best described as one of

A) apprehension.

B) ambivalence.

C) appreciation.

D) astonishment.

24

As used in line 20, "expert" most nearly means

A) knowledgeable.

B) professional.

C) capable.

D) trained.

25

What does the author suggest about the transgenic studies done in the 1980s and 1990s?

A) They were limited by the expensive nature of animal research.

B) They were not expected to yield products ready for human use.

C) They were completed when an anticoagulant compound was identified.

D) They focused only on the molecular properties of cows, goats, and sheep.

26

Which choice provides the best evidence for the answer to the previous question?

A) Lines 16-19 ("The trouble . . . need")

B) Lines 25-29 ("If they . . . milk")

C) Lines 35-36 ("At first . . . true")

D) Lines 37-40 ("That all . . . clots")

27

According to the passage, which of the following is true of antithrombin?

A) It reduces compounds that lead to blood clots.

B) It stems from a genetic mutation that is rare in humans.

C) It is a sequence of DNA known as a promoter.

D) It occurs naturally in goats' mammary glands.

28

Which choice provides the best evidence for the answer to the previous question?

A) Lines 12-16 ("Many . . . more")

B) Lines 42-44 ("It acts . . . bloodstream")

C) Lines 44-46 ("But as . . . antithrombin")

D) Lines 62-65 ("The researchers . . . production")

29

Which of the following does the author suggest about the "female goats" mentioned in line 59?

A) They secreted antithrombin in their milk after giving birth.

B) Some of their kids were not born with the antithrombin gene.

C) They were the first animals to receive microinjections.

D) Their cells already contained genes usually found in humans.

30

The most likely purpose of the parenthetical information in lines 63-64 is to

A) illustrate an abstract concept.

B) describe a new hypothesis.

C) clarify a claim.

D) define a term.

CONTINUE ➤

The phrase "liquid gold" (line 71) most directly suggests that

A) GTC has invested a great deal of money in the microinjection technique.

B) GTC's milking parlors have significantly increased milk production.

C) transgenic goats will soon be a valuable asset for dairy farmers.

D) ATryn has proved to be a financially beneficial product for GTC.

Questions 32-41 are based on the following passages.

Passage 1 is adapted from Edmund Burke, *Reflections on the Revolution in France*. Originally published in 1790. Passage 2 is adapted from Thomas Paine, *Rights of Man*. Originally published in 1791.

Passage 1

To avoid . . . the evils of inconstancy and versatility, ten thousand times worse than those of obstinacy and the blindest prejudice, we have
Line consecrated the state, that no man should approach
5 to look into its defects or corruptions but with due caution; that he should never dream of beginning its reformation by its subversion; that he should approach to the faults of the state as to the wounds of a father, with pious awe and trembling solicitude. By
10 this wise prejudice we are taught to look with horror on those children of their country who are prompt rashly to hack that aged parent in pieces, and put him into the kettle of magicians, in hopes that by their poisonous weeds, and wild incantations, they may
15 regenerate the paternal constitution, and renovate their father's life.

Society is indeed a contract. Subordinate contracts for objects of mere occasional interest may be dissolved at pleasure—but the state ought not to be
20 considered as nothing better than a partnership agreement in a trade of pepper and coffee, calico or tobacco, or some other such low concern, to be taken up for a little temporary interest, and to be dissolved by the fancy of the parties. It is to be looked on with
25 other reverence; because it is not a partnership in things subservient only to the gross animal existence of a temporary and perishable nature. It is a partnership in all science; a partnership in all art; a partnership in every virtue, and in all perfection.
30 As the ends of such a partnership cannot be obtained in many generations, it becomes a partnership not only between those who are living, but between those who are living, those who are dead, and those who are to be born. . . . The municipal corporations of
35 that universal kingdom are not morally at liberty at their pleasure, and on their speculations of a contingent improvement, wholly to separate and tear asunder the bands of their subordinate community, and to dissolve it into an unsocial, uncivil,
40 unconnected chaos of elementary principles.

CONTINUE

Passage 2

Every age and generation must be as free to act for
itself, *in all cases*, as the ages and generations which
preceded it. The vanity and presumption of
governing beyond the grave, is the most ridiculous
45 and insolent of all tyrannies.

Man has no property in man; neither has any
generation a property in the generations which are to
follow. The Parliament or the people of 1688, or of
any other period, had no more right to dispose of the
50 people of the present day, or to bind or to control
them in any shape whatever, than the parliament or
the people of the present day have to dispose of, bind,
or control those who are to live a hundred or a
thousand years hence.

55 Every generation is, and must be, competent
to all the purposes which its occasions require. It is
the living, and not the dead, that are to be
accommodated. When man ceases to be, his power
and his wants cease with him; and having no longer
60 any participation in the concerns of this world, he
has no longer any authority in directing who shall be
its governors, or how its government shall be
organized, or how administered. . . .

Those who have quitted the world, and those who
65 are not yet arrived at it, are as remote from each
other, as the utmost stretch of mortal imagination
can conceive. What possible obligation, then, can
exist between them; what rule or principle can be laid
down, that two nonentities, the one out of existence,
70 and the other not in, and who never can meet in this
world, that the one should control the other to the
end of time? . . .

The circumstances of the world are continually
changing, and the opinions of men change also; and
75 as government is for the living, and not for the dead,
it is the living only that has any right in it. That
which may be thought right and found convenient in
one age, may be thought wrong and found
inconvenient in another. In such cases, who is to
80 decide, the living, or the dead?

In Passage 1, Burke indicates that a contract between
a person and society differs from other contracts
mainly in its

A) brevity and prominence.

B) complexity and rigidity.

C) precision and usefulness.

D) seriousness and permanence.

As used in line 4, "state" most nearly refers to a

A) style of living.

B) position in life.

C) temporary condition.

D) political entity.

As used in line 22, "low" most nearly means

A) petty.

B) weak.

C) inadequate.

D) depleted.

It can most reasonably be inferred from Passage 2
that Paine views historical precedents as

A) generally helpful to those who want to change
society.

B) surprisingly difficult for many people to
comprehend.

C) frequently responsible for human progress.

D) largely irrelevant to current political decisions.

CONTINUE

36

How would Paine most likely respond to Burke's statement in lines 30-34, Passage 1 ("As the . . . born")?

A) He would assert that the notion of a partnership across generations is less plausible to people of his era than it was to people in the past.

B) He would argue that there are no politically meaningful links between the dead, the living, and the unborn.

C) He would question the possibility that significant changes to a political system could be accomplished within a single generation.

D) He would point out that we cannot know what judgments the dead would make about contemporary issues.

37

Which choice provides the best evidence for the answer to the previous question?

A) Lines 41-43 ("Every . . . it")

B) Lines 43-45 ("The vanity . . . tyrannies")

C) Lines 56-58 ("It is . . . accommodated")

D) Lines 67-72 ("What . . . time")

38

Which choice best describes how Burke would most likely have reacted to Paine's remarks in the final paragraph of Passage 2?

A) With approval, because adapting to new events may enhance existing partnerships.

B) With resignation, because changing circumstances are an inevitable aspect of life.

C) With skepticism, because Paine does not substantiate his claim with examples of governments changed for the better.

D) With disapproval, because changing conditions are insufficient justification for changing the form of government.

39

Which choice provides the best evidence for the answer to the previous question?

A) Lines 1-4 ("To avoid . . . state")

B) Lines 7-9 ("he should . . . solicitude")

C) Lines 27-29 ("It is . . . perfection")

D) Lines 34-38 ("The municipal . . . community")

40

Which choice best states the relationship between the two passages?

A) Passage 2 challenges the primary argument of Passage 1.

B) Passage 2 advocates an alternative approach to a problem discussed in Passage 1.

C) Passage 2 provides further evidence to support an idea introduced in Passage 1.

D) Passage 2 exemplifies an attitude promoted in Passage 1.

41

The main purpose of both passages is to

A) suggest a way to resolve a particular political struggle.

B) discuss the relationship between people and their government.

C) evaluate the consequences of rapid political change.

D) describe the duties that governments have to their citizens.

CONTINUE

Questions 42-52 are based on the following passage and supplementary material.

This passage is adapted from Carolyn Gramling, "Source of Mysterious Medieval Eruption Identified." ©2013 by American Association for the Advancement of Science.

About 750 years ago, a powerful volcano erupted somewhere on Earth, kicking off a centuries-long cold snap known as the Little Ice Age. Identifying the
Line volcano responsible has been tricky.

5   That a powerful volcano erupted somewhere in the world, sometime in the Middle Ages, is written in polar ice cores in the form of layers of sulfate deposits and tiny shards of volcanic glass. These cores suggest that the amount of sulfur the mystery
10 volcano sent into the stratosphere put it firmly among the ranks of the strongest climate-perturbing eruptions of the current geological epoch, the Holocene, a period that stretches from 10,000 years ago to the present. A haze of stratospheric sulfur
15 cools the climate by reflecting solar energy back into space.

In 2012, a team of scientists led by geochemist Gifford Miller strengthened the link between the mystery eruption and the onset of the Little Ice Age
20 by using radiocarbon dating of dead plant material from beneath the ice caps on Baffin Island and Iceland, as well as ice and sediment core data, to determine that the cold summers and ice growth began abruptly between 1275 and 1300 C.E. (and
25 became intensified between 1430 and 1455 C.E.). Such a sudden onset pointed to a huge volcanic eruption injecting sulfur into the stratosphere and starting the cooling. Subsequent, unusually large and frequent eruptions of other volcanoes, as well as
30 sea-ice/ocean feedbacks persisting long after the aerosols have been removed from the atmosphere, may have prolonged the cooling through the 1700s.

Volcanologist Franck Lavigne and colleagues now think they've identified the volcano in question:
35 Indonesia's Samalas. One line of evidence, they note, is historical records. According to Babad Lombok, records of the island written on palm leaves in Old Javanese, Samalas erupted catastrophically before the end of the 13th century, devastating surrounding
40 villages—including Lombok's capital at the time, Pamatan—with ash and fast-moving sweeps of hot rock and gas called pyroclastic flows.

The researchers then began to reconstruct the formation of the large, 800-meter-deep caldera [a
45 basin-shaped volcanic crater] that now sits atop the volcano. They examined 130 outcrops on the flanks of the volcano, exposing sequences of pumice—ash hardened into rock—and other pyroclastic material. The volume of ash deposited, and the estimated
50 height of the eruption plume (43 kilometers above sea level) put the eruption's magnitude at a minimum of 7 on the volcanic explosivity index (which has a scale of 1 to 8)—making it one of the largest known in the Holocene.

55 The team also performed radiocarbon analyses on carbonized tree trunks and branches buried within the pyroclastic deposits to confirm the date of the eruption; it could not, they concluded, have happened before 1257 C.E., and certainly happened
60 in the 13th century.

It's not a total surprise that an Indonesian volcano might be the source of the eruption, Miller says. "An equatorial eruption is more consistent with the apparent climate impacts." And, he adds, with sulfate
65 appearing in both polar ice caps—Arctic and Antarctic—there is "a strong consensus" that this also supports an equatorial source.

Another possible candidate—both in terms of timing and geographical location—is Ecuador's
70 Quilotoa, estimated to have last erupted between 1147 and 1320 C.E. But when Lavigne's team examined shards of volcanic glass from this volcano, they found that they didn't match the chemical composition of the glass found in polar ice cores,
75 whereas the Samalas glass is a much closer match. That, they suggest, further strengthens the case that Samalas was responsible for the medieval "year without summer" in 1258 C.E.

CONTINUE ▶

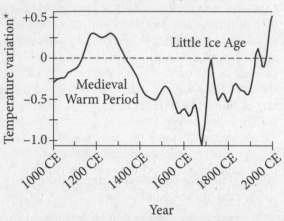

Estimated Temperature in Central England
1000 CE to 2000 CE

*Variation from the 1961-1990 average temperature, in °C,
represented at 0.

Adapted from John P. Rafferty, "Little Ice Age." Originally published
in 2011. ©2014 by Encyclopedia Britannica, Inc.

42

The main purpose of the passage is to

A) describe periods in Earth's recent geologic
history.

B) explain the methods scientists use in
radiocarbon analysis.

C) describe evidence linking the volcano Samalas to
the Little Ice Age.

D) explain how volcanic glass forms during volcanic
eruptions.

43

Over the course of the passage, the focus shifts from

A) a criticism of a scientific model to a new theory.

B) a description of a recorded event to its likely
cause.

C) the use of ice core samples to a new method of
measuring sulfates.

D) the use of radiocarbon dating to an examination
of volcanic glass.

44

Which choice provides the best evidence for the
answer to the previous question?

A) Lines 17-25 ("In 2012 . . . 1455 C.E.")

B) Lines 43-46 ("The researchers . . . atop the
volcano")

C) Lines 46-48 ("They examined . . . material")

D) Lines 55-60 ("The team . . . 13th century")

45

The author uses the phrase "is written in" (line 6)
most likely to

A) demonstrate the concept of the hands-on nature
of the work done by scientists.

B) highlight the fact that scientists often write about
their discoveries.

C) underscore the sense of importance that
scientists have regarding their work.

D) reinforce the idea that the evidence is there and
can be interpreted by scientists.

46

Where does the author indicate the medieval
volcanic eruption most probably was located?

A) Near the equator, in Indonesia

B) In the Arctic region

C) In the Antarctic region

D) Near the equator, in Ecuador

47

Which choice provides the best evidence for the
answer to the previous question?

A) Lines 1-3 ("About 750 . . . Ice Age")

B) Lines 26-28 ("Such a . . . the cooling")

C) Lines 49-54 ("The volume . . . the Holocene")

D) Lines 61-64 ("It's not . . . climate impacts")

Unauthorized copying or reuse of any part of this page is illegal.

688

CONTINUE

48

As used in line 68, the phrase "Another possible candidate" implies that

A) powerful volcanic eruptions occur frequently.

B) the effects of volcanic eruptions can last for centuries.

C) scientists know of other volcanoes that erupted during the Middle Ages.

D) other volcanoes have calderas that are very large.

49

Which choice best supports the claim that Quilotoa was not responsible for the Little Ice Age?

A) Lines 3-4 ("Identifying . . . tricky")

B) Lines 26-28 ("Such a . . . cooling")

C) Lines 43-46 ("The researchers . . . atop the volcano")

D) Lines 71-75 ("But . . . closer match")

50

According to the data in the figure, the greatest below-average temperature variation occurred around what year?

A) 1200 CE

B) 1375 CE

C) 1675 CE

D) 1750 CE

51

The passage and the figure are in agreement that the onset of the Little Ice Age began

A) around 1150 CE.

B) just before 1300 CE.

C) just before 1500 CE.

D) around 1650 CE.

52

What statement is best supported by the data presented in the figure?

A) The greatest cooling during the Little Ice Age occurred hundreds of years after the temperature peaks of the Medieval Warm Period.

B) The sharp decline in temperature supports the hypothesis of an equatorial volcanic eruption in the Middle Ages.

C) Pyroclastic flows from volcanic eruptions continued for hundreds of years after the eruptions had ended.

D) Radiocarbon analysis is the best tool scientists have to determine the temperature variations after volcanic eruptions.

STOP

If you finish before time is called, you may check your work on this section only.

Do not turn to any other section.

Writing and Language Test

35 MINUTES, 44 QUESTIONS

Turn to Section 2 of your answer sheet to answer the questions in this section.

DIRECTIONS

Each passage below is accompanied by a number of questions. For some questions, you will consider how the passage might be revised to improve the expression of ideas. For other questions, you will consider how the passage might be edited to correct errors in sentence structure, usage, or punctuation. A passage or a question may be accompanied by one or more graphics (such as a table or graph) that you will consider as you make revising and editing decisions.

Some questions will direct you to an underlined portion of a passage. Other questions will direct you to a location in a passage or ask you to think about the passage as a whole.

After reading each passage, choose the answer to each question that most effectively improves the quality of writing in the passage or that makes the passage conform to the conventions of standard written English. Many questions include a "NO CHANGE" option. Choose that option if you think the best choice is to leave the relevant portion of the passage as it is.

Questions 1-11 are based on the following passage.

Ghost Mural

In 1932 the well-known Mexican muralist David Alfaro Siqueiros was commissioned to paint a mural on the second-story exterior wall of a historic building in downtown Los Angeles. Siqueiros was asked to celebrate tropical America in his work, **1** he accordingly titled it "América Tropical." He painted the mural's first two sections, featuring images of a tropical rainforest and a Maya pyramid, during the day. **2** Also, to avoid

1
A) NO CHANGE
B) which he accordingly titled
C) accordingly he titled it
D) it was titled accordingly

2
A) NO CHANGE
B) However,
C) Although,
D) Moreover,

Unauthorized copying or reuse of any part of this page is illegal.

CONTINUE ➤

690

scrutiny, Siqueiros painted the final section of the mural, the [3] centerpiece at night.

[4] The reason for Siqueiros's secrecy became clear when the mural was [5] confided. The centerpiece of the work was dominated by images of native people being oppressed and [6] including an eagle symbolizing the United States. Siqueiros's political message did not please the wealthy citizens who had commissioned his work. They eventually ordered the mural to be literally whitewashed, or painted over with white paint.

However, by the 1970s, the white paint had begun to fade, and the bright colors of the mural were beginning to show through. At the same time, a social and civil rights movement for Mexican Americans was working to raise awareness of Mexican American cultural identity. Artists associated with [7] this began to rediscover and promote the work of the Mexican muralists, particularly Siqueiros. To them, "América Tropical" was an example of how art in public spaces could be used to celebrate Mexican American heritage while at the same time making a political statement. Inspired by Siqueiros and the other muralists, this new generation of artists strove to emulate the old mural masters.

3

A) NO CHANGE
B) centerpiece,
C) centerpiece;
D) centerpiece—

4

Which choice best connects the sentence with the previous paragraph?
A) NO CHANGE
B) All three sections of the mural were on display
C) The community turned out in large numbers
D) Siqueiros was informed of people's reactions

5

A) NO CHANGE
B) promulgated.
C) imparted.
D) unveiled.

6

A) NO CHANGE
B) included
C) includes
D) had included

7

A) NO CHANGE
B) it
C) them
D) this movement

CONTINUE →

8 The result was an explosion of mural painting that spread throughout California and the southwestern United States in the 1970s. It was the Chicano mural movement. Hundreds of large, colorful new murals depicting elements of Mexican American life and history appeared during this period, some in designated cultural locations but many more in abandoned lots, on unused buildings, or **9** painted on infrastructure such as highways and bridges. Many of these murals can still be seen today, although some have not been well maintained.

8

Which choice most effectively combines the underlined sentences?

A) The result was an explosion, the Chicano mural movement, of mural painting that spread throughout California and the southwestern United States in the 1970s.

B) The result was the Chicano mural movement, an explosion of mural painting that spread throughout California and the southwestern United States in the 1970s.

C) The explosion of mural painting that spread throughout California and the southwestern United States in the 1970s was the resulting Chicano mural movement.

D) An explosion of mural painting resulted and it spread throughout California and the southwestern United States in the 1970s; it was the Chicano mural movement.

9

A) NO CHANGE

B) they were painted on

C) on

D) DELETE the underlined portion.

CONTINUE

Fortunately, a new group of artists has discovered the murals, and efforts are underway to clean, restore, and repaint them. Once again, Siqueiros's "América Tropical" is **10** leading the way. After a lengthy and complex restoration process, this powerful work is now a tourist attraction, complete with a visitor center and a rooftop viewing platform. **11** Advocates hope that Siqueiros's mural will once more serve as an inspiration, this time inspiring viewers to save and restore an important cultural and artistic legacy.

Which choice most effectively sets up the information that follows?

A) NO CHANGE

B) being cleaned and restored.

C) at risk of destruction.

D) awaiting its moment of appreciation.

At this point, the writer is considering adding the following sentence.

> When it was painted in 1932, Siqueiros's mural was considered offensive, but now it is acclaimed.

Should the writer make this addition here?

A) Yes, because it provides historical context for the changes discussed in the passage.

B) Yes, because it provides a useful reminder of how people once viewed Siqueiros's work.

C) No, because it unnecessarily repeats information from earlier in the passage.

D) No, because it makes a claim about Siqueiros's work that is not supported by the passage.

CONTINUE ➤

Questions 12-22 are based on the following passage.

The Hype of Healthier Organic Food

Some people buy organic food because they believe organically grown crops are more nutritious and safer for consumption than [12] the people who purchase their conventionally grown counterparts, which are usually produced with pesticides and synthetic fertilizers. In the name of health, [13] spending $1.60 for every dollar they would have spent on food that is [14] grown in a manner that is considered conventional. Scientific evidence, [15] therefore, suggests that consumers do not reap significant benefits, in terms of either nutritional value or safety, from organic food.

12

A) NO CHANGE
B) the purchase of
C) purchasing
D) DELETE the underlined portion.

13

A) NO CHANGE
B) these consumers spend
C) having spent
D) to spend

14

A) NO CHANGE
B) grown with conventional methods, using pesticides and synthetic fertilizers.
C) conventionally and therefore not organically grown.
D) conventionally grown.

15

A) NO CHANGE
B) furthermore,
C) however,
D) subsequently,

CONTINUE

Although advocates of organic food **16** <u>preserve</u> that organic produce is healthier than conventionally grown produce because it has more vitamins and minerals, this assertion is not supported by scientific research. **17** <u>For instance,</u> one review published in *The American Journal of Clinical Nutrition* provided analysis of the results of comparative studies conducted over a span of 50 years; researchers consistently found no evidence that organic crops are more nutritious than conventionally grown ones in terms of their vitamin and mineral content. **18** Similarly, Stanford University researchers who examined almost 250 studies comparing the nutritional content of different kinds of organic foods with that of their nonorganic counterparts found very little difference between the two.

16

A) NO CHANGE
B) carry on
C) maintain
D) sustain

17

A) NO CHANGE
B) However,
C) In addition,
D) Likewise,

18

At this point, the writer is considering adding the following sentence.

> The United States Department of Agriculture (USDA) reports that organic agricultural products are now available in approximately 20,000 markets specializing in natural foods.

Should the writer make this addition here?

A) Yes, because it adds a relevant research finding from a government agency.

B) Yes, because it supports the passage's argument that organic food is less nutritious than conventionally grown food.

C) No, because it is not relevant to the paragraph's discussion of scientific evidence.

D) No, because it introduces a term that has not been defined in the passage.

CONTINUE

Evidence also undermines the claim that organic food is safer to eat. While researchers have found lower levels of pesticide residue in organic produce than in nonorganic produce, the pesticide residue detected in conventional produce falls within acceptable safety limits. According to such organizations as the US Environmental Protection Agency, the minute amounts of residue falling within such limits **19** <u>have</u> no negative impact on human health. **20**

19

A) NO CHANGE

B) is having

C) has had

D) has

20

At this point, the writer wants to further reinforce the paragraph's claim about the safety of nonorganic food. Which choice most effectively accomplishes this goal?

A) To be labeled organic, a product must meet certain standards determined and monitored by the US Department of Agriculture.

B) Organic food, however, is regulated to eliminate artificial ingredients that include certain types of preservatives, sweeteners, colorings, and flavors.

C) Moreover, consumers who are concerned about ingesting pesticide residue can eliminate much of it by simply washing or peeling produce before eating it.

D) In fact, the Environmental Protection Agency estimates that about one-fifth of the pesticides used worldwide are applied to crops in the United States.

Unauthorized copying or reuse of any part of this page is illegal.

696

CONTINUE

Based on scientific evidence, organic food offers neither significant nutritional nor safety benefits for consumers. Proponents of organic food, of course, are quick to add that [21] their are numerous other reasons to buy organic [22] food, such as, a desire to protect the environment from potentially damaging pesticides or a preference for the taste of organically grown foods. Research regarding these issues is less conclusive than the findings regarding nutritional content and pesticide residue safety limits. What is clear, though, is this: if a consumer's goal is to buy the healthiest and safest food to eat, the increased cost of organic food is a waste of money.

21

A) NO CHANGE
B) there are
C) there is
D) their is

22

A) NO CHANGE
B) food such as:
C) food such as,
D) food, such as

CONTINUE

Questions 23-33 are based on the following passage and supplementary material.

You Are Where You Say

Research on regional variations in English-language use has not only yielded answers to such [23] life-altering questions as how people in different parts of the United States refer to carbonated beverages ("soda"? "pop"? "coke"?) [24] it also illustrates how technology can change the very nature of research. While traditional, human-intensive data collection [25] has all but disappeared in language studies, the explosion of social media has opened new avenues for investigation.

[1] Perhaps the epitome of traditional methodology is the *Dictionary of American Regional English*, colloquially known as *DARE*. [2] Its fifth and final alphabetical volume—ending with "zydeco"—released in 2012, the dictionary represents decades of arduous work. [3] Over a six-year period from 1965 to 1970, university graduate students conducted interviews in more than a thousand communities across the nation. [4] Their goal was to determine what names people used for such everyday objects and concepts as a submarine sandwich

The writer wants to convey an attitude of genuine interest and to avoid the appearance of mockery. Which choice best accomplishes this goal?

A) NO CHANGE

B) galvanizing

C) intriguing

D) weird

A) NO CHANGE

B) and also illustrates

C) but also illustrates

D) illustrating

Which choice most effectively sets up the contrast in the sentence and is consistent with the information in the rest of the passage?

A) NO CHANGE

B) still has an important place

C) remains the only option

D) yields questionable results

Unauthorized copying or reuse of any part of this page is illegal.

698

CONTINUE

(a "hero" in New York City but a "dagwood" in many parts of Minnesota, Iowa, and Colorado) and a heavy rainstorm (variously a "gully washer," "pour-down," or "stump mover"). [5] The work that dictionary founder Frederic G. Cassidy had expected to be finished by 1976 was not, in fact, completed in his lifetime. [6] The wait did not dampen enthusiasm among **26** scholars. Scholars consider the work a signal achievement in linguistics. **27**

Not all research into regional English varieties **28** requires such time, effort, and resources, however. Today's researchers have found that the veritable army of trained volunteers traveling the country conducting face-to-face interviews can sometimes be **29** replaced by another army the vast array of individuals volunteering details about their lives—and, inadvertently, their language—through social media. Brice Russ of Ohio State University, for example, has employed software to sort through postings on one social media **30** cite in search of particular words and phrases of interest as well as the location from which users are posting. From these data,

26

A) NO CHANGE
B) scholars, and these scholars
C) scholars, but scholars
D) scholars, who

27

To improve the cohesion and flow of this paragraph, the writer wants to add the following sentence.

　　Data gathering proved to be the quick part of the project.

The sentence would most logically be placed after

A) sentence 2.
B) sentence 3.
C) sentence 4.
D) sentence 5.

28

A) NO CHANGE
B) are requiring
C) have required
D) require

29

A) NO CHANGE
B) replaced—by another army,
C) replaced by another army;
D) replaced by another army:

30

A) NO CHANGE
B) site in search of
C) sight in search for
D) cite in search for

CONTINUE

he was able, among other things, to confirm regional variations in people's terms for soft drinks. As the map shows, "soda" is commonly heard in the middle and western portions of the United States; "pop" is frequently used in many southern states; and "coke" is predominant in the northeastern and southwest regions but used elsewhere as well. **31** As interesting as Russ's findings are, though, **32** they're true value lies in their reminder that the Internet is not merely a sophisticated tool for collecting data but is also **33** itself a rich source of data.

Soft Drink Descriptions by State
Highest Percentage Reported

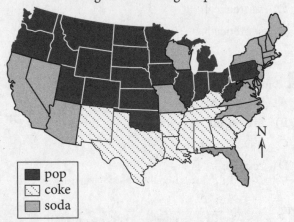

Adapted from Jennifer M. Smith, Department of Geography, The Pennsylvania State University, with data from www.popvssoda.com

31

The writer wants the information in the passage to correspond as closely as possible with the information in the map. Given that goal and assuming that the rest of the previous sentence would remain unchanged, in which sequence should the three terms for soft drinks be discussed?

A) NO CHANGE

B) "pop," "soda," "coke"

C) "pop," "coke," "soda"

D) "soda," "coke," "pop"

32

A) NO CHANGE

B) their true value lies in their

C) there true value lies in they're

D) their true value lies in there

33

Which choice most effectively concludes the sentence and paragraph?

A) NO CHANGE

B) where we can learn what terms people use to refer to soft drinks.

C) a useful way to stay connected to friends, family, and colleagues.

D) helpful to researchers.

CONTINUE

Questions 34-44 are based on the following passage.

Creating Worlds: A Career in Game Design

If you love video games and have thought about how the games you play might be changed or improved, or if you've imagined creating a video game of your own, you might want to consider a career as a video game designer. There [34] were a number of steps you can take to determine whether game design is the right field for you and, if it is, to prepare yourself for such a career.

Before making the choice, you should have some sense of what a video game designer does. Every video game, whether for a console, computer, or mobile device, starts with a concept that originates in the mind of a designer. The designer envisions the game's fundamental [35] elements: the settings, characters, and plots that make each game unique, and is thus a primary creative force behind a video game.

Conceptualizing a game is only the beginning of a video game designer's [36] job, however, no matter how good a concept is, it will never be translated into a video game unless it is communicated effectively to all the other members of the video game development team. [37] A designer must generate extensive documentation and

---

34

A) NO CHANGE
B) has been
C) are
D) was

35

A) NO CHANGE
B) elements: the settings, characters, and plots that make each game unique—
C) elements—the settings, characters, and plots that make each game unique—
D) elements; the settings, characters, and plots that make each game unique;

36

A) NO CHANGE
B) job, however. No
C) job—however, no
D) job however no

37

At this point, the writer is considering adding the following sentence.

> Successful communication is essential if a designer's idea is to become a reality.

Should the writer make this addition here?

A) Yes, because it supports the conclusion drawn in the following sentence.
B) Yes, because it illustrates a general principle discussed in the paragraph.
C) No, because it distracts from the focus of the paragraph by introducing irrelevant material.
D) No, because it merely reformulates the thought expressed in the preceding sentence.

38 explain his or her ideas clearly in order to ensure that the programmers, artists, and others on the team all share the same vision. **39** Likewise, anyone considering a career as a video game designer must be **40** skilled writers and speakers. In addition, because video game development is a collaborative effort and because the development of any one game may take months or even years, a designer must be an effective team player as well as detail oriented.

[1] A basic understanding of computer programming is essential. [2] In fact, many designers **41** initially begin their pursuits as programmers. [3] Consider taking some general computer science courses as well as courses in artificial intelligence and graphics in order to increase your understanding of the technical challenges involved in developing a video game. [4] Courses in psychology and human behavior may help you develop **42** emphatic collaboration skills, while courses in the humanities, such as in literature and film, should give you the background necessary to develop effective narrative structures. [5] A

38

Which choice results in a sentence that best supports the point developed in this paragraph?
A) NO CHANGE
B) possess a vivid imagination
C) assess his or her motivations carefully
D) learn to accept constructive criticism

39

A) NO CHANGE
B) Nevertheless,
C) Consequently,
D) However,

40

A) NO CHANGE
B) a skilled writer and speaker.
C) skilled both as writers and speakers.
D) both skilled writers and speakers.

41

A) NO CHANGE
B) start to begin their work
C) initiate their progression
D) begin their careers

42

A) NO CHANGE
B) paramount
C) eminent
D) important

CONTINUE

designer also needs careful educational preparation. [6] Finally, because a designer should understand the business aspects of the video game industry, such as budgeting and marketing, you may want to consider taking some business courses. [7] Although demanding and deadline driven, **43** video game design can be a lucrative and rewarding field for people who love gaming and have prepared themselves with the necessary skills and knowledge. **44**

43

A) NO CHANGE

B) the choice of video game design

C) you should choose video game design because it

D) choosing to design video games

44

To make this paragraph most logical, sentence 5 should be

A) placed where it is now.

B) placed before sentence 1.

C) placed after sentence 3.

D) DELETED from the paragraph.

STOP

If you finish before time is called, you may check your work on this section only.
Do not turn to any other section.

Math Test – No Calculator

25 MINUTES, 20 QUESTIONS

Turn to Section 3 of your answer sheet to answer the questions in this section.

DIRECTIONS

For questions 1-15, solve each problem, choose the best answer from the choices provided, and fill in the corresponding circle on your answer sheet. **For questions 16-20**, solve the problem and enter your answer in the grid on the answer sheet. Please refer to the directions before question 16 on how to enter your answers in the grid. You may use any available space in your test booklet for scratch work.

NOTES

1. The use of a calculator **is not permitted**.

2. All variables and expressions used represent real numbers unless otherwise indicated.

3. Figures provided in this test are drawn to scale unless otherwise indicated.

4. All figures lie in a plane unless otherwise indicated.

5. Unless otherwise indicated, the domain of a given function f is the set of all real numbers x for which $f(x)$ is a real number.

REFERENCE

$A = \pi r^2$ $A = \ell w$ $A = \frac{1}{2}bh$ $c^2 = a^2 + b^2$ Special Right Triangles
$C = 2\pi r$

$V = \ell wh$ $V = \pi r^2 h$ $V = \frac{4}{3}\pi r^3$ $V = \frac{1}{3}\pi r^2 h$ $V = \frac{1}{3}\ell wh$

The number of degrees of arc in a circle is 360.
The number of radians of arc in a circle is 2π.
The sum of the measures in degrees of the angles of a triangle is 180.

CONTINUE ▶

1

Which of the following expressions is equal to 0 for some value of x ?

A) $|x - 1| - 1$

B) $|x + 1| + 1$

C) $|1 - x| + 1$

D) $|x - 1| + 1$

2

$$f(x) = \frac{3}{2}x + b$$

In the function above, b is a constant. If $f(6) = 7$, what is the value of $f(-2)$?

A) -5

B) -2

C) 1

D) 7

3

$$\frac{x}{y} = 6$$
$$4(y + 1) = x$$

If (x, y) is the solution to the system of equations above, what is the value of y ?

A) 2

B) 4

C) 12

D) 24

4

If $f(x) = -2x + 5$, what is $f(-3x)$ equal to?

A) $-6x - 5$

B) $6x + 5$

C) $6x - 5$

D) $6x^2 - 15x$

CONTINUE

5

$$3(2x + 1)(4x + 1)$$

Which of the following is equivalent to the expression above?

A) $45x$

B) $24x^2 + 3$

C) $24x^2 + 18x + 3$

D) $18x^2 + 6$

6

If $\dfrac{a - b}{b} = \dfrac{3}{7}$, which of the following must also be

true?

A) $\dfrac{a}{b} = -\dfrac{4}{7}$

B) $\dfrac{a}{b} = \dfrac{10}{7}$

C) $\dfrac{a + b}{b} = \dfrac{10}{7}$

D) $\dfrac{a - 2b}{b} = -\dfrac{11}{7}$

7

While preparing to run a marathon, Amelia created a training schedule in which the distance of her longest run every week increased by a constant amount. If Amelia's training schedule requires that her longest run in week 4 is a distance of 8 miles and her longest run in week 16 is a distance of 26 miles, which of the following best describes how the distance Amelia runs changes between week 4 and week 16 of her training schedule?

A) Amelia increases the distance of her longest run by 0.5 miles each week.

B) Amelia increases the distance of her longest run by 2 miles each week.

C) Amelia increases the distance of her longest run by 2 miles every 3 weeks.

D) Amelia increases the distance of her longest run by 1.5 miles each week.

CONTINUE

8

Which of the following equations represents a line that is parallel to the line with equation
$y = -3x + 4$?

A) $6x + 2y = 15$

B) $3x - y = 7$

C) $2x - 3y = 6$

D) $x + 3y = 1$

9

$$\sqrt{x - a} = x - 4$$

If $a = 2$, what is the solution set of the equation above?

A) $\{3, 6\}$

B) $\{2\}$

C) $\{3\}$

D) $\{6\}$

10

If $\dfrac{t + 5}{t - 5} = 10$, what is the value of t ?

A) $\dfrac{45}{11}$

B) 5

C) $\dfrac{11}{2}$

D) $\dfrac{55}{9}$

11

$$x = 2y + 5$$
$$y = (2x - 3)(x + 9)$$

How many ordered pairs (x, y) satisfy the system of equations shown above?

A) 0

B) 1

C) 2

D) Infinitely many

CONTINUE

12

Ken and Paul each ordered a sandwich at a restaurant. The price of Ken's sandwich was x dollars, and the price of Paul's sandwich was \$1 more than the price of Ken's sandwich. If Ken and Paul split the cost of the sandwiches evenly and each paid a 20% tip, which of the following expressions represents the amount, in dollars, each of them paid? (Assume there is no sales tax.)

A) $0.2x + 0.2$

B) $0.5x + 0.1$

C) $1.2x + 0.6$

D) $2.4x + 1.2$

13

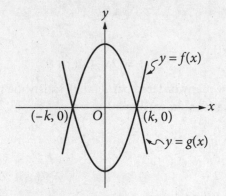

The functions f and g, defined by $f(x) = 8x^2 - 2$ and $g(x) = -8x^2 + 2$, are graphed in the xy-plane above. The graphs of f and g intersect at the points $(k, 0)$ and $(-k, 0)$. What is the value of k ?

A) $\dfrac{1}{4}$

B) $\dfrac{1}{2}$

C) 1

D) 2

14

$$\frac{8 - i}{3 - 2i}$$

If the expression above is rewritten in the form $a + bi$, where a and b are real numbers, what is the value of a ? (Note: $i = \sqrt{-1}$)

A) 2

B) $\dfrac{8}{3}$

C) 3

D) $\dfrac{11}{3}$

15

$$x^2 - \frac{k}{2}x = 2p$$

In the quadratic equation above, k and p are constants. What are the solutions for x ?

A) $x = \dfrac{k}{4} \pm \dfrac{\sqrt{k^2 + 2p}}{4}$

B) $x = \dfrac{k}{4} \pm \dfrac{\sqrt{k^2 + 32p}}{4}$

C) $x = \dfrac{k}{2} \pm \dfrac{\sqrt{k^2 + 2p}}{2}$

D) $x = \dfrac{k}{2} \pm \dfrac{\sqrt{k^2 + 32p}}{4}$

CONTINUE

DIRECTIONS

For questions 16–20, solve the problem and enter your answer in the grid, as described below, on the answer sheet.

1. Although not required, it is suggested that you write your answer in the boxes at the top of the columns to help you fill in the circles accurately. You will receive credit only if the circles are filled in correctly.
2. Mark no more than one circle in any column.
3. No question has a negative answer.
4. Some problems may have more than one correct answer. In such cases, grid only one answer.
5. **Mixed numbers** such as $3\frac{1}{2}$ must be gridded as 3.5 or 7/2. (If $\boxed{3\,1\,/\,2}$ is entered into the grid, it will be interpreted as $\frac{31}{2}$, not $3\frac{1}{2}$.)
6. **Decimal answers:** If you obtain a decimal answer with more digits than the grid can accommodate, it may be either rounded or truncated, but it must fill the entire grid.

Answer: $\frac{7}{12}$ Answer: 2.5

Write answer in boxes. ← Fraction line

← Decimal point

Grid in result.

Acceptable ways to grid $\frac{2}{3}$ are:

Answer: 201 – either position is correct

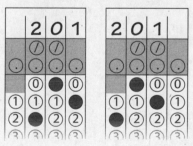

NOTE: You may start your answers in any column, space permitting. Columns you don't need to use should be left blank.

CONTINUE ➡

16

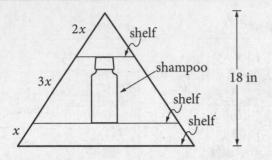

Jim has a triangular shelf system that attaches to his showerhead. The total height of the system is 18 inches, and there are three parallel shelves as shown above. What is the maximum height, in inches, of a shampoo bottle that can stand upright on the middle shelf?

17

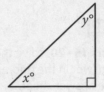

In the triangle above, the sine of $x°$ is 0.6. What is the cosine of $y°$?

18

$$x^3 - 5x^2 + 2x - 10 = 0$$

For what real value of x is the equation above true?

CONTINUE

19

$$-3x + 4y = 20$$
$$6x + 3y = 15$$

If (x, y) is the solution to the system of equations above, what is the value of x ?

20

The mesosphere is the layer of Earth's atmosphere between 50 kilometers and 85 kilometers above Earth's surface. At a distance of 50 kilometers from Earth's surface, the temperature in the mesosphere is $-5°$ Celsius, and at a distance of 80 kilometers from Earth's surface, the temperature in the mesosphere is $-80°$ Celsius. For every additional 10 kilometers from Earth's surface, the temperature in the mesosphere decreases by $k°$ Celsius, where k is a constant. What is the value of k ?

STOP

If you finish before time is called, you may check your work on this section only.
Do not turn to any other section.

Math Test – Calculator

55 MINUTES, 38 QUESTIONS

Turn to Section 4 of your answer sheet to answer the questions in this section.

DIRECTIONS

For questions 1-30, solve each problem, choose the best answer from the choices provided, and fill in the corresponding circle on your answer sheet. **For questions 31-38**, solve the problem and enter your answer in the grid on the answer sheet. Please refer to the directions before question 31 on how to enter your answers in the grid. You may use any available space in your test booklet for scratch work.

NOTES

1. The use of a calculator **is permitted**.

2. All variables and expressions used represent real numbers unless otherwise indicated.

3. Figures provided in this test are drawn to scale unless otherwise indicated.

4. All figures lie in a plane unless otherwise indicated.

5. Unless otherwise indicated, the domain of a given function f is the set of all real numbers x for which $f(x)$ is a real number.

REFERENCE

    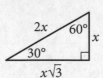

$A = \pi r^2$
$C = 2\pi r$

$A = \ell w$

$A = \dfrac{1}{2}bh$

$c^2 = a^2 + b^2$

Special Right Triangles

$V = \ell wh$

$V = \pi r^2 h$

$V = \dfrac{4}{3}\pi r^3$

$V = \dfrac{1}{3}\pi r^2 h$

$V = \dfrac{1}{3}\ell wh$

The number of degrees of arc in a circle is 360.
The number of radians of arc in a circle is 2π.
The sum of the measures in degrees of the angles of a triangle is 180.

CONTINUE

1

The monthly membership fee for an online television and movie service is $9.80. The cost of viewing television shows online is included in the membership fee, but there is an additional fee of $1.50 to rent each movie online. For one month, Jill's membership and movie rental fees were $12.80. How many movies did Jill rent online that month?

A) 1

B) 2

C) 3

D) 4

2

One of the requirements for becoming a court reporter is the ability to type 225 words per minute. Donald can currently type 180 words per minute, and believes that with practice he can increase his typing speed by 5 words per minute each month. Which of the following represents the number of words per minute that Donald believes he will be able to type m months from now?

A) $5 + 180m$

B) $225 + 5m$

C) $180 + 5m$

D) $180 - 5m$

3

If a 3-pound pizza is sliced in half and each half is sliced into thirds, what is the weight, in ounces, of each of the slices? (1 pound = 16 ounces)

A) 4

B) 6

C) 8

D) 16

4

Nick surveyed a random sample of the freshman class of his high school to determine whether the Fall Festival should be held in October or November. Of the 90 students surveyed, 25.6% preferred October. Based on this information, about how many students in the entire 225-person class would be expected to prefer having the Fall Festival in October?

A) 50

B) 60

C) 75

D) 80

CONTINUE

5

The density of an object is equal to the mass of the object divided by the volume of the object. What is the volume, in milliliters, of an object with a mass of 24 grams and a density of 3 grams per milliliter?

A)   0.125

B)   8

C)   21

D)   72

6

Last week Raul worked 11 more hours than Angelica. If they worked a combined total of 59 hours, how many hours did Angelica work last week?

A)   24

B)   35

C)   40

D)   48

7

Movies with Greatest Ticket Sales in 2012

MPAA rating	Type of movie				
	Action	Animated	Comedy	Drama	Total
PG	2	7	0	2	11
PG-13	10	0	4	8	22
R	6	0	5	6	17
Total	18	7	9	16	50

The table above represents the 50 movies that had the greatest ticket sales in 2012, categorized by movie type and Motion Picture Association of America (MPAA) rating. What proportion of the movies are comedies with a PG-13 rating?

A) $\frac{2}{25}$

B) $\frac{9}{50}$

C) $\frac{2}{11}$

D) $\frac{11}{25}$

8

Line ℓ in the xy-plane contains points from each of Quadrants II, III, and IV, but no points from Quadrant I. Which of the following must be true?

A) The slope of line ℓ is undefined.

B) The slope of line ℓ is zero.

C) The slope of line ℓ is positive.

D) The slope of line ℓ is negative.

CONTINUE

Number of Registered Voters
in the United States in 2012, in Thousands

Region	Age, in years					Total
	18 to 24	25 to 44	45 to 64	65 to 74	75 and older	
Northeast	2,713	8,159	10,986	3,342	2,775	27,975
Midwest	3,453	11,237	13,865	4,221	3,350	36,126
South	5,210	18,072	21,346	7,272	4,969	56,869
West	3,390	10,428	11,598	3,785	2,986	32,187
Total	14,766	47,896	57,795	18,620	14,080	153,157

The table above shows the number of registered voters in 2012, in thousands, in four geographic regions and five age groups. Based on the table, if a registered voter who was 18 to 44 years old in 2012 is chosen at random, which of the following is closest to the probability that the registered voter was from the Midwest region?

A) 0.10

B) 0.25

C) 0.40

D) 0.75

CONTINUE

Questions 10 and 11 refer to the following information.

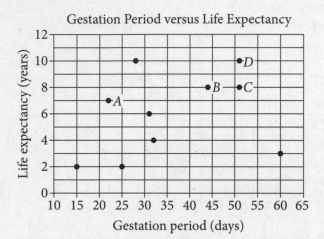

Gestation Period versus Life Expectancy

A curator at a wildlife society created the scatterplot above to examine the relationship between the gestation period and life expectancy of 10 species of animals.

10

What is the life expectancy, in years, of the animal that has the longest gestation period?

A) 3

B) 4

C) 8

D) 10

11

Of the labeled points, which represents the animal for which the ratio of life expectancy to gestation period is greatest?

A) A

B) B

C) C

D) D

12

In the xy-plane, the graph of function f has x-intercepts at -3, -1, and 1. Which of the following could define f ?

A) $f(x) = (x - 3)(x - 1)(x + 1)$

B) $f(x) = (x - 3)(x - 1)^2$

C) $f(x) = (x - 1)(x + 1)(x + 3)$

D) $f(x) = (x + 1)^2(x + 3)$

CONTINUE

13

The population of mosquitoes in a swamp is estimated over the course of twenty weeks, as shown in the table.

Time (weeks)	Population
0	100
5	1,000
10	10,000
15	100,000
20	1,000,000

Which of the following best describes the relationship between time and the estimated population of mosquitoes during the twenty weeks?

A) Increasing linear

B) Decreasing linear

C) Exponential growth

D) Exponential decay

14

$$1{,}000\left(1 + \frac{r}{1{,}200}\right)^{12}$$

The expression above gives the amount of money, in dollars, generated in a year by a $1,000 deposit in a bank account that pays an annual interest rate of r %, compounded monthly. Which of the following expressions shows how much additional money is generated at an interest rate of 5% than at an interest rate of 3% ?

A) $1{,}000\left(1 + \dfrac{5 - 3}{1{,}200}\right)^{12}$

B) $1{,}000\left(1 + \dfrac{\frac{5}{3}}{1{,}200}\right)^{12}$

C) $\dfrac{1{,}000\left(1 + \dfrac{5}{1{,}200}\right)^{12}}{1{,}000\left(1 + \dfrac{3}{1{,}200}\right)^{12}}$

D) $1{,}000\left(1 + \dfrac{5}{1{,}200}\right)^{12} - 1{,}000\left(1 + \dfrac{3}{1{,}200}\right)^{12}$

CONTINUE

15

Which of the following scatterplots shows a relationship that is appropriately modeled with the equation $y = ax^b$, where a is positive and b is negative?

A)

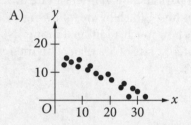

B)

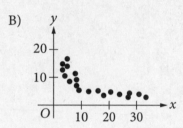

C)

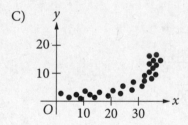

D)

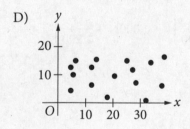

Questions 16 and 17 refer to the following information.

Mr. Martinson is building a concrete patio in his backyard and deciding where to buy the materials and rent the tools needed for the project. The table below shows the materials' cost and daily rental costs for three different stores.

Store	Materials' Cost, M (dollars)	Rental cost of wheelbarrow, W (dollars per day)	Rental cost of concrete mixer, K (dollars per day)
A	750	15	65
B	600	25	80
C	700	20	70

The total cost, y, for buying the materials and renting the tools in terms of the number of days, x, is given by $y = M + (W + K)x$.

16

For what number of days, x, will the total cost of buying the materials and renting the tools from Store B be less than or equal to the total cost of buying the materials and renting the tools from Store A ?

A) $x \le 6$

B) $x \ge 6$

C) $x \le 7.3$

D) $x \ge 7.3$

CONTINUE

17

If the relationship between the total cost, y, of buying the materials and renting the tools at Store C and the number of days, x, for which the tools are rented is graphed in the xy-plane, what does the slope of the line represent?

A) The total cost of the project

B) The total cost of the materials

C) The total daily cost of the project

D) The total daily rental costs of the tools

18

Jim has identical drinking glasses each in the shape of a right circular cylinder with internal diameter of 3 inches. He pours milk from a gallon jug into each glass until it is full. If the height of milk in each glass is about 6 inches, what is the largest number of full milk glasses that he can pour from one gallon of milk? (Note: There are 231 cubic inches in 1 gallon.)

A) 2

B) 4

C) 5

D) 6

19

If $3p - 2 \geq 1$, what is the least possible value of $3p + 2$?

A) 5

B) 3

C) 2

D) 1

CONTINUE

20

The mass of living organisms in a lake is defined to be the biomass of the lake. If the biomass in a lake doubles each year, which of the following graphs could model the biomass in the lake as a function of time? (Note: In each graph below, O represents $(0, 0)$.)

A)
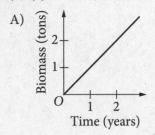

B)
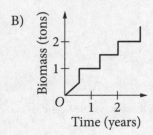

C)
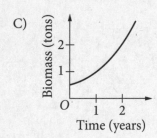

D)
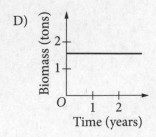

Questions 21 and 22 refer to the following information.

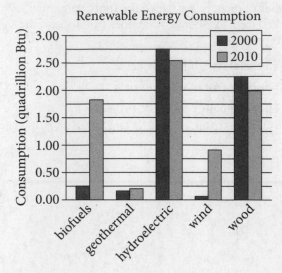

The bar graph above shows renewable energy consumption in quadrillions of British thermal units (Btu) in the United States, by energy source, for several energy sources in the years 2000 and 2010.

21

In a scatterplot of this data, where renewable energy consumption in the year 2000 is plotted along the x-axis and renewable energy consumption in the year 2010 is plotted along the y-axis for each of the given energy sources, how many data points would be above the line $y = x$?

A) 1

B) 2

C) 3

D) 4

CONTINUE

22

Of the following, which best approximates the percent decrease in consumption of wood power in the United States from 2000 to 2010 ?

A)   6%

B)   11%

C)   21%

D)   26%

23

The tables below give the distribution of high temperatures in degrees Fahrenheit (°F) for City A and City B over the same 21 days in March.

City A

Temperature (°F)	Frequency
80	3
79	14
78	2
77	1
76	1

City B

Temperature (°F)	Frequency
80	6
79	3
78	2
77	4
76	6

Which of the following is true about the data shown for these 21 days?

A) The standard deviation of temperatures in City A is larger.

B) The standard deviation of temperatures in City B is larger.

C) The standard deviation of temperatures in City A is the same as that of City B.

D) The standard deviation of temperatures in these cities cannot be calculated with the data provided.

CONTINUE

24

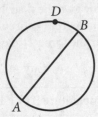

In the circle above, segment AB is a diameter. If the length of arc $\overset{\frown}{ADB}$ is 8π, what is the length of the radius of the circle?

A)   2

B)   4

C)   8

D) 16

25

$$f(x) = 2x^3 + 6x^2 + 4x$$
$$g(x) = x^2 + 3x + 2$$

The polynomials $f(x)$ and $g(x)$ are defined above. Which of the following polynomials is divisible by $2x + 3$?

A) $h(x) = f(x) + g(x)$

B) $p(x) = f(x) + 3g(x)$

C) $r(x) = 2f(x) + 3g(x)$

D) $s(x) = 3f(x) + 2g(x)$

26

Let x and y be numbers such that $-y < x < y$. Which of the following must be true?

    I. $|x| < y$

    II. $x > 0$

    III. $y > 0$

A) I only

B) I and II only

C) I and III only

D) I, II, and III

CONTINUE

The relative housing cost for a US city is defined to be the ratio $\dfrac{\text{average housing cost for the city}}{\text{national average housing cost}}$, expressed as a percent.

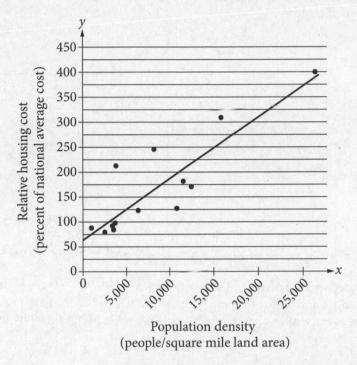

Population density
(people/square mile land area)

The scatterplot above shows the relative housing cost and the population density for several large US cities in the year 2005. The line of best fit is also shown and has equation $y = 0.0125x + 61$. Which of the following best explains how the number 61 in the equation relates to the scatterplot?

A) In 2005, the lowest housing cost in the United States was about $61 per month.

B) In 2005, the lowest housing cost in the United States was about 61% of the highest housing cost.

C) In 2005, even in cities with low population densities, housing costs were never below 61% of the national average.

D) In 2005, even in cities with low population densities, housing costs were likely at least 61% of the national average.

CONTINUE

28

$$f(x) = (x + 6)(x - 4)$$

Which of the following is an equivalent form of the function f above in which the minimum value of f appears as a constant or coefficient?

A) $f(x) = x^2 - 24$

B) $f(x) = x^2 + 2x - 24$

C) $f(x) = (x - 1)^2 - 21$

D) $f(x) = (x + 1)^2 - 25$

29

If x is the average (arithmetic mean) of m and 9, y is the average of $2m$ and 15, and z is the average of $3m$ and 18, what is the average of x, y, and z in terms of m ?

A) $m + 6$

B) $m + 7$

C) $2m + 14$

D) $3m + 21$

30

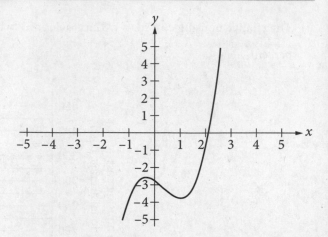

The function $f(x) = x^3 - x^2 - x - \dfrac{11}{4}$ is graphed in the xy-plane above. If k is a constant such that the equation $f(x) = k$ has three real solutions, which of the following could be the value of k ?

A) 2

B) 0

C) −2

D) −3

CONTINUE

DIRECTIONS

For questions 31–38, solve the problem and enter your answer in the grid, as described below, on the answer sheet.

1. Although not required, it is suggested that you write your answer in the boxes at the top of the columns to help you fill in the circles accurately. You will receive credit only if the circles are filled in correctly.
2. Mark no more than one circle in any column.
3. No question has a negative answer.
4. Some problems may have more than one correct answer. In such cases, grid only one answer.
5. **Mixed numbers** such as $3\frac{1}{2}$ must be gridded as 3.5 or 7/2. (If ⟨3 1 / 2⟩ is entered into the grid, it will be interpreted as $\frac{31}{2}$, not $3\frac{1}{2}$.)
6. **Decimal answers:** If you obtain a decimal answer with more digits than the grid can accommodate, it may be either rounded or truncated, but it must fill the entire grid.

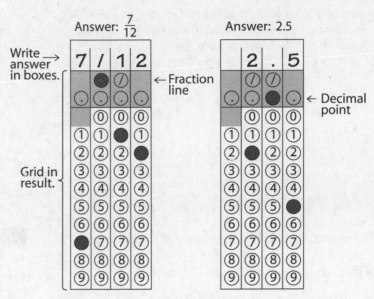

Unauthorized copying or reuse of any part of this page is illegal.

CONTINUE ▶

725

31

A partially filled pool contains 600 gallons of water. A hose is turned on, and water flows into the pool at the rate of 8 gallons per minute. How many gallons of water will be in the pool after 70 minutes?

32

The normal systolic blood pressure P, in millimeters of mercury, for an adult male x years old can be modeled by the equation $P = \dfrac{x + 220}{2}$. According to the model, for every increase of 1 year in age, by how many millimeters of mercury will the normal systolic blood pressure for an adult male increase?

33

The *pes*, a Roman measure of length, is approximately equal to 11.65 inches. It is also equivalent to 16 smaller Roman units called digits. Based on these relationships, 75 Roman digits is equivalent to how many <u>feet</u>, to the nearest hundredth? (12 inches = 1 foot)

34

In a study of bat migration habits, 240 male bats and 160 female bats have been tagged. If 100 more female bats are tagged, how many more male bats must be tagged so that $\dfrac{3}{5}$ of the total number of bats in the study are male?

CONTINUE

35

$$q = \frac{1}{2}nv^2$$

The dynamic pressure q generated by a fluid moving with velocity v can be found using the formula above, where n is the constant density of the fluid. An aeronautical engineer uses the formula to find the dynamic pressure of a fluid moving with velocity v and the same fluid moving with velocity $1.5v$. What is the ratio of the dynamic pressure of the faster fluid to the dynamic pressure of the slower fluid?

36

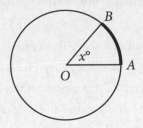

Note: Figure not drawn to scale.

In the figure above, the circle has center O and has radius 10. If the length of arc $\overset{\frown}{AB}$ (shown in bold) is between 5 and 6, what is one possible integer value of x ?

CONTINUE

Questions 37 and 38 refer to the following information.

The stock price of one share in a certain company is worth $360 today. A stock analyst believes that the stock will lose 28 percent of its value each week for the next three weeks. The analyst uses the equation $V = 360(r)^t$ to model the value, V, of the stock after t weeks.

37

What value should the analyst use for r ?

38

To the nearest dollar, what does the analyst believe the value of the stock will be at the end of three weeks? (Note: Disregard the $ sign when gridding your answer.)

STOP

If you finish before time is called, you may check your work on this section only.
Do not turn to any other section.

No Test Material On This Page

The SAT

GENERAL DIRECTIONS

- You may work on only one section at a time.
- If you finish a section before time is called, check your work on that section. You may NOT turn to any other section.

MARKING ANSWERS

- Be sure to mark your answer sheet properly.

COMPLETE MARK ●   EXAMPLES OF INCOMPLETE MARKS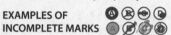

- You must use a No. 2 pencil.
- Carefully mark only one answer for each question.
- Make sure you fill the entire circle darkly and completely.
- Do not make any stray marks on your answer sheet.
- If you erase, do so completely. Incomplete erasures may be scored as intended answers.
- Use only the answer spaces that correspond to the question numbers.

USING YOUR TEST BOOK

- You may use the test book for scratch work, but you will not receive credit for anything that you write in your test book.
- After time has been called, you may not transfer answers from your test book to your answer sheet or fill in circles.
- You may not fold or remove pages or portions of a page from this book, or take the book or answer sheet from the testing room.

SCORING

- For each correct answer, you receive one point.
- You do not lose points for wrong answers; therefore, you should try to answer every question even if you are not sure of the correct answer.

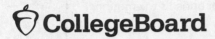

SAT® Practice Essay #4

 ESSAY BOOK

DIRECTIONS

The essay gives you an opportunity to show how effectively you can read and comprehend a passage and write an essay analyzing the passage. In your essay, you should demonstrate that you have read the passage carefully, present a clear and logical analysis, and use language precisely.

Your essay must be written on the lines provided in your answer booklet; except for the Planning Page of the answer booklet, you will receive no other paper on which to write. You will have enough space if you write on every line, avoid wide margins, and keep your handwriting to a reasonable size. Remember that people who are not familiar with your handwriting will read what you write. Try to write or print so that what you are writing is legible to those readers.

You have 50 minutes to read the passage and write an essay in response to the prompt provided inside this booklet.

REMINDERS

— Do not write your essay in this booklet. Only what you write on the lined pages of your answer booklet will be evaluated.

— An off-topic essay will not be evaluated.

Follow this link for more information on scoring your practice test: **www.sat.org/scoring**

This cover is representative of what you'll see on test day.

As you read the passage below, consider how Paul Bogard uses

- evidence, such as facts or examples, to support claims.
- reasoning to develop ideas and to connect claims and evidence.
- stylistic or persuasive elements, such as word choice or appeals to emotion, to add power to the ideas expressed.

Adapted from Paul Bogard, "Let There Be Dark." ©2012 by Los Angeles Times. Originally published December 21, 2012.

1 At my family's cabin on a Minnesota lake, I knew woods so dark that my hands disappeared before my eyes. I knew night skies in which meteors left smoky trails across sugary spreads of stars. But now, when 8 of 10 children born in the United States will never know a sky dark enough for the Milky Way, I worry we are rapidly losing night's natural darkness before realizing its worth. This winter solstice, as we cheer the days' gradual movement back toward light, let us also remember the irreplaceable value of darkness.

2 All life evolved to the steady rhythm of bright days and dark nights. Today, though, when we feel the closeness of nightfall, we reach quickly for a light switch. And too little darkness, meaning too much artificial light at night, spells trouble for all.

3 Already the World Health Organization classifies working the night shift as a probable human carcinogen, and the American Medical Association has voiced its unanimous support for "light pollution reduction efforts and glare reduction efforts at both the national and state levels." Our bodies need darkness to produce the hormone melatonin, which keeps certain cancers from developing, and our bodies need darkness for sleep. Sleep disorders have been linked to diabetes, obesity, cardiovascular disease and depression, and recent research suggests one main cause of "short sleep" is "long light." Whether we work at night or simply take our tablets, notebooks and smartphones to bed, there isn't a place for this much artificial light in our lives.

4 The rest of the world depends on darkness as well, including nocturnal and crepuscular species of birds, insects, mammals, fish and reptiles. Some examples are well known—the 400 species of birds that migrate at night in North America, the sea turtles that come ashore to lay their eggs—and some are not, such as the bats that save American farmers billions in pest control and the moths that pollinate 80% of the world's flora. Ecological light pollution is like the bulldozer of the night, wrecking habitat and disrupting ecosystems several billion years in the making. Simply put, without darkness, Earth's ecology would collapse. . . .

5   In today's crowded, louder, more fast-paced world, night's darkness can provide solitude, quiet and stillness, qualities increasingly in short supply. Every religious tradition has considered darkness invaluable for a soulful life, and the chance to witness the universe has inspired artists, philosophers and everyday stargazers since time began. In a world awash with electric light . . . how would Van Gogh have given the world his "Starry Night"? Who knows what this vision of the night sky might inspire in each of us, in our children or grandchildren?

6   Yet all over the world, our nights are growing brighter. In the United States and Western Europe, the amount of light in the sky increases an average of about 6% every year. Computer images of the United States at night, based on NASA photographs, show that what was a very dark country as recently as the 1950s is now nearly covered with a blanket of light. Much of this light is wasted energy, which means wasted dollars. Those of us over 35 are perhaps among the last generation to have known truly dark nights. Even the northern lake where I was lucky to spend my summers has seen its darkness diminish.

7   It doesn't have to be this way. Light pollution is readily within our ability to solve, using new lighting technologies and shielding existing lights. Already, many cities and towns across North America and Europe are changing to LED streetlights, which offer dramatic possibilities for controlling wasted light. Other communities are finding success with simply turning off portions of their public lighting after midnight. Even Paris, the famed "city of light," which already turns off its monument lighting after 1 a.m., will this summer start to require its shops, offices and public buildings to turn off lights after 2 a.m. Though primarily designed to save energy, such reductions in light will also go far in addressing light pollution. But we will never truly address the problem of light pollution until we become aware of the irreplaceable value and beauty of the darkness we are losing.

Write an essay in which you explain how Paul Bogard builds an argument to persuade his audience that natural darkness should be preserved. In your essay, analyze how Bogard uses one or more of the features listed in the box above (or features of your own choice) to strengthen the logic and persuasiveness of his argument. Be sure that your analysis focuses on the most relevant features of the passage.

Your essay should not explain whether you agree with Bogard's claims, but rather explain how Bogard builds an argument to persuade his audience.

This page represents the back cover of the Practice Essay.

DO NOT OPEN THIS BOOK UNTIL THE SUPERVISOR TELLS YOU TO DO SO.

CollegeBoard

| COMPLETE MARK ● | EXAMPLES OF INCOMPLETE MARKS | It is recommended that you use a No. 2 pencil. It is very important that you fill in the entire circle darkly and completely. If you change your response, erase as completely as possible. Incomplete marks or erasures may affect your score. |

■ TEST NUMBER   ■ SECTION 1

ENTER TEST NUMBER

For instance, for Practice Test #1, fill in the circle for 0 in the **first column** and for 1 in the **second column**.

0 ○ ○
1 ○ ○
2 ○ ○
3 ○ ○
4 ○ ○
5 ○ ○
6 ○ ○
7 ○ ○
8 ○ ○
9 ○ ○

	A B C D		A B C D		A B C D		A B C D
1	○ ○ ○ ○	14	○ ○ ○ ○	27	○ ○ ○ ○	40	○ ○ ○ ○
2	○ ○ ○ ○	15	○ ○ ○ ○	28	○ ○ ○ ○	41	○ ○ ○ ○
3	○ ○ ○ ○	16	○ ○ ○ ○	29	○ ○ ○ ○	42	○ ○ ○ ○
4	○ ○ ○ ○	17	○ ○ ○ ○	30	○ ○ ○ ○	43	○ ○ ○ ○
5	○ ○ ○ ○	18	○ ○ ○ ○	31	○ ○ ○ ○	44	○ ○ ○ ○
6	○ ○ ○ ○	19	○ ○ ○ ○	32	○ ○ ○ ○	45	○ ○ ○ ○
7	○ ○ ○ ○	20	○ ○ ○ ○	33	○ ○ ○ ○	46	○ ○ ○ ○
8	○ ○ ○ ○	21	○ ○ ○ ○	34	○ ○ ○ ○	47	○ ○ ○ ○
9	○ ○ ○ ○	22	○ ○ ○ ○	35	○ ○ ○ ○	48	○ ○ ○ ○
10	○ ○ ○ ○	23	○ ○ ○ ○	36	○ ○ ○ ○	49	○ ○ ○ ○
11	○ ○ ○ ○	24	○ ○ ○ ○	37	○ ○ ○ ○	50	○ ○ ○ ○
12	○ ○ ○ ○	25	○ ○ ○ ○	38	○ ○ ○ ○	51	○ ○ ○ ○
13	○ ○ ○ ○	26	○ ○ ○ ○	39	○ ○ ○ ○	52	○ ○ ○ ○

 Download the College Board SAT Practice app to instantly score this test.
Learn more at sat.org/scoring.

● ● ● ● ●   ● ●

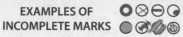
SAT PRACTICE ANSWER SHEET

COMPLETE MARK ●   EXAMPLES OF INCOMPLETE MARKS ⊘⊗⊜◓◔

It is recommended that you use a No. 2 pencil. It is very important that you fill in the entire circle darkly and completely. If you change your response, erase as completely as possible. Incomplete marks or erasures may affect your score.

■ **SECTION 2**

	A B C D		A B C D		A B C D		A B C D		A B C D
1	○○○○	10	○○○○	19	○○○○	28	○○○○	37	○○○○
2	○○○○	11	○○○○	20	○○○○	29	○○○○	38	○○○○
3	○○○○	12	○○○○	21	○○○○	30	○○○○	39	○○○○
4	○○○○	13	○○○○	22	○○○○	31	○○○○	40	○○○○
5	○○○○	14	○○○○	23	○○○○	32	○○○○	41	○○○○
6	○○○○	15	○○○○	24	○○○○	33	○○○○	42	○○○○
7	○○○○	16	○○○○	25	○○○○	34	○○○○	43	○○○○
8	○○○○	17	○○○○	26	○○○○	35	○○○○	44	○○○○
9	○○○○	18	○○○○	27	○○○○	36	○○○○		

 If you're scoring with our mobile app we recommend that you cut these pages out of the back of this book. The scoring does best with a flat page.

● ● ● ● ●   ●   ●

CollegeBoard

SAT PRACTICE ANSWER SHEET

| COMPLETE MARK ● | EXAMPLES OF INCOMPLETE MARKS ⊘⊗⊖◖ ◓✎✐⊛ | It is recommended that you use a No. 2 pencil. It is very important that you fill in the entire circle darkly and completely. If you change your response, erase as completely as possible. Incomplete marks or erasures may affect your score. |

■ SECTION 3

1 Ⓐ Ⓑ Ⓒ Ⓓ   4 Ⓐ Ⓑ Ⓒ Ⓓ   7 Ⓐ Ⓑ Ⓒ Ⓓ   10 Ⓐ Ⓑ Ⓒ Ⓓ   13 Ⓐ Ⓑ Ⓒ Ⓓ

2 Ⓐ Ⓑ Ⓒ Ⓓ   5 Ⓐ Ⓑ Ⓒ Ⓓ   8 Ⓐ Ⓑ Ⓒ Ⓓ   11 Ⓐ Ⓑ Ⓒ Ⓓ   14 Ⓐ Ⓑ Ⓒ Ⓓ

3 Ⓐ Ⓑ Ⓒ Ⓓ   6 Ⓐ Ⓑ Ⓒ Ⓓ   9 Ⓐ Ⓑ Ⓒ Ⓓ   12 Ⓐ Ⓑ Ⓒ Ⓓ   15 Ⓐ Ⓑ Ⓒ Ⓓ

Only answers that are gridded will be scored. You will not receive credit for anything written in the boxes.

16 **17** **18** **19** **20**

(grid-in answer bubbles for numbers 16–20, each with / and . and digits 0–9)

NO CALCULATOR ALLOWED

Did you know that you can print out these test sheets from the web? Learn more at sat.org/scoring.

● ● ● ● ●   ●   ●

737

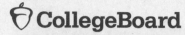
SAT PRACTICE ANSWER SHEET

COMPLETE MARK ●   EXAMPLES OF INCOMPLETE MARKS   It is recommended that you use a No. 2 pencil. It is very important that you fill in the entire circle darkly and completely. If you change your response, erase as completely as possible. Incomplete marks or erasures may affect your score.

■ SECTION 4

	A B C D		A B C D		A B C D		A B C D		A B C D
1	○ ○ ○ ○	7	○ ○ ○ ○	13	○ ○ ○ ○	19	○ ○ ○ ○	25	○ ○ ○ ○
2	○ ○ ○ ○	8	○ ○ ○ ○	14	○ ○ ○ ○	20	○ ○ ○ ○	26	○ ○ ○ ○
3	○ ○ ○ ○	9	○ ○ ○ ○	15	○ ○ ○ ○	21	○ ○ ○ ○	27	○ ○ ○ ○
4	○ ○ ○ ○	10	○ ○ ○ ○	16	○ ○ ○ ○	22	○ ○ ○ ○	28	○ ○ ○ ○
5	○ ○ ○ ○	11	○ ○ ○ ○	17	○ ○ ○ ○	23	○ ○ ○ ○	29	○ ○ ○ ○
6	○ ○ ○ ○	12	○ ○ ○ ○	18	○ ○ ○ ○	24	○ ○ ○ ○	30	○ ○ ○ ○

CALCULATOR ALLOWED

! If you're using our mobile app keep in mind that bad lighting and even shadows cast over the answer sheet can affect your score. Be sure to scan this in a well-lit area for best results.

● ● ● ● ●   ●   ●

CollegeBoard

■ SECTION 4 (Continued)

Only answers that are gridded will be scored. You will not receive credit for anything written in the boxes.

31   **32**   **33**   **34**   **35**

Only answers that are gridded will be scored. You will not receive credit for anything written in the boxes.

36   **37**   **38**

CALCULATOR ALLOWED

● ● ● ● ●　　● 　 ●

SECTION 5

IMPORTANT: **USE A NO. 2 PENCIL. DO NOT WRITE OUTSIDE THE BORDER!**
Words written outside the essay box or written in ink **WILL NOT APPEAR** in the copy sent to be scored, and your score will be affected.

PLANNING PAGE You may plan your essay in the unlined planning space below, but use only the lined pages following this one to write your essay. Any work on this planning page will not be scored.

Use pages 7 through 10 for your ESSAY ⟶

FOR PLANNING ONLY

Use pages 7 through 10 for your ESSAY ⟶

PLEASE DO NOT WRITE IN THIS AREA

○○○○○○○○○○○○○○○○○○○○○○○○○○○○○○○○○

SERIAL #

740

741

You may continue on the next page.

You may continue on the next page.

SERIAL #

STOP.

Answer Explanations

SAT Practice Test #4

Section 1: Reading Test

QUESTION 1.

Choice C is the best answer. The narrator initially expresses uncertainty, or uneasiness, over his decision to set out for the North Pole: "my motives in this undertaking are not entirely clear" (lines 9-10). At the end of the passage, the narrator recognizes that because of this journey he is "on the brink of knowing . . . not an ethereal mathematical spot," the North Pole, but himself (lines 56-57).

Choices A, B, and D are incorrect because the narrator does not suggest that he fears going on the expedition, doubts his own abilities, or feels disdain for the North Pole.

QUESTION 2.

Choice D is the best answer. Lines 56-57 provide evidence that the narrator eventually recognizes his motives for traveling to the North Pole: "What I am on the brink of knowing, I now see, is not an ephemeral mathematical spot but myself." The narrator initially was unsure of why he was traveling to the North Pole, but realizes that he has embarked on a journey to find himself.

Choices A, B, and C are incorrect because they do not provide the best evidence that the narrator eventually recognizes his motives for traveling to the North Pole. Rather, choices A, B, and C all focus on the narrator's preparations and expectations for the journey.

QUESTION 3.

Choice D is the best answer. In lines 1-6, the narrator says that he feels a "vast yearning" and that his emotions are "complicated." He explains that he does "not understand quite what it is that the yearning desires." In this context, his emotions are "not readily verifiable," or not completely understood.

Choices A, B, and C are incorrect because in this context, "not readily verifiable" does not mean unable to be authenticated, likely to be contradicted, or without empirical support.

QUESTION 4.

Choice C is the best answer. In lines 10-13, the narrator explains that "the machinery of [his] destiny has worked in secret" to prepare him for this journey, as "its clockwork" has propelled him to "this time and place." By using the phrases "the machinery" and "its clockwork," the narrator is showing that powerful and independent forces are causing him to journey to the North Pole.

Choices A, B, and D are incorrect because they do not indicate the main purpose of lines 10-13. While lines 10-13 mention that these powerful and independent forces have been working "for years, for a lifetime" to convince the narrator to journey to the North Pole, they do not expose a hidden side of the narrator, demonstrate the narrator's manner, or explain the amount of time the narrator has spent preparing for his expedition.

QUESTION 5.

Choice A is the best answer. In lines 20-21, the narrator states that many people have perished while journeying to the North Pole: "Nobody has succeeded in this thing, and many have died."

Choices B, C, and D are incorrect because the narrator does not indicate that previous explorers have made surprising discoveries, have failed to determine the exact location of the North Pole, or had different motivations than his own.

QUESTION 6.

Choice A is the best answer. In lines 20-21, the narrator provides evidence that many previous explorers seeking the North Pole have perished in the attempt: "Nobody has succeeded in this thing, and many have died."

Choices B, C, and D do not mention previous explorers; therefore, these lines do not provide the best evidence that explorers died while seeking the North Pole.

QUESTION 7.

Choice B is the best answer. In lines 27-39, the narrator states that he is "intent" on traveling to the North Pole but acknowledges that the journey is absurd: "Who wants the North Pole! What good is it! Can you eat it! Will it carry you from Gothenburg to Malmö like a railway?" By asking these questions, the narrator recognizes that the North Pole has no practical value.

Still, the narrator admits that finding the North Pole is necessary, as it "must nevertheless be sought for."

Choices A, C, and D are incorrect because the narrator does not view his expedition to the North Pole as immoral, socially beneficial, or scientifically important.

QUESTION 8.

Choice D is the best answer. In lines 27-31, the narrator asks a series of rhetorical questions about the North Pole: "Who wants the North Pole! What good is it! Can you eat it? Will it carry you from Gothenburg to Malmö like a railway?" In this context, the narrator is suggesting that reaching the North Pole has no foreseeable benefit or value to humanity; unlike trains that bring travelers to specific destinations, the North Pole does not provide humans with a specific benefit or form of convenience.

Choices A, B, and C are incorrect because the question posed in lines 30-31 does not debate modes of travel, examine the proximity of cities that can be reached by trains, or question how often people travel.

QUESTION 9.

Choice D is the best answer. In lines 48-49, the narrator states that the North Pole "is an abstraction, a mathematical fiction" and that "no one but a Swedish madman could take the slightest interest in it." In this context, the narrator is stating that people would not "take the slightest interest in," or be curious about, the North Pole.

Choices A, B, and C are incorrect because in this context, "take the slightest interest in" does not mean to accept responsibility for, to possess little regard for, or to pay no attention to something.

QUESTION 10.

Choice A is the best answer. In lines 49-51, the narrator describes his balloon journey toward the North Pole: "The wind is still from the south, bearing us steadily northward at the speed of a trotting dog." In this context, the wind is "bearing," or carrying, the narrator in a direction to the North.

Choices B, C, and D are incorrect because in this context, "bearing" does not mean affecting, yielding, or enduring.

QUESTION 11.

Choice C is the best answer. The author states that "demographic inversion is not a proxy for population growth" (lines 32-33). In other words, demographic inversion is distinct from population growth. The author also notes that demographic inversion is evident in many American cities, as it "can occur in cities that are growing, those whose numbers are flat, and even in those undergoing a modest decline in size" (lines 33-35).

Choices A, B, and D are incorrect because they do not summarize the first paragraph.

QUESTION 12.

Choice D is the best answer. The author notes that one of "the most powerful demographic events of the past decade [was] the movement of African Americans out of central cities" (lines 14-17).

Choices A, B, and C are incorrect because the author does not state that the unemployed, immigrants, or young professionals moved away from central-city areas in large numbers in the early 2000s.

QUESTION 13.

Choice A is the best answer. The author states that democratic inversion "can occur in cities that are growing, those whose numbers are flat, and even in those undergoing a modest decline in size" (lines 33-35). In this context, cities whose "numbers," or population size, are "flat" have static, or unchanging, populations.

Choices B, C, and D are incorrect because in this context, "flat" does not mean deflated, featureless, or obscure.

QUESTION 14.

Choice B is the best answer. The author states that many major American cities are currently experiencing economic hardship, or "enormous fiscal problems," because of "public pension obligations they incurred in the more prosperous years of the past two decades" (lines 36-39). The author then provides the example of Chicago, a city that can no longer afford to pay the "public services to which most of [its] citizens have grown to feel entitled" (lines 41-43). The author is arguing that many major American cities face economic hardship due to past promises (such as public services) they made to their constituents.

Choices A, C, and D are incorrect because the passage does not discuss expected tax increases, an inner-city tax base, or manufacturing production as they relate to the financial status of many major American cities.

QUESTION 15.

Choice A is the best answer. In lines 36-39, the author provides evidence that many major American cities are currently experiencing economic hardship due to promises made in past years: "America's major cities face enormous fiscal problems, many of them the result of public pension obligations they incurred in the more prosperous years of the past two decades." America's major cities made past promises, such as "public pension obligations," to their citizens, which caused their current financial situation.

Choices B, C, and D are incorrect because they do not provide evidence that many major American cities are currently experiencing economic hardship due to promises made in past years.

QUESTION 16.

Choice C is the best answer. The author explains how sociologist Ernest W. Burgess determined that urban areas have a traditional four-zone structure (lines 54-63). He then states that Burgess was "right about the urban America of 1974" (line 65) as it also followed the traditional four-zone structure: "Virtually every city in the country had a downtown, where the commercial life of the metropolis was conducted; it had a factory district just beyond; it had districts of working-class residences just beyond that; and it had residential suburbs for the wealthy and the upper middle class at the far end of the continuum" (lines 66-71).

Choices A, B, and D are incorrect because the passage does not imply that American cities in 1974 were witnessing the flight of minority populations to the suburbs, had begun to lose their manufacturing sectors, or were already experiencing demographic inversion.

QUESTION 17.

Choice C is the best answer. In lines 66-71, the author provides evidence that American cities in 1974 had a traditional four-zone structure: "Virtually every city in the country had a downtown, where the commercial life of the metropolis was conducted; it had a factory district just beyond; it had districts of working-class residences just beyond that; and it had residential suburbs for the wealthy and the upper middle class at the far end of the continuum."

Choices A, B, and D are incorrect because they do not provide evidence that American urban cities in 1974 had a traditional four-zone structure. Choice A references a seminal paper on the layout of American cities, choice B identifies Burgess's original theory, and choice D focuses on movement to the suburbs.

QUESTION 18.

Choice A is the best answer. In lines 66-68, the author notes that American cities in 1974 each had a "downtown, where the commercial life of the metropolis was conducted." In this context, the author is stating that these cities "conducted," or carried out, business, the "commercial life," in downtown areas.

Choices B, C, and D are incorrect because in this context, "conducted" does not mean supervised, regulated, or inhibited.

QUESTION 19.

Choice B is the best answer. Chart 1 shows the percentage of the US population in 2010 that lived in non-metro, small metro, and large metro areas. While the author cites census numbers, he notes that "when it comes to measuring demographic inversion, raw census numbers are an ineffective blunt instrument" (lines 11-13). Census data refer to the number of people living in a specific area and the demographic information that's been collected on them. The author would most likely consider the information in chart 1 to be possibly accurate but an "ineffective blunt instrument" that's not truly informative.

Choices A and C are incorrect because the author would not consider census data to be excellent or compelling. Choice D is incorrect because while the author does not believe the census completely explains demographic inversion, he would be unlikely to disagree with the census data.

QUESTION 20.

Choice A is the best answer. Chart 2 shows that the growth of all metropolitan areas in the 1990s was higher than the growth in all metropolitan areas in the 2000s: large metro areas experienced a growth of 14.3% in the 1990s versus a growth of 10.9% in the 2000s, small metro areas experienced a growth of 13.1% in the 1990s versus a growth of 10.3% in the 2000s, and non-metro areas experienced a growth of 9.0% in the 1990s versus a growth of 4.5% in the 2000s.

Choices B, C, and D are incorrect because they do not accurately characterize the US growth rate by metro size from 2000-2010 as illustrated in chart 2.

QUESTION 21.

Choice D is the best answer. Chart 2 shows that in the 1990s the US population increased in large metro, small metro, and non-metro areas when compared to the population growth experienced in the 1980s. Large metro areas experienced a growth of 12.5% in the 1980s versus a growth of 14.3% in the 1990s, small metro areas experienced a growth of 8.8% in the 1980s versus a growth of 13.1% in the 1990s, and non-metro areas experienced a growth of 1.8% in the 1980s versus a growth of 9.0% in the 1990s. Given this information, the population grew more in all metro areas in the 1990s when compared to the growth of those areas in the 1980s.

Choices A, B, and C are incorrect because they do not draw an accurate conclusion about the US growth rate in the 1990s.

QUESTION 22.

Choice A is the best answer. Lines 9-11 introduce the focus of the passage: "Welcome to the world of 'pharming,' in which simple genetic tweaks turn animals into living pharmaceutical factories." The passage then discusses the chronological development of "pharming," and describes ATryn, a useful drug produced after decades of laboratory experiments.

Choices B and C are incorrect because the passage does not primarily evaluate research or summarize long-term research findings. Choice D is incorrect because "pharming" is not a branch of scientific study.

QUESTION 23.

Choice C is the best answer. The author is appreciative of pharming and describes it as turning "animals into living pharmaceutical factories" (lines 10-11). She expresses a positive view of pharming in line 70, when she describes its end result: "*Et voilà*—human medicine!"

Choices A, B, and D are incorrect because the author's attitude about pharming is not accurately characterized as one of fear, disinterest, or surprise.

QUESTION 24.

Choice C is the best answer. In lines 19-21, the author explains that dairy animals are "expert," or capable, "protein producers."

Choices A, B, and D are incorrect because in this context "expert" does not mean knowledgeable, professional, or trained.

QUESTION 25.

Choice B is the best answer. In line 36, the author explains that the initial transgenic studies were "lab-bound thought experiments come true." Those first studies, in other words, were considered to be of theoretical value only. They were not expected to yield products ready for human use.

Choices A and D are incorrect because the cost of animal research and the molecular properties of certain animals are not discussed in the passage. Choice C is incorrect because the passage does not suggest that all of the transgenic studies were focused on anticoagulants.

QUESTION 26.

Choice C is the best answer. In lines 35-36, the author provides evidence that the transgenic studies done in the 1980s and 1990s were not expected to yield products ready for human use. The author explains that the initial transgenic studies were "merely gee-whiz, scientific geekery, lab-bound thought experiments come true."

Choices A, B, and D are incorrect because they do not provide evidence that the transgenic studies done in the 1980s and 1990s were not expected to yield products ready for human use. Choices A and B do not address the transgenic studies, and choice D focuses on ATryn, a drug that was intended for human use.

QUESTION 27.

Choice A is the best answer. Lines 42-44 explain that ATryn "acts as a molecular bouncer, sidling up to clot-forming compounds and escorting them out of the bloodstream." Antithrombin can thus be seen as an agent that reduces the amount of dangerous clots in the bloodstream.

Choices B, C, and D are incorrect because the passage does not suggest that antithrombin stems from a rare genetic mutation, is a sequence of DNA, or occurs naturally in goats' mammary glands.

QUESTION 28.

Choice B is the best answer. Lines 42-44 provide evidence that antithrombin reduces compounds that lead to blood clots, as it acts as a "molecular bouncer, sidling up to clot-forming compounds and escorting them out of the bloodstream."

Choices A, C, and D do not provide evidence that antithrombin reduces compounds that lead to blood clots; these lines describe proteins, people unable to produce antithrombin, and the production of ATryn.

QUESTION 29.

Choice B is the best answer. In lines 60-62, the description of female goats' kids mentions that "some of them proved to be transgenic, the human gene nestled safely in their cells." The statement "some of them" indicates that while a number of the newborn goats were transgenic, others were not.

Choices A, C, and D are incorrect because the passage does not suggest that the female goats used in the initial experiment secreted antithrombin in their milk after giving birth, were the first animals to receive the microinjections, or had cells that contained genes usually found in humans.

QUESTION 30.

Choice D is the best answer. In lines 63-64, the parenthetical is added after the phrase "a promoter," which is "(. . . a sequence of DNA that controls gene activity)." The parenthetical's purpose is to define the term "promoter."

Choices A, B, and C are incorrect because they do not correctly identify the purpose of the parenthetical information in lines 63-64.

QUESTION 31.

Choice D is the best answer. Gold is a valuable element that commands high prices, so calling something "liquid gold" implies that it has great value. Because the pharmaceutical company GTC was producing the drug in order to sell it, it can be inferred that describing ATryn as "liquid gold" means it proved to be a lucrative product for GTC.

Choices A, B, and C are incorrect because the phrase "liquid gold" does not refer to the microinjection technique, efficiency in dairy production, or transgenic goats being beneficial to dairy farmers.

QUESTION 32.

Choice D is the best answer. In lines 25-29, Burke describes the contract between a person and society as one that is "not a partnership in things subservient only to the gross animal existence of a temporary and perishable nature. It is a partnership in all science; a partnership in all art; a partnership in every virtue, and in all perfection." Describing that contract as a partnership in all things indicates its seriousness, while describing it as not being a "temporary and perishable nature" implies its permanence.

Choice A is incorrect because line 27 states that the contract between a person and society is not "temporary or perishable," meaning it is not brief. Choices B and C are incorrect because the passage does not compare the contracts in terms of complexity or precision.

QUESTION 33.

Choice D is the best answer. In lines 1-9, Burke explains that people have "consecrated the state" to "avoid . . . the evils of inconstancy and versatility," and that people should examine "the faults of the state . . . with pious awe and trembling solitude." Burke then explains that society is taught to "look with horror on those children of their country who want to hack that aged parent in pieces" (lines 10-12). Burke is arguing that children want to revise the state, or "this aged parent," by amending its faults. In this context, "state" refers to a political entity, or government, that attempts to protect its citizens from "the evils of inconstancy and versatility."

Choices A, B, and C are incorrect because in this context, "state" does not mean style of living, position in life, or temporary condition.

QUESTION 34.

Choice A is the best answer. In lines 17-29, Burke argues that "subordinate contracts," are simply business agreements over traded goods, while the state is not merely "a partnership agreement in a trade . . . or some other such low concern . . . but a partnership in all science; a partnership in all art;

a partnership in every virtue, and in all perfection." In this context, Burke is stating that the state is not a contract consisting of "low" or petty concerns.

Choices B, C, and D are incorrect because in this context, "low" does not mean weak, inadequate, or depleted.

QUESTION 35.

Choice D is the best answer. In lines 41-43, Paine asserts that "Every age and generation must be as free to act for itself, *in all cases*, as the ages and generations which preceded it." He later states that deceased citizens of a state should no longer have "any authority in directing who shall be its governors, or how its government shall be organized, or how administered" (lines 61-63). Paine doesn't believe, in other words, that the decisions of previous generations should dictate the conditions of modern life and government.

Choices A, B, and C are incorrect because they do not accurately characterize the way Paine views historical precedents.

QUESTION 36.

Choice B is the best answer. In lines 30-34, Burke describes societal contracts as long-term agreements that preserve the interests of past generations and link the living and the dead into a "partnership." Paine, however, states that past generations have no "control" over the decisions made by living (line 71) because the dead have "no longer any participation in the concerns of this world" (lines 59-60).

Choices A, C, and D are incorrect because they do not accurately characterize how Paine would respond to Burke's claim that societal contracts link past and current generations.

QUESTION 37.

Choice D is the best answer. Lines 67-72 provide the best evidence that Paine would respond to Burke's statement that society is a "partnership" between past and current generations (lines 30-34) with the explanation that the current generation cannot know what judgments the dead would make about contemporary issues. In these lines Paine explains: "What possible obligation, then, can exist between them; what rule or principle can be laid down, that two nonentities, the one out of existence, and the other not in, and who never can meet in this world, that the one should control the other to the end of time?"

Choices A, B, and C are incorrect because the lines cited do not provide the best evidence that Paine would respond to Burke's statement that society is a "partnership" between past and current generations (lines 30-34) by arguing that the current generation cannot know what judgments the dead would make about contemporary issues.

QUESTION 38.

Choice D is the best answer. Paine concludes Passage 2 with the argument that because social issues change over time, the living should not try to adhere to decisions made by former generations (lines 73-80). Burke, however, states that living citizens exist within a "universal kingdom" (line 35) comprised of the living, the dead, and those who are not yet born. Burke argues that the living do not have the right to change their government based on "their speculations of a contingent improvement" (lines 36-37). Therefore, Burke would disapprove of Paine's concluding argument, as he believes the living do not have sufficient justification for changing the existing governmental structure.

Choices A, B, and C are incorrect because they do not accurately describe how Burke would likely have responded to Paine's remarks in the final paragraph of Passage 2.

QUESTION 39.

Choice D is the best answer. Lines 34-38 provide the best evidence that Burke would disapprove of Paine's remarks in the final paragraph of Passage 2: "The municipal corporations of that universal kingdom are not morally at liberty at [the living's] pleasure, and on their speculations of a contingent improvement, wholly to separate and tear asunder the bands of their subordinate community." In these lines, Burke is arguing that the living do not have sufficient justification to change the existing governmental structure.

Choices A, B, and C do not provide the best evidence that Burke would disapprove of Paine's remarks in the final paragraph of Passage 2, as Burke believes the living do not have sufficient justification for changing the existing governmental structure.

QUESTION 40.

Choice A is the best answer. The primary argument of Passage 1 is that an inviolable contract exists between a people and its government, one that is to be "looked on with other reverence" (lines 24-25). Passage 1 suggests that this contract exists between past and future generations as well; in effect, current and future generations should be governed by decisions made in the past. Passage 2 challenges these points, as it argues that current and future generations are not obligated to preserve past generations' beliefs: "The Parliament or the people of 1688, or of any other period, had no more right to dispose of the people of the present day, or to bind or to control them in any shape whatever, than the parliament or the people of the present day have to dispose of, bind, or control those who are to live a hundred or a thousand years hence" (lines 48-54).

Choices B, C, and D are incorrect because Passage 2 does not offer an alternative approach to Passage 1, support an idea introduced in Passage 1, or exemplify an attitude promoted in Passage 1.

QUESTION 41.

Choice B is the best answer. Passage 1 argues that the government is sacred (lines 3-6) and that no person should interfere with it (lines 6-9). Passage 2 argues that people have the right to make changes to their government: "The circumstances of the world are continually changing, and the opinions of men change also; and as government is for the living, and not for the dead, it is the living only that has any right in it" (lines 73-76).

Choices A, C, and D are incorrect because they do not identify the main purpose of both passages.

QUESTION 42.

Choice C is the best answer. The author explains that a "powerful volcano" erupted around 750 years ago and caused "a centuries-long cold snap known as the Little Ice Age" (lines 1-3). The author then states that a group of scientists believe the volcano Samalas was this "powerful volcano," and she explains how the scientists' research supports this claim (lines 17-78).

Choices A, B, and D are incorrect because they do not identify the main purpose of the passage.

QUESTION 43.

Choice B is the best answer. The author begins the passage by explaining how the Little Ice Age was a "centuries-long cold snap" that was likely caused by a volcanic eruption (lines 1-3). The author then explains how scientists used radiocarbon analysis to determine when the Little Ice Age began and how a volcanic eruption triggered the cooling temperatures (lines 17-25).

Choices A, C, and D are incorrect because the passage does not criticize a scientific model, offer a new method of measuring sulfates, or shift from the use of radiocarbon dating to an examination of volcanic glass.

QUESTION 44.

Choice A is the best answer. In lines 17-25, the passage shifts focus from describing a recorded event to providing evidence that the Little Ice Age was likely caused by a volcanic eruption. The passage states that scientists used "radiocarbon dating of dead plant material from beneath the ice caps on Baffin Island and Iceland, as well as ice and sediment core data" to determine when the Little Ice Age began and how it was connected to the "mystery" volcanic eruption.

Choices B, C, and D are incorrect because they do not provide the best evidence that the passage shifts focus from a description of a recorded event to its likely cause. Choices B, C, and D all focus on the scientists' research but do not explain what caused the Little Ice Age.

QUESTION 45.

Choice D is the best answer. According to lines 5-8, "That a powerful volcano erupted somewhere in the world, sometime in the Middle Ages, is written in polar ice cores in the form of layers of sulfate deposits and tiny shards of volcanic glass." The phrase "is written in" reinforces the idea that the polar ice caps contain evidence of the volcanic eruption, and that scientists can interpret this evidence by examining the "sulfate deposits and tiny shards of volcanic glass."

Choices A, B, and C are incorrect because the author does not use the phrase "is written in" to demonstrate the concept of the hands-on nature of the scientists' work, highlight the fact that scientists often write about their work, or underscore the sense of importance scientists have about their work.

QUESTION 46.

Choice A is the best answer. The scientists believe the volcano Samalas, located in Indonesia, was most likely the medieval volcanic eruption (lines 33-35). The eruption likely occurred near the equator because an equatorial location is "consistent with the apparent climate impacts" the scientists observed (lines 61-67).

Choices B, C, and D are incorrect because the scientists do not suggest that the medieval volcanic eruption was located in the Arctic region, the Antarctic region, or Ecuador.

QUESTION 47.

Choice D is the best answer. In lines 61-64, the author cites geochemist Gifford Miller's findings that provide evidence that the medieval volcanic eruption most likely occurred in Indonesia near the equator: "It's not a total surprise that an Indonesian volcano might be the source of the eruption, Miller says. 'An equatorial eruption is more consistent with the apparent climate impacts.'"

Choices A, B, and C are incorrect because they do not provide evidence that the medieval volcanic eruption most likely occurred in Indonesia near the equator. Rather, choices A, B, and C focus on the medieval volcano's power, impact, and magnitude.

QUESTION 48.

Choice C is the best answer. In lines 68-71, the author states, "Another possible candidate—both in terms of timing and geographical location—is Ecuador's

Quilotoa, estimated to have last erupted between 1147 and 1320 C.E." The phrase "another possible candidate" implies that the scientists believe that in the Middle Ages a different volcanic eruption, such as an eruption from the volcano Quilotoa, could have been responsible for the onset of the Little Ice Age.

Choices A, B, and D are incorrect because the phrase "another possible candidate" does not imply the frequency or effects of volcanic eruptions, or that some volcanoes have large calderas.

QUESTION 49.

Choice D is the best answer. In lines 71-75, the author explains how Lavigne's team proved that Quilotoa's eruption did not cause the Little Ice Age:

"But when Lavigne's team examined shards of volcanic glass from this volcano, they found that they didn't match the chemical composition of the glass found in polar ice cores, whereas the Samalas glass is a much closer match." These findings show that Samalas, not Quilotoa, was responsible for the onset of the Little Ice Age.

Choices A, B, and C are incorrect because they focus on the difficulty of identifying the volcano responsible for the Little Ice Age, the magnitude of the volcanic eruption, and the researchers' experiment.

QUESTION 50.

Choice C is the best answer. The data in the figure show the greatest below-average temperature variation occurred in 1675 CE, as the temperature reached a variation of −1.0° Celsius.

Choice A is incorrect because the figure shows that the temperature in 1200 CE was above average (+0.25° Celsius). Choices B and D are incorrect because the below-average temperature variation reported in 1675 CE (at −1.0° Celsius) was greater than the below-average temperature variation reported for 1375 CE (around −0.25° Celsius) and 1750 CE (around (−0.5° Celsius).

QUESTION 51.

Choice B is the best answer. The passage says that the Little Ice Age began "about 750 years ago" (line 1) and that "the cold summers and ice growth began abruptly between 1275 and 1300 C.E." (lines 23-24). The figure indicates that average temperatures in central England began to drop around 1275 CE, and this drop in temperatures continued "through the 1700s" (line 32).

Choices A, C, and D are incorrect because the passage and figure do not indicate that the Little Ice Again began around 1150 CE, just before 1500 CE, or around 1650 CE.

QUESTION 52.

Choice A is the best answer. The figure shows that the greatest cooling period of the Little Ice Age occurred between 1500 and 1700 CE; it also shows that the greatest warming period of the Medieval Warm Period occurred between 1150 and 1250 CE. Therefore, the Little Ice Age's greatest cooling occurred a couple of centuries, or "hundreds of years," after the temperature peaks of the Medieval Warm Period.

Choices B, C, and D are incorrect because the figure does not focus on equatorial volcanic eruptions, pyroclastic flows, or radiocarbon analysis.

Section 2: Writing and Language Test

QUESTION 1.

Choice B is the best answer because the relative clause appropriately modifies the noun "work" in the preceding independent clause.

Choices A, C, and D are incorrect because each creates a comma splice.

QUESTION 2.

Choice B is the best answer because it creates the appropriate contrasting transition from the fact that the first two panels were painted during the day to the fact that the third panel was painted at night.

Choices A, C, and D are incorrect because each creates an inappropriate transition from the previous sentence. Choice A and choice D imply addition rather than contrast. Choice C results in an incomplete sentence.

QUESTION 3.

Choice B is the best answer because it creates an appropriate appositive to the subject "mural," and is correctly set off by commas on both sides.

Choices A, C, and D are incorrect because each is incorrectly punctuated. Choice A lacks a comma after "centerpiece," choice C unnecessarily introduces an independent clause, and choice D contains an em dash that has no parallel earlier in the sentence.

QUESTION 4.

Choice A is the best answer because it explicitly introduces the explanation for the behavior (painting at night) described in the previous paragraph.

Choices B, C, and D are incorrect because none alludes to the artist's painting at night, which is described at the end of the previous paragraph and explained in this paragraph.

QUESTION 5.

Choice D is the best answer because it refers to an action that can be performed on a physical object such as a mural.

Choices A, B, and C are incorrect because each refers to an action that is performed on information rather than on a physical object.

QUESTION 6.

Choice B is the best answer because it creates a past tense construction consistent with the verb "was dominated."

Choices A, C, and D are incorrect because none is consistent with the verb tense established earlier in the sentence.

QUESTION 7.

Choice D is the best answer because it is the most precise choice, specifying the noun that the demonstrative pronoun "this" refers to.

Choices A, B, and C are incorrect because each provides a vague, nonspecific pronoun that does not concretely define a referent.

QUESTION 8.

Choice B is the best answer because it correctly places and punctuates the appositive phrase that describes the "Chicano mural movement."

Choices A, C, and D are incorrect because each contains awkward syntax that obscures the relationship between the key noun phrases "an explosion of mural painting" and "the Chicano mural movement."

QUESTION 9.

Choice C is the best answer because it creates parallel construction within the list of locations ("*in* abandoned lots, *on* unused buildings, or *on* infrastructure").

Choices A, B, and D are incorrect because none follows the construction established within the list of locations.

QUESTION 10.

Choice A is the best answer because it alludes to the uniquely high level of investment, described in the next sentence, that the new group of artists is making in restoring and publicizing "América Tropical."

Choices B, C, and D are incorrect because each fails to express the connection between the general restoration efforts mentioned in the previous sentence and the specific role of "América Tropical" in these efforts, which is described in the next sentence.

SAT PRACTICE TEST #4

QUESTION 11.

Choice C is the best answer because details of the initial reaction to Siqueiros's mural and its subsequent rediscovery are given previously in the passage and are not needed to set up the forward-looking sentence that follows.

Choices A, B, and D are incorrect because each provides an inaccurate interpretation of the sentence that the writer is considering adding.

QUESTION 12.

Choice D is the best answer because without the underlined portion, the sentence contains an appropriate parallel contrast between the phrases "organically grown crops" and "conventionally grown counterparts," each of which describes crops.

Choices A, B, and C are incorrect because each creates an illogical comparison: crops to "people," crops to "purchase," and crops to "purchasing."

QUESTION 13.

Choice B is the best answer because it provides the subject "consumers," creating a complete sentence and providing a referent for the pronoun "they" that appears later in the sentence.

Choices A, C, and D are incorrect because each lacks the subject that the sentence requires and none provide a referent for "they."

QUESTION 14.

Choice D is the best answer because it efficiently creates a contrast with "organically grown."

Choices A, B, and C are incorrect because they are unnecessarily wordy and repeat information given in previous sentences.

QUESTION 15.

Choice C is the best answer because it sets up the contrast between the added expense of organic food and the evidence that suggests a lack of benefits from eating organic food.

Choices A, B, and D are incorrect because each fails to acknowledge the contrast between the last sentence in the paragraph and the previous sentences.

QUESTION 16.

Choice C is the best answer because "maintain" is commonly used to describe advocating a position in an argument.

Choices A, B, and D are incorrect because none is appropriate in the context of describing an opinion advocated by a group of people.

QUESTION 17.

Choice A is the best answer because the transitional phrase "For instance" sets up an example supporting the point, made in the previous sentence, that organic food may not contain more vitamins and minerals than conventionally grown food.

Choices B, C, and D are incorrect because none indicates that the sentence is providing an example supporting the point made in the previous sentence.

QUESTION 18.

Choice C is the best answer because it accurately identifies the reason that the writer should not add the proposed sentence: the paragraph is about evidence of nutritional content, not the availability of organic food.

Choices A, B, and D are incorrect because each provides an inaccurate interpretation of the proposed sentence's relationship to the passage.

QUESTION 19.

Choice A is the best answer because the plural verb "have" is consistent with the plural subject "amounts."

Choices B, C, and D are incorrect because each is a singular verb, which is inconsistent with the plural subject "amounts."

QUESTION 20.

Choice C is the best answer because the example it supplies, that pesticides can be minimized by washing or peeling produce, supports the claim that nonorganic food is safe.

Choices A, B, and D are incorrect because none supports the paragraph's claim about the safety of nonorganic food.

QUESTION 21.

Choice B is the best answer because the plural noun phrase "numerous other reasons" must be preceded by a plural verb and a pronoun that does not indicate possession: "there are."

Choices A, C, and D are incorrect because each contains the singular verb "is," the possessive pronoun "their," or both.

QUESTION 22.

Choice D is the best answer because a nonrestrictive clause must be preceded by a comma; in addition, "such as" is never followed by a comma.

In this case, the list of reasons supporting the claim that there are benefits to buying organic food is nonrestrictive; the list tells the reader something about organic food but does not restrict or place limits on organic food.

Choices A, B, and C are incorrect because each places erroneous punctuation after the phrase "such as." Choices B and C also lack the necessary comma preceding "such as."

QUESTION 23.

Choice C is the best answer because "intriguing" conveys a realistic level of interest for the entertaining but ultimately inconsequential question of regional differences in words for carbonated beverages.

Choices A, B, and D are incorrect because each mocks the topic of regional words for carbonated beverages.

QUESTION 24.

Choice C is the best answer because "but also" is the appropriate transition to complete the correlative pair "not only . . . but also," which begins earlier in the sentence.

Choices A, B, and D are incorrect because each fails to complete the phrase "not only . . . but also."

QUESTION 25.

Choice B is the best answer because it is consistent with the fact that there remains a "veritable army of trained volunteers traveling the country" and because it uses "still" to contrast this method with the "new avenues."

Choices A, C, and D are incorrect because none is consistent with the information contained later in the passage.

QUESTION 26.

Choice D is the best answer because it uses the relative pronoun "who" to avoid needless repetition of the word "scholars."

Choices A, B, and C are incorrect because each unnecessarily repeats the word "scholars."

QUESTION 27.

Choice C is the best answer because the new sentence provides a logical transition from sentences 3 and 4, which describe the data collection, to sentence 5, which explains that completing the dictionary took far longer than expected.

Choices A, B, and D are incorrect because each fails to create a logical transition between the preceding and subsequent sentences.

QUESTION 28.

Choice A is the best answer because the singular verb "requires" agrees with the singular subject "research."

Choices B, C, and D are incorrect because they do not create subject-verb agreement.

QUESTION 29.

Choice D is the best answer because a colon is the correct punctuation to introduce the elaborating phrase that follows the word "army."

Choices A, B, and C are incorrect because none provides the appropriate punctuation.

QUESTION 30.

Choice B is the best answer because it contains both the correct word to refer to an Internet location—"site"—and the correct preposition to complete the collocation "in search of."

Choices A, C, and D are incorrect because each contains a word that does not refer to an Internet location, and choices C and D contain the wrong preposition.

QUESTION 31.

Choice C is the best answer because it correctly associates each beverage term with the region described in the sentence according to the information contained in the map.

Choices A, B, and D are incorrect because each contradicts the information contained in the map.

QUESTION 32.

Choice B is the best answer because it contains the two plural possessive pronouns needed to refer to the subject "findings"—"their" and "their."

Choices A, C, and D are incorrect because each contains a word frequently confused with "their."

QUESTION 33.

Choice A is the best answer because it provides a summary and evaluation of gathering data from the Internet, which is the focus of the paragraph.

Choices B, C, and D are incorrect because each is either irrelevant to the main point of the paragraph or unnecessarily repeats information.

QUESTION 34.

Choice C is the best answer because it uses the present tense, which is consistent with the verbs that appear later in the sentence.

Choices A, B, and D are incorrect because they create awkward shifts in tense.

QUESTION 35.

Choice C is the best answer because the em dashes correctly bracket the examples of the types of elements.

Choices A, B, and D are incorrect because each uses either inconsistent or incorrect punctuation to set off the types of elements.

QUESTION 36.

Choice B is the best answer because a period is an appropriate way to separate the two independent clauses that meet at the underlined text.

Choices A, C, and D are incorrect because each either creates a comma splice or lacks necessary punctuation.

QUESTION 37.

Choice D is the best answer because the proposed sentence to be added is a paraphrase of the sentence before it, containing the same ideas.

Choices A, B, and C are incorrect because none fully acknowledges the relationship between the proposed sentence to be added and the other sentences in the paragraph.

QUESTION 38.

Choice A is the best answer because it highlights the importance of the game designer's communication with others, which is the paragraph's main point.

Choices B, C, and D are incorrect because none describes communication originating with the game designer, which is the main focus of the paragraph.

QUESTION 39.

Choice C is the best answer because the importance of communication is established in the previous sentences. The transition "consequently" best captures the fact that the designer must be skilled in this area.

Choices A, B, and D are incorrect because each contains a transition that either repeats information or creates an illogical relationship between this sentence and the previous sentences.

QUESTION 40.

Choice B is the best answer because it provides the singular nouns "writer" and "speaker" to agree with the singular pronoun "anyone."

Choices A, C, and D are incorrect because none creates pronoun-referent agreement.

QUESTION 41.

Choice D is the best answer because it expresses in the clearest, simplest way the idea that many game designers start out as programmers.

Choices A, B, and C are incorrect because each is unnecessarily wordy and obscures meaning.

QUESTION 42.

Choice D is the best answer because it logically and appropriately modifies the phrase "collaboration skills."

Choices A, B, and C are incorrect because none appropriately describes the value of collaboration skills.

QUESTION 43.

Choice A is the best answer because it provides a logical subject for the modifying phrase "demanding and deadline driven."

Choices B, C, and D are incorrect because each creates a dangling modifier.

QUESTION 44.

Choice B is the best answer because sentence 5 expresses the main point upon which the paragraph elaborates.

Choices A, C, and D are incorrect because none places sentence 5 in the appropriate position to set up the details contained in the paragraph.

Section 3: Math Test — No Calculator

QUESTION 1.

Choice A is correct. The expression $|x - 1| - 1$ will equal 0 if $|x - 1| = 1$. This is true for $x = 2$ and for $x = 0$. For example, substituting $x = 2$ into the expression $|x - 1| - 1$ and simplifying the result yields $|2 - 1| - 1 = |1| - 1 = 1 - 1 = 0$. Therefore, there is a value of x for which $|x - 1| - 1$ is equal to 0.

Choice B is incorrect. By definition, the absolute value of any expression is a nonnegative number. Substituting any value for x into the expression

$|x + 1|$ will yield a nonnegative number as the result. Because the sum of a nonnegative number and a positive number is positive, $|x + 1| + 1$ will be a positive number for any value of x. Therefore, $|x + 1| + 1 \neq 0$ for any value of x. Choice C is incorrect. By definition, the absolute value of any expression is a nonnegative number. Substituting any value for x into the expression $|1 - x|$ will yield a nonnegative number as the result. Because the sum of a nonnegative number and a positive number is positive, $|1 - x| + 1$ will be a positive number for any value of x. Therefore, $|1 - x| + 1 \neq 0$ for any value of x. Choice D is incorrect. By definition, the absolute value of any expression is a nonnegative number. Substituting any value for x into the expression $|x - 1|$ will yield a nonnegative number as the result. Because the sum of a nonnegative number and a positive number is positive, $|x - 1| + 1$ will be a positive number for any value of x. Therefore, $|x - 1| + 1 \neq 0$ for any value of x.

QUESTION 2.

Choice A is correct. Since $f(x) = \frac{3}{2}x + b$ and $f(6) = 7$, substituting 6 for x in $f(x) = \frac{3}{2}x + b$ gives $f(6) = \frac{3}{2}(6) + b = 7$. Then, solving the equation $\frac{3}{2}(6) + b = 7$ for b gives $\frac{18}{2} + b = 7$, or $9 + b = 7$. Thus, $b = 7 - 9 = -2$. Substituting this value back into the original function gives $f(x) = \frac{3}{2}x - 2$; therefore, one can evaluate $f(-2)$ by substituting -2 for x: $\frac{3}{2}(-2) - 2 = -\frac{6}{2} - 2 = -3 - 2 = -5$.

Choice B is incorrect as it is the value of b, not of $f(-2)$. Choice C is incorrect as it is the value of $f(2)$, not of $f(-2)$. Choice D is incorrect as it is the value of $f(6)$, not of $f(-2)$.

QUESTION 3.

Choice A is correct. The first equation can be rewritten as $x = 6y$. Substituting $6y$ for x in the second equation gives $4(y + 1) = 6y$. The left-hand side can be rewritten as $4y + 4$, giving $4y + 4 = 6y$. Subtracting $4y$ from both sides of the equation gives $4 = 2y$, or $y = 2$.

Choices B, C, and D are incorrect and may be the result of a computational or conceptual error when solving the system of equations.

QUESTION 4.

Choice B is correct. If $f(x) = -2x + 5$, then one can evaluate $f(-3x)$ by substituting $-3x$ for every instance of x. This yields $f(-3x) = -2(-3x) + 5$, which simplifies to $6x + 5$.

Choices A, C, and D are incorrect and may be the result of miscalculations in the substitution or of misunderstandings of how to evaluate $f(-3x)$.

QUESTION 5.

Choice C is correct. The expression $3(2x + 1)(4x + 1)$ can be simplified by first distributing the 3 to yield $(6x + 3)(4x + 1)$, and then expanding to obtain $24x^2 + 12x + 6x + 3$. Combining like terms gives $24x^2 + 18x + 3$.

Choice A is incorrect and may be the result of performing the term-by-term multiplication of $3(2x + 1)(4x + 1)$ and treating every term as an x-term. Choice B is incorrect and may be the result of correctly finding $(6x + 3)(4x + 1)$, but then multiplying only the first terms, $(6x)(4x)$, and the last terms, $(3)(1)$, but not the outer or inner terms. Choice D is incorrect and may be the result of incorrectly distributing the 3 to both terms to obtain $(6x + 3)(12x + 3)$, and then adding $3 + 3$ and $6x + 12x$ and incorrectly adding the exponents of x.

QUESTION 6.

Choice B is correct. The equation $\frac{a - b}{b} = \frac{3}{7}$ can be rewritten as $\frac{a}{b} - \frac{b}{b} = \frac{3}{7}$, from which it follows that $\frac{a}{b} - 1 = \frac{3}{7}$, or $\frac{a}{b} = \frac{3}{7} + 1 = \frac{10}{7}$.

Choices A, C, and D are incorrect and may be the result of calculation errors in rewriting $\frac{a - b}{b} = \frac{3}{7}$. For example, choice A may be the result of a sign error in rewriting $\frac{a - b}{b}$ as $\frac{a}{b} + \frac{b}{b} = \frac{a}{b} + 1$.

QUESTION 7.

Choice D is correct. In Amelia's training schedule, her longest run in week 16 will be 26 miles and her longest run in week 4 will be 8 miles. Thus, Amelia increases the distance of her longest run by 18 miles over the course of 12 weeks. Since Amelia increases the distance of her longest run each week by a constant amount, the amount she increases the distance of her longest run each week is $\frac{26 - 8}{16 - 4} = \frac{18}{12} = \frac{3}{2} = 1.5$ miles.

Choices A, B, and C are incorrect because none of these training schedules would result in increasing Amelia's longest run from 8 miles in week 4 to 26 miles in week 16. For example, choice A is incorrect because if Amelia increases the distance of her longest run by 0.5 miles each week and has her longest run of 8 miles in week 4, her longest run in week 16 would be $8 + 0.5 \cdot 12 = 14$ miles, not 26 miles.

QUESTION 8.

Choice A is correct. For an equation of a line in the form $y = mx + b$, the constant m is the slope of the line. Thus, the line represented by $y = -3x + 4$ has slope -3. Lines that are parallel have the same slope. To find out which of the given equations represents a line with the same slope as the line represented by $y = -3x + 4$, one can rewrite each equation in the form $y = mx + b$, that is, solve each equation for y. Choice A, $6x + 2y = 15$, can be rewritten as $2y = -6x + 15$ by subtracting $6x$ from each side of the equation. Then, dividing each side of $2y = -6x + 15$ by 2 gives $y = -\frac{6}{2}x + \frac{15}{2} = -3x + \frac{15}{2}$. Therefore, this line has slope -3 and is parallel to the line represented by $y = -3x + 4$. (The lines are parallel, not coincident, because they have different y-intercepts.)

Choices B, C, and D are incorrect and may be the result of common misunderstandings about which value in the equation of a line represents the slope of the line.

QUESTION 9.

Choice D is correct. The question states that $\sqrt{x - a} = x - 4$ and that $a = 2$, so substituting 2 for a in the equation yields $\sqrt{x - 2} = x - 4$. To solve for x, square each side of the equation, which gives $\left(\sqrt{x - 2}\right)^2 = (x - 4)^2$, or $x - 2 = (x - 4)^2$. Then, expanding $(x - 4)^2$ yields $x - 2 = x^2 - 8x + 16$, or $0 = x^2 - 9x + 18$. Factoring the right-hand side gives $0 = (x - 3)(x - 6)$, and so $x = 3$ or $x = 6$. However, for $x = 3$, the original equation becomes $\sqrt{3 - 2} = 3 - 4$, which yields $1 = -1$, which is not true. Hence, $x = 3$ is an extraneous solution that arose from squaring each side of the equation. For $x = 6$, the original equation becomes $\sqrt{6 - 2} = 6 - 4$, which yields $\sqrt{4} = 2$, or $2 = 2$. Since this is true, the solution set of $\sqrt{x - 2} = x - 4$ is $\{6\}$.

Choice A is incorrect because it includes the extraneous solution in the solution set. Choice B is incorrect and may be the result of a calculation or factoring error. Choice C is incorrect because it includes only the extraneous solution, and not the correct solution, in the solution set.

QUESTION 10.

Choice D is correct. Multiplying each side of $\frac{t + 5}{t - 5} = 10$ by $t - 5$ gives $t + 5 = 10(t - 5)$. Distributing the 10 over the values in the parentheses yields $t + 5 = 10t - 50$. Subtracting t from each side of the equation gives $5 = 9t - 50$, and then adding 50 to each side gives $55 = 9t$. Finally, dividing each side by 9 yields $t = \frac{55}{9}$.

Choices A, B, and C are incorrect and may be the result of calculation errors or using the distribution property improperly.

QUESTION 11.

Choice C is correct. Since $y = (2x - 3)(x + 9)$ and $x = 2y + 5$, it follows that $x = 2\left((2x - 3)(x + 9)\right) + 5 = 4x^2 + 30x - 49$. This can be rewritten as $4x^2 + 29x - 49 = 0$. Because the discriminant of this quadratic equation, $29^2 - 4(4)(-49) = 29^2 + 4(4)(49)$, is positive, this equation has 2 distinct roots. Using each of the roots as the value of x and finding y from the equation $x = 2y + 5$ gives 2 ordered pairs (x, y) that satisfy the given system of equations. Since no other value of x satisfies $4x^2 + 29x - 49 = 0$, there are no other ordered pairs that satisfy the given system. Therefore, there are 2 ordered pairs (x, y) that satisfy the given system of equations.

Choices A and B are incorrect and may be the result of either a miscalculation or a conceptual error. Choice D is incorrect because a system of one quadratic equation and one linear equation cannot have infinitely many solutions.

QUESTION 12.

Choice C is correct. Since the price of Ken's sandwich was x dollars, and Paul's sandwich was $1 more, the price of Paul's sandwich was $x + 1$ dollars. Thus, the total cost of the sandwiches was $2x + 1$ dollars. Since this cost was split evenly, Ken and Paul each paid $\frac{2x + 1}{2} = x + 0.5$ dollars plus a 20% tip. After adding the 20% tip, each of them paid $(x + 0.5) + 0.2(x + 0.5) = 1.2(x + 0.5) = 1.2x + 0.6$ dollars.

Choices A, B, and D are incorrect. These expressions do not model the given context. They may be the result of errors in setting up the expression or of calculation errors.

QUESTION 13.

Choice B is correct. One can find the intersection points of the two graphs by setting the functions $f(x)$ and $g(x)$ equal to one another and then solving for x. This yields $8x^2 - 2 = -8x^2 + 2$. Adding $8x^2$ and 2 to each side of the equation gives $16x^2 = 4$. Then dividing each side by 16 gives $x^2 = \frac{1}{4}$, and then taking the square root of each side gives $x = \pm\frac{1}{2}$. From the graph, the value of k is the x-coordinate of the point of intersection on the positive x-axis. Therefore, $k = \frac{1}{2}$.

Alternatively, since $(k, 0)$ lies on the graph of both f and g, it follows that $f(k) = g(k) = 0$. Thus, evaluating $f(x) = 8x^2 - 2$ at $x = k$ gives $0 = 8k^2 - 2$. Adding 2 to each side yields $2 = 8k^2$ and then dividing each side by 8 gives $\frac{1}{4} = k^2$. Taking the square root of each side then gives $k = \pm\frac{1}{2}$. From the graph, k is positive, so $k = \frac{1}{2}$.

Choices A, C, and D are incorrect and may be the result of calculation errors in solving for x or k.

QUESTION 14.

Choice A is correct. To rewrite $\frac{8 - i}{3 - 2i}$ in the standard form $a + bi$, multiply the numerator and denominator of $\frac{8 - i}{3 - 2i}$ by the conjugate, $3 + 2i$. This gives $\left(\frac{8 - i}{3 - 2i}\right)\left(\frac{3 + 2i}{3 + 2i}\right) = \frac{24 + 16i - 3i + (-i)(2i)}{3^2 - (2i)^2}$. Since $i^2 = -1$, this last fraction can be rewritten as $\dfrac{24 + 16i - 3i + 2}{9 - (-4)} = \dfrac{26 + 13i}{13}$, which simplifies to $2 + i$. Therefore, when $\dfrac{8 - i}{3 - 2i}$ is rewritten in the standard form $a + bi$, the value of a is 2.

Choices B, C, and D are incorrect and may be the result of errors in symbolic manipulation. For example, choice B could be the result of mistakenly rewriting $\dfrac{8 - i}{3 - 2i}$ as $\dfrac{8}{3} + \dfrac{1}{2}i$.

QUESTION 15.

Choice B is correct. The given quadratic equation can be rewritten as $2x^2 - kx - 4p = 0$. Applying the quadratic formula, $\dfrac{-b \pm \sqrt{b^2 - 4ac}}{2a}$, to this equation with $a = 2$, $b = -k$, and $c = -4p$ gives the solutions $\dfrac{k}{4} \pm \dfrac{\sqrt{k^2 + 32p}}{4}$.

Choices A, C, and D are incorrect and may be the result of errors in applying the quadratic formula.

QUESTION 16.

The correct answer is 9. Since the three shelves of the triangular shelf system are parallel, the three triangles in the figure are similar. Since the shelves divide the left side of the largest triangle in the ratio 2 to 3 to 1, the similarity ratios of the triangles are as follows.

▶ Smallest to middle: 2 to 5

▶ Smallest to largest: 2 to 6, or 1 to 3

▶ Middle to largest: 5 to 6

The height of the largest shampoo bottle that can stand upright on the middle shelf is equal to the height of the middle shelf. The height of the entire triangular shelf system is 18 inches. This is the height of the largest triangle. The height of the middle shelf is the height of the middle triangle minus the height of the smallest triangle. Since the similarity ratio of the middle triangle to the largest triangle is 5 to 6, the height of the middle shelf is $\dfrac{5}{6}(18) = 15$ inches. Since the similarity ratio of the smallest triangle to the largest triangle is 1 to 3, the height of the middle shelf is $\dfrac{1}{3}(18) = 6$ inches. Therefore, the height of the middle shelf is 9 inches.

QUESTION 17.

The correct answer is .6 or $\dfrac{3}{5}$. The angles marked $x°$ and $y°$ are acute angles in a right triangle. Thus, they are complementary angles. By the complementary angle relationship between sine and cosine, it follows that $\sin(x°) = \cos(y°)$. Therefore, the cosine of $y°$ is .6. Either .6 or the equivalent fraction $\dfrac{3}{5}$ may be gridded as the correct answer.

Alternatively, since the sine of $x°$ is .6, the ratio of the side opposite the $x°$ angle to the hypotenuse is .6. The side opposite the $x°$ angle is the side adjacent to the $y°$ angle. Thus, the ratio of the side adjacent to the $y°$ angle to the hypotenuse, which is equal to the cosine of $y°$, is equal to .6.

QUESTION 18.

The correct answer is 5. The four-term polynomial expression can be factored completely, by grouping, as follows:

$$\left(x^3 - 5x^2\right) + \left(2x - 10\right) = 0$$
$$x^2\left(x - 5\right) + 2\left(x - 5\right) = 0$$
$$\left(x - 5\right)\left(x^2 + 2\right) = 0$$

By the zero product property, set each factor of the polynomial equal to 0 and solve each resulting equation for x. This gives $x = 5$ or $x = \pm i\sqrt{2}$, respectively. Because the question asks for the real value of x that satisfies the equation, the correct answer is 5.

QUESTION 19.

The correct answer is 0. Multiplying each side of $-3x + 4y = 20$ by 2 gives $-6x + 8y = 40$. Adding each side of $-6x + 8y = 40$ to the corresponding side of $6x + 3y = 15$ gives $11y = 55$, or $y = 5$. Finally, substituting 5 for y in $6x + 3y = 15$ gives $6x + 3(5) = 15$, or $x = 0$.

QUESTION 20.

The correct answer is 25. In the mesosphere, an increase of 10 kilometers in the distance above Earth results in a decrease in the temperature by $k°$ Celsius where k is a constant. Thus, the temperature in the mesosphere is linearly dependent on the distance above Earth. Using the values provided and the slope formula, one can calculate the unit rate of change for the temperature in the mesosphere to be $\dfrac{-80 - (-5)}{80 - 50} = \dfrac{-75}{30} = \dfrac{-2.5}{1}$. The slope indicates that, within the mesosphere, if the distance above Earth increases by 1 kilometer, the temperature decreases by 2.5° Celsius. Therefore, if the distance above Earth increases by $(1 \times 10) = 10$ kilometers, the temperature will decrease by $(2.5 \times 10) = 25°$ Celsius. Thus, the value of k is 25.

Section 4: Math Test — Calculator

QUESTION 1.

Choice B is correct. Let m be the number of movies Jill rented online during the month. Since the monthly membership fee is $9.80 and there is an additional fee of $1.50 to rent each movie online, the total of the membership fee and the movie rental fees, in dollars, can be written as $9.80 + 1.50m$. Since the total of these fees for the month was \$12.80, the equation $9.80 + 1.50m = 12.80$ must be true. Subtracting 9.80 from each side and then dividing each side by 1.50 yields $m = 2$.

Choices A, C, and D are incorrect and may be the result of errors in setting up or solving the equation that represents the context.

QUESTION 2.

Choice C is correct. Donald believes he can increase his typing speed by 5 words per minute each month. Therefore, in m months, he believes he can increase his typing speed by $5m$ words per minute. Because he is currently able to type at a speed of 180 words per minute, he believes that in m months, he will be able to increase his typing speed to $180 = 5m$ words per minute.

Choice A is incorrect because the expression indicates that Donald currently types 5 words per minute and will increase his typing speed by 180 words per minute each month. Choice B is incorrect because the expression indicates that Donald currently types 225 words per minute, not 180 words per minute. Choice D is incorrect because the expression indicates that Donald will decrease, not increase, his typing speed by 5 words per minute each month.

QUESTION 3.

Choice C is correct. Because there are 16 ounces in 1 pound, a 3-pound pizza weighs $3 \times 16 = 48$ ounces. One half of the pizza weighs $\frac{1}{2} \times 48 = 24$ ounces, and one-third of the half weighs $\frac{1}{3} \times 24 = 8$ ounces.

Alternatively, since $\frac{1}{2} \times \frac{1}{3} = \frac{1}{6}$, cutting the pizza into halves and then into thirds results in a pizza that is cut into sixths. Therefore, each slice of the 48-ounce pizza weighs $\frac{1}{6} \times 48 = 8$ ounces.

Choice A is incorrect and is the result of cutting each half into sixths rather than thirds. Choice B is incorrect and is the result of cutting each half into fourths rather than thirds. Choice D is incorrect and is the result of cutting the whole pizza into thirds.

QUESTION 4.

Choice B is correct. Because Nick surveyed a random sample of the freshman class, his sample was representative of the entire freshman class. Thus, the percent of students in the entire freshman class expected to prefer the Fall Festival in October is appropriately estimated by the percent of students who preferred it in the sample, 25.6%. Thus, of the 225 students in the freshman class, approximately $225 \times 0.256 = 57.6$ students would be expected to prefer having the Fall Festival in October. Of the choices given, this is closest to 60.

Choices A, C, and D are incorrect. These choices may be the result of misapplying the concept of percent or of calculation errors.

QUESTION 5.

Choice B is correct. The density of an object is equal to the mass of the object divided by the volume of the object, which can be expressed as density $= \dfrac{\text{mass}}{\text{volume}}$. Thus, if an object has a density of 3 grams per milliliter and a mass of 24 grams, the equation becomes 3 grams/milliliter $= \dfrac{24 \text{ grams}}{\text{volume}}$. This can be rewritten as volume $= \dfrac{24 \text{ grams}}{3 \text{ grams/milliliter}} = 8$ milliliters.

Choice A is incorrect and be may be the result of confusing the density and the volume and setting up the density equation as $24 = \dfrac{3}{\text{volume}}$. Choice C is incorrect and may be the result of a conceptual error that leads to subtracting 3 from 24. Choice D is incorrect and may be the result of confusing the mass and the volume and setting up the density equation as $24 = \dfrac{\text{volume}}{3}$.

QUESTION 6.

Choice A is correct. Let a be the number of hours Angelica worked last week. Since Raul worked 11 more hours than Angelica, Raul worked $a + 11$ hours last week. Since they worked a combined total of 59 hours, the equation $a + (a + 11) = 59$ must hold. This equation can be simplified to $2a + 11 = 59$, or $2a = 48$. Therefore, $a = 24$, and Angelica worked 24 hours last week.

Choice B is incorrect because it is the number of hours Raul worked last week. Choice C is incorrect. If Angelica worked 40 hours and Raul worked 11 hours more, Raul would have worked 51 hours, and the combined total number of hours they worked would be 91, not 59. Choice D is incorrect and may be the result of solving the equation $a + 11 = 59$ rather than $a + (a + 11) = 59$.

QUESTION 7.

Choice A is correct. According to the table, of the 50 movies with the greatest ticket sales in 2012, 4 are comedy movies with a PG-13 rating. Therefore, the proportion of the 50 movies with the greatest ticket sales in 2012 that are comedy movies with a PG-13 rating is $\dfrac{4}{50}$, or equivalently, $\dfrac{2}{25}$.

Choice B is incorrect; $\dfrac{9}{50}$ is the proportion of the 50 movies with the greatest ticket sales in 2012 that are comedy movies, regardless of rating. Choice C is incorrect; $\dfrac{2}{11} = \dfrac{4}{22}$ is the proportion of movies with a PG-13 rating that are comedy movies. Choice D is incorrect; $\dfrac{11}{25} = \dfrac{22}{50}$ is the proportion of the 50 movies with the greatest ticket sales in 2012 that have a rating of PG-13.

QUESTION 8.

Choice D is correct. The quadrants of the xy-plane are defined as follows: Quadrant I is above the x-axis and to the right of the y-axis; Quadrant II is above the x-axis and to the left of the y-axis; Quadrant III is below the x-axis and to the left of the y-axis; and Quadrant IV is below the x-axis and to the right of the y-axis. It is possible for line ℓ to pass through Quadrants II, III, and IV, but not Quadrant I, only if line ℓ has negative x- and y-intercepts. This implies that line ℓ has a negative slope, since between the negative x-intercept and the negative y-intercept the value of x increases (from negative to zero) and the value of y decreases (from zero to negative); so the quotient of the change in y over the change in x, that is, the slope of line ℓ, must be negative.

Choice A is incorrect because a line with an undefined slope is a vertical line, and if a vertical line passes through Quadrant IV, it must pass through Quadrant I as well. Choice B is incorrect because a line with a slope of zero is a horizontal line and, if a horizontal line passes through Quadrant II, it must pass through Quadrant I as well. Choice C is incorrect because if a line with a positive slope passes through Quadrant IV, it must pass through Quadrant I as well.

QUESTION 9.

Choice B is correct. According to the table, in 2012 there was a total of $14{,}766 + 47{,}896 = 62{,}662$ registered voters between 18 and 44 years old, and $3{,}453 + 11{,}237 = 14{,}690$ of them were from the Midwest region. Therefore, the probability that a randomly chosen registered voter who was between 18 and 44 years old in 2012 was from Midwest region is $\dfrac{14{,}690}{62{,}662} \approx 0.234$. Of the given choices, 0.25 is closest to this value.

Choices A, C, and D are incorrect and may be the result of errors in selecting the correct proportion or in calculating the correct value.

QUESTION 10.

Choice A is correct. According to the graph, the animal with the longest gestation period (60 days) has a life expectancy of 3 years.

Choices B, C, and D are incorrect. All the animals that have a life expectancy of 4, 8, or 10 years have a gestation period that is shorter than 60 days, which is the longest gestation period.

QUESTION 11.

Choice A is correct. The ratio of life expectancy to gestation period for the animal represented by point A is approximately $\dfrac{7 \text{ years}}{23 \text{ days}}$, or about

0.3 years/day, which is greater than the ratio for the animals represented by the other labeled points (the ratios for points B, C, and D, in units of years of life expectancy per day of gestation, are approximately $\frac{8}{44}$, $\frac{8}{51}$, and $\frac{10}{51}$ respectively, each of which is less than 0.2 years/day).

Choices B, C, and D are incorrect and may be the result of errors in calculating the ratio or in reading the graph.

QUESTION 12.

Choice C is correct. All of the given choices are polynomials. If the graph of a polynomial function f in the xy-plane has an x-intercept at b, then $(x - b)$ must be a factor of $f(x)$. Since -3, -1, and 1 are each x-intercepts of the graph of f, it follows that $(x + 3)$, $(x +1)$, and $(x - 1)$ must each be a factor of $f(x)$. The factored polynomial function in choice C is the only polynomial given with these 3 factors.

Choices A, B, and D are incorrect because they do not contain all three factors that must exist if the graph of the polynomial function f has x-intercepts at -3, -1, and 1.

QUESTION 13.

Choice C is correct. The mosquito population starts at 100 in week 0 and then is multiplied by a factor of 10 every 5 weeks. Thus, if $P(t)$ is the mosquito population after t weeks, then based on the table, $P(t) = 100(10)^{\frac{t}{5}}$, which indicates an exponential growth relationship.

Choices A, B, and D are incorrect and may be the result of an incorrect interpretation of the relationship or errors in modeling the relationship.

QUESTION 14.

Choice D is correct. According to the given formula, the amount of money generated for a year at 5% interest, compounded monthly, is $1,000\left(1 + \frac{5}{1,200}\right)^{12}$, whereas the amount of money generated at 3% interest, compounded monthly, is $1,000\left(1 + \frac{3}{1,200}\right)^{12}$. Therefore, the difference between these two amounts, $1,000\left(1 + \frac{5}{1,200}\right)^{12} - 1,000\left(1 + \frac{3}{1,200}\right)^{12}$, shows how much additional money is generated at an interest rate of 5% than at an interest rate of 3%.

Choices A, B, and C are incorrect and may be the result of misinterpreting the given formula. For example, the expression in choice C gives how many times as much money, not how much additional money, is generated at an interest rate of 5% than at an interest rate of 3%.

QUESTION 15.

Choice B is correct. The graph of $y = ax^b$, where a is positive and b is negative, has a positive y-intercept and rapidly decreases (in particular, decreases at a faster rate than a linear function) toward the x-axis as x increases. Of the scatterplots shown, only the one in choice B would be appropriately modeled by such a function.

Choice A is incorrect, as this scatterplot is appropriately modeled by a linear function. Choice C is incorrect, as this scatterplot is appropriately modeled by an increasing function. Choice D is incorrect, as this scatterplot shows no clear relationship between x and y.

QUESTION 16.

Choice A is correct. The total cost y, in dollars, of buying the materials and renting the tools for x days from Store A and Store B is found by substituting the respective values for these stores from the table into the given equation, $y = M + (W + K)x$, as shown below.

$$\text{Store A: } y = 750 + (15 + 65)x = 750 + 80x$$

$$\text{Store B: } y = 600 + (25 + 80)x = 600 + 105x$$

Thus, the number of days, x, for which the total cost of buying the materials and renting the tools from Store B is less than or equal to the total cost of buying the materials and renting the tools from Store A can be found by solving the inequality $600 + 105x \leq 750 + 80x$. Subtracting $80x$ and 600 from each side of $600 + 105x \leq 750 + 80x$ and combining like terms yields $25x \leq 150$. Dividing each side of $25x \leq 150$ by 25 yields $x \leq 6$.

Choice B is incorrect. The inequality $x \geq 6$ is the number of days for which the total cost of buying the materials and renting the tools from Store B is <u>greater than</u> or equal to the total cost of buying the materials and renting the tools from Store A. Choices C and D are incorrect and may be the result of an error in setting up or simplifying the inequality.

QUESTION 17.

Choice D is correct. The total cost, y, of buying the materials and renting the tools in terms of the number of days, x, is given as $y = M + (W + K)x$. If this relationship is graphed in the xy-plane, the slope of the graph is equal to $W + K$, which is the daily rental cost of the wheelbarrow plus the daily rental cost of the concrete mixer, that is, the total daily rental costs of the tools.

Choice A is incorrect because the total cost of the project is y. Choice B is incorrect because the total cost of the materials is M, which is the y-intercept of the graph of $y = M + (W + K)x$. Choice C is incorrect because the total daily cost of the project is the total cost of the project divided by the total number of days the project took and, since materials cost more than 0 dollars, this is not the same as the total daily rental costs.

QUESTION 18.

Choice C is correct. The volume V of a right circular cylinder is given by the formula $V = \pi r^2 h$, where r is the base radius of the cylinder and h is the height of the cylinder. Since each glass has an internal diameter of 3 inches, each glass has a base radius of $\frac{3}{2}$ inches. Since the height of the milk in each glass is 6 inches, the volume of milk in each glass is $V = \pi\left(\frac{3}{2}\right)^2(6) \approx$ 42.41 cubic inches. The total number of glasses Jim can pour from 1 gallon is equal to $\dfrac{\text{number of cubic inches in 1 gallon}}{\text{number of cubic inches in 1 glass}} = \dfrac{231}{42.41}$, which is approximately 5.45 glasses. Since the question asks for the largest number of <u>full</u> glasses Jim can pour, the number of glasses needs to be rounded down to 5.

Choices A, B, and D are incorrect and may be the result of conceptual errors or calculation errors. For example, choice D is incorrect because even though Jim can pour more than 5 full glasses, he will not have enough milk to pour a full 6th glass.

QUESTION 19.

Choice A is correct. Adding 4 to each side of the inequality $3p - 2 \geq 1$ yields the inequality $3p + 2 \geq 5$. Therefore, the least possible value of $3p + 2$ is 5.

Choice B is incorrect because it gives the least possible value of $3p$, not of $3p + 2$. Choice C is incorrect. If the least possible value of $3p + 2$ were 2, then it would follow that $3p + 2 \geq 2$. Subtracting 4 from each side of this inequality would yield $3p - 2 \geq -2$. This contradicts the given inequality, $3p - 2 \geq 1$. Therefore, the least possible value of $3p + 2$ cannot be 2. Choice D is incorrect because it gives the least possible value of p, not of $3p + 2$.

QUESTION 20.

Choice C is correct. Since the biomass of the lake doubles each year, the biomass starts at a positive value and then increases exponentially over time. Of the graphs shown, only the graph in choice C is of an increasing exponential function.

Choice A is incorrect because the biomass of the lake must start at a positive value, not zero. Furthermore, this graph shows linear growth, not exponential growth. Choice B is incorrect because the biomass of the lake must start at a positive value, not zero. Furthermore, this graph has vertical segments and is not a function. Choice D is incorrect because the biomass of the lake does not remain the same over time.

QUESTION 21.

Choice C is correct. The exact coordinates of the scatterplot in the xy-plane cannot be read from the bar graph provided. However, for a data point to be above the line $y = x$, the value of y must be greater than the value of x. That is, the consumption in 2010 must be greater than the consumption in 2000. This occurs for 3 types of energy sources shown in the bar graph: biofuels, geothermal, and wind.

Choices A, B, and D are incorrect and may be the result of a conceptual error in presenting the data shown in a scatterplot. For example, choice B is incorrect because there are 2 data points in the scatterplot that lie <u>below</u> the line $y = x$.

QUESTION 22.

Choice B is correct. Reading the graph, the amount of wood power used in 2000 was 2.25 quadrillion BTUs and the amount used in 2010 was 2.00 quadrillion BTUs. To find the percent decrease, find the difference between the two numbers, divide by the original value, and then multiply by 100: $\frac{2.25 - 2.00}{2.25} \times 100 = \frac{0.25}{2.25} \times 100 \approx 11.1$ percent. Of the choices given, 11% is closest to the percent decrease in the consumption of wood power from 2000 to 2010.

Choices A, C, and D are incorrect and may be the result of errors in reading the bar graph or in calculating the percent decrease.

QUESTION 23.

Choice B is correct. The standard deviation is a measure of how far the data set values are from the mean. In the data set for City A, the large majority of the data are in three of the five possible values, which are the three values closest to the mean. In the data set for City B, the data are more spread out, with many values at the minimum and maximum values. Therefore, by observation, the data for City B have a larger standard deviation.

Alternatively, one can calculate the mean and visually inspect the difference between the data values and the mean. For City A the mean is $\frac{1,655}{21} \approx 78.8$, and for City B the mean is $\frac{1,637}{21} \approx 78.0$. The data for City A are closely clustered near 79, which indicates a small standard deviation. The data for City B are spread out away from 78, which indicates a larger standard deviation.

Choices A, C, and D are incorrect and may be the result of misconceptions about the standard deviation.

QUESTION 24.

Choice C is correct. Since segment AB is a diameter of the circle, it follows that arc $\overset{\frown}{ADB}$ is a semicircle. Thus, the circumference of the circle is twice the length of arc $\overset{\frown}{ADB}$ which is $2(8\pi) = 16\pi$. Since the circumference of a circle is 2π times the radius of the circle, the radius of this circle is 16π divided by 2π, which is equal to 8.

Choices A, B, and D are incorrect and may be the result of losing track of factors of 2 or of solving for the diameter of the circle instead of the radius. For example, choice D is the diameter of the circle.

QUESTION 25.

Choice B is correct. In $f(x)$, factoring out the greatest common factor, $2x$, yields $f(x) = 2x(x^2 + 3x + 2)$. It is given that $g(x) = x^2 + 3x + 2$, so using substitution, $f(x)$ can be rewritten as $f(x) = 2x \cdot g(x)$. In the equation $p(x) = f(x) + 3g(x)$, substituting $2x \cdot g(x)$ for $f(x)$ yields $p(x) = 2x \cdot g(x) + 3 \cdot g(x)$. In $p(x)$, factoring out the greatest common factor, $g(x)$, yields $p(x) = (g(x))(2x + 3)$. Because $2x + 3$ is a factor of $p(x)$, it follows that $p(x)$ is divisible by $2x + 3$.

Choices A, C, and D are incorrect because $2x + 3$ is not a factor of the polynomials $h(x)$, $r(x)$, or $s(x)$. Using the substitution $f(x) = 2x \cdot g(x)$, and factoring further, $h(x)$, $r(x)$, and $s(x)$ can be rewritten as follows:

$$h(x) = (x + 1)(x + 2)(2x + 1)$$

$$r(x) = (x + 1)(x + 2)(4x + 3)$$

$$s(x) = 2(x + 1)(x + 2)(3x + 1)$$

Because $2x + 3$ is not a factor of $h(x)$, $r(x)$, or $s(x)$, it follows that $h(x)$, $r(x)$, and $s(x)$ are not divisible by $2x + 3$.

QUESTION 26.

Choice C is correct. If $-y < x < y$, the value of x is either between $-y$ and 0 or between 0 and y, so statement I, $|x| < y$ is true. It is possible that the value of x is greater than zero, but x could be negative. For example, a counterexample to statement II, $x > 0$, is $x = -2$ and $y = 3$, yielding $-3 < -2 < 3$, so the given condition is satisfied. Statement III must be true since $-y < x < y$ implies that $-y < y$, so y must be greater than 0. Therefore, statements I and III are the only statements that must be true.

Choices A, B, and D are incorrect because each of these choices either omits a statement that must be true or includes a statement that could be false.

QUESTION 27.

Choice D is correct. To interpret what the number 61 in the equation of the line of best fit represents, one must first understand what the data in the scatterplot represent. Each of the points in the scatterplot represents a large US city, graphed according to its population density (along the horizontal axis) and its relative housing cost (along the vertical axis). The line of best fit for this data represents the expected relative housing cost for a certain population density, based on the data points in the graph. Thus, one might say, on average, a city of population density x is expected to have a relative housing cost of y%, where $y = 0.0125x + 61$. The number 61 in the equation represents the y-intercept of the line of best fit, in that when the population density, x, is 0, there is an expected relative housing cost of 61%. This might not make the best sense within the context of the problem, in that when the population density is 0, the population is 0, so there probably wouldn't be any housing costs. However, it could be interpreted that for cities with low population densities, housing costs were likely around or above 61% (since below 61% would be for cities with negative population densities, which is impossible).

Choice A is incorrect because it interprets the values of the vertical axis as dollars and not percentages. Choice B is incorrect because the lowest housing cost is about 61% of the national average, not 61% of the highest housing cost. Choice C is incorrect because one cannot absolutely assert that no city with a low population density had housing costs below 61% of the national average, as the model shows that it is unlikely, but not impossible.

QUESTION 28.

Choice D is correct. The minimum value of a quadratic function appears as a constant in the vertex form of its equation, which can be found from the standard form by completing the square. Rewriting $f(x) = (x + 6)(x - 4)$ in standard form gives $f(x) = x^2 + 2x - 24$. Since the coefficient of the linear term is 2, the equation for $f(x)$ can be rewritten in terms of $(x + 1)^2$ as follows:

$$f(x) = x^2 + 2x - 24 = (x^2 + 2x + 1) - 1 - 24 = (x + 1)^2 - 25$$

Since the square of a real number is always nonnegative, the vertex form $f(x) = (x + 1)^2 - 25$ shows that the minimum value of f is -25 (and occurs at $x = -1$). Therefore, this equivalent form of f shows the minimum value of f as a constant.

Choices A and C are incorrect because they are not equivalent to the given equation for f. Choice B is incorrect because the minimum value of f, which is -25, does not appear as a constant or a coefficient.

QUESTION 29.

Choice B is correct. Since the average of 2 numbers is the sum of the 2 numbers divided by 2, the equations $x = \dfrac{m + 9}{2}$, $y = \dfrac{2m + 15}{2}$ and $z = \dfrac{3m + 18}{2}$ are true. The average of x, y, and z is given by $\dfrac{x + y + z}{3}$. Substituting the preceding expressions in m for each variable gives $\dfrac{\dfrac{m + 9}{2} + \dfrac{2m + 15}{2} + \dfrac{3m + 18}{2}}{3}$. This fraction can be simplified to $\dfrac{6m + 42}{6}$, or $m + 7$.

Choices A, C, and D are incorrect and may be the result of conceptual errors or calculation errors. For example, choice D is the sum of x, y, and z, not the average.

QUESTION 30.

Choice D is correct. The equation $f(x) = k$ gives the solutions to the system of equations $y = f(x) = x^3 - x^2 - x - \dfrac{11}{4}$ and $y = k$. A real solution of a system of two equations corresponds to a point of intersection of the graphs of the two equations in the xy-plane. The graph of $y = k$ is a horizontal line that contains the point $(0, k)$. Thus, the line with equation $y = -3$ is a horizontal line that intersects the graph of the cubic equation three times, and it follows that the equation $f(x) = -3$ has three real solutions.

Choices A, B, and C are incorrect because the graphs of the corresponding equations are horizontal lines that do not intersect the graph of the cubic equation three times.

QUESTION 31.

The correct answer is 1160. The pool contains 600 gallons of water before the hose is turned on, and water flows from the hose into the pool at a rate of 8 gallons per minute. Thus, the number of gallons of water in the pool m minutes after the hose is turned on is given by the expression $600 + 8m$. Therefore, after 70 minutes, there will be $600 + 8(70) = 1160$ gallons of water in the pool.

QUESTION 32.

The correct answer is $\dfrac{1}{2}$ or .5. The equation that models the normal systolic blood pressure, in millimeters of mercury, for a male x years old, $P = \dfrac{x + 220}{2}$, can be rewritten as $P = \dfrac{1}{2}x + 110$. For each increase of 1 year in age, the value of x increases by 1; hence, P becomes $\dfrac{1}{2}(x + 1) + 110 = \left(\dfrac{1}{2}x + 110\right) + \dfrac{1}{2}$. That is, P increases by $\dfrac{1}{2}$ millimeter of mercury. Either the fraction $\dfrac{1}{2}$ or its decimal equivalent, .5, may be gridded as the correct answer.

QUESTION 33.

The correct answer is 4.55. Since there are 16 Roman digits in a Roman pes, 75 digits is equal to $\dfrac{75}{16}$ pes. Since 1 pes is equal to 11.65 inches, $\dfrac{75}{16}$ pes is equal to $\dfrac{75}{16}(11.65)$ inches. Since 12 inches is equal to 1 foot, $\dfrac{75}{16}(11.65)$ inches is equal to $\dfrac{75}{16}(11.65)\left(\dfrac{1}{12}\right)$ 4.55078125 feet. Therefore, 75 digits is equal to $\dfrac{75}{16}(11.65)\left(\dfrac{1}{12}\right) = 4.55078125$ feet. Rounded to the nearest hundredth of a foot, 75 Roman digits is equal to 4.55 feet.

QUESTION 34.

The correct answer is 150. In the study, 240 male and 160 plus another 100 female bats have been tagged, so that 500 bats have been tagged altogether. If x more male bats must be tagged for $\frac{3}{5}$ of the total number of bats to be male, the proportion $\frac{\text{male bats}}{\text{total bats}} = \frac{240 + x}{500 + x} = \frac{3}{5}$ must be true. Multiplying each side of $\frac{240 + x}{500 + x} = \frac{3}{5}$ by $5(500 + x)$ gives $5(240 + x) = 3(500 + x)$, which simplifies to $1200 + 5x = 1500 + 3x$. Therefore, $x = 150$, and 150 more male bats must be tagged; this will bring the total to 390 male bats out of 650 bats, which is equal to $\frac{3}{5}$.

QUESTION 35.

The correct answer is 2.25 or $\frac{9}{4}$. Let q_s be the dynamic pressure of the slower fluid moving with velocity v_s, and let q_f be the dynamic pressure of the faster fluid moving with velocity v_f. Then $v_f = 1.5v_s$.

Given the equation $q = \frac{1}{2}nv^2$, substituting the dynamic pressure and velocity of the faster fluid gives $q_f = \frac{1}{2}nv_f^2$. Since $v_f = 1.5v_s$, the expression $1.5v_s$ can be substituted for v_f in this equation, giving $q_f = \frac{1}{2}n(1.5v_s)^2$. This can be rewritten as $q_f = (2.25)\frac{1}{2}nv_s^2 = (2.25)q_s$. Therefore, the ratio of the dynamic pressure of the faster fluid is $\frac{q_f}{q_s} = \frac{2.25q_s}{q_s} = 2.25$. Either 2.25 or the equivalent improper fraction $\frac{9}{4}$ may be gridded as the correct answer.

QUESTION 36.

The correct answer is 29, 30, 31, 32, 33, or 34. Since the radius of the circle is 10, its circumference is 20π. The full circumference of a circle is 360°. Thus, an arc of length s on the circle corresponds to a central angle of $x°$, where $\frac{x}{360} = \frac{s}{20\pi}$, or $x = \frac{360}{20\pi}s$. Since $5 < s < 6$, it follows that $\frac{360}{20\pi}(5) < x < \frac{360}{20\pi}(6)$, which becomes, to the nearest tenth, $28.6 < x < 34.4$. Therefore, the possible integer values of x are 29, 30, 31, 32, 33, and 34. Any one of these numbers may be gridded as the correct answer.

QUESTION 37.

The correct answer is .72. According to the analyst's estimate, the value V, in dollars, of the stock will decrease by 28% each week for t weeks, where $t = 1$, 2, or 3, with its value being given by the formula $V = 360(r)^t$. This equation is an example of exponential decay. A stock losing 28% of its value each week is the same as the stock's value decreasing to 72% of its value from the previous week, since $V - (.28)V = (.72)V$. Using this information, after 1 week the value, in dollars, of the stock will be $V = 360(.72)$; after 2 weeks the value of the stock will be $V = 360(.72)(.72) = 360(.72)^2$; and after 3 weeks the value of the stock will be $V = 360(.72)(.72)(.72) = 360(.72)^3$. For all of the values of t in question, namely $t = 1$, 2, and 3, the equation $V = 360(.72)^t$ is true. Therefore, the analyst should use .72 as the value of r.

QUESTION 38.

The correct answer is 134. The analyst's prediction is that the stock will lose 28 percent of its value for each of the next three weeks. Thus, the predicted value of the stock after 1 week is $\$360 - (0.28)\$360 = \$259.20$; after 2 weeks, $\$259.20 - (0.28)\$259.20 \approx \$186.62$; and after 3 weeks, $\$186.62 - (0.28)\$186.62 \approx \$134.37$. Therefore, to the nearest dollar, the stock analyst believes the stock will be worth 134 dollars after three weeks.